Due Return Date Date	Due Return Date Date

The Critical Reader
REVISED EDITION

THE
Critical Reader

Essays »«« *Stories* »«« *Poems*

REVISED EDITION

Edited by

ROY LAMSON
MASSACHUSETTS INSTITUTE OF TECHNOLOGY

HALLETT SMITH
CALIFORNIA INSTITUTE OF TECHNOLOGY

HUGH N. MACLEAN
YORK UNIVERSITY, TORONTO

WALLACE W. DOUGLAS
NORTHWESTERN UNIVERSITY

W · W · NORTON & COMPANY · INC · *New York*

Contents

〜〜〜〜〜〜〜〜〜〜〜〜〜〜〜〜〜〜〜〜〜〜〜〜〜〜〜〜〜

The selections that are analyzed or provided
with exercises are marked with an asterisk.

The Stories

The Poems

Foreword

~~~~~~

THIS BOOK of essays, stories, and poems is based upon the proposition that reading is an art, and that it can be mastered by students who have enough maturity to go to college. Not all will practise it with the same facility, of course, but everybody can acquire some.

The medium of the art is words—a medium used by everyone and capable of an enormous range of effects. It goes without saying that the ability to respond to subtle or profound pieces of literature is not developed without exposure to examples of what might be called "difficult" writing. Many students never become critical readers because their reading assignments in English courses have been too easy for them. Happily this situation has been changing, and it is more common to find teachers now who think college freshmen are capable of reading Hopkins's "The Windhover" or Joyce's "The Dead" or an essay by Edmund Wilson than it was fifteen years ago.

But the ability to read well and critically, to be sensitive and discriminating, depends not only upon what is read but upon how it is read. The student who "reads to remember" and to pour out details in answer to an examination question may never become a critical reader because he does not proceed from fact to responsible judgment. Conversely, the reader who is so obsessed with his own likes and dislikes that he pays no attention to the shape of the work he is reading or its partly concealed motives, will never become a critical reader either. The well-trained reader will pay attention to those elements of language, imagery, and form; of style, scope, approach to material, attitude, proportion, and emphasis which reveal what we sometimes call, by a convenient fiction, the "intention" of the work. He will have learned to recognize and discount his own prejudices, whether of form or content, and to test his impulses and responses against an honest and thorough examination of the work itself.

Any art is learned partly by imitation and partly by practice. We have included in each section—the Essays, the Stories, and the Poems—a half-dozen or so samples of critical analysis. These are intended to help the student who has carefully read the essay or story or poem and thinks he understands it but still doesn't know how to go about making a critical analysis. But the great majority of the selections published here are "plain texts" providing the student with his own opportunity to practise the art of critical reading.

It should be evident that there is a relation between the art of reading and the art of writing. A student who analyzes carefully enough the traits of prose style in an essay assigned for analysis will inevitably find that his own prose will profit—but only if he has frequent occasions to practise that other art of writing and to have his work conscientiously criticized.

Critical reading, in the long run, yields pleasure. It should, since the purpose of most literature is to give pleasure. But how is this achieved? "Nothing can permanently please," said Coleridge, "which does not contain in itself the reason why it is so and not otherwise." If analysis destroys the pleasure of reading a work of literary art, then there is something wrong with the method of analysis, because surely there is a double pleasure in discovering what it is in something that gives it the power to please permanently.

The Revised Edition of *The Critical Reader* appears after more than a decade of classroom experience with the original edition. The changes made in the contents of the volume result from this experience and from the advice of many teachers and students who have used the book. These changes amount to less than one third of the total, and they occur mainly in the Essay section. The reason is obvious: essays lose their freshness, become dated, or seem labored and artificial, much sooner than poems and stories do. The fourteen new essays, as well as the seven new poems and four new stories, are intended to offer variety of subject and of complexity—writings of value in themselves which provide opportunities for the student to become a responsible and critical reader.

Acknowledgments

In the Revised Edition of *The Critical Reader* the editors are grateful to Professors James K. Robinson, Robert O. Payne, and Willard Thorp for helpful suggestions and criticism, and to Mrs. K. C. Liu and Mrs. Aida L. Blender for their help in preparing the manuscript. The editors also wish to thank the staffs of the libraries of York University, California Institute of Technology, and Massachusetts Institute of Technology.

The Critical Reader
REVISED EDITION

The Essays

~~~~~~

THE ESSAYS in this collection have been chosen for their varied illustration of three elements: style, structure, idea. Perhaps most readers will be initially stimulated by the essayists' ideas, and certainly the editors hope that students will want to discuss these in terms of their own experience. But such discussions, however rewarding they may be, will not do much for a student's prose style, nor for his knowledge of the architectonics of modern English and American prose. The critical comments appended to some essays, therefore, place particular stress on style and structure, with a view to indicating the connections between these and the "content" of the essay. Briefly, the collection is intended to show how essayists design and pattern their material to clarify and illuminate an idea.

Essays have often been sorted into two categories: formal and informal (although Montaigne might have thought the distinction a curious one). The criterion of difference has less to do with topic than with manner or style or tone. Thus Macaulay, dealing with Addison or Frederick the Great, adopted a pontifical tone to which the Ciceronian rhythms of his style were suited, while the opening sentences of even a relatively "formal" essay by Lamb ("On the Tragedies of Shakespeare," say) strike a personal and conversational note that is never quite abandoned. But broad distinctions of this sort are not very helpful to the student, especially in an age when many readers are likely to find Lamb rather formal and Macaulay virtually unreadable. As the "formal essay" seems to have moved steadily toward the special audience of the learned journal, the "informal essay" has widely extended its domain: almost every essay in this collection is "informal" in an older sense of the term. What matters for the critical reader is that he should come to grips with the factors conditioning each essay: its particular occasion, intention, context, and audience—not to mention the author's personality.

Most of the pieces collected here resist type-casting. The two by MacLeish and Cummings were both originally delivered as lectures to academic audiences, but only an uncritical reader will make anything of that; nor will easy distinctions between formal and informal lectures advance us much. Smith's essay, by definition a "learned article," is largely concerned with the excesses of its own kind. The essays by McNulty, Wilson, Agee, and Lawrence are in the widest sense "reportage," but the style of each obviously reflects a special point of view, intention, and conditioning milieu. One piece is not an essay at all, if traditional standards are to hold: Pati Hill's interview with Truman Capote is really a composite affair. Capote talked; the interviewer selected and arranged, bringing Capote's personality and outlook into relief, in much the same way as a gifted accompanist more than merely "accompanies" the soloist. National magazines regularly belabor and debase the form; for good or ill, the English essay of the future may assume some such unexpected shape as this. However that may be, the range of style and kind in the modern essay should make the reader wary of facile generalization—and it lends point to a comment made by Paul Valéry:

. . . style is not an unchanging rite, an everlasting mold cut once and for all—even by a Flaubert; it must adapt itself to the author's design and serve solely to prepare the final *fireworks*. It must be adequate for its object.[1]

The student who reads with an eye to the improvement of form and structure in his own writing—who expects, that is, to combine coherence with variety—will find a wide spectrum of method here. The essays by Nagel, Commager, and Cecil are

---

[1] *The Art of Poetry*, Vol. 7 of *Collected Works of Paul Valéry*, Bollingen Series XLV (New York, 1958), p. 351.

among the more readily grasped in this regard: logical argument, as one would expect of Nagel, directs and dominates the movement of his essay; those by Commager and Cecil are models of clarity and reasoned order. With Agee and (less obviously) Wilson, the imagination takes over as guiding principle, so that while clear narrative movement marks each essay, at bottom the structure turns on connotative language, metaphor and symbol. In the essay by Lawrence, an impressionistic manner may at first discourage the search for structural principle, but the series of vivid pictures is punctuated by paragraphs of an essentially emotional character; these hold the piece together, and indicate its meaning too. Different again are the essays by Cummings and McNulty, in which what Cummings might call "nonstructure" itself becomes a structural principle. Having said this much, however—and the student who is able to recognize the controlling movement at the heart of each essay will be at a tremendous advantage in his own expository writing—a note of caution is in order. Hemingway distinguishes between the serious and the solemn writer (who "is always a bloody owl"); the critical reader, unhappily, can degenerate into the critical over-reader, who is apt to present for inspection imaginary gardens with imaginary toads in them. Students are referred to the "Notice" that follows the title-page of *Huckleberry Finn:*

Persons attempting to find a motive in this narrative will be prosecuted; persons attempting to find a moral in it will be banished; persons attempting to find a plot in it will be shot.

As for the ideas in these essays, while no one can judge with much certainty what will seem dated or trivial by 1972—not to say 1963—the editors have singled out issues that seem likely to retain significance and interest for students working with this book. Snow's essay touches on some English origins of the "scientific age" we call our own; Ernest Nagel speaks of the role that science must, in his view, now assume in American education. Commager and van den Haag consider other educa-

tional issues in a changing America; the points they make
invite comparison with the views advanced by Nagel and Raymond Aron. Pieces by the Englishman Lawrence and the American Hemingway, both having to do with Mediterranean peoples, are balanced by Raymond Aron's cool assessment of
American society today. The authors of these essays glance
horizontally, as it were, at nations and customs not their own:
other voices, other rooms. The regard of Virginia Woolf and
Lord David Cecil is directed to their countrymen, but backward
in time; speaking with affectionate sympathy of two eras rather
different from ours, each writer reminds us of the uses of the
past. And Edmund Wilson shows how "ten men in a darkened
kitchen" may recurrently affirm man's force to persist, in spite
of time's passing and the pressures of modern society. The
imagination, of course, is explicitly or implicitly the central
concern of several essays, ranging from Thurber's musings on
bad eyesight to the views of Archibald MacLeish on poetry
and history. A number of pieces, finally, deal more or less
directly with the writer's craft: how a writer writes, for whom,
and to what end.

While the editors suppose that the critical reader of essays will
continuously attend to matters of style, structure, and idea (and
to the nature of their integration), to propose one unchanging
formula of attack as the way to eviscerate any essay is far from
their intention. That would be to

teach

> Bloody instructions, which being taught return
> To plague the inventor.

The "Suggestions for Study," then, are precisely that: suggestions deliberately various in kind from which discussion may
spring and the process of analysis develop. But it would be a
pity if students or instructors were to be satisfied with analysis
alone, and so leave each essay "all in pieces, all coherence gone."
To make analysis, formal or informal, subserve and lead to

comprehensive synthesis: this habit of mind will mark the truly critical reader.

The Admiral on the Wheel

JAMES THURBER (1894–1961)

WHEN THE COLORED maid stepped on my glasses the other morning, it was the first time they had been broken since the late Thomas A. Edison's seventy-ninth birthday. I remember that day well, because I was working for a newspaper then and I had been assigned to go over to West Orange that morning and interview Mr. Edison. I got up early and, in reaching for my glasses under the bed (where I always put them), I found that one of my more sober and reflective Scotch terriers was quietly chewing them. Both tortoiseshell temples (the pieces that go over your ears) had been eaten and Jeanie was toying with the lenses in a sort of jaded way. It was in going over to Jersey that day, without my glasses, that I realized that the disadvantages of defective vision (bad eyesight) are at least partially compensated for by its peculiar advantages. Up to that time I had been in the habit of going to bed when my glasses were broken and lying there until they were fixed again. I had believed I could not go very far without them, not more than a block, anyway, on account of the danger of bumping into things, getting a headache, losing my way. None of these things happened, but a lot of others did. I saw the Cuban flag flying over a national bank, I saw a gay old lady with a gray parasol walk right through the side of a truck, I saw a cat roll across a street in a small striped barrel, I saw bridges rise lazily into the air, like balloons.

I suppose you have to have just the right proportion of sight to encounter such phenomena: I seem to remember that oculists have told me I have only two-fifths vision without what one of them referred to as "artifical compensation" (glasses). With three-fifths vision or better, I suppose the Cuban flag would have been an American flag, the gay old lady a garbage man with a garbage can on his back, the cat a piece of butcher's paper blowing in the wind, the floating bridges smoke from tugs, hanging in the air. With perfect vision, one is extricably trapped in the workaday world, a prisoner of reality, as lost in the commonplace America of 1937 as Alexander Selkirk was lost on his lonely island. For the hawk-eyed person life has none of those soft edges which for me blur into fantasy; for such a person an electric welder is merely an electric welder, not a radiant fool setting off a sky-rocket by day. The kingdom of the partly blind is a little like Oz, a little like Wonderland, a little like Poictesme. Anything you can think of, and a lot you never would think of, can happen there.

For three days after the maid, in cleaning the apartment, stepped on my glasses—I had not put them far enough under the bed—I worked at home and did not go uptown to have them fixed. It was in this period that I made the acquaintance of a remarkable Chesapeake spaniel. I looked out my window and after a moment spotted him, a noble, silent dog lying on a ledge above the entrance to a brownstone house on lower Fifth Avenue. He lay there, proud and austere, for three days and nights, sleepless, never eating, the perfect watchdog. No ordinary dog could have got up on the high ledge above the doorway, to begin with; no ordinary people would have owned such an animal. The ordinary people were the people who walked by the house and did not see the dog. Oh, I got my glasses fixed finally and I know that now the dog has gone, but I haven't looked to see what prosaic object occupies the spot where he so staunchly stood guard over one of the last of the old New York houses on Fifth Avenue; perhaps an unpainted flowerbox or a cleaning cloth dropped from an upper window by a care-less menial. The moment of disenchantment would be too hard; I never look out that particular window any more.

Sometimes at night, even with my glasses on, I see strange and unbelievable sights, mainly when I am riding in an auto-mobile, which somebody else is driving (I never drive myself at night out of fear that I might turn up at the portals of some mystical monastery and never return). Only last summer I was riding with someone along a country road when suddenly I cried at him to look out. He slowed down and asked me sharply what was the matter. There is no worse experience than to have someone shout at you to look out for something you don't see. What this driver didn't see and I did see (two-fifths vision works a kind of magic in the night) was a little old admiral in full-dress uniform riding a bicycle at right angles to the car I was in. He might have been starlight behind a tree, or a bill-board advertising Moxie; I don't know—we were quickly past the place he rode out of; but I would recognize him if I saw him again. His beard was blowing in the breeze and his hat was set at a rakish angle, like Admiral Beatty's. He was having a swell time. The gentleman who was driving the car has been, since that night, a trifle stiff and distant with me. I suppose you can hardly blame him.

To go back to my daylight experiences with the naked eye, it was me, in case you have heard the story, who once killed fifteen white chickens with small stones. The poor beggars never had a chance. This happened many years ago when I was living at Jay, New York. I had a vegetable garden some seventy feet behind the house, and the lady of the house had asked me to keep an eye on it in my spare moments and to chase away any chickens from neighbouring farms that came pecking around. One morning, getting up from my typewriter, I wandered out behind the house and saw that a flock of white chickens had invaded the garden. I had, to be sure, misplaced my glasses for the moment, but I could still see well enough to let the chickens have it with ammunition from a pile of stones that I kept handy for the purpose. Before I could be stopped, I had riddled all the tomato plants in the garden, over the tops of which the lady of the house had, the twilight before, placed newspapers and paper bags to ward off the effects of frost. It was one of the darker experiences of my dimmer hours.

Some day, I suppose, when the clouds are heavy and the rain is coming down and the pressure of realities is too great, I shall deliberately take my glasses off and go wandering out into the streets. I daresay I may never be heard of again (I have always believed it was Ambrose Bierce's vision and not his whim that caused him to wander into oblivion). I imagine I'll have a remarkable time, wherever I end up.

Suggestions for Study

THIS ESSAY, less allusive and complex than some of its author's later pieces, remains a fine example of an early Thurber. The mildly ironic tone combines with a disarming air of vague and helpless concern in the face of "workaday life" and its harassing trivia to reinforce the serious idea at the heart of the essay.

Thurber's style isn't easily defined. Truman Capote speaks of Thurber as "a styleless stylist—which is very difficult, very admirable, and *always* very popular." Suitably for an essay about appearance and reality (and the ambiguities inherent in their relations), the style of this piece is marked especially by contrasts, striking comparisons, unexpected parallels. "As lost in the commonplace America of 1937 as Alexander Selkirk was lost on his lonely island," or ". . . for such a person an electric welder is merely an electric welder, not a radiant fool setting off a sky-rocket by day," depend for their initial effect on arresting imagery; but the delicate play of likeness and difference in each catch more subtly at the mind of the reader. Diction and sentence structure reflect this too:

His beard was blowing in the breeze and his hat was set at a rakish angle, like Admiral Beatty's. He was having a swell time. The gentleman who was driving the car has been, since that night, a trifle stiff and distant with me. . . .

Again, the three parenthetical phrases in the opening paragraph serve three separate purposes. What is the point of the third of these? Still another device is the unexpected adjective: "extricably trapped." Even when Thurber links broadly parallel phrases—"a little like Oz, a little like Wonderland, a little like Poictesme"—the varying connotations help the reader to imagine what the kingdom of the partly blind may really be like.

The latter part of the essay, especially the paragraph beginning, "To go back to my daylight experiences," is worth close attention. What, for instance, do such expressions as "It was me, in case you have heard the story, who . . . ," "The poor beggars never had a chance," and ". . . before I could be stopped," suggest about the author, who seems to have become someone else? What is the reason for this shift in point of view? Relate these matters to the last paragraph of the essay (and compare "The Secret Life of Walter Mitty").

The first topical allusion in the piece throws some light on structure and organization. At least two structural patterns hold the essay together: a movement from past, through present, to future time, and (within the other) the alternating rhythm of day and night.

If one is fond of isolating key phrases, either "With perfect vision, one is extricably trapped in the workaday world, a prisoner of reality," or "Anything you can think of, and a lot you never would think of, can happen there," will serve well enough. But the essay is really a series of variations on a theme of William Blake:

> We are led to Believe a Lie
> When we see not Thro' the Eye.

Progress and Change

E. B. WHITE (1899–   )

MY FRIENDS in the city tell me that the Sixth Avenue El is coming down, but that's a hard thing for anyone to believe who once lived in its fleeting and audible shadow. The El was the most distinguished and outstanding vein on the town's neck, a varicosity tempting to the modern surgeon. One wonders whether New York can survive this sort of beauty operation, performed in the name of civic splendor and rapid transit.

A resident of the city grew accustomed to the heavenly railroad which swung implausibly in air, cutting off his sun by day, wandering in and out of his bedchamber by night. The presence of the structure and the passing of the trains were by all odds the most pervasive of New York's influences. Here was a sound which, if it ever got in the conch of your ear, was ineradicable— forever singing, like the sea. It punctuated the morning with brisk tidings of repetitious adventure, and it accompanied the night with sad but reassuring sounds of life-going-on—the sort of threnody which cricket and katydid render for suburban people sitting on screened porches, the sort of lullaby which the whippoorwill sends up to the Kentucky farm wife on a summer evening.

I spent a lot of time, once, doing nothing in the vicinity of Sixth Avenue. Naturally I know something of the El's fitful charm. It was, among other things, the sort of railroad you would occasionally ride just for the hell of it, a higher existence into which you would escape unconsciously and without destination. Let's say you had just emerged from the Childs' on the west side of Sixth Avenue between 14th and 15th Streets, where you had

PROGRESS AND CHANGE is reprinted from *One Man's Meat* by E. B. White. Copyright 1930 by E. B. White. Reprinted by permission of Harper and Brothers.

had a bowl of vegetable soup and a stack of wheat cakes. The syrup still was a cloying taste on your tongue. You intended to go back to the apartment and iron a paragraph, or wash a sock. But miraculously, at the corner of 14th, there rose suddenly in front of you a flight of marble stairs all wrapt in celestial light, with treads of shining steel, and risers richly carved with the names of the great, and a canopy overhead where danced the dust in the shafts of golden sunshine. As in a trance, you mounted steadily to the pavilion above, where there was an iron stove and a man's hand visible through a mousehole. And the first thing you knew you were in South Ferry, with another of life's inestimable journeys behind you—and before you the dull, throbbing necessity of getting uptown again.

For a number of years I went to work every morning on the uptown trains of the Sixth Avenue El. I had it soft, because my journey wasn't at the rush hour and I often had the platform of the car to myself. It was a good way to get where you wanted to go, looking down on life at just the right speed, and peeking in people's windows, where the sketchy pantomime of potted plant and half-buttoned undershirt and dusty loft provided a curtain raiser to the day. The railroad was tolerant and allowed its passengers to loll outdoors if they wished; and on mornings when the air was heady that was the place to be—with the sudden whiff of the candy factory telling you that your ride was half over, and the quick eastward glance through 24th Street to check your time with the clock in the Metropolitan Tower, visible for the tenth part of a second.

The El always seemed to me to possess exactly the right degree of substantiality: it seemed reasonably strong and able to carry its load, and competent with that easy slovenly competence of an old drudge; yet it was perceptibly a creature of the clouds, the whole structure vibrating ever so slightly following the final grasping success of the applied brake. The El had giddy spells, too—days when a local train would shake off its patient, plodding manner and soar away in a flight of sheer whimsy, skipping stations in a drunken fashion and scaring the pants off everybody. To go roaring past a scheduled stop, hell bent for 53rd Street and the plunge into space, was an experience which befell every El rider more than once. On this line a man didn't have to be a locomotophobe to suffer from visions of a motorman's lifeless form slumped over an open throttle. And if the suspense got too great and you walked nervously to the front of the train the little window in the booth gave only the most tantalizing view of the driver—three inert fingers of a gloved hand, or a *Daily News* wedged in some vital cranny.

One thing I always admired about the El was the way it tormented its inexperienced customers. Veterans like myself, approaching a station stop, knew to a fraction of an inch how close it was advisable to stand to the little iron gates on the open type cars. But visitors to town had no such information. When the train halted and the guard, pulling his two levers, allowed the gates to swing in and take the unwary full in the stomach, there was always a dim pleasure in it for the rest of us. Life has little enough in the way of reward; these small moments of superiority are not to be despised.

The El turned the Avenue into an arcade. That, in a way, was its chief contribution. It made Sixth Avenue as distinct from Fifth as Fifth is from Jones Street. Its pillars, straddling the car tracks in the long channel of the night, provided the late cruising taxicab with the supreme challenge, and afforded the homing pedestrian, his wine too much with him, forest sanctuary and the friendly accommodation of a tree.

Of course I have read about the great days of the El, when it was the railroad of the élite and when financial giants rode elegantly home from Wall Street in its nicely appointed coaches. But I'm just as glad I didn't meet the El until after it had lost its money. Its lazy crescendos, breaking into one's dreams, will always stick in the mind—and the soiled hands of the guards on the bellcords, and the brusque, husky-throated bells that had long ago lost their voices, cuing each other along the whole length of the train. Yes, at this distance it's hard to realize that the Sixth Avenue El is just a problem in demolition. I can't for the life of me imagine what New York will have to offer in its place. It will have to be something a good deal racier, a good deal more open and aboveboard, than a new subway line.

Suggestions for Study

ONE DOESN'T need to be a New Yorker (although "risers richly carved with the names of the great" may call for expert advice) to enjoy this essay: people in every city and town will have experienced the wry combination of nostalgia and civic pride that the passing of some ugly and beloved landmark brings, whether it's the New Orleans Custom House, the Toronto City Hall or the old mill at Grover's Corners. Grimy and outmoded, the El had to go; yet the El in fact stimulated the free play in men of everything that isn't grimy and outmoded. Apparently transient, the El fostered what is permanent.

A particular feature of White's style, the subtle interweaving of fact and fancy, reinforces the point of the essay.

. . . that's a hard thing for anyone to believe who once lived in its fleeting and audible shadow.

To go roaring past a scheduled stop, hell bent for 53rd Street and the plunge into space, was an experience which befell every El rider more than once.

It was, among other things, the sort of railroad you would occasionally ride just for the hell of it, a higher existence into which you would escape unconsciously and without destination.

The diction, too, combines colloquialisms like "I had it soft" or "scaring the pants off everybody," with terms carefully chosen for their connotative suggestion in the context of the piece. Consider, for example, the adjectives in "life's inestimable journeys," "the homing pedestrian," and the pairing of "three inert fingers" with "some vital cranny."

Technically, the essay is an instance of "extended definition, developed by means of particulars and details." And it is true that each paragraph deals with a notable aspect of the El's appeal or imaginative role. But the structure depends more vitally on a series of metaphorical expressions: at the outset no more than "the most distinguished and outstanding vein on the town's neck," the El has by the end of the essay turned into the last of the big spenders, whose giddy spells and capacity for sheer whimsy quite naturally brought financial disaster. It is worth noticing that the El pulses with vitality throughout, and that in contrast with the guards and drivers (who are deliberately made to seem lifeless, like figures in a waxworks), gates, pillars, and "the brusque, husky-throated bells that had long ago lost their voices" are instinct with life. Why does White do this?

The piece has something in common with those fairy stories in which large green frogs turn into people (usually princes). To the objection that this can't happen in "real life," especially not in the jungles of cities, White would perhaps reply with a phrase from his essay: it can, if you're "looking down on life at just the right speed."

Bellevue Days

JOHN McNULTY (1895–1956)

ONE AFTERNOON recently, after visiting friends on Gramercy Park, I took a cab to go to East Seventy-second Street, where I live, and the driver chose to go up First Avenue. We were

halted by a light at Twenty-sixth Street, in front of Bellevue
Hospital. While we waited, both the driver and I looked at the
big, dull buildings and the many yards, and watched the flow
of people through the gates.

"Good old Bellevue!" I said.

"My wife's brother was in there once," the driver said before
the light changed and we started on our way again. "He had what
they call a sacroiliac, a very painful thing in the back. It must
be a tough spot to be in, that Bellevue."

"I was in there once, too," I said.

"No kidding?" the driver asked.

"No kidding," I said. "And you're right. It is kind of tough
in there sometimes. But just the same, I've got a soft spot in my
heart for old Bellevue."

"What was it—accident or something?" the driver asked.

"No," I said. "Heart attack. But I'm practically O.K. now.
That was a couple of years ago."

"You got to take it easy if you've had one of those," he said.

"They made me take it easy in Bellevue," I said. "And I want
to tell you I met some fine people in there and they all certainly
treated me first-rate."

"Now, that's a funny thing," said the driver. "My wife's
brother said almost the same words many a time. Said he met
some fine people in there, and the treatment he got from everybody was real good. Almost the same words you said."

When I got home that afternoon, it turned out that my wife
was still out shopping, so I made myself a cup of tea and sat
down to rest for a while, as I often do these days. I had to laugh
a little to myself at the idea of having said "Good old Bellevue!"
to a stranger. Yet that is the way I feel whenever I chance to
pass the place—almost as if it were some school I attended as a
youth and could not let slip lightly from my mind. Indeed, it
was almost that way—like an alma mater.

In the middle of May, 1947, our flat was being painted (for
the first time in three years), and the place was a mess. My wife

thought it would be a good opportunity to visit her mother, in Wakefield, Rhode Island. As for me, I had some work to do in town, and I also liked to go to the races at Belmont in the afternoon, when my work was through. So she went to the country, and I moved into an inexpensive room in a hotel on East Fortieth Street, near Lexington.

The night of May 22nd (I remember the dates well, because they have been on so many records since then) I had dinner alone—a steak and au gratin potatoes, with a drink before dinner and a bottle of beer with it. After dinner, it then being about ten o'clock, I bought the *Daily Racing Form* at Forty-second Street and Third Avenue, from a blind man, and walked to the hotel. Before I went up to my room on the fourth floor, I stopped at the desk to chat with Louis Schwartz, the night clerk, who was there early. He and I had struck up a friendship, based on the fact that we both were horseplayers. He had noticed me coming in nightly with the *Form* tucked under my arm, and one word had led to another until we found out that we were both "watching" the same horse, as horseplayers say. That is, we were both looking every day for a particular horse's name in the entries, and sometimes bet on him when he did run. The name of the horse we both happened to have singled out was *Deep Texas*. He was a pretty good sort of horse. He never got famous, but it is safe to say that thousands of horseplayers throughout the country were at that time "watching" *Deep Texas*. He won a few times, too.

"Our horse isn't going tomorrow," Louis said as he gave me my room key.

"No, I already looked," I said. "Well, I'll give you a ring if I see anything. I'm going upstairs and look them over."

"Good night," Louis said. "Ring me down here if you see anything you like for tomorrow. I drop four bucks today."

"Tomorrow's another day," I said, using a practically compulsory rejoinder among horseplayers.

No matter how much a man likes his own home, a week

or so by himself in a hotel room can be pretty nice, every year or so. I found it pleasant that night. To come into the small but comfortable room, nicely tidied up after I had left it in disarray, was pleasing, and the room's very smallness made things handy and matters manageable. Everything going fine, I thought, as I opened the window, fixed the bed light at the proper angle, and got into bed with the *Form*. For a moment, I considered spending seventy-five cents in calling my wife in Rhode Island, but then I decided that I didn't have seventy-five cents' worth of anything to say to her, except to tell her I was comfortable and ask if she was the same. I dismissed the notion and looked over nearly all the entries for the next day's racing. It seemed to be a most ordinary card, and there was no horse I had any great conviction about, so I let the *Form* drop to the floor, turned out the light, and went to sleep in two shakes of a lamb's tail. Didn't even have to count the shakes.

I awoke about six the next morning, too early for coffee to be sent up, so I figured I'd get shaved and dressed and go over to the Shack at Forty-first and Lexington for some coffee, and read the papers there. I changed from pajamas into underwear and started to shave. In the middle of that job, a pain came into the center of my chest. It was not a startling pain, not a dreadful one at all, just such a pain as anyone might have, but I thought I might lie down for a few minutes. Some little passing jiggeroo of the system, I told myself. After a while, when it didn't go away, I thought I might call Louis downstairs, for comfort and reassurance if for nothing else. I was glad I knew Louis, and that he was not just any old hotel clerk. I wouldn't have wanted to call any old hotel clerk if this little mishap turned out to be nothing at all, but with my horseplaying friend it would be all right to call anyway. I picked up the phone and waited until Louis answered. He handled the switchboard as well as the desk at that hour.

"Louis," I said, "I didn't see anything good in the entries, so I didn't call last night. But listen, Louis, I think I'm getting sick."

"What's the matter?" he asked.

"Well, I don't know, but could you come up? I'm not kidding, I'm feeling pretty sick," I said.

"You sound scared," he said. "Don't get scared. It'll only take me a couple of minutes. I'll put the elevator guy on the desk here and run the car myself. I'll be right up."

That smart Louis must have had a key with him, because he let himself in without making me come to the door. I said hello to him, and he said, "Geez, you don't look good. I think you better be quiet. There's a doctor lives upstairs. I'll run up and get him. Take it easy, now. I'll be right back." He was back in a very short time, but in that short interval I was thinking I might be making a hullaballoo over nothing. The doctor who came in with Louis was a jaunty fellow, wearing an undershirt, pants, and slippers. Because he was jaunty, I grinned rather foolishly at him, and started to sit up in bed. "Lie down," he said. "Lie still. What's the trouble?" He took my pulse and listened to my chest. He had no stethoscope—just put his head down and listened to my heartbeat. "Keep as quiet as you can," he said to me, and then spoke to Louis. "Call the cops," he said to him. "Don't try to get him into any fancy hospital. Tell the cops to get an ambulance from Bellevue right away."

Louis went out, and again I foolishly tried to grin at the doctor. He didn't grin back, he was very calm and on-the-level-looking. "You're having a heart attack," he said. "Don't move around at all." He took a vial from his pants' pocket, shook out two pills, and gave them to me, telling me to swallow them. "I'll get you some water," he said. "Lie still. They'll be here and take care of you. Don't get frightened, old boy."

Soon a white-coated interne and two young cops carrying a stretcher came in with Louis. The doctor talked with the interne in the bathroom, and one of the young cops said to me, most sympathetically, "Take it easy, Mac." (He didn't

know that "Mac" was right for my nickname; he probably
called everyone that.)

"*You* fellows take it easy," I said. "I'm going to be all right."

"Sure, Mac," the cop said.

"Here's your pants and shirt," Louis said to me. "Put them
on nice and easy. I got your topcoat and your other things."

The interne told me to lie down on the stretcher, and I did.
Before I had got used to the feeling of being carried, I was
lifted gently and skillfully into the ambulance. The siren began
to whine, and the ambulance swung around the corner of
Lexington and headed south.

Although I was lying down in the ambulance and unable to
see out, I could sense pleasurably that it was a fine, bright morning. My apprehension of a few minutes before was inexplicably
gone, perhaps only momentarily, but gone. I kept thinking
how many times I had heard ambulances sounding in the streets
of New York and had paid small attention. This time, it was
me who was in the ambulance, with its siren whining away at
seven o'clock or so of a May morning. This time, I was the
one, out of eight million people, who had suddenly been taken
sick. A night clerk, a casual doctor (whose name I still don't
know), two young cops, an interne, and an ambulance driver
were all pitching in to help the sick man. They didn't know
who he was, never saw him before, didn't give a damn, particularly. Man alive, but this is a great town, I was thinking as the
ambulance slowed down, went through some gates, and stopped
at an entrance, where they lifted me out on the stretcher and
carried me into Bellevue. I had heard and read about Bellevue
all my life, but I had never been in there before.

Inside the hospital, my anxiety returned. It seemed to me,
lying on one of those wheeled tables, that they were asking a vast number of questions before anything was done. Name
and address, of course, and age, which was fifty-one, and previous illnesses, of which there had been practically none. Dozens

of other statistics, too, it seemed. I answered as best I could, and
then I was taken to an elevator and up to a ward. The ward, I
heard a man say in the elevator, was B-1. The table I was on
was wheeled along between the long rows of beds, so close together, and when it reached the bed I was to occupy, down near
the end, I started to rise, to climb into bed.

"Hey!" the attendant shouted at me with authority. "Don't
you move an inch." A big, strong fellow, he lifted me into the
bed in a jiffy. "What time is it?" I asked him.

"The time doesn't make any difference, pal," he said. "It's
about twenty-five past seven." That's really pretty good, I
thought to myself. Only about an hour since this hit me, and
here I am in bed in Bellevue already. Two nurses were by my
bed, and they put a screen around it. But before they had done
so, I had time to notice men in bathrobes, walking patients,
strolling by. Each one looked intently at me for an instant,
studying the new man just brought in, the new member of the
ward. These passersby did not stop; they merely looked, in a
studious way, and then continued on to stand, with great idleness, looking out the big, arched window at the end of the ward,
through which I could see the East River. Tugboats were coming
prettily down the river, but in a moment the nurses and their
screen blocked all that from view.

Soon, two doctors, both young, were with me, doing things
with stethoscopes and, in a kindly but swift manner, asking
questions. Dozens of times, from the doctors and the nurses, and
even once from a passing bathrobed man, I heard the great
admonition of our town, "Take it easy, now." The doctors
gave me some medicine, and I lay back on the pillow, taking it
easy between trying to get squints at the East River, and then
I fell asleep.

The great joke among us men in Ward B-1, for all the twenty-
six days I was there, was to call the place the Vitamin Ward,
on account of B-1 being a famous vitamin. It was a simple joke,

but we all liked it, no matter how many times it was pulled. The Vitamin Ward contained mostly heart cases and pulmonary cases, but there were a few strays of other kinds. The capacity of the ward was thirty-four, and beds were seldom empty more than a few hours.

About the first fellow I became acquainted with was a big man—Princeton 1911, it turned out—who looked like an American version of the traditional British sergeant major. He had a whopper of a mustache, and walked around in his pajamas and bathrobe as if he were about to shake up the troops for regimental inspection. Also on the roster of our ward was Alfred the Armenian, a horseplayer on the outside, like me, who was permanently distressed because he had been saving up betting money all winter and had then wound up in Bellevue exactly on the day in April when the New York racing season opened, at Jamaica. And there was Olsen, a thirty-five-year-old baseball fan who seemed unable to keep from catching pneumonia; he'd been in and out of Bellevue for four or five years, pneumonia having caught him five times in that period. And there were a few others who, as the days passed, changed in my mind from units in a parade of washed-out bathrobes and pajamas into individual persons I knew.

Those bathrobes at Bellevue are honeys. They're curiously pink or purplish gray, and they've been washed a thousand times, and so have the pajamas. Nearly everyone lying in bed and looking at them go by, with people in them, has the commonplace thought that if the president of U.S. Steel and a scratch bum from a doorway were dressed in that Bellevue rig, it would be all even between them. Great levellers, those bathrobes. Most of the time, as I said, there were thirty-four of us in Ward B-1. Not all of us were stony-broke, but some were. Most were. That didn't make a particle of difference. All thirty-four of us were on the side lines of the city for as long as we were in B-1. Before we got there and after we got out again, we had done and would do different things to get by. One of us would be a dishwasher once more, as Alfred the Armenian had been. Another would push a hack around Brooklyn, the way Milton, who was three beds up from me, did. No matter what it was we had done or would do for a living, for the time it was all even among us. Whatever was going on outside the windows, in the city of New York, we had no part of it. We didn't even have any part in the affairs of our families, if we had any. Some didn't have any. Perhaps that sounds dismal, but it wasn't. There was a kind of serenity to it.

There was a man died in the bed next to me one night, and I think that to him it was like going through a door he didn't want to go through. He came in during the afternoon, and after the doctor talked to him and those who had brought him, I talked to the doctor about my new neighbour. "He's too late," the doctor said. The new man was gaunt and sepulchral. Later in the afternoon, his folks came in to see him. They sat, a woman and a young girl, whom I presumed to be his wife and daughter, in the narrow space between our beds. When families visit in Bellevue, they often have nothing to say. They sit in that space between the beds, and maybe once in a while the wife of the sick man touches his arm and strokes it, but stops quickly because she is a little ashamed, it being so public a place. They speak a few words, and then sit silently, and the sons and daughters usually look around at the other people more than they look at their father. There seems to be nothing the family can say, except to answer the sick man, who generally asks only the simplest questions, like "How is Willie?"

The gaunt man's folks left about six o'clock, and after that he lay in bed staring around a lot but not saying anything. Before the night came down and the dimmed ward lights went on, he began to talk. I couldn't understand the words, but I could see his eyes, and they were looking at me, because I was the nearest person to him. Later—it must have been two or three o'clock—he began to holler.

"Hey!" someone in the semidarkness down the ward shouted. "Shut up! We got to sleep. Shut up, pal!" The man didn't hear him, I guess. If he did, he kept on talking anyway. There was enough light for me to see him. He stretched out a bony arm toward me and said, "Hold me, hold me, somebody, I die." He wanted somebody to take his hand and keep him this side of the door. "Hold me, hold me, somebody, I die!" he hollered, loud this time, and he tried to get up. "Shut up," another voice down the ward said.

"Listen," I said to him. "Nobody who can yell as loud as you is going to die."

"Hold me, somebody," he said persistently.

The nurse came and put a screen around him. He died. In the morning, the bed was empty. We had all gone to sleep, despite the scurrying around the bed.

Mattie was a Negro woman attendant, fat and jolly. Not too fat, not too jolly. The day would hardly come up over the river, over there by Newtown Creek, before Mattie would be in to tidy up. First the dawn, then Mattie. They were alike— sure and certain. As she came in every morning, she would look over the ward with a glance to see that all her boys were still there.

"Aren't you ashamed of yourself?" she would ask. "Look the way you got your bed all rumped up. Push over, I'll fix it." And Mattie would fix the bed, straighten it out, make you feel somebody was taking care of you.

There was the time Olsen was gone. He was the pneumonia man—always getting pneumonia, and then, afterward, what the doctors call sequelae. That means what follows a disease. (A person picks up fragments of medicine while in Bellevue, mostly incorrect fragments.) To take care of one of Olsen's sequelae, they were going to perform an operation. He had a good chance of getting out of the hospital for a little while before the operation if he played his cards right. There was a ball game in

Brooklyn the night before his operation, and, sure enough, he was able to talk the doctors into giving him a pass to go out for the evening. "I'll be back by twelve o'clock, so tell the man at the gate to let me in," he said to them. Before he left, Olsen came around to see me and told me that, according to the afternoon papers, Ralph Branca was going to pitch. The Brooks had a chance, a pretty good chance, he said. I noticed that he called them the Brooks and not the Bums or any other name by which they are referred to on the sports pages.

It was quite a thing for all of us, Olsen's going to the night game over in Brooklyn. First, he had to sign a paper to get his clothes back. They were rumply when he got them. In Bellevue, ordinarily, they take a patient's clothes away when he comes in and steam them, take the lice, if any, out of them, and put them away until the patient is going to leave. But, even so, Olsen looked pretty good in his clothes, better than in his bathrobe. I don't know where he got the money for the night game, but out he went. "So long, boys," he yelled down the ward as he gave his hat a tap. "I think Branca will pin their ears back. See you in the morning."

He wasn't there the next morning. He had overstayed his leave. He was AWOL. Mattie made Olsen's bed up—hopefully, it seemed. Two days passed, and Olsen was still not back. On the third morning, Mattie came in, glanced around, gave a tug to the corner of Olsen's bed, and walked through the ward to the big, arched window at my end. It was a foggy morning, and the air was nearly rain. The dampness in the streets almost got into the ward. Mattie looked out at the river and the fog. "Man, oh, man, this will wash him in," she said. "He can't take this, the lungs he got. This will wash him right back in here." Then she went and gave a couple of more tugs to Olsen's bed. Olsen never came back, at least not while I was there. We talked about him. Most of us figured he must have got to drinking after the game. Branca won it.

One day, in the middle of a bright afternoon, I looked up and

Alfred the Armenian was standing by my bed. He said, "My name isn't Alfred. You got a schooling, I think. Well, my name is Mesrop. Alfred is easier, but my name is Mesrop. Do you know who Mesrop was?"

I told him I didn't know who Mesrop was.

"He was a hell of an Armenian," Alfred said. "Do you think that is much to be, a hell of an Armenian?"

"No," I said.

"Well, I think it is," said Alfred. "Do you know what Mesrop did?"

"Can't say as I do," I told him.

"He invented the alphabet, that's what he did," Alfred said.

"No kidding?" I said.

"Made up the whole alphabet," Alfred said. "He was a hell of an Armenian."

Alfred wandered away from my bed and went back to his own, across the ward and two down.

My wife came in to visit a few minutes afterward. She brought some cookies. While we were talking, I looked over and saw that Alfred was sitting in the straight-backed chair placed alongside his bed for the visitors who never came to see him. He had his hands folded on the bed, and his head was on his hands. "I think Alfred is crying," I said to my wife.

"Oh," she said. "I'll give him some cookies." She went over and nudged Alfred and gave him some cookies. I was right. He *was* crying.

He said thanks, ate a cookie, then strode over to me. Right in front of my wife, he said, "She thinks I'm a baby. She gave me some cookies to stop me crying."

"She's nuts," I said.

Alfred lit a cigarette and walked away.

The friends who come to visit a man when he is in a hospital like Bellevue become, for ever afterward, a special group in the man's mind. Even years later, whenever the man runs into

one of them, he will identify him with a sudden, swift, unspoken
thought: He came to see me at Bellevue. It isn't altogether
pleasant or easy to go visiting in Bellevue. It's such a big, sprawling place that getting from the gate to a certain bedside is a
task in itself. For us in the beds, our ward became the whole
hospital as the weeks passed, for we hardly knew of the existence
of the scores of other wards surrounding us, but to the visitor
Bellevue was enormous, mystifying, and tortuous. Then, too,
as the visitor makes his way through the place in crowded times
like the pneumonia season, he is apt to come upon whole corridors lined with beds, upon which lie men who are gravely ill,
and it sinks the visitor's heart. However contented we members
of B-1 effortlessly were, our visitors always seemed a little
depressed. After they had left, we often agreed that it was quite
a job cheering them up.

Apparently, there is not a great deal for medical men to do
about a heart case—or, to give it the name the cardiacs of the
Vitamin Ward always used, "a bum ticker." The basic idea seems
to be to keep the patient in bed and quiet. That is not to say
that care was lacking in Ward B-1. Sometimes we used to think
there was too much of it. It was not uncommon to be gone over
by doctors seven or eight times in a day. That came about not
wholly through solicitude for patients but largely because Bellevue is a teaching hospital as well as a healing hospital. The
medical students of Columbia, Cornell, and N.Y.U. gain practical
knowledge to supplement their classroom work by being taken
through the wards by their teachers, who are older men, of
medical eminence. Thus, the various wards are regarded as
provinces of Cornell, N.Y.U., or Columbia. Ward B-1 was a
Cornell ward.

At odd times of the day, we bed patients, always looking up
and down the ward to watch the goings on of our world, would
see a group of white-coated men gather around the nurses' desk,
near the door. "Here comes the two-o'clock show," the Prince-

ton 1911 man would say to me. Or perhaps it would be the four-o'clock show or the supper show. He knew, as we all knew, that the white-coated group was a professor of medicine (as well as a practicing notable, of course) and his students, and that they were about to come down the ward, stopping here and there and going over us.

To be sure, the medical lore a patient picks up in Bellevue is about comparable to the military law a soldier masters while he's a prisoner in the guardhouse—fragmentary, sometimes distorted, and often downright incorrect, yet to the soldier or the patient intensely interesting, since it concerns him pretty directly. Often enough, I was the subject of the teacher's brief talks and demonstrations ("the two-o'clock show"). A teacher that I remember was Dr. Cary Eggleston, who is one of the big cardiologists of the country. As he and the students stood around my bed, he would pick up one of my hands, for instance, turn it palm upward, and show it to his pupils. "Liver palm," he would say. That didn't sound any too complimentary, but I understood, as did the rest of us, that whatever was said in those sessions was really none of our business. We were eavesdropping, in a way.

There was some medicine administered during the routine of the day, of course, and what I heard about one particular drug caught my fancy. As a rule, neither nurses nor doctors, or anyone else, will let a patient know too much about the medicine he's getting, but sometimes they can be importuned into telling. A young technician, not a doctor, came in every day for a week or so and gave me capsules. Sometimes he gave me one, another time he would give me four, and a third time two. The range went all the way from one capsule to six. "Just what the hell are those capsules?" I asked him one day. He must have been feeling talky, because he told me. "It's an experimental thing," he said. "But don't let that alarm you. There's no danger."

"That's all right," I said.

"You know, don't you, that what caused your trouble was

a clot?" he asked.

"Yes," I said.

"The stuff in the capsules is called dicumerol," he said. "It's not exactly new, but they don't know as much about it as they would like to. They hope it will serve to keep blood from clotting. You notice we take a blood test every day?"

"Certainly I notice," I said.

"That test daily is to show us what the previous day's capsule or capsules of dicumerol have done to your blood. You see, we are trying to find out what level is best in your particular case. We don't really know. We'll help you eventually, we hope, but the bigger idea is to use you as a means of adding just one small thing more to the store of knowledge about hearts."

"I get it," I said.

"Want to know how they came upon this drug?" he asked. He seemed to be a fellow of a nosy turn of mind, as, I would say, befits a fellow in a scientific field.

"How?" I asked.

"On certain farms, an unusual number of cows were losing their calves," he said. "That is, losing them before they were born. They looked into that and found that these cows were eating a certain kind of weed that thinned out their blood so much that it caused them to lose their calves. From that weed, they extracted the agent that was causing the trouble, and that's dicumerol. Properly controlled, it could possibly stop blood from clotting dangerously. And that's what we're trying to learn from you guys, if you don't mind."

"Don't mind a bit," I said.

In time, I stopped getting those capsules, for reasons best known to the doctors, so I didn't see the young technician for more than a week. Then, one day, I spied him across the ward, giving medicine to another bum-ticker man.

"Hey!" I hollered over to him.

"Oh, hello there," he said, and when he was through with the other man, he came over to my bed. "How're you doing?"

he asked.

"All right, they say," I replied. "What did you learn from me about dicumerol?"

"Not a goddam thing," he said, and walked away.

We had one Bowery bum in Ward B-1. His name was Dooley, and he didn't weigh more than a hundred and two, give or take a pound. He was a panhandler on the outside. He made no bones about that. He was around sixty-three, and that is the way he had wound up, pan-handling. He had terrible arthritis in his legs, and the treatment he was getting required his legs to be in casts. He was in casts from the soles of his feet up to his thighs. Dooley was one of the fellows who didn't have any visitors. He shared other people's visitors. After your visitors had left, Dooley would ask, in a nice way, who they were. Conversation between Dooley and me had to be hollered, because we were so far apart in the ward.

"Hey, Mac!" Dooley hollered to me one morning. "Did I ever tell you how embarrassed I got once?"

"No," I hollered back.

"It was a time I twist my ankle," he said. "Come to think of it, I twist both of them, and I was drunk into the bargain. And on top of that it was the pneumonia season, and they were all jammed up in here. In the corridors, everywhere. They take me in, but they have to throw me out in two days. Give me crutches, though. Brand-new crutches. I never had crutches before. Geez, it was icy outside. I had a hell of a time working the crutches. I start down the avenue toward the Bowery, and up comes an old man and give me something. I wasn't used to handling crutches and taking money at the same time. So I just hang on to what he give me with my right hand and say thanks and go along. 'I got dough,' I say to myself. 'I guess I'll go to the movies.' Well, do you know what happens, Mac?"

"No," I said.

"I get up to that movie house—you know the one, on the

west side of the street?"

"I know where you mean," I said.

"I walk up on the crutches to the window where the lady sells the tickets, and I unclutch my hand, and geez, what I have is a cent," Dooley said. "I been thinking all the time the old man give me a dime, and in those days you could get in the movies for a dime. My God, was I embarrassed! I didn't know what to do, so I say 'Excuse me' to the lady and go on down the avenue."

In Ward B-1, we did considerable grousing about the food, like soldiers in the army. The food at Bellevue is skimpy, but it will keep body and soul together, and the way one of the young doctors explained it to me, the primary idea at the hospital is to mend the body and patch it up, and that is more a question of medicine and instruments and apparatus than it is of food. He meant that Bellevue would rather economize on the food and spend more of its narrow budget on medicine and equipment, and when we patients chewed the matter over (in lieu of something better to chew), we tended to agree with him.

One thing there always seemed to be plenty of, though, was eggs. Breakfast for us bed patients usually consisted of a small bowl of porridge, fairly thin; two eggs, usually hard-boiled; a slice or two of bread; and some coffee, kind of weak. The eggs were in comparative abundance for a good reason. Prisoners on penal farms are kept busy raising hens, among other things, and the eggs that derive from the prisoners' forced industry go to public institutions like Bellevue. We all used to squirrel away a few eggs. Each patient, in the narrow space between his bed and the next fellow's, had a metal table with several shelves. For the time a man is in there, his worldly possessions are encompassed by the small space of those shelves: a towel, some soap, toilet articles, a book, maybe a letter or two—and, thanks to amiable thievery, a couple of eggs, against emergency hunger. The hospital doesn't hand out eggs to be hoarded; they are acquired by benign larceny, which is prevalent in Bellevue. At least, it was in Ward B-1.

When the food comes up to the ward, on rolling steam tables, from the kitchens, the walking patients have to help hand it out, because the nurses have too much else to do. Well, shortly after breakfast was over, Olsen (or some other walking patient) would come strolling along, an uncommon look of innocence on his face. He'd saunter up to the bedside, engage in the most immaculate of small talk. Then, out of the corner of his mouth, in the manner of a prisoner talking to a fellow convict in a jail yard, he'd say, "Could you use an egg, Mac?"

"Certainly could, pal," I'd say, also corner-of-the-mouth. And in a jiffy Olsen would dexterously slip a couple of hard-boiled eggs into the folds of my towel, on the shelf of my bedside table. A minute or two later, I'd see him doing the same thing for Dooley, across the way. Olsen could hide more eggs more effectively than Fred Keating, the magician. It was a good feeling, I learned soon, to have a few eggs in reserve in Ward B-1.

Lucky lads, like myself, sometimes got help on the food problem from the outside. There was the matter of the steak. After a few weeks of Bellevue fare, a man actually dreams of steak, which is one item he doesn't get there. One day, when a friend of mine came to visit, I mentioned the steak mirages we all had. My friend keeps a tavern in the Forties, where I had assailed many a sirloin. "Don't eat any supper tomorrow," he said. "I'm coming in."

About six o'clock the next afternoon, I looked down the ward, as I had been doing every minute or two since five o'clock, and I saw my friend heading toward me in a great rush. He was burdened heavily with something ponderously wrapped in towels and napkins. He practically ran up to the bedside, and sweat was glistening on his face and his eyes were popping. He put his burden on the bed, hastily unwrapped it, and there was a steaming steak as big as a banjo, with onions and French fries beautifully girdling it. "Wade into this!" he said, and he whisked a sharp knife and fork out of his pocket, where he had had them, wrapped in a napkin. The smell of steak got into the air, and right away practically everybody in the ward was staring at my bed. "Man alive!" I said. "This is too much for me."

It really was, so I hailed Princeton 1911 and Olsen to join me in the steak, and got the nurse to cut off a couple of chunks and take them over to the encased Dooley. It was marvellous eating, we all agreed. "How in the world did you get that steak here piping hot and everything?" I asked my friend as I settled back luxuriously on the pillow.

He laughed. "Well, I guess I might get in bad if anyone found out," he said. "And maybe a cop would get the sack. But you got to maneuver things in this town; you got to get guys to rally around when somebody's in a jam."

"Explain yourself," I said to him. "I don't know what you're talking about."

He grinned at the sight of Princeton 1911, Olsen, Dooley, and myself so well fed, and said, "There's a motorcycle cop comes into the store [the saloon is always "the store" with my friend] for a little slug now and then. Especially on cold days, when it is bitter on one of those motorcycles. He has one slug and lets it go at that. Good cop, not a scrounger. Well, when you told me a steak would come in handy, I wondered at first how the hell I could get it all those twenty blocks and more and still have it hot for you. Then it came to me. I explained the situation to the motorcycle cop, and he said, 'This is official business on behalf of a bona fide taxpayer of the City of New York.' That's what he said. He told me have the steak ready at quarter of six on the dot. And at twenty to six he came and asked where's the steak? It was ready, and the cop said for me to wrap it up well and come on. He had a taxi waiting right outside the door, and what does he do, after I get into the cab with the steak, but jump on his motorcycle and speed off ahead of the cab. In two seconds, we were roaring down the street, with the siren howling. We went through lights fifty miles an hour, like nobody's business, and I bet it didn't take us four minutes to

get down here. Regular motorcycle escort. The cop beat it as
soon as the cab got to the gate. He stopped a minute and told
me not to say anything about what he did. The Commissioner
might not approve, he said, but what the hell! How was the
steak, anyway?"

"It was goddam good," I said.

"I'll say it was goddam good," said Princeton 1911.

"Me, too," Dooley hollered over.

"You can say that again," said Olsen.

One bird of passage blew into Ward B-1. He came in during
the night, while we were all asleep, and he was put in Olsen's bed
because this was the time when Olsen was AWOL. "Bird" is
not the right word for him. The poor man looked just like a
marmoset, his face was so small and he was so frail. He had the
same kind of darting, shoe-button eyes as a marmoset, and he
also had the same evident desire to ingratiate himself.

When we looked at this newcomer next morning, the first
thing we saw was a pip of a shiner. His right eye was in a setting
of black and purple and magenta, which made the eye itself
look all the more bright. His right forearm was in a splint.
Ordinarily, injured men didn't get into B-1, but this fellow was
only an overnight guest, so to speak, and Olsen's bed happened
to be empty.

Alfred the Armenian halted at his bed and asked him what
was the matter. "Something must have happened to me," the
little man said. "I got a kind of a black eye and what they call
a fractured noola." One half of this announcement—the black-
eye part—was an enormously unnecessary statement, and the
other half was mystifying. It was some time before we figured
it out. The marmoset man had evidently peeked at the description
of his injuries that the doctors had written down on his record,
and he had got a little balled up in his anatomical terms. He had
a fracture of the ulna, and the word must have looked to him,
through his black eye, like "nula," which he pronounced "noola."

They sent him out after lunch, and we all promptly forgot about
him, except to ask, once in a while during an idle moment, "I
wonder whatever became of the noola man?"

The evening and early morning were the best times in Ward
B-1. The food in Bellevue is scanty, as I said, so the snack that
came around on a rolling table at eight-fifteen at night was a big
event. Before Olsen went to the night game and never came back,
he was the one who pushed the table around. The nurses do
not have time for such chores, and so walking patients, like
Olsen, take over. About eight o'clock, nearly three hours after
dinner, we would begin thinking, and often talking, about the
snack.

"I hope they have cocoa tonight," Dooley would say.

"I think they *will* have cocoa," Milton, the Brooklyn cab-
driver, might reply. "They had grapefruit juice now two nights
hand-running. I think it will be cocoa."

The snack that Olsen wheeled around usually consisted of
a couple of slices of bread and something to drink—sometimes
it was grapefruit juice, occasionally plain milk, if some was left
over from dinner, and, on big nights, cocoa. I would watch Olsen
make his way along the ward to my bed, and all the while my
appetite would grow. Finally, the table would be in front of
my bed, and Olsen would say, "Cocoa, Mac, or what?"

"Cocoa," I would say.

"How about you, Mr. Darton?" Olsen would ask the Princeton 1911 man, in the bed on my right.

"Don't mind if I do," the Princeton man would say. And
in a minute we would all be having our slice of bread and our
cocoa, and talking bed to bed. "What a bunch of chumps up
there at the Racquet Club," the Princeton man said to me one
night. "They think they're living high. Chumps. That's what
they are, eh, Mac?"

"What could be better than this?" I said.

"Isn't that river pretty?" he asked, waving a chunk of bread at the arched window. "Look at all those lights." A tug was coming down in the dark, and strung above her were red and green lights, betokening to oncoming vessels what kind of tow she had behind her.

"Real handsome little river," I said. The cocoa was good, and we were all happy for a while.

Heart cases usually stay in the hospital for from six to eight weeks. When my day to go home came around, I found I was to go out as I had come in—on a stretcher. But the stretcher was now a precaution, rather than a necessity. The nurse brought my clothes, to be taken, but not worn, home. Right away, I noticed that they were un-wrinkled, and did not have that shrunken look that Olsen's had had. "How come my clothes aren't all rumpled up like Olsen's?" I asked her.

"I guess the attendant noticed that you were brought in from a good hotel, and figured he wouldn't bother to delouse them," she said.

"Caste system?" I asked. "Is that creeping in here?"

"No," the nurse said. "The man was merely saving wear and tear on the delousing machine, that's all."

My wife took charge of getting my clothes home, and I got onto the stretcher myself. On the way out, naturally, I was wheeled along between the rows of beds. We B-1 veterans had been talking for a couple of days about my going home. As well as we had known each other, we hadn't said anything about looking each other up sometimes on the outside. All of us were grown-up enough to know that such promises are never kept. Dooley hollered goodbye and good luck from his bed, and so did the others, as the stretcher went by. Bellevue fellows are always glad when somebody—anybody—has won out over whatever was the matter with him, and, thanks to what had been done for me (I had done nothing for myself except be obedient), I had won out. While they were hollering goodbye, I knew they were thinking about the day they'd go home, too. Even

Dooley, who could look forward only to going back to the Bowery, had told me that he had a couple of pals down there he'd like to say hello to once again.

Suggestions for Study

THE BOOK John McNulty loved most, according to James Thurber, was H. L. Mencken's *The American Language*. The dialogue of this essay bears out that view: the rhythms and special marks of New York speech, for which McNulty had a precise ear, are accurately reproduced and almost unencumbered with explanatory adverbs. McNulty lets his New Yorkers speak for themselves; the succession of "he said," "I asked," "he replied," is scarcely varied by elaboration of any kind. (Hemingway does this too.) Find the exceptions and account for them.

The essay is worked out chiefly at two levels of language. For himself, or at least for the "self" speaking here, McNulty ordinarily employs a rather flat manner, brightened by ironically urbane expressions (". . . where I had assailed many a sirloin"), to throw into relief the colloquialisms of other speakers. But the regular appearance of such terms as "some little passing jiggeroo of the system," "that smart Louis," or "a pip of a shiner," enlarge and complete "Mac's" personality. Some sentences decorously combine these levels: "He seemed to be a fellow of a nosy turn of mind, as, I would say, befits a fellow in a scientific field." Details of another sort contribute, directly or indirectly, to the projection of the narrator's character: "Branca won it," for instance; or the way Olsen addresses Princeton 1911.

A less honest writer might have yielded to a tired but tempting cliché potential in the situation: the rendering of Ward B-1 as a capsule version, or cross-section, of humanity (on the pattern of movies like *Lifeboat*, or *Twelve Angry Men*). The description of Mattie is one sign of McNulty's concern for the facts; can you find others? To be sure, escorted steaks aren't often encountered by hospital patients; but for the most part, McNulty confines himself to the day-to-day minutiae of ward life: faded bathrobes, "the two-o'clock show," the death of a patient.

McNulty deliberately sandwiches the account of the gaunt man's death between a description of Bellevue bathrobes and Olsen's departure for the ball game. Why does he place the episode just here in the essay? Why is there no other reference to death? Are the little vignettes making up the account of "Bellevue Days" arranged in any meaningful order? Or does a random succession itself reflect a principle of selective structure?

The musings, early in the piece, on Bellevue bathrobes as "great levellers," and the reference to "a kind of serenity" characteristic of life in the hospital, ought not to be given disproportionate weight by a reader concerned with identifying the theme of the essay. Any attempt to read the piece as a solemn equalitarian tract should be discouraged by the conversation about delousing machines. Still, the essay makes a serious and important point: it is the same point made by most of the novels of E. M. Forster, and epitomized by the epigraph to *Howard's End:* "Only connect——"

The Little Water Ceremony

EDMUND WILSON (1895–)

THE LITTLE Water Company is the most important of the Iroquois medicine societies: the most sacred and the most secret and the one that has been most rigorously cultivated. The mem-

THE LITTLE WATER CEREMONY is reprinted from *Apologies to the Iroquois* by Edmund Wilson, published in the U.S.A. by Farrar, Straus and Cudahy, and in Great Britain and the Commonwealth by W. H. Allen & Co. Ltd., London. Copyright © 1959 Edmund Wilson. Reprinted by permission of the author.

bers of this society are the guardians of a miraculous medicine which has the power to revive the dying, and they must sing to it three or four times a year in order to keep up its strength —a ceremony which, like the Dark Dance described above,[1] must always be performed in the dark. The members of this society are either people who have been cured by the medicine or people who have had a dream involving some part of the ceremony. They are likely to be men of high standing, and they ought, one would think, to have good voices. There is a tradition that they are able, without oral communication, to fix upon the dates for the ceremony, and they are supposed to need no rehearsals. They may not sing or hum the songs except when performing the ceremony. Non-members are rarely admitted to the room in which this takes place, but if the members approve, they may listen in an adjoining room or outside the house. Many Indians have never heard this ceremony. I was told by an old man at Tonawanda that, though his brother had been head of the society, he had never been allowed to attend and had never been able even to get his brother to "tell him what it was all about." In his case, it is probable that the reason for this was his having become a Christian.

I was fortunate enough, however, to be given an opportunity of hearing this rite in the Tonawanda Seneca reservation—again through the kindness and in the company of Fenton—and we were even invited to sit with the singers. As in the case of the Dark Dance, the Little Water Ceremony consists mainly of an elaborate series of song sequences, and since these, as with the Dark Dance, are based on a legend, I must begin by telling the story.

The theme of the Little Water legend is the familiar one of death and resurrection. There was once a young hunter—a chief —who was greatly respected by the animals on account of the

---

[1] *Editors' note:* Wilson gives an account of the "Dark Dance" in an earlier chapter of his book.

kindness he showed them. He never killed a deer that was swimming or a doe that had a fawn, or an animal that he took un-
awares or that was tired from long pursuit. For the predatory
birds and animals, he would always first kill a deer and skin
it and cut it open and cry, "Hear, all you meat-eaters. This is
for you." He would always leave some honey for the bears and
some corn in the fields for the crows. The tripes of the game he
killed he threw into the lakes and streams for the fish and the
water animals. One day, when cut off from his party, he was
captured and scalped by the Cherokees. When they had gone,
the Wolf smelled blood, and he came up and licked the bloody
head. But when he recognized the Good Hunter, he howled for
the rest of the animals, who all came and gathered around and
mourned for their lost friend. The Bear felt the body with his
paws and on the chest found a spot that was warm. The birds
had come, too, and they all held a council, while the Bear kept
him warm in his arms, as to how they could bring the young
hunter to life. The only dissenting voice was that of the Turkey
Buzzard, who said, "Let's wait till he gets ripe and eat him." And
they compounded a powerful medicine, to which each one contributed a "life-spark"—in some versions a bit of the brain, in
others a bit of the heart. But the mixture of all these ingredients
made an essence so concentrated that it could all be contained
in an acorn shell, and it is called for this reason the Little Water.

Now the Owl said, "A live man must have a scalp," and who
was to go for the scalp? In certain of the tellings of the story, a
long discussion takes place. One animal after another is decided
unfit. The quadrupeds will never do: what is needed is a clever
bird. The Dew Eagle is sometimes chosen. He is the ranking bird
of the Iroquois, who carries a pool of dew on his back and, when
rain falls, can spill it as mist. One variant makes it the Humming-
bird, who moves quickly and is almost invisible. But it is more
likely to be the Giant Crow (Gáh-ga-go-wa), the messenger for
all the birds, who plays a prominent role in the ceremony. He
flies to the Cherokee village, and there he sees the good hunter's

scalp, which has been stretched on a hoop and hung up to dry in the smoke that comes out of the smoke-hole. He swoops down and snatches it. The Cherokees see him and shoot their arrows at him, but the Crow flies so high that they cannot reach him.

When he has brought the scalp back to the council, they find it is too much dried out to be worn by a living man. The Great Crow has to vomit on it and the Dew Eagle sprinkle on it some drops of his dew before it is supple and moist enough to be made to grow back on the hunter's head. He has already been given the medicine, and he feels himself coming to life. As he lies with his eyes still closed, he realizes that he is now able to understand the language of the animals and birds. They are singing a wonderful song, and he listens to it and finds later on that he is able to remember every word. They tell him to form a company and to sing it when their help is needed. He asks how they make the medicine, and they say that they cannot tell him because he is not a virgin. But someone will be given the secret, and they will notify this person by singing their song. The Bear helps the youth to his feet, and when he opens his eyes, there is nobody there: only a circle of tracks. It is dawn. He goes back to his people.

We met the Little Water singers at about ten o'clock on the night of June 6, 1959. The hours of singing must coincide with the duration of the events of the story, so one has to sit up all night. The ceremony took place in an ample kitchen. No one may smoke cigarettes in the room, and no one may be present who has been drinking liquor; no menstruating woman may enter the house. Such impurities would spoil the medicine. It is possible for women to be "bundle-holders"—that is, guardians of the sacred powder, but on this occasion none was present. The lady of the house sometimes entered the kitchen, before the proceedings began, to attend to operations on the stove, but she always withdrew and, when the ceremony started—with doors closed and lights extinguished—she sat, with her young son and another woman (entertained, in this case, by no television), in a lighted adjacent room. On the other hand, the doors were not locked, with a sentinel posted outside, as, according to Arthur C. Parker, had formerly been the custom.[2]

The Senecas of Tonawanda are, as a group, perhaps the most self-confident and the proudest in the whole Iroquois world. Their dwellings range from pretty modern cottages to log-cabins with plastered cracks, and both kinds seem quite sound and well-kept. The man who presides at the Little Water ceremony—whose English name is Corbett Sundown—is a chief whose hereditary title is So-gant-dzo-wa, He Has a Large Forehead, and one of the dominating personalities at Tonawanda. He struck me as being more like the kind of Indian with whom the first settlers dealt than anyone else I had met: good-looking with trenchant features, speaking English with a strong accent, giving an impression of formidable strength in reserve. Chief Sundown likes to tell funny stories, and his laughter is somewhat harsh. (The Indians are extremely humorous, but as a rule they do not smile or laugh until one of their deadpan jokes makes *you* laugh, when the tone of the conversation may become quite jovial.) Corbett Sundown is both a foreman in a gypsum plant and a guardian of ancient tradition. In Tonawanda, the fires of nationalism do not seem to burn so fiercely as they do on certain other of the reservations; but, though we found Sundown rather noncommittal, it was evident that he was fully informed about everything that was going on in Iroquoia. He had sent a message to Fenton inviting him to attend the ceremony, but I had to be approved and invited before Fenton could bring me in, so we first went to his house to see him. My previous requests to be allowed to hear the ceremony had not met with any success, and he now told me that they did not want people who came simply out of curiosity, and that especially they did not want journalists who knew nothing about Indian life and who printed

[2] *Editors' note:* Arthur C. Parker (1881–1955), American archeologist and student of Senecan history and folklore.

preposterous stories. There was a television show going on in
the room next to that in which we sat, and the head of a young
boy presently peered in at the door to see who the visitors were,
then at once disappeared again. "That's *his* culture," said Corbett
Sundown. "He grew up with it." I wondered what the result
would be of growing up, in such an *echt* Indian household as
Sundown's apparently was, on a diet of white rubbish. It was
evident that TV was like the air he breathed. First he watched
on his back from the bed, then he listened on his face on a rug.
He left the table to go back to it while we were still eating supper.
For of course we were not allowed to leave without sharing the
Sundowns' supper—the only meal I had with the Indians that
included a distinctively Indian dish (except for succotash, which
we borrowed from them): something called Indian "cornbread,"
which, however, does not resemble our bread and which I took
at first for some sort of meatloaf. It is gray and has kidney beans
embedded in it; they fry it in thick slices.

In the kitchen of the other house where the ceremony was
to be performed, the conversation was mostly in Seneca, with
an occasional exchange in English with us. I noticed that the
time was always given in English: "eleven o'clock," etc. There
was a good deal of kidding and joking, with Corbett Sundown,
as it were, sparking off the laughs. Their voices are low and
their speech is rapid compared to those of other upstate New
Yorkers. They are said to complain of our loudness. Whenever
the door was opened, a swarm of mosquitoes came in, and these
provoked a good deal of mirth. When I was slapping my ankles
and the top of my head, a round-faced bespectacled chief remarked with a quiet grin, "If you don't bother them, they'll
leave you alone." Fenton told me that the mosquitoes at Tonawanda had always been famous for ferocity. One of the Senecas
had said that the Tonawanda mosquitoes were tri-motored. There
was a legend about their origin. There had at first been a single
huge mosquito. One day she chased a man, who ran for his life
and then dodged behind a tree. The proboscis of the monster

was thrust into the tree, and, swollen with blood, she exploded. From the myriad drops of her blood sprang the Tonawanda breed of mosquitoes, smaller but equally fierce. This set off a man from Canada—the only Indian present who wore a tie—to give us another version, in which the mosquito was shot with an arrow, and, evidently an experienced storyteller, he went on to other tales. An Indian had met a bear, and getting a tree between him and it, had seized the front paws of the bear on either side of the tree. But then he could do nothing more: he had to stand there holding the bear. At length his brother came by with another man, and he called out for them to help him. "Have you had your breakfast yet?" asked the brother of his companion. The companion answered yes. "Then *you* help him: I haven't had mine." —In Canada, a Member of Parliament was eating at a lunch-counter beside an Indian. "I wish I had your appetite," said the Member of Parliament. "I never have any appetite." "Take it," said the Indian. "Why don't you take it?" "What do you mean?" said the Member of Parliament. "You've taken my land, you've taken my freedom, you've taken my women," said the Indian. "You might as well take my appetite too."

The materials for the ceremony and the feast were brought in. The soup was in a copper washboiler; the pork for it was set on the stove. There were two or three baskets of fresh strawberries and some cans of frozen ones. Chief Sundown removed the stems of the former, and poured them all into two white enamelled pails, already partly filled with water, so that they floated in a kind of syrup. The rattles were carried in a big white bag. They are pale yellow polished gourds—some very large, some small—with dried cherrystones inside. Three reed flutes were laid on the table. The medicine, in two modern boxes, one of them a tin tea-caddy, was set on the same table and covered with a sheet of white muslin. This muslin is a part of the "quantity of goods of the value of $10,000" provided for in the Pickering Treaty of 1794, which the Iroquois still collect from the federal government. Everybody, including ourselves, brought in a small package of Indian tobacco, which, as one entered, was handed to Sundown. This tobacco is mixed in a single receptacle, and little piles of it—set down counterclockwise—are carefully placed on the table, two rows of four each, which represent the eight clans of the Senecas, to show that the medicine has been given for all. The singers sat on two long benches against two walls of the kitchen that met at a right angle. There were only ten Indians present (the number of the singers is not fixed). In the kitchen were a large wood stove, a washing machine and a white modern sink. On a shelf stood a big box of Corn Flakes.

At a quarter past eleven, the preliminaries to the ceremony began. Chief Sundown arose and, closing his eyes, with his hands held down and clasped, made a twenty-minute speech in Seneca —with many repetitions, I was told, announcing what they were going to do. Two friends from afar had come to help them. Then the food and the musical instruments were all placed on the stove or beside it, to be blessed to the use of the ceremony; the piles of tobacco were picked up from the table in the same order in which they had been laid; and Chief Sundown, taking off one of the stove-lids, began dropping tobacco in pinches into the red-burning fire below, invoking, as he did so, the Divinity and His deputies, the Sun, Moon, Stars, Winds, etc.:

> "Now I give you incense,
> You, the Great Darkness!
> You, our great-grand-parents, here tonight—
> We offer you incense!
> We assemble at certain times in the year
> That this may be done.
>   (We trust that all believe in this medicine,
>   For all are invited to partake of this medicine.) . . .
>   Now we offer you this incense!
> Some have had ill luck
> Endeavouring to give a human being.[3]
> We hope you will take hold

[3] In childbearing.

And help your grandchildren,
Nor be discouraged in us!
  Now we act as we offer you incense!
You love it the most of all offerings!
With it you will hear us better
And not tire of our talking,
But love us with all power
Beyond all treasures
Or spreading your words through the air!
  All men travelling under the great heavens,
You have invited your grandchildren and all nations!
  O you that make the noise,
You the great Thunderer!
Your grandchildren wish to thank you!
All your grandchildren have asked me
To offer this incense upon the mountain to you! . . .
  O you the Manager of All Things!
We ask you to help us,
To help us make this medicine strong!
You are the Creator,
The Most High,
The Best Friend of men!
We ask you to help us!
We implore your favor!
  I have spoken."

Then the rest of the tobacco was put into pipes, and they smoked for a few minutes in silence. Then the strawberry pails were passed in a ritualistic order, the guests being served last. This was done after each intermission, just before the new sequence was begun. Everyone drinks from a ladle; and they jokingly called out a word—"Nyon, nyon" (pronounced as in French *bon*)—which I did not understand but which reminded me of the traditional "*Gor'ko, gor'ko!*" that guests cry at Russian wedding parties. This, it seems, is the word for "You're welcome." The point is that—somewhat in the fashion that the English have abbreviated, "Thank you," to " 'Kyou"—the Senecas have averted it altogether by saying "You're welcome" first. The preliminary cries of this word eliminate the monotonous interchange. I had noticed that I was the only person present who said "Thank you" when I was offered the syrup.

Now the door to the next room was closed, the switch in the wall was turned off, and the ceremony proper began. The room with its Corn Flakes had vanished: you were at once in a different world. The single beat of a rattle is heard in the sudden blackness like the striking of a gigantic match, and it is answered by other such flashes that make rippings of sound as startling as a large-scale electric spark. Then the first of the two chief singers cries *"Wee yoh!"* and the second *"Yoh wee!"*, and the first of them now sets the rhythm for the rattles, which is picked up by the rest of the company. In this section the tempo is uniform, and it reminds one of the rapid jogging that is heard by the passenger on an express train. The rhythm is kept up, without raggedness or flagging, for a little less than an hour. Arthur Parker says that the pace is 150 a minute; but I do not know whether this applies to the section I am now describing or to the even faster passages in the later ones. The songs themselves are in slower time. Their structure has something in common with that of old English and Scottish ballads, as well as their nonsense refrains —like the English, "Benorio, benory"—and the wistfulness of their accent, as of human beings alone with nature, singing in unpeopled spaces. The first singer gives the couplet, and this is repeated by the second; then all take it up in a powerful chorus. A man and a woman are searching for the magical Little Water that has brought the Good Hunter to life but the receipt for compounding which, because he was not a virgin, the animals could not teach him. Now their song has been heard, and the man and the woman are obeying its summons to search. The first line of every couplet always applies to the woman—since the woman, among the Iroquois, is always given first place—and the second line to the man:

> "She went to the village.
> He went to the village."

—to the fields, to the little spring, to the edge of the wood, etc. In the climactic final couplet, they go to the top of a hill, and there they are left "standing under the clouds."

In the second section, the rhythms of the rattles are different. While the first and second singers are introducing the couplets, the rattles are going so fast that they seem to weave a kind of veil or screen—a scratching almost visible on the darkness—that hangs before the lyric voices; but when the chorus takes up the theme, this changes to a slow heavy beat that has something of the pound of a march. The shift is extremely effective. When it occurs, this accompaniment of the rattles—contrary to our convention—does not quite coincide with the song and the chorus but always overlaps a little. The big shimmer of the solo begins before the pound of the chorus has ended: in a moment, you are given notice, a fresh song will be springing up; and in the same way the lusty thump will commence before the song has quite finished. In this section, the animals assemble: "The She-Owl," and then "the He-Owl," "came bringing tobacco and joined the song." And presently these creatures begin to speak, as they are mentioned pair by pair in the couplets. They are mimicked by one or more singers—who have had their parts assigned them —as the arrival of each is announced. The effect of this is startling and eerie. The Gáhgagowa caws—the first half of his name is evidently onomatopoetic; the Bear and the Panther roar; the Owl has a soft four-note hoot: "Wu-wu, Wu-wu." There are many archaic words in the ritual that nobody now understands. Besides the Giant Crow, the Great Eagle, the Dew Eagle, the Great Phoebe, the Great Woodpecker and a bird which, after a moment's thought, had been identified for us by Sundown as the Kingbird, there are birds which can no longer be identified, and when one of these birds was mentioned, the cackle of a hen who has just laid an egg—followed by quiet laughter—was heard from the prehistoric darkness. A climax of animation occurs toward the end of this section. The She- and He-Wolves arrive. They are heralded as running along the rim of the hills, and afterwards through the meadows. They do not howl; since they are running, they bark like dogs. A queer kind of excitement is created here. The animals are supposed to be present, and I learn from Arthur Parker that the adepts are believed to see them. He hints at further mysteries which he is not allowed to reveal; and from reading Fenton's unpublished notes on the Little Water Ceremony, I get the impression that the singers are supposed to *become* the animals. They are forbidden to keep time with their feet—as they do in all the other ceremonies— since the quadrupeds go on pads and the tread of the birds is soundless. The men who serve the syrup are called Eagles, and the man who presides is the Giant Crow. The Wolf has also some special role. I did not see any animals nor did the medicine become visibly luminous, as it was formerly supposed to do when its power was renewed by the singing. I could not see that the boxes were even opened. Nor was I conscious of another phenomenon that Chief Sundown had told me to listen for. "You'll hear a woman's voice," he had said, "and there's no woman in the room." I have learned that the best first singers—who always sing the feminine lines—have a practice of outdoing the chorus by pitching each song in a sequence a little higher than the one before. If this singer starts the sequence off so high that it is sure at a later stage to get out of the range of the others, he is stopped, and they have to begin again—the worst *gaffe* that can be committed except for a singer's forgetting the words. (I noticed, in an intermission, that the first singer, who was younger than the others, was studying his lines in a notebook.)

It was delightful to go out in these intermissions. One was here in the cool June night of the green Tonawanda woodland. There was a fragrance of something blooming. The back lawn, where the grass had been cut, was revealed by a bulb with a reflector behind it that directed the light from the top of the house. The peelings of asbestos shingling, in imitation of brick, that were hanging away from this wall contrasted with the beauty of the landscape and the music that had been liberated inside the house. The Indians talked softly and smoked a little. The hoot of a real owl was heard; a mudhen croaked from nearby Salt Creek; a nighthawk flew away through the lighted air to the forest that made the background.

The third section is the climax of the symphony. Now the medicine at last is found. The questers have discovered that the marvellous song emanates from the top of a mountain—the mountain, I suppose, that the man and the woman have ascended at the end of the first sequence. But it ought to be explained that this couple do not appear in all versions of the ceremony, which differs somewhat in the different reservations. There is a version in which it is simply a man; and the account I shall give here of the search is taken from a telling of the *legend*—not always consistent with the songs—in which the searchers are two young men. These questers set out in the dark, and they are to endure a whole set of ordeals, to surmount a whole series of obstacles. At the start they are trapped in a "windfall," a place where the trees have been blown down, and they must break their way out of this. They feel that there are presences about them, that the animals are guiding them to the source of the song. Next they must plod through a swamp. Then they have to cross a ravine; then they hear the roaring of a cataract and are confronted with another ravine through which a swift river runs. One of the young men is "almost afraid"; but they go down and swim across it, though the waters are terribly cold. A mountain now rises before them, so steep that they think they can never climb it. The less hardy of the searchers proposes a rest, but the other says they have to go on, and when he has spoken, they hear a voice that sings "Follow me, follow me!" and a light comes flying over them. This is the Whippoorwill, whose song is the "flourish of the flute" mentioned to me by Nicodemus Bailey. Each of the sequences is opened and closed by this cry, but it is only in this third part, I think, that the flute intervenes in the narrative. It plays a role like the bird in *Siegfried* that will lead the hero to his lost mother. With effort, the young men scale the mountain, and at the top they find a great stalk of corn growing out of the barren rock, and from this stalk comes the song that has drawn them. They are told by the winged light to burn a tobacco offering and then to cut the root of the corn. When they do so, it bleeds human blood, but immediately the wound heals. They are now told by the voices of the animals how to collect the ingredients of the medicine, how to mix it and how to apply it.

This section is more complicated than the others, and it is said to be difficult to sing. In each of the first two sequences, the songs all follow a pattern; but in the third, they begin on unexpected notes and follow unfamiliar courses. This is magic, a force beyond nature is tearing itself free. There is a passage of reiteration that entirely departs from the ballad stanzas and that sounds like some sort of litany. A great structure is raised by the rattles that is neither the big shimmer, the express train nor the grand triumphal march. And a paean is let loose: it fills the room with its volume. One finds oneself surrounded, almost stupefied, as if the space between the four walls had become one of the tubes of a pipe organ and as if one were sitting inside it, almost drowned in a sustained diapason. How strange when the lights are turned on—strange, apparently, for the singers, too, who sit blinking and dazed at first, having to bring themselves up short in this kitchen, in this new electric-lighted world—to find oneself there in the room with these ten men who work in the daytime in the gypsum mines and plants of the neighbouring town of Akron, dressed in their unceremonious clothes: an assortment of physical types, some handsome, some not so handsome, some young and some old, some fat and some lean, some sallow, one almost black, some with spectacles, some with their teeth gone, who have just given body in the darkness to a creation which absorbed and transcended them all. A car had driven up to the house while the singing was going on; its headlights had glared toward the window. I saw the profile against it of a man turning round to look; but the singing was not interrupted, and the driver, when he heard it, withdrew.

This sequence, through which is expressed the whole mystery

and virtue of the Little Water, seems hard for even the well-informed outsider to follow, though the first two parts, apparently, for a student of Seneca, are plain enough sailing. The reports on it are rather scrappy and mutually inconsistent. Neither Parker nor Jesse Cornplanter, who has also touched on the Little Water, throws any light at all on its central episode. My description of this part of the quest is based upon the version of the legend given by Arthur Parker. In our earlier conversation with Chief Sundown, William Fenton had quoted songs from the first two sections, but said he could not remember the third. Sundown did nothing to help him out: he said simply, "Everything has a meaning. I'm not very good on songs." We questioned the second singer in the intermission that followed this section. He brought out some of the keywords in Seneca but his command of English was limited. "He goes to the swamp . . . He goes to the swamp . . ." he made an attempt to explain. "He [I do not know who this was] told us what everything meant." I learn from another source that a swamp is the place in which the searchers find saxifrage, the one plant included in the medicine. I do not know whether the saxifrage is a variant on the singing stalk of corn.

The singers had worked hard over this complicated section. One man declared that he was soaked with sweat. I should think they must all have been. But the next part is relatively relaxing. The music is the same as in the second sequence. The animals are thanked pair by pair, and they make their appropriate acknowledgements. The mood is one of calm jubilation.

This usually ends the ceremony, but on this occasion they sang a fifth sequence, which is used in the treatment of patients. In the old days the medicine powder was carried along in warfare to revivify the badly wounded. Today it is only applied in cases of accident or illness that are regarded as more or less desperate. At the bedside, three pinches of the powder are dropped in a cup of water so as to make the points of a triangle. (The water must have been dipped from the stream in the direction in which it is running.) If the powder sinks to the bottom, the patient must be given up; if the water is clouded, the results are doubtful; if it floats, the chances are good. The treatment goes on four days. The medicine man takes some of the water in his mouth and sprays it on the part afflicted, and the medicine songs are sung. Then the patient is protected by a white screen, and given nothing but white food to eat: white of chicken and white of egg—if possible, from a white fowl. I was told that a doctor who for many years had been attending a Seneca community would say, when he heard of an accident, "They won't call me in for four days, and by that time his leg will be all swollen and purple." After the doctor had set the leg, the Indians would claim that the medicine had healed it. The fifth sequence we heard was the ritual intended for broken bones, and, instead of being enlivened by animal cries, it was lacerated by shrieks and groans supposed to be coming from the patient.

We left—being extremely sleepy—without taking part in the final feast, at which the members, cawing like crows, eat the stew in the manner indicated by the verb which has already been mentioned in connection with the ceremony of the Dark Dance.[4]

But there is more to the Little Water Ceremony than the effort to renew the medicine. To have heard it is to understand its importance as a builder of morale, and why it has to be performed by a small group of men in a darkened room. The members of this medicine society really constitute a sort of elite, and they are making an affirmation of the will of the Iroquois people, of their vitality, their force to persist. These adepts have mastered the principle of life, they can summon it by the ceremony itself. Through this they surpass themselves, they prove to themselves their power. Ten men in a darkened kitchen, with an audience of four or five of whom the celebrants are hardly aware, make a core from which radiates conviction, of which the stoutness may sustain their fellows.

I knew that the Little Water—with its theme of near-death and resuscitation—was supposed to end just at daybreak. "It is

[4] *Editors' note:* That is, "they ate, old style, with their fingers."

brightening. Dawn is approaching. The morning star is already up," says one version of the Good Hunter legend of the hour when the hunter goes home. And I had wondered how precisely they would time it. When the lights were turned on, it was half past four. I had certainly at one point observed, glancing out of the torrent of sound, that the windows were becoming less dim; but when I thanked Corbett Sundown, I wished him good-night. "Not goodnight, good morning," he said, and he wished us a safe journey home. To Fenton he said, "You can tell your wife that you were up all night with us." And when we went out of the house to our car, I found that it was indeed dawn. The birds were now tuning up, the sun was just topping the forest and the woodland of the roadside was already quite green in the first soft and misty daylight.

Suggestions for Study

"IN REPORTING," says Truman Capote, "one is occupied with literalness and surfaces, with implication without comment." How completely does that statement apply to this essay?

Reportage the piece may be, but Wilson wears his press card with a difference. He employs three distinct styles, each appropriate to the structural development of the essay and suited to three successively assumed "masks": teller of Indian legends, anthropologist in the field, dazed witness of magic. For the Little Water legend itself he chooses the simple language and rather naïve manner of folk-tale; in the next section, describing the setting, participants, and materials of the ceremony, he adopts a dry, objective style: all the "facts" are solemnly set before us. "It is gray and has kidney beans embedded in it; they fry it in thick slices." The doors used to be locked, but nowadays they are not locked. When this straight-faced manner extends to Indian jokes, the reader perceives that the "scientific" approach is being exploited in an ironic way.

The brief account of preliminaries draws into focus all that has

gone before: the austere language of prayer suitably follows the
innocence of the legend as well as the various taboos ensuring
purity, while the joking reiteration of relatively meaningless conversational forms helps to assign the everyday world of gypsum
factory, television, and Corn Flakes to its proper place.

Innocent simplicity and empirical objectivity give way in the
description of the ceremony proper to a highly imaginative style,
as dependent on metaphor as previous sections were barren of it.
But the process is gradual. The "earnest anthropologist" continues to make notes and reasoned comparisons (although the
pace of the rattles already bewilders him) in the first section,
which reminds him of a modern express train. But in the next
section, clarity begins to be obscured. Solo and chorus overlap;
the dominant metaphor significantly becomes "a kind of veil or
screen"; baffled impatience marks the mood of the observer ("I
did not see any animals . . . I could not see that the boxes were
even opened"). The final section quite defies his efforts at analysis, as the recourse to legend (distinct from the overpowering
ceremony) makes clear. Triumphant metaphor encloses and "almost drowns" the observer, who blinks in the electric light as
dazedly as the singers. Nor can they explain what has happened.

The passage is organized in many linguistic and structural ways.
To which senses does its language progressively appeal? What is
the function, in terms of structure and of effect upon the reader,
of the "intermission" between second and third sections? Why
the continued insistence on various kinds of hard work required
by the ceremony? And why is the fourth section so briefly described?

As a sociologist might say, the ceremony is "utilized" to renew
the medicine. Wilson explicitly calls it something better than
that: an affirmation (not merely a symbolic one) of "the will of
the Iroquois people." But there is more; the reference to "music
that had been liberated inside the house," together with similar
expressions, should suggest the significance of the ceremony at a
deeper level still.

Cagliari

D. H. LAWRENCE (1885–1930)

THERE IS A very little crowd waiting on the quay: mostly men with their hands in their pockets. But, thank Heaven, they have a certain aloofness and reserve. They are not like the tourist-parasites of these post-war days, who move to the attack with a terrifying cold vindictiveness the moment one emerges from any vehicle. And some of these men look really poor. There are no poor Italians any more: at least, loafers.

Strange the feeling round the harbour: as if everybody had gone away. Yet there are people about. It is "festa" however, Epiphany. But it is so different from Sicily: none of the suave Greek-Italian charms, none of the airs and graces, none of the glamour. Rather bare, rather stark, rather cold and yellow— somehow like Malta, without Malta's foreign liveliness. Thank Goodness no one wants to carry my knapsack. Thank Goodness no one has a fit at the sight of it. Thank Heaven no one takes any notice. They stand cold and aloof, and don't move.

We make our way through the Customs: then through the Dazio, the City Customs-house. Then we are free. We set off up a steep, new, broad road, with little trees on either side. But stone, arid, new, wide stone, yellowish under the cold sky—and abandoned-seeming. Though, of course, there are people about. The north wind blows bitingly.

We climb a broad flight of steps, always upwards, up the wide, precipitous, dreary boulevard with sprouts of trees. Looking for the Hotel, and dying with hunger.

At last we find it, the Scala di Ferro: through a courtyard with
green plants. And at last a little man with lank, black hair, like
an esquimo, comes smiling. He is one brand of Sardinian—esquimo
looking. There is no room with two beds: only single rooms.
And thus we are led off, if you please, to the "bagnio": the
bathing-establishment wing, on the dank ground floor. Cubicles
on either side a stone passage, and in every cubicle a dark stone
bath, and a little bed. We can have each a little bath cubicle.
If there's nothing else for it, there isn't: but it seems dank and
cold and horrid, underground. And one thinks of all the un-
savory "assignations" at these old bagnio places. True, at the
end of the passage are seated two carabinieri. But whether to
ensure respectability or not, Heaven knows. We are in the baths,
that's all.

The esquimo returns after five minutes, however. There *is* a
bedroom in the house. He is pleased, because he didn't like putting us into the bagnio. Where he found the bedroom I don't
know. But there it was, large, sombre, cold, and over the kitchen
fumes of a small inner court like a well. But perfectly clean and
all right. And the people seemed warm and good-natured, like
human beings. One has got so used to the non-human ancient-
souled Sicilians, who are suave and so completely callous.

After a really good meal we went out to see the town. It was
after three o'clock and everywhere was shut up like an English
Sunday. Cold, stony Cagliari: in summer you must be sizzling
hot, Cagliari, like a kiln. The men stood about in groups, but
without the intimate Italian watchfulness that never leaves a
passer-by alone.

Strange, stony Cagliari. We climbed up a street like a corkscrew stairway. And we saw announcements of a children's fancy-
dress ball. Cagliari is very steep. Half-way up there is a strange
place called the bastions, a large, level space like a drill-ground
with trees, curiously suspended over the town, and sending off
a long shoot like a wide viaduct, across above the corkscrew street

that comes climbing up. Above this bastion place the town still rises steeply to the Cathedral and the fort. What is so curious is that this terrace or bastion is so large, like some big recreation ground, that it is almost dreary, and one cannot understand its being suspended in mid-air. Down below is the little circle of the harbour. To the left a low, malarial-looking sea plain, with tufts of palm trees and Arab-looking houses. From this runs out the long spit of land towards that black-and-white watch-fort, the white road trailing forth. On the right, most curiously, a long strange spit of sand runs in a causeway far across the shallows of the bay, with the open sea on one hand, and vast, end-of-the-world lagoons on the other. There are peaky, dark mountains beyond this—just as across the vast bay are gloomy hills. It is a strange, strange landscape: as if here the world left off. The bay is vast in itself; and all these curious things happening at its head: this curious, craggy-studded town, like a great stud of house-covered rock jutting up out of the bay flats: around it on one side the weary, Arab-looking palm-desolated malarial plain, and on the other side great salt lagoons, dead beyond the sand-bar: these backed again by serried, clustered mountains, suddenly, while away beyond the plain, hills rise to sea again. Land and sea both seem to give out, exhausted, at the bay head: the world's end. And into this world's end starts up Cagliari, and on either side, sudden, serpent-crest hills.

But it still reminds me of Malta: lost between Europe and Africa and belonging to nowhere. Belonging to nowhere, never having belonged to anywhere. To Spain and the Arabs and the Phœnicians most. But as if it had never really had a fate. No fate. Left outside of time and history.

The spirit of the place is a strange thing. Our mechanical age tries to override it. But it does not succeed. In the end the strange, sinister spirit of the place, so diverse and adverse in differing places, will smash our mechanical oneness into smithereens, and all that we think the real thing will go off with a pop, and we shall be left staring.

On the great parapet above the Municipal Hall and above the corkscrew high-street a thick fringe of people is hanging, looking down. We go to look too: and behold, below there is the entrance to the ball. Yes, there is a china shepherdess in pale blue and powdered hair, crook, ribbons, Marie Antoinette satin daintiness and all, slowly and haughtily walking up the road, and gazing superbly round. She is not more than twelve years old, moreover. Two servants accompany her. She gazes supremely from right to left as she goes, mincingly, and I would give her the prize for haughtiness. She is perfect—a little too haughty for Watteau, but "marquise" to a T. The people watch in silence. There is no yelling and screaming and running. They watch in a suitable silence.

Comes a carriage with two fat bay horses slithering, almost swimming up the corkscrew high-street. That in itself is a "tour-de-force": for Cagliari doesn't have carriages. Imagine a street like a corkscrew stair, paved with slippery stone. And imagine two bay horses rowing their way up it: they did not walk a single stride. But they arrived. And there fluttered out three strangely exquisite children, two frail, white satin Pierrots and a white satin Pierrette. They were like fragile winter butterflies with black spots. They had a curious, indefinable remote elegance, something conventional and "fin-de-siècle." But not our century. The wonderful artificial delicacy of the eighteenth. The boys had big, perfect ruffs round their necks: and behind were slung old, cream-colored Spanish shawls, for warmth. They were frail as tobacco flowers, and with remote, cold elegance they fluttered by the carriage, from which emerged a large black-satin Mama. Fluttering their queer little butterfly feet on the pavement, hovering round the large Mama like three frail-tissued ghosts, they found their way past the solid, seated Carabinieri into the hall.

Arrived a primrose-brocade beau, with ruffles, and his hat under his arm: about twelve years old. Walking statelily, without a qualm up the steep twist of the street. Or perhaps so perfect in his self-consciousness that it became an elegant "aplomb" in him. He was a genuine eighteenth-century exquisite, rather stiffer than the French, maybe, but completely in the spirit. Curious, curious children! They had a certain stand-offish superbness, and not a single trace of misgiving. For them, their "noblesse" was indisputable. For the first time in my life I recognized the true cold superbness of the old "noblesse." They had not a single qualm about their own perfect representing of the higher order of being.

Followed another white satin "marquise," with a maid-servant. They are strong on the eighteenth century in Cagliari. Perhaps it is the last bright reality to them. The nineteenth hardly counts.

Curious the children in Cagliari. The poor seem thoroughly poor-bare-footed urchins, gay and wild in the narrow dark streets. But the more well-to-do children are so fine: so extraordinarily elegantly dressed. It quite strikes one of a heap. Not so much the grown-ups. The children. All the "chic," all the fashion, all the originality is expended on the children. And with a great deal of success. Better than Kensington Gardens very often. And they promenade with Papa and Mama with such alert assurance, having quite brought it off, their fashionable get-up. Who would have expected it?

Oh narrow, dark, and humid streets going up to the Cathedral, like crevices. I narrowly miss a huge pail of slop-water which comes crashing down from heaven. A small boy who was playing in the street, and whose miss is not quite a clean miss, looks up with that naïve, impersonal wonder with which children stare at a star or a lamp-lighter.

The Cathedral must have been a fine old pagan stone fortress once. Now it has come, as it were, through the mincing machine of the ages, and oozed out baroque and sausagey, a bit like the horrible baldachins in St. Peter's at Rome. None the less it is homely and hole-and-cornery, with a rather ragged high mass trailing across the pavement towards the high altar, since it is almost sunset, and Epiphany. It feels as if one might squat in a corner and play marbles and eat bread and cheese and be at home: a comfortable old-time churchey feel.

There is some striking filet lace on the various altar-cloths. And St. Joseph must be a prime saint. He has an altar and a verse of invocation praying for the dying.

"Oh, St. Joseph, true potential father of Our Lord." What can it profit a man, I wonder, to be the potential father of anybody! For the rest I am not Baedeker.

The top of Cagliari is the fortress: the old gate, the old ramparts, of honey-combed, fine yellowish sandstone. Up in a great sweep goes the rampart wall, Spanish and splendid, dizzy. And the road creeping down again at the foot, down the back of the hill. There lies the country: that dead plain with its bunch of palms and a fainting sea, and inland again, hills. Cagliari must be on a single, loose, lost bluff of rock.

From the terrace just below the fortress, above the town, not behind it, we stand and look at the sunset. It is all terrible, taking place beyond the knotted, serpent-crested hills that lie, bluey and velvety, beyond the waste lagoons. Dark, sultry, heavy crimson the west is, hanging sinisterly, with those gloomy blue cloud-bars and cloud-banks drawn across. All behind the blue-gloomy peaks stretches the curtain of sinister, smouldering red, and away to the sea. Deep below lie the sea-meres. They seem miles and miles, and utterly waste. But the sand-bar crosses like a bridge, and has a road. All the air is dark, a sombre bluish tone. The great west burns inwardly, sullenly, and gives no glow, yet a deep red. It is cold.

We go down the steep streets, smelly, dark, dank, and very cold. No wheeled vehicle can scramble up them, presumably. People live in one room. Men are combing their hair or fastening their collars in the doorways. Evening is here, and it is a feast day.

At the bottom of the street we come to a little bunch of masked youths, one in a long yellow frock and a frilled bonnet, another like an old woman, another in red twill. They are arm in arm and are accosting the passers-by. The q-b [1] gives a cry, and looks for escape. She has a terror of maskers, a terror that comes from childhood. To say the truth, so have I. We hasten invisibly down the far side of the street, and come out under the bastions. Then we go down our own familiar wide, short, cold boulevard to the sea.

At the bottom, again, is a carriage with more maskers. Carnival is beginning. A man dressed as a peasant woman in native costume is clambering with his great wide skirts and wide strides on to the box, and, flourishing his ribboned whip, is addressing a little crowd of listeners. He opens his mouth wide and goes on with a long yelling harangue of taking a drive with his mother—another man in old-woman's gaudy finery and wig who sits already bobbing on the box. The would-be daughter flourishes, yells, and prances up there on the box of the carriage. The crowd listens attentively and mildly smiles. It all seems real to them. The q-b hovers in the distance, half-fascinated, and watches. With a great flourish of whip and legs—showing his frilled drawers—the masker pulls round to drive along the boulevard by the sea—the only place where one can drive.

The big street by the sea is the Via Roma. It has the cafés on one side and across the road the thick tufts of trees intervening between the sea and us. Among these thick tufts of sea-front trees the little steam tram, like a little train, bumps to rest, after having wound round the back of the town.

The Via Roma is all social Cagliari. Including the cafés with their outdoor tables on the one side of the road, and the avenue

[1] *Editors' note:* q-b: The queen-bee, Lawrence's wife.

strand on the other, it is very wide, and at evening it contains the whole town. Here, and here alone carriages can spank along, very slowly, officers can ride, and the people can promenade "en masse."

We were amazed at the sudden crowd we found ourselves amongst—like a short, dense river of people streaming slowly in a mass. There is practically no vehicular traffic—only the steady dense streams of human beings of all sorts, all on a human footing. It must have been something like this in the streets of imperial Rome, where no chariots might drive and humanity was all on foot.

Little bunches of maskers, and single maskers danced and strutted along in the thick flow under the trees. If you are a mask you don't walk like a human being: you dance and prance along extraordinaryily like the life-size marionettes, conducted by wires from above. That is how you go: with that odd jauntiness as if lifted and propelled by wires from the shoulders. In front of me went a charming coloured harlequin, all in diamond-shaped colours, and beautiful as a piece of china. He tripped with the light, fantastic trip, quite alone in the thick crowd, and quite blithe. Came two little children hand in hand in brilliant scarlet and white costumes sauntering calmly. They did not do the mask trip. After a while a sky-blue girl with a high hat and full skirts, very short, that went flip-flip-flip, as a ballet dancer's, whilst she strutted; after her a Spanish grandee capering like a monkey. They threaded among the slow stream of the crowd. Appeared Dante and Beatrice, in Paradise apparently, all in white sheet-robes, and with silver wreaths on their heads, arm in arm, and prancing very slowly and majestically, yet with the long lilt as if hitched along by wires from above. They were very good: all the well-known vision come to life, Dante incorporate, and white as a shroud, with his tow-haired, silver-crowned, immortal Beatrice on his arm, strutting the dark avenues. He had the nose and cheek-bones and banded cheek, and the stupid wooden look, and offered a modern criticism on the Inferno.

It had become quite dark, the lamps were lighted. We crossed the road to the Café Roma, and found a table on the pavement among the crowd. In a moment we had our tea. The evening was cold, with ice in the wind. But the crowd surged on, back and forth, back and forth, slowly. At the tables were seated mostly men, taking coffee or vermouth or aqua vitae, all familiar and easy, without the modern self-consciousness. There was a certain pleasant, natural robustness of spirit, and something of a feudal free-and-easiness. Then arrived a family, with children, and nurse in her native costume. They all sat at table together, perfectly easy with one another, though the marvellous nurse seemed to be seated below the salt. She was bright as a poppy, in a rose-scarlet dress of fine cloth, with a curious little waistcoat of emerald green and purple, and a bodice of soft, homespun linen with great full sleeves. On her head she had a rose-scarlet and white head-dress, and she wore great studs of gold filigree, and similar ear-rings. The feudal-bourgeois family drank its syrup-drinks and watched the crowd. Most remarkable is the complete absence of self-consciousness. They all have a perfect natural "sang-froid," the nurse in her marvellous native costume is as thoroughly at her ease as if she were in her own village street. She moves and speaks and calls to a passer-by without the slightest constraint, and much more, without the slightest presumption. She is below the invisible salt, the invisible but insuperable salt. And it strikes me the salt-barrier is a fine thing for both parties: they both remain natural and human on either side of it, instead of becoming devilish, scrambling and pushing at the barricade.

The crowd is across the road, under the trees near the sea. On this side stroll occasional pedestrians. And I see my first peasant in costume. He is an elderly, upright, handsome man, beautiful in the black-and-white costume. He wears the full-sleeved white shirt and the close black bodice of thick, native frieze, cut low. From this sticks out a short kilt or frill, of the same black frieze, a band of which goes between the legs, between

the full loose drawers of coarse linen. The drawers are banded
below the knee into tight black frieze gaiters. On his head he has
the long black stocking cap, hanging down behind. How handsome he is, and so beautifully male! He walks with his hands loose
behind his back, slowly, upright, and aloof. The lovely un-
approachableness, indomitable. And the flash of the black and
white, the slow stride of the full white drawers, the black gaiters
and black cuirass with the bolero, then the great white sleeves
and white breast again, and once more the black cap—what marvellous massing of the contrast, marvellous, and superb, as on a
magpie.—How beautiful maleness is, if it finds its right expression.—And how perfectly ridiculous it is made in modern clothes.

There is another peasant too, a young one with a swift eye and
hard cheek and hard, dangerous thighs. He has folded his stocking cap, so that it comes forward to his brow like a phrygian cap.
He wears close knee breeches and close sleeved waistcoat of
thick brownish stuff that looks like leather. Over the waistcoat
a sort of cuirass of black, rusty sheepskin, the curly wool outside. So he strides, talking to a comrade. How fascinating it is,
after the soft Italians, to see these limbs in their close knee-
breeches, so definite, so manly, with the old fierceness in them
still. One realises, with horror, that the race of men is almost extinct in Europe. Only Christ-like heroes and woman-worshipping
Don Juans, and rabid equality-mongrels. The old, hardy, indomitable male is gone. His fierce singleness is quenched. The
last sparks are dying out in Sardinia and Spain. Nothing left but
the herd-proletariat and the herd-equality mongrelism, and the
wistful poisonous self-sacrificial cultured soul. How detestable.

But that curious, flashing, black-and-white costume! I seem
to have known it before: to have worn it even: to have dreamed
it. To have dreamed it: to have had actual contact with it. It belongs in some way to something in me—to my past, perhaps. I
don't know. But the uneasy sense of blood-familiarity haunts me.
I *know* I have known it before. It is something of the same uneasiness I feel before Mount Eryx: but without the awe this time.

In the morning the sun was shining from a blue, blue sky, but the shadows were deadly cold, and the wind like a flat blade of ice. We went out running to the sun. The hotel could not give us coffee and milk: only a little black coffee. So we descended to the sea-front again, to the Via Roma, and to our café. It was Friday: people seemed to be bustling in from the country with huge baskets.

The Café Roma had coffee and milk, but no butter. We sat and watched the movement outside. Tiny Sardinian donkeys, the tiniest things ever seen, trotted their infinitesimal little paws along the road, drawing little wagons like handcarts. Their proportion is so small, that they make a boy walking at their side look like a tall man, while a natural man looks like a Cyclops stalking hugely and cruelly. It is ridiculous for a grown man to have one of these little creatures, hardly bigger than a fly, hauling his load for him. One is pulling a chest of drawers on a cart, and it seems to have a whole house behind it. Nevertheless it plods bravely, away beneath the load, a wee thing.

They tell me there used to be flocks of these donkeys, feeding half wild on the wild, moor-like hills of Sardinia. But the war —and also the imbecile wantonness of the war-masters—consumed these flocks too, so that few are left. The same with the cattle. Sardinia, home of cattle, hilly little Argentine of the Mediterranean, is now almost deserted. It is war, say the Italiana.— And also the wanton, imbecile, foul lavishness of the war-masters. It was not alone the war which exhausted the world. It was the deliberate evil wastefulness of the war-makers in their own countries. Italy ruined Italy.

Two peasants in black-and-white are strolling in the sun, flashing. And my dream of last evening was not a dream. And my nostalgia for something I know not what was not an illusion. I feel it again, at once, at the sight of the men in frieze and linen, a heart yearning for something I have known, and which I want back again.

It is market day. We turn up the Largo Carlo-Felice, the second wide gap of a street, a vast but very short boulevard, like the end of something. Cagliari is like that: all bits and bobs. And by the side of the pavement are many stalls, stalls selling combs and collar-studs, cheap mirrors, handkerchiefs, shoddy Manchester goods, bed-ticking, boot-paste, poor crockery, and so on. But we see also Madame of Cagliari going marketing, with a servant accompanying her, carrying a huge grass-woven basket: or returning from marketing, followed by a small boy supporting one of these huge grass-woven baskets—like huge dishes—on his head, piled with bread, eggs, vegetables, a chicken, and so forth. Therefore we follow Madame going marketing, and find ourselves in the vast market house, and it fairly glows with eggs: eggs in these great round dish-baskets of golden grass: but eggs in piles, in mounds, in heaps, a Sierra Nevada of eggs, glowing warm white. How they glow! I have never noticed it before. But they give off a warm, pearly effulgence into the air, almost a warmth. A pearly-gold heat seems to come out of them. Myriads of eggs, glowing avenues of eggs.

And they are marked—60 centimes, 65 centimes. Ah, cries the q-b, I must live in Cagliari—For in Sicily the eggs cost 1.50 each.

This is the meat and poultry and bread market. There are stalls of new, various-shaped bread, brown and bright: there are tiny stalls of marvellous native cakes, which I want to taste, there is a great deal of meat and kid: and there are stalls of cheese, all cheeses, all shapes, all whitenesses, all the cream-colours, on into daffodil yellow. Goat cheese, sheeps cheese, Swiss cheese, Parmegiano, stracchino, caciocavallo, torolone, how many cheeses I don't know the names of! But they cost about the same as in Sicily, eighteen francs, twenty francs, twenty-five francs the kilo. And there is lovely ham—thirty and thirty-five francs the kilo. There is a little fresh butter too—thirty or thirty-two francs the kilo. Most of the butter, however, is tinned in Milan. It costs the same as the fresh. There are splendid piles of salted black olives, and huge bowls of green salted olives. There are chickens and ducks and wild-fowl: at eleven and twelve and fourteen francs a kilo. There is mortadella, the enormous Bologna sausage, thick as a church pillar: 16 francs: and there are various sorts of smaller sausage, salami, to be eaten in slices. A wonderful abundance of food, glowing and shining. We are rather late for fish, especially on Friday. But a barefooted man offers us two weird objects from the Mediterranean, which teems with marine monsters.

The peasant women sit behind their wares, their home-woven linen skirts, hugely full, and of various colours, ballooning round them. The yellow baskets give off a glow of light. There is a sense of profusion once more. But alas no sense of cheapness: save the eggs. Every month, up goes the price of everything.

"I must come and live in Cagliari, to do my shopping here," says the q-b. "I must have one of those big grass baskets."

We went down to the little street—but saw more baskets emerging from a broad flight of stone stairs, enclosed. So up we went— and found ourselves in the vegetable market. Here the q-b was happier still. Peasant women, sometimes barefoot, sat in their tight little bodices and voluminous, coloured skirts behind the piles of vegetables, and never have I seen a lovelier show. The intense deep green of spinach seemed to predominate, and out of that came the monuments of curd-white and black-purple cauliflowers: but marvellous cauliflowers, like a flower-show, the purple ones intense as great bunches of violets. From this green, white, and purple massing struck out the vivid rose-scarlet and blue crimson of radishes, large radishes like little turnips, in piles. Then the long, slim, grey-purple buds of artichokes, and dangling clusters of dates, and piles of sugar-dusty white figs and sombre-looking black figs, and bright burnt figs: basketfuls and basketfuls of figs. A few baskets of almonds, and many huge walnuts. Basket-pans of native raisins. Scarlet peppers like trumpets: mag--nificent fennels, so white and big and succulent: baskets of new potatoes: scaly kohlrabi: wild asparagus in bunches, yellow-budding sparacelli: big, clean-fleshed carrots: feathery salads with white hearts: long, brown-purple onions and then, of course pyramids of big oranges, pyramids of pale apples, and baskets of brilliant shiny mandarini, the little tangerine oranges with their green-black leaves. The green and vivid-coloured world of fruit-gleams I have never seen in such splendour as under the market roof at Cagliari: so raw and gorgeous. And all quite cheap, the one remaining cheapness, except potatoes. Potatoes of any sort are 1.40 or 1.50 the kilo.

"Oh!" cried the q-b, "If I don't live at Cagliari and come and do my shopping here, I shall die with one of my wishes unfulfilled."

But out of the sun it was cold, nevertheless. We went into the streets to try and get warm. The sun was powerful. But alas, as in southern towns generally, the streets are sunless as wells.

So the q-b and I creep slowly along the sunny bits, and then perforce are swallowed by shadow. We look at the shops. But there is not much to see. Little, frowsy provincial shops, on the whole.

But a fair number of peasants in the streets, and peasant women in rather ordinary costume: tight-bodiced, volume-skirted dresses of hand-woven linen or thickish cotton. The prettiest is of dark-blue-and-red, stripes-and-lines, intermingled, so made that the dark-blue gathers round the waist into one colour, the myriad pleats hiding all the rosy red. But when she walks, the full-petticoated peasant woman, then the red goes flash-flash-flash, like a bird showing its colours. Pretty that looks in the sombre street. She has a plain, light bodice with a peak: sometimes a little vest, and great full white sleeves, and usually a handkerchief or shawl loose knotted. It is charming the way they walk, with quick, short steps. When all is said and done, the most attractive costume for women in my eye, is the tight little bodice and the many-pleated skirt, full and vibrating with movement. It has a charm which modern elegance lacks completely—a bird-like play in movement.

They are amusing, these peasant girls and women: so brisk and defiant. They have straight backs, like little walls, and decided, well-drawn brows. And they are amusingly on the alert. There is no eastern creeping. Like sharp, brisk birds they dart along the streets, and you feel they would fetch you a bang over the head as leave as look at you. Tenderness, thank heaven, does not seem to be a Sardinian quality. Italy is so tender—like cooked macaroni—yards and yards of soft tenderness ravelled round everything. Here men don't idealise women, by the looks of things. Here they don't make these great leering eyes, the inevitable yours-to-command look of Italian males. When the men from the country look at these women, then it is Mind-yourself, my lady. I should think the grovelling Madonna-worship is not much of a Sardinian feature. These women have to look out for themselves, keep their own back-bone stiff and their knuckles hard. Man is going to be male Lord if he can. And woman isn't going to give him too much of his own way, either. So there you have it, the fine old martial split between the sexes. It is tonic and splendid, really, after so much sticky intermingling and backboneless Madonna-worship. The Sardinian isn't looking for the "noble woman nobly planned." No, thank you. He wants that young madam over there, a young stiff-necked generation that she is. Far better sport than with the nobly-planned sort: hollow frauds that they are. Better sport too than with a Carmen, who gives herself away too much. In these women there is something shy and defiant and un-get-atable. The defiant, splendid split between the sexes, each absolutely determined to defend his side, her side, from assault. So the meeting has a certain wild, salty savour, each the deadly unknown to the other. And at the same time, each his own, her own native pride and courage, taking the dangerous leap and scrambling back.

Give me the old, salty way of love. How I am nauseated with sentiment and nobility, the macaroni slithery-slobbery mess of modern adorations.

One sees a few fascinating faces in Cagliari: those great dark
unlighted eyes. There are fascinating dark eyes in Sicily, bright,
big, with an impudent point of light, and a curious roll, and long
lashes: the eyes of old Greece, surely. But here one sees eyes of
soft, blank darkness, all velvet, with no imp looking out of them.
And they strike a stranger, older note: before the soul became
self-conscious: before the mentality of Greece appeared in the
world. Remote, always remote, as if the intelligence lay deep
within the cave, and never came forward. One searches into the
gloom for one second, while the glance lasts. But without being
able to penetrate to the reality. It recedes, like some unknown
creature deeper into its lair. There *is* a creature, dark and potent.
But what?

Sometimes Velasquez, and sometimes Goya gives us a suggestion of these large, dark, unlighted eyes. And they go with
fine, fleecy black hair—almost as fine as fur. I have not seen them
north of Cagliari.

The q-b spies some of the blue-and-red stripe-and-line cotton
stuff of which the peasants make their dress: a large roll in the
doorway of a dark shop. In we go, and begin to feel it. It is just
soft, thickish cotton stuff—twelve francs a metre. Like most
peasant patterns, it is much more complicated and subtle than appears: the curious placing of the stripes, the subtle proportion,
and a white thread left down one side only of each broad blue
block. The stripes, moreover, run *across* the cloth, not lengthwise
with it. But the width would be just long enough for a skirt—
though the peasant skirts have almost all a band at the bottom
with the stripes running round-ways.

The man—he is the esquimo type, simple, frank and amiable
—says the stuff is made in France, and this the first roll since the
war. It is the old, old pattern, quite correct—but the material not
quite so good. The q-b takes enough for a dress.

He shows us also cashmeres, orange, scarlet, sky-blue, royal blue: good, pure-wool cashmeres that were being sent to India, and were captured from a German mercantile submarine. So he says. Fifty francs a metre—very, very wide. But they are too much trouble to carry in a knapsack, though their brilliance fascinates.

So we stroll and look at the shops, at the filigree gold jewelling of the peasants, at a good bookshop. But there is little to see and therefore the question is, shall we go on? Shall we go forward?

There are two ways of leaving Cagliari for the north: the State railway that runs up the west side of the island, and the narrow-gauge secondary railway that pierces the centre. But we are too late for the big trains. So we will go by the secondary railway, wherever it goes.

There is a train at 2:30, and we can get as far as Mandas, some fifty miles in the interior. When we tell the queer little waiter at the hotel, he says he comes from Mandas, and there are two inns. So after lunch—a strictly fish menu—we pay our bill. It comes to sixty odd francs—for three good meals each, with wine, and the night's lodging, this is cheap, as prices now are in Italy.

Pleased with the simple and friendly Scala di Ferre, I shoulder my sack and we walk off to the second station. The sun is shining hot this afternoon—burning hot, by the sea. The road and the buildings look dry and desiccated, the harbour rather weary and end of the world.

There is a great crowd of peasants at the little station. And almost every man has a pair of woven saddle-bags—a great flat strip of coarse-woven wool, with flat pockets at either end, stuffed with purchases. These are almost the only carrying bags. The men sling them over their shoulder, so that one great pocket hangs in front, one behind.

These saddle bags are most fascinating. They are coarsely woven in bands of raw black-rusty wool, with varying bands of raw white wool or hemp or cotton—the bands and stripes of varying widths going crosswise. And on the pale bands are woven sometimes flowers in most lovely colours, rose-red and blue and green, peasant patterns—and sometimes fantastic animals, beasts, in dark wool again. So that these striped zebra bags, some wonderful gay with flowery colours on their stripes, some weird with fantastic, griffin-like animals, are a whole landscape in themselves.

The train has only first and third class. It costs about thirty francs for the two of us, third class to Mandas, which is some sixty miles. In we crowd with the joyful saddlebags, into the wooden carriage with its many seats.

And, wonder of wonders, punctually to the second, off we go, out of Cagliari. En route again.

Suggestions for Study

LIKE THE French Impressionists ("Les Fauves" to their contemporaries), Lawrence goes his own way in stylistic matters. *Cagliari* is full of unorthodoxies: even the basic subject-verb-object order of the English sentence is often obscured. "Arrived a primrose-brocade beau, with ruffles"; "Pretty that looks in the sombre street." Valéry's remark, previously quoted, is relevant: "Style . . . must adapt itself to the author's design. . . . It must be adequate for its object." Lawrence developed a style peculiarly adapted to his insistent emphasis on the individual's sense-experience.

This impressionistic style is by no means of a piece throughout. The "raw and gorgeous" description of Cagliari's market depends chiefly on highly connotative adjectives attached to each item in the display; but when eggs are in question, Lawrence turns conjurer, and presents a series of arranged patterns: "eggs in piles, in mounds, in heaps . . . glowing avenues of eggs." (Compare Melville on squeezing spermaceti, in Chapter XCIV of *Moby Dick*.) Particularly striking are the two views of Cagliari harbor: that beginning "Strange, stony Cagliari" emphasizes what is unusual and mysterious, but in the later passage ("From the terrace just below the fortress"), "It is all terrible." Analyze the diction and structure of each section to see how Lawrence secures these contrasting effects.

Three structural movements hold the piece together. One is sensuous. From the baths, the steep streets, the sunset—all cold—we move at length into sunshiny heat: "burning hot, by the sea" (although the harbor continues to suggest the end of the world). A second is personal and imaginative: Lawrence is struck first by the sinister quality of Cagliari, then by its quasi-nostalgic appeal, finally by its fathomless reality, older even than self-consciousness. The third movement is intellectually whimsical. At the outset Lawrence appears merely to set "natural" Cagliari and its people over against artifice, art, and "our mechanical age." But the ball, where Cagliarians easily achieve the "wonderful artificial delicacy" of a century at once real and remote, and the fair, where Dante and Beatrice come to life, show that the "nature" of Cagliari includes and masters art as well as artifice. And the back-country railway, so punctually keeping its appointments, is further proof of Cagliari's power to reproduce, if it pleases, the achievements of mechanistic progress. "Nature" does not simply oppose "art," but contains it.

Consider Lawrence's account of pattern in the peasants' cottons, and of their saddle-bags: how are these matters related to the theme and structure of the essay?

At the Gudgers'

JAMES AGEE (1909–1955)

RICKETTS HAD shown me tricks of driving I shouldn't have dared or imagined along the clay, and now retracing it, alone, with the

dark coming on, I followed my own ruts most of the time, often
with my hands off the steering-wheel, holding the car in a light
and somewhat swift second gear so that it seemed more to float
and sail than to go on the ground, catching it lightly as possible
in the instant of slewing and putting on speed rather than slow-
ing and guiding beforehand, as I should have been more likely to
do of myself. Half a dozen places we had come very near bog-
ging, and here the clay was so wrought-up it was necessary each
time to guess again. You can't afford to use brakes in this sort
of material, and whatever steering you do, it must be as light-
handed as possible; about the only thing to say of speed in such
situations is to go a full shade faster most of the time than you can
imagine is at all safe to go. It is different from snow and from
any other mud I know of, and it holds a dozen sudden differences
within itself, all requiring quick modifications of technique and
all more or less indescribably hidden among one another: driving,
you feel less like an "operator" than like a sort of passive-active
brain suspended at the center of a machine, careful to let it take
its own way, and to hold it at all in restraint only by little ticklings
of an end of a whip: your senses are translated, they pervade
the car, so that you are all four wheels as sensitively as if each
were a fingertip; and these feel out a safe way through rather
by force of will or wish than by any action. The joke of this
was that my forces of will or of wish were crossed on themselves
between the curiosity to manage this two miles of road, out of
amateurish pride, and the regret that I was not at the Gudgers'
and the desire to be there and to have a good excuse for being
there: so that each time I got through a particularly tough stretch,
it was in about as much amused regret as pleasure: so that at
length, feeling the right rear wheel slew deeply toward the ditch;
well, I didn't know then, and don't now, whether the things I
was doing to save it were "correct" or not, and whether or not
it was by my will that I wrung the wheel and drove so deep that
there was no longer any hope at all of getting it out: but I do
know that as I felt it settle it was a thorough pleasure to me, an

added pleased feeling of, well, I did all *I* could: I sat in the steep-tilted car maybe a full minute with the motor idling, feeling a smile all over the bones of my face as strange to me as grease-paint: set it in low, shifted the steering, gave it all modulations of power and of steering I could think of; they only foundered it deeper as I had begun to hope they might: and abruptly shut off the engine and the lights and lighted a cigarette and sat looking out at the country and at the sky, while the vanquished engine cooled with a tin noise of ticking.

There was the very darkest kind of daylight which can be called daylight at all, still on everything, and all through the air, a cold, blue-brown light of agate; and I was stationary in the middle of a world of which all members were stationary, and in this stasis, a sour odor of the earth and of night strengthened into me steadfastly until, at length, I felt an exact traction with this country in each twig and clod of it as it stood, not as it stood past me from a car, but to be stood in the middle of, or drawn through, passed, on foot, in the plain rhythm of a human being in his basic relation to his country. Each plant that fluted up in long rows out of the soil was native to its particular few square inches of rootage, and held relationship among these others to the work and living of some particular man and family, in a particular house, perhaps whose lamp I saw beneath this field; and each tree had now its own particular existence and personality, stood up branching out of its own special space in the spreading of its blood, and stayed there waiting, a marked man, a tree: as different as the difference between a conducted tour of a prison and the first hours there as a prisoner: and all the while, it grew darker.

I took off my shoes and changed to sneakers (there was no sense in this, and I don't understand why), rolled the legs of my pants to the knee, took out an extra pack of cigarettes, two pencils, a small notebook, rolled up the windows, and locked the car: looked how deeply to the hub the wheel was sunk, and started off down the road, looking back at the car frequently from changed dis-

tances as if at a picture of myself, tilted up there helpless with
its headlights and bumper taking what light was left. I began to
feel laughter toward it as if it were a new dealer, a county
dietitian, an editor of Fortune, or an article in the New Republic;
and so, too, at myself, marveling with some scorn by what mixture of things in nature good and beneath nausea I was now where
I was and in what purposes: but all the while I kept on walking,
and all the while the bone center of my chest was beating with
haste and hope, and I was watching for landmarks, less by need
(for all I needed was to follow this road to a branching and the
branch to its end) than for gratification in feeling them approach
me once more in a changed pace and purpose and depth of feeling and meaning: for I now felt shy of them yet somehow as if
I newly possessed or was soon to possess them, as if they silently
opened and stood quiet before me to watch and evaluate and
guard against me, yet at the same time, in a kind of grave aloofness
of the defenseless, to welcome me: and yet again in all this I felt
humble, and respectful, careful that I should not so much as
set my foot in this clay in a cheapness of attitude, and full of
knowledge, I have no right, here, I have no real right, much as
I want it, and could never earn it, and should I write of it, must
defend it against my kind: but I kept on walking: the crumpled
edge of the gravel pit, the two negro houses I twisted between,
among their trees; they were dark; and down the darkness under
trees, whose roots and rocks were under me in the mud, and
shin-deep through swollen water; and watched the steep-slanted
corn, all struck toward me from my left, and nearly motionless
now, while along my right and all upon me there was the rustling
second rain of a trillion leaves relaxing the aftermath of storm,
and a lithe, loud, rambling noise of replenished branches; thinking, how through this night what seepage in the porous earth
would soon express this storm in glanded springs, deep wells refreshed; odors all round so black, so rich, so fresh, they surpassed
in fecundity the odors of a woman; the cold and quiet sweating
of hard walking; and so at last to the darkness of that upward

ravine of road beyond which the land opens in a wave, and floats the house:

Up this ravine, realizing myself now near, I came stealthily, knowing now I had at least half-contrived this, and after a misunderstood refusal, and for the first time realizing that by now, a half-hour fully dark, you must likely be in bed, through supper, done with a day, so that I must surely cause disturbance: slower, and slower, and two thirds ready to turn back, to spend the night in the car; and out into the cleared yard, silently, standing vertical to the front center of the house; it is dead black; not alight; just stands there, darker than its surroundings, perfectly quiet; and standing here, silently, in the demeanour of the house itself I grow full of shame and of reverence from the soles of my feet up my body to the crest of my skull and the leaves of my hands like a vessel quietly spread full of water which has sprung from in the middle of my chest: and shame the more, because I do not yet turn away, but still stand here motionless and as if in balance, and am aware of a vigilant and shameless hope that— not that I shall move forward and request you, disorder you— but that "something shall happen," as it "happened" that the car lost to the mud: and so waiting, in doubt, desire and shame, in a drawing-back of these around a vacuum of passive waiting, as the six walls of an empty room might wait for a sound: and this, or my breathing, or the beating of my heart, must have been communicated, for there is a sudden forward rush to the ledge of the porch of bellowing barking, and a dog, shouting his soul out against me: nothing else: and I think how they are roused by it and feel I have done wrong enough already, and withdraw a little, hoping that will quiet him, and in the same hope hold forward my hand and speak very quietly. He subdues to a growled snarling of bragging hate and fear and I am ready to turn and leave when a shadow heavily shuffles behind him, and in a stooped gesture of peering me out, Gudger's voice asks, who is it: ready for trouble. I speak before I move, telling him who I am, then what has happened, why I am here, and walk toward him, and

how sorry I am to bother them. It's all right with him; come on
in; he had thought I was a nigger.

I come up onto the porch shamefacedly, telling him again how
sorry I am to have rousted them out like this. It's all right. They
were just got to bed, none of them asleep yet. He has pulled
on his overalls over nothing else and is barefooted. In the dark
I can see him stooping his square head a little forward to study
me. There is still antagonism and fear in his voice and in his eyes,
but I realize this is not toward me, but toward the negro he
thought I was: his emotions and his mind are slow to catch up
with any quick change in the actuality of a situation. In a little
more this antagonism has drained away and he is simply a tired
and not unkind man taking care of a half-stranger at night who
is also an anomaly; and thus he does as he has done before without
any affectation of social grace: people plain enough take a much
more profoundly courteous care of one another and of themselves
without much if any surprise and no flurry of fussiness and a
kind of respect which does not much ask questions. So it was
there was neither any fake warmth and heartiness nor any coldness in his saying, Sure, come on in, to my asking could he put
me up for the night after all, and he added, Better eat some supper. I was in fact very hungry, but I did all I was able to stop
this, finally trying to compromise it to a piece of bread and some
milk, that needn't be prepared; I'm making you enough bother
already; but no; Can't go to bed without no supper; you just
hold on a second or two; and he leans his head through the bedroom door and speaks to his wife, explaining, and lights the lamp
for her. After a few moments, during which I hear her breathing
and a weary shuffling of her heels, she comes out barefooted carrying the lamp, frankly and profoundly sleepy as a child; feeling
disgusted to wake her further with so many words I say, Hello,
Mrs. Gudger: say I want to tell you I'm *awful* sorry to give you
all this bother: you just, honest I don't need much of anything,
if you'd just tell me where a piece of bread is, it'll be *plenty*, I'd
hate for you to bother to cook anything up for me: but she

answers me while passing, looking at me, trying to get me into focus from between her sticky eyelashes, that 'taint no bother at all, and for me not to worry over that, and goes on into the kitchen; and how quickly I don't understand, for I am too much occupied to see, with Gudger, and with holding myself from the cardinal error of hovering around her, or of offering to help her, she has built a pine fire and set in front of me, on the table in the hall, warmed-over biscuit and butter and blackberry jam and a jelly-glass full of buttermilk, and warmed field peas, fried pork, and four fried eggs, and she sits a little away from the table out of courtesy, trying to hold her head up and her eyes open, until I shall have finished eating, saying at one time how it's an awful poor sort of supper and at another how it's awful plain, mean food; I tell her different, and eat as rapidly as possible and a good deal more than I can hold, in fact, all the eggs, a second large plateful of peas, most of the biscuit, feeling it is better to keep them awake and to eat too much than in the least to let them continue to believe I am what they assume I must be: "superior" to them or to their food, eating only so much as I need to be "polite"; and I see that they are, in fact, quietly surprised and gratified in my appetite.

But somehow I have lost hold of the reality of all this, I scarcely can understand how; a loss of the reality of simple actions upon the specific surface of the earth. This country, these roads, these odors and noises, the action of walking the dark in mud, the approach, just what a slow succession of certain trees past your walking can implant in you, can mean to you, the house as it stands there dark in darkness, the indecisiveness and the bellowing dog, the conversations of questioning, defense, assurance, acceptance, the subtle yet strong distinctions of attitude, the walking between the walls of wood and the sitting and eating, the tastes of the several foods, the weights of our bodies in our chairs, the look of us in the lamplight in the presence of the walls of the house and of the country night, the beauty and stress of our

tiredness, how we held quietness, gentleness, and care toward one
another like three mild lanterns held each at the met heads of
strangers in darkness: such things, and these are just a few, I have
not managed to give their truth in words, which are a soft, plain-
featured, and noble music, each part in the experience of it and
in the memory so cleanly and so simply defined in its own terms,
striking so many chords and relationships at once, which I can
but have blurred in the telling at all.

To say, then, how, as I sat between the close walls of this
hallway, which opened upon wide night at either end, between
these two somberly sleepy people in the soft smile of the light,
eating from unsorted plates with tin-tasting implements the heavy,
plain, traditional food which was spread before me, the feeling
increased itself upon me that at the end of a wandering and seeking, so long it had begun before I was born, I had apprehended
and now sat at rest in my own home, between two who were my
brother and my sister, yet less that than something else; these,
the wife my age exactly, the husband four years older, seemed
not other than my own parents, in whose patience I was so
different, so diverged, so strange as I was; and all that surrounded
me, that silently strove in through my senses and stretched me full,
was familiar and dear to me as nothing else on earth, and as if
well known in a deep past and long years lost; so that I could
wish that all my chance life was in truth the betrayal, the curable
delusion, that it seemed, and that this was my right home, right
earth, right blood, to which I would never have true right. For
half my blood is just this; and half my right of speech; and by
bland chance alone is my life so softened and sophisticated in
the years of my defenselessness, and I am robbed of a royalty I
can not only never claim, but never properly much desire or
regret. And so in this quiet introit, and in all the time we have
stayed in this house, and in all we have sought, and in each detail
of it, there is so keen, sad, and precious a nostalgia as I can
scarcely otherwise know; a knowledge of brief truancy into the
sources of my life, whereto I have no rightful access, having paid
no price beyond love and sorrow.

The biscuits are large and shapeless, not cut round, and are pale, not tanned, and are dusty with flour. They taste of flour and soda and damp salt and fill the mouth stickily. They are better with butter, and still better with butter and jam. The butter is pallid, soft, and unsalted, about the texture of cold-cream; it seems to taste delicately of wood and wet cloth; and it tastes "weak." The jam is loose, of little berries, full of light raspings of the tongue; it tastes a deep sweet purple tepidly watered, with a very faint sheen of a sourness as of iron. Field peas are olive-brown, the shape of lentils, about twice the size. Their taste is a cross between lentils and boiled beans; their broth is bright with seasoning of pork, and of this also they taste. The broth is soaked up in bread. The meat is a bacon, granular with salt, soaked in the grease of its frying: there is very little lean meat in it. What there is is nearly as tough as rind; the rest is pure salted stringy fat. The eggs taste of pork too. They are fried in it on both sides until none of the broken yolk runs, are heavily salted and peppered while they fry, so that they come to table nearly black, very heavy, rinded with crispness, nearly as dense as steaks. Of milk I hardly know how to say; it is skimmed, blue-lighted; to a city palate its warmth and odor are somehow dirty and at the same time vital, a little as if one were drinking blood. There is even in so clean a household as this an odor of pork, of sweat, so subtle it seems to get into the very metal of the cooking-pans beyond any removal of scrubbing, and to sweat itself out of newly washed cups; it is all over the house and all through your skin and clothing at all times, yet as you bring each piece of food to your mouth it is so much more noticeable, if you are not used to it, that a quiet little fight takes place on your palate and in the pit of your stomach; and it seems to be this odor, and a sort of wateriness and discouraged tepidity, which combine to make the food seem unclean, sticky, and sallow with some invisible sort of disease, yet this is the odor and consistency and temper and these are true tastes of home; I know this even of myself; and much as my reflexes are twitching in refusal of each mouthful a true homesick and simple fondness for it has so strong

hold of me that in fact there is no fight to speak of and no faking
of enjoyment at all. And even later, knowing well enough of such
food what an insult it is to those who must spend their lives eating it, and who like it well enough, and when I am sick with
it, I have also fondness for it, and when this fails, a funny kind
of self-scorning determination that I shall eat for a few weeks
what a million people spend their lives eating, and feel that
whatever discomfort it brings me is little enough and willingly
taken on, in the scale of all it could take to even us up.

All this while we are talking some: short of exact recording,
which is beyond my memory, I can hardly say how: the forms
of these plainest and most casual actions are the hardest I can
conceive of to set down straight as they happen; and each is
somewhat more beautiful and more valuable, I feel, than, say,
the sonnet form. This form was one in which two plain people
and one complex one who scarcely know each other discourse
while one eats and the others wait for him to finish so they may
get back to bed: it has the rhythms and inflections of this triple
shyness, of sleepiness, of fast eating, of minds in the influence of
lamplight between pine walls, of talk which means little or nothing of itself and much in its inflections: What is the use? What
is there I can do about it? Let me try just a few of the surfaces
instead. Just in the fact that they were drawn up out of bed to
do me this natural kindness, one in overalls and one in a house
dress slid on over nakedness, and were sitting here, a man and
his wife, in an hour whose lateness is uncommon to them, there
is a particular sort of intimacy between the three of us which is
not of our creating and which has nothing to do with our talk,
yet which is increased in our tones of voice, in small quiet turns
of humor, in glances of the eyes, in ways even that I eat my food,
in their knowledge how truly friendly I feel toward them, and
how seriously I am concerned to have caused them bother, and
to let them be done with this bother as quickly as possible. And
the best in this—it will be hard to explain unless you know something of women in this civilization—is the experiencing of

warmth and of intimacy toward a man and his wife at the same time (for this would seldom happen, it being the business of a wife to serve and to withdraw). I felt such an honor in her not just staying at more distance, waiting to clear up after me, but sitting near, almost equal in balance with her husband, and actually talking; and I began even through her deep exhaustion to see such pleasant and seldom warmth growing in her, in this shifted status and acceptance in it, and such a kindly and surprised current of warmth increasing through this between her husband and her, a new light and gentle novelty spreading a prettiness in her face that, beyond a first expostulation that she get back to her rest and leave me to clean off the table, I not only scarcely worried for her tiredness, or her husband's, but even somewhat prolonged the while we sat there, shamed though I was to do so, and they wakened, and warmed to talking, even while fatigue so much more heavily weighed them under, till it became in the scale of their sleeping an almost scandalously late-night conversation, in which we were all leaned toward each other in the lamplight secretly examining the growth of friendliness in one another's faces, they opening further speaking as often as I and more often: while nevertheless there stole up my quiet delight from the pit of my stomach a cold and sickening shame to be keeping them up, a feeling I had mistaken their interest and their friendliness, that it was only a desperate and nearly broken patience in a trap I had imposed in abuse of their goodness; and I broke through a little wait in what we were speaking, to say how sorry and ashamed I was, and that we must get to sleep; and this they received so genuinely, so kindly, that even in their exhaustion I was immediately healed, and held no fear of their feelings about it: and we drew back our chairs and got up and she cleared the table (no, beyond quickly stacking my dishes toward her I could not offer even to help her with this) and there followed a simple set of transitions which are beautiful in my remembrance and which I can scarcely set down: a telling me where I would sleep, in the front room; a spreading of pallets on the floor of the back bedroom; a waking and bringing-in of the children from their sleeping on the bed I was to have: they came sleepwalking, along bare floor toward lamplight, framed in the lighted upright planks of the door: the yielding-over to me of the lamp, which I accepted (there are courtesies you accept, though you are ashamed to), provided they should have used it first to get themselves to bed: they give me, meanwhile, their little tin night-light, which looks like the minutest kind of Roman lamp: I say good night to Mrs. Gudger and she to me, smiling sleepily and sadly in a way I cannot deduce, and goes on in; I button my door, that leads into their bedroom, and wait in this front room, new to me, with my night-light, sitting on the edge of the child-warmed bed, looking at the little sketches of carpentry I can see in my faint light, and at the light under their door and through seams in the wall, while in a confusion of shufflings and of muted voices which overspreads the sleeping of children like quiet wings; and rustlings of cloth, and sounding of bedsprings, they restore themselves for sleeping: then a shuffling, a sliding of light, a soft knock at the door; I come to it; Gudger and I exchange our lamps, speaking few words in nearly inaudible voices, while beyond his shoulder I feel the deep dark breathing a soft and quiet prostration of bodies: All right in year hain't you?—Ah, sure, fine. Sure am.—Annie Mae told me to say, she's sorry she ain't got no clean sheet, but just have to (*oh, no!*) make out best way you can.—Oh, no. No. You tell her I certainly do thank her, but, no, I'll be fine like this, *fine* like this—She just don't got none tell she does a warshin.—Sure; sure; I wouldn't want to dirty up a clean sheet for you, one night. Thanks a lot. Door, right head a yer bed, if you want to git out. I look, and nod:

Yeah; thanks.

Night:

Night:

The door draws shut.

.   .   .   .   .   .

The sun was not yet up, but the sky over the hill was like white china and it was full daylight now, everything hung with rain and letting it run off in large drops; the grain of wood in the wall of the house was yellow, red and fading blue-black (as of wet tortoise shell), which the sun would not bleach for several hours yet; the ground was drawn down hard on itself with a somehow blue-sheened surface that looked hard as iron. The lamp was no longer giving any light beyond its own daylighted chimney, and Mrs. Gudger put it out. Even now, with the hot load of the breakfast inside me, I was stiff with cold and was not yet well awake.

We cut up across the hill field by the path their walking had laid in it; the path was all but rained out. In some parts it was packed hard enough to be slippery, the rest of the time it let our feet down as deep as plowed dirt itself and we lifted them out in each step with one to three inches of clay hung on them. The cotton plants brushed us at the knees so that in no time we were drenched there.

It was only a chance that the road and the ditch clay would have hardened enough during the night to make it possible to get the car out. With about ten minutes work, that brought up a shallow, stickily drying sweat in the cool of this morning, we managed to do it, and moving precariously in low and second as if walking a slackwire, with a couple of sideslips that nearly ditched us again, we got the car out to the slag and swung right and made speed on its slow rollercoaster lifts and falls while around us fields, with which I found I felt a strong new kind of familiarity, lifted and relaxed upon our motion.

After not more than three miles, just within first sight of Cookstown, low and diminutive, Gudger told me to turn right just this side of the grismill.

It was dirt road again, but wider, and thick enough with sand to be possible, though it was still good and wet. I managed about thirty-five on it, and the tires were very loud under us. This was new country to me, still totally poor, yet with something loosened and pastoral about it and as if self-sufficient and less hopelessly lonesome and abandoned; the early light and the cleanness and silence after the rain may have been responsible for this impression. There were more small, privately owned farms than on many roads I had driven over, none of them any richer-looking than tenant farms; yet living was a little different on them and a little less pointless. Even in the smoke that wrinkled up out of their chimneys and lavished lazily like the tail of a pleased cat and in the keen odors of fire and breakfast that lay occasionally across the road, there was a little more security than in these same on a tenant farm, and a little more of the sense of a family planted in one place and coming up like a tree, even if it was a starved tree.

Strung along at two out of three mail boxes, thinly along the road, men stood smoking and waited. I started to slow for the first and Gudger said the truck would be along. With all the equipment in the back we had room only for one more anyway. They looked at us coldly and shyly as we went past. To three or four Gudger lifted a hand, and these lifted a hand, not smiling.

We ran sharply up a hill with small black pines on it and at the top a small unpainted church and clay burial ground, and the hill ran down much more slowly. Gudger said turn right down there at the bottom. I swung right through a snowlike sludge of clay and righted the car along a rut between the deep ones and a light rut in the grass. It was harder going again. Wet blackberry brambles laid water on the windshield. In two hundred yards more the woods were up to one side of us, a high field to the other, and the road was sand again, and Gudger said to take the right fork, and it was as subduing as going into a tunnel. The pines and the soft-wooded and high trees and the oaks and hickories were thick all around us and over us now, so that the air was cold, dark and clear, and noisily hushed as I remember when, a child, I used to crawl into a culvert, and sat down and listened. The sand road was drenching wet and there was the mark of one car that had been ahead of us, and ahead there was the rattling of a wagon, and we rounded a heavy bush and saw it and slowed; the men looked round, two black, one white, who lifted his hand as Gudger lifted his; the negroes nodded. The whipped mules dragged the wagon on through a flooded branch that submerged thirty yards of the road and stood up around the bushes and tree-trunks on either side so that they had no rootage, and I watched where and how deep the wheels went while I idled the motor and lighted Gudger's and my own cigarette. It was twenty-one past six. Gudger said, 'We got here in good time.' They got the wagon on through and drew up along a patch of grass and roots at the side of the road. I said thanks with hand and head, put the car into low and then into second and, following their trail, which still creased the water a little, went through pretty fast with a loud cold splitting and crashing noise of the new water and was on solid land again. The white man and I lifted hands as I went by and the negroes nodded again, but more slightly. They were all three looking at us curiously and tentatively. 'Left up yer ahead'; where there was wide light on the wet road. We swung as if into the face of a powerful searchlight into a long grassy clearing stacked down the middle with wet yellow lumber and full of light which had, since we lost it to woods, greatly increased and which came straight and low at us from the far end; we went past another wagon and drew up at the side of the road in the heavy grass halfway down the clearing. The wagon passed alongside and Gudger and the men on the wagon lifted their hands and the men looked back noncommittally at me and Gudger and the sedan and the Tennessee license. Gudger's watch made twenty-three past six.

The sawmill was at the far end; it was still in the morning shadow of the woods. The sun had just cleared the tops of the pines beyond it so that they were still burnt away. Rising and twisting all through these close-growing pines, and on the high glittering grass and in long streams in the air, was the white smoke of the cold, now swiftly heating, early morning, which the sun drew up, and the sun struck through this smoke and diffused it so that the air was clear, transparent and all but blinding bright, as if it had been polished. The wagon that had drawn aside from us in the woods road had come up and let off its men, and a truckload of negroes and white men arrived from Cookstown, and the clearing was thickening but not by any means crowded with men and the sound of their talk and the noises of the beginning of a day's work: nearly every one of these men glanced at us more than once, carefully and with candor, yet they did not stare, and were only careful, not hostile. Over by the toolshed of fresh pine a negro, harnessing his team, threw back his head and looked into the sun and sang, shouting, a phrase which sprang out of his throat like a wet green branch. Gudger said he was agoin to have to git on to work now. I told him I sure was obliged to him for taking me in last night and he said he was glad to have holp me.

Suggestions for Study

ARCHIBALD MACLEISH hankers after "the feel of the facts" (p. 239); to Agee, "the aspect of a street in sunlight can roar in the heart of itself as a symphony, perhaps as no symphony can," and his style reflects an intensely concentrated effort to say just how the world roars. "He worked in what looked like a rush and a rage," says Walker Evans. The lengthy narrative sentences, depending heavily on colons and semi-colons, and struck through with introspective asides, suggest Faulkner; the sensual detail, braced by alliterative devices, of such passages as the one beginning, "The biscuits are large and shapeless," recalls Thomas Wolfe. But the expression, "I felt an exact traction with this country in each twig and clod of it," brings one back to Agee's own obsessive concern with the feel of the facts, and his own way of communicating that.

For Agee, the power of words to communicate took third place, after the power of the camera, and that of music (fourth place, perhaps: "A piece of the body torn out by the roots might be more to the point," he once wrote). Photographs are integral to the book from which this passage is taken; much of the text has been called "a camera moving through rooms." Beginning with Agee's amused backward look at the mired car, go through the piece and find evidence of "the photographer at work," in tableau and in the contrast of light and shade. Even Agee's affinity for capping an extended passage of rather plain diction with a startling and suggestive figure of speech ("a smile all over the bones of my face as strange to me as greasepaint") is, perhaps, analogous to the art of a few gifted photographers like Cartier-Bresson, who evoke from "realistic" detail subtle and unexpected effects.

Agee calls words "a soft, plain-featured, and noble music"; the comparison is relevant to the structure of this passage, although one should be wary of facile parallels to specific musical forms. Balance and counterpoint are regularly in evidence. The first paragraph is a maze of patterned movement between opposed themes: heavy mud and the delicacy of touch required to maneuver in it, will to manage the road vs. will to get stuck, violent slewing action succeeded by "vanquished" stillness; and, at a deeper level, the act of hopeless foundering which allows meaningful freedom of action, or the scarcely-suggested matching of this episode to the main business of the passage (for which Agee is now freed). Notice that each of these sets of "oppositions" thrusts especially at one faculty: sense, will, emotion, intellect, imagination.

Analyze the structure of the second paragraph, attending carefully to its rhythms, which are not those of the first.

What seems to be the central symbol in terms of which the passage develops? Having identified that, consider the propriety of the scene at the heart of the passage:

. . . an almost scandalously late-night conversation in which we were all leaned toward each other in the lamplight secretly examining the growth of friendliness in one another's faces, they opening further speaking as often as I and more often.

Nonlecture Two: i and their son

E.E. CUMMINGS (1894–   )

You will perhaps pardon me, as a nonlecturer, if I begin my second nonlecture with an almost inconceivable assertion: I was born at home.

For the benefit of those of you who can't imagine what the word "home" implies, or what a home could possibly have been like, I should explain that the idea of home is the idea of privacy. But again—what is privacy? You probably never heard of it. Even supposing that (from time to time) walls exist around you, those walls are no longer walls; they are merest pseudo-solidities, perpetually penetrated by the perfectly predatory collective organs of sight and sound. Any apparent somewhere which you may inhabit is always at the mercy of a ruthless and omnivorous everywhere. The notion of a house, as one single definite particular and unique place to come into, from the anywhereish and everywhereish world outside—that notion must strike you as fantastic. You have been brought up to believe that a house, or a universe, or a you, or any other object, is only seemingly solid: really (and you are realists, whom nobody and nothing can deceive) each seeming solidity is a collection of large holes—and, in the case of a house, the larger the holes the better; since the principal function of a modern house is to admit whatever might otherwise remain outside. You haven't the least or feeblest conception of being here, and now, and alone, and yourself. Why (you ask) should anyone want to be here, when (simply by pressing a button) anyone can be in fifty places at once? How could anyone want to be now, when anyone can

NONLECTURE TWO: I AND THEIR SON is reprinted from *i: Six Nonlectures* by E.E. Cummings. Copyright 1953 by E.E. Cummings. Reprinted by permission of Harvard University Press.

92

go whening all over creation at the twist of a knob? What could induce anyone to desire aloneness, when billions of soi-disant dollars are mercifully squandered by a good and great government lest anyone anywhere should ever for a single instant be alone? As for being yourself—why on earth should you be yourself; when instead of being yourself you can be a hundred, or a thousand, or a hundred thousand thousand, other people? The very thought of being oneself in an epoch of interchangeable selves must appear supremely ridiculous.

Fine and dandy: but, so far as I am concerned, poetry and every other art was and is and forever will be strictly and distinctly a question of individuality. If poetry were anything— like dropping an atombomb—which anyone did, anyone could become a poet merely by doing the necessary anything; whatever that anything might or might not entail. But (as it happens) poetry is being, not doing. If you wish to follow, even at a distance, the poet's calling (and here, as always, I speak from my own totally biased and entirely personal point of view) you've got to come out of the measurable doing universe into the immeasurable house of being. I am quite aware that, wherever our socalled civilization has slithered, there's every reward and no punishment for unbeing. But if poetry is your goal, you've got to forget all about punishments and all about rewards and all about selfstyled obligations and duties and responsibilities etcetera ad infinitum and remember one thing only: that it's you—nobody else—who determine your destiny and decide your fate. Nobody else can be alive for you; nor can you be alive for anybody else. Toms can be Dicks and Dicks can be Harrys, but none of them can ever be you. There's the artist's responsibility; and the most awful responsibility on earth. If you can take it, take it—and be. If you can't, cheer up and go about other people's business; and do (or undo) till you drop.

My own home faced the Cambridge world as a finely and solidly constructed mansion, preceded by a large oval lawn and ringed with an imposing white-pine hedge. Just in front of the house itself stood two huge appletrees; and faithfully, every spring, these giants lifted their worlds of fragrance toward the room where I breathed and dreamed. Under one window of this room flourished (in early summer) a garden of magnificent roses: the gift of my parents' dear friend "stubby" Child—who (I learned later) baptized me and who (I still later discovered) was the Child of English And Scottish Ballads. As a baby, I sported a white sweater; on which my mother had embroidered a red H, for Harvard.

Our nearest neighbour, dwelling (at a decent distance) behind us, was Roland Thaxter; primarily the father of my loveliest playmate and ultimately the professor of cryptogamic botany. To our right, on Irving Street, occurred professors James and Royce and Warren; to our left, on Scott Street, transpired professor of economics Taussig. Somewhat back of the Taussig house happened professor Lanman—"known and loved throughout India" as my mother would say, with a pensive smile. She had been slightly astonished by an incident which embellished her official introduction to Mr and Mrs Lanman: the celebrated Sanscrit scholar having, it seems, seized his would-be interlocutor's hand, yanked her aside, and violently whispered "do you see anything peculiar about my wife?"—then (without giving my mother time to reply) "she has new shoes on" professor Lanman hissed "and they hurt her!" I myself experienced astonishment when first witnessing a spectacle which frequently thereafter repeated itself at Professor Royce's gate. He came rolling peacefully forth, attained the sidewalk, and was about to turn right and wander up Irving, when Mrs Royce shot out of the house with a piercing cry "Josie! Josie!" waving something string-like in her dexter fist. Mr Royce politely paused, allowing his spouse to catch up with him; he then shut both eyes, while she snapped around his collar a narrow necktie possessing a permanent bow; his eyes thereupon opened, he bowed, she smiled, he advanced, she retired, and the scene was over. As for professor Taussig, he had a cocker spaniel named Hamlet; and the Taussig family always put Hamlet out when they played their pianola—no doubt the first law of economics—but Hamlet's hearing was excellent, and he yodelled heartrendingly as long as the Hungarian Rhapsody persisted. Genial professor Warren's beautiful wife (whose own beautiful name was Salomé Machado) sometimes came to call on my maternal grandmother; and Salomé always brought her guitar. I remember sitting spellbound on our upstairs porch among appleblossoms, one heavenly spring afternoon, adoring the quick slim fingers of Salomé Machado's exquisite left hand—and I further remember how, as Salomé sang and played, a scarlet tanager alighted in the blossoms; and listened, and disappeared.

One of the many wonderful things about a home is that it can be as lively as you please without ever becoming public. The big Cambridge house was in this respect, as in all other respects, a true home. Although I could be entirely alone when I wished, a varied social life awaited me whenever aloneness palled. A father and mother—later, a sister—two successive grandmothers and an aunt (all three of whom sang, or played the piano, or did both, extremely well) and one uncle, plus three or four hearty and jovial servants, were at my almost unlimited disposal. The servants—and this strikes me as a more than important point—very naturally enjoyed serving; for they were not ignobly irresponsible impersons, they were not shamelessly overpaid and mercilessly manipulated anonymities, they were not pampered and impotent particles of a greedy and joyless collective obscenity. In brief: they were not slaves. Actually, these good and faithful servants (of whom I speak) were precisely everything which no slave can ever be—they were alive; they were loved and loving human beings. From them, a perfect ignoramus could and did learn what any unworld will never begin to begin to so much as suspect: that slavery, and the only slavery, is service without love.

After myself and my father and mother, I loved most dearly my mother's brother George. He was by profession a lawyer, by inclination a bon vivant, and by nature a joyous human being. When this joyous human being wasn't toiling in his office, or hobnobbing with socalled swells at the Brookline country club, he always became my playfellow. No more innocently good-hearted soul ever kissed the world goodnight; but when it came to literature, bloodthirsty was nothing to him. And (speaking of bloodthirstiness) I here devoutly thank a beneficent Providence for allowing me to live my childhood and my boyhood and even my youth without ever glimpsing that typical item of an era of at least penultimate confusion—the uncomic nonbook. No paltry supermen, no shadowy space-cadets, no trifling hyperjungle-queens and pantless pantherwomen insulted my virginal imagination. I read or was read, at an early age, the most immemorial myths, the wildest wild animal stories, lots of Scott and quantities of Dickens (including the immortal Pickwick Papers), Robinson Crusoe and The Swiss Family Robinson, Gulliver's Travels, Twenty Thousand Leagues Under the Sea, poetry galore, The Holy Bible, and The Arabian Nights. One city winter I floated through chivalry with Malory and Foissart: the following country summer—we had by then acquired a farm—I dressed as a Red Indian, slept in a teepee, and almost punctured our best Jersey cow with a random arrow; in emulation of the rightful inhabitants of my wrongful native land.

A gruesome history of the Tower Of London had been conscientiously compiled by a prominent British prelate, endowed with what would now be termed sadistic trends; and suddenly this fearful opus burgeoned in our midst. Every night after dinner, if George were on deck, he would rub his hands and wink magnificently in my direction and call to my maiden aunt "Jane, let's have some ruddy gore!" whereupon Jane would protestingly join us in the parlour; and George would stealthily produce the opus; and she would blushfully read; and I would cling to the sofa in exquisite terror. We also read—for sheer relaxation—

Lorna Doone (with whom I fell sublimely in love) and Treasure Island (as a result of which, the blind pirate Pew followed me upstairs for weeks; while for months, if not years, onelegged John Silver stood just behind me as my trembling fingers fumbled the electric light chain).

Out of Brookline's already mentioned country club, I readily conjured a gorgeous and dangerous play-world: somewhat resembling the three ring circus of the five Ringling brothers; and dedicated by dashing gentlemen to fair ladies and fine horses and other entrancing symbols of luxurious living. George had not been born into this fashionable cosmos, but he loved it so much that he learned to smoke cigars; and if he hadn't learned anything, the cosmos would certainly have welcomed him for his own abundant self's sake. His own abundant self wrote vers de société; which he recited at orgies or banquets—I was never sure which —but also, for my benefit, chez lui. And no sooner had George discovered my liking for verse than he presented me with an inestimable treasure entitled The Rhymester—opening which totally unostentatious masterpiece, I entered my third poetic period.

Poetic period number one had been nothing if not individualistic; as two almost infantile couplets, combining fearless expression with keen observation, amply testify. The first of these primeval authenticities passionately exclaims

> O, the pretty birdie, O;
> with his little toe, toe, toe!

while the second mercilessly avers

> there was a little farder
> and he made his mudder harder

—but, alas! a moribund mental cloud soon obscured my vital psychic sky. The one and only thing which mattered about any poem (so ran my second poetic period's credo) was what the poem said; its socalled meaning. A good poem was a poem which did good, and a bad poem was a poem which didn't: Julia Ward Howe's Battle Hymn Of The Republic being a good poem because it helped free the slaves. Armed with this ethical immutability, I composed canticles of comfort on behalf of the grief-stricken relatives of persons recently deceased; I implored healthy Christians to assist poor-whites afflicted with The Curse Of The Worm (short for hookworm); and I exhorted right-minded patriots to abstain from dangerous fireworks on the 4th of July. Thus it will be seen that, by the year 1900, one growing American boy had reached exactly that state of "intellectual development" beyond which every ungrowing Marxist adult of today is strictly forbidden, on pain of physical disappearance, ever to pass.

The Rhymester diverted my eager energies from what to how: from substance to structure. I learned that there are all kinds of intriguing verse-forms, chiefly French; and that each of these forms can and does exist in and of itself, apart from the use to which you or I may or may not put it. A rondel is a rondel, irrespective of any idea which it may be said to embody; and whatever a ballade may be about, it is always a ballade—never a villanelle or a rondeau. With this welcome revelation, the mental cloud aforesaid ignominiously dissolved; and my psychic sky joyfully reappeared, more vital even than before.

One ever memorable day, our ex-substantialist (deep in structural meditation) met head-on professor Royce; who was rolling peacefully home from a lecture. "Estlin" his courteous and gentle voice hazarded "I understand that you write poetry." I blushed. "Are you perhaps" he inquired, regarding a particular leaf of a particular tree "acquainted with the sonnets of Dante Gabriel Rossetti?" I blushed a different blush and shook an ignorant head. "Have you a moment?" he shyly suggested, less than half looking at me; and just perceptibly appended "I rather imagine you might enjoy them." Shortly thereafter, sage and ignoramus were sitting opposite each other in a diminutive study (marvellously smelling of tobacco and cluttered with student notebooks of a menacing bluish shade)—the ignoramus listening, enthralled; the sage intoning, lovingly and beautifully, his favorite poems. And very possibly (though I don't, as usual, know) that is the reason—or more likely the unreason—I've been writing sonnets ever since.

En route to a university whose name begins with H, our unhero attended four Cambridge schools: the first, private—where everybody was extraordinarily kind; and where (in addition to learning nothing) I burst into tears and nosebleeds—the other three, public; where I flourished like the wicked and learned what the wicked learn, and where almost nobody cared about somebody else. Two figures emerge from this almost: a Miss Maria Baldwin and a Mr Cecil Derry. Miss Baldwin, the dark lady mentioned in my first nonlecture (and a lady if ever a lady existed) was blessed with a delicious voice, charming manners, and a deep understanding of children. Never did any demidivine dictator more gracefully and easily rule a more unruly and less graceful populace. Her very presence emanated an honour and a glory: the honour of spiritual freedom—no mere freedom from—and the glory of being, not (like most extant mortals) really undead, but actually alive. From her I marvellingly learned that the truest power is gentleness. Concerning Mr. Derry, let me say only that he was (and for me will always remain) one of those blessing and blessed spirits who deserve the name of teacher: predicates who are utterly in love with their subject; and who, because they would gladly die for it, are living for it gladly. From him I learned (and am still learning) that gladness is next to godliness. He taught me Greek. This may be as apt a moment as any to state that in the world of my boyhood—long, long ago; before time was space and Oedipus was a complex and religion was the opiate of the people and pigeons had learned to play pingpong—social stratification not merely existed but luxuriated. All women were not, as now, ladies; a gentleman was a gentleman; and a mucker (as the professorial denizens of Irving and Scott streets knew full well: since their lofty fragment of Cambridge almost adjoined plebeian Somerville) was a mucker. Being

myself a professor's (& later a clergyman's) son, I had every
socalled reason to accept these conventional distinctions without
cavil; yet for some unreason I didn't. The more implacably a
virtuous Cambridge drew me toward what might have been her
bosom, the more sure I felt that soi-disant respectability com-
prised nearly everything which I couldn't respect, and the more
eagerly I explored sinful Somerville. But while sinful Somerville
certainly possessed a bosom (in fact, bosoms) she also possessed
fists which hit below the belt and arms which threw snowballs
containing small rocks. Little by little and bruise by teacup, my
doubly disillusioned spirit made an awe-inspiring discovery;
which (on more than several occasions) has prevented me from
wholly misunderstanding socalled humanity: the discovery,
namely, that all groups, gangs, and collectivities—no matter how
apparently disparate—are fundamentally alike; and that what
makes any world go round is not the trivial difference between
a Somerville and a Cambridge, but the immeasurable difference
between either of them and individuality. Whether this discovery
is valid for you, I can't pretend to say: but I can and do say,
without pretending, that it's true for me—inasmuch as I've found
(and am still finding) authentic individuals in the most varied
environments conceivable. Nor will anything ever persuade me
that, by turning Somerville into Cambridge or Cambridge into
Somerville or both into neither, anybody can make an even
slightly better world. Better worlds (I suggest) are born, not
made; and their birthdays are the birthdays of individuals. Let
us pray always for individuals; never for worlds. "He who would
do good to another" cries the poet and painter William Blake
"must do it in Minute Particulars"—and probably many of you
are familiar with this greatly pitying line. But I'll wager that not
three of you could quote me the line which follows it

General Good is the plea of the scoundrel, hypocrite, & flatterer

for that deeply terrible line spells the doom of all unworlds;
whatever their slogans and their strategies, whoever their heroes
or their villains.

The Picador

ERNEST HEMINGWAY (1898–1961)

You READ of bulls in the old days accepting thirty, forty, fifty and even seventy pics from the picadors while to-day a bull that can take seven pics is an amazing animal, and it seems as though things were very different in those days and the bullfighters must have been such men as were the football players on the high-school team when we were still in grammar school. Things change very much and instead of great athletes only children play on the high-school teams now and if you sit with the older men at the café you know there are no good bullfighters now either; they are all children without honor, skill or virtue, much the same as those children who now play football, a feeble game it has become, on the high-school team and nothing like the great, mature, sophisticated athletes in canvas-elbowed jerseys, smelling vinegary from sweated shoulder pads, carrying leather headguards, their moleskins clotted with mud, that walked on leather-cleated shoes that printed in the earth along beside the sidewalk in the dusk, a long time ago.

There were always giants in those days and the bulls really did accept that many pics, the contemporary accounts prove, but the pics were different. In the oldest old days the pic had a very small steel triangular tip so wrapped and protected that only that small tip could go into the bull. The picadors received the bull with their horse straight toward him, drove the pic at him and as they held him off pivoted the horse to the left freeing him from the charge and letting the bull go by. A bull, even a modern bull, could accept a large number of those pics since the steel did not cut into him deeply and it was a move of address on the part of the picador rather than a deliberately sought shock and punishment.

The present pic is very destructive even though properly placed. It is especially destructive since the picador does not place it, shoot the stick it is called, until the bull has reached the horse. The bull must then make the effort of lifting the horse at the same time the man is leaning his weight on the shaft and driving the steel into the bull's neck muscle or his withers. If all of the picadors were as skillful as a few are there would be no need to let the bull reach the horse before shooting the stick. But the majority of the picadors, because it is a poorly paid occupation that leads only to concussion of the brain, are not even capable of sinking the pic into a bull properly. They rely on a lucky drive and the certain effort the bull must make in tossing horse and rider to tire the bull's neck muscles and do the work that a real picador could accomplish without losing either his horse or his seat in the saddle. The wearing of protective mattresses by the horses has made the picadors' work much more difficult and hazardous. Without the mattress the bull's horn can get into the horse and he can lift him, or, sometimes, satisfied with the damage he is doing with his horn, be held off by the man's pic; with the mattress he butts into the horse, there is nothing for his horn to go into and he crashes horse and rider over in a heap. The use of the protective mattress has led to another abuse in bullfighting. Horses that are no longer killed in the ring may be offered by the horse contractor again and again. They are so afraid of the bulls and become so panic stricken on smelling them that they are almost impossible to manage. The new government regulation provides that the picadors may refuse such horses and that they must be marked so that they cannot be used or offered by any horse contractor, but since the picador is so poorly paid, this regulation too will probably be destroyed by the propina, or tip, which makes up a regular part of the picador's income and which he accepts from the contractor for riding the animals he is given the right and duty, by the government regulations, to refuse.

The propina is responsible for almost every horror in bullfighting. The regulations provide for the size, sturdiness and fitness of the horses used in the bull ring and if proper horses are used and the picadors well trained there would be no need for any horses to be killed except accidentally and against the will of the riders as they are killed, for instance, in steeple-chasing. But the enforcing of these regulations for his own protection is left to the picador as the most interested party and the picador is so poorly paid for the danger he undergoes that, for a small addition to this pay, he is willing to accept horses that make his work even more difficult and dangerous. The horse contractor must furnish or have available thirty-six horses for each fight. He is paid a fixed sum no matter what happens to his horses. It is to his interest to furnish the cheapest animals he can get and see that as few of them are used as possible.

This is about how it works out; the picadors arrive the day before the fight or in the morning of the fight at the corrals of the bull ring to choose and test the horses they are to ride. There is a piece of iron set in the stone wall of the corral that marks the minimum height at the shoulder that a horse must have to be accepted. A picador has the big saddle put on a horse, mounts, tests whether the horse minds bit and spur, backs, wheels and riding toward the corral wall drives against it with the shaft of a pic to see if the horse is sound and solid on his feet. He then dismounts and says to the contractor, "I wouldn't risk my life on that lousy skate for a thousand dollars."

"What's the matter with that horse?" says the contractor. "You'll go a long way before you'll find a horse like that."

"Too long a way," says the picador.

"What's the matter with him? That's a handsome little horse."

"He's got no mouth," the picador says. "He won't back. Besides he's short."

"He's just the right size. Look at him. Just the right size."

"Just the right size for what?"

"Just the right size to ride."

"Not me," says the picador turning away.

"You won't find a better horse."

"I believe that," says the picador.

"What's your real objection?"

"He's got glanders."

"Nonsense. That isn't glanders. That's just dandruff."

"You ought to spray him with flit," says the picador. "That would kill him."

"What's your real objection?"

"I have a wife and three children. I wouldn't ride him for a thousand dollars."

"Be sensible," the contractor says. They talk in low tones. He gives the picador fifteen pesetas.

"All right," says the picador. "Mark up the little horse."

So, in the afternoon you see the picador ride out the little horse and if the little horse gets ripped and, instead of killing him, the red-jacketed bull ring servant runs with him toward the horse gate to get him back where he can be patched up so the contractor can send him in again, you may be sure the bull ring servant has received or been promised a propina for every horse he can bring alive out of the ring, instead of killing them mercifully and decently when they are wounded.

I have known some fine picadors, honest, honorable, brave and in a bad business, but you may have all the horse contractors I have ever met, although some of them were nice fellows. If you wish and will take them, you may have all the bull ring servants too. They are the only people I have found in bullfighting that are brutalized by it and they are the only ones who take an active part who undergo no danger. I have seen several of them, two especially that are father and son, that I would like to shoot. If we ever have a time when for a few days you may shoot any one you wish I believe that before starting out to bag various policemen, Italian statesmen, government functionaries, Massachusetts judges, and a couple of companions of my youth I would shove in a clip and make sure of that pair of bull ring servants. I do not want to identify them any more closely because if I ever should bag them this would be evidence of premeditation. But of all the filthy cruelty I have ever seen they have furnished the most. Where you see gratuitous cruelty most often is in police brutality; in the police of all countries I have ever been in, including, especially, my own. These two Pamplona and San Sebastian monosabios should be, by rights, policemen and policemen on the radical squad, but they do the best they can with their talents in the bull ring. They carry on their belts puntillas, broad-headed knives, with which they can give the gift of death to any horse that is badly wounded, but I have never seen them kill a horse that could possibly be gotten on his feet and made to move toward the corrals. It is not only a question of the money they could make by salvaging horses to be taxidermed while alive so they may be reintroduced into the ring, for I have seen them refuse to kill, until forced to by the public, a horse there was no hope of getting onto his feet or of bringing back into the ring purely from pleasure in exerting their power to refuse to perform a merciful act as long as possible. Most bull ring servants are poor devils that perform a miserable function for a mean wage and are entitled to pity if not sympathy. If they save a horse or two that they should kill they do it with fear that outruns any pleasure and earn their money as well as the men do who pick up cigar butts, say. But these two that I speak of are both fat, well-fed and arrogant. I once succeeded in landing a large, heavy one-peseta-fifty rented, leather cushion alongside the head of the younger one during a scene of riotous disapproval in a bull ring in the north of Spain and I am never at the ring without a bottle of Manzanilla which I hope yet I will be able to land, empty, on one or the other at any time rioting becomes so general that a single bottle stroke may pass unperceived by the authorities. After one comes, through contact with its administrators, no longer to cherish greatly the law as a remedy in abuses, then the bottle becomes a sovereign means of direct action. If you cannot throw it at least you can always drink out of it.

In bullfights now a good pic is not one in which the picador, pivoting, protects his horse completely. That is what it should be, but you might go a long time and never see one. All you can expect in a good pic now is that the picador will place his stick properly, that is drive the point into the morillo, or hump of muscle that rises from the back of the bull's neck to his shoulders, that he will try to hold the bull off and that he will not twist his pic or turn it to try and make a deep wound in the bull in order that he may lose blood and so weaken, to make the danger less for the matador.

A bad pic is one that is placed anywhere else but in the morillo, one which rips or opens a big wound, or one in which the picador lets the bull reach the horse, then when the horn is in, pushes, drives and twists on the pic which is in the bull and tries to give the impression he is protecting his horse when he is really only injuring the bull to no good purpose.

If picadors had to own their own horses and were well paid they would protect them and the horse part of bullfighting would become one of the most brilliant and skillful of all rather than a necessary evil. For my own part if horses are to be killed the worse the horses are the better. For the picadors' part an old horse with big feet is much more useful to them in the way they pic now than would be a thoroughbred in good condition. To be useful in the bull ring a horse must be either old or well-tired. It is as much to tire the horses as to provide transportation for the picadors that the animals are ridden from the ring into town to the picadors' boarding house and back. In the provinces the bull ring servants ride the horses in the morning to tire them. The rôle of the horse has become that of providing something the bull will charge so that his neck muscles will be tired and of supporting the man who receives the charge and places his pic in such a manner as to force the bull to tire those muscles. His duty is to tire the bull rather than weaken him by wounds. The wound made by the pic is an incident rather than an end. Whenever it becomes an end it is censurable.

Used for this purpose the worst horses possible, that is those past any other usefulness, but which are solid on their feet and moderately manageable, are the best. I have seen thoroughbreds killed in their prime in other places than the bull ring and it is always a sad and disturbing business. The bull ring is a death's business for horses and the worse horses they are the better.

As I say, having the picadors own their own horses would change the whole spectacle. But I would rather see a dozen old worthless horses killed on purpose than one good horse killed by accident.

What about the Old Lady? She's gone. We threw her out of the book, finally. A little late you say. Yes, perhaps a little late. What about the horses? They are what people always like to talk about in regard to the bullfight. Has there been enough about the horses? Plenty about the horses, you say. They like it all but the poor horses. Should we try to raise the general tone? What about higher things?

Mr. Aldous Huxley writing in an essay entitled "Foreheads Villainous Low" commences: "In [naming a book by this writer] Mr. H. ventures, once, to name an Old Master. There is a phrase, quite admirably expressive [here Mr. Huxley inserts a compliment], a single phrase, no more, about 'the bitter nailholes' of Mantegna's Christs; then quickly, quickly, appalled by his own temerity, the author passes on (as Mrs. Gaskell might hastily have passed on, if she had somehow been betrayed into mentioning a water-closet), passes on, shamefacedly, to speak once more of Lower Things.

"There was a time, not so long ago, when the stupid and uneducated aspired to be thought intelligent and cultured. The current of aspiration has changed its direction. It is not at all uncommon now to find intelligent and cultured people doing their best to feign stupidity and to conceal the fact that they have received an education"—and more; more in Mr. Huxley's best educated vein which is a highly educated vein indeed.

What about that, you say? Mr. Huxley scores there, all right, all right. What have you to say to that? Let me answer truly. On reading that in Mr. Huxley's book I obtained a copy of the volume he refers to and looked through it and could not find the quotation he mentions. It may be there, but I did not have the patience nor the interest to find it, since the book was finished and nothing to be done. It sounds very much like the sort of thing one tries to remove in going over the manuscript. I believe it is more than a question of the simulation or avoidance of the appearance of culture. When writing a novel a writer should create living people; people not characters. A *character* is a caricature. If a writer can make people live there may be no great characters in his book, but it is possible that his book will remain as a whole; as an entity; as a novel. If the people the writer is making talk of old masters; of music; of modern painting; of letters; or of science then they should talk of those subjects in the novel. If they do not talk of those subjects and the writer makes them talk of them he is a faker, and if he talks about them himself to show how much he knows then he is showing off. No matter how good a phrase or a simile he may have if he puts it in where it is not absolutely necessary and irreplaceable he is spoiling his work for egotism. Prose is architecture, not interior decoration, and the Baroque is over. For a writer to put his own intellectual musings, which he might sell for a low price as essays, into the mouths of artificially constructed characters which are more remunerative when issued as people in a novel is good economics, perhaps, but does not make literature. People in a novel, not skillfully constructed *characters*, must be projected from the writer's assimilated experience, from his knowledge, from his head, from his heart and from all there is of him. If he ever has luck as well as seriousness and gets them out entire they will have more than one dimension and they will last a long time. A good writer should know as near everything as possible. Naturally he will not. A great enough writer seems to be born with knowledge. But he really is not; he has only been born with the ability to learn in a quicker ratio to the passage of time than other men and without conscious application, and with an intelligence to accept or reject what is already presented as knowledge. There are some things which cannot be learned quickly and time, which is all we have, must be paid heavily for their acquiring. They are the very simplest things and because it takes a man's life to know them the little new that each man gets from life is very costly and the only heritage he has to leave. Every novel which is truly written contributes to the total of knowledge which is there at the disposal of the next writer who comes, but the next writer must pay, always, a certain nominal percentage in experience to be able to understand and assimilate what is available as his birthright and what he must, in turn, take his departure from. If a writer of prose knows enough about what he is writing about he may omit things that he knows and the reader, if the writer is writing truly enough, will have a feeling of those things as strongly as though the writer had stated them. The dignity of movement of an ice-berg is due to only one-eighth of it being above water. A writer who omits things because he does not know them only makes hollow places in his writing. A writer who appreciates the seriousness of writing so little that he is anxious to make people see he is formally educated, cultured or well-bred is merely a popinjay. And this too remember; a serious writer is not to be confounded with a solemn writer. A serious writer may be a hawk or a buzzard or even a popinjay, but a solemn writer is always a bloody owl.

Suggestions for Study

NOWADAYS ALMOST every schoolboy knows all about the bull-fight, enabled by national magazines and bad movies; but Hemingway's *Death in the Afternoon*, written before terms like "the

moment of truth" had become popular, retains much of its original
force and impact. That is partly because the book is not just
about bulls and the men who fight them, but about the complexity
of human experience (which requires the writer to write "from
his knowledge, from his head, from his heart and from all there
is of him"); and partly because of the style. Dr. Johnson had some
advice for authors who, in the course of making revisions, encountered a passage that seemed "particularly fine": "Strike it
out!" Hemingway's style also reflects a concern with eliminating
needless decoration together with nonsense and cant. The language is simple and colloquial: "A good writer should know as
near everything as possible"; "This is about how it works out:
the picadors arrive the day before the fight or in the morning
of the fight at the corrals of the bull ring to choose and test
the horses they are to ride." Hemingway regularly ignores copy-
book dogmatics for the sake of directness ("If a writer of prose
knows enough about what he is writing about . . ."); nor does
he recoil from sentences that end with prepositions. What he
talks about are facts, mostly, and his sparse manner allows these
their full eloquence: the true writer "may omit things that he
knows and the reader, if the writer is writing truly enough, will
have a feeling of those things as strongly as though the writer
had stated them."

Structurally, the piece combines analysis (or extended definition) with analogy. The opening paragraph, frankly nostalgic
in tone, turns on the clause "it seems as though things were very
different in those days. . . ." Time, apparently, is absolute lord
of human actions: what is past was bigger and better than its
modern counterpart. The first sentence of the second paragraph
confirms this to a degree. But "the pics were different": qualita-
tively, then, past and present cannot so simply be related. There
follows the analysis of the picador's work. A good picador ought
to have knowledge, technique, experience: today the profession
is corrupted by cruelty, poor craftsmanship, greed. But if picadors owned their horses, all would change, and (given the dif-

ferent pics) modern pic-ing would match that of the past.

So with writers. "Artificially constructed characters . . . are more remunerative" than real people; showing off and fakery take the place of craftsmanship and technique; "hollow places" (like gaps defacing a tapestry) betray lack of knowledge. One might say that the last paragraph of this selection sets forth as theory what Hemingway practiced in his short stories and novels. The white hunter Wilson will not shoot lions from cars, and the hoodlums of "The Killers" take pride in their work; the writer also, by "writing truly enough," may meet the timeless demands of his craft.

The Age of Rutherford

SIR CHARLES SNOW (1905–   )

IN 1923, at the meeting of the British Association for the Advancement of Science in Liverpool, Lord Rutherford [1] announced, at the top of his enormous voice: "We are living in the heroic age of physics." He went on saying the same thing, loudly and exuberantly, until he died, fourteen years later.

The curious thing was, all he said was absolutely true. There had never been such a time. The year 1932 was the most spectacular year in the history of science. Living in Cambridge, one could not help picking up the human, as well as the intellectual, excitement in the air. Sir James Chadwick, gray-faced after a fortnight of work with three hours' sleep a night, telling the

THE AGE OF RUTHERFORD by Sir Charles Snow is reprinted from *The Atlantic Monthly*, November 1958, by permission of the author.

[1] *Editors' note:* Ernest Rutherford, first Baron Rutherford (1871–1937), a native of New Zealand, received the Nobel Prize for Chemistry in 1908. Later he became known chiefly for his pioneering research in nuclear physics.

Kapitza Club how he had discovered the neutron; P. M. S. Blackett, the most handsome of men, not quite so authoritative as usual, because it seemed too good to be true, showing plates which demonstrated the existence of the positive electron; Sir John Cockcroft, normally about as given to emotional display as the Duke of Wellington, skimming down King's Parade and saying to anyone whose face he recognized: "We've split the atom! We've split the atom!"

It meant an intellectual climate different in kind from anything else in England at the time. The tone of science was the tone of Rutherford: magniloquently boastful—boastful because the major discoveries were being made—creatively confident, generous, argumentative, lavish, and full of hope. The tone differed from the tone of literary England as much as Rutherford's personality differed from that of T. S. Eliot or F. R. Leavis. During the twenties and thirties, Cambridge was the metropolis of physics for the entire world. Even in the late nineteenth century, during the professorships of Clerk Maxwell and J. J. Thomson, it had never quite been that. "You're always at the crest of the wave," someone said to Rutherford. "Well, after all, I made the wave, didn't I?" Rutherford replied.

I remember seeing him a good many times before I first spoke to him. I was working on the periphery of physics at the time, and so didn't come directly under him. I already knew that I wanted to write novels, and that that was how I should finish, and this gave me a kind of ambivalent attitude to the scientific world; but, even so, I could not avoid feeling some sort of excitement, or enhancement of interest, whenever I saw Rutherford walking down Free School Lane.

He was a big rather clumsy man, with a substantial bay window that started in the middle of the chest. I should guess that he was less muscular than at first sight he looked. He had large staring blue eyes and a damp and pendulous lower lip. He didn't look in the least like an intellectual. Creative people of his abundant kind never do, of course, but all the talk of Rutherford looking like a farmer was unperceptive nonsense. His was really the kind of face and physique that often goes with great weight of character and gifts. It could easily have been the soma of a great writer. As he talked to his companions in the street, his voice was three times as loud as any of theirs, and his accent was bizarre. In fact, he came from the very poor: his father was an odd-job man in New Zealand and the son of a Scottish emigrant. But there was nothing Antipodean or Scottish about Rutherford's accent; it sounded more like a mixture of West Country and Cockney.

In my first actual meeting with him, perhaps I could be excused for not observing with precision. It was early in 1930; I had not yet been elected a Fellow of my own college, and so had put in for the Stokes studentship at Pembroke. One Saturday afternoon I was summoned to an interview. When I arrived at Pembroke, I found that the short list was only two, Philip Dee and I. Dee was called in first; as he was being interviewed, I was reflecting without pleasure that he was one of the brightest of Rutherford's young men.

Then came my turn. As I went in, the first person I saw, sitting on the right hand of the Master, was Rutherford himself. While the Master was taking me through my career, Rutherford drew at his pipe, not displaying any excessive interest in the proceedings. The Master came to the end of his questions, and said: "Professor Rutherford?"

Rutherford took out his pipe and turned onto me an eye which was blue, cold, and bored. He was the most spontaneous of men; when he felt bored, he showed it. That afternoon he felt distinctly bored. Wasn't his man, and a very good man, in for this job? What was this other fellow doing there? Why were we all wasting our time?

He asked me one or two indifferent questions, in an irritated, impatient voice. What was my present piece of work? What could spectroscopy tell us anyway? Wasn't it just "putting things into boxes"?

I thought that was a bit rough. Perhaps I realized that I had nothing to lose. Anyway, as cheerfully as I could manage, I asked if he couldn't put up with a few of us not doing nuclear physics. I went on, putting a case for my kind of subject.

A note was brought round to my lodgings that evening. Dee had got the job. The electors wished to say that either candidate could properly have been elected. That sounded like a bit of politeness, and I felt depressed. I cheered up a day or two later when I heard that Rutherford was trumpeting that I was a young man of spirit. Within a few months he backed me for another studentship. Incidentally, Dee was a far better scientist than I was or could have been, and neither Rutherford nor anyone else had been unjust.

From that time until he died, I had some opportunities of watching Rutherford at close quarters. Several of my friends knew him intimately, which I never did. It is a great pity that Tizard has not written about him at length. But I belonged to a dining club which he attended, and I think I had serious conversations with him three times, the two of us alone together.

The difficulty is to separate the inner man from the Rutherfordiana, much of which is quite genuine. From behind a screen in a Cambridge tailor's, a friend and I heard a reverberating voice: "That shirt's too tight round the neck. Every day I grow in girth. *And* in mentality." Yet his physical make-up was more nervous than it seemed. In the same way, his temperament, which seemed exuberantly, powerfully, massively simple, rejoicing with childish satisfaction in creation and fame, was not quite so simple as all that. His was a personality of Johnsonian scale. As with Johnson, the façade was overbearing and unbroken. But there were fissures within.

No one could have enjoyed himself more, either in creative work or the honors it brought him. He worked hard, but with immense gusto; he got pleasure not only from the high moments, but also from the hours of what to others would be drudgery, sitting in the dark counting the alpha particle scintillations on the screen. His insight was direct, his intuition, with one curious exception, infallible. No scientist has made less mistakes. In the corpus of his published work, one of the largest in scientific history, there was nothing he had to correct afterwards. By thirty, he had already set going the science of nuclear physics—single-handed, as a professor on five hundred pounds a year, in the isolation of late-Victorian Montreal. By forty, now in Manchester, he had found the structure of the atom on which all modern nuclear physics depends.

It was not done without noise; it was done with anger and storms—but also with an overflow of creative energy, with abundance and generosity, as though research were the easiest and most natural avocation in the world. He had deep sympathy with the creative arts, particularly literature; he read more novels than most literary people manage to do. He had no use for critics of any kind. He felt both suspicion and dislike of the people who invested scientific research or any other branch of creation with an aura of difficulty, who used long, methodological words to explain things which he did perfectly by instinct. "Those fellows," he used to call them. "Those fellows" were the logicians, the critics, the metaphysicians. They were clever; they were usually more lucid than he was; in argument against them he often felt at a disadvantage. Yet somehow they never produced a serious piece of work, whereas he was the greatest experimental scientist of the age.

I have heard greater claims made for him. I remember one discussion in particular, a few years after his death, by half a dozen men, all of whom had international reputations in science. Was Rutherford the greatest experimental scientist since Michael Faraday? Without any doubt. Greater than Faraday? Almost certainly so. And then—it is interesting, as it shows the anonymous Tolstoyan nature of organized science—how many years difference would it have made if he had never lived? How much longer before the nucleus would have been understood as we now understand it? Perhaps ten years. More likely only five.

Rutherford's intellect was so strong that he would, in the long run, have accepted that judgment. But he would not have liked it. His estimate of his own powers was realistic, but if it erred at all, it did not err on the modest side. "There is no room for this particle in the atom as designed by *me*," I once heard him assure a large audience. It was part of his nature that, stupendous as his work was, he should consider it 10 per cent more so. It was also part of his nature that, quite without acting, he should behave constantly as though he were 10 per cent larger than life. Worldly success? He loved every minute of it: flattery, titles, the company of the high official world. He said in a speech: "As I was standing in the drawing room at Trinity, a *clergyman* came in. And I said to him: 'I'm Lord Rutherford.' And he said to me: 'I'm the Archbishop of York.' And I don't suppose either of us believed the other."

He was a great man, a very great man, by any standards which we can apply. He was clever as well as creatively gifted, magnanimous (within the human limits) as well as hearty. He was also superbly and magnificently vain as well as wise—the combination is commoner than we think when we are young. He enjoyed a life of miraculous success. On the whole he enjoyed his own personality. But I am sure that, even quite late in his life, he felt stabs of a sickening insecurity.

Somewhere at the roots of that abundant and creative nature there was a painful, shrinking nerve. One has only to read his letters as a young man to discern it. There are passages of self-doubt which are not to be explained completely by a humble colonial childhood and youth. He was uncertain in secret, abnormally so for a young man of his gifts. He kept the secret as his personality flowered and hid it. But there was a mysterious diffidence behind it all. He hated the faintest suspicion of being patronized, even when he was a world figure. Archbishop Lang was once tactless enough to suggest that he supposed a famous scientist had no time for reading. Rutherford immediately felt that he was being regarded as an ignorant roughneck. He produced a formidable list of his last month's reading. Then, half innocently, half malevolently: "And what do you manage to read, your Grice?" "I am afraid," said the Archbishop, somewhat out of his depth, "that a man in my position really doesn't have the leisure . . ." "Ah, yes, your Grice," said Rutherford in triumph, "it must be a dog's life! It must be a dog's life!"

Once I had an opportunity of seeing that diffidence face to face. In the autumn of 1934 I published my first novel, which was called *The Search* and the background of which was the scientific world. Not long after it came out, Rutherford met me in King's Parade. "What have you been doing to us, young man?" he asked vociferously. I began to describe the novel, but it was not necessary; he announced that he had read it with care. He went on to invite, or rather command, me to take a stroll with him round the Backs. Like most of my scientific friends, he was good-natured about the book, which has some descriptions of the scientific experience which are probably somewhere near the truth. He praised it. I was gratified. It was a sunny October afternoon. Suddenly he said: "I didn't like the erotic bits. I suppose it's because we belong to different generations."

The book, I thought, was reticent enough. I did not know how to reply.

In complete seriousness and simplicity, he made another suggestion. He hoped that I was not going to write all my novels about scientists. I assured him that I was not—certainly not another for a long time.

He nodded. He was looking gentler than usual, and thoughtful. "It's a small world, you know," he said. He meant the world of science. "Keep off us as much as you can. People are bound to think that you are getting at some of us. And I suppose we've all got things that we don't want anyone to see."

I mentioned that his intuitive foresight went wrong just once. As a rule, he was dead right about the practical applications of science just as much as about the nucleus. But his single boss shot sounds ironic now. In 1933 he said, in another address to the British Association, "These transformations of the atom are of extraordinary interest to scientists, but we cannot control atomic energy to an extent which would be of any value commercially, and I believe we are not likely ever to be able to do so. A lot of nonsense has been talked about transmutations. Our interest in the matter is purely scientific."

That statement, which was made only nine years before the first pile worked, was not intended to be either optimistic or pessimistic. It was just a forecast, and it was wrong.

That judgment apart, people outside the scientific world often felt that Rutherford and his kind were optimistic—optimistic right against the current of the twentieth-century literary-intellectual mood, offensively and brazenly optimistic. This feeling was not quite unjustified, but the difference between the scientists and the nonscientists was subtler than that. When the scientists talked of the individual human condition, they did not find it any more hopeful than the rest of us. Does anyone really imagine that Bertrand Russell, G. H. Hardy, Rutherford, Blackett, and the rest were bemused by cheerfulness as they faced their own individual state? Very few of them had any of the consolations of religion: they believed, with the same certainty that they believed in Rutherford's atom, that they were going, after the loneliness of this mortal life, into annihilation. Intellectually they had an unqualified comprehension, without any cushions at all, of the tragic condition of individual man.

Nevertheless it is true that, of the kinds of people I have lived among, the scientists were much the happiest. Somehow scientists were buoyant at a time when other intellectuals could not keep away despair. The reasons for this are complex. Partly, the nature of a scientific activity, its complete success on its own terms, is itself a source of happiness; partly, people who are drawn to scientific activity tend to be happier in temperament than other clever men. By the nature of their vocation and also by the nature of their own temperament, the scientists did not think constantly of the individual human predicament. Since they could not alter it, they let it alone. When they thought about people, they thought most of what could be altered, not what couldn't. So they gave their minds not to the individual condition but to the social one.

There, science itself was the greatest single force for change. The scientists were themselves part of the deepest revolution in human affairs since the discovery of agriculture. They could accept what was happening, while other intellectuals shrank away. They not only accepted it, they rejoiced in it. It was difficult to find a scientist who did not believe that the scientific-technical-industrial revolution, accelerating under his eyes, was not doing incomparably more good than harm.

This was the characteristic optimism of scientists in the twenties and thirties. It still is. In some ways it was too easy an optimism, but the counterattitude of the nonscientific intellectuals was too easy a pessimism. Between Rutherford and Blackett on the one hand, and, say, Wyndham Lewis and Ezra Pound on the other, who are on the side of their fellow human beings? The only people who would have any doubt about the answer are those who dislike the human race.

So, in Rutherford's scientific world, the liberal decencies were taken for granted. It was a society singularly free from class or national or racial prejudice. Rutherford called himself alternatively conservative or nonpolitical, but the men he wanted to have jobs were those who could do physics. Niels Bohr, Otto Hahn, Georg von Hevesy, Hans Geiger were men and brothers, whether they were Jews, Germans, Hungarians—men and brothers whom he would much rather have near him than the Archbishop of Canterbury or one of "those fellows" or any damned English philosopher. It was Rutherford who, after 1933, took the lead in opening English academic life to Jewish refugees. In fact, scientific society was wide open, as it may not be again for many years. There was coming and going among laboratories all over the world, including Russia. Peter Kapitza, Rutherford's favorite pupil, contrived to be in good grace with the Soviet authorities and at the same time a star of the Cavendish. With a touch of genius and of the inspired Russian clown, he backed both horses for fifteen years until, on one of his holiday trips to Russia, the Soviet bosses blandly told him that they now wanted his services full time.

Kapitza flattered Rutherford outrageously, and Rutherford loved it. Kapitza was as impudent as Peter Lebedev; he had great daring and scientific insight. He once asked a friend of mine whether a foreigner could become an English peer; we strongly suspected that his ideal career would see him established simultaneously in the Soviet Academy of Sciences and as Rutherford's successor in the House of Lords.

Between Leningrad and Cambridge, Kapitza oscillated. Between Copenhagen and Cambridge, there was a stream of travelers, all the nuclear physicists of the world. Copenhagen had become the second scientific metropolis on account of the personal influence of one man, Niels Bohr, who was complementary to Rutherford as a person—patient, reflective, any thought hedged with Proustian qualifications—just as the theoretical quantum physics of which he was the master was complementary to Rutherford's experimental physics. He had been a pupil of Rutherford's and they loved and esteemed each other like father and son. (Rutherford was a paterfamilias born, and the death of his only daughter seems to have been the greatest sorrow of his personal life. In his relations with Bohr and Kapitza and others, there was a strong vein of paternal emotion diverted from the son he never had.) But, strong as Rutherford's liking for Bohr was, it was not strong enough to put up with Bohr's idea of a suitable length for a lecture. In the Cavendish lecture room, Bohr went past the hour and a half; Rutherford began plucking at his sleeve and muttering in a stage whisper about "another five minutes." Blandly, patiently, determined not to leave a qualification unsaid, Bohr went past the two hours; Rutherford was beginning to trumpet about "bringing the lecture to a close." Soon they were both on their feet at once.

Throughout the twenties and thirties, the quantum physics seemed as exciting as the experiments of the Rutherford school. At times it seemed more so. Looking at young Paul Dirac, in his middle twenties, pale and black-moustached like the bridegroom in an Italian wedding photograph, walking with his arms behind him along the Backs, people wondered if he had now written down the fundamental laws of physics and chemistry forever. Thirty years later, the revolution in theory still seems wonderful, but not quite so final as it did then. At the time, it was part, and in some ways the most dramatic part, of the general air of intellectual triumph which spread, of course, much further than physics—it touched almost all natural science. In physics the triumph was clearest and most dramatic, that was all.

Thus the climate in which English scientists went about their work was crammed full of confidence, socially well-intentioned and, in a serious working sense, international. But coming upon them was the distress of the thirties, the emergence of National Socialism, and the prospect of a war.

People outside the scientific world got the impression that, as soon as the trouble broke, the scientists moved to the Left as one man. That is not true, and yet the impression is not wholly false. More unanimously than any other intellectual group, the scientists were anti-Nazi. There were none of the ambiguous relations with Fascism into which Yeats and T. S. Eliot found themselves entering, none of those uncapitalized references to "the jew." Rutherford and his contemporaries mostly voted Conservative, but they regarded that kind of utterance as intellectually and morally contemptible. In fact, the literary neo-classics, the "men of 1914," made scientists think all the worse of the aesthetic world; in some ways, unfairly so. The social attitudes of Pound, Lewis, and T. E. Hulme are not, of course, representative of all artists. Their importance is symbolic, not statistical. This was a moral debasement the scientist did not know; many of them have not forgotten, and it has widened the gap between the cultures.

In his political attitudes, Rutherford was typical of a large fraction of scientists. He welcomed the Jewish refugees and put himself out for them; he presumably went on voting Conservative but was getting restive and sympathetic to the Churchill wing. He did not dislike Russia nearly as much as a nonscientific Conservative would have done. Like all scientists, conservative or radical, he had, almost without thinking what it meant, the future in his bones. In all those ways the respectable older scientists felt and acted with him. Some of them were already active in preparing for war, such as Tizard, perhaps the ablest scientist who ever devoted himself to military affairs; more than any other man he was responsible for the scientific thinking which lay behind the Battle of Britain.

But an overwhelming majority of the younger scientists had committed themselves to the Left. This was partly due to the social crisis; it was partly that science itself, in its new triumphant phase, was working inside young men's minds. Like their seniors, the young scientists had the future in their bones. Unlike their seniors, they found it natural to look for a political correlative. By the mid-thirties, it was very rare to find a physicist under forty whose sympathies were not on the Left.

This process of political crystallization had begun years before, when the leaders of the young radical scientists had already emerged: J. D. Bernal, Blackett, J. B. S. Haldane. All three were men of tough character and immense intellectual ability. The two Communists, Bernal and Haldane, suffered from the vagaries of the party line and were as late as 1935 leading a pacifist movement among scientists which they shortly after put into reverse. Nevertheless, Bernal, through charm, courage, and more learning than anyone else in England, became the most powerful intellectual force on the extreme Left; more than anyone else, he made Communism intellectually respectable. It was, however, rare for scientists, even the most radical, to enter the party. For most of them, Blackett—firmly planted on the Left but not a Communist, and a scientist of much greater achievement than Bernal or Haldane—was the chosen symbol. In fact, he spoke for the younger generation of scientists in the thirties very much as Rutherford spoke for the older.

My guess is that if one had taken a poll of the two hundred brightest physicists under the age of forty in 1936, about five would have been Communists, ten fellow travelers, fifty somewhere near the Blackett position, a hundred passively sympathetic to the Left. The rest would have been politically null, with perhaps five (or possibly six) oddities on the Right.

Of those two hundred, a number have since occupied positions of eminence. It is interesting that none of them has drastically altered his political judgment. There has just been a slight stagger, a place and a half to the Right, no more. The scientists who got under the shadow of the Communist Party have come out but have stayed (like Haldane) on the extreme Left. A few who were vaguely Left in the thirties would now be vaguely sympathetic to R. A. Butler. The changes have not been any more dramatic than that. There have not been any renunciations or swings to religious faith, such as a number of writers of the same age, once Left Wing, have gone in for. The scientists' radicalism had deeper roots.

Before Rutherford's death, a number of the younger scientists were already preparing for the war. Blackett, as usual giving them the lead, had been getting himself used to military problems for some years before. He had been put on the Air Defence Council by Tizard, who wanted talent regardless of politics and who was a specially good judge of talent when it came his way. It was for such reasons—and because England had just gone through its greatest age of physics—that the English scientists were by and large more effective than those of any other country throughout the war with Hitler.

That was one of the legacies of the age of Rutherford. The other legacy was that, after the war, some of the same scientists took Britain into the atomic age and got her a standing there which will retain her as a major power, if anything can.

Suggestions for Study

THE CONVERSATION of Oxford and Cambridge common-rooms has a reputation for urbane wit and the gleam of barbed anecdote; Snow's novels reflect their author's familiarity with that aspect of English university life. For about half of this essay, Snow maintains an essentially conversational style, focused on a series of anecdotes—rather as if he were in the company of a congenial group of dons. It is worth noticing that, unlike John McNulty, Snow is reluctant to allow his audience its head: Rutherford speaks "loudly and exuberantly," "in an irritated, impatient voice," "half innocently, half malevolently." This part of the essay depends for its effect primarily on the spoken word, or on the speaker's tone of voice. Rutherford's "enormous voice" announces the affair, and a good many paragraphs rise to a spoken climax. When conversations are not directly reproduced, they are likely to be paraphrased; now and again the device of rhetorical question enables the author to vary his manner without departing from its central effect. The comparison of Rutherford to Dr. Samuel Johnson is, under these circumstances, sufficiently apt.

With the sentence, "I mentioned that his intuitive foresight went wrong just once," the style is gradually altered: why and how does this take place? What stylistic elements assume primary importance in the latter portion of the essay? You might consider the piece as an exercise in the combination of "decorated" and "plain" styles; in that light, how completely has integration between style and subject been achieved?

A determinedly critical reader might certainly take exception to some features of the essay, which does not (for example) everywhere give evidence of ruthless revision: "In the autumn of 1934 I published my first novel, which was called *The Search* and the background of which was the scientific world." Again, the references to Rutherford's "fissures within" and the "one curious exception" to his ordinarily infallible intuition raise expectations only to disappoint them; neither Rutherford's "self-doubt" nor his "one boss shot," after all, have much to do with the central argument. Still, we are not to expect very delicately chiseled prose in an "informal" piece of meditative reminiscence such as this; further, the diction admirably reflects Rutherford's own distaste for "long, methodological" terms. "Boss shot" and "soma" will send most readers to the dictionary; for the rest, the language is plain enough.

The fact of Rutherford's "deep sympathy with the creative arts, particularly literature," is, or seems intended to have been, a key idea in the piece, for it indicates the point of the essay. Structurally, the argument turns on a central analogy: as Rutherford the great scientist personified and guided an age of great scientific advance, so, as "great liberal," he might have personified and guided an age of "true" liberalism. How successfully is this implied analogy worked out in the essay? Consider the relevance to this matter of the two concluding paragraphs.

The essay is stocked with stimulating opinions, any one of which might start a lively discussion. One at least ought to be quite fruitful:

People who are drawn to scientific activity tend to be happier in temperament than other clever men.

Science and the Humanities

ERNEST NAGEL (1901–   )

THE PLACE of science in a program of liberal education is not a new problem; it has been at the focus of reflection on educational philosophy and practice since Plato. Nevertheless, although the basic issues may not have undergone radical transformation with the passage of centuries, the problem has acquired new dimensions and fresh complexities in contemporary American society.

Until comparatively recent times, the theoretical sciences were regarded as branches of philosophical inquiry, having for their ultimate objective knowledge of man's supreme good in the light of his place in the universe; education designed for developing enlightened and cultivated minds was reserved for small minorities in relatively small populations; and the organization of human life did not require large groups of highly trained scientific personnel. Under the circumstances, it was easy enough for Plato and his successors to argue persuasively for a conception of liberal education in which the study of science occupied a prominent place. But these circumstances are no longer present. It is in consequence more difficult today to win effective general agreement that a solid grounding in natural and social science is an indispensable part of a humanistically oriented education, and that such grounding is no less essential for the formation of a liberal intelligence than is thorough exposure to the materials traditionally classified as belonging to the humanities.

What are the distinctive contributions the study of science

SCIENCE AND THE HUMANITIES by Ernest Nagel is reprinted from *Education in the Age of Science*, edited by Brand Blanshard. Copyright © 1959 by Basic Books, Inc.; © 1959 by the American Academy of Arts and Sciences. Reprinted by permission of Basic Books, Inc.

can make toward realizing the objectives of a liberal education? Let me outline what I regard as the three cardinal contributions.

THE THEORETICAL AND MORAL VALUE OF SCIENCE

It has been the perennial aim of theoretical science to make the world intelligible by disclosing fixed patterns of regularity and orders of dependence in events. This aim may never be fully realized. But it has been partly realized in the scientific exploration of both animate and inanimate subject matter. The knowledge that is thus progressively achieved—of general truths about various sectors in nature as well as of particular processes and events in them—is intrinsically delightful to many minds. In any event, the quest for such knowledge is an expression of a basic impulse of human nature, and it represents a distinctive variety of human experience. It is a history of magnificent victories as well as of tragic defeats for human intelligence in its endless war against native ignorance, childish superstitions, and baseless fears. If to be a humanist is to respond perceptively to all dimensions of man's life, an informed study of the findings and of the development of science must surely be an integral part of a humanistic education.

There is the further point that knowledge acquired by scientific inquiry is indispensable for a responsible assessment of moral ideals and for a rational ordering of human life. Ideals and values are not self-certifying; they are not established as valid by appeals to dogmatic authority, to intuitions of moral imperatives, or to undisciplined preference. Moral ideals must be congruous with the needs and capacities of human beings, both as biological individuals and as historically conditioned members of cultural groups, if those ideals are to serve as satisfactory guides to a rich and satisfying human life. The adequacy of proposed moral norms must therefore be evaluated on the basis of reliable knowledge acquired through controlled scientific inquiry. It is simply grotesque to imagine that anyone today can exercise genuine wisdom in human affairs without some mastery of the relevant conclusions of natural and social science.

I am not unaware that there have been great moral seers who possessed little if any scientific knowledge of the world or of man, and who nevertheless spoke with understanding about the paths of human virtue. However, though such men may have expressed profound insights into the ways of the human heart, merely to proclaim an insight does not establish its wisdom; and it is by no means self-evident that their vision of the human good, though generous and wise for their time, is really adequate for men living in different climes and with different opportunities for developing their powers. Insight and imagination are undoubtedly necessary conditions for moral wisdom, but they are not sufficient. For insights and visions may differ, and knowledge of the world and human circumstance must be introduced for adjudicating between conflicting moral ideas. It would be absurd to deny the exquisite perceptions and the stimuli to reflection that are often found in the pronouncements of scientifically untutored moral seers. But I do not believe their pronouncements can be taken at face value, or that in the light of the scientific knowledge we now possess those pronouncements are invariably sound. In short, apart from the intellectual joys accompanying the enlarged understanding of the world that scientific knowledge may bring, such knowledge is indispensable if the ideals and the conduct we adopt are to be based neither on illusion nor on uninformed parochial preferences. It is not an exaggeration to claim that the theoretical understanding that the sciences provide is the foundation for a liberal civilization and a humane culture.

SCIENCE AS INTELLECTUAL METHOD

The conclusions of science are the products of an intellectual method, and in general they cannot be properly understood or evaluated without an adequate grasp of the logic of scientific inquiry. I am not maintaining, of course, that there are fixed rules for devising experiments or making theoretical discoveries.

There are no such rules; and it is in large measure because it is commonly supposed that there are, that scientific inquiry is frequently believed to be a routine grubbing for facts, and unlike literature and the arts to require no powers of creative imagination. Indeed, science has fallen into understandable though undeserved disrepute among many humanistic thinkers because students of human affairs have sometimes permitted this misconception to control their inquiries and their literary productions. Nor am I asserting that the sciences share a common set of techniques of inquiry, so that disciplines not employing those techniques are not properly scientific. Except for the ability to use a language, it is doubtful whether there is such a set of common techniques. Certainly the techniques required for making astronomical observations are different from those used in the study of cellular division; mathematically formulated laws are relatively recent developments in chemistry, biology, and the social sciences; and though quantitative distinctions are widely used in many sciences, the techniques of measurement are often quite different for different subject matters.

On the other hand, I am suggesting that what is distinctive of all science, not merely of natural science such as physics, and what assures the general reliability of scientific findings, is the use of a *common intellectual method* for assessing the weight of the available evidence for a proposed solution of a problem, and for accepting or rejecting a tentative conclusion of an inquiry. Scientific method, in my use of this phrase, is a procedure of applying logical canons for *testing* claims to knowledge.

These logical canons have been adopted neither as arbitrary conventions, nor because there are no conceivable alternatives to them, nor because they can be established by appeals to self-evidence. They are themselves the distilled residue of a long series of attempts to win reliable knowledge, and they may be modified and improved in the course of further inquiries. They owe their authority to the fact that conclusions obtained in accordance with their requirements have agreed better with data

of observation, and have in the main withstood further critical
testing more successfully, than have conclusions obtained in other
ways. The use of scientific method does not guarantee the truth
of every conclusion reached by that method. But scientific
method does give rational assurance that conclusions conforming
to its canons are more likely to approximate the truth than beliefs held on other grounds. To accept the conclusions of science
without a thorough familiarity with its method of warranting
them is to remain ignorant of the critical spirit that is the life
of science. Not every claim to knowledge is a valid claim; and
without a clear grasp of the standards that evidence for a conclusion must meet, the risk is large of becoming a slave to every
rhetorical appeal, to every plausible though specious argument,
and to every intellectual fashion.

A firm grasp of the logical grounds upon which the sciences
rest their conclusions serves to show that the sciences can make
no dogmatic claims for the finality of their findings; that their
procedure nevertheless provides for the progressive corrections
of their cognitive claims; that they can achieve reliable knowledge even though they are fallible; and that however impressive
the achievements of science have been in giving us intellectual
mastery over many segments of existence, we cannot justifiably
assume that we have exhaustively surveyed the variety and the
depths of nature. The critical temper, the confidently constructive rationality, and the manly intellectual humility that
are essential for the practice of scientific method are not simply
adornments of a well-balanced mind; they are of its essence.

SCIENCE AS THE CODE OF A COMMUNITY

This brings me to the final point I want to make in this context. Viewed in broad perspective, science is an enterprise carried
on by a self-governing community of inquirers who conduct
themselves in accordance with an unwritten but binding code.
Each member of this republic has the right and the obligation
to make the most of his capacities for original and inventive re-

search, to make full use of his powers of imagination and insight, to be independent in his analyses and assessments, and to dissent from the views of others if in his judgment the evidence requires him to do so. In return for this he must submit his own investigations to examination by his scientific peers, and he must be prepared to defend his claims by reasoned argument against all competent critics, even if he should believe himself their superior in knowledge and insight. Accordingly, no question of fact or theory is in principle finally closed. The career of science is a continuing free exchange of ideas, and its enduring intellectual products are in the end the fruits of a refining process of mutual criticism. This does not mean that individual scientists do not possess passions and vanities, which are often obstacles to dispassionate judgment and which may hamper the advance of knowledge. It does mean that the institution of science provides a mechanism for discovering the truth irrespective of personal idiosyncrasies, but without curtailing the rights of its members to develop freely their own insights and to dissent from accepted beliefs. The organization of science as a community of free, tolerant, yet alertly critical inquirers embodies in remarkable measure the ideals of liberal civilization. The discipline that fosters these qualities of mind therefore must have an important place in an educational program designed to develop members for such a society.

I must now discuss some of the obstacles in modern American society that stand in the way of adequate realization of the values that are obtainable from training in science.

THE DANGER OF THE MOLE'S-EYE VIEW

In the first place, there is the high degree of specialization now required for exploration in most branches of science. Much of the indispensable day-by-day work of the scientist, even when he engages in fundamental research, has in consequence a relatively narrow scope. It is work which for the most part can be carried on successfully without thinking about the basic assumptions and issues. Accordingly, most scientists, whether in academic life or in one of the engineering professions, have at best only a perfunctory interest in the philosophical aspects of their discipline.

To be sure, in the course of solving their own technical problems many of the creative minds in science have felt themselves compelled to give close attention to the structure of scientific ideas, to examine the significance of scientific statements, or to analyze the logic of scientific inquiry. Indeed, revolutionary advances in scientific theory sometimes have been the consequences of just such comprehensive reflections. But to a large fraction of practicing scientists, concern with such matters is a luxury for which their immersion in detailed technical problems leaves them little time.

In consequence, the intellectual climate in which the sciences are taught is not generally favorable to the study of science as part of a liberal education. Courses in so-called "general science," designed in the main for those not contemplating a scientific career, are frequently so empty of scientific content, as well as of competent philosophical commentary, that they are viewed with merited contempt by scientists and humanists alike. On the other hand, the more traditional courses in science are normally organized so as to provide training mainly in professional skills. Unless he is guided by an exceptional teacher, it is only an exceptional student who acquires from such courses a just appreciation of the structure of scientific ideas, or of the logic and the civilizing significance of scientific procedure.

A second reason for the current difficulty in developing a satisfactory program of liberal education is rooted in the fact that in the popular, as in the Marxist, image of science, even fundamental research is primarily a hand-maiden to technology. The major financial rewards and positions of influence go for the most part to the applied scientist, such as the engineer and the physician, rather than to those engaged in basic research. Under such circumstances it is by no means easy to secure adequate recognition for the conception that the pursuit of pure science is one of the glories of a liberal civilization. I am not suggesting for a moment that the practical values of training in the sciences are of no serious importance and should be ignored in considering the place of science in liberal education; and I have never encountered a good reason for maintaining that there is no room in a humanistically oriented education for anything in the curriculum of scientific studies that will prepare students for some practical profession. I am urging, however, that primary or exclusive emphasis upon the development of specialized skills is a disservice to the student, to the future of both pure and applied science, and to the prospects of a liberal society.

THE FEAR OF SCIENCE AS INHUMANE

While science is currently prized for contributions to technology, paradoxically it is also condemned as the ultimate source of many of our major evils. The invention of the terrifying instruments of mass destruction has evoked widespread distrust of science, and has reinforced deep-seated doubts whether the benefits of scientific progress outweigh the miseries and the fears that apparently must be included in the price for advances in knowledge. Further, many critics of contemporary society attack science for having made possible the rise of so-called "mass culture" and its alleged consequences: the severe restrictions upon individual freedoms, the loss of a sense of individual inner purpose, the use of techniques for manipulating the minds as well as the bodies of men, the decline in standards of human excellence, and the general vulgarization of the quality of human life. Moreover, it is argued that science is inherently amoral and therefore likely to develop in the student a trained incapacity for distinguishing between good and evil and a callous indifference to humane values. In short, many humanistic thinkers view with concern the assignment to science of any large role in liberal education.

I shall try to meet some of the strictures made in the name

of humanism against science and its influence; and to suggest what could be done to emphasize the humanistic and philosophic import of science, without depriving science instruction of substantive content.

It is undoubtedly true that the existence of mass cultures depends upon the technical fruits of theoretical and engineering research. It is also undoubtedly the case that many of these techniques have been put to reprehensible uses. On the other hand, it is absurdly unilluminating to make science therefore responsible for the failings of contemporary society, as unilluminating as it would be to place the blame for Hitler's moral inadequacies upon the procreative act of his parents. Scientific discoveries and inventions indeed have created opportunities which frequently have been misused, whether by design or by inadvertence. But an opportunity does not determine the use that men make of it. It is childish to bewail the expansion of science as the chief source of our current evils, and sheer sentimentality to look with longing to earlier days when science played a less conspicuous role in the human economy—as if living under such earlier conditions were an option now open to us, and as if societies less complex than ours exhibit no failings comparable with those of our own.

It is not possible to deny that, despite improvements in the material conditions of life for an increasing fraction of the populace, much of our energy is directed toward the realization of shoddy ideals, and that relatively few men lead lives of creative self-fulfillment and high satisfaction. It is difficult to demur at such indictments without appearing to act the part of a Philistine. Nevertheless, the failings noted are not unique to our own culture. Critics of American mass culture tend to forget that only comparatively small elite groups in the great civilizations of the past were privileged to share in the high achievements of those cultures, and that even those groups had only limited opportunities for appreciating the supreme products of the human spirit. In our own society, on the other hand, modern science and technology have made available to unprecedented numbers the major resources of the great literature and of the arts of the past and present, never accessible before in such variety even to the highly privileged and cultivated members of earlier societies. I do not claim that these benefits are of passionate interest to the great majority. But there seems to me ample evidence that an increasing number in our society has come to value them, and that as a consequence of exposure to such things tastes have become more discriminating and less provincial.

Discriminating tastes cannot be formed overnight. In view of the size and the heterogeneous character of the American population, and of the fact that adequate leisure and training for developing and pursuing rational ideals is a fairly recent acquisition for most of its members, it is perhaps remarkable how rapid has been the growth of sensitivity in our society to the great works of literary, scientific, and artistic imagination. It is simply not the case that the mechanisms of our alleged mass culture are all geared to enforcing meretricious standards of excellence, or that there is today a decreasing number of opportunities for men to cultivate their individual talents. The evidence seems to me overwhelming that the growth of scientific intelligence has helped to bring about not only improvements in the material circumstances of life, but also an enhancement in its quality.

HUMANISTS NOT IMMUNE TO PROVINCIALISM

If thorough exposure to the discipline of science is essential for the development of a liberal intelligence, familiarity with the subjects traditionally classified as the humanities is no less essential. The values implicit in the study of the humanities are too well known to require extended comment. Their study acquaints us with a range of human aspirations and passions to which we can be strangers only if we remain provincial members of the human race; they transmit to us visions of human excellence that have stirred men throughout the centuries and that make men kindred spirits despite accidents of birth and circumstance; and they make us conscious of our cultural heritage, and so potentially more discriminatingly aware of its virtues and limitations. But there is no inherent incompatibility between the liberal values implicit in the study of the sciences and those fostered by the humanities.

Nevertheless, professional humanists often display a snobbish traditionalism, a condescension toward everything modern, and an impatience with the critical standards of scientific thought. There have been humanists whose enthusiasm for the aqueducts of ancient Rome had no bounds but for whom contemporary systems of water supply were undeserving of a cultivated man's serious interest. There are self-proclaimed humanists who are profoundly affected by the tragic heroism of the Spartans at Thermopylae but who dismiss the Warsaw uprising against the Nazi oppressor as merely a sordid incident. There are humanists who claim a special kind of truth for knowledge about human values and who reject as sheer presumption the view that ordinary canons of scientific validity are pertinent for assessing the worth of moral insights. Needless to say, I am not suggesting that attachment to the classical tradition of humanistic thought is invariably associated with the narrowness of spirit some of these attitudes exhibit. However, the fact that they are sometimes manifested suffices to show that professional scientists have no monopoly on snobbery and provincialism, and that training in the humanities does not insure breadth of perspective.

Since the claim that the humanities represent a distinctive mode of knowledge is a frequent source of antagonism between scientifically oriented thinkers and spokesmen for the humanities, I must deal with it briefly. The claim seems to me to rest partly on a misunderstanding of what is covered by the label "scientific method," partly on a confusion of knowledge with other forms of experience, and partly on what I regard as a mistaken belief in the efficacy of human reason to establish absolutely certain and necessary truths about empirical subject matter. I have already indicated that the label "scientific method" does not signify either a set of rules for making discoveries or the use of certain techniques in conducting inquiries. In any case, I am in full agreement with those who maintain that distinctive subject matters require distinct modes of investigation; that the techniques employed in the natural sciences are not paradigmatic for the study of human affairs; and that though there are physical, biological, and socio-psychological conditions for the occurrence of preferences and valuations, trustworthy judgments about moral ideals cannot be deduced simply from statements about those conditions.

The disciplines constituting the humanities in some cases supply instruction which is no different in kind, though it is different in specific content, from the knowledge obtained in various special areas of natural science. This is patently the case for history and biography, and for much descriptive literature about the habits, customs, and aspirations of men. The factual claims of such literature must be tested by reference to the available evidence. Though standards of proof in these inquiries may be less stringent than in other areas, cognitive claims are validated through the use of logical canons common to all discursive thought about empirical subject matter. On the other hand, there are other humanistic disciplines, among them poetry, painting, and music, which are sometimes alleged to be sources of a special kind of knowledge, to which the canons of scientific method are said to be irrelevant. Now undoubtedly these disciplines can be instructive, in ways different from the way propositions are instructive. They can provide objects for reflection and perception; they can acquaint us with works of imagination that develop our sensibilities and heighten our powers of discrimination; they can present us with patterns of sound, color, and rhythm which evoke, intensify, and discipline emotional responses; and they can confront us with embodied visions of human virtue and human destiny. These are all important and instructive forms of experience. But since nothing is stated by these objects in propositional form, in no intelligible sense can they be regarded as conveying truth or falsity. They are therefore not sources of a special kind of knowledge, though they may be occasions or subject matters for knowledge.

Men who are equipped by native endowment and training to be successful investigators in one area are usually not equally successful in other areas. In any event, the capacity for making contributions to moral enlightenment is not uniformly distributed; and insofar as humanists are capable conservers and purifiers of the conscience of mankind, they require powers of moral imagination and insight which are as specialized as are the powers of imagination and insight into physical processes that the competent physicist must possess. However, as has already been argued, imagination and insight are not sufficient for establishing a cognitive claim, whether in morals or in physics. For insights must be tested. In a manner analogous to the procedure in physics, a test of a moral insight consists in formulating a hypothesis, comparing the consequences of the hypothesis with alternative assumptions and with empirical data relevant to the problem, and finally evaluating the adequacy of the hypothesis as a solution of the moral problem in the light of the evidence. Those who reject this procedure as not suitable for the adjudication of moral issues, and who also reject authoritarian justifications of moral judgments, attempt to validate moral principles by appealing to an alleged rational intuition of their necessary truth. I do not think this approach is tenable, among other reasons because of the historical fact that men have claimed intuitive certainty for incompatible moral principles. Accordingly, though there are as many distinct true statements as there are situations about which predications can be made, there are not several *kinds* of truth, and there is only one reliable *method* for establishing claims to truth. In short, the contention that the humanities employ a distinctive conception of truth and represent a mode of knowledge different from scientific knowledge seems to me to be the consequence of a failure in analysis.

I have already indicated what I take to be the humanistic values fostered by science. Finally, I want to suggest briefly how some of these values might be conveyed through the teaching of scientific subjects. The prospects for a liberal society depend upon the teaching of science as part of a liberal education which is dominated neither by a narrow utilitarianism nor by a comparably myopic professionalism. We cannot afford the folly of killing the goose that lays the golden eggs. Whatever be the urgencies of foreign or domestic politics, we must not institute a system of science education whose primary aim is to prepare students for careers in applied science. We must aim also to develop capacities which will contribute to the pursuit of the disinterested love of learning along the entire front. But above all, somewhere in their education we must equip the future laymen in science, as well as the future engineers and the future pure scientists, with mature conceptions concerning the nature of the scientific enterprise and the logic of scientific inquiry.

My main suggestion is that the liberal values of science can be best exhibited by teaching science with a strong emphasis upon methodological issues. I most certainly do not mean by this the institution of courses in the methodology of science, separate from or in lieu of work in the substantive materials of the sciences. Such courses, though they have a place in the curriculum, convey little to those unfamiliar with the subject matter of the sciences. I do mean that the materials of a discipline should be so presented that the logical principles controlling the analysis, the organization, the validation, and the modification of scientific statements are kept in full view, and that the findings of the sciences are exhibited as the products of a creative but critical intelligence.

THE IMPORTANCE OF METHOD

The student should be disabused of the common misconception that a collection of facts is either the beginning or the goal of scientific inquiry. Emphasis must be placed on the theoretical motivations that underlie the gathering of data, upon the selective character of observation and experiment, and upon the need to analyze and interpret the primary data of observation before they can be admitted as significant fact. Moreover, the student should be made to recognize that the concepts to which he is introduced have not been obtained by a process of simple abstraction from empirical data, but that they are intellectual creations, often *suggested* by the data, and are the products of a constructive imagination. Accordingly, the structures and functions of scientific concepts need special attention, and the logical as well as overt operations that relate concepts to crude experience must be discussed. In view of the increasing role that quantitative notions play in modern natural and social sciences, the logic of measurement and the major types of quantitative measures occurring in a given discipline deserve particular consideration. The student should be made aware that the introduction of quantitative distinctions is not a denial of qualitative differences, but on the contrary is a means for identifying such differences in a more discriminating manner than is customary in everyday affairs. The chief objective of these methodological emphases is to make explicit that science is not a mechanical routine, and that even at the most elementary levels of achievement it involves the use of a disciplined but sophisticated imagination.

THE FUNCTION OF THEORY IN SCIENCE

A second group of considerations to which attention needs to be given is the various ways in which the materials of a subject matter are organized and explained. The student should come to understand that natural history is not natural science, and he should be taught to appreciate the difference in this respect between, say, classificatory botany and genetics. Here again the realization should be enforced that theories are not extracted from empirical data, that they are not inductive generalizations or extrapolations from the observed facts, that they are indeed free creations of the mind. On the other hand, it should be made clear that theories are not just arbitrary inventions, and that they must meet a variety of conditions to be satisfactory. Accordingly, attention needs to be given to the function of theories both as guiding principles for further inquiry and as unified systems of explanation and prediction. It is essential in this connection to note the limitations of a crude empiricism and to stress the intellectual and practical advantages that follow from theories which enable us to subsume under a few principles a vast array of apparently disparate facts. Furthermore, the student should be enlightened on what really takes place when a theory, initially adopted to account for a limited range of similar phenomena, eventually absorbs into its scope of application quite different phenomena. Such extensions of theories occur repeatedly in the history of thought, and they effect important unifications in our knowledge. But such unifications are often construed to signify that science has somehow managed to diminish the variety of nature and to destroy apparent distinctions. In consequence, science comes to be conceived as a form of black magic which converts the world into an alien mystery and makes incoherent the procedures of science itself. Surely one thing a student ought not to carry away with him from his exposure to science is the belief that the universe becomes less intelligible the more science advances.

SCIENCE AS THE DISCIPLINE OF JUDGMENT

Finally—and this seems to me of greatest importance—the substantive materials of every science should be so expounded that the student acquires a habitual sense of the difference between competent and doubtful evidence, and between well-grounded conclusions and those that have a precarious foundation. The basic ideas of the logic of sampling procedure and the rationale of experimental control groups must therefore be brought home to the student. It thus should become clear to him that the mere agreement of a given hypothesis with empirical data does not constitute a sound basis for accepting the hypothesis, and that unless evidence is produced and analyzed with a view to determining what alternative assumptions are compatible with the facts, one has not even begun to think scientifically. It is not an unreasonable conjecture that if these elementary but basic points in the logic of proof were transmitted through the teaching of science, there would not be such a dishearteningly large number of victims to specious claims and preposterous intellectual fads. But however this may be, the student should also become aware that evidence can have different degrees of probative force, depending on the composition and the mode of obtaining the evidence as well as upon the character of the conclusion the evidence is used to support. Accordingly, no one has received an adequate education in science who does not realize not only that science does not claim definitive finality for its conclusions, but also why such claims cannot be made. Those who acquire such a realization also understand the nature of the continuing critical reflection that is essential to scientific inquiry.

Let me add that such methodological emphases in the teaching of science can be achieved only at a price. A large fraction of the price is that such courses cannot be encyclopedic compendia of whatever might be useful for a professional career in science. Some traditional subject matter must therefore be eliminated. I am convinced it can be done without serious loss if the remainder is effectively presented with a stress on those traits that distinguish science as a method of inquiry. But the price is not too high if the teaching of science contributes vitally to a liberal education.

Is Ivy Necessary?

HENRY STEELE COMMAGER (1902–   )

HISTORICALLY and traditionally the university is urban. Bologna and Padua, Paris and Toulouse, Prague and Cracow, Heidelberg

Is Ivy Necessary? by Henry Steele Commager is reprinted from *Saturday Review*, September 17, 1960, by permission of the author and of *Saturday Review*.

and Leipzig, Copenhagen and Leyden—these set the pattern. By the eighteenth century almost every major city on the Continent, and every capital except Stockholm and London, boasted a university. The urban tradition persisted into the nineteenth century with the foundation of London and Manchester, Berlin and Bonn, Christiania and Toronto.

Oxford and Cambridge were the most notable exceptions to this association of the university with a major city, and they remained the only English universities until well into the nineteenth century. American colleges were modeled on these; the first was planted not in Boston or Salem, but in the village of Newtown, hopefully renamed Cambridge. Some of the later colonial foundations were located in towns—the College of Pennsylvania, for example, and King's College in New York—but for the most part circumstances reinforced the inclination to fix the American college in a rural frame. The circumstances were, and remained, decisive; after all, the nation was rural, and as colleges followed the westward-moving frontier, they blossomed in villages and in the countryside.

But the rural setting of our universities resulted from preference as well. Land was cheap in country villages, and space ample. Students were young, and it was thought easier to protect boys—and, by the nineteenth century, girls—from moral temptations and frivolous distractions in the countryside than in the city. Furthermore, there were, or came to be, political considerations as well: farmers and villagers were jealous of cities, and demanded that universities—like asylums and penitentiaries—be located for the benefit of local interests. Thus, in the nineteenth century, state universities were commonly established in small towns: at Ann Arbor, not Detroit; Urbana, not Chicago; Columbia, not St. Louis; Boulder, not Denver; Amherst, not Boston.

This combination of circumstances—the English rather than the Continental background, the colonial and frontier experience, the American passion for prolonging youth, the early advent of co-education, the habit of exploiting education for local profit

—all went to create a pervasive pastoral stereotype for the American college and university. And to this day the pastoral image persists; the less sophisticated among us still think of college in terms of spreading lawns and giant elms, of ivy-clad halls, of cozy rooms festooned with pennants, of happy, carefree students. The French, the German, the Italian student is not supposed to be carefree; when he is, it is at a café on some boulevard, or in a beer cellar, or perhaps engaged in a duel or a riot; but the American undergraduate is perpetually young and carefree, perpetually lounging on a well-cropped lawn, strolling beneath oaks and elms, straddling a traditional fence, cheering on brightly clad warriors to crash right through the line. So powerful is this stereotype, so powerful the pastoral urge, that most of our urban universities yearn to be rural and try to provide themselves with the trappings of a country college. A few—such as Goucher, or Colby, or Johns Hopkins—have moved physically to what they hoped would be the countryside; others try to create islands of peace within the grim urban surroundings.

Yet Harvard, Columbia and Pennsylvania flourished in or near large cities, and new universities sprang up in cities all through the nineteenth century: Pittsburgh, the City College, Boston, Buffalo, Rochester, and others. The twentieth century has seen as enormous expansion of older urban universities, and an enormous increase in the foundation of new ones; today it is the urban university that most faithfully represents higher education in America. Of the fifty-two universities confessing to more than 10,000 students, thirty-two are in large cities, fifteen in smaller cities, and only five in the countryside. The population of the great city universities is twice that of the others. The typical American college and university student is—in his physical surroundings—not unlike the typical English or Italian university student.

There is every reason to believe that this urban pattern, already typical, will become dominant in the next generation. Not only are urban universities growing most rapidly, but cities are growing out to embrace—or engulf—suburban and rural institutions.

It is time we gave up our pastoral image here—as elsewhere—and accepted the fact of urbanization and made the best of it. We can neither return to the pastoral world of the nineteenth century, nor can we spread a pastoral patina over our city institutions. Perhaps we can even be persuaded to give up Oxford Gothic: In the 1890's no one seemed to ask why the University of Chicago's "*battlemented* towers should rise, beneath the hopeful western skies." Perhaps we are today more conscious that Berlin and London universities manage to command prestige even without battlemented towers.

How can the urban university best play the educational role which history and circumstances have assigned to it?

A university is a community of scholars, old and young, and its function is to provide scholars with the environment and the facilities conducive to the discovery and transmission of ideas and to their application to the larger community, present and future. But this requires that the university be a physical as well as an intellectual organization; that it provide the physical facilities for the meeting of minds, for research and study, for social intercourse. Education is in part the imaginative relationship between old and young, and the university must provide for that—in classrooms, in more spacious studies (let us abandon the business term, "office"), in libraries and laboratories, and—what is so commonly overlooked—in facilities for ceremonial occasions as well. Students educate each other—that may be the most important part of college education—and the university must make that possible: by residence halls, club rooms, theatres, music rooms, browsing rooms, pleasant dining facilities, and playing fields.

Clearly our city universities cannot hope to house all their students, or even a large portion of them, but they should house a nucleus of full-time students who would constitute the core of the community and provide continuity. Clearly, too, the urban university has to make a special effort to keep the rest of the student body on the campus—a term we may fairly use, as it was originally applied to cities. It can do this by building student unions, and making them more than convenient places to install juke boxes; by providing for sports and recreation, music, drama, lectures, conferences, exhibits—all the things designed to catch the imagination of the young.

More than students are involved. The urban university must make a determined effort to keep faculty members on or near the campus in order to enable them to play their role in the maintenance of the intellectual community. Oxford and Cambridge think this so important that they have long required residence within four or five miles of the university. Continental universities rarely face the problem: scholars live, by preference, in Paris itself, in Vienna, in Turin or Bologna, in Copenhagen or Stockholm, and are part of both the university and the urban communities. But the American scholar is like other members of the professional classes; he lives—by choice or by necessity— in the suburbs. And since few of our city universities provide adequate studies, club houses, dining halls or other amenities, he tends to spend as little time as possible on the campus. He is part neither of a university nor of an urban community, nor do circumstances encourage him to fulfill his duties in the educational enterprise.

Universities must make strenuous efforts to reconstruct the academic community. This may call for large-scale faculty housing; it may even call for university initiative and cooperation in the rehabilitation of extensive parts of cities: Chicago, Columbia, and Pennsylvania have already embarked on such programs. It may involve university schools for faculty children, and playing grounds and recreation facilities for young and old alike. Given the cultural aridity of most of our cities, it will probably involve responsibility for a wide range of cultural and social activities and amenities. One of these, important to student and scholar alike, is a good bookshop. What with first-rate libraries, and floods of paperbacks, the bookshop is almost an anachronism in America. We have only to reflect on what Blackwell's and Parker's mean to Oxford, what Heffers and Bowes & Bowes mean to Cambridge, what Thin's and Grant's mean to Edinburgh, what the scores of bookshops on the left bank, or in the university quarters of London or Copenhagen or Utrecht mean to these communities to realize what we are missing. The bookshop is as essential a part of the university community as the library or the laboratory, and a good deal more important than the stadium. American universities should maintain bookshops even at a loss, just as they maintain theatres and music and athletics at a loss.

The distressing fact is that most of our urban universities are singularly lacking in any of the amenities of cultural life. How unlovely, how discouraging, are most of our great urban universities! The "bookstores" filled with textbooks and athletic equipment and toilet articles. The hideous cafeterias with their clutter and noise and dirt, the food antiseptic but tiresome; service non-existent; popular music piped in relentlessly to drown out all conversation. If there must be music why not Beethoven and Bach? The residence halls with their Coca-Cola machines (the impoverished English provide every student with facilities for making tea), and their television, and the students packed three to a room. The student unions designed to look and feel like hotel lobbies, with the local paper (never the *Times*) and *Playboy* for sale at the newsstand and a bowling alley in the basement. The student newspaper invariably featuring the most recent athletic contest or the forthcoming prom. You would as soon look at a Hearst paper for news of the world scholarship as to a university paper! Even the playing fields are closed to all but members of the varsity teams; the best facilities of the gymnasium set aside for teams; the hours of access to swimming pool or squash court rigidly fixed for the convenience of the coaches or of the teams.

What is the explanation of what must be called the mucker pose in so much of higher education in America—of its anti-academic and anti-intellectual character? It is twofold. First is the widespread illusion that education is something that goes on in the classroom, something that comes by way of a "course" that a professor "gives" and a student "takes." This leads to the natural conclusion that when the classroom is closed, the process of education is over, and that the professor might as well go home and tend to his garden, the student might as well go to the Union and watch television. It is no exaggeration to say that if all lectures were abandoned, Oxford and Cambridge would go on much as they have been going on for centuries; perhaps the time is coming when we, too, will have to abandon "courses" as a kind of desperate gesture to prove that education consists in more than taking notes and accumulating credits. An educational system centered on the lecture course will, inevitably, disparage and neglect those other and more significant aspects of the educational enterprise, and this is particularly true of urban universities, where all the material circumstances encourage such disparagement and neglect.

The second explanation is one common to all higher education in America, but whose effectiveness—or burden—increases almost geometrically with the size of the institution. I refer to the elementary consideration that while European universities are run by their faculties, American universities are run by administrative bureaucracies, many of whose members have not the remotest notion what a university is about. The power elite of many of our large city and state universities consists of the deans (often only the dean or the vice president in charge of education is supposed to be interested in that enterprise), the personnel of the buildings and grounds department, the public relations officers, the coaches and athletic staff, the scores of minor officials who keep the machinery running. We take for granted that bureaucracy takes over in politics, and perhaps we should not be too surprised that it so often takes over in education as well. It is important to insist, however, that a substantial part of this administrative bureaucracy makes no perceptible contribution to education. Oxford and Cambridge, Paris and Heidelberg have managed without public relations offices for a good many centuries, and seem to get along pretty well. No universities outside America maintain paid coaches for sports, or fritter away money and energy on stadia and field houses. And clearly, most of the bureaucrats who fix the dining hour (five to five forty-five!), who work out complicated techniques of entry and exit from their bookshops, who permit only one door into the library, who assign air-conditioned offices to administrators and cubbyholes to professors, who make so many of the ground rules that control university life, are concerned primarily with their own convenience and not with education. Just as we will never eliminate the gross evils of intercollegiate athletics until we resolutely give the games and the playing fields back to the students, so we will never eliminate the crudenesses, the anti-intellectual rules, the mucker pose in higher education, until we give the universities back to faculty and students. One reason why Oxford and Cambridge colleges are admired by the whole world is that they are wholly administered by their dons—in finances, gardens, student life, libraries, playing fields, food and drink. The first act of any university president who wishes to restore academic amenities to an urban institution will be to put the bureaucracy in its place.

Yet no matter how enterprising or imaginative our urban universities are, they are nevertheless conditioned by the elementary fact of their location. American students who go by preference to semi-rural colleges, such as Smith or Leland Stanford, gladly spend a junior year (and sometimes more) in Paris or Madrid or Florence. Distinguished scholars who can rarely be lured to teach in Syracuse or Dayton, Kansas City or Denver, Houston or San Diego, cheerfully accept a call to Bologna or Turin, Heidelberg or Edinburgh or Copenhagen. What is it that attacts the American student and scholar to urban universities in Europe?

It is not the universities alone. It is in part the chance to be abroad, the chance to have a different kind of life. But when Americans go abroad for study or for teaching they do not search out the universities in smaller towns—Exeter, let us say, or St. Andrews, or Aarhus, or Pau. They head for the big cities. And this is because they know that they can count on an exciting relationship between university and community in almost every country of the Old World. What lures the American student is the life of the boulevards, the cafés, the bistros; it is the Latin Quarter; it is the opera and the ballet, the theatre and the experimental film; it is the bookshop on every corner, the dozen newspapers in every city; it is the mature student body, educating itself, joining in the risks of life, taking an active part in literature, journalism, art, and politics. It is, too, the beauty of the cities that they know they can count on—not just the beauty stored away in museums, but the beauty of houses that have been allowed to grow old, of parks and squares instead of parking lots, of riverbanks not given over to industry, but to pleasure, of gardens in the heart of town, of bridges that you can walk across without risk of life, of bicycle paths that parallel busy boulevards, of sidewalk cafés, and of carnivals on street corners.

This is not the place to inquire into the causes of the blight that has fallen on American cities, but it is relevant to emphasize one or two considerations that concern the position of the university. One of them is—like the rural college—in part an inheritance from England; in part, too, it is a consequence of a classless society and over-rapid industrialization. I have in mind the elementary fact that we have neither a patriciate, happy to identify itself with the cities, nor an aristocracy rich enough to maintain great town houses. It is the patriciate that gave character and culture to so many of the proud cities of the Continent: think of the burghers who beautified Florence and Venice, Frankfurt and Hamburg, Geneva and Copenhagen and Bordeaux and Prague and a hundred other places. For centuries now the patrician class has been content to identify itself with its city, to reside in the city, to take responsibility for the government, the schools, and the cultural life of its community. There are no private houses with gardens in the very heart of New York or Chicago or Philadelphia (Boston and Washington are still exceptions), but think of the private houses, the mansions and palaces, that grace the heart of London and Paris and Vienna and Rome!

The European patriciate usually patronized the urban university, and rejoiced in its scholars and its opportunities. Not always, to be sure, or universally. Oxford and Cambridge got in the way of London and some of the other "provincial" universities, but the first families of Manchester, Edinburgh, and Glasgow identify themselves gladly with their universities. So, too, with the patriciates of cities like Bologna or Dresden, the cities of the low countries or of Scandinavia. And everywhere—even in London and Paris—the relationship between the university scholars and the community is intimate and lively.

Not so in the United States. New York City is an exception, to be sure, and possibly—though not certainly—Boston and San Francisco. But elsewhere urban universities make very little impact on their communities. What effect do the local universities have on the newspapers of Chicago or Detroit? What role do the newspapers play in the musical or theatrical life of Los Angeles? To what extent are university scholars a significant part of the social or club life of Pittsburgh or Houston? It is impossible to imagine Edinburgh society without its contingent of university scholars, or the government of Sweden without the contributions from the universities, or the journals and publishing houses of Paris aside from the scholars of the Sorbonne, or even the financial and corporate life of Copenhagen without the university contribution. But where in America do universities play a comparable role?

It is not enough for academicians to wring their hands and look wistfully to Edinburgh and Zurich and Stockholm. Most of our urban universities, it is safe to say, command just about the position they merit in their communities. If they cut themselves off from their communities and try to ape rural and ivy-clad colleges, they should not be surprised if the community ignores them. If they adopt the mucker pose of playing up athletics and social activities and playing down matters intellectual, they should not expect to command intellectual prestige. If they fail to maintain high academic standards or to attract a first-rate faculty, they should not be astonished if that segment of the community interested in education invests its loyalties in older or better colleges and universities. If they place their public relations in the hands of people who think a baseball victory more newsworthy than a translation of Horace, they must not be surprised if the community takes them at their word. Many of the problems that now afflict the urban university will take care of themselves if the university first sets its intellectual house in order.

But there remains the question of the nature of the relationship between the university and the community. That relationship should be intimate, but not dependent. How far can the university assimilate to the city without becoming parochial in its character? How far can it identify itself with the city without becoming a service station for local interests? These are difficult problems —more difficult with new American than with older European universities, more difficult in a framework that regards the university as primarily vocational than in one that takes for granted its scientific and philosophical character. Yet the experience of such institutions as Harvard, Columbia, the Hopkins, Chicago, Minnesota, and California suggest that these problems are by no means insuperable.

The first responsibility of the university is not to serve its immediate community but to serve the much larger community of learning of which it is a part; not to serve its immediate generation, but future generations. It is reassuring to reflect that those urban universities that resolutely act on this principle are also those that command the most ardent and generous support from their communities—London and Paris, let us say, or Harvard and Columbia and the Hopkins. The first purpose of the university is not to serve the practical and vocational needs of the local community—to turn out hotel managers or pharmacists, or to investigate the supposed needs of local industry ("Both the University of South Carolina and Clemson College, as well as the private institutions, have made known their willingness to make their facilities available for industrial research programs of *practically every kind*," read an advertisement in the New York Times last year), but to serve the needs of society at large and in the realms of basic research. It is reassuring that the universities which act on this principle are those which, in the end, enjoy both affection and prestige.

Yet the obligation to be part of the community remains. Perhaps the simplest formula here is that while the university itself must not merge its identity with the city that houses it, the individual members of the university should be far more active in, and take far more responsibility for, community affairs. They should live in the city; they should participate actively in the cultural life in the city—its music, art, and theatre, its newspapers and periodicals. They should be encouraged to take an active part in politics and public affairs. In all of these activities the university itself should cooperate, by making it convenient for its members to live in the city; by making its facilities available for civic purposes; by encouraging political or journalistic or even economic responsibility by members of its faculty. All of this requires a bit more boldness than most of our urban universities now display. It means that (as in Italy, for example) members of the faculty might be encouraged to edit newspapers. Perhaps that would give us better newspapers—who knows? It means that university administrations should not be frightened if their economists play an active role in labor unions, or help run the local Civil Liberties Union, or the local branch of the Foreign Policy Association. It means that the university should work closely with the local libraries, museums, and other cultural institutions.

If our universities are to enjoy the advantages of their urban position, if they are to be to American society what the great urban universities of Europe have been to their societies, they must assume responsibility for the development of urban and regional civilization. They have, most of them, a large domain and immense potential wealth: think how the urban universities of Italy and Germany jostled each other; think what they have contributed to the civilization of those people and countries! They have, most of them, great cultural resources in the cities themselves. What they need is an awareness of their opportunities and potentialities; what they need is a philosophy. They should foster the spirit that animated Pericles and his fellow Athenians:

Ours is no work-a-day city. No other provides so many recreations for the spirit. . . . We are lovers of beauty without extravagance and lovers of wisdom without unmanliness. Wealth to us is not mere material for vainglory, but an opportunity for achievement. . . . Our citizens attend both to public and private duties, and do not allow absorption in their own various affairs to interfere with their knowledge of the city's. . . . Let us draw strength not merely from twice told arguments—how fair and noble a thing it is to show courage in battle—but from the busy spectacle of our great city's life as we have it before us day by day, falling in love with her as we see her and remembering that all this greatness she owes to men with the fighter's daring, the wise man's understanding of his duty, and the good man's self-discipline in its performance.

In Search of the Real Shakespeare

HALLETT SMITH (1907–   )

SOME YEARS AGO two English critics, Ivor Brown and George Fearon, surveyed the fuss the modern world makes about Shakespeare in a book they called "The Amazing Monument." With a proper sense of wonder and detachment they contemplated the results of an idolatry which began in the eighteenth century and has continued down to the present time. Despite such occasional outbursts as Margaret Halsey's "I'm a big girl now and I don't believe in Shakespeare," the mid-twentieth century is as fascinated by the great mystery as the mid-nineteenth century was. The avenues of approach have changed, but the destination is still the same. What kind of person was it who wrote the plays and the poems? Can we form any picture of him which we would all recognize? Is it anyone we know?

According to Freud, God is a projection of the father-image, and so is the devil. This principle perhaps accounts for the wide variety to be found in the projections of Shakespeare. For the accounts of Shakespeare the man, whether given by the respectable orthodox academic authorities or by the extravagant and erring spirits who support Bacon, Oxford, Derby, or Dyer, are all projections. Shakespeare is not only fantastical himself, but the cause that fantasy is in other men.

To the late Miss Caroline Spurgeon, who investigated with admirable thoroughness the images in Shakespeare's plays as a clue to the tastes and personality of the author, Shakespeare was "in character what one can only describe as Christ-like; that is,

IN SEARCH OF THE REAL SHAKESPEARE by Hallett Smith is reprinted from *The Yale Review*, March 1951. Copyright Yale University Press. Reprinted by permission of *The Yale Review*.

gentle, kindly, honest, brave and true, with deep understanding and quick sympathy for all living things." Miss Spurgeon also discovered that Shakespeare had a sensitive nose and "intensely disliked bad smells," and that he was a neat and handy man around the house. In contrast, Logan Pearsall Smith declared that the one valuable service performed by Frank Harris was that he pointed out what other critics have not liked to mention—that if any deductions about his nature are to be made from Shakespeare's writings, an excessive and almost morbid sensuality must have been part of his equipment. John Dover Wilson, the most eminent modern editor of Shakespeare, seems to agree, for he identifies Shakespeare's tastes with those of a circle of young noblemen at court. "We must make it clear," says Mr. Wilson in a cautious tone, "that poetic and dramatic genius has no necessary connexion with moral propriety at all, and that Shakespeare right up to the end of his life was never a very decorous person."

These projections of Shakespeare often tell us more about the projector than they do about the Swan of Avon, whether the modern projector gives us a picture like himself or the opposite. The differences between any two Shakespeares we are asked to believe in may derive from the scholars' differing temperaments, or from differing theories of the nature of creative genius. These differences are difficult to trace, because they are often a mere matter of inference. But projections of Shakespeare are also a reflection of the period in which they were made, and every century has its own Shakespeare—not, perhaps, the Shakespeare it deserves, but the Shakespeare which can best be accommodated to that century's ideas about genius.

The Victorians, for example, were much concerned with the double life which great persons must lead. They realized that the newspaper, the popular magazine, the education of the masses, and the triumph of parliamentary democracy all demanded that great men, as a social force, must symbolize in public and private life the ideals to which a middle class subscribes. Carlyle was of the opinion that "Loyalty, Discipleship, all that was ever meant by *Hero-worship*, lives perennially in the human bosom, and waits, even in these dead days, only for occasions to unfold it, and inspire all men with it, and again make the world alive!" But Carlyle was much more willing than most of his contemporaries to accept "the contradiction which yawns wide enough in every life." Generally the Victorians were nervous about great men; they were afraid they would be Found Out. Thackeray reflects the contemporary concern, even when he is being humorous, in an essay "On Being Found Out." In it he was perhaps feeling in earnest while thinking in jest. Was it complete confidence, or was there just a touch of nervousness in Tennyson's lines, when he proclaimed, about the Duke of Wellington:

> Whatever record leap to light
> He never shall be shamed?

And so of Shakespeare. The records seemed fairly meager, and gave only dry reports of christenings, marriages, property arrangements, and deaths. Nothing personal. Charles Dickens approved of this state of affairs but he was worried that it might not last. "It is a great comfort, to my thinking," he wrote about Shakespeare to a friend, "that so little is known concerning the poet. It is a fine mystery; and I tremble every day lest something should come out."

The worry was needless, even if we remember Samuel Butler and Frank Harris. Nothing much has come out, except the projections of the critics, or perhaps their father-images, divine or infernal. Viscount Bryce, looking ahead in 1916 on the occasion of the tercentenary of Shakespeare's death, thought that the questions we ask about the relation of the genius to the man may be no nearer solution when the next centenary arrives. But the assurance that there is no gold has never stopped prospectors. Matthew Arnold's apostrophe to Shakespeare, "thou smilest and art still, out-topping knowledge," did not discourage Dowden, or Lee, or Raleigh, or Sir Edmund Chambers.

What kind of knowledge could be applied to Shakespeare the

man? Knowledge of one's own self, of course: I am a writer, he
was a writer, so his life must have been essentially like mine.
James Joyce was an exile, and he was interested in exiles, whether
from Stratford to London or from Dublin to Paris. Accordingly,
he found that "the note of banishment, banishment from the heart,
banishment from home, sounds uninterruptedly from *The Two
Gentlemen of Verona* onward till Prospero breaks his staff, buries
it certain fathoms in the earth and drowns his book." This strain,
once found, cannot be a mere literary effect; it must be autobiographical. So Joyce's Stephen Dedalus sums up the personality
of the old artificer from Stratford: "Christfox in leather trews,
a runaway in blighted treeforks from hue and cry. Knowing no
vixen, walking lonely in the chase. Women he won to him, tender
people, a whore of Babylon, ladies of justices, bully tapsters'
wives."

Bernard Shaw, whose vision of the world was strongly conditioned, according to H. N. Brailsford, by the destruction of
an ideal father-image by his own drunkard father, projected a
notorious picture of Shakespeare. How much of Shaw's "Shake-
spear" is merely a comic device for self-dramatization in the Pref-
aces is of course a problem for the critic of Shaw, but the picture
of the poet himself concerns us. He is, according to Shaw, a
snapper-up of unconsidered trifles, a literary jackdaw, a man who
could show much but teach little. As the projection of a father-
image, this is interesting, and we observe that when Shaw can,
he eagerly falls back upon conformity with the Bard, as when
he says, in the epistle dedicatory to "Man and Superman," that
Shakespeare had no conscience, and neither has he.

The general tendencies in Shakespeare projection have, however, changed somewhat in recent years. Before the first World
War the great concern was to draw a picture of the man who
could have written the plays, and either to reconcile this picture
with the known facts in the life of William Shakespeare of Stratford, actor and sharer in the company of players known as the
Chamberlain's, and later the King's Men; or else to show that

the two did not fit, and find some other candidate for the authorship. The latter course appealed to a large number of zealous men and women, beginning with Hawthorne's friend Delia Bacon of New Haven and coming down to the members of societies in England and America which still publish obscure journals devoted to the cause of Bacon or Oxford as the author of the plays. These people have been almost all amateurs in literary scholarship, though some have been distinguished in other fields. This makes them vulnerable to such dry remarks as that of Pearsall Smith: "I do not wish, however, to speak with any disrespect" (he has just compared the Baconians to the Gadarene swine) "of that view of the authorship of Shakespeare's plays which is so firmly held by officers in the Navy and the Army, by one of His Majesty's judges, and the manager of more than one large drapery establishment, and is corroborated by the authority of Mark Twain, Mrs. Henry Pott, Prince Bismarck, John Bright, the late Mr. Crump, K.C., and several thoughtful baronets."

Such a reply, for all its wit, is mere snobbery, of course. The Baconians, the Oxfordians, can be refuted; they have been refuted, over and over, but they never recognize the refutation. In fact, it is one of their constant complaints that their arguments are ignored by the professional academic authorities. A decade ago Professor O. J. Campbell, of Columbia University, met directly and demolished the Oxfordian thesis, but the editors of undergraduate newspapers still get letters asking them to demand from their English teachers an explanation of why they do not discuss with their students the proofs of Oxford's authorship. Several offers have been made to American universities to endow a chair for the teaching of one or another of the Shakespeare heresies. When these offers are refused, the professors are commonly charged with a conspiracy to keep the truth from light. So the temptation to reply by wit and snobbery is very great.

The adherents of Bacon, Oxford, or Derby, though perhaps as numerous since 1920 as before, are somehow less prominent today. One is more likely to encounter Mrs. Henry Pott than

Mark Twain. And since the issue has quieted down somewhat
for the time being, it might be instructive to look at the heretics
and see what we can learn from them.

The most powerful argument to win converts to the heresy
is of course the argument from education. Shakespeare's plays
were thought, in the nineteenth century, to show a mastery of
law, of seamanship, of history, of politics, of society, of natural
science, and of philosophy and the arts which a rude untutored
boor from the market town of Stratford could not possibly possess. The modern refutation of this argument has been two-fold.
In the first place, Shakespeare's plays show no very unusual
amount of learning, if they are judged by Elizabethan standards;
the works of Ben Jonson, the stepson of a bricklayer, show a great
deal more. In fact, there are contemporary references to show
that in his own time Shakespeare was considered remarkable for
his freedom from learning:

> Here I would let slip,
> If I had any in me, scholarship,
> And from all learning keep these lines as clear,
> As Shakespeare's best are, which our heirs shall hear
> Preachers apt to their auditors to show
> How far sometimes a mortal man may go
> By the dim light of Nature.

So writes Francis Beaumont about 1615.

The other refutation of the argument from education is complementary. It is an examination of the curriculum of the Elizabethan grammar school to show that if Shakespeare went to the
school at Stratford he could have accumulated a knowledge of
classical rhetoric, poetic, and philosophy which would put to
shame a classics major in a modern American college. Professor
Baldwin, of the University of Illinois, has recently published three
volumes, amounting to some 1700 pages, describing Shakespeare's
education. The reader may well wonder, when he finishes, how
the poet ever happened to be described as warbling his native
woodnotes wild. If he was exposed to all this, no wonder he speaks

of the whining schoolboy, with his satchel and shining morning face, creeping like a snail unwillingly to school.

So the heretical claim that the plays show much learning and William Shakespeare of Stratford little has been devastatingly refuted, perhaps over-refuted. It need trouble us no more. But before we leave the point, it is worth notice how many of the heretics were also self-made men. What they doubted it was possible for Shakespeare to do was merely an enlargement of what they had themselves done. Mark Twain could not credit the rustic from Stratford, though when he looked in the mirror he saw a boy from the Mississippi River boats who charmed and entertained the world. Ignatius Donnelly was himself the great orator of backwoods Minnesota but could not believe in the great dramatist from remote Warwickshire. Senator Albert J. Beveridge, himself an example of a gifted American provincial, thought it required a man of the cosmopolitan experience of Sir Walter Raleigh to write the plays. So the projection of Shakespeare which any man makes is often enough that of his opposite, not of himself. And this seems to hold true for some of the orthodox Shakespearians as well. Sir Sidney Lee was for long the standard authority on Shakespeare's life. His image of Shakespeare has been described as that of "a typical English manufacturer who happened to deal in *Twelfth Nights* and *Lears* instead of brass tacks." Now, says Dover Wilson, who made this summary of Lee, "Lee himself was not in the least like this. Where then did his image come from?" Where, indeed? Where do all images come from?

Dover Wilson himself, engaged in editing all the plays, volume by volume, with an occasional additional volume or two on such matters as Hamlet and Falstaff, found that he was forced to project his Shakespeare. The Bard was, says Wilson, fascinating, with charming manners, a good mixer: "The silent man is never popular and whatever else the man Shakespeare may have been he was certainly popular." This, of course, it would be pleasant to believe. But we are given pause by the testimony of J. J. Jusserand, scholar and ambassador and man of the world, surely himself an example of the type Mr. Wilson thinks Shakespeare represented. According to Jusserand, the chief thing distinctive about Shakespeare was his aloofness.

About a century ago the picture of Shakespeare as a businessman, interested in his plays only as a means to gain a fortune and found a family—the picture which receives its classical expression in Sidney Lee's biography (1898, 1915)—was already causing some worry. And oddly enough, it is the bourgeois who worries about Shakespeare's being too bourgeois. The snobbery which makes the Shakespeare heretics search for an author who is in the peerage is an evidence of this. As the authors of "The Amazing Monument" say, the attitude is fairly constant and runs something like this: "Why do we pay up thumping fees for these Etons and Magdalens and the rest if they cannot stop us from being represented by such plebeians as Shakespeare of old and later on by Dickens, Hardy, Wells and Shaw?"

The businessman's worry about Shakespeare's being too much of a businessman and too little of a poet was perhaps most happily answered in 1853 by Walter Bagehot, who was a banker. Bagehot insisted that Shakespeare was none of your literary-academic fellows; he must have led an active life, and you can see it in his works. Quoting the passage from "Venus and Adonis" about the hunted hare, Bagehot proclaimed, "It is absurd . . . to say we know nothing about the man who wrote that; we know that he had been after a hare." In fact Bagehot, who combined banking, economics, and literature in his own career, constantly emphasized that a sedentary or literary life does not make a good writer. "It is only people who have had a tooth out that really know the dentist's waiting-room."

The Principle of the Dentist's Waiting-Room does not seem to be permanently satisfactory. The trouble with it is that it leaves too little room for the imagination. The theory that because Shakespeare describes a shipwreck in "The Tempest" very vividly he must have been in a shipwreck leads to such an enormous amount of Dentist's Waiting-Room experience that it is difficult to see how Shakespeare could have found time to write the plays, the poems, and the sonnets, even supposing that he wrote with that facility attributed to him by the Folio editors. So the received modern view is very cautious and tentative on this matter, trying to strike a balance between a writer's own participating experience and what he can get from books, the talk of friends, and his own imagination.

Sir Edmund Chambers, our generation's standard authority, has summed it up. He realizes that for most readers it would be intolerable to suppose these plays anonymous, or the work of a ghost as elusive as the one in his own drama which legend says William Shakespeare played. It is better, we feel, to have an implausible author than an intangible one. But Chambers is concerned with "Facts and Problems," and he is scrupulous about allowing the facts no heavier burden than they are able to bear. "We are entitled to assume," he says, "a roving and apperceptive mind, conversant in some way with many men and manners, and gifted with that felicity in the selection and application of varied knowledge, which is one of the secrets of genius. What has perhaps puzzled readers most is the courtesy of Shakespeare; his easy movement in the give and take of social intercourse among persons of good breeding. We have not, indeed, to think of the well-to-do inhabitants of Stratford as boors; but the courtesy of a provincial town is not quite the courtesy of a Portia. Probably the true explanation is that, once more, it is a matter of apperceptiveness, of a temper alive, not only to facts, but to human values."

Since this summary of twenty years ago, the pursuit of Shakespeare the man has taken a somewhat different direction. It has been argued with some plausibility, by Miss Spurgeon especially, that the way to track Shakespeare is to watch him when he is intent upon something else—at such times he may reveal himself unconsciously. When he was writing a play, his conscious mind was concerned with problems of dramatic technique—exposition,

characterization, emotional contrasts, exits and entrances, solil-
oquies and asides. But he wrote in verse; the speeches are poetry,
and they are full of images, most significantly metaphors. These
images, thrown off in the speed of composition, may show us
something about the man himself.

Chambers, writing in 1944, finds this technique useful in re-
inforcing our belief that the author of the plays was an actor,
a man who simply could not help reverting to images from the
theater: "That Shakespeare's mind was permeated by the atmosphere of the stage, in which he lived and moved and had his
being, seems to me indisputable." But this is hardly revolutionary,
or new. Anyone who contributes 36 or 38 plays to the stage
is obviously interested in it, whether he be an actor or an aristocrat. His nature is subdued to what it works in, like the dyer's
hand.

The real test of the image-technique as a source of knowledge
of the man Shakespeare is its ability to tell us something new,
unexpected, perhaps even irrelevant (if anything about him can
be called irrelevant) about the man. Here Miss Spurgeon seems
to have scored some victories. She brings together several passages in which the subject of flattery and fawning calls up the
same image—one which is not traditional or literary, but seems
peculiar to Shakespeare and derived from his own experience.
Hamlet says to Horatio:

> Why should the poor be flatter'd?
> No, let the candied tongue lick absurd pomp,
> And crook the pregnant hinges of the knee
> Where thrift may follow fawning.

And in "Henry IV Part I" Hotspur recalls bitterly the flattering
behavior of Bolingbroke before he became king:

> Why, what a candy deal of courtesy
> This fawning greyhound then did proffer me!

In still a third play, Antony comments on the desertion of some
of his allies:

> The hearts
> That spaniel'd me at heels, to whom I gave
> Their wishes, do discandy, melt their sweets
> On blossoming Caesar.

The similarity of these passages was noticed by a commentator as early as 1794. The explanation of the flattery-dog-candy image, which seems to be distinctively Shakespeare's, relatively independent of general context, and powerful enough to be evoked in the mind of the dramatist over a period of ten years, was first given by Miss Spurgeon: "It was the habit in Elizabethan times to have dogs, which were chiefly of the spaniel and greyhound type, at the table, licking the hands of the guests, fawning and begging for sweetmeats with which they were fed, and of which, if they were like dogs today, they ate too many, dropping them in a semi-melting condition all over the place. Shakespeare, who was unusually fastidious, hated the habit, as he disliked all dirt and messiness, especially connected with food."

The possibilities of investigating image-clusters to find out something about Shakespeare the man seemed very promising in the light of Miss Spurgeon's observations. We might not be able to discover the specific sources of Shakespeare's peculiar responses, but if we could discover what these responses were, we could find something more important—how he felt, what were his likes and dislikes, what kind of man he was inside.

The most ambitious successor of Miss Spurgeon, Mr. E. A. Armstrong, has discovered other image-clusters and has tried to explain the whole thing on a psychological basis. And the most he can give us, aside from the image-clusters, is a warning: we must recognize that there are various ways in which motifs come to be associated. "Some," he says, "are there because of their emotional significance and others are conjoined by reason of some similarity of sound or sense, or even because of mere contiguity in the past." Punning and rhyming, we recall, are both modes of association by sound, and a man so accustomed to both these kinds of linkage must have often found his mind or imagination guided by them. Such associations would not account for the fawning-candy image, but Mr. Armstrong points out that the last of the three quoted passages is followed immediately by another metaphor:

> and this *pine* is *bark'd*
> That overtopp'd them all.

The sudden jump from the dinner table to the stripped forest tree is really only a step, we are told, because "the thought of the spaniel aroused a memory of the dog's bark and 'bark' suggested the stripped pine metaphor."

Linkages of words, sounds, and images provide material for the psychologist, of course, and we may expect further and more adventurous essays by the adherents of the various schools. Freud's work on Leonardo led to Dr. Ernest Jones's explanation of "Hamlet" in terms of the Oedipus complex, but it remained for the late Miss Ella Sharpe to find in "King Lear" evidence of early trauma induced in William Shakespeare the child by his mother's pregnancies in 1566 and 1568-9. One is dazzled by such revelations, and somewhat alarmed, for instead of knowing too little about Shakespeare the man it seems possible that we may soon know too much. What kind of curse would the Stratford gentleman have ordered for his tomb if he had foreseen disinterment by psychoanalysts as well as by sextons? (*Good friend, for Jesus' sake forbear!*)

The direction of the most recent approach to Shakespeare, then, is interesting because it is a more literary or verbal one. This is, I suppose, just what we should expect, since in recent years literary criticism in general has concerned itself more closely with words and their functions. Whether this approach, with its auxiliary of psychology, will tell us any more about the mystery of the man remains to be seen. There will always be people who say the peculiarities of the man do not matter: what is valuable is the works. But they will probably always be a minority, for the instinct of curiosity about personality will not be stilled, even when the means of finding an answer seem to be exhausted by repeated trials.

We can console ourselves, however. The projectors of Shakespeare make a fine show of their creations, if we are in the proper mood. Theseus, in "A Midsummer Night's Dream," has some difficulty in persuading Hippolyta, that tough and serious Amazon, to enjoy herself watching the efforts of Bottom, Snug, and the rest of the rude mechanicals to produce a play. To her, the desperate devices of the Athenian laborers, caught between the demands of symbol and realism, are only "the silliest stuff that ever I heard." This may be the feeling of many in the mid-twentieth century about the efforts to visualize William Shakespeare the man. But Hippolyta is answered, as perhaps the impatient skeptics should be answered now: "The best in this kind are but shadows; and the worst are no worse, if imagination amend them."

Reflections on Mass Culture

ERNEST VAN DEN HAAG (1914–)

BY AND LARGE, people seriously concerned with mass culture fall into three groups. There is first a nucleus of artists and literary men, supported by a few theoreticians. They feel isolated, alienated, submerged and pushed aside by mass culture; their hopes are dim and they detest it. The literati and the theoreticians are opposed by another group—the practical men, who have decided it is their duty to work for the mass media in spite of the opulent

REFLECTIONS ON MASS CULTURE by Ernest van den Haag is reprinted from *The American Scholar*, Vol. 29, No. 2, Spring 1960. Copyright © 1960 by the United Chapters of Phi Beta Kappa. Reprinted by permission of the publisher.

salaries pressed on them. Sedulously aided by academic fellow travellers, they resolutely defend popular culture and their own *sacrificium intellectus.*

The third and largest group stays squarely in the middle, although for motley reasons. Most sociologists are located here; they have been taught that to be anywhere else, particularly when cultural matters are involved, is unscientific. Besides, many of them lack the trained sensibility that would discriminate between, say, English prose and their own writing. Liberal philosophers, on the other hand, have investigated the impossibilities of justifying value judgments for so long that they regard anyone criticizing mass culture for moral or aesthetic reasons as bold but naive. There is no evidence, they seem to say, for practically any view; hence, let's close our eyes and discuss methodology.

With all that, liberal philosophers seem to stress, somewhat unilaterally, the lack of evidence for negative views of mass culture. Perhaps they feel uneasy with rejections of mass culture because of political fears—misplaced ones, in my opinion. They seem unable to free themselves from the suspicion that a rejection of mass culture implies a rejection of the masses (although the contrary is no less logical) and is, therefore, antidemocratic. However, this is a *non sequitur.* One might think little of the cultural capacity of the masses but not therefore of their political capacity.* But even if one thinks little of their political competence, one might still feel that there is no reason why they should not suffer, benefit and possibly learn from its use (and no more is needed to argue for democracy). Finally, although one might be somewhat pessimistic about the masses, one might be even more so about the political capacity of restricted groups. At any rate, neither mass culture nor objections to it seem to promote specific political views: fascists and communists, as often as liberals, favor mass culture, although they occasionally

---

* Conversely, I have not found cultivated people to be politically very sagacious. (I'd prefer to entrust my political destiny to farmers or workers rather than to professors as a group.)

borrow some phrases from its opponents.

Historians, who of all men might be expected to discern the uniqueness of mass culture, seldom do. When they pay heed to mass culture as a historical phenomenon, they seem to take the wrong cue. Thus, Stuart Hughes recently observed, in a perceptive paper, that "our students yawn over the classics" because they have "very little to do with their own lives." He implies that we might as well forget about the classics. This seems odd. Students have always yawned over the classics—only, in times past, teachers were not so sensitive to their own popularity rating nor so eager to entertain their students as to be willing to drop the classics. They dropped some yawning students instead and kept the interested ones. An immature mind cannot understand the classics; and it matures, in part, by learning to understand them—or, at least, to know them so that they may be understood later. Students brought up in an age of rapid technological change may be convinced that literature, like machinery, is subject to obsolescence—a conviction some teachers share or dare not oppose enough to crack the shell. Perhaps this is what makes the classics seem irrelevant.

Yet the classics, if truly classic, cannot be irrelevant, for they deal with subjects relevant to the universal human predicament in ways to be re-experienced perennially. Of course, it is possible that we have become irrelevant to the classics: if our lives have lost all meaning, then no literature worthy of that name can be meaningful to us. For it is the possible meaning of human life that classic literature explores; and we cannot be interested without any experience of meaning and style in our own lives. If we have no such experience, then entertainment bereft of meaning—diversion from boredom, time killing, mass culture—is all that remains. In this case, the relevant must become irrelevant, and only what is irrelevant to begin with can be absorbed. But I'm not yet willing to give up altogether. Under favorable conditions, the study of literature helps us see the possibilities of man's career on earth.

While some are ready to yield to those bored by high culture, others are convinced that the mass media can serve, indeed do serve, to bring high culture to the masses, and that in doing so they justify their existence or, at least, render an important service. Popular magazines may have authors such as Norman Vincent Peale, the argument goes, but don't they also publish an occasional uncensored article by Bertrand Russell? They do. However, a piece by a major philosopher does not make a philosophical magazine out of *Look*—it may make a popular journalist out of the philosopher. In the stream of, at best, diverting banalities, the worth-while piece tends to disappear without impact. It may seduce a Russell to lower his standards and write more such pieces, becoming less worth while and more acceptable in the process. It won't lure *Look* readers into the *Principia Mathematica*. Mass culture can be decorated with high culture pieces without being otherwise changed.

Note further that Russell's opinions are not offered to *Look* readers because of their intrinsic merit; they are offered because they are *his* opinions. Russell is by now a public figure, which means that he can be published without being taken seriously. Had I written the same words, I could not have broken into *Look*, precisely because people might have taken the utterance seriously instead of gobbling it up with the rest of the fare, while captivated by the utterer's fame.

Not everybody defends the mass media as vehicles that bring elements of high culture to the masses. Some depict the culture of the masses, articulated by the mass media in their normal offerings, as superior to high culture to begin with. Thus, one of mass culture's most faithful admirers, Mr. Gilbert Seldes, recently explained that he thinks more highly of Charlie Chaplin than of Marcel Proust because the former has brought more happiness to more people than the latter. Now happiness is hard to measure, and I am not sure that it makes sense to compare the feeling of a person reading Proust to that of another seeing Chaplin. We may grant, however, that more persons have been amused and diverted by Chaplin than by Proust. Still more people are made happy or are diverted by whiskey, apple pie, penicillin, Marilyn Monroe or, perhaps, by a movie that Mr. Seldes and I might agree is thoroughly bad. In short, making people happy is a criterion only if that is what one sets out to do—and I doubt that this was Proust's purpose or the purpose of any serious writer. Surely more persons enjoy Rodgers and Hammerstein than Bach—more enjoy Liberace than Glenn Gould. By definition, popular culture is enjoyed by more people than high culture. Mr. Seldes' view would sanction the elimination of art in favor of entertainment—high-class entertainment, at best.

And this is precisely what I am afraid of. Mass culture demands entertainment and so extravagantly rewards those who provide it with money, prestige and power that serious artists become isolated—and tempted. To be sure, such tendencies have always existed; but now they prevail. The strength of the offerings of mass culture, compared with those of art, has risen immensely, and the dividing line has been blurred.

The chances for the values of mass culture to be internalized in childhood also have greatly increased, so that what I have described as temptation is not felt to be such, but, on the contrary, as the due reward for well-directed, talented efforts. The view held by Mr. Seldes in all innocence is widely accepted by less articulate persons. It is a very basic American view, a naively pragmatic and philanthropic view that refuses to recognize what cannot be tangibly measured in terms at once hedonistic and altruistic.* The measurement for art thus becomes the number of people made happy—and as soon as this becomes the end of art, art ends.

The answer to those who oppose pessimistic views on mass

---

* When the Puritan American heritage collided with the more hedonistic attitudes of later immigrants, an interesting fusion resulted. Pleasure, the Puritans implied, is bad; sacrifice, good. The immigrants wanted to pursue happiness. The resulting attitude is: the pleasure sacrificed and given to others is all right, as is the happiness shared and given. What is bad becomes good if it is not enjoyed by oneself but produced for others.

culture lies here. They argue that there is no evidence that the masses are culturally worse off. (I suspect they are far from well off, but comparisons are nearly impossible.) As far as the elite is concerned, they ask what prevents it from being as creative as ever? Why can't it coexist with mass culture? Haven't there always been several coexisting levels of culture? Can't we have a pluralistic society?

This reasonable argument overlooks the historically most distinctive and important characteristic of mass culture: the dominant power of the mass of consumers over production, public opinion and prestige. The elite in the past was sufficiently isolated and protected from the masses (which, properly speaking, did not exist as such) to be able to cultivate its own garden. And the mass market (hardly in existence) had nothing much to offer. Further, power, income and prestige distribution being what they were, the masses had no desire to impinge on the culture of the elite; on the contrary, they made room for it. At any rate, if they had a wish to participate or encroach, they had no way of making their demands felt and of articulating them. (Even political revolutions, before Hitler, were led and inspired by members of the elite.) But this has changed. We all now cultivate cash crops in market gardens. Mass culture is manufactured according to the demands of the mass market. No *independent* elite culture is left, for mass culture is far too pervasive to permit it. Cultivated individuals and islands of high culture remain, of course. But they are interstitial and on the defensive even when admired and respected; indeed, then more than ever, for they easily may be "taken up" and typecast. The intellect when alive is not part of our social structure, nor does it have its own domicile.

A convinced egalitarian may ask, So what? No more elite, no more high culture; but the great majority of people—who never belonged—have what they wish. To be sure, most people never were, are not now, and are unlikely ever to be interested in high culture. Yet, it does not follow that high culture is unimportant.

Its importance cannot be measured by the number of people to whom it is important. Political issues may be decided by majority vote (or, at least, by letting the majority choose who is to decide them). This is surely not a good way, but nevertheless, I think, the best available.

However, the analogy between political issues and cultural issues (or, for that matter, moral ones) is inappropriate. Political issues, by whatever means they are decided, require collective action. Taxes cannot be levied only on those who feel they benefit proportionately from a pattern of public expenditure, or on individuals who are willing to vote for them. With art and literature it is otherwise, or it was. They could be cultivated by intellectual elites, without mass participation. This is becoming less possible every day. Mass culture threatens to decide cultural issues by a sort of universal suffrage. This is a threat to culture, not an occasion for rejoicing. For once cultural issues are regarded as indivisible, the majority view will prevail—and the majority prefers entertainment to art. Yet, unlike properly political matters, cultural ones do not require collective action, but rather that the mass of people and the law do not interfere. Culture cannot be created by political actions, although it can be destroyed by them. (The support of social groups is required, of course, but not that of society—or the masses—except inasmuch as it makes the existence of the social groups possible.) There would never have been any serious art, philosophy or literature if a majority vote had decided whether a given work was to be created and presented.

Yet, even if these things are important only to a few people, they are the best and most important people, the saving remnant. Actually, these things and these people are important even to those who ignorantly sneer at them. Such feelings as love; such experiences as wit, beauty or moral obligation; or styles of congress, housing and living—all, however degenerate they may become, are brought into existence and elaborated by artists and intellectuals. Without them, life is formless. With them, there is, at least, a paradigm. The most common of human experiences and the most trite still depend on artists and intellectuals to become fully conscious and articulate. Even the silliest entertainer and his public are part of, or are parasites of, a long line of creators of cultural expression—artists, philosophers, writers, composers, et cetera. For as Bernard Berenson suggested, "Popular art is always a derivation from professional individual art." Just as the technician depends on pure scientists he may never have heard of, so civilized nations in general depend on the creators of cultural expression—intellectuals and artists. The relation of the cultural elite to the masses may be compared to the relation of the saints and the cloistered to the faithful at large. Or, the cultural elite may be compared to the playwrights and the actors on stage, whose words, actions, costumes and settings are of significance to the spectators across the footlights, even though they are but spectators.

Although few people become outstanding mathematicians, scholars and artists, or understand what these are doing, society must permit those who cultivate such activities their separate existence or cease to be civilized. And the loss and degeneration of civilization injures everyone—the living and the unborn generations for whom we should hold in trust their rightful heritage. It is not enough, either, to permit some individual specialists to go their way. We need an intellectual and artistic elite (joined, of course, by merit) supported by a necessarily restricted and therefore discriminating public, both with reasonably continuous traditions. If this elite is not allowed autonomy and self-cultivation, if instead it is induced to follow mass tastes and to cater to them, there can be no cultural creation. We may parasitically ring a few changes on the culture of the past; we may find ways to entertain ourselves; but we won't have a style and an experience of our own.

I should not object to cultural pluralism—to mass culture coexisting with high culture—if it were possible. (Folk culture is long dead—although many people don't know a zombie when they see one.) A universally shared high culture is, of course, absurd and self-contradictory. This may sound snobbish, but I didn't make the world; I'm merely describing it. Talents as well as intelligence and sensitivity to various values are differentially distributed. We are lucky if 1 or 2 per cent of the population can be creative in any sense and 15 to 20 per cent can cultivate some sensibility. The remainder benefits indirectly.

The trouble with mass culture is that in various direct and indirect ways it tends to make the existence of high culture impossible. In our eagerness to open opportunity to everybody, we have greatly diminished the prizes available to anybody. Good wine is hard to cultivate when it is habitually diluted and we are brought up to be indiscriminate. We might do well to abandon the sterile and injurious attempts to "improve" mass culture, for its main effect is to debase high culture by "bringing it to the masses." What we must do is to bring some gifted people—not masses—to transmit high culture independently of the culture of mass society. My own view is pessimistic. I should like nothing better than to be proved wrong.

From France

RAYMOND ARON (1905–   )

In the course of half a dozen trips to the United States since 1950 I have never had time to linger there for long. I have stayed in New York, Washington, San Francisco, Cambridge, and have passed through Detroit and Montgomery. I know America's

From France by Raymond Aron is reprinted from *As Others See Us*, edited by Franz M. Joseph. Copyright © 1959 by Princeton University Press. Reprinted by permission of the publisher. Translated from the French by Anita Tenzer.

streets better than its homes. I know opinion-makers better than the common man. In that country that prides itself on not emulating its intellectuals, I know the latter better than the big businessmen. I have not explored the seamy side of American life, the areas of shadow and unhappiness.

Is this to say that my visits have taught me nothing I could not have learned in books? That would be going too far. Something essential is lacking in our view of the United States if we have not seen the people, the sky, the houses; if we have not dined in private homes, visited the national shrines; if we have not elbowed citizens in the street, in the trains, in the subways. Only experience enables us to sense how the institutions, the values, and the habits that we had come to know through books actually come to life. Only experience helps to place in proper perspective ideas that are at once true and apparently contradictory. Concepts, whether scientific or superficial, remain abstract, without flesh and blood, unless "one has seen for oneself."

For example, direct experience in the United States emphasizes certain economic considerations of which one is not unaware but which there is a tendency, from a distance, to underestimate. The hostility of the French workman toward "American capitalism" stems to a large extent from ignorance and ideological prejudices. Actually, it is the non-privileged classes, the workers, who profit most from American-style capitalism; a high standard of living changes their lot much more than that of the privileged; the middle class in the United States lives no better than the middle class of an averagely developed European country, and in certain respects it has a more difficult existence. And although the benefits of American wealth are less unequally distributed than many French leftists think, for many Americans, particularly for the young people, life is not so easy as is often imagined. In the United States, as everywhere else, one must work, and work hard.

American wealth manifests itself in two ways that are equally striking to the visitor. On the one hand, people speak of dollars, of price, more than anywhere else in the world. In France a suspension bridge would be singled out for the tourist's admiration by reason of its length, height, possibly the difficulties of construction and the genius of the architect; in San Francisco and elsewhere people rave about the sixty-million-dollar bridge. On the other hand, though everything is reckoned in dollars and cents, primary commodities such as electricity are squandered with a prodigality that scarcely ceases to surprise one. Strict economic calculation based on abundance of material and scarcity of manpower—this abstract formula found in all the books becomes a concrete reality.

After a few days this reality combines with numerous other impressions that converge toward a controversial proposition: American society was built by Europeans but is today, in many of its prinicpal aspects, different from European societies. In a word: while I was with Americans in Europe I was above all struck by the European background to their way of thinking, feeling, and living, but in the United States I was above all struck by the originality of American society.

The first reason for this impression stems, it seems to me, from the scale of natural phenomena. Europe, from Saint Andrews to Naples, from Brest to Warsaw, exists within certain norms: the rivers, the plains, the fields seem to be on the same scale. American norms are different. It takes one night to go by train from Paris to Berlin, three days and three nights to cross the American Republic from east to west. The airplane was necessary to make it possible to go from New York to San Francisco as one would go from Calais to Marseilles. Assuredly, if one thinks of it, the agglomeration of Paris or London is as excessive as that of New York—in fact even more monstrous, when considered in relation to the size of France or Great Britain. Nevertheless, in New York, the vertical architecture, in Washington the distances from one section of the city to another, give you the physical sensation of this "difference in scale" between the European nations and the United States.

There has been so much emphasis on the conformism and at the same time heterogeneity of American society that I hesitate to take up this theme. One has the feeling that there is greater religious, moral, and family diversity in the United States than in any European country. But superimposed on the national and racial differences, which depend on the origin of a family and the length of time it has been in the country, is a homogeneous façade. It is created in the first instance by the diffusion throughout the country of certain tools of technical civilization—drugstores, milk bars, service stations, and the like. The large-scale standardized production of objects in current usage spreads a uniform social veneer on the surface of American life; it is this technique of the "American way of life" that separates the majority of American tourists, in uniform or in civilian clothes, from the peoples among whom they live or visit. Also, a certain typical manner of behavior in social relations is shown you—by waitresses, gas-station attendants, salesgirls. A stereotyped smile greets you that at first delights, then irritates, and finally leaves you indifferent. In American society everyone contrives to wear a happy expression and to disguise the impersonality of social relations by greeting the stranger as though he, and he alone, were the only one expected. Adaptation to the environment is a virtue taught in the schools. Obedience to social demands becomes a necessity whose acceptance gives a feeling not of constraint but of merit.

This dialectic of plurality and conformism lies at the core of American life, making for the originality of the social structure, and raising the most contradictory evaluations. One speaks of a classless society while finding aggravated in it all the conflicts that tear European nations apart. Americanism assures the maintenance of the national community because this Americanism, while denying the reality of class struggle, admits as normal the rivalry between individuals and groups and accepts a hierarchy of money and prestige that is never definite, never crystallized, but at the same time never absent. In France, Great Britain, Italy,

Germany the sense of nationality takes different forms, but all the European countries seem to me to belong to the same general order; American society belongs to a different order. Its colonial history, its vast territories, the varied backgrounds of its people have given it characteristics that make it seem essentially different today from the nations of the old continent.

Let me make myself clear. One could easily enumerate a great number of phenomena, institutions, amusements from across the Atlantic that have acquired citizen's rights in France, elsewhere in Europe, and even throughout the world. This process of "Americanization" is looked upon by many with horror. But in some respects the battle is not so much against Americanism as against the universalizing of phenomena linked to the development of material civilization. If the effort toward increased productivity and the subordination of all usages to the imperatives of greater output is termed Americanization, then the whole of Europe, including France, is indeed in the process of becoming Americanized. In this connection it has to be remembered, though, that not all the secrets of American productivity are transferable.

II

International politics, for the first time in history, embraces the five continents. The United States is the first authentic world power. Since it is also the richest and most powerful country, it cannot but inspire mixed feelings—envy and resentment combined with admiration or fear.

I myself belong to the group of Frenchmen described as pro-American. In my view, American diplomacy, which seemed to me deplorable during the Second World War, has been fundamentally sound during the postwar period, at least in Europe. Reconciliation with a reconstructed Germany seemed to me in the best interests of France, and therefore I had no reason to agree with those who accused the leaders of the United States of a plot in favor of defeated Germany and against victimized

France. But it was not so much in Europe as in Africa and Asia that American policy was irritating to French public opinion. The chief reproach leveled by many Frenchmen at the Americans in the years following the second war was their anti-colonialism, their intervention in the French empire against French sovereignty. The fate of the Indians and Negroes has become the weapon used against the United States to counter the accusation of French colonialism.

I shall not attempt to investigate here in what proportion the defenders and the indicters are justified. It is true that the French are less race-conscious than the Americans, and that the latter are more impatient to grant self-government to all peoples, whether developed or underdeveloped. In certain areas there are real and often well-founded differences of interest or of feeling between the two countries. On the other hand, contact with the United States shows not only these differences but also the inevitable contrast between the attitude of a European or Asiatic country and the attitude of one that is of necessity global.

Glance at the map: the east coast of the United States faces toward Europe, the west toward Asia. In Washington the Secretary of State, the President, the journalists, feel just as much sense of responsibility toward South Korea or the Philippines as toward Berlin or Greece. Inevitably, those who are responsible react to news from a continent not only in terms of their friends and enemies on that continent, but also in terms of their allies on the other side of the world. During the Suez crisis in 1956 the positions taken by India or Burma weighed as heavily as those of Great Britain or France. The two latter countries were friends and allies of the United States, while Burma and India belong to the "unaffiliated third party," the vast group that, having acquired independence a few years ago, is passionately anti-colonial and wants to retain an active neutrality between the Soviet bloc and the free world.

The visitor to Washington gets a physical impression of the United States' world-wide mission when he consults the list of distinguished guests received by the President. The Austrian Chancellor succeeds the President of Indonesia; the President of South Vietnam or the President of Tunisia succeeds the Premier of France. One visitor is reminded that the United States has always sympathetically followed the struggles for independence of the peoples of Asia and Africa, which is true. The other is solemnly assured of the traditional friendship that exists between his country and Americans, which is not false either. Thus American leaders are convinced that their point of view on the world is less unilateral, more complex, than that of any of their allies. They are sincerely shocked that a tendency toward excessive simplification is attributed to them when they are consciously striving to encompass the whole earth.

There is no doubt that they have a global perspective, but the criticism of their penchant for simplification is not refuted because of it. In Europe, as in Asia, many observers face American leaders with the same reproach: that of bringing everything back to rivalry with Communism. And I think there is another more profound explanation for this oversimplification criticism. In politics Americans—average Americans even more than their leaders—seem to me to apply a method of "technical" thinking that expresses itself in terms of problems to be solved and a search for means to reach an end. Every situation is a problem; every problem admits of a solution. In the eyes of a fair number of Frenchmen every problem is a situation, and situations admit not of solution but of clear perception, a gradual inurement, possibly a transformation effected by man—above all by the great master of man and things, time. The allies of the United States are often much more perturbed by the manner and the language of American leaders than by their acts. Members of Congress, generals, journalists, sometimes express themselves as though the Communist problem could be taken care of by a radical solution—whereas for years, for decades, perhaps for centuries, it will be a reality with which we shall have to live, avoiding both "shooting war" and "appeasement."

This tendency to confuse political thinking with technical thinking sometimes leads Americans to assume implicitly that they can change the world at will—as if they were able to manipulate men, their feelings and their aspirations, on command. And it may be granted that the technical method of approach, while it risks impatience and oversimplification in analysis, is not without its advantages, for it is at least a stimulus to action. The French tendency—to analyze a situation, to note that each possible decision clashes against insurmountable obstacles, to wait until time wears away the obstacles or events remove them—is quite the opposite: it has the virtues of apparent lucidity, of real subtlety, but it risks the confusion of action with awareness.

Something that strikes a foreigner and has often impressed my compatriots is the spectacle offered by the capital of the United States, where the policy of the leading world power is elaborated. Washington, unlike London or Paris, lives only through politics. Federal capital though it is, it has practically no theatrical productions or concerts. Nothing there distracts the professional politicians from their vocation. The inhabitants of Washington, civil servants, diplomats, politicians, journalists, have nothing to do outside business hours but to meet for cocktail and dinner parties. Inevitably, they talk. President, Secretary of State, members of Congress, generals, admirals, talk among themselves and from one group to another, talk to journalists and before radio or television microphones. News released in the morning has made the rounds of the city by sundown. Exclusively political, it is the most gossip-ridden city in the world. As for the innumerable statements that are registered by press agencies each day and reverberate through all corners of the earth, they form part of the political game. The spectacle includes competition among the interest groups, factions within the parties, factions within the civil service and the military. Washington never speaks unanimously. One always wonders who speaks in the name of the United States. In periods of crisis these contradictions among the American voices lend themselves to interpretations that may be sincere or insincere but are rarely favorable: "war mongering," "men of straw," "lack of unified action." One must step back to acquire perspective; one must have had direct experience with the "American way of conducting politics" in order to discern—beyond the spectacular episodes, the delirious polemics, the great debates—the continuity of a moderate policy that is neither imaginative nor grandiose but does not lean toward war or toward capitulation.

Let me add that three categories of Frenchmen cannot share my view: professional diplomats; champions of certain French national interests that American policy ignores or vehemently attacks; and those who see the United States by way of categories (capitalism, imperialism) that in themselves inspire hostile judgments. No experience will change judgments that stem less from raw facts than from the historical and moral interpretation they are accorded.

III

While the concept the French have of the United States as a political power depends essentially on their individual political bent, it is entirely different in regard to American civilization. Here the admirers and detractors are not distributed in a parliamentary hemicycle, one group to the right, the other to the left. The American way of life inspires liking, indifference, hostility, according to criteria that seem not to be political.

Since 1944 the relationship between French and Americans has been closer than at any time in the past. Thousands of American soldiers have lived in France, thousands of French people have had contacts with them, and other thousands have themselves been to the United States. But let us remember that partial knowledge does not necessarily carry with it deep understanding. Even if French and Americans were to exert themselves to be fair to each other, they would not reach a good understanding unless they accepted each other's differences. If one ponders what the two peoples have to learn from each other, the first answer, the most banal and perhaps the most important, is that each, through the discovery of the other, should learn that it is not alone in the world and that its own sense of what is obvious is not necessarily universally shared.

The Frenchman does not always regard as charming the American child whose parents apparently grant him complete freedom; frequently he considers him insufferable. He is not always aware of the meaning of the collective life that Americanism develops, but is struck by what he considers a mediocre level of intellectual development. The optimism of Americans sometimes seems to him an attractive sign of youth, at other times a sign of puerility. The refusal to think of death, to make room for it in the awareness of human destiny, seems surprising and almost pitiable to many cultured Frenchmen. But the well-brought-up French child surprises and shocks American parents a little. The American observer does not regard as necessarily admirable the abstract, theoretical, sometimes encyclopaedic nature of the training received by French students. The American soldier is too affected by the discomfort of the houses and the dirtiness of the street in French villages; the French visitor in the United States is too affected by the facile smile of the salesgirl, the abundance of cars, the vulgarity of the television. Each makes the mistake of comparing the worst of what he sees abroad with the best he knows at home.

What types of Frenchmen manifest the most lively hostility to the American way of life? Without laying claims to exhaustiveness of scientific precision, I shall enumerate four types. One is the "cultured Frenchman," enamored of a certain style of living, who detests big industry, mass production, the lowering of standards in favor of the masses. (Georges Duhamel in *Scènes de la vie future* seems to me to epitomize the ideal of the "craftsman civilization" versus "industrial barbarism." His picture of the United States is a caricature, but M. Duhamel is also less the picture than the caricature of the Frenchman hostile to American life.) The second type, of which M. Étiemble is an example, is

above all struck by the race-consciousness that Americans con-
demn but have not yet surmounted.[1] A third type is not unaware
of industrial barbarism and race-consciousness, but lays greater
stress on the character of human relations, and on the impersonality of most of these relationships in the United States, the
tendency to be satisfied with the superficial and to ignore the
deep ties of love and friendship; thereupon unfolds a description
of the boredom and emptiness of American life, and the reaction
to it—violence, speed, sexuality, and so on. A fourth type is
struck above all by the intellectual fodder offered to the American masses, from scandal magazines to digests of books, even of
great books.

These four types are not absolutely distinct, one from another.
It goes without saying that the representative of the first type
also invokes race-consciousness, impersonality in human relations, and cultural poverty. But those of the second and third
groups do not lay the blame on "industrial barbarism," for most
of them are aware that economic progress is indispensable to
the raising of the standard of living. The exponents of the last
three types make free use of the same arguments, but they do
not place emphasis on the same aspects of American life. Race-
consciousness, pragmatism and superficiality in human relations,
or the vulgarity of mass culture appear as the major and characteristic factor, depending on the psychological makeup or
attention of the observer.

Are these critics of American civilization typical of French
opinion? There is no dearth of enthusiastic descriptions of the
United States, the latest being that of Renée and Pierre Gosset.[2]
It is probable that the French lower classes, the laborers and
petits bourgeois, would be more impressed by the advantages of
the "American way of life" than the middle class and the intel-

---

[1] Editors' note: Georges Duhamel, M.D. (1884–   ), novelist and essayist:
Scènes de la vie future (Paris, 1930). René Étiemble (1909–   ), Professor
of Comparative Literature at the Sorbonne: see his Hygiène des lettres (Paris,
1952–   ).
[2] Editors' note: L'Amérique aux Américains (Paris, 1953).

lectuals, since the European middle class already enjoys most of the advantages of industrial civilization and, in addition, certain of the advantages of incompletely industrialized countries. Nonetheless, a good number of the French who actually visit the United States, especially among those who express their views and offer them to their compatriots in book form, belong to the pessimistic rather than to the optimistic school of thought, to the critics rather than the admirers.

The picture of the United States held by a great many Frenchmen who have never crossed the Atlantic—probably a vague picture, and perhaps constituted or deformed by prejudice or political conviction—is neither false nor true. A young dynamic country with a high standard of living: the description is insufficient but not untrue, not an obstacle to mutual understanding. On the other hand, the antipathy manifested toward the United States by many French intellectuals who have been there is a reality that must be taken into consideration and that cannot simply be eliminated on grounds of prejudice, emotionalism, or misunderstanding. It is not enough to know each other in order to like each other; this axiom is no less true for peoples than for individuals.

No argument invoked by the critics is without a certain weight. It is true that race-consciousness exists in the United States, and not only in the South. It is also true that the attenuation of class distinctions has been countered by the accentuation of national or racial differences. The hierarchy among national groups is subtle, and it thins out slowly as the latest arrivals, the Poles, the Italians, the Balkan peoples, gradually, in their turn, move up the social scale. It does not disappear completely, because the desire to be distinguished by virtue of the length of one's American roots, by religion, by nationality of origin, combines with the ideology of human equality. With regard to color, the barrier continues.

Many Europeans have a fantastic conception of the lot of the Negroes in the United States. Actually their social and intellectual level is continually rising. There are universities for colored people, a Negro middle class. An increasing proportion of Negroes live in the North, where race-consciousness takes different forms from those in the South. Compared to the majority of the world's Negroes, those in the United States are probably the most highly privileged, at least in the material order, for they participate in the country's exceptional standard of living. But when the myths have been brushed aside, the main fact remains. The contradiction has not yet been resolved between what the American ideal demands and what American society's actual attitude is toward the Negroes. Would those people who pride themselves on not being race-conscious succeed in avoiding this contradiction if, in their own countries, they had a proportionate percentage of colored peoples? Should the inability of the Americans to put their consciences in order be indignantly denounced, or should one sympathize with their efforts to regulate their conduct according to their principles? Each will decide for himself.

By the same token, the other French criticisms—the impersonality of human relations, mass culture—are not, and cannot be dismissed as, the result of ignorance or bad faith. The fact is that many French people, especially in the cultured class, believe that human relations in the United States are deformed by pragmatism, emptied, so to speak, of all intensity and depth by concern with self-adaptation and immediate unqualified cordiality. Is the victim of half-knowledge worse than the victim of ignorance? Is he deceived by the surface of American life and thus unable to discover the friendships, the love—just as singular and rich in the United States as elsewhere—that are cloaked across the Atlantic under apparent absence of reserve and openness toward strangers, as they are cloaked in France under the seclusion of family life and reticence on first acquaintance? I shall not attempt an answer, but shall only suggest that this Franco-American colloquy contains certain elements of well-founded criticism, founded not necessarily on the real situation in America but on the reality of certain French reactions to the United States.

Perhaps the decisive question concerns what is termed, on both sides of the Atlantic, "mass culture." Delight is taken in confusing this with American culture in general—and isn't this culture-for-all, this bargain culture, the very antithesis of real culture? Productivity, industrialization, rise in living standards, do these terms that are associated with modern civilization conceal a drift of the rich and in certain respects democratic societies toward barbarism? A Frenchman who visits the United States cannot fail to be struck by certain facts: the style, which seems vulgar to him, of much of the radio and television, the sordidness of the sensational and scandal-oriented press, the provincialism of much of the news, the widespread use of rewrites and digests, the mediocrity of many of the films. But these facts would be acknowledged by the majority of Americans. Once again, it is a question of the place they occupy in the whole of American life, the significance they assume. Are they typically American, or are they linked to some degree to phenomena typical everywhere of modern civilization?

It must be admitted that the mass-circulation papers in France or Great Britain have no need to look to the United States for their ignoble proceedings. Not that they haven't borrowed a few from American models, but they have found quite enough on their own. Such French and English publications have proportionally as many readers as the American. The French love-stories press is perhaps of a higher caliber than the American crime or sex press, but this is not altogether sure. Soviet censorship eliminates excesses of crime, sex, and sentimentality, but this puritanism has, as a counterpart, an edifying literature of "positive" heroes and idylls in the shade of a tractor. For the time being, the fact that everyone knows how to read has resulted in the creation not of a single world of culture, but of two, perhaps as far apart from each other as were formerly the world of unwritten popular culture and that of the select.

Is the American case exceptional because the duality is more marked? Personally, I am inclined to reply that the duality is less marked. What most shocks the European intellectual is a certain continuity between the two cultural worlds. The kind of entertainment that the American child absorbs daily, even in intellectual families, the kind of literature he devours, in other words the vulnerability of cultured circles to the masses' lack of culture—this is the phenomenon that strikes so many European observers and occasions their condemnation. The practice of producing résumés of masterpieces is another example of this admixture of the two worlds that shocks and disquiets them. (In addition, of course, there is the problem of differences of opinion—the occasional refusal of the average American to subscribe to a hierarchy of values that seems obvious to the Frenchman.)

The observer favorably disposed toward American life replies that never have so many Americans (and young Americans) frequented the museums; never have there been so many good orchestras and good concerts. In the last analysis the amount of live art (music, painting) offered in most American cities far surpasses that offered in French cities or provinces. Never, thanks to radio and "hi-fi," have so many Americans heard good music. Never, thanks to reproductions, have they admired so much great painting. The indictment denounces the sliding of higher culture toward mass culture; the defense shows how a growing number of average Americans are reaching the higher world. I do not think one can entirely reject either thesis. American life supports both this risk and this opportunity. Depending on his sympathies or temperament, a person will stress the one or the other. At the moment, the allegation of American lack of culture, very widespread in French intellectual circles, is based on two aspects of American life.

The first of these is that in the United States the scale of values of the "highbrows" is not officially accepted by the general public (even the cultured public). The French, even when cultured (except for literary quasi-professionals), are far from being convinced of the genius of Baudelaire, Claudel, or Kafka, but for the most part they do not hesitate to appreciate the avant-garde. Whether in literature or in painting, the pseudo-enthusiasts tend to subscribe to the judgments of the authentic enthusiasts. The heretics have become orthodox. In France one may try in vain to cause a scandal or to provoke the philistines. By way of intellectual comfort, the middle class has apparently become converted to the values of bohemia or of maligned authors. Perhaps there are still some unrecognized geniuses, but never has there been such fear of not recognizing genius. The United States has not yet reached the indisputable reign of the avant-garde.

The second basis of criticism is the indifference manifested by Americans to cultural values, especially aesthetic values, in the course of everyday life. Concern with beauty is apparently ignored, or at least subordinated to utility, to preoccupation with income. The beauty that stems from the functional architecture in American structures strikes a discordant note in a harmony whose inspiration seems entirely different. The suburbs of European cities, especially in France, are not beautiful; the sense of town planning is too often absent. And nevertheless the cult of form, of aesthetic values, remains inseparable from the spirit of French culture—as it is in Japan, where concern with beauty touches every incident in existence, every piece of work, every garden, the fish-platter, the house. This cult seems, in the United States, to be superimposed on a radically different spirit.

Will an industrialized France, concerned with productivity, become a mediocre replica of the United States? Will the qualities that enchant so many foreigners in French life be irreparably destroyed by the modernization of the economy? And on the other side of the Atlantic, will the United States go ever farther in its own direction—production, pragmatism, awareness of the future rather than of the past? These are, I believe, the two questions that dominate the Franco-American colloquy, a dialogue of men and of cultures, the background for the polemics of the public square.

Barring ever possible catastrophes, I myself think that the charm of the French provinces is less linked to the slowness of economic development than it is said to be. It is not the low yield of labor but the art of living that is exemplary in France, and industry will not ruin the art of living, provided the French keep faith with themselves. And in the United States the growing expansion of the economy is, as of now, attenuating rather than aggravating the obsession with income. Since it has become the world's leading power, by force of circumstances rather than voluntarily, the United States has been forced to overcome that insularity in which all peoples delight. In the principal universities the number of professors and students devoted to the study of other worlds has multiplied. General culture has assumed a wider place in the curriculum, even in the technical schools. The younger generation wants to explore the world, and it seems to me is more interested in the arts than were former generations. According to my way of thinking, American society is maturing, and little by little broadening the pragmatism of the colonists resolved to conquer rebellious natural forces. It is acquiring a sense of history.

Is this to say that France modernized and the United States grown up will meet each other halfway? It would be ridiculous to substitute this new mythology for the old ones. The Franco-American colloquy originates not only in the supposed French refusal of technical civilization, the supposed youth of the United States, indifferent to the past and without experience of suffering. The soil, the sky, the dimensions, the population, the religion, are different on the two sides of the Atlantic. French culture is conspicuous for its catholicity, its profound pessimism, its undefined tension between faith and skepticism. National consciousness in the United States is pragmatic and moral; it will stay that way in the foreseeable future, at whatever stage of economic progress.

Alexis de Tocqueville thought he saw in American democracy the common destiny of all peoples. Many observers—with enthusiasm or with dismay—think they see in the technical civilization of the United States the picture of the industrial society that will be the common destiny of all peoples. Undeniably, we are all caught up in the same adventure, condemned to push ever farther in the direction of industrialization, urbanization, rationalization. Will ways of living and thinking, social relations, and ideologies tend in like manner toward uniformity?

I should not like to reply either yes or no. There are certain general implications inherent in technical progress. On the other hand, when it comes to attitudes toward life, death, the social hierarchy, or society, to questions of philosophy or of religion— here I have not seen the picture of our future in the United States. I think I discern there, beyond a transferable Americanism, the traits of a national community in process of formation that will be neither the ruin nor the salvation of the whole of humanity, but one among others.

The Pastons and Chaucer

VIRGINIA WOOLF (1892-1941)

THE TOWER of Caister Castle still rises ninety feet into the air, and the arch still stands from which Sir John Fastolf's barges sailed out to fetch stone for the building of the great castle. But now jackdaws nest on the tower, and of the castle, which once

covered six acres of ground, only ruined walls remain, pierced
by loop-holes and surmounted by battlements, though there are
neither archers within nor cannon without. As for the "seven
religious men" and the "seven poor folk" who should, at this
very moment, be praying for the souls of Sir John and his
parents, there is no sign of them nor sound of their prayers. The
place is a ruin. Antiquaries speculate and differ.

Not so very far off lie more ruins—the ruins of Bromholm
Priory, where John Paston was buried, naturally enough, since
his house was only a mile or so away, lying on low ground by
the sea, twenty miles north of Norwich. The coast is dangerous,
and the land, even in our time, inaccessible. Nevertheless the little
bit of wood at Bromholm, the fragment of the true Cross, brought
pilgrims incessantly to the Priory, and sent them away with eyes
opened and limbs straightened. But some of them with their
newly-opened eyes saw a sight which shocked them—the grave
of John Paston in Bromholm Priory without a tombstone. The
news spread over the country-side. The Pastons had fallen; they
that had been so powerful could no longer afford a stone to put
above John Paston's head. Margaret, his widow, could not pay
her debts; the eldest son, Sir John, wasted his property upon
women and tournaments, while the younger, John also, though
a man of greater parts, thought more of his hawks than of his
harvests.

The pilgrims of course were liars, as people whose eyes have
just been opened by a piece of the true Cross have every right
to be; but their news, none the less, was welcome. The Pastons
had risen in the world. People said even that they had been bondmen not so very long ago. At any rate, men still living could remember John's grandfather Clement tilling his own land, a hard-
working peasant; and William, Clement's son, becoming a judge
and buying land; and John, William's son, marrying well and
buying more land and quite lately inheriting the vast new castle
at Caister, and all Sir John's lands in Norfolk and Suffolk. People said that he had forged the old knight's will. What wonder,

then, that he lacked a tombstone? But, if we consider the character of Sir John Paston, John's eldest son, and his upbringing
and his surroundings, and the relations between himself and his
father as the family letters reveal them, we shall see how difficult
it was, and how likely to be neglected—this business of making
his father's tombstone.

For let us imagine, in the most desolate part of England
known to us at the present moment, a raw, new-built house,
without telephone, bathroom, or drains, arm-chairs or newspapers, and one shelf perhaps of books, unwieldy to hold, expensive to come by. The windows look out upon a few cultivated fields and a dozen hovels, and beyond them there is the
sea on one side, on the other a vast fen. A single road crosses
the fen, but there is a hole in it, which, one of the farm hands
reports, is big enough to swallow a carriage. And, the man adds,
Tom Topcroft, the mad bricklayer, has broken loose again and
ranges the country half-naked, threatening to kill any one who
approaches him. That is what they talk about at dinner in the
desolate house, while the chimney smokes horribly, and the
draught lifts the carpets on the floor. Orders are given to lock
all gates at sunset, and, when the long dismal evening has worn
itself away, simply and solemnly, girt about with dangers as they
are, these isolated men and women fall upon their knees in
prayer.

In the fifteenth century, however, the wild landscape was
broken suddenly and very strangely by vast piles of brand-new
masonry. There rose out of the sandhills and heaths of the Norfolk coast a huge bulk of stone, like a modern hotel in a watering-
place; but there was no parade, no lodging houses, and no pier
at Yarmouth then, and this gigantic building on the outskirts of
the town was built to house one solitary old gentleman without
any children—Sir John Fastolf, who had fought at Agincourt
and acquired great wealth. He had fought at Agincourt and
got but little reward. No one took his advice. Men spoke ill of

him behind his back. He was well aware of it; his temper was none the sweeter for it. He was a hot-tempered old man, powerful, embittered by a sense of grievance. But whether on the battlefield or at court he thought perpetually of Caister, and how, when his duties allowed, he would settle down on his father's land and live in a great house of his own building.

The gigantic structure of Caister Castle was in progress not so many miles away when the little Pastons were children. John Paston, the father, had charge of some part of the business, and the children listened, as soon as they could listen at all, to talk of stone and building, of barges gone to London and not yet returned, of the twenty-six private chambers, of the hall and chapel; of foundations, measurements, and rascally work-people. Later, in 1454, when the work was finished and Sir John had come to spend his last years at Caister, they may have seen for themselves the mass of treasure that was stored there; the tables laden with gold and silver plate; the wardrobes stuffed with gowns of velvet and satin and cloth of gold, with hoods and tippets and beaver hats and leather jackets and velvet doublets; and how the very pillow-cases on the beds were of green and purple silk. There were tapestries everywhere. The beds were laid and the bedrooms hung with tapestries representing sieges, hunting and hawking, men fishing, archers shooting, ladies playing on their harps, dallying with ducks, or a giant "bearing the leg of a bear in his hand." Such were the fruits of a well-spent life. To buy land, to build great houses, to stuff these houses full of gold and silver plate (though the privy might well be in the bedroom), was the proper aim of mankind. Mr. and Mrs. Paston spent the greater part of their energies in the same exhausting occupation. For since the passion to acquire was universal, one could never rest secure in one's possessions for long. The outlying parts of one's property were in perpetual jeopardy. The Duke of Norfolk might covet this manor, the Duke of Suffolk that. Some trumped-up excuse, as for instance that the Pastons were bondmen, gave them the right to seize the house and batter down the lodges in the owner's absence. And how could the owner of Paston and Mauteby and Drayton and Gresham be in five or six places at once, especially now that Caister Castle was his, and he must be in London trying to get his rights recognised by the King? The King was mad too, they said; did not know his own child, they said; or the King was in flight; or there was civil war in the land. Norfolk was always the most distressed of counties and its country gentlemen the most quarrelsome of mankind. Indeed, had Mrs. Paston chosen, she could have told her children how when she was a young woman a thousand men with bows and arrows and pans of burning fire had marched upon Gresham and broken the gates and mined the walls of the room where she sat alone. But much worse things than that had happened to women. She neither bewailed her lot nor thought herself a heroine. The long, long letters which she wrote so laboriously in her clear cramped hand to her husband, who was (as usual) away, make no mention of herself. The sheep had wasted the hay. Heyden's and Tuddenham's men were out. A dyke had been broken and a bullock stolen. They needed treacle badly, and really she must have stuff for a dress.

But Mrs. Paston did not talk about herself.

Thus the little Pastons would see their mother writing or dictating page after page, hour after hour, long, long letters, but to interrupt a parent who writes so laboriously of such important matters would have been a sin. The prattle of children, the lore of the nursery or schoolroom, did not find its way into these elaborate communications. For the most part her letters are the letters of an honest bailiff to his master, explaining, asking advice, giving news, rendering accounts. There was robbery and manslaughter; it was difficult to get in the rents; Richard Calle had gathered but little money; and what with one thing and another Margaret had not had time to make out, as she should have done, the inventory of the goods which her husband desired. Well might old Agnes, surveying her son's affairs rather grimly from a distance, counsel him to contrive it so that "ye may have less to do in the world; your father said, In little business lieth much rest. This world is but a thoroughfare, and full of woe; and when we depart therefrom, right nought bear with us but our good deeds and ill."

The thought of death would thus come upon them in a clap. Old Fastolf, cumbered with wealth and property, had his vision at the end of Hell fire, and shrieked aloud to his executors to distribute alms, and see that prayers were said "in perpetuum," so that his soul might escape the agonies of purgatory. William Paston, the judge, was urgent too that the monks of Norwich should be retained to pray for his soul "for ever." The soul was no wisp of air, but a solid body capable of eternal suffering, and the fire that destroyed it was as fierce as any that burnt on mortal grates. For ever there would be monks and the town of Norwich, and for ever the Chapel of Our Lady in the town of Norwich. There was something matter-of-fact, positive, and enduring in their conception both of life and of death.

With the plan of existence so vigorously marked out, children of course were well beaten, and boys and girls taught to know their places. They must acquire land; but they must obey their parents. A mother would clout her daughter's head three times a week and break the skin if she did not conform to the laws of behaviour. Agnes Paston, a lady of birth and breeding, beat her daughter Elizabeth. Margaret Paston, a softer-hearted woman, turned her daughter out of the house for loving the honest bailiff Richard Calle. Brothers would not suffer their sisters to marry beneath them, and "sell candle and mustard in Framlingham." The fathers quarrelled with the sons, and the mothers, fonder of their boys than of their girls, yet bound by all law and custom to obey their husbands, were torn asunder in their efforts to keep the peace. With all her pains, Margaret failed to prevent rash acts on the part of her eldest son John, or the bitter words with which his father denounced him. He was a "drone among bees," the father burst out, "which labour for gathering honey in the fields, and the drone doth naught but taketh his part of it." He treated his parents with insolence, and yet was fit for no charge of responsibility abroad.

But the quarrel was ended, very shortly, by the death (22nd May 1466) of John Paston, the father, in London. The body was brought down to Bromholm to be buried. Twelve poor men trudged all the way bearing torches beside it. Alms were distributed; masses and dirges were said. Bells were rung. Great quantities of fowls, sheep, pigs, eggs, bread, and cream were devoured, ale and wine drunk, and candles burnt. Two panes were taken from the church windows to let out the reek of the torches. Black cloth was distributed, and a light set burning on the grave. But John Paston, the heir, delayed to make his father's tombstone.

He was a young man, something over twenty-four years of age. The discipline and the drudgery of a country life bored him. When he ran away from home, it was, apparently, to attempt to enter the King's household. Whatever doubts, indeed, might be cast by their enemies on the blood of the Pastons, Sir John was unmistakably a gentleman. He had inherited his lands; the honey was his that the bees had gathered with so much labour. He had the instincts of enjoyment rather than of acquisition, and with his mother's parsimony was strangely mixed something of his father's ambition. Yet his own indolent and luxurious temperament took the edge from both. He was attractive to women, liked society and tournaments, and court life and making bets, and sometimes, even, reading books. And so life, now that John Paston was buried, started afresh upon rather a different foundation. There could be little outward change indeed. Margaret still ruled the house. She still ordered the lives of the younger children as she had ordered the lives of the elder. The boys still needed to be beaten into book-learning by their tutors, the girls still loved the wrong men and must be married to the right. Rents had to be collected; the interminable lawsuit for the Fastolf property dragged on. Battles were fought; the roses of York and Lancaster alternately faded and flourished. Norfolk was full of poor people seeking redress for their grievances, and Margaret worked

for her son as she had worked for her husband, with this significant change only, that now, instead of confiding in her husband, she took the advice of her priest.

But inwardly there was a change. It seems at last as if the hard
outer shell had served its purpose and something sensitive, appreciative, and pleasure-loving had formed within. At any rate
Sir John, writing to his brother John at home, strayed sometimes
from the business on hand to crack a joke, to send a piece of gossip,
or to instruct him, knowingly and even subtly, upon the conduct
of a love affair. Be "as lowly to the mother as ye list, but to the
maid not too lowly, nor that ye be too glad to speed, nor too
sorry to fail. And I shall always be your herald both here, if she
come hither, and at home, when I come home, which I hope
hastily within XI. days at the furthest." And then a hawk was to
be bought, a hat, or new silk laces sent down to John in Norfolk,
prosecuting his suit, flying his hawks, and attending with considerable energy and not too nice a sense of honesty to the affairs
of the Paston estates.

The lights had long since burnt out on John Paston's grave.
But still Sir John delayed; no tomb replaced them. He had his
excuses; what with the business of the lawsuit, and his duties at
Court, and the disturbance of the civil wars, his time was occupied and his money spent. But perhaps something strange had
happened to Sir John himself, and not only to Sir John dallying
in London, but to his sister Margery falling in love with the bailiff,
and to Walter making Latin verses at Eton, and to John flying
his hawks at Paston. Life was a little more various in its pleasures.
They were not quite so sure as the elder generation had been of
the rights of man and of the dues of God, of the horrors of
death, and of the importance of tombstones. Poor Margaret Paston scented the change and sought uneasily, with the pen which
had marched so stiffly through so many pages, to lay bare the
root of her troubles. It was not that the lawsuit saddened her;
she was ready to defend Caister with her own hands if need be,
"though I cannot well guide nor rule soldiers," but there was

something wrong with the family since the death of her husband and master. Perhaps her son had failed in his service to God; he had been too proud or too lavish in his expenditure; or perhaps he had shown too little mercy to the poor. Whatever the fault might be, she only knew that Sir John spent twice as much money as his father for less result; that they could scarcely pay their debts without selling land, wood, or household stuff ("It is a death to me to think of it"); while every day people spoke ill of them in the country because they left John Paston to lie without a tombstone. The money that might have bought it, or more land, and more goblets and more tapestry, was spent by Sir John on clocks and trinkets, and upon paying a clerk to copy out Treatises upon Knighthood and other such stuff. There they stood at Paston—eleven volumes, with the poems of Lydgate and Chaucer among them, diffusing a strange air into the gaunt, comfortless house, inviting men to indolence and vanity, distracting their thoughts from business, and leading them not only to neglect their own profit but to think lightly of the sacred dues of the dead.

For sometimes, instead of riding off on his horse to inspect his crops or bargain with his tenants, Sir John would sit, in broad daylight, reading. There, on the hard chair in the comfortless room with the wind lifting the carpet and the smoke stinging his eyes, he would sit reading Chaucer, wasting his time, dreaming—or what strange intoxication was it that he drew from books? Life was rough, cheerless, and disappointing. A whole year of days would pass fruitlessly in dreary business, like dashes of rain on the window pane. There was no reason in it as there had been for his father; no imperative need to establish a family and acquire an important position for children who were not born, or if born, had no right to bear their father's name. But Lydgate's poems or Chaucer's, like a mirror in which figures move brightly, silently, and compactly, showed him the very skies, fields, and people whom he knew, but rounded and complete. Instead of waiting listlessly for news from London or piecing out from his mother's gossip some country tragedy of love and jealousy, here, in a few pages, the whole story was laid before him. And then as he rode or sat at table he would remember some description or saying which bore upon the present moment and fixed it, or some string of words would charm him, and putting aside the pressure of the moment, he would hasten home to sit in his chair and learn the end of the story.

To learn the end of the story—Chaucer can still make us wish to do that. He has pre-eminently that story-teller's gift, which is almost the rarest gift among writers at the present day. Nothing happens to us as it did to our ancestors; events are seldom important; if we recount them, we do not really believe in them; we have perhaps things of greater interest to say, and for these reasons natural story-tellers like Mr. Garnett, whom we must distinguish from self-conscious story-tellers like Mr. Masefield, have become rare. For the story-teller, besides his indescribable zest for facts, must tell his story craftily, without undue stress or excitement, or we shall swallow it whole and jumble the parts together; he must let us stop, give us time to think and look about us, yet always be persuading us to move on. Chaucer was helped to this to some extent by the time of his birth; and in addition he had another advantage over the moderns which will never come the way of English poets again. England was an unspoilt country. His eyes rested on a virgin land, all unbroken grass and wood except for the small towns and an occasional castle in the building. No villa roofs peered through Kentish tree-tops; no factory chimney smoked on the hillside. The state of the country, considering how poets go to Nature, how they use her for their images and their contrasts even when they do not describe her directly, is a matter of some importance. Her cultivation or her savagery influences the poet far more profoundly than the prose writer. To the modern poet, with Birmingham, Manchester, and London the size they are, the country is the sanctuary of moral excellence in contrast with the town which is the sink of vice. It is a retreat, the haunt of modesty and virtue, where men go to hide and moralise. There is something morbid, as if shrinking from human contact, in the nature worship of Wordsworth, still more in the microscopic devotion which Tennyson lavished upon the petals of roses and the buds of lime trees. But these were great poets. In their hands, the country was no mere jeweller's shop, or museum of curious objects to be described, even more curiously, in words. Poets of smaller gift, since the view is so much spoilt, and the garden or the meadow must replace the barren heath and the precipitous mountain-side, are now confined to little landscapes, to birds' nests, to acorns with every wrinkle drawn to the life. The wider landscape is lost.

But to Chaucer the country was too large and too wild to be altogether agreeable. He turned instinctively, as if he had painful experience of their nature, from tempests and rocks to the bright May day and the jocund landscape, from the harsh and mysterious to the gay and definite. Without possessing a tithe of the virtuosity in word-painting which is the modern inheritance, he could give, in a few words, or even, when we come to look, without a single word of direct description, the sense of the open air.

> And se the fresshe floures how they sprynge

—that is enough.

Nature, uncompromising, untamed, was no looking-glass for happy faces, or confessor of unhappy souls. She was herself; sometimes, therefore, disagreeable enough and plain, but always in Chaucer's pages with the hardness and the freshness of an actual presence. Soon, however, we notice something of greater importance than the gay and picturesque appearance of the mediæval world—the solidity which plumps it out, the conviction which animates the characters. There is immense variety in the *Canterbury Tales*, and yet, persisting underneath, one consistent type. Chaucer has his world; he has his young men; he has his young women. If one met them straying in Shakespeare's world one would know them to be Chaucer's, not Shakespeare's. He wants to describe a girl, and this is what she looks like:

> Ful semely hir wimpel pinched was,
> Hir nose tretys; hir eyen greye as glas;
> Hir mouth ful smal, and ther-to soft and reed;
> But sikerly she hadde a fair foreheed;
> It was almost a spanne brood, I trowe;
> For, hardily, she was nat undergrowe.

Then he goes on to develop her; she was a girl, a virgin, cold in her virginity:

> I am, thou woost, yet of thy companye,
> A mayde, and love hunting and venerye,
> And for to walken in the wodes wilde,
> And noght to been a wyf and be with childe.

Next he bethinks him how

> Discreet she was in answering alway;
> And though she had been as wise as Pallas
> No countrefeted termes hadde she
> To seme wys; but after hir degree
> She spak, and alle hir wordes more and lesse
> Souninge in vertu and in gentillesse.

Each of these quotations, in fact, comes from a different Tale, but they are parts, one feels, of the same personage, whom he had in mind, perhaps unconsciously, when he thought of a young girl, and for this reason, as she goes in and out of the *Canterbury Tales* bearing different names, she has a stability which is only to be found where the poet has made up his mind about young women, of course, but also about the world they live in, its end, its nature, and his own craft and technique, so that his mind is free to apply its force fully to its object. It does not occur to him that his Griselda might be improved or altered. There is no blur about her, no hesitation; she proves nothing; she is content to be herself. Upon her, therefore, the mind can rest with that un-conscious ease which allows it, from hints and suggestions, to endow her with many more qualities than are actually referred to. Such is the power of conviction, a rare gift, a gift shared in

our day by Joseph Conrad in his earlier novels, and a gift of supreme importance, for upon it the whole weight of the building
depends. Once believe in Chaucer's young men and women and
we have no need of preaching or protest. We know what he finds
good, what evil; the less said the better. Let him get on with his
story, paint knights and squires, good women and bad, cooks, ship-
men, priests, and we will supply the landscape, give his society its
belief, its standing towards life and death, and make of the journey to Canterbury a spiritual pilgrimage.

This simple faithfulness to his own conceptions was easier
then than now in one respect at least, for Chaucer could write
frankly where we must either say nothing or say it slyly. He
could sound every note in the language instead of finding a great
many of the best gone dumb from disuse, and thus, when struck
by daring fingers, giving off a loud discordant jangle out of keeping with the rest. Much of Chaucer—a few lines perhaps in each
of the Tales—is improper and gives us as we read it the strange
sensation of being naked to the air after being muffled in old
clothing. And, as a certain kind of humour depends upon being
able to speak without self-consciousness of the parts and functions of the body, so with the advent of decency literature lost
the use of one of its limbs. It lost its power to create the Wife of
Bath, Juliet's nurse, and their recognisable though already colour-
less relation, Moll Flanders. Sterne, from fear of coarseness, is
forced into indecency. He must be witty, not humorous. He must
hint instead of speaking outright. Nor can we believe, with Mr.
Joyce's *Ulysses* before us, that laughter of the old kind will ever
be heard again.

> But, lord Christ! When that it remembreth me
> Up-on my yowthe, and on my Iolitee,
> It tikleth me aboute myn herte rote.
> Unto this day it doth myn herte bote
> That I have had my world as in my tyme.

The sound of that old woman's voice is still.

But there is another and more important reason for the surprising brightness, the still effective merriment of the *Canterbury
Tales*. Chaucer was a poet; but he never flinched from the life
that was being lived at the moment before his eyes. A farmyard,
with its straw, its dung, its cocks and its hens is not (we have come
to think) a poetic subject; poets seem either to rule out the farmyard entirely or to require that it shall be a farmyard in Thes-
saly and its pigs of mythological origin. But Chaucer says outright:

> Three large sowes hadde she, and namo,
> Three kyn, and eek a sheep that highte Malle;

or again,

> A yard she hadde, enclosed al aboute
> With stikkes, and a drye ditch with-oute.

He is unabashed and unafraid. He will always get close up to his
object—an old man's chin—

> With thikke bristles of his berde unsofte,
> Lyk to the skin of houndfish, sharp as brere;

or an old man's neck—

> The slakke skin about his nekke shaketh
> Whyl that he sang;

and he will tell you what his characters wore, how they looked,
what they ate and drank, as if poetry could handle the common
facts of this very moment of Tuesday, the sixteenth day of April,
1387, without dirtying her hands. If he withdraws to the time of
the Greeks or the Romans, it is only that his story leads him there.
He has no desire to wrap himself round in antiquity, to take
refuge in age, or to shirk the associations of common grocer's
English.

Therefore when we say that we know the end of the journey,
it is hard to quote the particular lines from which we take our
knowledge. He fixed his eyes upon the road before him, not upon

the world to come. He was little given to abstract contemplation. He deprecated, with peculiar archness, any competition with the scholars and divines:

> The answere of this I lete to divynis,
> But wel I woot, that in this world grey pyne is.

> What is this world? What asketh men to have?
> Now with his love, now in the colde grave
> Allone, withouten any companye,

he asks, or ponders

> O cruel goddes, that governe
> This world with binding of your worde eterne,
> And wryten in the table of athamaunt
> Your parlement, and your eterne graunt,
> What is mankinde more un-to yow holde
> Than is the sheepe, that rouketh in the folde?

Questions press upon him; he asks questions, but he is too true a poet to answer them; he leaves them unsolved, uncramped by the solution of the moment, thus fresh for the generations that come after him. In his life, too, it would be impossible to write him down a man of this party or of that, a democrat or an aristocrat. He was a staunch churchman, but he laughed at priests. He was an able public servant and a courtier, but his views upon sexual morality were extremely lax. He sympathised with poverty, but did nothing to improve the lot of the poor. It is safe to say that not a single law has been framed or one stone set upon another because of anything that Chaucer said or wrote; and yet, as we read him, we are of course absorbing morality at every pore. For among writers there are two kinds: there are the priests who take you by the hand and lead you straight up to the mystery; there are the laymen who imbed their doctrines in flesh and blood and make a complete model of the world without excluding the bad or laying stress upon the good. Wordsworth, Coleridge, and Shelley are among the priests; they give us text after text to be hung upon the wall, saying after saying to be laid upon the heart like an amulet against disaster—

> Farewell, farewell, the heart that lives alone

> He prayeth best that loveth best
> All things both great and small

—such lines of exhortation and command spring to memory instantly. But Chaucer lets us go our ways doing the ordinary things with the ordinary people. His morality lies in the way men and women behave to each other. We see them eating, drinking, laughing, and making love, and come to feel without a word being said what their standards are and so are steeped through and through with their morality. There can be no more forcible preaching than this where all actions and passions are represented, and instead of being solemnly exhorted we are left to stray and stare and make out a meaning for ourselves. It is the morality of ordinary intercourse, the morality of the novel, which parents and librarians rightly judge to be far more persuasive than the morality of poetry.

And so, when we shut Chaucer, we feel that without a word being said the criticism is complete; what we are saying, thinking, reading, doing has been commented upon. Nor are we left merely with the sense, powerful though that is, of having been in good company and got used to the ways of good society. For as we have jogged through the real, the unadorned country-side, with first one good fellow cracking his joke or singing his song and then another, we know that though this world resembles, it is not in fact our daily world. It is the world of poetry. Everything happens here more quickly and more intensely, and with better order than in life or in prose; there is a formal elevated dullness which is part of the incantation of poetry; there are lines speaking half a second in advance what we were about to say, as if we read our thoughts before words cumbered them; and lines

which we go back to read again with that heightened quality,
that enchantment which keeps them glittering in the mind long
afterwards. And the whole is held in its place, and its variety and
divagations ordered by the power which is among the most impressive of all—the shaping power, the architect's power. It is the
peculiarity of Chaucer, however, that though we feel at once
this quickening, this enchantment, we cannot prove it by quotation. From most poets quotation is easy and obvious; some metaphor suddenly flowers; some passage breaks off from the rest. But
Chaucer is very equal, very even-paced, very unmetaphorical. If
we take six or seven lines in the hope that the quality will be contained in them it has escaped.

> My lord, ye woot that in my fadres place,
> Ye dede me strepe out of my povre wede,
> And richely me cladden, o your grace.
> To yow broghte I noght elles, out of drede,
> But feyth and nakedness and maydenhede.

In its place that seemed not only memorable and moving but fit
to set beside striking beauties. Cut out and taken separately it
appears ordinary and quiet. Chaucer, it seems, has some art by
which the most ordinary words and the simplest feelings when
laid side by side make each other shine; when separated lose their
lustre. Thus the pleasure he gives us is different from the pleasure
that other poets give us, because it is more closely connected with
what we have ourselves felt or observed. Eating, drinking and
fine weather, the May, cocks and hens, millers, old peasant women,
flowers—there is a special stimulus in seeing all these common
things so arranged that they affect us as poetry affects us, and are
yet bright, sober, precise as we see them out of doors. There is
a pungency in this unfigurative language; a stately and memorable beauty in the undraped sentences which follow each other
like women so slightly veiled that you see the lines of their bodies
as they go—

> And she set down hir water pot anon
> Biside the threshold in an oxe's stall.

And then, as the procession takes its way, tranquilly, beautifully, out from behind peeps the face of Chaucer, grinning, malicious, in league with all foxes, donkeys, and hens, to mock the pomp and ceremonies of life—witty, intellectual, French, at the same time based upon a broad bottom of English humour.

So Sir John read his Chaucer in the comfortless room with the wind blowing and the smoke stinging, and left his father's tombstone unmade. But no book, no tomb, had power to hold him long. He was one of those ambiguous characters who haunt the boundary line where one age merges in another and are not able to inhabit either. At one moment he was all for buying books cheap; next he was off to France and told his mother, "My mind is now not most upon books." In his own house, where his mother Margaret was perpetually making out inventories or confiding in Gloys the priest, he had no peace or comfort. There was always reason on her side; she was a brave woman, for whose sake one must put up with the priest's insolence and choke down one's rage when the grumbling broke into open abuse, and "Thou proud priest" and "Thou proud Squire" were bandied angrily about the room. All this, with the discomforts of life and the weakness of his own character, drove him to loiter in pleasanter places, to put off coming, to put off writing, to put off, year after year, the making of his father's tombstone.

Yet John Paston had now lain for twelve years under the bare ground. The Prior of Bromholm sent word that the grave cloth was in tatters, and he had tried to patch it himself. Worse still, for a proud woman like Margaret Paston, the country people murmured at the Pastons' lack of piety, and other families she heard, of no greater standing than theirs, spent money in pious restoration in the very church where her husband lay unremembered. At last, turning from tournaments and Chaucer and Mistress Anne Hault, Sir John bethought him of a piece of cloth of gold which had been used to cover his father's hearse and might now be sold to defray the expenses of his tomb. Margaret had it in safe keeping; she had hoarded it and cared for it, and spent twenty marks on its repair. She grudged it; but there was no help for it. She sent it him, still distrusting his intentions or his power to put them into effect. "If you sell it to any other use," she wrote, "by my troth I shall never trust you while I live."

But this final act, like so many that Sir John had undertaken in the course of his life, was left undone. A dispute with the Duke of Suffolk in the year 1479 made it necessary for him to visit London in spite of the epidemic of sickness that was abroad; and there, in dirty lodgings, alone, busy to the end with quarrels, clamorous to the end for money, Sir John died and was buried at Whitefriars in London. He left a natural daughter; he left a considerable number of books; but his father's tomb was still unmade.

The four thick volumes of the Paston letters, however, swallow up this frustrated man as the sea absorbs a raindrop. For, like all collections of letters, they seem to hint that we need not care overmuch for the fortunes of individuals. The family will go on whether Sir John lives or dies. It is their method to heap up in mounds of insignificant and often dismal dust the innumerable trivialities of daily life, as it grinds itself out, year after year. And then suddenly they blaze up; the day shines out, complete, alive, before our eyes. It is early morning and strange men have been whispering among the women as they milk. It is evening, and there in the churchyard Warne's wife bursts out against old Agnes Paston: "All the devils of Hell draw her soul to Hell." Now it is the autumn in Norfolk and Cecily Dawne comes whining to Sir John for clothing. "Moreover, Sir, liketh it your mastership to understand that winter and cold weather draweth nigh and I have few clothes but of your gift." There is the ancient day, spread out before us, hour by hour.

But in all this there is no writing for writing's sake; no use of the pen to convey pleasure or amusement or any of the million shades of endearment and intimacy which have filled so many English letters since. Only occasionally, under stress of anger for the most part, does Margaret Paston quicken into some shrewd saw or solemn curse. "Men cut large thongs here out of other men's leather. . . . We beat the brushes and other men have the birds. . . . Haste reweth . . . which is to my heart a very spear." That is her eloquence and that her anguish. Her sons, it is true, bend their pens more easily to their will. They jest rather stiffly; they hint rather clumsily; they make a little scene like a rough puppet show of the old priest's anger and give a phrase or two directly as they were spoken in person. But when Chaucer lived he must have heard this very language, matter of fact, un-metaphorical, far better fitted for narrative than for analysis, capable of religious solemnity or of broad humour, but very stiff material to put on the lips of men and women accosting each other face to face. In short it is easy to see, from the Paston letters, why Chaucer wrote not *Lear* or *Romeo and Juliet,* but the *Canterbury Tales.*

Sir John was buried; and John the younger brother succeeded in his turn. The Paston letters go on; life at Paston continues much the same as before. Over it all broods a sense of discomfort and nakedness; of unwashed limbs thrust into splendid clothing; of tapestry blowing on the draughty walls; of the bedroom with its privy; of winds sweeping straight over land unmitigated by hedge or town; of Caister Castle covering with solid stone six acres of ground, and of the plain-faced Pastons indefatigably accumulating wealth, treading out the roads of Norfolk, and persisting with an obstinate courage which does them infinite credit in furnishing the bareness of England.

The Whig World

LORD DAVID CECIL (1902–)

THE GREAT Whig country houses of the eighteenth and early nineteenth centuries are among the most conspicuous monuments of
English history. Ornate and massive, with their pedimented por-
ticoes, their spreading balustraded wings, they dominate the
landscape round them with a magnificent self-assurance. Nor are
their interiors less imposing. Their colonnaded entrance halls,
whence the Adam staircase sweeps up beneath a fluted dome; their
cream and gilt libraries piled with sumptuous editions of the
classics; their orangeries peopled with casts from the antique;
their saloons hung with yellow silk, and with ceiling and doorways painted in delicate arabesque by Angelica Kauffmann, all
combine to produce an extraordinary impression of culture and
elegance and established power.

Yet, they are not palaces. There is something easy-going and
unofficial about them. Between library and saloon one comes on
little rooms, full of sporting prints and comfortable untidiness;
the bedrooms upstairs are friendly with chintz and flowered wall-
paper. Even the great rooms themselves, with their roomy writing tables, their armchairs, their tables piled with albums and commonplace books, seem designed less for state occasions than for
private life: for leisure and lounging, for intimate talk, and desultory reading. And the portraits that glow down from the walls
exhibit a similar character. The gentlemen lean back in their
hunting coats, the ladies stroll in their parks with spaniels snapping at the ribbons that dangle from the garden hats, slung on their
arms. In big and in detail these houses convey an effect of splendid

THE WHIG WORLD is reprinted from *The Young Melbourne* by Lord David
Cecil. Copyright 1939. Used by permission of the publishers, The Bobbs-Merrill
Company.

naturalness. In this they are typical of the society which was their creator.

The Whig aristocracy was a unique product of English civilization. It was before all things a governing class. At a time when economic power was concentrated in the landed interest, the Whigs were among the biggest landowners: their party was in office for the greater part of the eighteenth century; during this period they possessed a large proportion of the seats in the House of Commons; they produced more ambassadors and officers of state than the rest of England put together. And they lived on a scale appropriate to their power. "A man," said one of their latest representatives, "can jog along on £40,000 a year." And jog very well they did. They possessed, most of them, a mansion in London and two or three in the country; they moved through the world attended by a vast retinue of servants, of secretaries and chaplains, of companions, librarians and general hangers-on; they never travelled but in their own carriages; they kept open house to a continuous stream of guests, whom they entertained in the baroque and lavish style approved by their contemporaries.

For the elaboration of their life was increased by the period they lived in. The eighteenth century, that accomplished age, did not believe in the artless and the austere. In its view the good man or, as they would have phrased it, "the man of sense and taste," was he whose every activity was regulated in the light of a trained judgment and the experience of the wise in his own and former ages. From his earliest years the Whig nobleman was subjected to a careful education. He was grounded in the classics first by a tutor, then at Eton, then at the University. After this he went abroad for two years' grand tour to learn French and good manners in the best society of the continent. His sisters learnt French and manners equally thoroughly at home; and their demeanour was further improved by a course of deportment. The Whigs' taste was in harmony with the ideal that guided their education. They learnt to admire the grand style in painting, the "correct" in letters, the Latin tradition in oratory. And in everything they paid strict attention to form. Since life to them was so secure and so pleasant, the Whig aristocrats tended to take its fundamental values very much for granted; they concentrated rather on how to live. And here again, their ideal was not an artless one. Their customs, their mode of speech, their taste in decoration, their stylish stiff clothes, are alike marked by a character at once polished and precise, disciplined and florid. If one of them writes a note it is rounded with a graceful phrase, their most extempore speeches are turned with a flourish of rotund rhetoric.

Yet—and here it is that it differs from those of similar societies on the continent—theirs was not an unreal life; no Watteau-like paradise of exquisite trifling and fastidious idleness. For one thing it had its roots in the earth. Founded as their position was on landed property, the Whig aristocracy was never urban. They passed at least half the year in their country seats; and there they occupied themselves in the ordinary avocations of country life. The ladies interested themselves in their children, and visited the poor; the gentlemen looked after their estates, rode to hounds, and administered from the local bench justice to poachers and pilferers. Their days went by, active out-of-door, unceremonious; they wore riding-boots as often as silk stockings. Moreover, they were always in touch with the central and serious current of contemporary life. The fact that they were a governing class meant that they had to govern. The Whig lord was as often as not a minister, his eldest son an M.P., his second attached to a foreign embassy. So that their houses were alive with the effort and hurry of politics. Red Foreign Office boxes strewed the library tables; at any time of day or night a courier might come galloping up with critical news, and the minister must post off to London to attend a Cabinet meeting. He had his work in the country too. He was a landlord and magistrate, often a lord lieutenant. While every few years would come a general election when his sons, if not himself, might have to sally forth to stand on the hustings and be pelted with eggs and dead cats by the free and independent electors of the neighbouring borough. Indeed his was not a protected existence. The eighteenth century was the age of clubs; and Whig society itself was a sort of club, exclusive, but in which those who managed to achieve membership lived on equal terms; a rowdy, rough-and-tumble club, full of conflict and plain speaking, where people were expected to stand up for themselves and take and give hard knocks. At Eton the little dukes and earls cuffed and bullied each other like street urchins. As mature persons in their country homes, or in the pillared rooms of Brooks's Club, their intercourse continued more politely, yet with equal familiarity. While their House of Commons life passed in a robust atmosphere of combat and crisis and defeat. The Whigs despised the royal family; and there was certainly none of the hush and punctilio of court existence about them. Within the narrow limits of their world they were equalitarians.

Their life, in fact, was essentially a normal life, compounded of the same elements as those of general humanity, astir with the same clamour and clash and aspiration and competition as filled the streets round their august dwellings. Only, it was normal life played out on a colossal stage and with magnificent scenery and costumes. Their houses were homes, but homes with sixty bedrooms, set in grounds five miles round; they fought to keep their jobs, but the jobs were embassies and prime ministerships; their sons went to the same universities as humbler students, but were distinguished from them there by a nobleman's gold-tasselled mortarboard. When the Duke of Devonshire took up botany, he sent out a special expedition to the East Indies to search for rare plants; Lord Egremont liked pictures, so he filled a gallery with Claudes and Correggios; young Lord Palmerston was offered the Chancellorship of the Exchequer a year or two after entering Parliament.

This curiously blended life produced a curiously blended type of character. With so many opportunities for action, its interests were predominantly active. Most of the men were engaged in

politics. And the women—for they lived to please the men—
were political too. They listened, they sympathized, they advised;
through them two statesmen might make overtures to each other,
or effect a reconciliation. But politics then were not the life sentence to hard labour that in our iron age they have become.
Parliament only sat for a few months in the year; and even during the session, debates did not start till the late afternoon. The
Whigs had the rest of their time to devote to other things. If they
were sporting they raced and hunted; if interested in agriculture
they farmed on an ambitious scale; if artistic they collected marbles and medals; if intellectual they read history and philosophy;
if literary they composed compliments in verse and sonorous,
platitudinous orations. But the chief of their spare time was given
up to social life. They gave balls, they founded clubs, they played
cards, they got up private theatricals: they cultivated friendship,
and every variety, platonic and less platonic, of the art of love.
Their ideal was the Renaissance ideal of the whole man, whose
aspiration it is to make the most of every advantage, intellectual
and sensual, that life has to offer.

In practice, of course, this ideal was not so broad as it sounds.
The Whigs could not escape the limitations imposed by the
splendour of their circumstances. Like all aristocrats they tended
to be amateurs. When life is so free and so pleasant, a man is not
likely to endure the drudgery necessary to make himself really
expert in any one thing. Even in those affairs of state which took
up most of the Whigs' time, they troubled little with the dry
details of economic theory or administrative practice. Politics
to them meant first of all personalities, and secondly general
principles. And general principles to them were an occasion for
expression rather than thought. They did not dream of questioning the fundamental canons of Whig orthodoxy. All believed
in ordered liberty, low taxation and the enclosure of land; all disbelieved in despotism and democracy. Their only concern was
to restate these indisputable truths in a fresh and effective fashion.

Again, their taste was a little philistine. Aristocratic taste nearly always is. Those whose ordinary course of life is splendid and satisfying, find it hard to recognize the deeper value of the exercises of the solitary imagination; art to them is not the fulfilment of the soul, but an ornamental appendage to existence. Moreover, the English nobility were too much occupied with practical affairs to achieve the fullest intellectual life. They admired what was elegant, sumptuous and easy to understand; portraits that were good likenesses and pleasing decorations; architecture which appropriately housed a stately life. In books, they appreciated acute, wittily phrased observation of human nature, or noble sentiments expressed in flowing periods; Cicero, Pope, Horace, Burke. The strange and the harsh they dismissed immediately. Among contemporary authors they appreciated Jane Austen, condemned Crabbe, for the most part, as sordid and low; and neglected Blake almost entirely. If they had read him, they would not have liked him. For—it is another of their limitations—they were not spiritual. Their education did not encourage them to be; and, anyway, they found this world too absorbing to concern themselves much with the next. The bolder spirits among them were atheists. The average person accepted Christianity, but in a straightforward spirit, innocent alike of mysticism and theological exactitude.

Further, their circumstances did not encourage the virtues of self-control. Good living gave them zest; wealth gave them opportunity; and they threw themselves into their pleasures with an animal recklessness at once terrifying and exhilarating to a modern reader. The most respectable people often drank themselves under the table without shocking anyone. "Colonel Napier came in to-night as drunk as an owl," remarks Lady Sarah Napier, of the staid middle-aged gentleman who was her husband. And their drinking was nothing to their gambling. Night after night they played loo and faro from early evening till the candles guttered pale in the light of the risen sun. Lord Stavordale lamented he had not been playing higher, on a night when he won £11,000 in a single hand at hazard. Georgiana, Duchess of Devonshire, cost her husband nearly £1,000,000 in card debts. Rich as they were,

they often ruined themselves. The letters of the time are loud
with lamentations about the duns coming in and the furniture
going out. Nor was their sexual life of a kind to commend them to
an austere morality. "I was afraid I was going to have the gout
the other day," writes Lord Carlisle to a friend, "I believe I live
too chaste: it is not a common fault with me." It was not a common fault with any of them. In fact an unmarried man was
thought unpleasantly queer, if he did not keep under his protection some sprightly full-bosomed Kitty Clive or Mrs. Bellamy,
whose embraces he repaid with a house in Montpelier Square, a
box at the opera, and a smart cabriolet in which to drive her down
to Brighthelmstone for a week's amorous relaxation. Nor did he
confine himself to professional ladies of pleasure. Even unmarried girls like Lady Hester Stanhope were suspected of having
lovers; among married women the practice was too common to
stir comment. The historian grows quite giddy as he tries to dis-
entangle the complications of heredity consequent on the free
and easy habits of the English aristocracy. The Harley family,
children of the Countess of Oxford, were known as the Harleian
Miscellany on account of the variety of fathers alleged to be responsible for their existence. The Duke of Devonshire had three
children by the Duchess and two by Lady Elizabeth Foster, the
Duchess one by Lord Grey; and most of them were brought up
together in Devonshire House, each set of children with a surname of its own. "Emily, does it never strike you," writes Miss
Pamela Fitzgerald in 1816, "the vices are wonderfully prolific
among Whigs? There are such countless illegitimates, such a tribe
of children of the mist." It is noteworthy that the author of this
lively comment was a carefully brought up young lady of the
highest breeding. The free habits of these days encouraged free
speech. "Comfortable girls," remarks a middle-aged lady of her
growing nieces, "who like a dirty joke." And the men, as can
be imagined, were a great deal freer than the women. For all their
polish the Whigs were not refined people in the Victorian sense
of the word.

It appears in other aspects of their lives. They could be extremely arrogant; treating their inferiors with a patrician insolence which seems to us the reverse of good breeding. Lady Catherine de Bourgh was not the caricature that an ignorant person might suppose. Fashionable young men of refined upbringing amused themselves by watching fights where the Game Chicken battered the Tutbury Pet into unconsciousness with bare and blood-stained fists. And the pamphlets, the squibs, the appalling political cartoons that lay open in the most elegant drawing-rooms show that the ladies of the day were not squeamish either.

Still, unseemly as some of its manifestations were, one must admit that there is something extremely attractive in this earthy exuberance. And, as a matter of fact, it was the inevitable corollary of their virtues. English society had the merits of its defects. Its wide scope, its strong root in the earth, gave it an astounding, an irresistible vitality. For all their dissipation there was nothing decadent about these eighteenth century aristocrats. Their excesses came from too much life, not too little. And it was the same vitality that gave them their predominance in public life. They took on the task of directing England's destinies with the same self-confident vigour, that they drank and diced. It was this vigour that made Pitt Prime Minister at twenty-four years old,[1] that enabled the Foxites to keep the flag of liberty flying against the united public opinion of a panic-stricken nation. Nor did they let their pleasures interfere with these more serious activities. After eighteen hours of uninterrupted gambling, Charles Fox would arrive at the House of Commons to electrify his fellow members by a brilliant discourse on American taxation. Rakes and ladies of fashion intersperse their narratives of intrigue with discussions on politics, on literature, even on morals. For they were not unmoral. Their lapses came from passion not from principle; and they are liable at any time to break out in contrite acknowledgments of guilt, and artless resolutions for future improvement.

[1] Pitt diverged from the Whigs in later life: but he was brought up among them; and is, so far, representative of the Whig tradition.

Indeed it was one of the paradoxes created by their mixed composition that, though they were worldly, they were not sophisticated. Their elaborate manners masked simple reactions. Like
their mode of life their characters were essentially natural; spontaneous, unintrospective, brimming over with normal feelings,
love of home and family, loyalty, conviviality, desire for fame,
hero-worship, patriotism. And they showed their feelings too.
Happy creatures! They lived before the days of the stiff upper
lip and the inhibited public school Englishman. A manly tear
stood in their eye at the story of a heroic deed: they declared
their loves in a strain of flowery hyperbole. They were the more
expressive from their very unselfconsciousness. It never struck
them that they needed to be inarticulate to appear sincere. They
were equally frank about their less elevated sentiments. Eighteenth
century rationalism combined with rural common sense to make
them robustly ready to face unedifying facts. And they declared
their impressions with a brusque honesty, outstandingly characteristic of them. From Sir Robert Walpole who encouraged
coarse conversation on the ground that it was the only form of
talk which everyone enjoyed, down to the Duke of Wellington
who described the army of his triumphs as composed of "the scum
of the earth, enlisted for drink," the Augustan aristocracy, Whig
and Tory alike, said what they thought with a superb disregard
for public opinion. For if they were not original they were
independent-minded. The conventions which bounded their lives
were conventions of form only. Since they had been kings of
their world from birth they were free from the tiresome inhibi-
tions that are induced by a sense of inferiority. Within the locked
garden of their society, individuality flowered riotous and ramp-
ant. Their typical figures show up beside the muted introverts of
to-day as clear-cut and idiosyncratic as characters in Dickens.
They took for granted that you spoke your mind and followed
your impulses. If these were odd they were amused but not disapproving. They enjoyed eccentrics; George Selwyn who never
missed an execution, Beau Brummel who took three hours to tie

his cravat. The firm English soil in which they were rooted, the
spacious freedom afforded by their place in the world, allowed
personality to flourish in as many bold and fantastic shapes as it
pleased.

But it was always a garden plant, a civilized growth. Whatever
their eccentricities, the Whig nobles were never provincial and
never uncouth. They had that effortless knowledge of the world
that comes only to those, who from childhood have been accustomed to move in a complex society; that delightful unassertive
confidence possible only to people who have never had cause to
doubt their social position. And they carried to the finest degree
of cultivation those social arts which engaged so much of their
time. Here we come to their outstanding distinction. They were
the most agreeable society England has ever known. The character of their agreeability was of a piece with the rest of them;
mundane, straightforward, a trifle philistine, largely concerned
with gossip, not given to subtle analyses or flights of fancy. But
it had all their vitality and all their sense of style. It was incomparably racy and spontaneous and accomplished; based solidly on
a wide culture and experience, yet free to express itself in bursts
of high spirits, in impulses of appreciation, in delicate movements
of sentiment, in graceful compliments. For it had its grace; a
virile classical grace like that of the Chippendale furniture which
adorned its rooms, lending a glittering finish to its shrewd humour, its sharp-eyed observation, its vigorous disquisitions on
men and things. Educated without pedantry, informal but not
slipshod, polished but not precious, brilliant without fatigue, it
combined in an easy perfection the charms of civilization and nature. Indeed the whole social life of the period shines down the
perspective of history like some masterpiece of natural art; a
prize bloom, nurtured in shelter and sunshine and the richest
soil, the result of generations of breeding and blending, that
spreads itself to the open sky in strength and beauty.

It was at its most characteristic in the middle of the century,
it was at its most dazzling towards its close. By 1780 a new spirit

was rising in the world. Ossian had taught people to admire ruins and ravines, Rousseau to examine the processes of the heart; with unpowdered heads and the ladies in simple muslin dresses, they paced the woods meditating, in Cowperlike mood, on the tender influences of nature. Though they kept the style and good sense of their fathers, their sympathies were wider. At the same time their feelings grew more refined. The hardness, which had marred the previous age, dwindled. Gainsborough, not Hogarth, mirrored the taste of the time; sensibility became a fashionable word. For a fleeting moment Whig society had a foot in two worlds and made the best of both of them. The lucid outline of eighteenth-century civilization was softened by the glow of the romantic dawn.

Dawn—but for them it was sunset. The same spirit that tinged them with their culminating glory was also an omen of their dissolution. For the days of aristocratic supremacy were numbered. By the iron laws which condition the social structure of man's existence, it could only last as long as it maintained an economic predominance. With the coming of the Industrial Revolution this predominance began to pass from the landlords to other ranks of the community. Already by the close of the century, go-ahead manufacturers in the north were talking of Parliamentary reform; already, in the upper rooms of obscure London alleys, working men met together to clamour for liberty, equality, and fraternity. Within forty years of its zenith, the Whig world was completely swept away. Only a few survivors lingered on to illustrate to an uncomprehending generation the charm of the past. Of these the most distinguished was William Lamb, second Viscount Melbourne.[2]

---

[2] *Editors' note:* "The Whig World" is the opening chapter of Cecil's biography of Lord Melbourne; hence this sentence, which is not so much a conclusion of the chapter as a forecast of the subject of the book.

Suggestions for Study

MOST OF this piece seems to be plain statement; Cecil only occasionally allows himself an obviously decorative sentence: "Night
after night they played loo and faro from early evening till the
candles guttered pale in the light of the risen sun"; or "Indeed
the whole social life of the period shines down the perspective of
history like some masterpiece of natural art; a prize bloom, nurtured in shelter and sunshine and the richest soil, the result of generations of breeding and blending that spreads itself to the open
sky in strength and beauty." In each of these sentences there is
a conspicuous heightening of the rhythm: *pale* (not *palely*) and
risen in the first sentence, and the repeated *and*'s in "shelter and
sunshine and the richest soil" in the second sentence were probably chosen for their effect on the rhythm. There is an archaic
formality about both *pale* and *risen;* and this, along with the
elaborate sentence pattern and the alliteration and assonance
(e. g., "shelter and sunshine," "breeding and blending"), deep-
ens the tone of these sentences, in an admirable contrast with the
generally rather astringent style.

On the whole Cecil seems to write like a historian, telling us
facts, giving us conclusions. The sentences are short, with a tone
of finality; and we are not much aware of subsidiary clauses that
might take the emphasis off the fact that each sentence carries. The
paragraph beginnings seem to be part of a complex argument:
"Yet they are not"; "For the elaboration of their life"; "Yet—
and here it is that it differs"; "Their life, in fact, was essentially";
"In practice, of course, this ideal was not so broad"; and so on.
Many abstract conceptions suggest a historian's appraisal of a
period; but note how nicely these are balanced by concrete allusions and examples. Many abstract or Latinate words suggest the
scholar's aridity of style; but again, note how these are balanced
by concrete or English words.

Yet Cecil does not achieve his effect by the logic of his argument, or by the control of his style. For he is not really trying to convince us of some new interpretation of Whig society, or to present us with new facts about it. Rather he is asking us to understand this "masterpiece of natural art," to understand this paradox of "splendid naturalness." And when he says, "Here we come to their outstanding distinction," we are aware at last that we have been led, or cajoled, to accept his statement that "they were the most agreeable society England has ever known." Cecil's facts are indeed facts, but facts of an especially amusing or dramatic kind, which exemplify the incongruities of human nature while at the same time they record the special qualities of the Augustan age.

Cecil's sentences are indeed short and somewhat dry, but there is a wonderful variation in their attack and in their pattern. After several sentences that seem merely informative, we are given one like this: "Since life to them was so secure and so pleasant, the Whig aristocrats tended to take its fundamental values very much for granted; they concentrated rather on how to live," in which the argument is at once summed up and expanded. Or a sentence like this: "And general principles to them were an occasion for expression rather than thought," in which the wit and the epigrammatic structure compress a good deal of acute criticism of eighteenth-century thinking. Neither the style nor the content of the essay is florid or sentimental; there is about it only the "easy perfection" of civilization.

The Poet and the Press

ARCHIBALD MacLEISH (1892–   )

It is an axiom of our civilization, if that is the proper name for
the chaos of ideas in which we live, that poetry is the opposite of
journalism and that journalism is the opposite of poetry. The two
are about as likely to meet in an evening's conversation as John
Keats and Arthur Krock, and each becomes, when applied to
the other, a pejorative term. If you want to insult Scotty Reston,
as a number of people in Washington now do, you will refer to
those superb pieces of diplomatic correspondences of his as
"poetry"—meaning piffle. If you want to insult Thomas Stearns
Eliot, as nobody in Washington or anywhere else would now
dream of doing, you will call *The Waste Land* "journalism"—
meaning journalism. Elder writers addressing younger writers
in those invaluable interviews in the *Paris Review* advise them to
avoid the practice of journalism as they would wet socks and
gin before breakfast, and the New York *Mirror* returns the
compliment by announcing in an editorial as solemn as a sermon
that anyone who does not regard Robert W. Service as a great
poet is a fancy pants, and may even be an intellectual. In short,
the two limits of the typewriter keyboard in our time, the two
extremes which will never meet, the East and West of our fractured world, are poetry and journalism. But why, if you really
stop to think of it, should poetry and journalism be the two poles
of the world of words in our time? Why should they appear to
us as each other's opposites? There are manifest differences be-

tween the two—differences which any of us could tick off—
but are they really as manifest as all that? Poetry is an art, yes;
or should be. But is journalism the opposite of art?

No one would claim that the usual news story in the, let us
say, Chicago *Tribune* is a work of art, at least in the ordinary
sense of that term. But no one would deny either that great works
of journalism exist and that when they exist they exist within a
discipline of their own—a discipline which reveals itself, as the
disciplines of art always reveal themselves, in form. The style of
a great work of journalism is not, as the glib phrase goes, the
man. The style of a great work of journalism is the man in terms
of the purpose: a man working at the utmost intensity of which
he is capable toward an end to which he is wholly committed.
But this, of course, is precisely the characteristic of the style of
any work of art—the precise characteristic which distinguishes
a work of art from a mere indulgence of personality on one hand
or an impersonal "job" on the other.

You cannot, in other words, distinguish journalism from
poetry, to the extreme degree in which we distinguish them,
merely by saying that one is an art and the other is not. And
neither, I think, can you justify their antipodal relationship by
the device used in most college catalogues, where courses in expository writing are courses in expository writing, but courses in
the writing of poems are courses in creative writing. The theory
would be, I imagine, that the poet is supposed to create a world
in his poems, whereas the journalist is supposed not to create one
but stick as closely as he can to the world he's got. This means
that the poet makes something new, but the journalist describes
something old, or in any case something that has already happened, for if it has not already happened he is no journalist. More
precisely, this means that the journalist selects from among things
that already are: events that have in fact befallen, actions actually
acted, objects seen, sounds heard; whereas the poet must spin his
chronicle out of himself like a spider. But if we leave the theory
and look at the practice—specific poems, specific journalisms—
will this distinction as between creative and selective hold?

Take the first poem that walks into your mind: for of course all of us have such visitors. "Old favorites" we call them because they are free of the house and enter without knocking. Some of you—quite a few, I should guess—will find yourselves thinking of Herrick's "Daffodils," not only because it is one of the finest of English lyrics and one of the poems most frequently taught to children, but because its tune, once echoed in the corridors of the ear, will never stop:

> Fair daffodils, we weep to see
>   You haste away so soon:
> As yet the early-rising sun
>   Has not attain'd his noon.
>   Stay, stay,
>   Until the hasting day
>   Has run
>   But to the even-song;
> And, having pray'd together, we
>   Will go with you along.
>
> We have short time to stay, as you.
>   We have as short a Spring;
> As quick a growth to meet decay,
>   As you, or any thing.
>   We die,
> As your hours do, and dry
>   Away,
>   Like to the Summer's rain;
> Or as the pearls of morning's dew
>   Ne'er to be found again.

Or some of you will fish up Keats's murex because those five long "I" sounds at the beginning of the "Ode on a Grecian Urn" have held an instant of your mind motionless since the day in your childhood when you first heard them:

> Thou still unravished bride of quietness!
>   Thou foster-child of Silence and slow Time,
> Sylvan historian.

For myself, I always think, when I look for touchstones such as these, of a poem I cannot read, written in a tongue no man living can now pronounce—the poem the Emperor Wu Ti wrote in the second century B.C. for his dead mistress, Li Fu Jen. Arthur Waley's translation goes like this:

> The sound of her silk skirt has stopped
> On the marble pavement dust grows
> Her empty room is cold and still
> Fallen leaves are piled against the door
> > Longing for that lovely lady
> How can I bring my aching heart to rest?

But whatever poem you call back to mind, the question I would put to you would be the same: Does your poem seem to you, as you contemplate it in your imagination, to be "created" in the sense in which we use that word of the events described in the book of Genesis? Is there not rather a selection and ordering, as there is a selection and ordering in the art of history and in the practice of journalism? The selection is of a different kind, yes: things are chosen which history would find too trivial to touch and which journalism, in its passionate haste to get on with the story, would have no time for. The organization of the fragments selected is also different. Things are put together in poetry which history would never put together because of its addiction to the logic of cause and effect and which journalism would never put together because of its commitment to the lucidities of common sense. Men do not pray with daffodils in history if they care for the opinion in which posterity will contemplate them, and grief in journalism is sobs, not dead leaves at a door sill or the silence of the sound of silk—the silence after the ceasing of the sound. But granted all this—granted, too, that the structure of words in poetry is very different, far more orderly, immeasurably more strict, than the structure of words in the prose of journalism or of history—does it really follow that the enormous gulf we have dug between the conception of journalism and the conception of poetry is explained away by calling poetry a creative art?

I should not say so. I should say that an examination of actual poems and actual journalisms would lead any reader to the conclusion that the difference between them, wide though it is, cannot be stated in terms of creation. Both are re-creations, different in degree but not different in kind, for the material in each case is our human experience of the world and of ourselves; and not fundamentally different in method or even in purpose, since the method of poetry like the method of journalism is selection from the chaotic formlessness of experience, and the purpose of both is the recording of the fragments selected in a sequence that makes sense.

It is perfectly true that the sense which poetry makes of its fragments is not the sense which journalism makes. No reporter in America or anywhere else would organize fragments of the experience of a divorce case to read: "love is not love which alters when it alteration finds or bends with the remover to remove. O, no! it is an ever-fixed mark that looks on tempests and is never shaken; it is the star to every wand'ring bark, whose worth's unknown, although his height be taken." In journalism this summation of experience is not sensible at all. It is not even true. Love, in journalism, does not bear "it out even to the edge of doom."

And the opposite is also obvious. The sense which journalism makes of the life of a man and the life of a woman, or the life of a man and the lives of two women, is not sensible or even true in poetry. But the fact remains that both Shakespeare's sonnet and the news story of the broken marriage are re-creations of fragments selected from the confusion of human experience in an effort to give them order and to make them comprehensible. The purpose in one case may merely be to make them comprehensible to human curiosity, whereas the purpose in the other is very evidently to reach the human intelligence at its most perceptive and most alive: Shakespeare's sonnet has undertones of irony which only a most subtly listening ear can hear. But in both cases and however different their levels, the end is comprehension, understanding.

Poetry, despite the almost magical powers of the greatest poets, is a human labor, and what humanity most desperately needs is not the creation of new worlds but the re-creation, in terms of human comprehension, of the world we have, and it is to this task that all the arts are committed. Indeed, it is for this reason that the arts go on from generation to generation in spite of the fact that Phidias has already carved and Homer has already sung. The Creation, we are informed, was accomplished in seven days with Sunday off, but the re-creation will never be accomplished because it is always to be accomplished anew for each new generation of living men. To hold the vast, whirling, humming, buzzing, boggling confusion of the Greek world still long enough to see it is not to hold the vast, whirling, humming, buzzing, boggling confusion of our world still. New charms are necessary, new spells, new artifices. Whether they know it or not, the young men forgather in Paris in one generation, in San Francisco in another, because the world goes round, the light changes, and the old jugs will not carry living water. New jugs must be devised which the generation past will reject as monstrosities and the generation to come will, when it arrives, reject for other reasons: as banalities and bores.

But the essential point is that this labor does not differ in kind from the continuing labor of generations of journalists and historians who also face a new and turning world and who must also find new ways to speak of it. The materials of poetry, whatever the miracles accomplished with them, are gathered where the materials of history, present and past, are gathered, in what Keats called the arable field of events. Poetry transforms these materials by a faculty the use of which is discouraged in journalism, the faculty of imagination, but the product of the metamorphosis is not an opposite thing from the product of the process.

known in journalism as reporting. It is not what our grandfathers used to say it was: a "fancy" as opposed to the sober "facts" of practical men. For one thing, the constructions of the imagination are not fancies and never were. For another, facts are not what our grandfathers supposed them to be in those happy far-off Victorian generations when science picked facts out of life like grits out of porridge and marshaled them in patterns on a page.

The re-creations of the imagination do correspond to the experience of the real physical world. Poetry may take liberties with the materials of that experience which history and journalism are not free to take. It may translate them into unexpected and even improbable forms. But it neither will nor can disguise their origins in experience, for the moment it did so it would cease to be an art. It would become a sorcery, a magic. Those Grecian centaurs, half man, half horse, those Oriental mother goddesses all arms and breasts—these derive from nature. It is only the arrangement of the parts which is unnatural! The parts themselves—the horse, the man, the arms, the breasts—have been discovered in the world the senses know. Even what we call "abstraction" in the art of our own day is not new creation in the sense in which the world of Genesis is new. Vision reduced to line, balance, color, proportion is still vision and still belongs in a world in which line, balance, color and proportion exist.

Indeed, this dependence of all poetry, of all art, on human experience of the actual world is only made the more obvious by the attempts of art, which have been made frequently in our time, to escape from the actual world. Poems, for example, which derive from the subconscious mind as the poems of the early Surrealists did, or purported to do, are still poems of experience and still poems composed by a process of selection from among the moments of experience. The only difference is that the selecting sieve is set up somewhere outside the conscious mind. But the poem does not become, in consequence, a parentless, pristine creation. On the contrary, it is even more obviously and immediately derived from the common human reality than a

poem made, as the Greeks made poems, under the selective direction of a conscious intelligence. The proof lies in the experiments of those contemporary psychiatrists who have attempted
to work their way back through completed poems to their roots
in experience. They have made very little of the poems of, say,
John Donne, but they have had a harvest home with the works
of the Surrealists. A Surrealist poem is a direct recording of the
experiencing mind on the tape of speech, and all that need be
done to make one's way to the unhappy childhood or the illicit
love is to play the recording back. John Donne is another matter.
The conscious act of art is there to make a mechanical playback
impossible. All you will get if you try is that series of garbled
screams and whinnies with which the amateurs of tape recording are familiar.

But one need not go to the Surrealists or their successors to
make this point. The most apparently fanciful of all familiar
poems will testify, if you will truly read them, that their fancies
are no less substantial, no less true, no less (if the word is still
permitted) real—at least no less authenticated by experience—
than the most substantial facts. Consider Prospero's great trope in
The Tempest: those cloud-capped towers, gorgeous palaces,
solemn temples, the great globe itself, which "like this insubstantial pageant faded" dissolve, "leave not a rack behind." Consider Rimbaud's pianos in the Alps, his hares praying to the rainbow through the spider's web, his little boy waving his arms
to the weather vanes "Après le Deluge," after the Deluge had
subsided, in the *Illuminations.* Compare these extravagant fancies
with the hard facts of history and journalism. You will find it
difficult, I think, to say just what the substantial difference is.
You may even find yourself concluding that, if anything, the
fancies are harder than the facts. We are, we are indeed, "such
stuff as dreams are made on," and any man who has not yet
learned that "our little life is rounded with a sleep" has not yet
begun to live that little life. We do, after every Deluge which
drowns the world, whether for one man or for many, come upon

that moment when everything is new again and possible, even the impossible; when little boys and weather vanes salute each other. There can scarcely be a man or a woman in my generation, if he has really shared that generation's life, who has not known that moment—and then lost it, as Rimbaud's poem loses it. Are these fancies not as substantial as our facts? Are they not as real as murder or the World Series or Governor Faubus, to say nothing of our China policy or a Dow-Jones average? Has anyone ever met a Dow-Jones average on a Sunday afternoon, or bathing, or anywhere else in the world? And as for our China policy, would anyone know its face if it walked onto this platform and sat down and arranged its smile?

I am not suggesting that the facts of journalism are insubstantial. I am merely suggesting that there is no such difference between the facts of journalism and the fancies of poetry as we assume when we turn them into each other's opposites. You can prove it to yourself in either way: by reading poems or by reading newspapers. What do you remember about the recent revolution in Iraq—in some ways the most important news story of the year, though not the best reported? What I remember is the account of the assassination of the old Premier, the famous desert fox and the most powerful man in the valley of the two rivers, who was shot in the dress of an old woman. Why do I remember that? Because the fact becomes something more than fact in the telling. Because I understand something of the man —and of those who killed him. Because the political event becomes a human event and casts a shadow far beyond Baghdad, far beyond the desert, far beyond the Middle East. It is only when the scattered and illegible fragments in which we pick up our experience of the world are recomposed in such a way that they make sense *as* human experience that great journalism can result. And the same thing is true in the same words of poetry. What poetry composes of its fragments is more lasting than what journalism composes. It is larger. It goes deeper. It is more meaningful. It has beauty. But it is not contrary in kind. Poetry and journalism—to put it in more inclusive terms, poetry and history—are not opposites and cannot be opposites, and the notion that they are is a delusion.

Something more than error is involved in this respectable and sanctified confusion. There are popular errors of various kinds. Some are harmful. Some are merely silly. This one is harmful. It has hurt poetry. It has altered journalism. And its effect, or the effect of the deeper delusions which have fathered it, on our unhappy civilization has been and continues to be disastrous. What really distinguishes poetry from journalism, aside from the obvious distinctions of form—uses of words, patterns of words, sequences of words—is not a difference in kind but a difference in focus. Journalism is concerned with events, poetry with feelings. Journalism is concerned with the look of the world: poetry with the feel of the world. Journalism wishes to tell what it is that has happened everywhere as though the same things had happened for every man. Poetry wishes to say what it is like for any man to be himself in the presence of a particular occurrence as though only he were alone there.

The best definition of journalism appears daily in the New York *Times:* "All the News that's Fit to Print." The best definition of poetry is spelled out in Coleridge's *Biographia Literaria:* "the balance or reconcilement of discordant qualities . . . a more than usual state of emotion with more than usual order." To separate journalism and poetry, therefore—history and poetry —to set them up at opposite ends of the world of discourse, is to separate seeing from the feel of seeing, emotion from the acting of emotion, knowledge from the realization of knowledge.

The poet, with us, stops his horse at twilight at the wood's edge in falling snow and yields for a moment to that longing for sleep in the cold, white, drifting stillness which is also another and deeper longing all reflective men have known, but the journalist permits himself to see only a man in a buggy stopping in inclement weather at a remote and unlikely spot; since nothing has "happened," he publishes nothing. And the same thing is true in reverse. The journalist dodges hand grenades in the bazaar of a hot, dusty, dirty, flea-bitten desert city to report an obscure war which may be the beginning of the ultimate war, but the poet, because all this is merely happening, does not write at all; because nothing is felt, he has nothing to say.

I exaggerate, of course. There have been journalists of our generation, men like Elmer Davis as well as men like Ernie Pyle, who would not have separated the feel of things from the look of them if they could, and there are contemporary poets who not only felt but saw the war in Spain—saw it, in fact, far more clearly than the journalists or the foreign offices or the professional observers of world affairs. Indeed, the greatest of contemporary poets was also one of the most exact and penetrating observers of the history of his time, if not always the most intelligent interpreter of that history.

> Turning and turning in the widening gyre
> The falcon cannot hear the falconer;
> Things fall apart; the centre cannot hold;
> Mere anarchy is loosed upon the world,
> The blood-dimmed tide is loosed, and everywhere
> The ceremony of innocence is drowned;
> The best lack all conviction, while the worst
> Are full of passionate intensity.

No journalist writing of the tragic events with which the name of the late Senator McCarthy is associated ever defined that aspect of contemporary life as precisely as Yeats had defined it some thirty years before:

> The best lack all conviction, while the worst
> Are full of passionate intensity.

But Yeats is an exception in this as in many other things. And not even Yeats was able to bring the event and the feel of the event together as they were brought in Homer's time and Dante's and Shakespeare's. Journalism, with us, tends more and more toward an admirably dispassionate objectivity which presents the event in the colorless air of intellectual detachment at the cost of its emotional significance, and poetry, reacting to the same divisive influence but in an opposite direction, turns more and more to the emotional significance divorced from the event. I do not know that it is possible to say that this fracture of the word is bad for journalism as such, for the great modern newspapers are, as newspapers, far superior to their predecessors. They collect more news faster and present it more accurately. It is only too possible to say, however, that it is bad for poetry and bad for the civilization.

Great poems are instruments of knowledge—a knowledge carried alive into the heart by passion, but knowledge nevertheless. Feeling without knowing never made a work of art and never will. And the attempt which contemporary poetry increasingly makes to detach feelings from their occasions—to pursue feelings as themselves and for their own sakes, resolutely ignoring the events from which they derive—can only be harmful to the art. Poems so composed are like kites without strings. They cannot bear up against the carrying away of time, because they have no attachment to a point in time.

The consequences to poetry itself of its increasing inwardness are of concern, unhappily, only to poets. What the rest of us might wish to think of is the effect of all this on our civilization. It is not difficult to define. Some time ago, Lewis Mumford, certainly one of the most intelligent of living Americans, wrote a letter to the New York *Times* expressing his horror at the apathy of his countrymen in the face of the dangers inherent in our policy and conduct in the Straits of Formosa. Here we were, he said, on a brink from which we might at any moment be shoved by the Chinese Nationalists or dragged by the Chinese Communists, with a war yawning before us which could only be fought by the horrible weapons of genocide and with the end of human life on the earth as a very possible consequence. And yet we neither protested nor objected. We merely sat there in numb indifference, leaving the decision of life or death to a Secretary of State whose previous decisions or indecisions were responsible for our predicament.

It was an angry letter, and one with which men of certain opinions might differ. But what struck me about it was not its statement of the facts, which seemed to me only too painfully correct, but its explanation of the reason for our national indifference to the facts. Our apathy, Mr. Mumford suggested—I do not know how seriously—could only be the consequence of our enormous consumption of tranquilizers and sedatives. Only a nation doped into unreality could possibly contemplate in silence a series of events and declarations which might at any moment lead to the extermination of enormous numbers of peaceful human beings, first in Asia and then throughout the world, including the part of the world in which we live ourselves.

I say I was struck by this explanation. I was struck by it because I found myself wishing the real explanation might be as simple and ironic. For the truth is, of course, that our apathy with regard to the incredible and terrifying events in Amoy Harbor and the disastrous consequences which might at any moment follow was the result not of our habits in the taking of pills but of our habits in the thinking of thoughts. And the further truth is that this strange dislocation in the thinking of thoughts by which we can "know" what we cannot feel—by which we can know that the consequence of a merely diplomatic maneuver may be the atomizing of the city of Peiping and then Tokyo and then Moscow and then New York, but cannot imagine in our live emotions what this knowing would feel like—this dislocation is the consequence of a deeper dislocation not only in ourselves but in our civilization.

For this divorce between knowing and feeling is not anything we Americans can claim as our own peculiar prerogative. The Germans have exhibited the same curious capacity: the

"good Germans" who knew about the gas ovens of the concentration camps but were nevertheless able to live with their knowledge in tranquillity and good conscience until they began to go
in crowded, silent audiences to performances of *The Diary of
Anne Frank*. And we ourselves—shall .we call ourselves the "good
Americans"?—are guilty of the same peace of mind. We know
what happened at Hiroshima. We have read, or read about,
John Hersey's account of the results of the atomic bombing of
that city. Most of us are at least aware of the specters which
crawl through Dr. Hachiya's book: "Their faces and hands were
burnt and swollen and great sheets of skin had peeled away from
their tissues to hang down like rags on a scarecrow. They moved
like a line of ants. All through the night they went past our
house, but this morning they had stopped. I found them lying
on both sides of the road so thick that it was impossible to pass
without stepping on them." We know all this. But do we feel
our knowledge? Could we even *think* about risking the possibility of a world-wide atomic war as a matter of face or official
vanity if we did?

I am not going to discuss foreign policy—if that is the right
term for our recent behavior off the China coast. But nothing
could better illustrate the flaw at the heart of our civilization
than this strange chapter of our history. Nothing could more
convincingly demonstrate that knowledge without feeling is not
knowledge and can lead only to public irresponsibility and
indifference, and conceivably to ruin. Nothing could more
clearly prove that when the fact is disassociated from the feel of
the fact in the minds of an entire people—in the common mind
of a civilization—that people, that civilization, is in danger.

Some of you, I have no doubt, will think the terms I have been
using throughout this discussion are inadequate to so serious an
indictment. Journalism seems, to most of us, a profession like
another, and poetry seems remote indeed from matters of such
moment as the survival of the world. But the fact is, of course,
that the survival of the world—at least the survival of a world

which has prepared as ingeniously for its own suicide as the world we live in—depends, madmen and accidents aside, solely on the knowledge of the men and women who inhabit it. And that knowledge is composed precisely of the two increments which journalism and poetry provide. Information is essential to the kind of knowledge on which an opinion relevant to the situation on Quemoy can be based. But the feel of the facts which that information communicates is also essential if the knowledge and the opinions it fathers are to be trustworthy and reliable. What has happened with us is that the first has outrun the second. We are, as we are constantly and justly being reminded, the best informed people on an earth which is better informed now than it ever was before in its history. But though we are provided with more facts than any previous generation, we are not necessarily possessed of more knowledge of those facts.

On the contrary, we seem to be less and less capable of receiving our facts into our imaginations, where they can come alive with feeling. Benjamin Franklin's contemporaries were not told within a few hours that some hundreds of coal miners had been trapped in a mine in what is now Yugoslavia, but when, after many months, the news of such a disaster at last came through, it would have come as a human tragedy with its human significance about it. The news of Napoleon's retreat from Moscow would be broadcast today minute-by-minute, photographed, columnized, interpreted, recorded to the last detail. When Napoleon actually turned back, the news was brought to New York in a brig commanded by my great-grandfather months after the event and in an individual witness's report, but it loomed in the New York newspapers of the next morning like news from Troy, which, in a sense, it was. What the Greeks knew about Troy, they knew through a man's slow telling.

I am not deploring the advances of journalism. They are miraculous. No man who has grown used to the news coverage of an expertly managed paper could live without it. But every improvement, and particularly every improvement made possible by mechanical invention, exacts its price, as we are discovering in our increasingly mechanized country. Often the price is exacted at the cost of nature and sometimes even at the cost of human nature. We are deluged with facts, but we have lost, or are losing, our human ability to feel them. Poetry still survives with us, survives with vigor and inventiveness, throwing up new masters capable of standing with the old. But the poem itself has lost its power in men's minds. We have not discarded the art as Herbert Spencer thought men would when the machine had come to flower, but we have impaired the practice of the skill the art can give, the skill of feeling truly and so truly knowing. We know with the head now, by the facts, by the abstractions. We seem unable to know as Shakespeare knew, who makes King Lear cry out to blinded Gloucester on the heath, "you see how this world goes," and Gloucester answers, "I see it feelingly."

Why we are thus impotent, I do not know. I know only that this impotence exists and that it is dangerous, increasingly dangerous. I know, too, or think I know, that whatever the underlying cause of the divorce of feeling from knowing, that divorce reveals itself most vividly in the strange and ignorant belief that the life of the imagination lies at an opposite pole from the life of the inquiring mind—that men can live and know and master their experience of this darkling earth by accumulating information and no more.

Men who believe that have, in effect, surrendered their responsibilities as men. They have gone over to the enemy, to those unhappy hordes, victims of the new and terrible tyranny of our time, who are not meant to know for themselves and with their whole beings but only to accept the daily ration of news and hates which Peiping or Moscow issues to them. Slavery begins when men give up the human need to know with the whole heart, to know for themselves, to bear the burden for themselves—the "burden," as Wordsworth called it, "of the mystery." To acquiesce, as the Russians and the Chinese and the Poles—even the Hungarians—have had to acquiesce in someone else's knowing is to acquiesce in someone else's deciding, and at that point, whatever the society is called, it is not free.

The real defense of freedom is imagination, that feeling life of the mind which actually knows because it involves itself in its knowing, puts itself in the place where its thought goes, walks in the body of the little Negro girl who feels the spittle dribbling on her cheek, follows in that line of ants whose skin is ragged tatters. The man who knows with his heart knows himself to be a man, feels as himself, cannot be silenced. He is free no matter where he lives, as Boris Pasternak has shown that he is free even in Russia. The man who knows with his mind only, who will not commit himself beyond his wits, who will not feel the thing he knows, or know the thing he feels—that man has no freedom anywhere. He is tugged by the string of whatever is told him, maneuvered by slogans. Sooner or later his life will seem indifferent to him, something managed by others, and he will acquiesce in the management, think about it as little as possible, occupy himself with the only things near enough to seem real—his car, his front lawn, those shadows on the television screen—symbolic shadows.

To me—not many others think so—the real crisis in the life of our society is the crisis of the life of the imagination. Far more than we need an intercontinental missile or a moral rearmament or a religious revival, we need to come alive again, to recover the virility of the imagination on which all earlier civilizations have been based: Coleridge's "synthetic and magical power" by which "the whole soul of man" may be brought to activity and knowledge may be *known*. It is for this reason that I have permitted myself to speak of my concern in a great university. I do not mean that I think education is wholly responsible for the flaw which has split knowledge of heart from knowledge of head, though it has surely its fair share of the blame. I mean rather that it is principally by the process of education that the flaw can be healed. The need for a review of the relation between education and the arts was never greater than at this moment, when our whole attention is fixed on the relation between education and the sciences. A society which has so lost the capacity to see the world feelingly that it can watch in silence while the possibility of nuclear extermination is employed as a diplomatic maneuver may stand in need of thousands of young manufacturing scientists sooner than it thinks. But even sooner, it will need to learn to know.

The Well of English Now Defiled

WILLARD THORP (1899–   )

WHEN Edmund Spenser paused for a moment in the fourth book of his *Faerie Queene* to refer reverently to an earlier poet, Geoffrey Chaucer, as that "well of English undefiled," he was implying, I gather, that the English of his own day had become poisoned with ink-horn terms and Italianate expressions. This allusion ought to comfort one in a discussion of the evidences of defilement in English prose to-day (and more particularly as English teachers see them in the writing we receive from our students). But I am not much comforted, because Spenser and fifty other influential writers of Elizabethan England were busy removing the poison from the well. I am not sure we can again accomplish this kind of sanitary engineering. By 1959 the incidence of poison in the well may have passed the safety mark.

I have been red-pencilling student papers for a good many years and I ought by now to have become resigned or cynical.

THE WELL OF ENGLISH NOW DEFILED by Willard Thorp is reprinted from *Encounter*, December 1959, by permission of the author.

But I am not, and the reason for my present concern is a sinister change in the kind of writing we have lately been getting. It used to be that we could do our duty and even bring about reforms by sprinkling in the margins of themes those cabalistic signs *"coh."* (for coherence), *"sp."* (for spelling), and *"gr."* (for grammar). But these traditional correctives will no longer serve. We are now too often presented with a kind of prose—if that is the name for it—which is inviolable. A red-pencil used against it becomes as impotent as a sword in a folk-tale which has had a spell put on it. Sometimes this prose resembles remotely a bad translation from a foreign language. Sometimes it suggests that the writer has squeezed together under pressure the jagged ends of several assorted ideas. The only name I have for this monstrosity is No-English.

The writer of No-English is unconscious of the fact that his pages resemble nothing else under the sun. If you say to him, "This is not English. You must tear this up and try again," he will answer plaintively: "But you know what I *mean*, don't you?" He will be indignant if you reply, "I can *guess*, but only because I know what you are supposed to mean."

Let me cite a few choice samples of No-English. These come, alas, from examination papers in my course in American literature.

A change from the optimastic view of the individual man as put forth in trancendentic philosophy to the pessimistic view of man kind frought with invalid morals living a superficial life with no direction such as T. S. Eliot flitting bug-eyed from Antwerp to Brussels to London.

He was a man who had dispared to the nature of a man and although he had these tendencies of subjection he soon gained aspirations and broke away from the school of disparants and strove on his own beliefs.

When Twain was writing *Huckleberry Finn* he decided to implement the voyage as a cohesive catalyst. Twain used a general local. Faulkner has a restrictive local, and Thoreau wrote for every-body in the universal.

Huck Finn sets out in a cimilar direction, away from society. He also floats on the sea of life and has periodic relations with the surrounding society. The Grangerfords put Huck up, for instance, and promptly acquaint him with social disorganization and bitterness.

The American ideal seemed to hang void in the twenties, a shame-ful thing because Americans must forage ahead. Eliot was not the gung-ho American as Whitman. Whitman was one of the best ex-amples of this "nature into thought" angle.

To one who cares about the well-forged instrument by which those who use English communicate with one another there are, I submit, some very alarming symptoms of decay and defilement in these passages of No-English. Listened to with half an ear they sound impressive, authoritative, and even powerful. Though their authors were composing complete nonsense, they put down these jumbled words with the self-assurance of an advertising copy-writer or an editor of *Time*.

Why is the tide of No-English flooding in with such power that we cannot stand against it?

First in importance is the influence of officialese. This is the age of the official statement from the government, of com-muniqués, of press releases from public relations officers. All writing of this sort must sound impressive and authoritative, for it is composed to be believed in without dissent.

Here is a prime example of officialese (which originated, I am happy to say, not in America but England):

It will be apparent that the draining away of senior experienced men will be of such proportions for some years to come as to con-stitute a serious factor to be contended with in providing for the adequate staffing of State departments. The difficulty in this respect is aggravated by the expansion of governmental activities which has been a feature during the last few years, and which seems likely to persist for some time. This expansion has already imposed considerable strain upon the personnel of the public service and, coupled with the progressive wastage in the ranks of the senior officers to which reference has been made, tends to produce conditions which, on occasion, border on the acute. The Commission is giving its particular attention to the problems contained in and engendered by the circumstances already present and those which it is anticipated will develop in future.

These fourteen lines of "twisted, pretentious, long-winded and down-at-heel" officialese, can, with a little labour, be shortened to six lines.* You can always condense officialese by about two-thirds; this is one of the ways you recognize it.

So many senior and experienced officers will leave the service during the next few years that State departments will be short of staff; and the difficulties this will cause will be aggravated if, as seems possible, the State's activities continue to expand. The Commission is giving this matter attention.

More often than not the young are trying to write officialese. And why not? This is the way very important people in our society "reveal" or "announce" what are supposed to be matters of life-or-death. This is the interminable voice of the age—or one of its voices.

The evident desire of the writers of No-English to pack power into their prose can, I think, be traced to another defiler of the well of English. Almost every popular magazine nowadays is likely to be written in a hot-rod style which bursts with energy in every sentence. Authors who wish to sell their wares to *Time*, *Look*, and *Life*, must write in a 500-horsepower style. And their editors, as well, seem to live in constant fear that if they take the foot off the accelerator the reader will drop off to sleep between

---

* This example of officialese and the condensation of it I have borrowed from Eric Partridge and John W. Clark, *British and American English Since 1900* (1951), p. 44.

sentences or, bored and indifferent, turn on the television set.

Two qualities of *Time*-style exert an especially subtle influence. The supercharged *Time*- (or *Newsweek*-) sentence teaches the student that his prose should never be quiet. It must always shock with the hot-foot. One cannot imagine, for instance, *Time*'s printing one of the calm and witty essays of E. B. White; it would be as much out of place as a preacher at a jitterbug contest.

The souped-up article also teaches the student-reader that certain words are absolute as definitions of attributes of mind and body. No variations or gradations are possible and so none need be sought. Take, for instance, one of *Time*'s pet words—"paunchy." As one whose paunchiness is increasingly distressful to him, I resent this word's invariability. There was a time when I had a little professorial pot; later I was "stout" (as we used to say, in a politer era); then I became, I suppose, definitely potbellied. But in *Time*'s view I have always been paunchy; there is no need for other words to describe my long struggle with the flesh, my triumphs and my eventual defeat. Consider another of *Time*'s favourites—"bug-eyed." Gone are the possibilities of playing with such fine old words as startled, a-feared, aghast, agog, spellbound, open-mouthed, thunderstruck. Nor is there any way of knowing whether the man affected with bug-eyedness inherited his condition or is a hyperthyroid case or is exophthalmic. He is just "bug-eyed"—that's all.

Much more to be feared than the poison vials of officialese or of *Time* is the expensively distilled poison of advertising-style. Students cannot escape it—nor can we. As the poet Karl Shapiro put it in his poem, "Drug Store":

> And every nook and cranny of the flesh
> Is spoken to by packages with wiles.
> "Buy me, buy me," they whimper and cajole;
> The hectic range of lipstick pouts,
> Revealing the wicked and the simple mouth.

One of the most insidious things about advertising-style is that it burns up the language at a furious rate because there is so much oxygen in it. The new Plymouth, the ad-man says, is *newest, most modern* of the low-price three. Also *biggest*. Its Power-Flow 117 motor is *brilliant*. Its Power-Flite no-clutch transmission is the *finest made*. The next ad-writer for Plymouth is going to find ashes all over his cubicle. What can he dig out of the dictionary which is newer than "newest," bigger than "biggest," higher than "highest horsepower in the field?"

Consider the consumption of debased advertising metaphors which goes on in one issue of *Look* or *Life*. We note that "a new day has dawned for the car owners of America." Can this startling statement mean that the atomic-powered automobile has arrived? Not at all. Firestone is merely marketing a new tyre. And how are we to "open the door on to-morrow?" By such exciting experiences as getting married? having a baby? a plane trip to Europe? Certainly not. That "door on to-morrow" will open if you make an itsy-bitsy deposit on a Dodge. And what is this on the next page?—"Like all great ideas, this one's slightly marvellous—yet so simple." Can it be we are about to hear something of the order of magnitude of the second law of thermo-dynamics or Leibnitz's theory of the monads? We are not so easily fooled. We know instinctively, after years of indoctrination, that this great idea will prove, alas, to be only Sta-Flat's creation of a new girdle, with extra strength where you need it most ("midriff, waist, tummy").

There is another defiler of modern prose whose poisoning is carried out under the cover of darkness. I find it difficult to identify him. Professor John Clark declares the culprit to be the second-rate newspaper reporter. I am not sure he is the chief offender; but I am certain that some person or persons unknown have put over on us lately a most peculiar, very limited vocabulary which serves, unfortunately, to cover every situation in modern life. In listing these words—about forty in number

—Professor Clark notes that "if an historical novelist of fifty or a hundred years from now should wish to give his readers a fairly realistic illusion of the flavour of everyday American English of the 1950's, he could adopt no more economical means than to sprinkle his dialogue with these expressions."

To prove to myself how constantly these words turn up and how unthinkingly we ourselves resort to them, I used every one of them in a little descriptive scene which took less than ten minutes to compose, so easily did these words fall into place.

A teen-ager dropped into my office to-day much worried about his inferiority complex and anxious to adjust. He seemed to think I was a sincere-type professor and had some know-how in inter-personal relations. He said there was a campus-inspired rumour that I am good at human engineering and so thought he'd contact me and get a few constructive angles. First I tried to fit him into some frame of reference and then I processed him by screening him with some questions, and so got the overall picture. (I discovered, by the way, that his mother is a low-grade home-maker.) I then briefed him on the need for grasping our most unique set-up here and seeing how we are geared for modern living. Next I made him the proposi-tion that he be less negative, more relaxed, and mix with a few of the outstanding youth at the top-flight level of our student body. He would be sure, I said, to find them like-minded, percentagewise. When we finished off, he thanked me for our little streamlined get-together and said he would try to integrate better. I found the ex-perience so educational that I think I'll author an article about it after I've researched the matter further.

Some of the offensive expressions are hand-me-downs from pseudo-scientific writing; some derive from the writing of sociologists and psychologists; some emanate from the sales-conference and the business convention. Several reveal the codified anxieties of modern life, while others are the slogans of "positive thinking" which are supposed to cure these anxieties. Because these expressions make up an important part of the vocabulary of his time, the modern student is compelled to use them. But while this fictional professor was having his cosy little streamlined interview with this hypothetical student, neither of them was a human being—a person, as Shakespeare once said, with hands, organs, dimensions, senses, affections, passions; fed with food, subject to diseases, warmed and cooled with winter and summer. The student was an intelligence test to be taken and scored; the professor was a machine to grind out medians, percentiles, and normal distribution curves.

There is one predicament in our present kind of collegiate education which, I am convinced, confuses the student who desires to write good English, which may, indeed, lead him to believe that there is no necessity for trying to write in the great tradition of English prose. Because the fields of learning now share very little common ground, they (and we) no longer possess a common language. The historian cannot understand the equations of the physicist and the physicist cannot understand the new vocabulary developed by the sociologist. The professor of literature who lectures about "levels of meaning," the "texture and tension of poetry," the wonderful "ambiguities" in Melville's prose, and the "personal symbolism" in the poetry of Robert Frost, opens the eyes but not the ears of his colleague in chemistry who had no idea literature was *that* difficult. This impenetrability of our particular subjects to the uninitiated does not worry us—as professors—to any great extent. We go our separate ways, happy in our isolation. We rejoice in our own jargon. We suppose that our colleagues in other fields understand.

But I have begun to notice lately that our better students take an unholy pride in the vocabularies they encounter as they move through their academic day. Imagine what the impact of specialised subjects and the vocabularies by which they are presented may be on a conscientious young man who really wishes to comprehend what his lecturers, hour after hour, are telling him. At 8.30 in his physics class he hears this:

BARRIER DESIGN

At atmospheric pressure the mean free path of a molecule is of the order of a ten-thousandth of a millimeter or one-tenth of a micron. To ensure true "diffusive" flow of the gas, the diameter of the myriad holes in the barrier must be less than one-tenth the mean free path. Therefore, the barrier material must have almost no holes which are appreciably larger than 0.01 micron (4×10^{-7} inch), but must have billions of holes of this size or smaller. These holes must not enlarge or plug up as the result of direct corrosion or dust coming from corrosion elsewhere in the system. The barrier must be able to withstand a pressure "head" of one atmosphere.

At 9.30 our young man is in his place in his music class in Elementary Harmony. His professor has been talking about triads in minor keys. After the late-comers have got to their seats he begins:

When the dominant and sub-mediant triads (V and VI) are connected in the minor mode, the voices have to move along certain *fixed* lines in order to avoid consecutive 5ths and octaves and the augmented 2nd. The leading-tone always ascends to the tonic (or descends from it). Two of the upper voices must move in contrary motion to the bass, and the *3rd is always to be doubled* in the triad on the sixth degree, *in four-part writing*.

Our earnest friend has a much-needed coke in the Student Centre at 10.30 but at 11.30 he is in the Psychology building.

When two simple stimuli are combined in some total perception, the hedonic tone of the resultant depends upon the sum of the hedonic tones of the two stimuli. We must, however, limit this principle in two ways. (*a*) It holds only when it can operate without interference by some of the other hedonic laws [I have explained]. (*b*) It holds only when the relative importances of the different constituents in the sum are determined and taken into account.

After a breather at lunch (and fifteen minutes at the pool-table) he is back in place at 1.30, listening to the Professor of Religion on the relations between mysticism and magic.

To the two dogmas of the "Astral Light" or universal agent and the "power of the will" there is to be added a third: the doctrine of Analogy, or implicit correspondence between appearance and reality, the microcosm of man and the macrocosm of the universe, the seen and the unseen worlds. In this, occultism finds the basis of all its transcendental speculations. *Quod superius sicut quod inferius* —the first words of that Emerald Table which was once attributed to Hermes Trismegistus himself—is an axiom which must be agreeable to all Platonists.*

Finally, at 2.30, the last lecture of the day. The course is American Literature, and the professor is talking about the pamphleteers of the American Revolution. He does up Tom Paine neatly in the last ten minutes of the hour and concludes by saying: "The opening paragraph of Paine's great propaganda pamphlet, 'The Crisis,' which put heart into Washington's ragged little army in December, 1776, and turned the fortunes of war in our favour, contains one of the most eloquent passages of prose written in the 18th century."

These are the times that try men's souls. The summer soldier and the sunshine patriot will, in this crisis, shrink from the service of their country; but he that stands it *now*, deserves the love and thanks of man and woman. Tyranny, like hell, is not easily conquered; yet we have this consolation with us, that the harder the conflict, the more glorious the triumph. What we obtain too cheap, we esteem too lightly: it is dearness only that gives everything its value. Heaven knows how to put a proper price upon its goods; and it would be strange indeed if so celestial an article as FREEDOM should not be highly rated.

What does our young man think of this, if he can think at all, after the day's barrage of special terms and concepts? "It's eloquent, so what?" Who is there to tell him that although it is

---

* These four quotations have been cribbed, verbatim, from: Henry DeWolf Smyth, *Atomic Energy for Military Purposes* (Princeton University Press, 1945), p. 177; Arthur Foote and Walter R. Spalding, *Modern Harmony* (Schmidt Co., 1924), p. 41; Baring, Langfeld, and Weld, *Psychology, A Factual Textbook* (Wiley and Sons, 1935), pp. 376–377; and Evelyn Underhill, *Mysticism* (Dutton, 1926), p. 191.

important to know all he has learned during the day, and that the beginning of wisdom is the certitude of fact, nevertheless there is something beyond fact which is of the utmost importance. If, in his pride of knowledge, he refuses to learn how to communicate his knowledge, his ideas, and his aspirations, in language that is simple, sensuous, passionate, direct, honest, precise, varied, strong though quiet, *and* eloquent, he will never bring men to his way of thinking. He will have condemned himself to the prison of the public relations officer, or the life of the Madison Avenue ad-man, or to the drudgery, without the final reward, of the narrow specialist-scholar. He deserves to win a better fate. But who among us is ready to speak sternly to him, our pride and our hope, though he still writes No-English?

An Interview With Truman Capote

TRUMAN CAPOTE (1924–   )
Interviewer: Pati Hill

TRUMAN CAPOTE lives in a big yellow house in Brooklyn Heights, which he has recently restored with the taste and elegance that is generally characteristic of his undertakings. As I entered he was head and shoulders inside a newly arrived crate containing a wooden lion.

"There!" he cried as he tugged it out to a fine birth amid a welter of sawdust and shavings. "Did you ever see anything so splendid? Well, that's that. I saw him and I bought him. Now he's all mine."

"He's large," I said. "Where are you going to put him?"

"Why, in the fireplace, of course," said Capote. "Now come along into the parlor while I get someone to clear away this mess."

The parlor is Victorian in character and contains Capote's most intimate collection of art objects and personal treasures, which, for all their orderly arrangement on polished tables and bamboo bookcases, somehow remind you of the contents of a very astute little boy's pockets. There is, for instance, a golden Easter egg brought back from Russia, an iron dog, somewhat the worse for wear, a Fabergé pillbox, some marbles, blue ceramic fruit, paper-weights, Battersea boxes, picture postcards, and old photographs. In short everything that might seem useful or handy in a day's adventuring around the world.

Capote himself fits in very well with this impression at first glance. He is small and blond, with a forelock that persists in falling down into his eyes, and his smile is sudden and sunny. His approach to anyone new is one of open curiosity and friend- liness. He might be taken in by anything and, in fact, seems only too ready to be. There is something about him, though, that makes you feel that for all his willingness it would be hard to pull any wool over his eyes and maybe it is better not to try.

There was a sound of scuffling in the hall and Capote came in, preceded by a large bulldog with a white face.

"This is Bunky," he said.

Bunky sniffed me over and we sat down.

INTERVIEWER: When did you first start writing?

CAPOTE: When I was a child of about ten or eleven and lived near Mobile.

I had to go into town on Saturdays to the dentist and I joined the Sunshine Club that was organized by the Mobile Press Register. There was a children's page with contests for writing and for coloring pictures, and then every Saturday afternoon they had a party with free Nehi and Coca-Cola. The prize for the short-story writing contest was either a pony or a dog, I've forgotten which, but I wanted it badly. I had been noticing the activities of some neighbors who were up to no good, so I wrote a kind of *roman à clef* called "Old Mr. Busybody" and entered it in the contest. The first installment appeared one Sunday, under my real name of Truman Streckfus Persons. Only somebody suddenly realized that I was serving up a local scandal as fiction, and the second installment never appeared. Naturally, I didn't win a thing.

INTERVIEWER: Were you sure then that you wanted to be a writer?

CAPOTE: I realized that I *wanted* to be a writer. But I wasn't sure I *would* be until I was fifteen or so. At that time I had immodestly started sending stories to magazines and literary quarterlies. Of course no writer ever forgets his first acceptance; but one fine day when I was seventeen, I had my first, second, and third, all in the same morning's mail. Oh, I'm here to tell you, dizzy with excitement is no mere phrase!

INTERVIEWER: What did you first write?

CAPOTE: Short stories. And my more unswerving ambitions still revolve around this form. When seriously explored, the short story seems to me the most difficult and disciplining form of prose writing extant. Whatever control and technique I may have I owe entirely to my training in this medium.

INTERVIEWER: What do you mean exactly by "control"?

CAPOTE: I mean maintaining a stylistic and emotional upper hand over your material. Call it precious and go to hell, but I believe a story can be wrecked by a faulty rhythm in a sentence—especially if it occurs toward the end—or a mistake in paragraphing, even punctuation. Henry James is the maestro of the semi-colon. Hemingway is a first-rate paragrapher. From the point of view of ear, Virginia Woolf never wrote a bad sentence. I don't mean to imply that I successfully practice what I preach. I try, that's all.

INTERVIEWER: How does one arrive at short-story technique?

CAPOTE: Since each story presents its own technical problems, obviously one can't generalize about them on a two-times-two-equals-four basis. Finding the right form for your story is simply to realize the most *natural* way of telling the story. The test of whether or not a writer has divined the natural shape of his story is just this: after reading it, can you imagine it differently, or does it silence your imagination and seem to you absolute and final? As an orange is final. As an orange is something nature has made just right.

INTERVIEWER: Are there devices one can use in improving one's technique?

CAPOTE: Work is the only device I know of. Writing has laws of perspective, of light and shade, just as painting does, or music. If you are born knowing them, fine. If not, learn them. Then re-arrange the rules to suit yourself. Even Joyce, our most extreme disregarder, was a superb craftsman; he could write *Ulysses* *because* he could write *Dubliners*. Too many writers seem to consider the writing of short stories as a kind of finger exercise. Well, in such cases, it is certainly only their fingers they are exercising.

INTERVIEWER: Did you have much encouragement in those early days, and if so, by whom?

CAPOTE: Good Lord! I'm afraid you've let yourself in for quite a saga. The answer is a snake's nest of no's and a few yes's. You see, not altogether but by and large, my childhood was spent in parts of the country and among people unprovided with any semblance of a cultural attitude. Which was probably not a bad thing, in the long view. It toughened me rather too soon to swim against the current—indeed, in some areas I developed the muscles of a veritable barracuda, especially in the art of dealing with one's enemies, an art no less necessary than knowing how to appreciate one's friends.

But to go back. Naturally, in the milieu aforesaid, I was thought somewhat *eccentric*, which was fair enough, and *stupid*, which I suitably resented. Still, I despised school—or schools, for I was always changing from one to another—and year after year failed the simplest subjects out of loathing and boredom. I played hooky at least twice a week and was always running away from home. Once I ran away with a friend who lived across the street—a girl much older than myself who in later life achieved a certain fame. Because she murdered a half-dozen people and was electrocuted at Sing Sing. Someone wrote a book about her. They called her the Lonely Hearts Killer. But there, I'm wandering again. Well, finally, I guess I was around twelve, the principal at the school I was attending paid a call on my family, and told them that in his opinion, and in the opinion of the faculty, I was "subnormal." He thought it would be sensible, the humane action, to send me to some special school equipped to handle backward brats. Whatever they may have privately felt, my family as a whole took official umbrage, and in an effort to prove I wasn't subnormal, pronto packed me off to a psychiatric study clinic at a university in the East where I had my I.Q. inspected. I enjoyed it thoroughly and—guess what?—came home a genius, so proclaimed by science. I don't know who was the more appalled: my former teachers, who refused to believe it, or my family, who didn't want to believe it —they'd just hoped to be told I was a nice normal boy. Ha ha! But as for me, I was exceedingly pleased—went around staring at myself in mirrors and sucking in my cheeks and thinking over in my mind, my lad, you and Flaubert—or Maupassant or Mansfield or Proust or Chekhov or Wolfe, whoever was the idol of the moment.

I began writing in fearful earnest—my mind zoomed all night every night, and I don't think I really slept for several years. Not until I discovered that whisky could relax me. I was too young, fifteen, to buy it myself, but I had a few older friends who were most obliging in this respect and I soon accumulated a suitcase full of bottles, everything from blackberry brandy to bourbon. I kept the suitcase hidden in a closet. Most of my drinking was done in the late afternoon; then I'd chew a handful of Sen Sen and go down to dinner, where my behavior, my glazed silences, gradually grew into a source of general consternation. One of my relatives used to say, "Really, if I didn't know better, I'd swear he was dead drunk." Well, of course, this little comedy, if such it was, ended in discovery and some disaster, and it was many a moon before I touched another drop. But I seem to be off the track again. You asked about encouragement. The first person who ever really helped me was, strangely, a teacher. An English teacher I had in high school, Catherine Wood, who backed my ambitions in every way, and to whom I shall always be grateful. Later on, from the time I first began to publish, I had all the encouragement anyone could ever want, notably from Margarita Smith, fiction editor of *Mademoiselle*, Mary Louise Aswell of *Harper's Bazaar*, and Robert Linscott of Random House. You would have to be a glutton indeed to ask for more good luck and fortune than I had at the beginning of my career.

INTERVIEWER: Did the three editors you mention encourage you simply by buying your work, or did they offer criticism, too?

CAPOTE: Well, I can't imagine anything *more* encouraging than having someone buy your work. I never write—indeed, am physically incapable of writing—anything that I don't think will be paid for. But, as a matter of fact, the persons mentioned, and some others as well, were all very generous with advice.

INTERVIEWER: Do you like anything you wrote long ago as well as what you write now?

CAPOTE: Yes. For instance, last summer I read my novel *Other Voices, Other Rooms* for the first time since it was published eight years ago, and it was quite as though I were reading something by a stranger. The truth is, I am a stranger to that book; the person who wrote it seems to have so little in common with my present self. Our mentalities, our interior temperatures are entirely different. Despite awkwardness, it has an amazing intensity, a real voltage. I am very pleased I was able to write the

book when I did, otherwise it would never have been written.
I like *The Grass Harp* too, and several of my short stories, though
not "Miriam," which is a good stunt but nothing more. No, I
prefer "Children on Their Birthdays" and "Shut a Final Door,"
and oh, some others, especially a story not too many people
seemed to care for, "Master Misery," which was in my collection *A Tree of Night.*

INTERVIEWER: You recently published a book about the *Porgy
and Bess* trip to Russia. One of the most interesting things about
the style was its unusual detachment, even by comparison to the
reporting of journalists who have spent many years recording
events in an impartial way. One had the impression that this
version must have been as close to the truth as it is possible to
get through another person's eyes, which is surprising when you
consider that most of your work has been characterized by its
very personal quality.

CAPOTE: Actually, I don't consider the style of this book, *The
Muses Are Heard*, as markedly different from my fictional style.
Perhaps the content, the fact that it is about real events, makes
it seem so. After all, *Muses* is straight reporting, and in reporting one is occupied with literalness and surfaces, with implication without comment—one can't achieve immediate depths the
way one may in fiction. However, one of the reasons I've wanted
to do reportage was to prove that I could apply my style to the
realities of journalism. But I believe my fictional method is equally
detached—emotionality makes me lose writing control: I have
to exhaust the emotion before I feel clinical enough to analyze
and project it, and as far as I'm concerned that's one of the
laws of achieving true technique. If my fiction seems more personal it is because it depends on the artist's most personal and
revealing area: his imagination.

INTERVIEWER: How do you exhaust the emotion? Is it only a
matter of thinking about the story over a certain length of time,
or are there other considerations?

CAPOTE: No, I don't think it is merely a matter of time. Suppose you ate nothing but apples for a week. Unquestionably you would exhaust your appetite for apples and most certainly know what they taste like. By the time I write a story I may no longer have any hunger for it, but I feel that I thoroughly know its flavor. The *Porgy and Bess* articles are not relevant to this issue. That was reporting, and "emotions" were not much involved— at least not the difficult and personal territories of feeling that I mean. I seem to remember reading that Dickens, as he wrote, choked with laughter over his own humor and dripped tears all over the page when one of his characters died. My own theory is that the writer should have considered his wit and dried his tears long, long before setting out to evoke similar reactions in a reader. In other words, I believe the greatest intensity in art in all its shapes is achieved with a deliberate, hard, and cool head. For example, Flaubert's *A Simple Heart*. A warm story, warmly written; but it could only be the work of an artist muchly aware of true techniques, i.e., necessities. I'm sure, at some point, Flaubert must have felt the story very deeply— but *not* when he wrote it. Or, for a more contemporary example, take that marvelous short novel of Katherine Anne Porter's, *Noon Wine*. It has such intensity, such a sense of happening-now, yet the writing is so controlled, the inner rhythms of the story so immaculate, that I feel fairly certain Miss Porter was at some distance *from* her material.

INTERVIEWER: Have your best stories or books been written at a comparatively tranquil moment in your life or do you work better because, or in spite, of emotional stress?

CAPOTE: I feel slightly as though I've never lived a tranquil moment, unless you count what an occasional Nembutal induces. Though, come to think of it, I spent two years in a very romantic house on top of a mountain in Sicily, and I guess this period could be called tranquil. God knows, it was quiet. That's where I wrote *The Grass Harp*. But I must say an iota of stress, striving toward deadliness, does me good.

INTERVIEWER: You have lived abroad for the last eight years.

Why did you decide to return to America?

CAPOTE: Because I'm an American, and never could be, and have no desire to be, anything else. Besides, I like cities, and New York is the only real city-city. Except for a two-year stretch, I came back to America every one of those eight years, and I never entertained expatriate notions. For me, Europe was a method of acquiring perspective and an education, a stepping stone toward maturity. But there *is* the law of diminishing returns, and about two years ago it began to set in: Europe had given me an enormous lot, but suddenly I felt as though the process were reversing itself—there seemed to be a taking away. So I came home, feeling quite grown up and able to settle down where I belong—which doesn't mean I've bought a rocking chair and turned to stone. No indeed. I intend to have footloose escapades as long as frontiers stay open.

INTERVIEWER: Do you read a great deal?

CAPOTE: Too much. And anything, including labels and recipes and advertisements. I have a passion for newspapers—read all the New York dailies every day, and the Sunday editions, and several foreign magazines too. The ones I don't buy I read standing at the news stands. I average about five books a week—the normal-length novel takes me about two hours. I enjoy thrillers and would like someday to write one. Though I prefer first-rate fiction, for the last few years my reading seems to have been concentrated on letters and journals and biographies. It doesn't bother me to read while I am writing—I mean, I don't suddenly find another writer's style seeping out of my pen. Though once, during a lengthy spell of James, my own sentences *did* get awfully long.

INTERVIEWER: What writers have influenced you the most?

CAPOTE: So far as I consciously know, I've never been aware of direct literary influence, though several critics have informed me that my early works owe a debt to Faulkner and Welty and McCullers. Possibly. I'm a great admirer of all three; and Katherine Anne Porter, too. Though I don't think, when really ex-

amined, that they have much in common with each other, or
me, except that we were all born in the South. Between thirteen
and sixteen are the ideal if not the only ages for succumbing to
Thomas Wolfe—he seemed to me a great genius then, and still
does, though I can't read a line of it now. Just as other youthful
flames have guttered: Poe, Dickens, Stevenson. I love them in
memory, but find them unreadable. These are the enthusiasms
that remain constant: Flaubert, Turgenev, Chekhov, Jane Austen,
James, E. M. Forster, Maupassant, Rilke, Proust, Shaw, Willa
Cather—oh the list is too long, so I'll end with James Agee, a
beautiful writer whose death over two years ago was a real
loss. Agee's work, by the way, was much influenced by the
films. I think most of the younger writers have learned and
borrowed from the visual, structural side of movie technique.
I have.

INTERVIEWER: You've written for the films, haven't you? What
was that like?

CAPOTE: A lark. At least the one picture I wrote, *Beat the Devil*,
was tremendous fun. I worked on it with John Huston while
the picture was actually being made on location in Italy. Sometimes scenes that were just about to be shot were written right
on the set. The cast were completely bewildered—even Huston
sometimes didn't seem to know what was going on. Naturally
the scenes had to be written out of a sequence, and there were
peculiar moments when I was carrying around in my head the
only real outline of the so-called plot. You never saw it? Oh,
you should. It's a marvelous joke. Though I'm afraid the pro-
ducer didn't laugh. The hell with them. Whenever there's a
revival I go to see it and have a fine time.

  Seriously, though, I don't think a writer stands much chance
of imposing himself on a film unless he works in the warmest
rapport with the director or is himself the director. It's so much
a director's medium that the movies have developed only one
writer who, working exclusively as a scenarist, could be called
a film genius. I mean that shy, delightful little peasant, Zavattini.

What a visual sense! Eighty percent of the good Italian movies were made from Zavattini scripts—all of the De Sica pictures, for instance. De Sica is a charming man, a gifted and deeply sophisticated person; nevertheless he's mostly a megaphone for Zavattini, his pictures are absolutely Zavattini's creations; every nuance, mood, every bit of business is clearly indicated in Zavattini's scripts.

INTERVIEWER: What are some of your writing habits? Do you use a desk? Do you write on a machine?

CAPOTE: I am a completely horizontal author. I can't think unless I'm lying down, either in bed or stretched on a couch and with a cigarette and coffee handy. I've got to be puffing and sipping. As the afternoon wears on, I shift from coffee to mint tea to sherry to martinis. No, I don't use a typewriter. Not in the beginning. I write my first version in longhand (pencil). Then I do a complete revision, also in longhand. Essentially I think of myself as a stylist, and stylists can become notoriously obsessed with the placing of a comma, the weight of a semicolon. Obsessions of this sort, and the time I take over them, irritate me beyond endurance.

INTERVIEWER: You seem to make a distinction between writers who are stylists and writers who aren't. Which writers would you call stylists and which not?

CAPOTE: What is style? And "what" as the Zen Koan asks, "is the sound of one hand?" No one really *knows;* yet either you *know* or you don't. For myself, if you will excuse a rather cheap little image, I suppose style is the mirror of an artist's sensibility —more so than the *content* of his work. To some degree all writers have style—Ronald Firbank, bless his heart, had little else, and thank God he realized it. But the possession of style, *a* style, is often a hindrance, a negative force, not as it should be, and as it is—with, say, E. M. Forster and Colette and Flaubert and Mark Twain and Hemingway and Isak Dinesen—a reinforcement. Dreiser, for instance, has *a* style—but oh, *Dio buono!* And Eugene O'Neill. And Faulkner, brilliant as he is. They all seem to me triumphs over strong but negative styles, styles that do not really add to the communication between writer and reader. Then there is the styleless stylist—which is very difficult, very admirable, and *always* very popular: Graham Greene, Maugham, Thornton Wilder, John Hersey, Willa Cather, Thurber, Sartre (remember, we're *not* discussing content), J. P. Marquand, and so on. But yes, there *is* such an animal as a nonstylist. Only they're not writers; they're typists. Sweaty typists blacking up pounds of bond paper with formless, eyeless, earless messages. Well, who are some of the younger writers who seem to know that style exists? P. H. Newby, Francoise Sagan, somewhat. Bill Styron, Flannery O'Connor—she has some fine moments, that girl. James Merrill. William Goyen— if he'd stop being hysterical. J. D. Salinger—especially in the colloquial tradition. Colin Wilson? Another typist.

INTERVIEWER: You say that Ronald Firbank had little else but style. Do you think that style alone can make a writer a great one?

CAPOTE: No, I don't think so—though, it could be argued, what happens to Proust if you separate him from his style? Style has never been a strong point with American writers. This though some of the best have been Americans. Hawthorne got us off to a fine start. For the past thirty years Hemingway, stylistically speaking, has influenced more writers on a world scale than anyone else. At the moment, I think our own Miss Porter knows as well as anyone what it's all about.

INTERVIEWER: Can a writer learn style?

CAPOTE: No, I don't think that style is consciously arrived at, any more than one arrives at the color of one's eyes. After all, your style is you. At the end the personality of a writer has so much to do with the work. The personality has to be humanly there. Personality is a debased word, I know, but it's what I mean. The writer's individual humanity, his word or gesture toward the world, has to appear almost like a character that makes contact with the reader. If the personality is vague or

confused or merely literary, *ça ne va pas*. Faulkner, McCullers
—they project their personality at once.

INTERVIEWER: It is interesting that your work has been so widely
appreciated in France. Do you think style can be translated?

CAPOTE: Why not? Provided the author and the translator are
artistic twins.

INTERVIEWER: Well, I'm afraid I interrupted you with your
short story still in penciled manuscript. What happens next?

CAPOTE: Let's see, that was second draft. Then I type a third
draft on yellow paper, a very special certain kind of yellow
paper. No, I don't get out of bed to do this. I balance the machine
on my knees. Sure, it works fine; I can manage a hundred words
a minute. Well, when the yellow draft is finished, I put the
manuscript away for a while, a week, a month, sometimes
longer. When I take it out again, I read it as coldly as possible,
then read it aloud to a friend or two, and decide what changes
I want to make and whether or not I want to publish it. I've
thrown away rather a few short stories, an entire novel, and
half of another. But if all goes well, I type the final version on
white paper and that's that.

INTERVIEWER: Is the book organized completely in your head
before you begin it or does it unfold, surprising you as you go
along?

CAPOTE: Both. I invariably have the illusion that the whole play
of a story, its start and middle and finish, occur in my mind
simultaneously—that I'm seeing it in one flash. But in the work-
ing-out, the writing-out, infinite surprises happen. Thank God,
because the surprise, the twist, the phrase that comes at the right
moment out of nowhere, is the unexpected dividend, that joyful
little push that keeps a writer going.

At one time I used to keep notebooks with outlines for stories.
But I found doing this somehow deadened the idea in my imagination. If the notion is good enough, if it truly belongs to
you, then you can't forget it—it will haunt you till it's written.

INTERVIEWER: How much of your work is autobiographical?

CAPOTE: Very little, really. A little is *suggested* by real incidents or personages, although everything a writer writes is in some way autobiographical. *The Grass Harp* is the only true thing I ever wrote, and naturally everybody thought it all invented, and imagined *Other Voices, Other Rooms* to be autobiographical.

INTERVIEWER: Do you have any definite ideas or projects for the future?

CAPOTE (*meditatively*): Well, yes, I believe so. I have always written what was easiest for me until now: I want to try something else, a kind of controlled extravagance. I want to use my mind more, use many more colors. Hemingway once said anybody can write a novel in the first person. I know now exactly what he means.

INTERVIEWER: Were you ever tempted by any of the other arts?

CAPOTE: I don't know if it's art, but I was stage-struck for years and more than anything I wanted to be a tap-dancer. I used to practice my buck-and-wing until everybody in the house was ready to kill me. Later on, I longed to play the guitar and sing in night clubs. So I saved up for a guitar and took lessons for one whole winter, but in the end the only tune I could really play was a beginner's thing called "I Wish I Were Single Again." I got so tired of it that one day I just gave the guitar to a stranger in a bus station. I was also interested in painting, and studied for three years, but I'm afraid the fervor, *la vrai chose*, wasn't there.

INTERVIEWER: Do you think criticism helps any?

CAPOTE: Before publication, and if provided by persons whose judgement you trust, yes, of course criticism helps. But after anything is published, all I want to read or hear is praise. Anything less is a bore, and I'll give you fifty dollars if you produced a writer who can honestly say he was ever helped by the prissy carpings and condescensions of reviewers. I don't mean to say that none of the professional critics are worth paying attention to—but few of the good ones review on a regular basis. Most of all, I believe in hardening yourself against opinion.

I've had, and I continue to receive, my full share of abuse, some
of it extremely personal, but it doesn't faze me any more. I can
read the most outrageous libel about myself and never skip a
pulsebeat. And in this connection, there is one piece of advice I
strongly urge: never demean yourself by talking back to a
critic, never. Write those letters to the editor in your head, but
don't put them on paper.

INTERVIEWER: What are some of your personal quirks?

CAPOTE: I suppose my superstitiousness could be termed a quirk.
I have to add up all numbers: there are some people I never
telephone because their number adds up to an unlucky figure.
Or I won't accept a hotel room for the same reason. I will not
tolerate the presence of yellow roses—which is sad because
they're my favorite flower. I can't allow three cigarette butts
in the same ashtray. Won't travel on a plane with two nuns.
Won't begin or end anything on a Friday. It's endless, the things
I can't and won't. But I derive some curious comfort from obeying these primitive concepts.

INTERVIEWER: You have been quoted as saying your preferred
pastimes are "conversation, reading, travel, and writing, in that
order." Do you mean that literally?

CAPOTE: I think so. At least I'm pretty sure conversation will
always come first with me. I like to listen, and I like to talk.
Heavens, girl, can't you *see* I like to talk?

The Stories

ONE MIGHT argue that for enjoyment of the short story the average reader does not have to be a critical reader, that he does not need to see how the characters, the action, the ideas, the effects he has enjoyed have been communicated through form, through language, through imagery. The argument may be easier to advance for the short story than for poetry, but since the short story is an art form, the opportunity for increased enjoyment through an understanding of its art always awaits the critical reader. Enjoyment not only of fiction but of any art is limited only to the capacity of the reader or viewer to respond and understand.

It is true that the short story is a less concentrated form of art than the poem, and generally it uses language in a more limited way than poetry. Because its language is less highly arranged and systematized, it will probably communicate more readily to the average reader than poetry. Yet as art it can give pleasure because it appeals to any reader who is interested in and concerned with people in the wide range of their lives from the heroic to the ridiculous. A basic and simple appeal of all narrative, the short story, the novel, the tale is the unfolding of event—the answer to "What happens next?" But were such an appeal the only one, the short story would stultify as an art form. What distinguishes the modern short story of artistic intent is its variety of form, action, and content and its penetration into human character and emotion. The fifteen stories selected for this volume will illustrate this comment.

"What is the ideal short story?" the critical reader with a philosophical turn of mind might ask. There is no simple answer to the question. Indeed there is no "ideal short story." For the sake of discussion one might say that a good short story is built around a theme or interesting content, expressed through valid characters, and communicated in fitting language—all proportioned to provide a calculated and understandable effect. The core of the short story, then, is some kind of relatable experience of existence. It is obvious that the themes and substance of short stories are as many as life can exhibit and imagination invent. Within a reasonable compass the writer selects those elements of life and imagination which will create and sustain interest, develop some desired effect, and provide pleasure to the reader. The story may deal with the tensions of men and women and the ultimate issues of the human lot, as does Joyce's "The Dead." It may communicate both the funny and sad qualities of life through its revelation of two people who live thousands of miles apart and in vastly different societies, as in John Updike's "Dear Alexandros." It may be based on the most painful and pressing of realities, the injustice of "Dry September," the waste and loss of "Babylon Revisited," and yet contain flashes of the fantastic—the nightmare idiocy of the lynching party, the feverish dream of Paris in the Jazz Age—which lead one to question the nature of reality. The very theme itself may be fantastic, as in "The Celestial Omnibus" and "The Rocking-Horse Winner," and yet render cogent comment on the verities of existence, such as the inviolability of art, the need for love.

Some of the stories are primarily stories of character and not of theme. "The Short Happy Life of Francis Macomber," "Noon Wine," "Goodbye, My Brother," and "In the Zoo" are examples. Francis Macomber, his wife, and the English hunter are first portrayed rather fully; then their characters develop in action and the action is developed through their characters; not even the excitement of the events in big-game hunting interferes with the gradual revelation of character, which leads subtly and painfully to an apparently inevitable end. "Noon Wine," rather than tracing the effect of character on event, shows the effect of event on character. It stems not from the observation that if people are thus, they must act so, but rather that if events are thus, they must have these results on these people. It moves toward its final effect with pace fully controlled and calculated.

"Goodbye, My Brother," traces the fundamental tension arising from the characters and ways of life of two brothers against a detailed background of a family on summer vacation. Throughout "In the Zoo," Mrs. Placer's suspicious and unhappy nature leaves its mark on everyone around her. She even changes the character of a pet dog from a friendly animal to a vicious defender of his mistress, "from an easy-going Gael to a loud-voiced Teuton." In both these stories, the settings are carefully used to support and intensify the main emphasis on character.

There is no "ideal" theme; there is also no "ideal" style. Each theme or group of characters demands in its conception a treatment suitable to it, and the ability of the artist is tested in meeting that demand. The structure of a story may be very simple and yet afford great opportunity for complexity and subtlety in characterization, as in "The Dead." The story may remain virtually stationary, as does "The Secret Life of Walter Mitty," which, through the clever description of one man's dreams, comments obliquely on the pitiful impotence and drab confined existence of an average man in our times, while, delightfully, it mocks the curious consolations and aspirations of humanity. Or it may move swiftly and inconspicuously through act after act of a highly personal and eventful drama as it focuses the reader's final attention on the eternal, philosophical joke of human littleness, as does "The Gioconda Smile."

The treatment of "The Lumber-Room" is slight and delicate as the child it concerns, cool, remote, and contemptuous as he is; yet the story sparkles with the secret joy of a boy's triumph over the coarse, obtuse adult world. "Keela, the Outcast Indian Maiden" deals with two men's memory of a cruelty; it is told for the most part by these two men themselves, one in words, the other in expressed, though unspoken, thoughts. The tale as such is not the important thing; told objectively it would be nothing. What is skillfully pointed up is the difference in attitude between the tellers, and it is pointed up by the technique of a story within a story.

The critical reader will not be satisfied with the "what happens next?" level of reading alone, nor should he be content simply with an analysis of technique. Again, as in the reading of poetry, the total effect and how it is accomplished should be the broad outline for study. With this in mind the reader will come to see the degrees of artistry represented in the stories. He will look upon the short-story writer as one who faces the problems of selection, emphasis, and medium in his art, as do poets, painters, and composers. He will understand that a good story is always under the complete control of the writer, and that suggestion rather than statement is a master tool of the short-story writer (here he might contrast stories such as Wagner's "Beat Down Frigid Rome" and Joyce's "The Dead").

More specifically, the understanding of style and method involves a study of several technical aspects of the art of the short story, some of which have been mentioned already. The critical reader should be aware of such important technical matters as narrative method and point of view. Who tells the story? Is it a character in the story or is it the author with an omniscient view of characters and action? Is the author or the narrator close to the events or at a distance, and for what reasons? What are the advantages of the narrative method and point of view selected?

Other questions of how the story is told follow readily. How does the story begin? What means are used to introduce characters and establish setting? If the story is one in which mood is of major importance, how is that mood or atmosphere created?

The scope and the emphasis of the story deserve careful attention, for herein the writer practices the difficult arts of selection and suggestion. How much in time, space, and idea does the story encompass? Does it place emphasis on character, on theme, on atmosphere, or on plot? Where and how has the author centered the reader's interest and attention within the story? What is the key moment in the story, and where is it placed? How has the author developed event, action, conflict, and character to build toward a key moment? Where and how has the author presented the climax of the story? How does the story end, and to what effect? Other elements such as pace or speed of the narrative and the disposition of details also fall under any critical view of the scope and emphasis of the story. Pace is perhaps one of the more difficult elements to understand and evaluate, but it is an important factor by which an author exercises control over the story and the reader's reactions. Ultimately, the study of scope and emphasis will reveal the structure, the pattern or design of a story. The question for the critical reader is the value of that total arrangement.

Of other elements which might be studied, the reader should not fail to look closely at dialogue and monologue. How do characters talk to each other and to themselves? What are the characteristics of their language, and how much of the narrative is carried by dialogue? What is the nature and effectiveness of monologue, both external and internal? What psychological aspects of the story are expressed through internal monologue?

The kind and use of symbols in a story also demand attention. Every story does not have to use symbols, of course, but if they are used what is their function and what do they contribute? Another powerful element, of drama and fiction particularly, is irony. To what effect does the writer employ irony? (Both for the use of symbols and irony Stafford's "In the Zoo" deserves careful study.)

Perhaps the critical reader will accept one more question. What is the nature of "knowledge" in the story? How convincingly has the author presented both the general and detailed qualities of character, setting, and atmosphere? Does the sheer force of *recognition* provided by realistic detail serve the story well or stand apart as an almost separate interest for the reader? How does the author gain the reader's acceptance of realistic or fantastic detail?

The editors do not mean to say that every short-story writer asks himself all these questions. The questions are for the critical reader. It is a commonplace observation about literary craftsmanship that an author may be aware of all the elements of interest to the student or critic without ever bothering to analyze what he has consciously or unconsciously chosen in every instance. The important thing for the user of this book is that he *see* thoroughly and understandingly what the author has done and how he has

done it. To that end the questions raised should be useful; they
are not offered, however, as the only approach to analysis.

The order of the stories very loosely represents an effort to
move from the less difficult to the more difficult, but the editors
have no intention of setting up a critical obstacle course of
increasingly complex traps and pitfalls. They would prefer to
have the reader begin where he will but to read at the level that
the stories themselves demand. Lastly, and without moralizing,
the editors remind the reader that intelligent analysis does not
destroy the short story or the poem; it is a step toward greater
appreciation and understanding of an art.

The Lumber-Room

"SAKI" (H. H. MUNRO, 1870–1916)

THE CHILDREN were to be driven, as a special treat, to the sands
at Jagborough. Nicholas was not to be of the party; he was in
disgrace. Only that morning he had refused to eat his wholesome bread-and-milk on the seemingly frivolous ground that
there was a frog in it. Older and wiser and better people had told
him that there could not possibly be a frog in his bread-and-milk
and that he was not to talk nonsense; he continued, nevertheless,
to talk what seemed the veriest nonsense, and described with much
detail the colouration and markings of the alleged frog. The
dramatic part of the incident was that there really was a frog
in Nicholas' basin of bread-and-milk; he had put it there himself, so he felt entitled to know something about it. The sin of
taking a frog from the garden and putting it into a bowl of wholesome bread-and-milk was enlarged on at great length, but the
fact that stood out clearest in the whole affair, as it presented
itself to the mind of Nicholas, was that the older, wiser, and better

people had been proved to be profoundly in error in matters about which they had expressed the utmost assurance.

"You said there couldn't possibly be a frog in my bread-and-milk; there *was* a frog in my bread-and-milk," he repeated, with the insistence of a skilled tactician who does not intend to shift from favourable ground.

So his boy-cousin and girl-cousin and his quite uninteresting younger brother were to be taken to Jagborough sands that afternoon and he was to stay at home. His cousins' aunt, who insisted, by an unwarranted stretch of imagination, in styling herself his aunt also, had hastily invented the Jagborough expedition in order to impress on Nicholas the delights that he had justly forfeited by his disgraceful conduct at the breakfast table. It was her habit, whenever one of the children fell from grace, to improvise something of a festival nature from which the offender would be rigorously debarred; if all the children sinned collectively they were suddenly informed of a circus in a neighbouring town, a circus of unrivalled merit and uncounted elephants, to which, but for their depravity, they would have been taken that very day.

A few decent tears were looked for on the part of Nicholas when the moment for the departure of the expedition arrived. As a matter of fact, however, all the crying was done by his girl-cousin, who scraped her knee rather painfully against the step of the carriage as she was scrambling in.

"How she did howl," said Nicholas cheerfully, as the party drove off without any of the elation of high spirits that should have characterized it.

"She'll soon get over that," said the *soi-disant* aunt; "it will be a glorious afternoon for racing about over those beautiful sands. How they will enjoy themselves!"

"Bobby won't enjoy himself much, and he won't race much either," said Nicholas with a grim chuckle; "his boots are hurting him. They're too tight."

"Why didn't he tell me they were hurting?" asked the aunt with some asperity.

"He told you twice, but you weren't listening. You often don't listen when we tell you important things."

"You are not to go into the gooseberry garden," said the aunt, changing the subject.

"Why not?" demanded Nicholas.

"Because you are in disgrace," said the aunt loftily.

Nicholas did not admit the flawlessness of the reasoning; he felt perfectly capable of being in disgrace and in a gooseberry garden at the same moment. His face took on an expression of considerable obstinacy. It was clear to his aunt that he was determined to get into the gooseberry garden, "only," as she remarked to herself, "because I have told him he is not to."

Now the gooseberry garden had two doors by which it might be entered, and once a small person like Nicholas could slip in there he could effectually disappear from view amid the masking growth of artichokes, raspberry canes, and fruit bushes. The aunt had many other things to do that afternoon, but she spent an hour or two in trivial gardening operations among flower beds and shrubberies, whence she could keep a watchful eye on the two doors that led to the forbidden paradise. She was a woman of few ideas, with immense powers of concentration.

Nicholas made one or two sorties into the front garden, wriggling his way with obvious stealth of purpose towards one or other of the doors, but never able for a moment to evade the aunt's watchful eye. As a matter of fact, he had no intention of trying to get into the gooseberry garden, but it was extremely convenient for him that his aunt should believe that he had; it was a belief that would keep her on self-imposed sentry-duty for the greater part of the afternoon. Having thoroughly confirmed and fortified her suspicions, Nicholas slipped back into the house and rapidly put into execution a plan of action that had long germinated in his brain. By standing on a chair in the library one could reach a shelf on which reposed a fat, important-looking key. The key was as important as it looked; it was the instrument which kept the mysteries of the lumber-room secure from unauthorized

intrusion, which opened a way only for aunts and such-like privileged persons. Nicholas had not had much experience of the
art of fitting keys into keyholes and turning locks, but for some
days past he had practised with the key of the schoolroom door;
he did not believe in trusting too much to luck and accident.
The key turned stiffly in the lock, but it turned. The door opened,
and Nicholas was in an unknown land, compared with which the
gooseberry garden was a stale delight, a mere material pleasure.

Often and often Nicholas had pictured to himself what the
lumber-room might be like, that region that was so carefully
sealed from youthful eyes and concerning which no questions
were ever answered. It came up to his expectations. In the first
place it was large and dimly lit, one high window opening on
to the forbidden garden being its only source of illumination. In
the second place it was a storehouse of unimagined treasures.
The aunt-by-assertion was one of those people who think that
things spoil by use and consign them to dust and damp by way
of preserving them. Such parts of the house as Nicholas knew best
were rather bare and cheerless, but here there were wonderful
things for the eye to feast on. First and foremost there was a piece
of framed tapestry that was evidently meant to be a fire-screen.
To Nicholas it was a living, breathing story; he sat down on a roll
of Indian hangings, glowing in wonderful colours beneath a layer
of dust, and took in all the details of the tapestry picture. A man,
dressed in the hunting costume of some remote period, had just
transfixed a stag with an arrow; it could not have been a difficult
shot because the stag was only one or two paces away from him;
in the thickly growing vegetation that the picture suggested it
would not have been difficult to creep up to a feeding stag, and
the two spotted dogs that were springing forward to join in the
chase had evidently been trained to keep to heel till the arrow
was discharged. That part of the picture was simple, if interesting, but did the huntsman see, what Nicholas saw, that four galloping wolves were coming in his direction through the wood?
There might be more than four of them hidden behind the trees,

and in any case would the man and his dogs be able to cope with the four wolves if they made an attack? The man had only two arrows left in his quiver, and he might miss with one or both of them; all one knew about his skill in shooting was that he could hit a large stag at a ridiculously short range. Nicholas sat for many golden minutes revolving the possibilities of the scene; he was inclined to think that there were more than four wolves and that the man and his dogs were in a tight corner.

But there were other objects of delight and interest claiming his instant attention: there were quaint twisted candlesticks in the shape of snakes, and a teapot fashioned like a china duck, out of whose open beak the tea was supposed to come. How dull and shapeless the nursery teapot seemed in comparison! And there was a carved sandal-wood box packed tight with aromatic cotton-wool, and between the layers of cotton-wool were little brass figures, hump-necked bulls, and peacocks and goblins, delightful to see and to handle. Less promising in appearance was a large square book with plain black covers; Nicholas peeped into it, and, behold, it was full of coloured pictures of birds. And such birds! In the garden, and in the lanes when he went for a walk, Nicholas came across a few birds, of which the largest were an occasional magpie or wood-pigeon; here were herons and bustards, kites, toucans, tiger-bitterns, brush turkeys, ibises, golden pheasants, a whole portrait gallery of undreamed-of creatures. And as he was admiring the colouring of the mandarin duck and assigning a life-history to it, the voice of his aunt in shrill vociferation of his name came from the gooseberry garden without. She had grown suspicious at his long disappearance, and had leapt to the conclusion that he had climbed over the wall behind the sheltering screen of the lilac bushes; she was now engaged in energetic and rather hopeless search for him among the artichokes and raspberry canes.

"Nicholas, Nicholas!" she screamed, "you are to come out of this at once. It's no use trying to hide there; I can see you all the time."

It was probably the first time for twenty years that any one had smiled in that lumber-room.

Presently the angry repetitions of Nicholas' name gave way to a shriek, and a cry for somebody to come quickly. Nicholas shut the book, restored it carefully to its place in a corner, and shook some dust from a neighbouring pile of newspapers over it. Then he crept from the room, locked the door, and replaced the key exactly where he had found it. His aunt was still calling his name when he sauntered into the front garden.

"Who's calling?" he asked.

"Me," came the answer from the other side of the wall; "didn't you hear me? I've been looking for you in the gooseberry garden, and I've slipped into the rain-water tank. Luckily there's no water in it, but the sides are slippery and I can't get out. Fetch the little ladder from under the cherry tree—"

"I was told I wasn't to go into the gooseberry garden," said Nicholas promptly.

"I told you not to, and now I tell you that you may," came the voice from the rain-water tank, rather impatiently.

"Your voice doesn't sound like aunt's," objected Nicholas; "you may be the Evil One tempting me to be disobedient. Aunt often tells me that the Evil One tempts me and that I always yield. This time I'm not going to yield."

"Don't talk nonsense," said the prisoner in the tank; "go and fetch the ladder."

"Will there be strawberry jam for tea?" asked Nicholas innocently.

"Certainly there will be," said the aunt, privately resolving that Nicholas should have none of it.

"Now I know that you are the Evil One and not aunt," shouted Nicholas gleefully; "when we asked aunt for strawberry jam yesterday she said there wasn't any. I know there are four jars of it in the store cupboard, because I looked, and of course you know it's there, but *she* doesn't, because she said there wasn't any. Oh, Devil, you *have* sold yourself!"

There was an unusual sense of luxury in being able to talk to an aunt as though one was talking to the Evil One, but Nicholas knew, with childish discernment, that such luxuries were not to be over-indulged in. He walked noisily away, and it was a kitchen-maid, in search of parsley, who eventually rescued the aunt from the rain-water tank.

Tea that evening was partaken of in a fearsome silence. The tide had been at its highest when the children had arrived at Jagborough Cove, so there had been no sands to play on—a circumstance that the aunt had overlooked in the haste of organizing her punitive expedition. The tightness of Bobby's boots had had disastrous effect on his temper the whole of the afternoon, and altogether the children could not have been said to have enjoyed themselves. The aunt maintained the frozen muteness of one who has suffered undignified and unmerited detention in a rain-water tank for thirty-five minutes. As for Nicholas, he, too, was silent, in the absorption of one who has much to think about; it was just possible, he considered, that the huntsman would escape with his hounds while the wolves feasted on the stricken stag.

The Secret Life of Walter Mitty

JAMES THURBER (1894–1961)

"WE'RE GOING through!" The Commander's voice was like thin ice breaking. He wore his full-dress uniform, with the heavily braided white cap pulled down rakishly over one cold gray eye. "We can't make it, sir. It's spoiling for a hurricane, if you ask

THE SECRET LIFE OF WALTER MITTY is reprinted by permission. Copyright 1939, James Thurber. Originally published in *The New Yorker*.

me." "I'm not asking you, Lieutenant Berg," said the Commander. "Throw on the power light! Rev her up to 8,500! We're going through!" The pounding of the cylinders increased: ta-pocketa-pocketa-pocketa-*pocketa-pocketa*. The Commander stared at the ice forming on the pilot window. He walked over and twisted a row of complicated dials. "Switch on No. 8 auxiliary!" he shouted. "Switch on No. 8 auxiliary!" repeated Lieutenant Berg. "Full strength in No. 3 turret!" shouted the Commander. "Full strength in No. 3 turret!" The crew, bending to their various tasks in the huge, hurtling eight-engined Navy hydroplane, looked at each other and grinned. "The Old Man'll get us through," they said to one another. "The Old Man ain't afraid of Hell!" . . .

"Not so fast! You're driving too fast!" said Mrs. Mitty. "What are you driving so fast for?"

"Hmm?" said Walter Mitty. He looked at his wife, in the seat beside him, with shocked astonishment. She seemed grossly unfamiliar, like a strange woman who had yelled at him in a crowd. "You were up to fifty-five," she said. "You know I don't like to go more than forty. You were up to fifty-five." Walter Mitty drove on toward Waterbury in silence, the roaring of the SN202 through the worst storm in twenty years of Navy flying fading in the remote, intimate airways of his mind. "You're tensed up again," said Mrs. Mitty. "It's one of your days. I wish you'd let Dr. Renshaw look you over."

Walter Mitty stopped the car in front of the building where his wife went to have her hair done. "Remember to get those overshoes while I'm having my hair done," she said. "I don't need overshoes," said Mitty. She put her mirror back into her bag. "We've been all through that," she said, getting out of the car. "You're not a young man any longer." He raced the engine a little. "Why don't you wear your gloves? Have you lost your gloves?" Walter Mitty reached in a pocket and brought out the gloves. He put them on, but after she had turned and gone into the building and he had driven on to a red light, he took them off again. "Pick it up, brother!" snapped a cop as the light changed, and

Mitty hastily pulled on his gloves and lurched ahead. He drove around the streets aimlessly for a time, and then he drove past the hospital on his way to the parking lot.

. . . "It's the millionaire banker, Wellington McMillan," said the pretty nurse. "Yes?" said Walter Mitty, removing his gloves slowly. "Who has the case?" "Dr. Renshaw and Dr. Benbow, but there are two specialists here, Dr. Remington from New York and Mr. Pritchard-Mitford from London. He flew over." A door opened down a long, cool corridor and Dr. Renshaw came out. He looked distraught and haggard. "Hello, Mitty," he said. "We're having the devil's own time with McMillan, the millionaire banker and close personal friend of Roosevelt. Obstreosis of the ductal tract. Tertiary. Wish you'd take a look at him." "Glad to," said Mitty.

In the operating room there were whispered introductions: "Dr. Remington, Dr. Mitty. Mr. Pritchard-Mitford, Dr. Mitty." "I've read your book on streptothricosis," said Pritchard-Mitford, shaking hands. "A brilliant performance, sir." "Thank you," said Walter Mitty. "Didn't know you were in the States, Mitty," grumbled Remington. "Coals to Newcastle, bringing Mitford and me up here for a tertiary." "You are very kind," said Mitty. A huge, complicated machine, connected to the operating table, with many tubes and wires, began at this moment to go pocketa-pocketa-pocketa. "The new anesthetizer is giving way!" shouted an interne. "There is no one in the East who knows how to fix it!" "Quiet, man!" said Mitty, in a low, cool voice. He sprang to the machine, which was now going pocketa-pocketa-queep-pocketa-queep. He began fingering delicately a row of glistening dials. "Give me a fountain pen!" he snapped. Someone handed him a fountain pen. He pulled a faulty piston out of the machine and inserted the pen in its place. "That will hold for ten minutes," he said. "Get on with the operation." A nurse hurried over and whispered to Renshaw, and Mitty saw the man turn pale. "Coreopsis has set in," said Renshaw nervously. "If you would take over, Mitty?" Mitty looked at him and at the craven figure of

Benbow, who drank, and at the grave, uncertain faces of the two great specialists. "If you wish," he said. They slipped a white gown on him; he adjusted a mask and drew on thin gloves; nurses handed him shining . . .

"Back it up, Mac! Look out for that Buick!" Walter Mitty jammed on the brakes. "Wrong lane, Mac," said the parking-lot attendant, looking at Mitty closely. "Gee. Yeh," muttered Mitty. He began cautiously to back out of the lane marked "Exit Only." "Leave her sit there," said the attendant. "I'll put her away." Mitty got out of the car. "Hey, better leave the key." "Oh," said Mitty, handing the man the ignition key. The attendant vaulted into the car, backed it up with insolent skill, and put it where it belonged.

They're so damn cocky, thought Walter Mitty, walking along Main Street; they think they know everything. Once he had tried to take his chains off, outside New Milford, and he had got them wound around the axles. A man had had to come out in a wrecking car and unwind them, a young, grinning garageman. Since then Mrs. Mitty always made him drive to a garage to have the chains taken off. The next time, he thought, I'll wear my right arm in a sling; they won't grin at me then. I'll have my right arm in a sling and they'll see I couldn't possibly take the chains off myself. He kicked at the slush on the sidewalk. "Over-shoes," he said to himself, and he began looking for a shoe store.

When he came out into the street again, with the overshoes in a box under his arm, Walter Mitty began to wonder what the other thing was his wife had told him to get. She had told him twice, before they set out from their house for Waterbury. In a way he hated these weekly trips to town—he was always getting something wrong. Kleenex, he thought, Squibb's, razor blades? No. Toothpaste, toothbrush, bicarbonate, carborundum, initiative and referendum? He gave it up. But she would remember it. "Where's the what's-its-name?" she would ask. "Don't tell me you forgot the what's-its-name." A newsboy went by shouting something about the Waterbury trial.

. . . "Perhaps this will refresh your memory." The District

Attorney suddenly thrust a heavy automatic at the quiet figure on the witness stand. "Have you ever seen this before?" Walter Mitty took the gun and examined it expertly. "This is my Webley-Vickers 50.80," he said calmly. An excited buzz ran around the courtroom. The judge rapped for order. "You are a crack shot with any sort of firearms, I believe?" said the District Attorney, insinuatingly. "Objection!" shouted Mitty's attorney. "We have shown that the defendant could not have fired the shot. We have shown that he wore his right arm in a sling on the night of the fourteenth of July." Walter Mitty raised his hand briefly and the bickering attorneys were stilled. "With any known make of gun," he said evenly, "I could have killed Gregory Fitzhurst at three hundred feet *with my left hand*." Pandemonium broke loose in the courtroom. A woman's scream rose above the bedlam and suddenly a lovely, dark-haired girl was in Walter Mitty's arms. The District Attorney struck at her savagely. Without rising from his chair, Mitty let the man have it on the point of the chin. "You miserable cur!" . . .

"Puppy biscuit," said Walter Mitty. He stopped walking and the buildings of Waterbury rose up out of the misty courtroom and surrounded him again. A woman who was passing laughed. "He said 'Puppy biscuit,' " she said to her companion. "That man said 'Puppy biscuit' to himself." Walter Mitty hurried on. He went into an A. & P., not the first one he came to but a smaller one farther up the street. "I want some biscuit for small, young dogs," he said to the clerk. "Any special brand, sir?" The greatest pistol shot in the world thought a moment. "It says 'Puppies Bark for It' on the box," said Walter Mitty.

His wife would be through at the hairdresser's in fifteen minutes, Mitty saw in looking at his watch, unless they had trouble drying it; sometimes they had trouble drying it. She didn't like to get to the hotel first; she would want him to be there waiting for her as usual. He found a big leather chair in the lobby, facing a window, and he put the overshoes and the puppy biscuit on the floor beside it. He picked up an old copy of *Liberty* and sank down into the chair. "Can Germany Conquer the World Through the Air?" Walter Mitty looked at the pictures of bombing planes and of ruined streets.

. . . "The cannonading has got the wind up in young Raleigh, sir," said the sergeant. Captain Mitty looked up at him through tousled hair. "Get him to bed," he said wearily. "With the others. I'll fly alone." "But you can't, sir," said the sergeant anxiously. "It takes two men to handle that bomber and the Archies are pounding hell out of the air. Von Richtman's circus is between here and Saulier." "Somebody's got to get that ammunition dump," said Mitty. "I'm going over. Spot of brandy?" He poured a drink for the sergeant and one for himself. War thundered and whined around the dugout and battered at the door. There was a rending of wood and splinters flew through the room. "A bit of a near thing," said Captain Mitty carelessly. "The box barrage is closing in," said the sergeant. "We only live once, Sergeant," said Mitty, with his faint, fleeting smile. "Or do we?" He poured another brandy and tossed it off. "I never see a man could hold his brandy like you, sir," said the sergeant. "Begging your pardon, sir." Captain Mitty stood up and strapped on his huge Webley-Vickers automatic. "It's forty kilometers through hell, sir," said the sergeant. Mitty finished one last brandy. "After all," he said softly, "what isn't?" The pounding of the cannon increased; there was the rat-tat-tatting of machine guns, and from somewhere came the menacing pocketa-pocketa-pocketa of the new flame-throwers. Walter Mitty walked to the door of the dugout humming "Auprès de Ma Blonde." He turned and waved to the sergeant. "Cheerio!" he said. . . .

Something struck his shoulder. "I've been looking all over this hotel for you," said Mrs. Mitty. "Why do you have to hide in this old chair? How did you expect me to find you?" "Things close in," said Walter Mitty vaguely. "What?" Mrs. Mitty said. "Did you get the what's-its-name? The puppy biscuit? What's in that box?" "Overshoes," said Mitty. "Couldn't you have put them on in the store?" "I was thinking," said Walter Mitty. "Does it ever occur to you that I am sometimes thinking?" She looked at him. "I'm going to take your temperature when I get you home," she said.

They went out through the revolving doors that made a faintly derisive whistling sound when you pushed them. It was two blocks to the parking lot. At the drugstore on the corner she said, "Wait here for me. I forgot something. I won't be a minute." She was more than a minute. Walter Mitty lighted a cigarette. It began to rain, rain with sleet in it. He stood up against the wall of the drugstore, smoking. . . . He put his shoulders back and his heels together. "To hell with the handkerchief," said Walter Mitty scornfully. He took one last drag on his cigarette and snapped it away. Then, with that faint, fleeting smile playing about his lips, he faced the firing squad; erect and motionless, proud and disdainful, Walter Mitty the Undefeated, inscrutable to the last.

Beat Down Frigid Rome

ESTHER WAGNER (1917–   )

THE BELL HAD just rung for the first period, and old Latimer threw open the door with one of his long-armed, extravagant, precisely controlled gestures. He stood back to supervise with his cold ancient-looking smile the entry of his Latin I class from the Gothic marches of the corridors to the centurion atmosphere of his classroom. He had a trick of fixing his eyes on the feet of his students as they crossed the doorsill, an elaborately blank

Reprinted from *The Atlantic Monthly*, April 1958, by permission of the author.

glance which stilled the last flap of every loafer, deadened the last clump of every ski boot. At the end of this morning's stream of feet came a pair of unobtrusively foreign-made, cordovan-polished brogues, and old Latimer shifted his gaze to the unlined pleasant face of his colleague, Mr. Merton, English teacher and Administrative Assistant to the Dean of Boys.

All the faculty felt rather sorry for Merton, who had to handle the college admissions correspondence and was continually writing hopeful, covertly pleading letters to the deans of admission of the great Eastern colleges. Merton had to give them the hard sell on sons of three generations of Harvard or Yale or Hurstleigh men who now found themselves doubtful candidates because they had made a couple of C's in junior year. He resented this, remembering his own easy admission to the most august of colleges during the depression years, and sometimes thinking almost savagely of their jowled fathers, survivors of the Cretaceous age of the gentleman's C. Worst of all, he couldn't even be certain that his sure-fire candidates would get just where they wanted to go.

He now brought in to old Latimer a sheaf of application papers and a student's dossier in a battered manila folder, from which a wild-eyed photograph unpromisingly slopped over at the top.

"Lang's application for the Hurstleigh scholarship, sir," he muttered, looking warily at the nearest amorphous little countenances staring apprehensively at the assignment on the blackboard or bowed in swift vocabulary review. "Here's their stuff about qualifications, and Lang's papers. The Head would like to have your letter today if it's at all possible."

"Fourth period, or end of third," said old Latimer with the effortless laconic air which marked everything he said and did. He could make long speeches or perform the most complex personal rituals without ever letting go his characteristic effects of concision, condensation, compression. No one ever analyzed these effects or dissected his techniques; the Head never sent student teachers to work under him, though they were always assigned to visit his classes in the capacity of audience. His authority was beyond formulation. The Head was the Head; the Dean was the Little Corporal or the Boss-man; the Old Man was Latimer, who had no administrative position whatever, no connection with the faculty council, was never put on committees or made Sponsor of anything. He was the Old Man of the Mountain, the Old Man of the Sea. The funny thing was that he wasn't even very old: fifty-five at the most, with thick silver-fox hair.

Merton left and the freshmen were silent. The door swung to with a click, and there rose behind it the great strange atmosphere of the Latin room, haunting to generations of students, compounded of the smell of Latimer's old beautiful tweeds, the wild fragrance of the ferns in his extravagant window boxes, the stone eyes of the Roman senators in prints on the front wall, the glint of gold letters on the leather bindings ranged on the desk, the complex lines of the small, fiercely exact reproduction of a Roman trireme encased in glass.

Old Latimer's classes always began quietly enough. The students lifted their faces to him, confident, expecting something to happen. Some waited for the great gusts of temper that swept the room rhythmically, periodically, like the rise and fall of some giant breathing chest. Some hoped for a dramatic chastisement, in baritone shout or chill sibilant whisper, of some classmate; some simply wished to escape this. Old Latimer never had any trouble with discipline and never thought about it.

Now he ran rapidly over the vocabulary, asking for meanings of words, principal parts of verbs, suddenly swooping to demand a whole declension, the total conjugation of one of the hard tenses, like the future passive of the -io verbs. For good answers he gave his swift wolfish smile, baring an astonishingly long, sharp left incisor. For a slow one he waited in impassive, gentlemanly patience or in the most ill-concealed ennui, rolling up his eyes, shaking his chalk in his hand. The choice of manner

depended on the personality of the student, the past performances, known ability, standing of the student after some scene
of the day before, and so on.

Over kitten-like, earnest little Emily Rushmore in the front
row, struggling with the forms of the infinitive in her accustomed
style of mixed timidity and stubbornness, valor and misgiving,
he lingered long, hinting, grinning, exhorting, correcting, suddenly thrusting his large-boned brilliant-eyed countenance within
one inch of hers to hiss an ending at her, bowing with a genuine
smiling courtesy when she hit happily on a correct form. The
little girl's face lit and shadowed, her eyelids drooped or lifted,
following this peculiar orchestration. Latimer pressed her on to
the fifth declension, new for the day; her maunderings over this
caused him suddenly to throw up his hands, throw out his arms,
throw back his head, and shout: "Emily Rushmore! Emily
Rushmore!" Out came the rush of eloquence all knew would
come, this time untinged with violence, just ringing with passion, elevated, sincere. In the great hills of North Dakota, he
informed her, where the Sioux thought there abided forever the
spirits of the dead, there was a great slab of mountain which
bore her name. He called to her mind the images of great men
hewn there by tremendous effort. Even so, he told her, he had
hewn into the great slabs of her blank child's mind the forms
of the four great Latin declensions, "complete, Emily, with
mutations and characteristic variations from the norm—the -i
of the ablative of *mare, insigne, animal, exemplar.*" The low
beautiful baritone rose to a deep shout as he showered on her
the epithets of Slab, Granite Hillside, Erstwhile Smooth Expanse. "And now you boggle at the second -i in *diei,*" he added,
suddenly in a normal, conversational voice, and smiled.

Emily began to relax; a delicate little giggle escaped her and
a deep chortle spread through the class.

"Now, the translation," said old Latimer, smothering a yawn.
"It's a simplified little anecdote taken from the *Aeneid,* which
you—*some* of you, I mean—will be reading late next year."

He piloted them through the short story of Aeneas' landing on the coast near Carthage, Dido's reception of him, the banquet, and the beginning of the tale. He excoriated someone for making a passive active, praised someone for making the historical present a past, explained neatly and lucidly the Roman attitude toward the order of words, reminded everyone that some ablatives of manner take *cum* and some do not take *cum*, assigned a lesson dealing with the comparison of irregular adjectives, pointed out to everyone that the translation for that lesson described the love of Dido for Aeneas and incarnated the idea of romantic love which most appealed to the ancient world, "not *exactly* a valentine affair! June and moon were not its symbols, but chains and fire and destroying disease; naked force and terrible pain. Here is great Virgil telling about Dido wandering through the city, burned with it, pierced with it, sick with it . . ." and the deep beautiful voice rolled over the classroom in a tide of unintelligible sound, as strongly marked by rhythm as any music they had ever heard:

> Heu vatum ignarae mentes! quid vota furentem,
> quid delubra iuvant? Est mollis flamma medullas
> interea, et tacitum vivit sub pectore volnus.
> Uritur infelix Dido . . .

Over the faces of two or three, the incantation seekers, who would never forget this face or room, this sound, so long as they lived, came the drop-jawed, feeble-minded look of total acceptance they habitually wore at these moments. The bell rang; old Latimer seemed suddenly to forget the whole thing, smiled his briskest smile, said, "All right, now *watch those irregulars*," and flung open his door.

In every school there is one teacher concerning whom a rumor circulates that he has a large personal fortune and teaches not for money but from some obscure disinterested motive. In Latimer's school this role fell naturally to him, and each generation increased the collection of wild stories about his personal life and background. The man's clothes, bearing, accent, all suggested some world of personal autonomy and distinction totally foreign to their own world of hard-working, commuting, cocktail-drinking, sense-talking older men, with their ordinary expensive suits, their speech full of flat *a*'s, slurred consonants, dulled vowels (*guv'munt*), and familiar well-understood words.

He seemed also a fortuitous ambassador from some world quite different from that represented by their other teachers. All this was augmented by the fact that nobody really did know anything much about Latimer. The students all knew that he was an accomplished athlete; he played an almost embarrassingly good game of tennis for one so old, was seen with his wife on golf links and on the bridle paths. He skated on the school pond once or twice a year, with great competence, using a fine pair of Austrian skates. But he coached no teams, never talked of sports or went to football games.

The faculty knew with a fair degree of certainty that he had taught in several Eastern colleges and in at least one of the great prep schools, and that there was some quite exciting story about his marriage to the mother of one of his pupils. The tall dashing-looking woman whom everybody knew only as Mrs. Latimer certainly was not a very representative faculty wife. She was more than merely civil, really friendly in a fast-talking, brilliantly smiling way. She gave a large cocktail party once a year for all the faculty and served very good food and drinks. She wore dark red or dark green or purple tweeds in the daytime and black silk in the evening. It was thought that she had many friends "in town"—not in the suburb where the school was located—and that these were not suburban types. Nobody ever saw her in the summer. She and her husband simply disappeared off the Middle Western map, to return always just in time for the opening reception given by the Head, coming into it as though they had never been away, hard and precise in physical outline, clipped of speech, vague and uninformative in conversation.

Parents and other teachers quite often felt that Latimer did not take as much personal interest in the students as was the prevailing mode at the school. Certainly he spent little time on his inept and failing students. But no one dared reproach him with this, in view of the long fanatical hours he devoted to helping the middle range of his students, lavishing upon them his burning gaze, his infinite powers of dramatization, his gifts of lucid explanation and varied repetition, in an impassioned effort to bring them out of their uncertainties and into that state of life where they could translate with confidence, decline and conjugate with aplomb, recognize without hesitation the landmarks of early Latin studies, indirect discourse, purpose clauses, and the like. He never spoke to these students or to any others about their outside life, never allowed them to speak of their family routines or their home atmospheres. They could not feel that he was interested in them as human beings; it seemed unlikely that he ever thought of them as such, and probable that he did not consider them people as they had been taught to expect that their teachers would.

Not one of them resented this. Indeed, it seemed to relieve them, a cool, sharp, stinging astringent applied to the irritations of their adolescence. And for all his lack of interest in their personal existences, when he turned that deep brilliant glance upon them to see what they knew about the passive periphrastic or whether they had studied the vocabulary, they felt *noticed* as in few other departments of their lives.

Old Latimer cared no more for himself as a human being than he did for them. His mad histrionics and Dionysian outbursts were not designed to compel their admiration nor to impose upon them a sense of his autocracy and difference. They were teaching devices. For all his personal complexities and the baroque, even rococo fabric of his individual being, he was the one person of power in their lives who wished and demanded of them something really simple and clear in outline. He wanted them to learn Latin.

He now looked down at the little mess of papers on his desk. The face of his best student, Robert Lang, looked wildly up at him from the photograph, denuded of its habitual steel-rimmed glasses. He picked up the Hurstleigh folder on the classical scholarship, prepared by a man he knew well and coldly disliked, a representative at classical meetings and archaeological congresses of the billboard world of Rotarianism, adjustment, genial cooperation, and general group dynamics. Latimer narrowed his eyes and tossed the folder aside. Next he picked up the general statement of Hurstleigh's Dean of Admissions on the college's admission policies. His eye fell on the phrase "breadth of extracurricular interests" and, further on, "ability to function effectively in the group," and a savage scowl twisted the upper part of his face. It disappeared as he looked up to see Lang entering the room and quietly closing the door behind him.

The exotic airs generated in the classroom during the freshman class were dissipated in an instant as Latimer's senior student took his seat immediately opposite the master's chair and smiled his thin smile. Anything less "all-round" than the appearance and personal atmosphere of Robert Lang would be difficult to imagine. From head to foot of his physical being the general stigmata of unattractive adolescence were surcharged by the presence of an imposing array of particularities. Behind a fierce hedge of skin disorders and scattered bristle, under a layer of impermanent childish flesh, slept a fine regular profile and a nobly sculptured jawbone. But the boy's pale eyes shone with the fanaticisms of the early-blooming specialist; his encrusted shirt collar, bedraggled Fair Isle sweater, smudged shoes spoke of the sacrifice of one order of fastidiousness to another.

Latimer always sat at his desk during his conferences with

Lang. He spoke in even, courteous tones, both friendly and remote, as one gentleman addressing another slightly younger. "What is it today, Bob?" he asked quietly, taking up his green Cicero and leafing through its opening pages.

"The peroration from the *Pro Cluentio*, sir," said Lang, and began to translate from his little student's edition. The flowery and passionate appeal for the life of an upright man unjustly charged with a low murder, the crown of the great lawyer's defense against a prosecution which had moved almost exclusively in the territories of political and class prejudice, took shape in effortless English. Here and there Lang paused for a moment to comment on a series of gerundives, to mention the names of less familiar grammatical constructions, to guess at the reason for a curious ordering of phrases.

Latimer listened in silence, inclining his head, turning the pages, catching the boy's eye from time to time over the top of his book and communicating assent. At the end he nodded gravely and said, "All right. Now read a bit of the Latin, Bob, and remember the trouble we had last time with the long *i*'s." Lang looked up from his page and did not look back at it as he recited the last section from memory, his eyes plunged deep into Latimer's. *"Orat vos Habitus, iudices, et flens obsecrat"*—his voice sank and deepened at the end of the clause, in imitation not of Latimer but of his own notion of Cicero's tones at this melodramatic moment. Latimer permitted himself a discreet smile.

"Well, Bob?" he asked, as the dying fall faded away. Lang's smile, as discreet as his own, commented restrainedly on the last measures of the speech.

"Well, sir . . . of course you can't miss the Old Silvertongue in it, the Clarence Darrow touch; naturally he had to overdo it, with that jury, and all the emotion hung over from the other trial, eight years before. But you can't help admiring his judgment. He brings it out about old Sassia being an unnatural mother and rubs it in about her coming up for the trial, such a terrible old bitch that nobody could miss it, even in the country towns. Then he pulls out the stops about Cluentius 'weeping begs you to restore him to his life, his kinsmen' and the rest of it, and then to bring up the old prejudice from the other trial when Cluentius bribed the jury—that really took nerve. Nobody else would have dared; they would have ended with the boo-hoo stuff. I think he's great. The trouble is, you can feel him thinking it, too. And you can tell he despised the jury and the court and the whole system. But it's good. You feel he knows his business. It's the thing you really can like about him in these straight law cases where he's just *being* a lawyer, the best in Rome, and forgetting the rest of it."

"The rest of it?"

"Yes, being the great philosopher and the father of his country and all that stuff that spoils him later on. The pleasures of old age part, the hysterical old woman part, all that."

"Bob," said Latimer in a soft idle voice, twirling a gold pencil, "what do you want at Hurstleigh with that scholarship? What are you going to do in college?"

"I don't know exactly, sir," said Lang, surprised. "Just learn Greek, I guess. Read the other Latin stuff. Try archaeology and history. Just be a classicist—learn to be one, I mean."

"Is that what you want? Just to *be* a classicist?"

"Well . . . I don't know yet what part of it I can go in for permanently. I've got to find that out."

"What, do you suppose," inquired the Old Man, a sharp, flinty note edging into his voice, "is the role of the classicist in our present society?" Bob Lang caught and held his eyes in another of those long, profoundly calm gazes. He shrugged, without impertinence. "I don't know much about it. I only know about a couple: Professor Hanley, I guess, and Ladislaw."

"Hanley! Yes, Hanley lives like a duke at what passes for a great university. He has his cigarettes and his jackets made for him in London, and he makes a large thing out of teaching the boys the names of the wines they ought to like. He does give good parties, that I'll say for him, and he keeps his invitation cards piled up on his mantel, and they *do* pile up. Everybody asks him to write introductions for their new little translation or their new little historical novel. But that, my dear Lang, is not a classicist. That is the Master of Hixon House. That is—uh, let's say, a personality."

Lang looked slightly alarmed, not so much at this novel portrait of an august figure, hitherto a name on a title page and in a catalogue, as at the sudden crackling tone in the Old Man's voice. Since he had been taken out of the regular Latin class in the middle of his second year, two years ago, he had not seen any of Latimer's famous histrionics. There was a code drawn silently between the two. It was understood that this sort of thing was not necessary.

"Ladislaw!" continued the Old Man, his voice picking up speed, though still low-pitched. "You are probably unaware, Lang, that Ladislaw reaches the age of retirement next year. Last year he had performed on himself a brain operation known as a frontal lobotomy, calculated to remove from the sufferer all traces of the anxieties and tensions which have been disordering his personality, and with them all sense of responsibility and involvement in the knottier questions of life. I understand the result has been quite striking. Both Ladislaw and his administration can envisage the next year with fortitude, if not exactly with equanimity. Equanimity is, I am afraid, quite out of the question in the Ladislaw affair. But at any rate, the enrollment in classical studies at his university has for the past decade been such that it will not be necessary to replace him."

A violent silence fell. He resumed, speaking now with great weariness, "My friend, the poet Raphael Stein, maintains a very good position at Essex Academy. His students graduate with distinction, are joyously accepted everywhere simply on his say-so, and go on to major in government, history, economics, journalism —on his advice. The knowledge of Greek and Roman letters with which he has equipped them often stays with them, as a sort of interior decoration of the mind, for quite a while before it is relegated to the mental attic where, in most of their cases, one can only admit that it belongs. But Stein is not a classicist; he is a poet, who has found an agreeable, even quite sympathetic means of support.

"Throckmorton instructs young ladies in the number of half a dozen or so annually; he retires this year, and they are replacing him with a Scotchman who will devote most of his energies to the teaching of theology. Interest in religion and anthropology grows; the classics departments are, my boy, becoming more and more interdepartmental. It may perhaps be possible for you to make use of these bodies of knowledge as stalking horses, or as ritual masks, behind which you may carry on undisturbed your classicist's freakish endeavors."

"What about the department at Hurstleigh, sir?" asked Lang in the manner of one who more or less changes the subject. There was no answer. Latimer snapped off the point of his gold pencil, looked out the window, and let the matter drop. Feeling the need to get the conference back on that impersonal level which had for years now been the scene of his most profoundly enjoyable experiences, Lang introduced another theme.

"I was reading a poem of Yeats's last night," he said cautiously, feeling his way a bit. "It goes at the end: *Whence had they come, The hand and lash that beat down frigid Rome?* [1] I couldn't quite make it out. Why 'frigid'?"

"Oh, just to suggest something cold and resistant, not easily beaten down, I imagine," said the Old Man in the same low weary tone. "Good question, that *Whence had they come?* He has a poem about Whiggery, too: *All's Whiggery now . . .*"

"Can't get what he's trying to bring out with that 'Whiggery,' either," said Lang. "Mr. Fletcher told us what the Whigs were, and all, but it doesn't help much."

"The man himself tells you, boy! 'A levelling, rancorous, rational sort of mind.' You read a lot, don't you? Tell me what you see in Latin! What's *in* it for you?"

[1] *Editors' note:* Yeats's poem is printed below, p. 732.

At it again, thought Lang. But with perfect aplomb he began to look round for something true to tell the Old Man. "Well, at first I thought it was the language itself, the constructions and all that. I like the syntax, and thinking about the forms. Take that motto, for instance, they're always using in the Renaissance: *Nec spe nec metu.* You see it in the corner of old maps all the time. Well, if it's an ablative of manner it would mean 'with neither hope nor fear,' and just bring out a kind of stoicism, a stiff-upper-lip attitude, ready to take the rough with the smooth. But it shouldn't be an ablative of manner: no *cum,* and no adjective to let them off the *cum.* Some exceptions, like *dolo*—but not many. So if it's an ablative of cause, it changes the whole thing: 'Neither because of hope nor because of fear,' and it means the man's doing whatever he's doing not because he wants to get something out of it, not because he's afraid of what will happen if he doesn't, but just because he wants to. Probably because of the thing itself. That sort of thing is interesting to think about; interesting to me, anyway. But this year, and last year with Virgil, there's a lot more to it. You start to get an idea of what it was like, with them. I guess I just *like* the Romans. They're my type, I mean." He grinned suddenly and added, "*Romani nil me alienum puto,* you could say."

Latimer grinned back at him over the pun. The bell rang. Lang snapped out of it, gathered up his books and papers, looked curiously at his folder on Latimer's desk, snuffled a bit, and lurched out of the room.

The Old Man stared after him, then turned his glance to the pile of papers. He took up the recommendation blank, unscrewed his fine gold fountain pen, and began to write rapidly.

Gentlemen:

I am requested to write in support of the application of my student Robert Lang for admission to your freshman class as Wroxbury Scholar. As I read your statements concerning your freshman class and concerning this scholarship, I find myself rather at a loss. It seems unlikely to me that Robert Lang will satisfy your most important requirements. It is with regret that I write this, but I feel that candor is in order.

The boy is the most brilliant scholar I have ever prepared. There is small doubt that his performance on the College Board will be as near perfect as the circumstances of the examination allow. His mastery of the language is complete, or nearly so; his acquaintance with Roman civilization of the late republican and early imperial period is broad and his understanding of it sensitive. He can compose sensible and elegant Latin sentences. His translations are unexceptionable both in accuracy and in grace. In short, it is difficult to imagine him as a member of your first-year Latin class under Professor Speidel.

Furthermore, it would be idle to pretend that he has profited from or enjoyed his experience as manager of the basketball squad here this winter. The duties of the position demanded nothing but a little correspondence, and attendance at the games; when Lang had fulfilled these obligations, which he found tedious but not difficult, he considered that he had done what was required. His participation in the group emotions and satisfactions made available to him through this experience was, in fact, minimal.

The truth is that Lang's extracurricular interests are not broad in the sense you intend. His grasp of three languages, Latin, French, *and* English, and his continually expanding acquaintance with the literature and histories, ancient and modern, preserved in these languages, have made it somewhat difficult for him to "function effectively in the group," if I may be forgiven for borrowing a phrase of yours. In fact, Lang's group considers him very odd indeed, and rightly so.

His complexion falls far short of the Hurstleigh ideal, and I fear his posture is inelegant. Should you wish me to supply you with any further relevant information, and should this information be in my possession, I shall of course be happy to furnish you with more details.

Very truly yours.

As the Old Man signed this letter, the door opened to admit Mr. Merton, hands full of folders and papers as usual. The young man smiled with satisfaction as he saw that the recommendation was complete and ready for the Head. Remembering with pleasure that Lang had made the highest score on record in the entire country on the junior College Board in Latin the last year, and permitting himself to hope for at least one easy admission, he stretched out his hand for the paper and let his eye run quickly over it. His expression changed rapidly as he took in the sense of the clear fine writing. Amusement and irritation gave way to a real indignation as he suddenly imagined himself showing this thing to the Head. He scowled and drew in his breath to launch his protest; then his eyes fell on Latimer, staring up at him, a muscle fluttering wildly near the temple, perspiration standing coldly at the hairline. The passion in the clawed old face was appalling.

Merton's voice stopped in his throat, and for a moment he heard nothing but the bumping, plunging of his heart. Horrified, he watched tears gather in Latimer's eyes. Silent, he left the room, clutching the sheet of paper with his others. As the bell screamed through the hall he darted on an impulse into the boys' washroom, happily empty, and leaned against the wall for a moment. He was quite young, an English teacher of the new school, full of ideas about communication; but he was not stupid, not unread, and above all not insensitive. He simply felt that it wasn't normal to be invaded by this kind of thing at ten thirty in the morning. He waited passively, unresentfully, for the harsh grip of pity and terror to relax, before he should plunge again into the whirling, clattering corridor of the last period before Morning Exercise.

Dear Alexandros

JOHN UPDIKE (1932–   )

TRANSLATION *of a letter written by Alexandros Koundouriotis, Needy Child No. 6,511 in the records of Hope, Incorporated, an international charity with headquarters in New York.*

July 1959

Dear Mr. and Mrs. Bentley:

Dear American Parents, first of all I want to inquire about your good health, and then, if you ask me, tell you that I am keeping well, for which I thank God, and hope that it is the same with you. May God keep you always well, and grant you every happiness and joy. With great eagerness I was looking forward again this month to receiving a letter from you, but unfortunately I have again not received one. So I am worried about you, for I am longing to hear about you, dear American Parents. You show such a great interest in me, and every month I receive your help. Over here it is very hot at this time of the year, for we are in the heart of the summer. The work out in the fields is very tiring, as I hear the older people saying. As for me, when I have no work at home I go down to the sea for a swim, and enjoy the sea with my friends. For at this time of the year the sea is lovely. So much for my news. Vacations continue, until it is time for the schools to reopen, when with new strength and joy we shall begin our lessons again. Today that I am writing to you I received again the $8.oo that you sent me, for the month of July, and I thank you very much. With this money I shall buy whatever I need, and we shall also buy some flour for our bread. In closing, I send you greetings from my granny and my sister, and hope that my letter finds you in good health and joy. I shall be looking forward to receiving a letter from you, to hear about you and how you are spending your summer. I greet you with much affection.

Your son,
Alexandros

REPLY *from Kenneth Bentley, American Parent No. 4,638.*
September 25

Dear Alexandros:

We are all sorry that you should worry about us because you have not received a letter from us. I fear we are not as regular in writing as you are, but the pretentiously named organization which delivers our letters seems to be very slow, they take about three months as far as I can tell. Perhaps they send them by way of China.

You describe the Greek summer very beautifully. It is autumn now in New York City. The sad little trees along the somewhat sad little street where I live now are turning yellow, the ones that are not already dead. The pretty girls that walk along the main streets are putting on hats again. In New York the main streets run north and south so that there is usually a sunny side and a shady side and now people cross the street to be on the sunny side because the sun is no longer too warm. The sky is very blue and some evenings after I eat in a luncheonette or restaurant I walk a few blocks over to the East River to watch the boats and look at Brooklyn, which is another section of this immense city.

Mrs. Bentley and I no longer live together. I had not intended to tell you this but now the sentence is typed and I see no harm in it. Perhaps already you were wondering why I am writing from New York City instead of from Greenwich. Mrs. Bentley and little Amanda and Richard all still live in our nice home in Greenwich and the last time I saw them looked very well. Amanda now is starting kindergarten and was very excited and will never wear dungarees or overalls any more but insists on wearing dresses because that is what makes little girls look nice, she thinks. This makes her mother rather angry, especially on Saturdays and Sundays when Amanda plays mostly in the dirt with the neighbor children. Richard walks very well now and does not like his sister teasing him. As who does? I go to see them once a week and pick up my mail and your last letter was one of the letters I picked up and was delighted to read. Mrs. Bentley asked me to answer it, which I was delighted to do, because she had written you the last time. In fact I do not think she did, but writing letters was one thing she was not good at, although it was her idea for us to subscribe to Hope, Incorporated, and I know she loves you very much, and was especially happy to learn that you plan to begin school with "new strength and joy."

There has been much excitement in the United States over the visit of the head of Soviet Russia, Mr. Khrushchev. He is a very talkative and self-confident man and in meeting some of our own talkative and self-confident politicians there has been some friction, much of it right on television where everybody could see. My main worry was that he would be shot but I don't think he will be shot any more. His being in the country has been a funny feeling, as if you have swallowed a penny, but the American people are so anxious for peace that they will put up with small discomforts if there is any chance it will do any good. The United States, as perhaps you will learn in school, was for many years an isolated country and there still is a perhaps childish wish that other nations, even though we are a great power, just let us alone, and then the sun will shine.

That was not a very good paragraph and perhaps the man or woman who kindly translates these letters for us will kindly omit it. I have a cold in my chest that mixes with a great deal of cigarette smoke and makes me very confused, especially after I have been sitting still for a while.

I am troubled because I imagine I hear you asking, "Then were Mr. and Mrs. Bentley, who sent me such happy letters from

America, and photographs of their children, and a sweater and
a jackknife at Christmas, telling lies? Why do they not live together any more?" I do not wish you to worry. Perhaps in your
own village you have husbands and wives who quarrel. Perhaps
they quarrel but continue to live together but in America where
we have so much plumbing and fast automobiles and rapid high-
ways we have forgotten how to live with inconveniences, although I admit that my present mode of life is something of an
inconvenience to me. Or perhaps in your schooling, if you keep
at it, and I hope you will, the priests or nuns will have you read
the very great Greek poem The Iliad, in which the poet Homer
tells of Helen who left her husband to live with Paris among the
Trojans. It is something like that with the Bentleys, except that I,
a man, have gone to live among the Trojans, leaving my wife
at home. I do not know if the Iliad is a part of your schooling,
and would be curious to know. Your nation should be very
proud of producing masterpieces which the whole world can
enjoy. In the United States the great writers produce works
which people do not enjoy, because they are so depressing to
read.

But we were not telling lies, Mrs. Bentley and Amanda and
Richard and I were very happy and to a degree are yet. Please
continue to send us your wonderful letters, they will go to
Greenwich, and we will all enjoy them. We will continue to
send you the money for which you say you are grateful, though
the money we give you this way is not a fourth of the money we
used to spend for alcoholic drinks. Not that Mrs. Bentley and
I drank all these alcoholic drinks. We had many friends who
helped us, most of them very tedious people, although perhaps
you would like them more than I do. Certainly they would like
you more than they liked me.

I am so happy that you live near the sea where you can swim
and relax from the tiring work of the fields. I was born far inland in America, a thousand miles from any ocean, and did not
come to love the sea until I was grown up and married. So in that

sense you are luckier than I. Certainly to be near the sea is a
great blessing, and I remember often thinking how nice it was
that my own children should know what it was to run on the
sand of the pretty though not large beach at Greenwich, and to
have that great calm horizon over their shoulders.

Now I must end, for I have agreed to take a young woman
out to dinner, a young woman who, you will be interested to
hear, is herself Greek in origin, though born an American, and
who has much of the beauty of your race. But I have already
cruelly burdened our translator. My best wishes to your granny,
who has taken such good care of you since your mother died,
and to your sister, whose welfare and good health is such a large
concern in your heart.

Sincerely,
Kenneth Bentley

P.S.: In looking back at the beginning of my letter I see with
regret that I have been unkind to the excellent organization
which has made possible our friendship with you, which has
produced your fine letters, which we are always happy to receive
and which we read and reread. If we have not written as often
as we should have it is our fault and we ask you to forgive us.

Goodbye, My Brother

JOHN CHEEVER (1912–   )

WE ARE a family that has always been very close in spirit. Our
father was drowned in a sailing accident when we were young,
and our mother has always stressed the fact that our familial

relationships have a kind of permanence that we will never meet with again. I don't think about the family much, but when I remember its members and the coast where they lived and the sea salt that I think is in our blood, I am happy to recall that I am a Pommeroy—that I have the nose, the coloring, and the promise of longevity—and that while we are not a distinguished family, we enjoy the illusion when we are together, that the Pommeroys are unique. I don't say any of this because I'm interested in family history or because this sense of uniqueness is deep or important to me but in order to advance the point that we are loyal to one another in spite of our differences, and that any rupture in this loyalty is a source of confusion and pain.

We are four children; there is my sister Diana and the three men—Chaddy, Lawrence, and myself. Like most families in which the children are out of their twenties, we have been separated by business, marriage, and war. Helen and I live on Long Island now, with our four children. I teach in a secondary school, and I am past the age where I expect to be made headmaster—or principal, as we say—but I respect the work. Chaddy, who has done better than the rest of us, lives in Manhattan, with Odette and their children. Mother lives in Philadelphia, and Diana, since her divorce, has been living in France, but she comes back to the States in the summer to spend a month at Laud's Head. Laud's Head is a summer place on the shore of one of the Massachusetts islands. We used to have a cottage there, and in the twenties our father built the big house. It stands on a cliff above the sea and, excepting St. Tropez and some of the Apennine villages, it is my favorite place in the world. We each have an equity in the place and we contribute some money to help keep it going.

Our youngest brother, Lawrence, who is a lawyer, got a job with a Cleveland firm after the war, and none of us saw him for four years. When he decided to leave Cleveland and go to work for a firm in Albany, he wrote Mother that he would, between jobs, spend ten days at Laud's Head, with his wife and their two children. This was when I had planned to take my vacation—I

had been teaching summer school—and Helen and Chaddy and
Odette and Diana were all going to be there, so the family would
be together. Lawrence is the member of the family with whom
the rest of us have least in common. We have never seen a great
deal of him, and I suppose that's why we still call him Tifty—a
nickname he was given when he was a child, because when he
came down the hall toward the dining room for breakfast, his
slippers made a noise that sounded like "Tifty, tifty, tifty."
That's what Father called him, and so did everyone else. When
he grew older, Diana sometimes used to call him Little Jesus, and
Mother often called him The Croaker. We had disliked Lawrence, but we looked forward to his return with a mixture of
apprehension and loyalty, and with some of the joy and delight
of reclaiming a brother.

Lawrence crossed over from the mainland on the four-o'clock
boat one afternoon late in the summer, and Chaddy and I went
down to meet him. The arrivals and departures of the summer
ferry have all the outward signs that suggest a voyage—whistles,
bells, hand trucks, reunions, and the smell of brine—but it is a
voyage of no import, and when I watched the boat come into the
blue harbor that afternoon and thought that it was completing a
voyage of no import, I realized that I had hit on exactly the kind
of observation that Lawrence would have made. We looked for
his face behind the windshields as the cars drove off the boat,
and we had no trouble in recognizing him. And we ran over and
shook his hand and clumsily kissed his wife and the children.
"Tifty!" Chaddy shouted. "Tifty!" It is difficult to judge
changes in the appearance of a brother, but both Chaddy and
I agreed, as we drove back to Laud's Head, that Lawrence still
looked very young. He got to the house first, and we took the
suitcases out of his car. When I came in, he was standing in the
living room, talking with Mother and Diana. They were in their
best clothes and all their jewelry, and they were welcoming him
extravagantly, but even then, when everyone was endeavoring to

seem most affectionate and at a time when these endeavors come easiest, I was aware of a faint tension in the room. Thinking about this as I carried Lawrence's heavy suitcases up the stairs, I realized that our dislikes are as deeply ingrained as our better passions, and I remembered that once, twenty-five years ago, when I had hit Lawrence on the head with a rock, he had picked himself up and gone directly to our father to complain.

I carried the suitcases up to the third floor, where Ruth, Lawrence's wife, had begun to settle her family. She is a thin girl, and she seemed very tired from the journey, but when I asked her if she didn't want me to bring a drink upstairs to her, she said she didn't think she did.

When I got downstairs, Lawrence wasn't around, but the others were all ready for cocktails, and we decided to go ahead. Lawrence is the only member of the family who has never enjoyed drinking. We took our cocktails onto the terrace, so that we could see the bluffs and the sea and the islands in the east, and the return of Lawrence and his wife, their presence in the house, seemed to refresh our responses to the familiar view; it was as if the pleasure they would take in the sweep and the color of that coast, after such a long absence, had been imparted to us. While we were there, Lawrence came up the path from the beach.

"Isn't the beach fabulous, Tifty?" Mother asked. "Isn't it fabulous to be back? Will you have a Martini?"

"I don't care," Lawrence said. "Whisky, gin—I don't care what I drink. Give me a little rum."

"We don't have any *rum*," Mother said. It was the first note of asperity. She had taught us never to be indecisive, never to reply as Lawrence had. Beyond this, she is deeply concerned with the propriety of her house, and anything irregular by her standards, like drinking straight rum or bringing a beer can to the dinner table, excites in her a conflict that she cannot, even with her capacious sense of humor, surmount. She sensed the asperity and worked to repair it. "Would you like some Irish, Tifty dear?" she said. "Isn't Irish what you've always liked? There's some Irish on the sideboard. Why don't you get yourself some Irish?" Lawrence said that he didn't care. He poured himself a Martini, and then Ruth came down and we went in to dinner.

In spite of the fact that we had, through waiting for Lawrence, drunk too much before dinner, we were all anxious to put our best foot forward and to enjoy a peaceful time. Mother is a small woman whose face is still a striking reminder of how pretty she must have been, and whose conversation is unusually light, but she talked that evening about a soil-reclamation project that is going on up-island. Diana is as pretty as Mother must have been; she is an animated and lovely woman who likes to talk about the dissolute friends that she has made in France, but she talked that night about the school in Switzerland where she had left her two children. I could see that the dinner had been planned to please Lawrence. It was not too rich, and there was nothing to make him worry about extravagance.

After supper, when we went back onto the terrace, the clouds held that kind of light that looks like blood, and I was glad that Lawrence had such a lurid sunset for his homecoming. When we had been out there a few minutes, a man named Edward Chester came to get Diana. She had met him in France, or on the boat home, and he was staying for ten days at the inn in the village. He was introduced to Lawrence and Ruth, and then he and Diana left.

"Is that the one she's sleeping with now?" Lawrence asked.

"What a horrid thing to say!" Helen said.

"You ought to apologize for that, Tifty," Chaddy said.

"I don't know," Mother said tiredly. "I don't know, Tifty. Diana is in a position to do whatever she wants, and I don't ask sordid questions. She's my only daughter. I don't see her often."

"Is she going back to France?"

"She's going back the week after next."

Lawrence and Ruth were sitting at the edge of the terrace, not in the chairs, not in the circle of chairs. With his mouth set, my brother looked to me then like a Puritan cleric. Sometimes, when I try to understand his frame of mind, I think of the beginnings of our family in this country, and his disapproval of Diana and her lovers reminded me of this. The branch of the Pommeroys to which we belong was founded by a minister who was eulogized by Cotton Mather for his untiring abjuration of the Devil. The Pommeroys were ministers until the middle of the nineteenth century, and the harshness of their thought—man is full of misery, and all earthly beauty is lustful and corrupt—has been preserved in books and sermons. The temper of our family changed somewhat and became more lighthearted, but when I was of school age, I can remember a cousinage of old men and women who seemed to hark back to the dark days of the ministry and to be animated by perpetual guilt and the deification of the scourge. If you are raised in this atmosphere—and in a sense we were—I think it is a trial of the spirit to reject its habits of guilt, self-denial, taciturnity, and penitence, and it seemed to me to have been a trial of the spirit in which Lawrence had succumbed.

"Is that Cassiopeia?" Odette asked.

"No, dear," Chaddy said. "That isn't Cassiopeia."

"Who was Cassiopeia?" Odette said.

"She was the wife of Cepheus and the mother of Andromeda," I said.

"The cook is a Giants fan," Chaddy said. "She'll give you even money that they win the pennant."

It had grown so dark that we could see the passage of light through the sky from the lighthouse at Cape Herion. In the dark below the cliff, the continual detonations of the surf sounded. And then, as she often does when it is getting dark and she has drunk too much before dinner, Mother began to talk about the improvements and additions that would someday be made on the house, the wings and bathrooms and gardens.

"This house will be in the sea in five years," Lawrence said.

"Tifty the Croaker," Chaddy said.

"Don't call me Tifty," Lawrence said.

"Little Jesus," Chaddy said.

"The sea wall is badly cracked," Lawrence said. "I looked at it this afternoon. You had it repaired four years ago, and it cost eight thousand dollars. You can't do that every four years."

"Please, Tifty," Mother said.

"Facts are facts," Lawrence said, "and it's a damned-fool idea to build a house at the edge of a cliff on a sinking coast-line. In my lifetime, half the garden has washed away and there's four feet of water where we used to have a bathhouse."

"Let's have a very *general* conversation," Mother said bitterly. "Let's talk about politics or the boat-club dance."

"As a matter of fact," Lawrence said, "the house is probably in some danger now. If you had an unusually high sea, a hurricane sea, the wall would crumble and the house would go. We could all be drowned."

"I can't *bear* it," Mother said. She went into the pantry and came back with a full glass of gin.

I have grown too old now to think that I can judge the sentiments of others, but I was conscious of the tension between Lawrence and Mother, and I knew some of the history of it. Lawrence couldn't have been more than sixteen years old when he decided that Mother was frivolous, mischievous, destructive, and overly strong. When he had determined this, he decided to separate himself from her. He was at boarding school then, and I remember that he did not come home for Christmas. He spent Christmas with a friend. He came home very seldom after he had made his unfavorable judgment on Mother, and when he did come home, he always tried, in his conversation, to remind her of his estrangement. When he married Ruth, he did not tell Mother. He did not tell her when his children were born. But in spite of these principled and lengthy exertions he seemed, unlike the rest of us, never to have enjoyed any separation, and when they are together, you feel at once a tension, an unclearness.

And it was unfortunate, in a way, that Mother should have

picked that night to get drunk. It's her privilege, and she doesn't get drunk often, and fortunately she wasn't bellicose, but we were all conscious of what was happening. As she quietly drank her gin, she seemed sadly to be parting from us; she seemed to be in the throes of travel. Then her mood changed from travel to injury, and the few remarks she made were petulant and irrelevant. When her glass was nearly empty, she stared angrily at the dark air in front of her nose, moving her head a little, like a fighter. I knew that there was not room in her mind then for all the injuries that were crowding into it. Her children were stupid, her husband was drowned, her servants were thieves, and the chair she sat in was uncomfortable. Suddenly she put down her empty glass and interrupted Chaddy, who was talking about baseball. "I know one *thing*," she said hoarsely. "I know that if there is an afterlife, I'm going to have a very different kind of family. I'm going to have nothing but fabulously rich, witty, and enchanting children." She got up and, starting for the door, nearly fell. Chaddy caught her and helped her up the stairs. I could hear their tender good nights, and then Chaddy came back. I thought that Lawrence by now would be tired from his journey and his return, but he remained on the terrace, as if he were waiting to see the final malfeasance, and the rest of us left him there and went swimming in the dark.

When I woke the next morning, or half woke, I could hear the sound of someone rolling the tennis court. It is a fainter and a deeper sound than the iron buoy bells off the point—an unrhythmic iron chiming—that belongs in my mind to the beginnings of a summer day, a good portent. When I went downstairs, Lawrence's two kids were in the living room, dressed in ornate cowboy suits. They are frightened and skinny children. They told me their father was rolling the tennis court but that they did not want to go out because they had seen a snake under the doorstep. I explained to them that their cousins—all the other children—ate breakfast in the kitchen and that they'd better run along in there. At this announcement, the boy began to cry. Then his sister joined him. They cried as if to go in the kitchen and eat would destroy their most precious rights. I told them to sit down with me. Lawrence came in, and I asked him if he wanted to play some tennis. He said no, thanks, although he thought he might play some singles with Chaddy. He was in the right here, because both he and Chaddy play better tennis than I, and he did play some singles with Chaddy after breakfast, but later on, when the others came down to play family doubles, Lawrence disappeared. This made me cross—unreasonably so, I suppose—but we play darned interesting family doubles and he could have played in a set for the sake of courtesy.

Late in the morning, when I came up from the court alone, I saw Tifty on the terrace, prying up a shingle from the wall with his jackknife. "What's the matter, Lawrence?" I said. "Termites?" There are termites in the wood and they've given us a lot of trouble.

He pointed out to me, at the base of each row of shingles, a faint blue line of carpenter's chalk. "This house is about twenty-two years old," he said. "These shingles are about two hundred years old. Dad must have bought shingles from all the farms around here when he built the place, to make it look venerable. You can still see the carpenter's chalk put down where these antiques were nailed into place."

It was true about the shingles, although I had forgotten it. When the house was built, our father, or his architect, had ordered it covered with lichened and weather-beaten shingles. I didn't follow Lawrence's reasons for thinking that this was scandalous.

"And look at these doors," Lawrence said. "Look at these doors and window frames." I followed him over to a big Dutch door that opens onto the terrace and looked at it. It was a relatively new door, but someone had worked hard to conceal its newness. The surface had been deeply scored with some metal implement, and white paint had been rubbed into the incisions to imitate brine, lichen, and weather rot. "Imagine spending thousands of dollars to make a sound house look like a wreck," Lawrence said. "Imagine the frame of mind this implies. Imagine wanting to live so much in the past that you'll pay men carpenters' wages to disfigure your front door." Then I remembered Lawrence's sensitivity to time and his sentiments and opinions about our feelings for the past. I had heard him say, years ago, that we and our friends and our part of the nation, finding ourselves unable to cope with the problems of the present, had, like a wretched adult, turned back to what we supposed was a happier and a simpler time, and that our taste for reconstruction and candlelight was a measure of this irremediable failure. The faint blue line of chalk had reminded him of these ideas, the scarified door had reinforced them, and now clue after clue presented itself to him—the stern light at the door, the bulk of the chimney, the width of the floorboards and the pieces set into them to resemble pegs. While Lawrence was lecturing me on these frailties, the others came up from the court. As soon as Mother saw Lawrence, she responded, and I saw that there was little hope of any rapport between the matriarch and the changeling. She took Chaddy's arm. "Let's go swimming and have Martinis on the beach," she said. "Let's have a *fabulous* morning."

The sea that morning was a solid color, like verd stone. Everyone went to the beach but Tifty and Ruth. "I don't mind *him*," Mother said. She was excited, and she tipped her glass and spilled some gin into the sand. "I don't mind *him*. It doesn't matter to me how *rude* and *horrid* and *gloomy* he is, but what I can't bear are the faces of his wretched little children, those fabulously unhappy little children." With the height of the cliff between us, everyone talked wrathfully about Lawrence; about how he had grown worse instead of better, how unlike the rest of us he was, how he endeavored to spoil every pleasure. We drank our gin; the abuse seemed to reach a crescendo, and then, one by one, we went swimming in the solid green water. But when we came out no one mentioned Lawrence unkindly; the line of abusive conversation had been cut, as if swimming had the cleansing force claimed for baptism. We dried our hands and lighted cigarettes, and if Lawrence was mentioned, it was only to suggest, kindly, something that might please him. Wouldn't he like to sail to Barin's cove, or go fishing?

And now I remember that while Lawrence was visiting us, we went swimming oftener than we usually do, and I think there was a reason for this. When the irritability that accumulated as a result of his company began to lessen our patience, not only with Lawrence but with one another, we would all go swimming and shed our animus in the cold water. I can see the family now, smarting from Lawrence's rebukes as they sat on the sand, and I can see them wading and diving and surface-diving and hear in their voices the restoration of patience and the rediscovery of inexhaustible good will. If Lawrence noticed this change—this illusion of purification—I suppose that he would have found in the vocabulary of psychiatry, or the mythology of the Atlantic, some circumspect name for it, but I don't think he noticed the change. He neglected to name the curative powers of the open sea, but it was one of the few chances for diminution that he missed.

The cook we had that year was a Polish woman named Anna Ostrovick, a summer cook. She was first rate—a big, fat, hearty, industrious woman who took her work very seriously. She liked to cook and to have the food she cooked appreciated and eaten, and whenever we saw her, she always urged us to eat. She cooked hot bread—crescents and brioches—for breakfast two or three times a week, and she would bring these into the dining room herself and say, "Eat, eat, eat!" When the maid took the serving dishes back into the pantry, we could sometimes hear Anna, who was standing there, say, "Good! They eat." She fed the garbage man, the milkman, and the gardener. "Eat!" she told them. "Eat, eat!" On Thursday afternoons, she went to the movies with the maid, but she didn't enjoy the movies, because the actors were all so thin. She would sit in the dark theatre for an hour and a half watching the screen anxiously for the appearance of someone who had enjoyed his food. Bette Davis merely left with Anna the impression of a woman who has not eaten well. "They are all so skinny," she would say when she left the movies. In the evenings, after she had gorged all of us, and washed the pots and pans, she would collect the table scraps and go out to feed the creation. We had a few chickens that year, and although they would have roosted by then, she would dump food into their trough and urge the sleeping fowl to eat. She fed the songbirds in the orchard and the chipmunks in the yard. Her appearance at the edge of the garden and her urgent voice—we could hear her calling "Eat, eat, eat"—had become, like the sunset gun at the boat club and the passage of light from Cape Herion, attached to that hour. "Eat, eat, eat," we could hear Anna say. "Eat, eat . . ." Then it would be dark.

When Lawrence had been there three days, Anna called me into the kitchen. "You tell your mother," she said, "that *he* doesn't come into my kitchen. If *he* comes into my kitchen all the time, I go. *He* is always coming into my kitchen to tell me what a sad woman I am. He is always telling me that I work too hard and that I don't get paid enough and that I should belong to a union with vacations. Ha! He is so skinny but he is always coming into my kitchen when I am busy to pity me, but I am as good as him, I am as good as *anybody*, and I do not have to have people like that getting into my way all the time and feeling sorry for me. I am a famous and a wonderful cook and I have jobs everywhere and the only reason I come here to work this summer is because I was never before on an island, but I can have other jobs tomorrow, and if he is always coming into my kitchen to pity me, you tell your mother I am going. I am as good as *anybody* and I do not have to have that skinny all the time telling how poor I am."

I was pleased to find that the cook was on our side, but I felt that the situation was delicate. If Mother asked Lawrence to stay out of the kitchen, he would make a grievance out of the request. He could make a grievance out of anything, and it sometimes seemed that as he sat darkly at the dinner table, every word of disparagement, wherever it was aimed, came home to him. I didn't mention the cook's complaint to anyone, but somehow there wasn't any more trouble from that quarter.

The next cause for contention that I had from Lawrence came over our backgammon games.

When we are at Laud's Head, we play a lot of backgammon. At eight o'clock, after we have drunk our coffee, we usually get out the board. In a way, it is one of our pleasantest hours. The lamps in the room are still unlighted, Anna can be seen in the dark garden, and in the sky above her head there are continents of shadow and fire. Mother turns on the light and rattles the dice as a signal. We usually play three games apiece, each with the others. We play for money, and you can win or lose a hundred dollars on a game, but the stakes are usually much lower. I think that Lawrence used to play—I can't remember— but he doesn't play any more. He doesn't gamble. This is not because he is poor or because he has any principles about gambling but because he thinks the game is foolish and a waste of time. He was ready enough, however, to waste his time watching the rest of us play. Night after night, when the game began, he pulled a chair up beside the board, and watched the checkers and the dice. His expression was scornful, and yet he watched carefully. I wondered why he watched us night after night, and, through watching his face, I think that I may have found out.

Lawrence doesn't gamble, so he can't understand the excitement of winning and losing money. He has forgotten how to play the game, I think, so that its complex odds can't interest him. His observations were bound to include the facts that backgammon is an idle game and a game of chance, and that the board, marked with points, was a symbol of our worthlessness. And since he doesn't understand gambling or the odds of the game, I thought that what interested him must be the members of his family. One night when I was playing with Odette—I had won thirty-seven dollars from Mother and Chaddy—I think I saw what was going on in his mind.

Odette has black hair and black eyes. She is careful never to expose her white skin to the sun for long, so the striking contrast of blackness and pallor is not changed in the summer. She needs and deserves admiration—it is the element that contents her—and she will flirt, unseriously, with any man. Her shoulders were bare that night, her dress was cut to show the division of her breasts and to show her breasts when she leaned over the board to play. She kept losing and flirting and making her losses seem like a part of the flirtation. Chaddy was in the other room. She lost three games, and when the third game ended, she fell back on the sofa and, looking at me squarely, said something about going out on the dunes to settle the score. Lawrence heard her. I looked at Lawrence. He seemed shocked and gratified at the same time, as if he had suspected all along that we were not playing for anything so insubstantial as money. I may be wrong, of course, but I think that Lawrence felt that in watching our backgammon he was observing the progress of a mordant tragedy in which the money we won and lost served as a symbol for more vital forfeits. It is like Lawrence to try to read significance and finality into every gesture that we make, and it is certain of Lawrence that when he finds the inner logic to our conduct, it will be sordid.

Chaddy came in to play with me. Chaddy and I have never liked to lose to each other. When we were younger, we used to be forbidden to play games together, because they always ended in a fight. We think we know each other's mettle intimately. I think he is prudent; he thinks I am foolish. There is always bad blood when we play anything—tennis or backgammon or softball or bridge—and it does seem at times as if we were playing for the possession of each other's liberties. When I lose to Chaddy, I can't sleep. All this is only half the truth of our competitive relationship, but it was the half-truth that would be discernible to Lawrence, and his presence at the table made me so self-conscious that I lost two games. I tried not to seem angry when I got up from the board. Lawrence was watching me. I went out onto the terrace to suffer there in the dark the anger I always feel when I lose to Chaddy.

When I came back into the room, Chaddy and Mother were playing. Lawrence was still watching. By his lights, Odette had lost her virtue to me, I had lost my self-esteem to Chaddy, and now I wondered what he saw in the present match. He watched raptly, as if the opaque checkers and the marked board served for an exchange of critical power. How dramatic the board, in its ring of light, and the quiet players and the crash of the sea outside must have seemed to him! Here was spiritual cannibalism made visible; here, under his nose, were the symbols of the rapacious use human beings made of one another.

Mother plays a shrewd, an ardent, and an interfering game. She always has her hands in her opponent's board. When she plays with Chaddy, who is her favorite, she plays intently. Lawrence would have noticed this. Mother is a sentimental woman. Her heart is good and easily moved by tears and frailty, a characteristic that, like her handsome nose, has not been changed at all by age. Grief in another provokes her deeply, and she seems at times to be trying to divine in Chaddy some grief, some loss, that she can succor and redress, and so reëstablish the relationship that she enjoyed with him when he was sickly and young. She loves defending the weak and the childlike, and now that we are old, she misses it. The world of debts and business, men and war, hunting and fishing has on her an exacerbating effect. (When Father drowned, she threw away his fly rods and his guns.) She has lectured us all endlessly on self-reliance, but when we come back to her for comfort and for help—particularly Chaddy—she seems to feel most like herself. I suppose Lawrence thought that the old woman and her son were playing for each other's soul.

She lost. "Oh *dear*," she said. She looked stricken and bereaved, as she always does when she loses. "Get my glasses, get me my checkbook, get me something to drink." Lawrence got up at last and stretched his legs. He looked at us all bleakly. The wind and the sea had risen, and I thought that if he heard the waves, he must hear them only as a dark answer to all his dark questions; that he would think that the tide had expunged the embers of our picnic fires. The company of a lie is unbearable, and he seemed like the embodiment of a lie. I couldn't explain to him the simple and intense pleasures of playing for money, and it seemed to me hideously wrong that he should have sat on the edge of the board and concluded that we were playing for one another's soul. He walked restlessly around the room two or three times and then, as usual, gave us a parting shot. "I should think you'd go crazy," he said, "cooped up with one another like this, night after night. Come on, Ruth, I'm going to bed."

That night, I dreamed about Lawrence. I saw his plain face magnified into ugliness, and when I woke in the morning, I felt sick, as if I had suffered a great spiritual loss while I slept, like the loss of courage and heart. It was foolish to let myself be troubled by my brother. I needed a vacation. I needed to relax. At school, we live in one of the dormitories, we eat at the house table, and we never get away. I not only teach English winter and summer but I work in the principal's office and fire the pistol at track meets. I needed to get away from this and from every other form of anxiety, and I decided to avoid my brother. Early that day, I took Helen and the children sailing, and we stayed out until suppertime. The next day, we went on a picnic. Then I had to go to New York for a day, and when I got back, there was the costume dance at the boat club. Lawrence wasn't going to this, and it's a party where I always have a wonderful time.

The invitations that year said to come as you wish you were. After several conversations, Helen and I had decided what to wear. The thing she most wanted to be again, she said, was a bride, and so she decided to wear her wedding dress. I thought this was a good choice—sincere, lighthearted, and inexpensive. Her choice influenced mine, and I decided to wear an old football uniform. Mother decided to go as Jenny Lind, because there was an old Jenny Lind costume in the attic. The others decided to rent costumes, and when I went to New York, I got the clothes. Lawrence and Ruth didn't enter into any of this.

Helen was on the dance committee, and she spent most of Friday decorating the club. Diana and Chaddy and I went sailing. Most of the sailing that I do these days is in Manhasset, and I am used to setting a homeward course by the gasoline barge and the tin roofs of the boat shed, and it was a pleasure that afternoon, as we returned, to keep the bow on a white church spire in the village and to find even the inshore water green and clear. At the end of our sail, we stopped at the club to get Helen. The committee had been trying to give a submarine appearance to the ballroom, and the fact that they had nearly succeeded in accomplishing this illusion made Helen very happy. We drove back to Laud's Head. It had been a brilliant afternoon, but on the way home we could smell the east wind—the dark wind, as Lawrence would have said—coming in from the sea.

My wife, Helen, is thirty-eight, and her hair would be gray, I guess, if it were not dyed, but it is dyed an unobtrusive yellow —a faded color—and I think it becomes her. I mixed cocktails that night while she was dressing, and when I took a glass upstairs to her, I saw her for the first time since our marriage in her wedding dress. There would be no point in saying that she looked to me more beautiful than she did on our wedding day, but because I have grown older and have, I think, a greater depth of feeling, and because I could see in her face that night both youth and age, both her devotion to the young woman that she had been and the positions that she had yielded graciously to time, I think I have never been so deeply moved. I had already put on the football uniform, and the weight of it, the heaviness of the pants and the shoulder guards, had worked a change in me, as if in putting on these old clothes I had put off the reasonable anxieties and troubles of my life. It felt as if we had both returned to the years before our marriage, the years before the war.

The Collards had a big dinner party before the dance, and our family—excepting Lawrence and Ruth—went to this. We drove over to the club, through the fog, at about half past nine. The orchestra was playing a waltz. While I was checking my raincoat, someone hit me on the back. It was Chucky Ewing, and the funny thing was that Chucky had on a football uniform. This seemed comical as hell to both of us. We were laughing when we went down the hall to the dance floor. I stopped at the door to look at the party, and it was beautiful. The committee had hung fish nets all around the sides and over the high ceiling. The nets on the ceiling were filled with colored balloons. The light was soft and uneven, and the people—our friends and neighbors—dancing in the soft light to "Three O'Clock in the Morning" made a pretty picture. Then I noticed the number of women dressed in white, and I realized that they, like Helen, were wearing wedding dresses. Patsy Hewitt and Mrs. Gear and the Lackland girl waltzed by, dressed as brides. Then Pep Talcott came over to where Chucky and I were standing. He was dressed to be Henry VIII, but he told us that the Auerbach twins and Henry Barrett and Dwight MacGregor were all wearing uniforms, and that by the last count there were ten brides on the floor.

This coincidence, this funny coincidence, kept everybody laughing, and made this one of the most lighthearted parties we've ever had at the club. At first I thought that the women had planned with one another to wear wedding dresses, but the ones that I danced with said it was a coincidence and I'm sure that Helen had made her decision alone. Everything went smoothly for me until a little before midnight. I saw Ruth standing at the edge of the floor. She was wearing a long red dress. It was all wrong. It wasn't in the spirit of the party at all. I danced with her, but no one cut in, and I was darned if I'd spend the rest of the night dancing with her and I asked her where Lawrence was. She said he was out on the dock, and I took her over to the bar and left her and went out to get Lawrence.

The east fog was thick and wet, and he was alone on the dock. He was not in costume. He had not even bothered to get himself up as a fisherman or a sailor. He looked particularly saturnine. The fog blew around us like a cold smoke. I wished that it had been a clear night, because the easterly fog seemed to play into my misanthropic brother's hands. And I knew that the buoys—the groaners and bells that we could hear then— would sound to him like half-human, half-drowned cries, although every sailor knows that buoys are necessary and reliable fixtures, and I knew that the foghorn at the lighthouse would mean wanderings and losses to him and that he could misconstrue the vivacity of the dance music. "Come on in, Tifty," I said, "and dance with your wife or get her some partners."

"Why should I?" he said. "Why should I?" And he walked to the window and looked in at the party. "Look at it," he said. "Look at that . . ."

Chucky Ewing had got hold of a balloon and was trying to organize a scrimmage line in the middle of the floor. The others were dancing a samba. And I knew that Lawrence was looking bleakly at the party as he had looked at the weather-beaten shingles on our house, as if he saw here an abuse and a distortion of time; as if in wanting to be brides and football players we exposed the fact that, the lights of youth having been put out in us, we had been unable to find other lights to go by and, destitute of faith and principle, had become foolish and sad. And that he was thinking this about so many kind and happy and generous people made me angry, made me feel for him such an unnatural abhorrence that I was ashamed, for he is my brother and a Pommeroy. I put my arm around his shoulders and tried to force him to come in, but he wouldn't.

I got back in time for the Grand March, and after the prizes had been given out for the best costumes, they let the balloons down. The room was hot, and someone opened the big doors onto the dock, and the easterly wind circled the room and went out, carrying across the dock and out onto the water most of the balloons. Chucky Ewing went running out after the balloons, and when he saw them pass the dock and settle on the water, he took off his football uniform and dove in. Then Eric Auerbach dove in and Lew Phillips dove in and I dove in, and you know how it is at a party after midnight when people start jumping into the water. We recovered most of the balloons and dried off and went on dancing, and we didn't get home until morning.

The next day was the day of the flower show. Mother and Helen and Odette all had entries. We had a pickup lunch, and Chaddy drove the women and children over to the show. I took a nap, and in the middle of the afternoon I got some trunks and a towel and, on leaving the house, passed Ruth in the laundry. She was washing clothes. I don't know why she should seem to have so much more work to do than anyone else, but she is always washing or ironing or mending clothes. She may have been taught, when she was young, to spend her time like this, or she may be at the mercy of an expiatory passion. She seems to scrub and iron with a penitential fervor, although I can't imagine what it is that she thinks she's done wrong. Her children were with her in the laundry. I offered to take them to the beach, but they didn't want to go.

It was late in August, and the wild grapes that grow profusely all over the island made the land wind smell of wine. There is a little grove of holly at the end of the path, and then you climb the dunes, where nothing grows but that coarse grass. I could hear the sea, and I remember thinking how Chaddy and I used to talk mystically about the sea. When we were young, we had decided that we could never live in the West because we would miss the sea. "It is very nice here," we used to say politely when we visited people in the mountains, "but we miss the Atlantic." We used to look down our noses at people from Iowa and

JOHN CHEEVER 323

Colorado who had been denied this revelation, and we scorned the Pacific. Now I could hear the waves, whose heaviness sounded like a reverberation, like a tumult, and it pleased me as it had pleased me when I was young, and it seemed to have a purgative force, as if it had cleared my memory of, among other things, the penitential image of Ruth in the laundry.

But Lawrence was on the beach. There he sat. I went in without speaking. The water was cold, and when I came out, I put on a shirt. I told him that I was going to walk up to Tanners Point, and he said that he would come with me. I tried to walk beside him. His legs are no longer than mine, but he always likes to stay a little ahead of his companion. Walking along behind him, looking at his bent head and his shoulders, I wondered what he could make of that landscape.

There were the dunes and cliffs and then, where they declined, there were some fields that had begun to turn from green to brown and yellow. The fields were used for pasturing sheep, and I guess Lawrence would have noticed that the soil was eroded and that the sheep would accelerate this decay. Beyond the fields there are a few coastal farms, with square and pleasant buildings, but Lawrence could have pointed out the hard lot of an island farmer. The sea, at our other side, was the open sea. We always tell guests that there, to the east, lies the coast of Portugal, and for Lawrence it would be an easy step from the coast of Portugal to the tyranny in Spain. The waves broke with a noise like a "hurrah, hurrah, hurrah," but to Lawrence they would say "Vale, vale." I suppose it would have occurred to his baleful and incisive mind that the coast was terminal moraine, the edge of the prehistoric world, and it must have occurred to him that we walked along the edge of the known world in spirit as much as in fact. If he should otherwise have overlooked this, there were some Navy planes bombing an uninhabited island to remind him.

That beach is a vast and preternaturally clean and simple landscape. It is like a piece of the moon. The surf had pounded the floor solid, so it was easy walking, and everything left on the sand had been twice changed by the waves. There was the spine of a shell, a broomstick, part of a bottle and part of a brick, both of them milled and broken until they were nearly unrecognizable, and I suppose Lawrence's sad frame of mind—for he kept his head down—went from one broken thing to another. The company of his pessimism began to infuriate me, and I caught up with him and put a hand on his shoulder. "It's only a summer day, Tifty," I said. "It's only a summer day. What's the matter? Don't you like it here?"

"I don't like it here," he said blandly, without raising his eyes. "I'm going to sell my equity in the house to Chaddy. I didn't expect to have a good time. The only reason I came back was to say goodbye."

I let him get ahead again and I walked behind him, looking at his shoulders and thinking of all the goodbyes he had made. When Father drowned, he went to church and said goodbye to Father. It was only three years later that he concluded that Mother was frivolous and said goodbye to her. In his freshman year at college, he had been very good friends with his roommate, but the man drank too much, and at the beginning of the spring term Lawrence changed roommates and said goodbye to his friend. When he had been in college for two years, he concluded that the atmosphere was too sequestered and he said goodbye to Yale. He enrolled at Columbia and got his law degree there, but he found his first employer dishonest, and at the end of six months he said goodbye to a good job. He married Ruth in City Hall and said goodbye to the Protestant Episcopal Church; they went to live on a back street in Tuckahoe and said goodbye to the middle class. In 1938, he went to Washington to work as a government lawyer, saying goodbye to private enterprise, but after eight months in Washington he concluded that the Roosevelt administration was sentimental and he said goodbye to it. They left Washington for a suburb of Chicago, where he said goodbye to his neighbors, one by one, on counts of drunkenness, boorishness, and stupidity. He said goodbye to Chicago and went to Kansas; he said goodbye to Kansas and went to Cleveland. Now he had said goodbye to Cleveland and come East again, stopping at Laud's Head long enough to say goodbye to the sea.

It was elegiac and it was bigoted and narrow, it mistook circumspection for character, and I wanted to help him. "Come out of it," I said. "Come out of it, Tifty."

"Come out of what?"

"Come out of this gloominess. Come out of it. It's only a summer day. You're spoiling your own good time and you're spoiling everyone else's. We need a vacation, Tifty. I need one. I need to rest. We all do. And you've made everything tense and unpleasant. I only have two weeks in the year. Two weeks. I need to have a good time and so do all the others. We need to rest. You think that your pessimism is an advantage, but it's nothing but an unwillingness to grasp realities."

"What are the realities?" he said. "Diana is a foolish and a promiscuous woman. So is Odette. Mother is an alcoholic. If she doesn't discipline herself, she'll be in a hospital in a year or two. Chaddy is dishonest. He always has been. The house is going to fall into the sea." He looked at me and added, as an afterthought, "You're a fool."

"You're a gloomy son of a bitch," I said. "You're a gloomy son of a bitch."

"Get your fat face out of mine," he said. He walked along.

Then I picked up a root and, coming at his back—although I have never hit a man from the back before—I swung the root, heavy with sea water, behind me, and the momentum sped my arm and I gave him, my brother, a blow on the head that forced him to his knees on the sand, and I saw the blood come out and begin to darken his hair. Then I wished that he was dead, dead and about to be buried, not buried but about to be buried, because I did not want to be denied ceremony and decorum in putting him away, in putting him out of my consciousness, and I saw the rest of us—Chaddy and Mother and Diana and Helen—in mourning in the house on Belvedere Street that was torn down twenty years ago, greeting our guests and our relatives

at the door and answering their mannerly condolences with
mannerly grief. Nothing decorous was lacking, so that even if
he had been murdered on a beach, one would feel before the
tiresome ceremony ended that he had come into the winter of
his life and that it was a law of nature, and a beautiful one, that
Tifty should be buried in the cold, cold ground.

He was still on his knees. I looked up and down. No one
had seen us. The naked beach, like a piece of the moon, reached
to invisibility. The spill of a wave, in a glancing run, shot up to
where he knelt. I would still have liked to end him, but now I
had begun to act like two men, the murderer and the Samaritan.
With a swift roar, like hollowness made sound, a white wave
reached him and encircled him, boiling over his shoulders, and
I held him against the undertow. Then I led him to a higher
place. The blood had spread all through his hair, so that it looked
black. I took off my shirt and tore it to bind up his head. He
was conscious, and I didn't think he was badly hurt. He didn't
speak. Neither did I. Then I left him there.

I walked a little way down the beach and turned to watch
him, and I was thinking of my own skin then. He had got to
his feet and he seemed steady. The daylight was still clear, but
on the sea wind fumes of brine were blowing in like a light
fog, and when I had walked a little way from him, I could
hardly see his dark figure in this obscurity. All down the beach
I could see the heavy salt air blowing in. Then I turned my
back on him, and as I got near to the house, I went swimming
again, as I seem to have done after every encounter with Lawrence that summer.

When I got back to the house, I lay down on the terrace.
The others came back. I could hear Mother defaming the flower
arrangements that had won prizes. None of ours had won anything. Then the house quieted, as it always does at that hour.
The children went into the kitchen to get supper and the others
went upstairs to bathe. Then I heard Chaddy making cocktails,
and the conversation about the flower-show judges was resumed.
Then Mother cried, "Tifty! Tifty! Oh, Tifty!"

He stood in the door, looking half dead. He had taken off the bloody bandage and he held it in his hand. "My brother did this," he said. "My brother did it. He hit me with a stone —something—on the beach." His voice broke with self-pity. I thought he was going to cry. No one else spoke. "Where's Ruth?" he cried. "Where's Ruth? Where in hell is Ruth? I want her to start packing. I don't have any more time to waste here. I have important things to do. I have *important* things to do." And he went up the stairs.

They left for the mainland the next morning, taking the six-o'clock boat. Mother got up to say goodbye, but she was the only one, and it is a harsh and an easy scene to imagine—the matriarch and the changeling, looking at each other with a dismay that would seem like the powers of love reversed. I heard the children's voices and the car go down the drive, and I got up and went to the window, and what a morning that was! Jesus, what a morning! The wind was northerly. The air was clear. In the early heat, the roses in the garden smelled like strawberry jam. While I was dressing, I heard the boat whistle, first the warning signal and then the double blast, and I could see the good people on the top deck drinking coffee out of fragile paper cups, and Lawrence at the bow, saying to the sea, "*Thalassa, thalassa*," while his timid and unhappy children watched the creation from the encirclement of their mother's arms. The buoys would toll mournfully for Lawrence, and while the grace of the light would make it an exertion not to throw out your arms and swear exultantly, Lawrence's eyes would trace the black sea as it fell astern; he would think of the bottom, dark and strange, where full fathom five our father lies.

Oh, what can you do with a man like that? What can you do? How can you dissuade his eye in a crowd from seeking out the cheek with acne, the infirm hand; how can you teach him to respond to the inestimable greatness of the race, the harsh surface beauty of life; how can you put his finger for him on the obdurate truths before which fear and horror are power-

less? The sea that morning was iridescent and dark. My wife
and my sister were swimming—Diana and Helen—and I saw
their uncovered heads, black and gold in the dark water. I saw
them come out and I saw that they were naked, unshy, beautiful,
and full of grace, and I watched the naked women walk out
of the sea.

The Gioconda Smile

ALDOUS HUXLEY (1894–   )

"Miss Spence will be down directly, sir."

"Thank you," said Mr. Hutton, without turning round. Janet
Spence's parlourmaid was so ugly—ugly on purpose, it always
seemed to him, malignantly, criminally ugly—that he could not
bear to look at her more than was necessary. The door closed. Left
to himself, Mr. Hutton got up and began to wander round the
room, looking with meditative eyes at the familiar objects it contained.

Photographs of Greek statuary, photographs of the Roman
Forum, coloured prints of Italian masterpieces, all very safe and
well known. Poor, dear Janet, what a prig—what an intellectual
snob! Her real taste was illustrated in that water-colour by the
pavement artist, the one she had paid half a crown for (and thirty-
five shillings for the frame). How often he had heard her tell the
story, how often expatiate on the beauties of that skilful imitation of an oleograph! "A real Artist in the streets," and you could
hear the capital A in Artist as she spoke the words. She made
you feel that part of his glory had entered into Janet Spence when

The Gioconda Smile is reprinted from *Mortal Coils*, copyright 1921 by
Aldous Huxley, by permission of Harper and Brothers, publishers.

she tendered him that half-crown for the copy of the oleograph. She was implying a compliment to her own taste and penetration. A genuine Old Master for half a crown. Poor, dear Janet!

Mr. Hutton came to a pause in front of a small oblong mirror. Stooping a little to get a full view of his face, he passed a white, well-manicured finger over his moustache. It was as curly, as freshly auburn as it had been twenty years ago. His hair still retained its colour, and there was no sign of baldness yet—only a certain elevation of the brow. "Shakespearean," thought Mr. Hutton, with a smile, as he surveyed the smooth and polished expanse of his forehead.

Others abide our question, thou art free. . . . Footsteps in the sea . . . Majesty . . . Shakespeare, thou shouldst be living at this hour. No, that was Milton, wasn't it? Milton, the Lady of Christ's. There was no lady about him. He was what the women would call a manly man. That was why they liked him—for the curly auburn moustache and the discreet redolence of tobacco. Mr. Hutton smiled again; he enjoyed making fun of himself. Lady of Christ's? No, no. He was the Christ of Ladies. Very pretty, very pretty. The Christ of Ladies. Mr. Hutton wished there were somebody he could tell the joke to. Poor, dear Janet wouldn't appreciate it, alas!

He straightened himself up, patted his hair, and resumed his peregrination. Damn the Roman Forum; he hated those dreary photographs.

Suddenly he became aware that Janet Spence was in the room, standing near the door. Mr. Hutton started, as though he had been taken in some felonious act. To make these silent and spectral appearances was one of Janet Spence's peculiar talents. Perhaps she had been there all the time, had seen him looking at himself in the mirror. Impossible! But, still, it was disquieting.

"Oh, you gave me such a surprise," said Mr. Hutton, recovering his smile and advancing with outstretched hand to meet her.

Miss Spence was smiling too: her Gioconda smile, he had once called it in a moment of half-ironical flattery. Miss Spence had taken the compliment seriously, and had always tried to live up to the Leonardo standard. She smiled on his silence while Mr. Hutton shook hands; that was part of the Gioconda business.

"I hope you're well," said Mr. Hutton. "You look it."

What a queer face she had! That small mouth pursed forward by the Gioconda expression into a little snout with a round hole in the middle as though for whistling—it was like a penholder seen from the front. Above the mouth a well-shaped nose, finely aquiline. Eyes large, lustrous, and dark, with the largeness, lustre, and darkness that seems to invite sties and an occasional bloodshot suffusion. They were fine eyes, but unchangingly grave. The penholder might do its Gioconda trick, but the eyes never altered in their earnestness. Above them, a pair of boldly arched, heavily pencilled black eyebrows lent a surprising air of power, as of a Roman matron, to the upper portion of the face. Her hair was dark and equally Roman; Agrippina from the brows upward.

"I thought I'd just look in on my way home," Mr. Hutton went on. "Ah, it's good to be back here"—he indicated with a wave of his hand the flowers in the vases, the sunshine and greenery beyond the windows—"it's good to be back in the country after a stuffy day of business in town."

Miss Spence, who had sat down, pointed to a chair at her side.

"No, really, I can't sit down," Mr. Hutton protested. "I must get back to see how poor Emily is. She was rather seedy this morning." He sat down, nevertheless. "It's these wretched liver chills. She's always getting them. Women—" He broke off and coughed, so as to hide the fact that he had uttered. He was about to say that women with weak digestions ought not to marry; but the remark was too cruel, and he didn't really believe it. Janet Spence, moreover, was a believer in eternal flames and spiritual attachments. "She hopes to be well enough," he added, "to see you at luncheon to-morrow. Can you come? Do!" He smiled persuasively. "It's my invitation too, you know."

She dropped her eyes, and Mr. Hutton almost thought that he

detected a certain reddening of the cheek. It was a tribute; he stroked his moustache.

"I should like to come if you think Emily's really well enough to have a visitor."

"Of course. You'll do her good. You'll do us both good. In married life three is often better company than two."

"Oh, you're cynical."

Mr. Hutton always had a desire to say "Bow-wow-wow" whenever that last word was spoken. It irritated him more than any other word in the language. But instead of barking he made haste to protest.

"No, no. I'm only speaking a melancholy truth. Reality doesn't always come up to the ideal, you know. But that doesn't make me believe any the less in the ideal. Indeed, I believe in it passionately —the ideal of a matrimony between two people in perfect accord. I think it's realisable. I'm sure it is."

He paused significantly and looked at her with an arch expression. A virgin of thirty-six, but still unwithered; she had her charms. And there was something really rather enigmatic about her. Miss Spence made no reply but continued to smile. There were times when Mr. Hutton got rather bored with the Gioconda. He stood up.

"I must really be going now. Farewell, mysterious Gioconda." The smile grew intenser, focused itself, as it were, in a narrower snout. Mr. Hutton made a Cinquecento gesture, and kissed her extended hand. It was the first time he had done such a thing; the action seemed not to be resented. "I look forward to to-morrow."

"Do you?"

For answer Mr. Hutton once more kissed her hand, then turned to go. Miss Spence accompanied him to the porch.

"Where's your car?" she asked.

"I left it at the gate of the drive."

"I'll come and see you off."

"No, no." Mr. Hutton was playful, but determined. "You must do no such thing. I simply forbid you."

"But I should like to come," Miss Spence protested, throwing a rapid Gioconda at him.

Mr. Hutton held up his hand. "No," he repeated, and then, with a gesture that was almost the blowing of a kiss, he started to run down the drive, lightly on his toes, with long, bounding strides like a boy's. He was proud of that run; it was quite marvellously youthful. Still, he was glad the drive was no longer. At the last bend, before passing out of sight of the house, he halted and turned round. Miss Spence was still standing on the steps, smiling her smile. He waved his hand, and this time quite definitely and overtly wafted a kiss in her direction. Then, breaking once more into his magnificent canter, he rounded the last dark promontory of trees. Once out of sight of the house he let his high paces decline to a trot, and finally to a walk. He took out his handkerchief and began wiping his neck inside his collar. What fools, what fools! Had there ever been such an ass as poor, dear Janet Spence? Never, unless it was himself. Decidedly he was the more malignant fool, since he, at least, was aware of his folly and still persisted in it. Why did he persist? Ah, the problem that was himself, the problem that was other people.

He had reached the gate. A large, prosperous-looking motor was standing at the side of the road.

"Home, M'Nab." The chauffeur touched his cap. "And stop at the cross-roads on the way, as usual," Mr. Hutton added, as he opened the door of the car. "Well?" he said, speaking into the obscurity that lurked within.

"Oh, Teddy Bear, what an age you've been!" It was a fresh and childish voice that spoke the words. There was the faintest hint of Cockney impurity about the vowel sounds.

Mr. Hutton bent his large form and darted into the car with the agility of an animal regaining its burrow.

"Have I?" he said, as he shut the door. The machine began to move. "You must have missed me a lot if you found the time so long." He sat back in the low seat; a cherishing warmth enveloped him.

"Teddy Bear . . ." and with a sigh of contentment a charming little head declined on to Mr. Hutton's shoulder. Ravished, he looked down sideways at the round, babyish face.

"Do you know, Doris, you look like the pictures of Louise de Kerouaille." He passed his fingers through a mass of curly hair.

"Who's Louise de Kera-whatever-it-is?" Doris spoke from remote distances.

"She was, alas! *Fuit*. We shall all be 'was' one of these days. Meanwhile . . ."

Mr. Hutton covered the babyish face with kisses. The car rushed smoothly along. M'Nab's back, through the front window, was stonily impassive, the back of a statue.

"Your hands," Doris whispered. "Oh, you mustn't touch me. They give me electric shocks."

Mr. Hutton adored her for the virgin imbecility of the words. How late in one's existence one makes the discovery of one's body!

"The electricity isn't in me, it's in you." He kissed her again, whispering her name several times: Doris, Doris, Doris. The scientific appellation of the sea-mouse, he was thinking as he kissed the throat, she offered him, white and extended like the throat of a victim awaiting the sacrificial knife. The sea-mouse was a sausage with iridescent fur: very peculiar. Or was Doris the sea cucumber, which turns itself inside out in moments of alarm? He would really have to go to Naples again, just to see the aquarium. These sea creatures were fabulous, unbelievably fantastic.

"Oh, Teddy Bear!" (More zoology; but he was only a land animal. His poor little jokes!) "Teddy Bear, I'm so happy."

"So am I," said Mr. Hutton. Was it true?

"But I wish I knew if it were right. Tell me, Teddy Bear, is it right or wrong?"

"Ah, my dear, that's just what I've been wondering for the last thirty years."

"Be serious, Teddy Bear. I want to know if this is right; if it's right that I should be here with you and that we should love one another, and that it should give me electric shocks when you touch me."

"Right? Well, it's certainly good that you should have electric shocks rather than sexual repressions. Read Freud; repressions are the devil."

"Oh, you don't help me. Why aren't you ever serious? If only you knew how miserable I am sometimes, thinking it's not right. Perhaps, you know, there is a hell, and all that. I don't know what to do. Sometimes I think I ought to stop loving you."

"But could you?" asked Mr. Hutton, confident in the powers of his seduction and his moustache.

"No, Teddy Bear, you know I couldn't. But I could run away, I could hide from you, I could lock myself up and force myself not to come to you."

"Silly little thing!" He tightened his embrace.

"Oh, dear, I hope it isn't wrong. And there are times when I don't care if it is."

Mr. Hutton was touched. He had a certain protective affection for this little creature. He laid his cheek against her hair and so, interlaced, they sat in silence, while the car, swaying and pitching a little as it hastened along, seemed to draw in the white road and the dusty hedges towards it devouringly.

"Good-bye, good-bye."

The car moved on, gathered speed, vanished round a curve, and Doris was left standing by the sign-post at the cross-roads, still dizzy and weak with the languor born of those kisses and the electrical touch of those gentle hands. She had to take a deep breath, to draw herself up deliberately, before she was strong enough to start her homeward walk. She had half a mile in which to invent the necessary lies.

Alone, Mr. Hutton suddenly found himself the prey of an appalling boredom.

II

Mrs. Hutton was lying on the sofa in her boudoir, playing Patience. In spite of the warmth of the July evening a wood fire was burning on the hearth. A black Pomeranian, extenuated by the heat and the fatigues of digestion, slept before the blaze.

"Phew! Isn't it rather hot in here?" Mr. Hutton asked as he entered the room.

"You know I have to keep warm, dear." The voice seemed breaking on the verge of tears. "I get so shivery."

"I hope you're better this evening."

"Not much, I'm afraid."

The conversation stagnated. Mr. Hutton stood leaning his back against the mantelpiece. He looked down at the Pomeranian lying at his feet, and with the toe of his right boot he rolled the little dog over and rubbed its white-flecked chest and belly. The creature lay in an inert ecstasy. Mrs. Hutton continued to play Patience. Arrived at an *impasse*, she altered the position of one card, took back another, and went on playing. Her Patiences always came out.

"Dr. Libbard thinks I ought to go to Llandrindod Wells this summer."

"Well—go, my dear—go, most certainly."

Mr. Hutton was thinking of the events of the afternoon: how they had driven, Doris and he, up to the hanging wood, had left the car to wait for them under the shade of the trees, and walked together out into the windless sunshine of the chalk down.

"I'm to drink the waters for my liver, and he thinks I ought to have massage and electric treatment, too."

Hat in hand, Doris had stalked four blue butterflies that were dancing together round a scabious flower with a motion that was like the flickering of blue fire. The blue fire burst and scattered into whirling sparks; she had given chase, laughing and shouting like a child.

"I'm sure it will do you good, my dear."

"I was wondering if you'd come with me, dear."

"But you know I'm going to Scotland at the end of the month."

Mrs. Hutton looked up at him entreatingly. "It's the journey," she said. "The thought of it is such a nightmare. I don't know if I can manage it. And you know I can't sleep in hotels. And then there's the luggage and all the worries. I can't go alone."

"But you won't be alone. You'll have your maid with you." He spoke impatiently. The sick woman was usurping the place of the healthy one. He was being dragged back from the memory of the sunlit down and the quick, laughing girl, back to this unhealthy, overheated room and its complaining occupant.

"I don't think I shall be able to go."

"But you must, my dear, if the doctor tells you to. And, besides, a change will do you good."

"I don't think so."

"But Libbard thinks so, and he knows what he's talking about."

"No, I can't face it. I'm too weak. I can't go alone." Mrs. Hutton pulled a handkerchief out of her black silk bag, and put it to her eyes.

"Nonsense, my dear, you must make the effort."

"I had rather be left in peace to die here." She was crying in earnest now.

"O Lord! Now do be reasonable. Listen now, please." Mrs. Hutton only sobbed more violently. "Oh, what is one to do?" He shrugged his shoulders and walked out of the room.

Mr. Hutton was aware that he had not behaved with proper patience; but he could not help it. Very early in his manhood he had discovered that not only did he not feel sympathy for the poor, the weak, the diseased, and deformed; he actually hated them. Once, as an undergraduate, he spent three days at a mission in the East End. He had returned, filled with a profound and ineradicable disgust. Instead of pitying, he loathed the unfortunate. It was not, he knew, a very comely emotion; and he had been ashamed of it at first. In the end he had decided that it was temperamental, inevitable, and had felt no further qualms. Emily had been healthy and beautiful when he married her. He had loved her then. But now—was it his fault that she was like this?

Mr. Hutton dined alone. Food and drink left him more benevolent than he had been before dinner. To make amends for his show of exasperation he went up to his wife's room and offered to read to her. She was touched, gratefully accepted the offer, and Mr. Hutton, who was particularly proud of his accent, suggested a little light reading in French.

"French? I am so fond of French." Mrs. Hutton spoke of the language of Racine as though it were a dish of green peas.

Mr. Hutton ran down to the library and returned with a yellow volume. He began reading. The effort of pronouncing perfectly absorbed his whole attention. But how good his accent was! The fact of its goodness seemed to improve the quality of the novel he was reading.

At the end of fifteen pages an unmistakable sound aroused him. He looked up; Mrs. Hutton had gone to sleep. He sat still for a little while, looking with a dispassionate curiosity at the sleeping face. Once it had been beautiful; once, long ago, the sight of it, the recollection of it, had moved him with an emotion profounder, perhaps, than any he had felt before or since. Now it was lined and cadaverous. The skin was stretched tightly over the cheekbones, across the bridge of the sharp, bird-like nose. The closed eyes were set in profound bone-rimmed sockets. The lamplight striking on the face from the side emphasized with light and shade its cavities and projections. It was the face of a dead Christ by Morales.

> *Le squelette était invisible*
> *Au temps heureux de l'art païen.*

He shivered a little, and tiptoed out of the room.

On the following day Mrs. Hutton came down to luncheon. She had had some unpleasant palpitations during the night, but she was feeling better now. Besides, she wanted to do honour to

her guest. Miss Spence listened to her complaints about Llandrindod Wells, and was loud in sympathy, lavish with advice.
Whatever she said was always said with intensity. She leaned
forward, aimed, so to speak, like a gun, and fired her words. Bang!
the charge in her soul was ignited, the words whizzed forth at the
narrow barrel of her mouth. She was a machine-gun riddling her
hostess with sympathy. Mr. Hutton had undergone similar bom-
bardments, mostly of a literary or philosophic character—bom-
bardments of Maeterlinck, of Mrs. Besant, of Bergson, of William
James. To-day the missiles were medical. She talked about in-
somnia, she expatiated on the virtues of harmless drugs and
beneficent specialists. Under the bombardment Mrs. Hutton
opened out, like a flower in the sun.

Mr. Hutton looked on in silence. The spectacle of Janet Spence
evoked in him an unfailing curiosity. He was not romantic enough
to imagine that every face masked an interior physiognomy of
beauty or strangeness, that every woman's small talk was like a
vapour hanging over mysterious gulfs. His wife, for example, and
Doris; they were nothing more than what they seemed to be. But
with Janet Spence it was somehow different. Here one could be
sure that there was some kind of a queer face behind the Gioconda smile and the Roman eyebrows. The only question was:
What exactly was there? Mr. Hutton could never quite make out.

"But perhaps you won't have to go to Llandrindod after all,"
Miss Spence was saying. "If you get well quickly Dr. Libbard
will let you off."

"I only hope so. Indeed, I do really feel rather better to-day."

Mr. Hutton felt ashamed. How much was it his own lack of
sympathy that prevented her from feeling well every day? But
he comforted himself by reflecting that it was only a case of feeling, not of being better. Sympathy does not mend a diseased liver
or a weak heart.

"My dear, I wouldn't eat those red currants if I were you," he
said, suddenly solicitous. "You know that Libbard has banned
everything with skins and pips."

"But I am so fond of them," Mrs. Hutton protested, "and I feel so well to-day."

"Don't be a tyrant," said Miss Spence, looking first at him and then at his wife. "Let the poor invalid have what she fancies; it will do her good." She laid her hand on Mrs. Hutton's arm and patted it affectionately two or three times.

"Thank you, my dear." Mrs. Hutton helped herself to the stewed currants.

"Well, don't blame me if they make you ill again."

"Do I ever blame you, dear?"

"You have nothing to blame me for," Mr. Hutton answered playfully. "I am the perfect husband."

They sat in the garden after luncheon. From the island of shade under the old cypress tree they looked out across a flat expanse of lawn, in which the parterres of flowers shone with a metallic brilliance.

Mr. Hutton took a deep breath of the warm and fragrant air. "It's good to be alive," he said.

"Just to be alive," his wife echoed, stretching one pale, knot-jointed hand into the sunlight.

A maid brought the coffee; the silver pots and the little blue cups were set on a folding table near the group of chairs.

"Oh, my medicine!" exclaimed Mrs. Hutton. "Run in and fetch it, Clara, will you? The white bottle on the sideboard."

"I'll go," said Mr. Hutton. "I've got to go and fetch a cigar in any case."

He ran in towards the house. On the threshold he turned round for an instant. The maid was walking back across the lawn. His wife was sitting up in her deck-chair, engaged in opening her white parasol. Miss Spence was bending over the table, pouring out the coffee. He passed into the cool obscurity of the house.

"Do you like sugar in your coffee?" Miss Spence inquired.

"Yes, please. Give me rather a lot. I'll drink it after my medicine to take the taste away."

Mrs. Hutton leaned back in her chair, lowering the sunshade

over her eyes, so as to shut out from her vision the burning sky.

Behind her, Miss Spence was making a delicate clinking among the coffee-cups.

"I've given you three large spoonfuls. That ought to take the taste away. And here comes the medicine."

Mr. Hutton had reappeared, carrying a wine-glass, half full of a pale liquid.

"It smells delicious," he said, as he handed it to his wife.

"That's only the flavouring." She drank it off at a gulp, shuddered, and made a grimace. "Ugh, it's so nasty. Give me my coffee."

Miss Spence gave her the cup; she sipped at it. "You've made it like syrup. But it's very nice, after that atrocious medicine."

At half-past three Mrs. Hutton complained that she did not feel as well as she had done, and went indoors to lie down. Her husband would have said something about the red currants, but checked himself; the triumph of an "I told you so" was too cheaply won. Instead, he was sympathetic, and gave her his arm to the house.

"A rest will do you good," he said. "By the way, I shan't be back till after dinner."

"But why? Where are you going?"

"I promised to go to Johnson's this evening. We have to discuss the war memorial, you know."

"Oh, I wish you weren't going." Mrs. Hutton was almost in tears. "Can't you stay? I don't like being alone in the house."

"But, my dear, I promised—weeks ago." It was a bother having to lie like this. "And now I must get back and look after Miss Spence."

He kissed her on the forehead and went out again into the garden. Miss Spence received him aimed and intense.

"Your wife is dreadfully ill," she fired off at him.

"I thought she cheered up so much when you came."

"That was purely nervous, purely nervous. I was watching her closely. With a heart in that condition and her digestion wrecked —yes, wrecked—anything might happen."

"Libbard doesn't take so gloomy a view of poor Emily's health." Mr. Hutton held open the gate that led from the garden into the drive; Miss Spence's car was standing by the front door.

"Libbard is only a country doctor. You ought to see a specialist."

He could not refrain from laughing. "You have a macabre passion for specialists."

Miss Spence held up her hand in protest. "I am serious. I think poor Emily is in a very bad state. Anything might happen—at any moment."

He handed her into the car and shut the door. The chauffeur started the engine and climbed into his place, ready to drive off.

"Shall I tell him to start?" He had no desire to continue the conversation.

Miss Spence leaned forward and shot a Gioconda in his direction. "Remember, I expect you to come and see me again soon."

Mechanically he grinned, made a polite noise, and, as the car moved forward, waved his hand. He was happy to be alone.

A few minutes afterwards Mr. Hutton himself drove away. Doris was waiting at the cross-roads. They dined together twenty miles from home, at a roadside hotel. It was one of those bad, expensive meals which are only cooked in country hotels frequented by motorists. It revolted Mr. Hutton, but Doris enjoyed it. She always enjoyed things. Mr. Hutton ordered a not very good brand of champagne. He was wishing he had spent the evening in his library.

When they started homewards Doris was a little tipsy and extremely affectionate. It was very dark inside the car, but looking forward, past the motionless form of M'Nab, they could see a bright and narrow universe of forms and colours scooped out of the night by the electric head-lamps.

It was after eleven when Mr. Hutton reached home. Dr.

Libbard met him in the hall. He was a small man with delicate hands and well-formed features that were almost feminine. His brown eyes were large and melancholy. He used to waste a great deal of time sitting at the bedside of his patients, looking sadness through those eyes and talking in a sad, low voice about nothing in particular. His person exhaled a pleasing odour, decidedly antiseptic but at the same time suave and discreetly delicious.

"Libbard?" said Mr. Hutton in surprise. "You here? Is my wife ill?"

"We tried to fetch you earlier," the soft, melancholy voice replied. "It was thought you were at Mr. Johnson's, but they had no news of you there."

"No, I was detained. I had a breakdown," Mr. Hutton answered irritably. It was tiresome to be caught out in a lie.

"Your wife wanted to see you urgently."

"Well, I can go now." Mr. Hutton moved towards the stairs.

Dr. Libbard laid a hand on his arm. "I am afraid it's too late."

"Too late?" He began fumbling with his watch; it wouldn't come out of the pocket.

"Mrs. Hutton passed away half an hour ago."

The voice remained even in its softness, the melancholy of the eyes did not deepen. Dr. Libbard spoke of death as he would speak of a local cricket match. All things were equally vain and equally deplorable.

Mr. Hutton found himself thinking of Janet Spence's words. At any moment—at any moment. She had been extraordinarily right.

"What happened?" he asked. "What was the cause?"

Dr. Libbard explained. It was heart failure brought on by a violent attack of nausea, caused in its turn by the eating of something of an irritant nature. Red currants? Mr. Hutton suggested. Very likely. It had been too much for the heart. There was chronic valvular disease: something had collapsed under the strain. It was all over; she could not have suffered much.

III

"It's a pity they should have chosen the day of the Eton and Harrow match for the funeral," old General Grego was saying as he stood, his top hat in his hand, under the shadow of the lych gate, wiping his face with his handkerchief.

Mr. Hutton overheard the remark and with difficulty restrained a desire to inflict grievous bodily pain on the General. He would have liked to hit the old brute in the middle of his big red face. Monstrous great mulberry, spotted with meal! Was there no respect for the dead? Did nobody care? In theory he didn't much care; let the dead bury their dead. But here, at the graveside, he had found himself actually sobbing. Poor Emily, they had been pretty happy once. Now she was lying at the bottom of a seven-foot hole. And here was Grego complaining that he couldn't go to the Eton and Harrow match.

Mr. Hutton looked round at the groups of black figures that were drifting slowly out of the churchyard towards the fleet of cabs and motors assembled in the road outside. Against the brilliant background of the July grass and flowers and foliage, they had a horribly alien and unnatural appearance. It pleased him to think that all these people would soon be dead, too.

That evening Mr. Hutton sat up late in his library reading the life of Milton. There was no particular reason why he should have chosen Milton; it was the book that first came to hand, that was all. It was after midnight when he had finished. He got up from his armchair, unbolted the French windows, and stepped out on to the little paved terrace. The night was quiet and clear. Mr. Hutton looked at the stars and at the holes between them, dropped his eyes to the dim lawns and hueless flowers of the garden, and let them wander over the farther landscape, black and grey under the moon.

He began to think with a kind of confused violence. There were the stars, there was Milton. A man can be somehow the peer of stars and night. Greatness, nobility. But is there seriously a difference between the noble and the ignoble? Milton, the stars, death, and himself—himself. The soul, the body; the higher and the lower nature. Perhaps there was something in it, after all. Milton had a god on his side and righteousness. What had he? Nothing, nothing whatever. There were only Doris's little breasts. What was the point of it all? Milton, the stars, death, and Emily in her grave, Doris and himself—always himself . . .

Oh, he was a futile and disgusting being. Everything convinced him of it. It was a solemn moment. He spoke aloud: "I will, I will." The sound of his own voice in the darkness was appalling; it seemed to him that he had sworn that infernal oath which binds even the gods: "I will, I will." There had been New Year's days and solemn anniversaries in the past, when he had felt the same contritions and recorded similar resolutions. They had all thinned away, these resolutions, like smoke, into nothingness. But this was a greater moment and he had pronounced a more fearful oath. In the future it was to be different. Yes, he would live by reason, he would be industrious, he would curb his appetites, he would devote his life to some good purpose. It was resolved and it would be so.

In practice he saw himself spending his mornings in agricultural pursuits, riding round with the bailiff, seeing that his land was farmed in the best modern way—silos and artificial manures and continuous cropping, and all that. The remainder of the day should be devoted to serious study. There was that book he had been intending to write for so long—*The Effect of Diseases on Civilization.*

Mr. Hutton went to bed humble and contrite, but with a sense that grace had entered into him. He slept for seven and a half hours, and woke to find the sun brilliantly shining. The emotions of the evening before had been transformed by a good night's rest into his customary cheerfulness. It was not until a good many seconds after his return to conscious life that he remembered his resolution, his Stygian oath. Milton and death seemed somehow different in the sunlight. As for the stars, they were not there. But the resolutions were good; even in the daytime he could see that. He had his horse saddled after breakfast, and rode round the farm with the bailiff. After luncheon he read Thucydides on the plague at Athens. In the evening he made a few notes on malaria in Southern Italy. While he was undressing he remembered that there was a good anecdote in Skelton's jest-book about the Sweating Sickness. He would have made a note of it if only he could have found a pencil.

On the sixth morning of his new life Mr. Hutton found among his correspondence an envelope addressed in that peculiarly vulgar handwriting which he knew to be Doris's. He opened it, and began to read. She didn't know what to say; words were so inadequate. His wife dying like that, and so suddenly—it was too terrible. Mr. Hutton sighed, but his interest revived somewhat as he read on:

"Death is so frightening, I never think of it when I can help it. But when something like this happens, or when I am feeling ill or depressed, then I can't help remembering it is there so close, and I think about all the wicked things I have done and about you and me, and I wonder what will happen, and I am so frightened. I am so lonely, Teddy Bear, and so unhappy, and I don't know what to do. I can't get rid of the idea of dying, I am so wretched and helpless without you. I didn't mean to write to you; I meant to wait till you were out of mourning and could come and see me again, but I was so lonely and miserable, Teddy Bear, I had to write. I couldn't help it. Forgive me, I want you so much; I have nobody in the world but you. You are so good and gentle and understanding; there is nobody like you. I shall never forget how good and kind you have been to me, and you are so clever and know so much, I can't understand how you ever came to pay any attention to me, I am so dull and stupid, much less like me and love me, because you do love me a little, don't you, Teddy Bear?"

Mr. Hutton was touched with shame and remorse. To be thanked like this, worshipped for having seduced the girl—it was too much. It had just been a piece of imbecile wantonness. Imbecile, idiotic: there was no other way to describe it. For, when all was said, he had derived very little pleasure from it. Taking all things together, he had probably been more bored than amused. Once upon a time he had believed himself to be a hedonist. But to be a hedonist implies a certain process of reasoning, a deliberate choice of known pleasures, a rejection of known pains. This had been done without reason, against it. For he knew beforehand—so well, so well—that there was no interest or pleasure to be derived from these wretched affairs. And yet each time the vague itch came upon him he succumbed, involving himself once more in the old stupidity. There had been Maggie, his wife's maid, and Edith, the girl on the farm, and Mrs. Pringle, and the waitress in London, and others—there seemed to be dozens of them. It had all been so stale and boring. He knew it would be; he always knew. And yet, and yet . . . Experience doesn't teach.

Poor little Doris! He would write to her kindly, comfortingly, but he wouldn't see her again. A servant came to tell him that his horse was saddled and waiting. He mounted and rode off. That morning the old bailiff was more irritating than usual.

Five days later Doris and Mr. Hutton were sitting together on the pier at Southend; Doris, in white muslin with pink garnishings, radiated happiness; Mr. Hutton, legs outstretched and chair tilted, had pushed the panama back from his forehead, and was trying to feel like a tripper. That night, when Doris was asleep, breathing and warm by his side, he recaptured, in this moment of darkness and physical fatigue, the rather cosmic emotion which had possessed him that evening, not a fortnight ago, when he had made his great resolution. And so his solemn oath had already gone the way of so many other resolutions. Unreason had triumphed;

at the first itch of desire he had given way. He was hopeless, hopeless.

For a long time he lay with closed eyes, ruminating his humiliation. The girl stirred in her sleep. Mr. Hutton turned over and looked in her direction. Enough faint light crept in between the half-drawn curtains to show her bare arm and shoulder, her neck, and the dark tangle of hair on the pillow. She was beautiful, desirable. Why did he lie there moaning over his sins? What did it matter? If he were hopeless, then so be it; he would make the best of his hopelessness. A glorious sense of irresponsibility suddenly filled him. He was free, magnificently free. In a kind of exaltation he drew the girl towards him. She woke, bewildered, almost frightened under his rough kisses.

The storm of his desire subsided into a kind of serene merriment. The whole atmosphere seemed to be quivering with enormous silent laughter.

"Could anyone love you as much as I do, Teddy Bear?" The question came faintly from distant worlds of love.

"I think I know somebody who does," Mr. Hutton replied. The submarine laughter was swelling, rising, ready to break the surface of silence and resound.

"Who? Tell me. What do you mean?" The voice had come very close; charged with suspicion, anguish, indignation, it belonged to this immediate world.

"A—ah!"

"Who?"

"You'll never guess." Mr. Hutton kept up the joke until it began to grow tedious, and then pronounced the name "Janet Spence."

Doris was incredulous. "Miss Spence of the Manor? That old woman?" It was too ridiculous. Mr. Hutton laughed too.

"But it's quite true," he said. "She adores me." Oh, the vast joke. He would go and see her as soon as he returned—see and conquer. "I believe she wants to marry me," he added.

"But you wouldn't . . . you don't intend . . ."

The air was fairly crepitating with humour. Mr. Hutton laughed aloud. "I intend to marry you," he said. It seemed to him the best joke he had ever made in his life.

When Mr. Hutton left Southend he was once more a married man. It was agreed that, for the time being, the fact should be kept secret. In the autumn they would go abroad together, and the world should be informed. Meanwhile he was to go back to his own house and Doris to hers.

The day after his return he walked over in the afternoon to see Miss Spence. She received him with the old Gioconda.

"I was expecting you to come."

"I couldn't keep away," Mr. Hutton gallantly replied.

They sat in the summer-house. It was a pleasant place—a little old stucco temple bowered among dense bushes of evergreen. Miss Spence had left her mark on it by hanging up over the seat a blue-and-white Della Robbia plaque.

"I am thinking of going to Italy this autumn," said Mr. Hutton. He felt like a ginger-beer bottle, ready to pop with bubbling humorous excitement.

"Italy. . . ." Miss Spence closed her eyes ecstatically. "I feel drawn there too."

"Why not let yourself be drawn?"

"I don't know. One somehow hasn't the energy and initiative to set out alone."

"Alone. . . ." Ah, sound of guitars and throaty singing! "Yes, travelling alone isn't much fun."

Miss Spence lay back in her chair without speaking. Her eyes were still closed. Mr. Hutton stroked his moustache. The silence prolonged itself for what seemed a very long time.

Pressed to stay to dinner, Mr. Hutton did not refuse. The fun had hardly started. The table was laid in the loggia. Through its arches they looked out on to the sloping garden, to the valley below and the farther hills. Light ebbed away; the heat and silence were oppressive. A huge cloud was mounting up the sky, and

there were distant breathings of thunder. The thunder drew
nearer, a wind began to blow, and the first drops of rain fell. The
table was cleared. Miss Spence and Mr. Hutton sat on in the growing darkness.

Miss Spence broke a long silence by saying meditatively:

"I think everyone has a right to a certain amount of happiness,
don't you?"

"Most certainly." But what was she leading up to? Nobody
makes generalisations about life unless they mean to talk about
themselves. Happiness: he looked back on his own life, and saw a
cheerful, placid existence disturbed by no great griefs or discomforts or alarms. He had always had money and freedom; he
had been able to do very much as he wanted. Yes, he supposed he
had been happy—happier than most men. And now he was not
merely happy; he had discovered in irresponsibility the secret of
gaiety. He was about to say something about his happiness when
Miss Spence went on speaking.

"People like you and me have a right to be happy some time
in our lives."

"Me?" said Mr. Hutton surprised.

"Poor Henry! Fate hasn't treated either of us very well."

"Oh, well, it might have treated me worse."

"You're being cheerful. That's brave of you. But don't think I
can't see behind the mask."

Miss Spence spoke louder and louder as the rain came down
more and more heavily. Periodically the thunder cut across her
utterances. She talked on, shouting against the noise.

"I have understood you so well and for so long."

A flash revealed her, aimed and intent, leaning towards him.
Her eyes were two profound and menacing gun-barrels. The
darkness re-engulfed her.

"You were a lonely soul seeking a companion soul. I could
sympathise with you in your solitude. Your marriage . . ."

The thunder cut short the sentence. Miss Spence's voice became audible once more with the words:

". . . could offer no companionship to a man of your stamp. You needed a soul mate."

A soul mate—he! a soul mate. It was incredibly fantastic. "Georgette Leblanc, the ex-soul mate of Maurice Maeterlinck." He had seen that in the paper a few days ago. So it was thus that Janet Spence had painted him in her imagination—a soul-mater. And for Doris he was a picture of goodness and the cleverest man in the world. And actually, really, he was what?—Who knows?

"My heart went out to you. I could understand; I was lonely, too." Miss Spence laid her hand on his knee. "You were so patient." Another flash. She was still aimed, dangerously. "You never complained. But I could guess—I could guess."

"How wonderful of you!" So he was an *âme incomprise*. "Only a woman's intuition . . ."

The thunder crashed and rumbled, died away, and only the sound of the rain was left. The thunder was his laughter, magnified, externalised. Flash and crash, there it was again, right on top of them.

"Don't you feel that you have within you something that is akin to this storm?" He could imagine her leaning forward as she uttered the words. "Passion makes one the equal of the elements."

What was his gambit now? Why, obviously, he should have said "Yes," and ventured on some unequivocal gesture. But Mr. Hutton suddenly took fright. The ginger beer in him had gone flat. The woman was serious—terribly serious. He was appalled.

Passion? "No," he desperately answered. "I am without passion."

But his remark was either unheard or unheeded, for Miss Spence went on with a growing exaltation, speaking so rapidly, however, and in such a burningly intimate whisper that Mr. Hutton found it very difficult to distinguish what she was saying. She was telling him, as far as he could make out, the story of her life. The lightning was less frequent now, and there were long intervals of darkness. But at each flash he saw her still aiming towards him, still yearning forward with a terrifying intensity. Darkness, the rain, and then flash! her face was there, close at hand. A pale mask, greenish white; the large eyes, the narrow barrel of the mouth, the heavy eyebrows. Agrippina, or wasn't it rather—yes, wasn't it rather George Robey?

He began devising absurd plans for escaping. He might suddenly jump up, pretending he had seen a burglar—Stop thief! stop thief!—and dash off into the night in pursuit. Or should he say that he felt faint, a heart attack? or that he had seen a ghost—Emily's ghost—in the garden? Absorbed in his childish plotting, he had ceased to pay any attention to Miss Spence's words. The spasmodic clutching of her hand recalled his thoughts.

"I honoured you for that, Henry," she was saying.

Honoured him for what?

"Marriage is a sacred tie, and your respect for it, even when the marriage was, as it was in your case, an unhappy one, made me respect you and admire you, and—shall I dare say the word?—"

Oh, the burglar, the ghost in the garden! But it was too late.

". . . yes, love you, Henry, all the more. But we're free now, Henry."

Free? There was a movement in the dark, and she was kneeling on the floor by his chair.

"Oh, Henry, Henry, I have been unhappy too."

Her arms embraced him, and by the shaking of her body he could feel that she was sobbing. She might have been a suppliant crying for mercy.

"You mustn't, Janet," he protested. Those tears were terrible, terrible. "Not now, not now! You must be calm; you must go to bed." He patted her shoulder, then got up, disengaging himself from her embrace. He left her still crouching on the floor beside the chair on which he had been sitting.

Groping his way into the hall, and without waiting to look for his hat, he went out of the house, taking infinite pains to close the front door noiselessly behind him. The clouds had blown over, and the moon was shining from a clear sky. There were puddles all along the road, and a noise of running water rose from the gutters and ditches. Mr. Hutton splashed along, not caring if he got wet.

How heartrendingly she had sobbed! With the emotions of pity and remorse that the recollection evoked in him there was a certain resentment: why couldn't she have played the game that he was playing—the heartless, amusing game? Yes, but he had known all the time that she wouldn't, she couldn't play that game; he had known and persisted.

What had she said about passion and the elements? Something absurdly stale, but true, true. There she was, a cloud black bosomed and charged with thunder, and he, like some absurd little Benjamin Franklin, had sent up a kite into the heart of the menace. Now he was complaining that his toy had drawn the lightning.

She was probably still kneeling by that chair in the loggia, crying.

But why hadn't he been able to keep up the game? Why had his irresponsibility deserted him, leaving him suddenly sober in a cold world? There were no answers to any of his questions. One idea burned steady and luminous in his mind—the idea of flight. He must get away at once.

IV

"What are you thinking about, Teddy Bear?"

"Nothing."

There was a silence. Mr. Hutton remained motionless, his elbows on the parapet of the terrace, his chin in his hands, looking down over Florence. He had taken a villa on one of the hilltops to the south of the city. From a little raised terrace at the end of the garden one looked down a long fertile valley on to the town and beyond it to the bleak mass of Monte Morello and, eastward of it, to the peopled hill of Fiesole, dotted with white houses. Everything was clear and luminous in the September sunshine.

"Are you worried about anything?"

"No, thank you."

"Tell me, Teddy Bear."

"But, my dear, there's nothing to tell." Mr. Hutton turned round, smiled, and patted the girl's hand. "I think you'd better go in and have your siesta. It's too hot for you here."

"Very well, Teddy Bear. Are you coming too?"

"When I've finished my cigar."

"All right. But do hurry up and finish it, Teddy Bear." Slowly, reluctantly, she descended the steps of the terrace and walked towards the house.

Mr. Hutton continued his contemplation of Florence. He had need to be alone. It was good sometimes to escape from Doris and the restless solicitude of her passion. He had never known the pains of loving hopelessly, but he was experiencing now the pains of being loved. These last weeks had been a period of growing discomfort. Doris was always with him, like an obsession, like a guilty conscience. Yes, it was good to be alone.

He pulled an envelope out of his pocket and opened it; not without reluctance. He hated letters; they always contained something unpleasant—nowadays, since his second marriage. This was from his sister. He began skimming through the insulting home-truths of which it was composed. The words "indecent haste," "social suicide," "scarcely cold in her grave," "person of the lower classes," all occurred. They were inevitable now in any communication from a well-meaning and right-thinking relative. Impatient, he was about to tear the stupid letter to pieces when his eye fell on a sentence at the bottom of the third page. His heart beat with uncomfortable violence as he read it. It was too monstrous! Janet Spence was going about telling everyone that he had poisoned his wife in order to marry Doris. What damnable malice! Ordinarily a man of the suavest temper, Mr. Hutton found himself trembling with rage. He took the childish satisfaction of calling names—he cursed the woman.

Then suddenly he saw the ridiculous side of the situation. The notion that he should have murdered anyone in order to marry Doris! If they only knew how miserably bored he was. Poor, dear Janet! She had tried to be malicious; she had only succeeded in being stupid.

A sound of footsteps aroused him; he looked round. In the garden below the little terrace the servant girl of the house was picking fruit. A Neapolitan, strayed somehow as far north as Florence, she was a specimen of the classical type—a little debased. Her profile might have been taken from a Sicilian coin of a bad period. Her features, carved floridly in the grand tradition, expressed an almost perfect stupidity. Her mouth was the most beautiful thing about her; the calligraphic hand of nature had richly curved it into an expression of mulish bad temper. . . . Under her hideous black clothes, Mr. Hutton divined a powerful body, firm and massive. He had looked at her before with a vague interest and curiosity. To-day the curiosity defined and focused itself into a desire. An idyll of Theocritus. Here was the woman; he, alas, was not precisely like a goatherd on the volcanic hills. He called to her.

"Armida!"

The smile with which she answered him was so provocative, attested so easy a virtue, that Mr. Hutton took fright. He was on the brink once more—on the brink. He must draw back, oh! quickly, quickly, before it was too late. The girl continued to look up at him.

"*Ha chiamato?*" she asked at last.

Stupidity or reason? Oh, there was no choice now. It was imbecility every time.

"*Scendo,*" he called back to her. Twelve steps led from the garden to the terrace. Mr. Hutton counted them. Down, down, down, down. . . . He saw a vision of himself descending from one circle of the inferno to the next—from a darkness full of wind and hail to an abyss of stinking mud.

V

For a good many days the Hutton case had a place on the front page of every newspaper. There had been no more popular murder trial since George Smith had temporarily eclipsed the European War by drowning in a warm bath his seventh bride. The public imagination was stirred by this tale of a murder brought to light months after the date of the crime. Here, it was felt, was one of those incidents in human life, so notable because they are so rare, which do definitely justify the ways of God to man. A wicked man had been moved by an illicit passion to kill his wife. For months he had lived in sin and fancied security—only to be dashed at last more horribly into the pit he had prepared for himself. Murder will out, and here was a case of it. The readers of the newspapers were in a position to follow every movement of the hand of God. There had been vague, but persistent, rumours in the neighbourhood; the police had taken action at last. Then came the exhumation order, the post-mortem examination, the inquest, the evidence of the experts, the verdict of the coroner's jury, the trial, the condemnation. For once Providence had done its duty, obviously, grossly, didactically, as in a melodrama. The newspapers were right in making of the case the staple intellectual food of a whole season.

Mr. Hutton's first emotion when he was summoned from Italy to give evidence at the inquest was one of indignation. It was a monstrous, a scandalous thing that the police should take such idle, malicious gossip seriously. When the inquest was over he would bring an action for malicious prosecution against the Chief Constable; he would sue the Spence woman for slander.

The inquest was opened; the astonishing evidence unrolled itself. The experts had examined the body, and had found traces of arsenic; they were of opinion that the late Mrs. Hutton had died of arsenic poisoning.

Arsenic poisoning. . . . Emily had died of arsenic poisoning?

After that, Mr. Hutton learned with surprise that there was enough arsenicated insecticide in his greenhouses to poison an army.

It was now, quite suddenly, that he saw it: there was a case against him. Fascinated, he watched it growing, growing, like some monstrous tropical plant. It was enveloping him, surrounding him; he was lost in a tangled forest.

When was the poison administered? The experts agreed that it must have been swallowed eight or nine hours before death. About lunch-time? Yes, about lunch-time. Clara, the parlour-maid, was called. Mrs. Hutton, she remembered, had asked her to go and fetch her medicine. Mr. Hutton had volunteered to go instead; he had gone alone. Miss Spence—ah, the memory of the storm, the white aimed face! the horror of it all!—Miss Spence confirmed Clara's statement, and added that Mr. Hutton had come back with the medicine already poured out in a wineglass, not in the bottle.

Mr. Hutton's indignation evaporated. He was dismayed, frightened. It was all too fantastic to be taken seriously, and yet this nightmare was a fact—it was actually happening.

M'Nab had seen them kissing, often. He had taken them for a drive on the day of Mrs. Hutton's death. He could see them reflected in the wind-screen, sometimes out of the tail of his eye.

The inquest was adjourned. That evening Doris went to bed with a headache. When he went to her room after dinner, Mr. Hutton found her crying.

"What's the matter?" He sat down on the edge of her bed and began to stroke her hair. For a long time she did not answer, and he went on stroking her hair mechanically, almost unconsciously; sometimes, even he bent down and kissed her bare shoulder. He had his own affairs, however, to think about. What had happened? How was it that the stupid gossip had actually come true? Emily had died of arsenic poisoning. It was absurd, impossible. The order of things had been broken, and he was at the mercy of an irresponsibility. What had happened, what was going to happen? He was interrupted in the midst of his thoughts.

"It's my fault—it's my fault!" Doris suddenly sobbed out. "I shouldn't have loved you; I oughtn't to have let you love me. Why was I ever born?"

Mr. Hutton didn't say anything, but looked down in silence at the abject figure of misery lying on the bed.

"If they do anything to you I shall kill myself."

She sat up, held him for a moment at arm's length, and looked at him with a kind of violence, as though she were never to see him again.

"I love you, I love you, I love you." She drew him, inert and passive, towards her, clasped him, pressed herself against him. "I didn't know you loved me as much as that, Teddy Bear. But why did you do it—why did you do it?"

Mr. Hutton undid her clasping arms and got up. His face became very red. "You seem to take it for granted that I murdered my wife," he said. "It's really too grotesque. What do you all take me for? A cinema hero?" He had begun to lose his temper. All the exasperation, all the fear and bewilderment of the day, was transformed into a violent anger against her. "It's all such damned stupidity. Haven't you any conception of a civilised man's mentality? Do I look the sort of man who'd go about slaughtering people? I suppose you imagined I was so insanely in love with you that I could commit any folly. When will you women understand that one isn't insanely in love? All one asks for is a quiet life, which you won't allow one to have. I don't know what the devil ever induced me to marry you. It was all a damned stupid, practical joke. And now you go about saying I'm a murderer. I won't stand it."

Mr. Hutton stamped towards the door. He had said horrible things, he knew—odious things that he ought speedily to unsay. But he wouldn't. He closed the door behind him.

"Teddy Bear!" He turned the handle; the latch clicked into place. "Teddy Bear!" The voice that came to him through the closed door was agonised. Should he go back? He ought to go back. He touched the handle, then withdrew his fingers and quickly walked away. When he was halfway down the stairs he halted. She might try to do something silly—throw herself out of the window or God knows what! He listened attentively; there was no sound. But he pictured her very clearly, tiptoeing across the room, lifting the sash as high as it would go, leaning out into the cold night air. It was raining a little. Under the window lay the paved terrace. How far below? Twenty-five or thirty feet? Once, when he was walking along Piccadilly, a dog had jumped out of a third-story window of the Ritz. He had seen it fall; he had heard it strike the pavement. Should he go back? He was damned if he would; he hated her.

He sat for a long time in the library. What had happened? What was happening? He turned the question over and over in his mind and could find no answer. Suppose the nightmare dreamed itself out to its horrible conclusion. Death was waiting for him. His eyes filled with tears; he wanted so passionately to live. "Just to be alive." Poor Emily had wished it too, he remembered: "Just to be alive." There were still so many places in this astonishing world unvisited, so many queer delightful people still unknown, so many lovely women never so much as seen. The huge white oxen would still be dragging their wains along the Tuscan roads, the cypresses would still go up, straight as pillars, to the blue heaven; but he would not be there to see them. And the sweet southern wines—Tear of Christ and Blood of Judas—others would drink them, not he. Others would walk down the obscure and narrow lanes between the bookshelves in the London Library, sniffing the dusty perfume of good literature, peering at strange titles, discovering unknown names, exploring the fringes of vast domains of knowledge. He would be lying in a hole in the ground. And why, why? Confusedly he felt that some extraordinary kind of justice was being done. In the past he had been wanton and imbecile and irresponsible. Now Fate was playing as wantonly, as irresponsibly, with him. It was tit for tat, and God existed after all.

He felt that he would like to pray. Forty years ago he used to kneel by his bed every evening. The nightly formula of his childhood came to him almost unsought from some long unopened chamber of the memory. "God bless Father and Mother, Tom and Cissie and the Baby, Mademoiselle and Nurse, and everyone that I love, and make me a good boy. Amen." They were all dead now—all except Cissie.

His mind seemed to soften and dissolve; a great calm descended upon his spirit. He went upstairs to ask Doris's forgiveness. He found her lying on the couch at the foot of the bed. On the floor beside her stood a blue bottle of liniment, marked "Not to be taken"; she seemed to have drunk about half of it.

"You didn't love me," was all she said when she opened her eyes to find him bending over her.

Dr. Libbard arrived in time to prevent any very serious consequences. "You mustn't do this again," he said while Mr. Hutton was out of the room.

"What's to prevent me?" she asked defiantly.

Dr. Libbard looked at her with his large, sad eyes. "There's nothing to prevent you," he said. "Only yourself and your baby. Isn't it rather bad luck on your baby, not allowing it to come into the world because you want to go out of it?"

Doris was silent for a time. "All right," she whispered. "I won't."

Mr. Hutton sat by her bedside for the rest of the night. He felt himself now to be indeed a murderer. For a time he persuaded himself that he loved this pitiable child. Dozing in his chair, he woke up, stiff and cold, to find himself drained dry, as it were, of every emotion. He had become nothing but a tired and suffering carcase. At six o'clock he undressed and went to bed for a couple of hours' sleep. In the course of the same afternoon the coroner's jury brought in a verdict of "Wilful Murder," and Mr. Hutton was committed for trial.

VI

Miss Spence was not at all well. She had found her public appearances in the witness-box very trying, and when it was all over she had something that was very nearly a breakdown. She slept badly, and suffered from nervous indigestion. Dr. Libbard used to call every other day. She talked to him a great deal—mostly about the Hutton case. . . . Her moral indignation was always on the boil. Wasn't it appalling to think that one had had a murderer in one's house. Wasn't it extraordinary that one could have been for so long mistaken about the man's character? (But she had had an inkling from the first.) And then the girl he had gone off with—so low class, so little better than a prostitute. The news that the second Mrs. Hutton was expecting a baby— the posthumous child of a condemned and executed criminal— revolted her; the thing was shocking—an obscenity. Dr. Libbard answered her gently and vaguely, and prescribed bromide.

One morning he interrupted her in the midst of her customary tirade. "By the way," he said in his soft, melancholy voice, "I suppose it was really you who poisoned Mrs. Hutton."

Miss Spence stared at him for two or three seconds with enormous eyes, and then quietly said, "Yes." After that she started to cry.

"In the coffee, I suppose."

She seemed to nod assent. Dr. Libbard took out his fountain-pen, and in his neat, meticulous calligraphy wrote out a prescription for a sleeping-draught.

Critical Analysis

AT THE outset it is important to consider the tone of "The Gioconda Smile." What might be a murder-mystery thriller becomes a vehicle for brilliant wit and satirical characterization, expressing a derisive view of human nature. Everyone is ridiculed. Huxley's characters live in a world where they either shun responsibility or step in arbitrarily to solve the problems of others. In either case they become fools, and eventually lose what they want. Mr. Hutton's and Janet Spence's views of themselves and others about them bring death and frustration. Huxley's attitude toward his characters and his manner of presenting that attitude provide the satirical and witty tone of "The Gioconda Smile."

The story is told in six parts, not to block out neatly the narrative of events but to provide episodes and incidents which give Huxley the best opportunity for satiric effects and ironical situations. Expected "big scenes" of action of the conventional type are usually merely stated in passing. What ordinary murder story, for example, would omit the trial of Mr. Hutton? The parts vary in range, intensity, and satiric force but all contribute to the total effect of irony and satire. The first part introduces Mr. Hutton and, mainly through his observation, Janet Spence. Notice how the story begins—with Mr. Hutton's monologue on Janet Spence and a reverie of self-admiration as he gazes into the mirror. Mr. Hutton's own proud approval of his long, bounding strides and his "youth" gives the reader a strong hint of his physical quality and his egocentricity. The ironic contrast between what Mr. Hutton protests: "I must get back to see how poor Emily is," and the truth of Doris, waiting in the "obscurity" of the back seat of the car for her "Teddy Bear," provides a humorous surprise—and a view of the true Mr. Hutton.

The section is primarily used to introduce character but not in a plain expository manner. Wit and satire supply the tone, especially in the description of Janet's taste in art and in Doris's baby talk. Actually, the only plot development is the invitation for Janet Spence, Mr. Hutton's "mysterious Gioconda," to come to luncheon. Part II might be called the life and death of sickly, though once pretty, Mrs. Hutton; now her cadaverous, lifeless mien is in strong contrast to Mr. Hutton and to the frolicsome

Doris, who even at this moment occupies his thoughts. To Mr. Hutton Janet Spence is an enigma, but, ironically, the probing of the riddle is to be his doom.

The irony of contrasting situation is again stressed in the activities of Mr. Hutton. Supposedly on a visit to the Johnsons "to discuss the war memorial, you know," he is actually with Doris, bored with his rendezvous at a roadside hotel, while at home his wife has died (poisoned by a woman in love with him!).

The penitence of Mr. Hutton opens the third section, but the penitence is not only short-lived; it is too late. His plan to take personal interest in his estate and also to write his great work on *The Effect of Diseases on Civilization* fails quickly. Reason is defeated; Doris wins. Mr. Hutton's intention of marrying Doris "seemed to him the best joke he had ever made in his life"; yet it is a joke which is to have ironic payment in Part IV. Janet Spence's confession of love allows him one more opportunity for grim "fun," but Mr. Hutton, "like some absurd little Benjamin Franklin, had sent up a kite in the heart of the menace. Now he was complaining that his toy had drawn lightning." The very simile is a good example of Huxley's witty laughter at the character.

It might be useful here to notice that Huxley up to this point has set up incidents and situations from which the story is to be completed. From the view of plot, the reader might well remember that Miss Spence had given Mrs. Hutton the fatal coffee at the luncheon (page 340) and had remarked to Mr. Hutton:

"I think Emily is in a very bad state. Anything might happen—at any moment."

Important both for plot and character are the actions and attitudes of Mr. Hutton, Doris, and Janet. The boredom which Doris can arouse in Mr. Hutton (page 334) is a mere sample of what married life with the lady was to be. Mr. Hutton's horror at the proposal to be Janet's "soul mate" has left a potential avenger in the story.

Part IV shifts the scene to Florence, to Mr. Hutton's life with Doris, and to his continued sensual drive. Bored with the lusty Doris, he sees Armida, the Neapolitan girl, standing enticingly before him, and he makes the decision for "imbecility." Huxley's wit in the treatment of character is carefully expressed in Mr. Hutton's intellectualized literary vision of his descent to Armida.

"*Scendo*," he called back to her. Twelve steps led from the garden to the terrace. Mr. Hutton counted them. Down, down, down, down. . . . He saw a vision of himself descending from one circle of the inferno to the next—from a darkness full of wind and hail to an abyss of stinking mud.

The tone for the conclusion of the story is set by the second sentence of Section V: "There had been no more popular murder trial since George Smith had temporarily eclipsed the European War by drowning in a warm bath his seventh bride." Huxley handles the detail briskly and briefly. What he wishes to stress most in the chapter is the final irony, the real irony of the story. To Mr. Hutton's disgust, Doris looks upon him as a murderer of the cinema-hero type, but he is psychologically and morally a murderer as he realizes what action Doris might take. Yet then follows the confession of his desire to live: "His eyes filled with tears; he wanted so passionately to live." And note what Mr. Hutton wants to live for—travel, new scenes, rare wines, the old volumes, "so many lovely women never so much as seen." The derisive laughter of Huxley at Mr. Hutton is here at its height. The formula of penitence, late and absurd, is repeated. The plot, whose elements have been in secondary position, becomes important in the brevity of its expression: "In the course of the same afternoon the coroner's jury brought in a verdict of 'Wilful Murder,' and Mr. Hutton was committed for trial."

At the very end of Part VI is Janet's confession, briefly given, but this short section shows Huxley's skill in drawing the final ironic portrait of a ridiculous, revengeful woman. He does it simply by a short mocking display of her point of view.

Her moral indignation was always on the boil. Wasn't it appalling to think that one had had a murderer in one's house? Wasn't it extraordinary that one could have been for so long mistaken about the man's character? (But she had had an inkling from the first.) And then the girl he had gone off with—so low class, so little better than a prostitute. The news that the second Mrs. Hutton was expecting a baby—the posthumous child of a condemned and executed criminal—revolted her; the thing was shocking—an obscenity.

Dr. Libbard, an observer in the story, has seen Mr. Hutton and the three women who affected his life. He knows all; he has the true key to the mystery of the "murderer," Mr. Hutton, and to the mind and action of Janet Spence. But he is a scrupulously "professional" soul, apparently beyond positive moral action. The conventional narrative would not have ended with Janet Spence's confession to her doctor. Why does Huxley end the story in this way? He has accomplished all he set out to do—to show his people caught in their own actions and ideas of life. Mr. Hutton is his main interest, and in Mr. Hutton's career the irony of the story is concentrated.

Huxley has paraded his fools. Mr. Hutton is torn between passion and reason and always does the absurd thing. Janet is a self-centred romantic, volatile and revengeful. Through her action the title, "The Gioconda Smile," becomes clear. The enticing, enigmatic charm of the smile of the wife of Francesco del Giocondo captivated Leonardo da Vinci, who painted her portrait, known as the Mona Lisa. Janet Spence's studied Gioconda smile has led Mr. Hutton, the polite, playfully chivalric sensualist, to his death. Doris, who in Mr. Hutton's opinion resembles a mistress of Charles II, is the flesh, the glorifier of conventional melodramatic action. Mrs. Hutton is the rose faded, the self-indulgent invalid in mind and body.

The irony and comic satire of "The Gioconda Smile" are at once an expression of and a part of the wit with which the story is conceived and executed. Wit best serves character and idea rather than plot and creates the final comic ironic tone of the tale. Huxley has paid most attention to Mr. Hutton, both as Mr. Hutton reveals himself and as he sees others. Though self-revealed as a sensualist and an egocentric, he has a curious intellectualized imagination which occasionally expresses itself wittily in references to philology, marine biology, literature, and art. To Janet's remark that he is cynical, he has the desire to answer "Bow-wow-wow," a philological retort stemming from the literal meaning of "cynical," doglike (Greek, kynikos). When he tells Doris that the "electricity" is in *her,* he recalls her as the sea-mouse, a sea worm of the genus *Aphrodite* or as a sea-cucumber, "which turns itself inside out in moments of alarm." His remarks about Milton's being called the "Lady of Christ's" (i.e. Christ's College, Cambridge) give him a neat opportunity to call himself "Christ of Ladies." The ailing Mrs. Hutton has in Mr. Hutton's view "the face of a dead Christ by Morales." But many times Mr. Hutton's intellectual byplay and descriptive power seem more a product of Huxley's own style than anything developed from the established character of Mr. Hutton. In one case, although the reader is led to believe that he is observing Janet Spence through Mr. Hutton's consciousness, the witty description of the lady seems to be Huxley's own.

What a queer face she had! That small mouth pursed forward by the Gioconda expression into a little snout with a round hole in the middle as though for whistling—it was like a penholder seen from the front. Above the mouth a well-shaped nose, finely aquiline. Eyes large, lustrous, and dark, with the largeness, lustre, and darkness that seems to invite sties and an occasional bloodshot suffusion. They were fine eyes, but unchangingly grave. The penholder might do its Gioconda trick, but the eyes never altered in their earnestness. Above them, a pair of boldly arched, heavily pencilled black eyebrows lent a surprising air of power, as of a Roman matron, to the upper portion of the face. Her hair was dark and equally Roman; Agrippina from the brows upward.

Huxley has other useful tricks. Mr. Hutton is always *Mr.* Hutton, except for the moments of his greatest emotional fervor in his scene with Janet—when he becomes "Henry," "Poor Henry." To Doris he is always "Teddy Bear," and she scarcely addresses a sentence to him without the nickname. By repetition these comic-satiric devices become very effective tags. Other examples are the "old Gioconda" which Janet throws at Mr. Hutton, and the characterization of Janet as Agrippina, or as Huxley devastatingly asks in the height of Janet's crisis, "Wasn't it rather George Robey?" The undertone of laughter runs through the description both of event and of character. The thunderstorm which rages during Janet's confession of love provides intensity, but of a comic-opera sort.

Huxley's brilliant verbal virtuosity, although it occasionally draws too much attention to itself, is derived from his whole approach to the story. This is not a story of plot. It is a skillfully ironic, brilliantly written portrait of an irresponsible sensualist, trying to live, but getting caught in a world which absurdly glorifies or condemns his actions. The characters in "The Gioconda Smile" are in mortal coils and Huxley laughs at each one of them.

Babylon Revisited

F. SCOTT FITZGERALD (1896-1940)

"AND where's Mr. Campbell?" Charlie asked.

"Gone to Switzerland. Mr. Campbell's a pretty sick man, Mr. Wales."

"I'm sorry to hear that. And George Hardt?" Charlie inquired.

"Back in America, gone to work."

"And where is the Snow Bird?"

"He was in here last week. Anyway, his friend, Mr. Schaeffer, is in Paris."

Two familiar names from the long list of a year and a half ago. Charlie scribbled an address in his notebook and tore out the page.

"If you see Mr. Schaeffer, give him this," he said. "It's my brother-in-law's address. I haven't settled on a hotel yet."

He was not really disappointed to find Paris was so empty. But the stillness in the Ritz bar was strange and portentous. It was not an American bar any more—he felt polite in it, and not as if he owned it. It had gone back into France. He felt the stillness from the moment he got out of the taxi and saw the doorman, usually in a frenzy of activity at this hour, gossiping with a *chasseur* by the servants' entrance.

Passing through the corridor, he heard only a single, bored voice in the once-glamorous women's room. When he turned into the bar he travelled the twenty feet of green carpet with his eyes fixed straight ahead by old habit; and then, with his foot firmly on the rail, he turned and surveyed the room, encountering only a single pair of eyes that fluttered up from a newspaper in the corner. Charlie asked for the head barman, Paul, who in the

BABYLON REVISITED is reprinted from *Taps at Reveille* by F. Scott Fitzgerald. Copyright 1931, 1935 by Charles Scribner's Sons. Used by permission of the publisher.

latter days of the bull market had come to work in his own custom-built car—disembarking, however, with due nicety at the nearest corner. But Paul was at his country house today and Alix giving him information.

"No, no more," Charlie said, "I'm going slow these days."

Alix congratulated him: "You were going pretty strong a couple of years ago."

"I'll stick to it all right," Charlie assured him. "I've stuck to it for over a year and a half now."

"How do you find conditions in America?"

"I haven't been to America for months. I'm in business in Prague, representing a couple of concerns there. They don't know about me down there."

Alix smiled.

"Remember the night of George Hardt's bachelor dinner here?" said Charlie. "By the way, what's become of Claude Fessenden?"

Alix lowered his voice confidentially: "He's in Paris, but he doesn't come here any more. Paul doesn't allow it. He ran up a bill of thirty thousand francs, charging all his drinks and his lunches, and usually his dinner, for more than a year. And when Paul finally told him he had to pay, he gave him a bad check."

Alix shook his head sadly.

"I don't understand it, such a dandy fellow. Now he's all bloated up—" He made a plump apple of his hands.

Charlie watched a group of strident queens installing themselves in a corner.

"Nothing affects them," he thought. "Stocks rise and fall, people loaf or work, but they go on forever." The place oppressed him. He called for the dice and shook with Alix for the drink.

"Here for long, Mr. Wales?"

"I'm here for four or five days to see my little girl."

"Oh-h! You have a little girl?"

Outside, the fire-red, gas-blue, ghost-green signs shone smokily through the tranquil rain. It was late afternoon and the streets were in movement; the *bistros* gleamed. At the corner of the Boulevard des Capucines he took a taxi. The Place de la Concorde moved by in pink majesty; they crossed the logical Seine, and Charlie felt the sudden provincial quality of the Left Bank.

Charlie directed his taxi to the Avenue de l'Opéra, which was out of his way. But he wanted to see the blue hour spread over the magnificent façade, and imagine that the cab horns, playing endlessly the first few bars of *Le Plus que Lent*, were the trumpets of the Second Empire. They were closing the iron grill in front of Brentano's Book-store, and people were already at dinner behind the trim little bourgeois hedge of Duval's. He had never eaten at a really cheap restaurant in Paris. Five-course dinner, four francs fifty, eighteen cents, wine included. For some odd reason he wished that he had.

As they rolled on to the Left Bank and he felt its sudden provincialism, he thought, "I spoiled this city for myself. I didn't realize it, but the days came along one after another, and then two years were gone, and everything was gone, and I was gone."

He was thirty-five, and good to look at. The Irish mobility of his face was sobered by a deep wrinkle between his eyes. As he rang his brother-in-law's bell in the Rue Palatine, the wrinkle deepened till it pulled down his brows; he felt a cramping sensation in his belly. From behind the maid who opened the door darted a lovely little girl of nine who shrieked "Daddy!" and flew up, struggling like a fish, into his arms. She pulled his head around by one ear and set her cheek against his.

"My old pie," he said.

"Oh, daddy, daddy, daddy, daddy, dads, dads, dads!"

She drew him into the salon, where the family waited, a boy and girl his daughter's age, his sister-in-law and her husband. He greeted Marion with his voice pitched carefully to avoid either feigned enthusiasm or dislike, but her response was more frankly tepid, though she minimized her expression of unalterable distrust by directing her regard toward his child. The two men clasped hands in a friendly way and Lincoln Peters rested his for a moment on Charlie's shoulder.

The room was warm and comfortably American. The three children moved intimately about, playing through the yellow oblongs that led to other rooms; the cheer of six o'clock spoke in the eager smacks of the fire and the sounds of French activity in the kitchen. But Charlie did not relax; his heart sat up rigidly in his body and he drew confidence from his daughter, who from time to time came close to him, holding in her arms the doll he had brought.

"Really extremely well," he declared in answer to Lincoln's question. "There's a lot of business there that isn't moving at all, but we're doing even better than ever. In fact, damn well. I'm bringing my sister over from America next month to keep house for me. My income last year was bigger than it was when I had money. You see, the Czechs—"

His boasting was for a specific purpose; but after a moment, seeing a faint restiveness in Lincoln's eye, he changed the subject:

"Those are fine children of yours, well brought up, good manners."

"We think Honoria's a great little girl too."

Marion Peters came back from the kitchen. She was a tall woman with worried eyes, who had once possessed a fresh American loveliness. Charlie had never been sensitive to it and was always surprised when people spoke of how pretty she had been. From the first there had been an instinctive antipathy between them.

"Well, how do you find Honoria?" she asked.

"Wonderful. I was astonished how much she's grown in ten months. All the children are looking well."

"We haven't had a doctor for a year. How do you like being back in Paris?"

"It seems very funny to see so few Americans around."

"I'm delighted," Marion said vehemently. "Now at least you can go into a store without their assuming you're a millionaire.

We've suffered like everybody, but on the whole it's a good deal pleasanter."

"But it was nice while it lasted," Charlie said. "We were a sort of royalty, almost infallible, with a sort of magic around us. In the bar this afternoon"—he stumbled, seeing his mistake—"there wasn't a man I knew."

She looked at him keenly. "I should think you'd have had enough of bars."

"I only stayed a minute. I take one drink every afternoon, and no more."

"Don't you want a cocktail before dinner?" Lincoln asked.

"I take only one drink every afternoon, and I've had that."

"I hope you keep to it," said Marion.

Her dislike was evident in the coldness with which she spoke, but Charlie only smiled; he had larger plans. Her very aggressiveness gave him an advantage, and he knew enough to wait. He wanted them to initiate the discussion of what they knew had brought him to Paris.

At dinner he couldn't decide whether Honoria was most like him or her mother. Fortunate if she didn't combine the traits of both that had brought them to disaster. A great wave of protectiveness went over him. He thought he knew what to do for her. He believed in character; he wanted to jump back a whole generation and trust in character again as the eternally valuable element. Everything wore out.

He left soon after dinner, but not to go home. He was curious to see Paris by night with clearer and more judicious eyes than those of other days. He bought a *strapontin* for the Casino and watched Josephine Baker go through her chocolate arabesques.

After an hour he left and strolled toward Montmartre, up the Rue Pigalle into the Place Blanche. The rain had stopped and there were a few people in evening clothes disembarking from taxis in front of cabarets, and *cocottes* prowling singly or in pairs, and many Negroes. He passed a lighted door from which issued music, and stopped with the sense of familiarity; it was Bricktop's, where he had parted with so many hours and so much money. A few doors farther on he found another ancient rendez-vous and incautiously put his head inside. Immediately an eager orchestra burst into sound, a pair of professional dancers leaped to their feet and a maître d'hôtel swooped toward him, crying, "Crowd just arriving, sir!" But he withdrew quickly.

"You have to be damn drunk," he thought.

Zelli's was closed, the bleak and sinister cheap hotels surround-ing it were dark; up in the Rue Blanche there was more light and a local, colloquial French crowd. The Poet's Cave had dis-appeared, but the two great mouths of the Café of Heaven and the Café of Hell still yawned—even devoured, as he watched, the meagre contents of a tourist bus—a German, a Japanese, and an American couple who glanced at him with frightened eyes.

So much for the effort and ingenuity of Montmartre. All the catering to vice and waste was on an utterly childish scale, and he suddenly realized the meaning of the word "dissipate"—to dissi-pate into thin air; to make nothing out of something. In the little hours of the night every move from place to place was an enor-mous human jump, an increase of paying for the privilege of slower and slower motion.

He remembered thousand-franc notes given to an orchestra for playing a single number, hundred-franc notes tossed to a door-man for calling a cab.

But it hadn't been given for nothing.

It had been given, even the most wildly squandered sum, as an offering to destiny that he might not remember the things most worth remembering, the things that now he would always remem-ber—his child taken from his control, his wife escaped to a grave in Vermont.

In the glare of a *brasserie* a woman spoke to him. He bought her some eggs and coffee, and then, eluding her encouraging stare, gave her a twenty-franc note and took a taxi to his hotel.

II

He woke upon a fine fall day—football weather. The depression of yesterday was gone and he liked the people on the streets. At noon he sat opposite Honoria at Le Grand Vatel, the only restaurant he could think of not reminiscent of champagne dinners and long luncheons that began at two and ended in a blurred and vague twilight.

"Now, how about vegetables? Oughtn't you to have some vegetables?"

"Well, yes."

"Here's *épinards* and *chou-fleur* and carrots and *haricots*."

"I'd like *chou-fleur*."

"Wouldn't you like to have two vegetables?"

"I usually only have one at lunch."

The waiter was pretending to be inordinately fond of children. *"Qu'elle est mignonne, la petite! Elle parle exactement comme une française."*

"How about dessert? Shall we wait and see?"

The waiter disappeared. Honoria looked at her father expectantly.

"What are we going to do?"

"First, we're going to that toy store in the Rue Saint-Honoré and buy you anything you like. And then we're going to the vaudeville at the Empire."

She hesitated. "I like it about the vaudeville, but not the toy store."

"Why not?"

"Well, you brought me this doll." She had it with her. "And I've got lots of things. And we're not rich any more, are we?"

"We never were. But today you are to have anything you want."

"All right," she agreed resignedly.

When there had been her mother and a French nurse he had been inclined to be strict; now he extended himself, reached out for a new tolerance; he must be both parents to her and not shut any of her out of communication.

"I want to get to know you," he said gravely. "First let me introduce myself. My name is Charles J. Wales, of Prague."

"Oh, daddy!" her voice cracked with laughter.

"And who are you, please?" he persisted, and she accepted a rôle immediately: "Honoria Wales, Rue Palatine, Paris."

"Married or single?"

"No, not married. Single."

He indicated the doll. "But I see you have a child, madame."

Unwilling to disinherit it, she took it to her heart and thought quickly: "Yes, I've been married, but I'm not married now. My husband is dead."

He went on quickly, "And the child's name?"

"Simone. That's after my best friend at school."

"I'm very pleased that you're doing so well at school."

"I'm third this month," she boasted. "Elsie"—that was her cousin—"is only about eighteenth, and Richard is about at the bottom."

"You like Richard and Elsie, don't you?"

"Oh, yes. I like Richard quite well and I like her all right."

Cautiously and casually he asked: "And Aunt Marion and Uncle Lincoln—which do you like best?"

"Oh, Uncle Lincoln, I guess."

He was increasingly aware of her presence. As they came in, a murmur of ". . . adorable" followed them, and now the people at the next table bent all their silences upon her, staring as if she were something no more conscious than a flower.

"Why don't I live with you?" she asked suddenly. "Because mamma's dead?"

"You must stay here and learn more French. It would have been hard for daddy to take care of you so well."

"I don't really need much taking care of any more. I do everything for myself."

Going out of the restaurant, a man and a woman unexpectedly hailed him.

"Well, the old Wales!"

"Hello there, Lorraine. . . . Dunc."

Sudden ghosts out of the past: Duncan Schaeffer, a friend from college. Lorraine Quarrles, a lovely, pale blonde of thirty; one of a crowd who had helped them make months into days in the lavish times of three years ago.

"My husband couldn't come this year," she said, in answer to his question. "We're poor as hell. So he gave me two hundred a month and told me I could do my worst on that. . . . This your little girl?"

"What about coming back and sitting down?" Duncan asked.

"Can't do it." He was glad for an excuse. As always, he felt Lorraine's passionate, provocative attraction, but his own rhythm was different now.

"Well, how about dinner?" she asked.

"I'm not free. Give me your address and let me call you."

"Charlie, I believe you're sober," she said judicially. "I honestly believe he's sober, Dunc. Pinch him and see if he's sober."

Charlie indicated Honoria with his head. They both laughed.

"What's your address?" said Duncan sceptically.

He hesitated, unwilling to give the name of his hotel.

"I'm not settled yet. I'd better call you. We're going to see the vaudeville at the Empire."

"There! That's what I want to do," Lorraine said. "I want to see some clowns and acrobats and jugglers. That's just what we'll do, Dunc."

"We've got to do an errand first," said Charlie. "Perhaps we'll see you there."

"All right, you snob. . . . Good-by, beautiful little girl."

"Good-by."

Honoria bobbed politely.

Somehow, an unwelcome encounter. They liked him because he was functioning, because he was serious; they wanted to see him, because he was stronger than they were now, because they wanted to draw a certain sustenance from his strength.

At the Empire, Honoria proudly refused to sit upon her father's folded coat. She was already an individual with a code of her own, and Charlie was more and more absorbed by the desire of putting a little of himself into her before she crystallized utterly. It was hopeless to try to know her in so short a time.

Between the acts they came upon Duncan and Lorraine in the lobby where the band was playing.

"Have a drink?"

"All right, but not up at the bar. We'll take a table."

"The perfect father."

Listening abstractedly to Lorraine, Charlie watched Honoria's eyes leave their table, and he followed them wistfully about the room, wondering what they saw. He met her glance and she smiled.

"I liked that lemonade," she said.

What had she said? What had he expected? Going home in a taxi afterward, he pulled her over until her head rested against his chest.

"Darling, do you ever think about your mother?"

"Yes, sometimes," she answered vaguely.

"I don't want you to forget her. Have you got a picture of her?"

"Yes, I think so. Anyhow, Aunt Marion has. Why don't you want me to forget her?"

"She loved you very much."

"I loved her too."

They were silent for a moment.

"Daddy, I want to come and live with you," she said suddenly.

His heart leaped; he had wanted it to come like this.

"Aren't you perfectly happy?"

"Yes, but I love you better than anybody. And you love me better than anybody, don't you, now that mummy's dead?"

"Of course I do. But you won't always like me best, honey.

You'll grow up and meet somebody your own age and go marry him and forget you ever had a daddy."

"Yes, that's true," she agreed tranquilly.

He didn't go in. He was coming back at nine o'clock and he wanted to keep himself fresh and new for the thing he must say then.

"When you're safe inside, just show yourself in that window."

"All right. Good-by, dads, dads, dads, dads."

He waited in the dark street until she appeared, all warm and glowing, in the window above and kissed her fingers out into the night.

III

They were waiting. Marion sat behind the coffee service in a dignified black dinner dress that just faintly suggested mourning. Lincoln was walking up and down with the animation of one who had already been talking. They were as anxious as he was to get into the question. He opened it almost immediately:

"I suppose you know what I want to see you about—why I really came to Paris."

Marion played with the black stars on her necklace and frowned.

"I'm awfully anxious to have a home," he continued. "And I'm awfully anxious to have Honoria in it. I appreciate your taking in Honoria for her mother's sake, but things have changed now"—he hesitated and then continued more forcibly—"changed radically with me, and I want to ask you to reconsider the matter. It would be silly for me to deny that about three years ago I was acting badly—"

Marion looked up at him with hard eyes.

"—but all that's over. As I told you, I haven't had more than a drink a day for over a year, and I take that drink deliberately, so that the idea of alcohol won't get too big in my imagination. You see the idea?"

"No," said Marion succinctly.

"It's a sort of stint I set myself. It keeps the matter in proportion."

"I get you," said Lincoln. "You don't want to admit it's got any attraction for you."

"Something like that. Sometimes I forget and don't take it. But I try to take it. Anyhow, I couldn't afford to drink in my position. The people I represent are more than satisfied with what I've done, and I'm bringing my sister over from Burlington to keep house for me, and I want awfully to have Honoria too. You know that even when her mother and I weren't getting along well we never let anything that happened touch Honoria. I know she's fond of me and I know I'm able to take care of her and— well, there you are. How do you feel about it?"

He knew that now he would have to take a beating. It would last an hour or two hours, and it would be difficult, but if he modulated his inevitable resentment to the chastened attitude of the reformed sinner, he might win his point in the end.

Keep your temper, he told himself. You don't want to be justified. You want Honoria.

Lincoln spoke first: "We've been talking it over ever since we got your letter last month. We're happy to have Honoria here. She's a dear little thing, and we're glad to be able to help her, but of course that isn't the question—"

Marion interrupted suddenly. "How long are you going to stay sober, Charlie?" she asked.

"Permanently, I hope."

"How can anybody count on that?"

"You know I never did drink heavily until I gave up business and came over here with nothing to do. Then Helen and I began to run around with—"

"Please leave Helen out of it. I can't bear to hear you talk about her like that."

He stared at her grimly; he had never been certain how fond of each other the sisters were in life.

"My drinking only lasted about a year and a half—from the time we came over until I—collapsed."

"It was time enough."

"It was time enough," he agreed.

"My duty is entirely to Helen," she said. "I try to think what she would have wanted me to do. Frankly, from the night you did that terrible thing you haven't really existed for me. I can't help that. She was my sister."

"Yes."

"When she was dying she asked me to look out for Honoria. If you hadn't been in a sanitarium then, it might have helped matters."

He had no answer.

"I'll never in my life be able to forget the morning when Helen knocked at my door, soaked to the skin and shivering, and said you'd locked her out."

Charlie gripped the sides of the chair. This was more difficult than he expected; he wanted to launch out into a long expostulation and explanation, but he only said: "The night I locked her out—" and she interrupted, "I don't feel up to going over that again."

After a moment's silence Lincoln said: "We're getting off the subject. You want Marion to set aside her legal guardianship and give you Honoria. I think the main point for her is whether she has confidence in you or not."

"I don't blame Marion," Charlie said slowly, "but I think she can have entire confidence in me. I had a good record up to three years ago. Of course, it's within human possibilities I might go wrong any time. But if we wait much longer I'll lose Honoria's childhood and my chance for a home." He shook his head, "I'll simply lose her, don't you see?"

"Yes, I see," said Lincoln.

"Why didn't you think of all this before?" Marion asked.

"I suppose I did, from time to time, but Helen and I were getting along badly. When I consented to the guardianship, I was flat on my back in a sanitarium and the market had cleaned me out. I knew I'd acted badly, and I thought if it would bring any peace to Helen, I'd agree to anything. But now it's different. I'm functioning, I'm behaving damn well, so far as—"

"Please don't swear at me," Marion said.

He looked at her, startled. With each remark the force of her dislike became more and more apparent. She had built up all her fear of life into one wall and faced it toward him. This trivial reproof was possibly the result of some trouble with the cook several hours before. Charlie became increasingly alarmed at leaving Honoria in this atmosphere of hostility against himself; sooner or later it would come out, in a word here, a shake of the head there, and some of that distrust would be irrevocably implanted in Honoria. But he pulled his temper down out of his face and shut it up inside him; he had won a point, for Lincoln realized the absurdity of Marion's remark and asked her lightly since when she had objected to the word "damn."

"Another thing," Charlie said: "I'm able to give her certain advantages now. I'm going to take a French governess to Prague with me. I've got a lease on a new apartment—"

He stopped, realizing that he was blundering. They couldn't be expected to accept with equanimity the fact that his income was again twice as large as their own.

"I suppose you can give her more luxuries than we can," said Marion. "When you were throwing away money we were living along watching every ten francs. . . . I suppose you'll start doing it again."

"Oh, no," he said. "I've learned. I worked hard for ten years, you know—until I got lucky in the market, like so many people. Terribly lucky. It didn't seem any use working any more, so I quit. It won't happen again."

There was a long silence. All of them felt their nerves straining, and for the first time in a year Charlie wanted a drink. He was sure now that Lincoln Peters wanted him to have his child.

Marion shuddered suddenly; part of her saw that Charlie's feet were planted on the earth now, and her own maternal feeling recognized the naturalness of his desire; but she had lived for a long time with a prejudice—a prejudice founded on a curious disbelief in her sister's happiness, and which, in the shock of one terrible night, had turned to hatred for him. It had all happened at a point in her life where the discouragement of ill health and adverse circumstances made it necessary for her to believe in tangible villainy and a tangible villain.

"I can't help what I think!" she cried out suddenly. "How much you were responsible for Helen's death, I don't know. Its something you'll have to square with your own conscience."

An electric current of agony surged through him; for a moment he was almost on his feet, an unuttered sound echoing in his throat. He hung on to himself for a moment, another moment.

"Hold on there," said Lincoln uncomfortably. "I never thought you were responsible for that."

"Helen died of heart trouble," Charlie said dully.

"Yes, heart trouble." Marion spoke as if the phrase had another meaning for her.

Then, in the flatness that followed her outburst, she saw him plainly and she knew he had somehow arrived at control over the situation. Glancing at her husband, she found no help from him, and as abruptly as if it were a matter of no importance, she threw up the sponge.

"Do what you like!" she cried, springing up from her chair. "She's your child. I'm not the person to stand in your way. I think if it were my child I'd rather see her—" She managed to check herself. "You two decide it. I can't stand this. I'm sick. I'm going to bed."

She hurried from the room; after a moment Lincoln said:

"This has been a hard day for her. You know how strongly she feels—" His voice was almost apologetic: "When a woman gets an idea in her head."

"Of course."

"It's going to be all right. I think she sees now that you—can provide for the child, and so we can't very well stand in your way or Honoria's way."

"Thank you, Lincoln."

"I'd better go along and see how she is."

"I'm going."

He was still trembling when he reached the street, but a walk down the Rue Bonaparte to the quais set him up, and as he crossed the Seine, fresh and new by the quai lamps, he felt exultant. But back in his room he couldn't sleep. The image of Helen haunted him. Helen whom he had loved so until they had senselessly begun to abuse each other's love, tear it into shreds. On that terrible February night that Marion remembered so vividly, a slow quarrel had gone on for hours. There was a scene at the Florida, and then he attempted to take her home, and then she kissed young Webb at a table; after that there was what she had hysterically said. When he arrived home alone he turned the key in the lock in wild anger. How could he know she would arrive an hour later alone, that there would be a snowstorm in which she wandered about in slippers, too confused to find a taxi? Then the aftermath, her escaping pneumonia by a miracle, and all the attendant horror. They were "reconciled," but that was the beginning of the end, and Marion, who had seen with her own eyes and who imagined it to be one of many scenes from her sister's martyrdom, never forgot.

Going over it again brought Helen nearer, and in the white, soft light that steals upon half sleep near morning he found himself talking to her again. She said that he was perfectly right about Honoria and that she wanted Honoria to be with him. She said she was glad he was being good and doing better. She said a lot of other things—very friendly things—but she was in a swing in a white dress, and swinging faster and faster all the time, so that at the end he could not hear clearly all that she said.

IV

He woke up feeling happy. The door of the world was open again. He made plans, vistas, futures for Honoria and himself, but suddenly he grew sad, remembering all the plans he and Helen had made. She had not planned to die. The present was the thing—work to do and someone to love. But not to love too much, for he knew the injury that a father can do to a daughter or a mother to a son by attaching them too closely: afterward, out in the world, the child would seek in the marriage partner the same blind tenderness and, failing probably to find it, turn against love and life.

It was another bright, crisp day. He called Lincoln Peters at the bank where he worked and asked if he could count on taking Honoria when he left for Prague. Lincoln agreed that there was no reason for delay. One thing—the legal guardianship. Marion wanted to retain that a while longer. She was upset by the whole matter, and it would oil things if she felt that the situation was still in her control for another year. Charlie agreed, wanting only the tangible, visible child.

Then the question of a governess. Charlie sat in a gloomy agency and talked to a cross Bernaise and to a buxom Breton peasant, neither of whom he could have endured. There were others whom he would see tomorrow.

He lunched with Lincoln Peters at Griffons, trying to keep down his exultation.

"There's nothing quite like your own child," Lincoln said. "But you understand how Marion feels too."

"She's forgotten how hard I worked for seven years there," Charlie said. "She just remembers one night."

"There's another thing." Lincoln hesitated. "While you and Helen were tearing around Europe throwing money away, we were just getting along. I didn't touch any of the prosperity because I never got ahead enough to carry anything but my insurance. I think Marion felt there was some kind of injustice in it—you not even working toward the end, and getting richer and richer."

"It went just as quick as it came," said Charlie.

"Yes, a lot of it stayed in the hands of *chasseurs* and saxophone players and maîtres d'hôtel—well, the big party's over now. I just said that to explain Marion's feeling about those crazy years. If you drop in about six o'clock tonight before Marion's too tired, we'll settle the details on the spot."

Back at his hotel, Charlie found a *pneumatique* that had been redirected from the Ritz bar where Charlie had left his address for the purpose of finding a certain man.

DEAR CHARLIE: You were so strange when we saw you the other day that I wondered if I did something to offend you. If so, I'm not conscious of it. In fact, I have thought about you too much for the last year, and it's always been in the back of my mind that I might see you if I came over here. We *did* have such good times that crazy spring, like the night you and I stole the butcher's tricycle, and the time we tried to call on the president and you had the old derby rim and the wire cane. Everybody seems so old lately, but I don't feel old a bit. Couldn't we get together some time today for old time's sake? I've got a vile hang-over for the moment, but will be feeling better this afternoon and will look for you about five in the sweat-shop at the Ritz.

Always devotedly,

LORRAINE.

His first feeling was one of awe that he had actually, in his mature years, stolen a tricycle and pedalled Lorraine all over the Étoile between the small hours and dawn. In retrospect it was a nightmare. Locking out Helen didn't fit in with any other act of his life, but the tricycle incident did—it was one of many. How many weeks or months of dissipation to arrive at that condition of utter irresponsibility?

He tried to picture how Lorraine had appeared to him then—very attractive; Helen was unhappy about it, though she said nothing. Yesterday, in the restaurant, Lorraine had seemed trite, blurred, worn away. He emphatically did not want to see her, and he was glad Alix had not given away his hotel address. It was a relief to think, instead, of Honoria, to think of Sundays spent with her and of saying good morning to her and of knowing she was there in his house at night, drawing her breath in the darkness.

At five he took a taxi and bought presents for all the Peters—a piquant cloth doll, a box of Roman soldiers, flowers for Marion, big linen handkerchiefs for Lincoln.

He saw, when he arrived in the apartment, that Marion had accepted the inevitable. She greeted him now as though he were a recalcitrant member of the family, rather than a menacing outsider. Honoria had been told she was going; Charlie was glad to see that her tact made her conceal her excessive happiness. Only on his lap did she whisper her delight and the question "When?" before she slipped away with the other children.

He and Marion were alone for a minute in the room, and on an impulse he spoke out boldly:

"Family quarrels are bitter things. They don't go according to any rules. They're not like aches or wounds; they're more like splits in the skin that won't heal because there's not enough material. I wish you and I could be on better terms."

"Some things are hard to forget," she answered. "It's a question of confidence." There was no answer to this and presently she asked, "When do you propose to take her?"

"As soon as I can get a governess. I hoped the day after tomorrow."

"That's impossible. I've got to get her things in shape. Not before Saturday."

He yielded. Coming back into the room, Lincoln offered him a drink.

"I'll take my daily whisky," he said.

It was warm here, it was a home, people together by a fire. The children felt very safe and important; the mother and father were serious, watchful. They had things to do for the children more important than his visit here. A spoonful of medicine was, after all, more important than the strained relations between Marion and himself. They were not dull people, but they were very much in the grip of life and circumstances. He wondered if he couldn't do something to get Lincoln out of his rut at the bank.

A long peal at the door-bell; the *bonne de toute faire* passed through and went down the corridor. The door opened upon another long ring, and then voices, and the three in the salon looked up expectantly; Richard moved to bring the corridor within his range of vision, and Marion rose. Then the maid came back along the corridor, closely followed by the voices, which developed under the light into Duncan Schaeffer and Lorraine Quarrles.

They were gay, they were hilarious, they were roaring with laughter. For a moment Charlie was astounded; unable to understand how they ferreted out the Peters' address.

"Ah-h-h!" Duncan wagged his finger rougishly at Charlie. "Ah-h-h!"

They both slid down another cascade of laughter. Anxious and at a loss, Charlie shook hands with them quickly and presented them to Lincoln and Marion. Marion nodded, scarcely speaking. She had drawn back a step toward the fire; her little girl stood beside her, and Marion put an arm about her shoulder.

With growing annoyance at the intrusion, Charlie waited for them to explain themselves. After some concentration Duncan said:

"We came to invite you out to dinner. Lorraine and I insist that all this shishi, cagy business 'bout your address got to stop."

Charlie came closer to them, as if to force them backward down the corridor.

"Sorry, but I can't. Tell me where you'll be and I'll phone you in half an hour."

This made no impression. Lorraine sat down suddenly on the side of a chair, and focussing her eyes on Richard, cried, "Oh, what a nice little boy! Come here, little boy." Richard glanced at his mother, but did not move. With a perceptible shrug of her shoulders, Lorraine turned back to Charlie:

"Come and dine. Sure your cousins won' mine. See you so sel'om. Or solemn."

"I can't," said Charlie sharply. "You two have dinner and I'll phone you."

Her voice became suddenly unpleasant. "All right, we'll go. But I remember once when you hammered on my door at four A.M. I was enough of a good sport to give you a drink. Come on, Dunc."

Still in slow motion, with blurred, angry faces, with uncertain feet, they retired along the corridor.

"Good night," Charlie said.

"Good night!" responded Lorraine emphatically.

When he went back into the salon Marion had not moved, only now her son was standing in the circle of her other arm. Lincoln was still swinging Honoria back and forth like a pendulum from side to side.

"What an outrage!" Charlie broke out. "What an absolute outrage!"

Neither of them answered. Charlie dropped into an armchair, picked up his drink, set it down again and said:

"People I haven't seen for two years having the colossal nerve—"

He broke off. Marion had made the sound "Oh!" in one swift, furious breath, turned her body from him with a jerk and left the room.

Lincoln set down Honoria carefully.

"You children go in and start your soup," he said, and when they obeyed, he said to Charlie:

"Marion's not well and she can't stand shocks. That kind of people make her really physically sick."

"I didn't tell them to come here. They wormed your name out of somebody. They deliberately—"

"Well, it's too bad. It doesn't help matters. Excuse me a minute."

Left alone, Charlie sat tense in his chair. In the next room he could hear the children eating, talking in monosyllables, already oblivious to the scene between their elders. He heard a murmur of conversation from a farther room and then the ticking bell of a telephone receiver picked up, and in a panic he moved to the other side of the room and out of earshot.

In a minute Lincoln came back. "Look here, Charlie. I think we'd better call off dinner for tonight. Marion's in bad shape."

"Is she angry with me?"

"Sort of," he said, almost roughly. "She's not strong and—"

"You mean she's changed her mind about Honoria?"

"She's pretty bitter right now. I don't know. You phone me at the bank tomorrow."

"I wish you'd explain to her I never dreamed these people would come here. I'm just as sore as you are."

"I couldn't explain anything to her now."

Charlie got up. He took his coat and hat and started down the corridor. Then he opened the door of the dining room and said in a strange voice, "Good night, children."

Honoria rose and ran around the table to hug him.

"Good night, sweetheart," he said vaguely, and then trying to make his voice more tender, trying to conciliate something, "Good night, dear children."

V

Charlie went directly to the Ritz bar with the furious idea of finding Lorraine and Duncan, but they were not there, and he realized that in any case there was nothing he could do. He had not touched his drink at the Peters', and now he ordered a whisky-and-soda. Paul came over to say hello.

"It's a great change," he said sadly. "We do about half the business we did. So many fellows I hear about back in the States lost everything, maybe not in the first crash, but then in the second. Your friend George Hardt lost every cent, I hear. Are you back in the States?"

"No, I'm in business in Prague."

"I heard that you lost a lot in the crash."

"I did," and he added grimly, "but I lost everything I wanted in the boom."

"Selling short."

"Something like that."

Again the memory of those days swept over him like a nightmare—the people they had met travelling; the people who couldn't add a row of figures or speak a coherent sentence. The little man Helen had consented to dance with at the ship's party, who had insulted her ten feet from the table; the women and girls carried screaming with drink or drugs out of public places—

—The men who locked their wives out in the snow, because the snow of twenty-nine wasn't real snow. If you didn't want it to be snow, you just paid some money.

He went to the phone and called the Peters' apartment; Lincoln answered.

"I called up because this thing is on my mind. Has Marion said anything definite?"

"Marion's sick," Lincoln answered shortly. "I know this thing isn't altogether your fault, but I can't have her go to pieces about it. I'm afraid we'll have to let it slide for six months; I can't take the chance of working her up to this state again."

"I see."

"I'm sorry, Charlie."

He went back to his table. His whisky glass was empty, but he shook his head when Alix looked at it questioningly. There wasn't much he could do now except send Honoria some things; he would send her a lot of things tomorrow. He thought rather angrily that this was just money—he had given so many people money. . . .

"No, no more," he said to another waiter. "What do I owe you?"

He would come back some day; they couldn't make him pay forever. But he wanted his child, and nothing was much good now, beside that fact. He wasn't young any more, with a lot of nice thoughts and dreams to have by himself. He was absolutely sure Helen wouldn't have wanted him to be so alone.

Critical Questions

THE ACTION of the story takes place against the background of the prosperity of the twenties and the great depression of the thirties. But the interest of the story is focused on Charlie Wales' personal problem: will he get his daughter? To what extent does the success of the story depend on the reader's having lived through the period in which it is set? How much does Fitzgerald count on his reader's knowledge to recreate a period and an attitude, when stimulated by a few key references?

What connection does Fitzgerald make between the social framework of the story and Charlie Wales' problem? The answer to this question involves, of course, a definition of Wales' character, and an analysis of the causes of his failure. On this point consider the following passages:

Charlie felt the sudden provincial quality of the Left Bank. [Page 369.]

But he wanted to see the blue hour spread over the magnificent façade, and imagine that the cab horns . . . were the trumpets of the Second Empire. [Page 369.]

He believed in character; he wanted to jump back a whole generation and trust in character again as the eternally valuable element. Everything else wore out. [Page 371.]

"You know I never did drink heavily until I gave up business and came over here with nothing to do." [Page 378.]

"I worked hard for ten years, you know—until I got lucky in the market, like so many people." [Page 380.]

He was absolutely sure Helen wouldn't have wanted him to be alone. [Page 390.]

The Short Happy Life of
Francis Macomber

ERNEST HEMINGWAY (1898–1961)

IT WAS NOW lunch time and they were all sitting under the double green fly of the dining tent pretending that nothing had happened.

"Will you have lime juice or lemon squash?" Macomber asked.

"I'll have a gimlet," Robert Wilson told him.

"I'll have a gimlet too. I need something," Macomber's wife said.

"I suppose it's the thing to do," Macomber agreed. "Tell him to make three gimlets."

The mess boy had started them already, lifting the bottles out of the canvas cooling bags that sweated wet in the wind that blew through the trees that shaded the tents.

"What had I ought to give them?" Macomber asked.

"A quid would be plenty," Wilson told him. "You don't want to spoil them."

"Will the headman distribute it?"

"Absolutely."

Francis Macomber had, half an hour before, been carried to his tent from the edge of the camp in triumph on the arms and shoulders of the cook, the personal boys, the skinner and the porters. The gun-bearers had taken no part in the demonstration. When the native boys put him down at the door of his tent, he had shaken all their hands, received their congratulations, and then gone into the tent and sat on the bed until his wife came in.

She did not speak to him when she came in and he left the tent at once to wash his face and hands in the portable wash basin outside and go over to the dining tent to sit in a comfortable canvas chair in the breeze and the shade.

"You've got your lion," Robert Wilson said to him, "and a damned fine one too."

Mrs. Macomber looked at Wilson quickly. She was an extremely handsome and well-kept woman of the beauty and social position which had, five years before, commanded five thousand dollars as the price of endorsing, with photographs, a beauty product which she had never used. She had been married to Francis Macomber for eleven years.

"He is a good lion, isn't he?" Macomber said. His wife looked at him now. She looked at both these men as though she had never seen them before.

One, Wilson, the white hunter, she knew she had never truly seen before. He was about middle height with sandy hair, a stubby mustache, a very red face and extremely cold blue eyes with faint white wrinkles at the corners that grooved merrily when he smiled. He smiled at her now and she looked away from his face at the way his shoulders sloped in the loose tunic he wore with the four big cartridges held in loops where the left breast pocket should have been, at his big brown hands, his old slacks, his very dirty boots and back to his red face again. She noticed where the baked red of his face stopped in a white line that marked the circle left by his Stetson hat that hung now from one of the pegs of the tent pole.

"Well, here's to the lion," Robert Wilson said. He smiled at her again and, not smiling, she looked curiously at her husband.

Francis Macomber was very tall, very well built if you did not mind that length of bone, dark, his hair cropped like an oarsman, rather thin-lipped, and was considered handsome. He was dressed in the same sort of safari clothes that Wilson wore except that his were new, he was thirty-five years old, kept himself very fit, was good at court games, had a number of big-game fishing records, and had just shown himself, very publicly, to be a coward.

"Here's to the lion," he said. "I can't ever thank you for what you did."

Margaret, his wife, looked away from him and back to Wilson.

"Let's not talk about the lion," she said.

Wilson looked over at her without smiling and now she smiled at him.

"It's been a very strange day," she said. "Hadn't you ought to put your hat on even under the canvas at noon? You told me that, you know."

"Might put it on," said Wilson.

"You know you have a very red face, Mr. Wilson," she told him and smiled again.

"Drink," said Wilson.

"I don't think so," she said. "Francis drinks a great deal, but his face is never red."

"It's red today," Macomber tried a joke.

"No," said Margaret. "It's mine that's red today. But Mr. Wilson's is always red."

"Must be racial," said Wilson. "I say, you wouldn't like to drop my beauty as a topic, would you?"

"I've just started on it."

"Let's chuck it," said Wilson.

"Conversation is going to be so difficult," Margaret said.

"Don't be silly, Margot," her husband said.

"No difficulty," Wilson said. "Got a damn fine lion."

Margot looked at them both and they both saw that she was going to cry. Wilson had seen it coming for a long time and he dreaded it. Macomber was past dreading it.

"I wish it hadn't happened. Oh, I wish it hadn't happened," she said and started for her tent. She made no noise of crying but they could see that her shoulders were shaking under the rose-colored, sun-proofed shirt she wore.

"Women upset," said Wilson to the tall man. "Amounts to nothing. Strain on the nerves and one thing'n another."

"No," said Macomber. "I suppose that I rate that for the rest of my life now."

"Nonsense. Let's have a spot of the giant killer," said Wilson. "Forget the whole thing. Nothing to it anyway."

"We might try," said Macomber. "I won't forget what you did for me though."

"Nothing," said Wilson. "All nonsense."

So they sat there in the shade where the camp was pitched under some wide-topped acacia trees with a boulder-strewn cliff behind them, and a stretch of grass that ran to the bank of a boulder-filled stream in front with forest beyond it, and drank their just-cool lime drinks and avoided one another's eyes while the boys set the table for lunch. Wilson could tell that the boys all knew about it now and when he saw Macomber's personal boy looking curiously at his master while he was putting dishes on the table he snapped at him in Swahili. The boy turned away with his face blank.

"What were you telling him?" Macomber asked.

"Nothing. Told him to look alive or I'd see he got about fifteen of the best."

"What's that? Lashes?"

"It's quite illegal," Wilson said. "You're supposed to fine them."

"Do you still have them whipped?"

"Oh, yes. They could raise a row if they chose to complain. But they don't. They prefer it to the fines."

"How strange!" said Macomber.

"Not strange, really," Wilson said. "Which would you rather do? Take a good birching or lose your pay?"

Then he felt embarrassed at asking it and before Macomber could answer he went on, "We all take a beating every day, you know, one way or another."

This was no better. "Good God," he thought. "I am a diplomat, aren't I?"

"Yes, we take a beating," said Macomber, still not looking at him. "I'm awfully sorry about that lion business. It doesn't have to go any further, does it? I mean no one will hear about it, will they?"

"You mean will I tell it at the Mathaiga Club?" Wilson looked at him now coldly. He had not expected this. So he's a bloody four-letter man as well as a bloody coward, he thought. I rather liked him too until today. But how is one to know about an American?

"No," said Wilson. "I'm a professional hunter. We never talk about our clients. You can be quite easy on that. It's supposed to be bad form to ask us not to talk though."

He had decided now that to break would be much easier. He would eat, then, by himself and could read a book with his meals. They would eat by themselves. He would see them through the safari on a very formal basis—what was it the French called it? Distinguished consideration—and it would be a damn sight easier than having to go through this emotional trash. He'd insult him and make a good clean break. Then he could read a book with his meals and he'd still be drinking their whisky. That was the phrase for it when a safari went bad. You ran into another white hunter and you asked, "How is everything going?" and he answered, "Oh, I'm still drinking their whisky," and you knew everything had gone to pot.

"I'm sorry," Macomber said and looked at him with his American face that would stay adolescent until it became middle-aged, and Wilson noted his crew-cropped hair, fine eyes only faintly shifty, good nose, thin lips and handsome jaw. "I'm sorry I didn't realize that. There are lots of things I don't know."

So what could he do, Wilson thought. He was all ready to break it off quickly and neatly and here the beggar was apologizing after he had just insulted him. He made one more attempt. "Don't worry about me talking," he said. "I have a living to make. You know in Africa no woman ever misses her lion and no white man ever bolts."

"I bolted like a rabbit," Macomber said.

Now what in hell were you going to do about a man who talked like that, Wilson wondered.

Wilson looked at Macomber with his flat, blue, machine-gunner's eyes and the other smiled back at him. He had a pleasant smile if you did not notice how his eyes showed when he was hurt.

"Maybe I can fix it up on buffalo," he said. "We're after them next, aren't we?"

"In the morning if you like," Wilson told him. Perhaps he had been wrong. This was certainly the way to take it. You most certainly could not tell a damned thing about an American. He was all for Macomber again. If you could forget the morning. But, of course, you couldn't. The morning had been about as bad as they come.

"Here comes the Memsahib," he said. She was walking over from her tent looking refreshed and cheerful and quite lovely. She had a very perfect oval face, so perfect that you expected her to be stupid. But she wasn't stupid, Wilson thought, no, not stupid.

"How is the beautiful red-faced Mr. Wilson? Are you feeling better, Francis, my pearl?"

"Oh, much," said Macomber.

"I've dropped the whole thing," she said, sitting down at the table. "What importance is there to whether Francis is any good at killing lions? That's not his trade. That's Mr. Wilson's trade. Mr. Wilson is really very impressive killing anything. You do kill anything, don't you?"

"Oh, anything," said Wilson. "Simply anything." They are, he thought, the hardest in the world; the hardest, the cruelest, the most predatory and the most attractive and their men have softened or gone to pieces nervously as they have hardened. Or is it that they pick men they can handle? They can't know that much at the age they marry, he thought. He was grateful that he had gone through his education on American women before now because this was a very attractive one.

"We're going after buff in the morning," he told her.

"I'm coming," she said.

"No, you're not."

"Oh, yes, I am. Mayn't I, Francis?"

"Why not stay in camp?"

"Not for anything," she said. "I wouldn't miss something like today for anything."

When she left, Wilson was thinking, when she went off to cry, she seemed a hell of a fine woman. She seemed to understand, to realize, to be hurt for him and for herself and to know how things really stood. She is away for twenty minutes and now she is back, simply enamelled in that American female cruelty. They are the damnedest women. Really the damnedest.

"We'll put on another show for you tomorrow," Francis Macomber said.

"You're not coming," Wilson said.

"You're very mistaken," she told him. "And I want *so* to see you perform again. You were lovely this morning. That is if blowing things' heads off is lovely."

"Here's the lunch," said Wilson. "You're very merry, aren't you?"

"Why not? I didn't come out here to be dull."

"Well, it hasn't been dull," Wilson said. He could see the boulders in the river and the high bank beyond with the trees and he remembered the morning.

"Oh, no," she said. "It's been charming. And tomorrow. You don't know how I look forward to tomorrow."

"That's eland he's offering you," Wilson said.

"They're the big cowy things that jump like hares, aren't they?"

"I suppose that describes them," Wilson said.

"It's very good meat," Macomber said.

"Did you shoot it, Francis?" she asked.

"Yes."

"They're not dangerous, are they?"

"Only if they fall on you," Wilson told her.

"I'm so glad."

"Why not let up on the bitchery just a little, Margot," Macomber said, cutting the eland steak and putting some mashed potato, gravy and carrot on the down-turned fork that tined through the piece of meat.

"I suppose I could," she said, "since you put it so prettily."

"Tonight we'll have champagne for the lion," Wilson said. "It's a bit too hot at noon."

"Oh, the lion," Margot said. "I'd forgotten the lion!"

So, Robert Wilson thought to himself, she *is* giving him a ride, isn't she? Or do you suppose that's her idea of putting up a good show? How should a woman act when she discovers her husband is a bloody coward? She's damn cruel but they're all cruel. They govern, of course, and to govern one has to be cruel sometimes. Still, I've seen enough of their damn terrorism.

"Have some more eland," he said to her politely.

That afternoon, late, Wilson and Macomber went out in the motor car with the native driver and the two gun-bearers. Mrs. Macomber stayed in the camp. It was too hot to go out, she said, and she was going with them in the early morning. As they drove off Wilson saw her standing under the big tree, looking pretty rather than beautiful in her faintly rosy khaki, her dark hair drawn back off her forehead and gathered in a knot low on her neck, her face as fresh, he thought, as though she were in England. She waved to them as the car went off through the swale of high grass and curved around through the trees into the small hills of orchard bush.

In the orchard bush they found a herd of impala, and leaving the car they stalked one old ram with long, wide-spread horns and Macomber killed it with a very creditable shot that knocked the buck down at a good two hundred yards and sent the herd off bounding wildly and leaping over one another's backs in long, leg-drawn-up leaps as unbelievable and as floating as those one makes sometimes in dreams.

"That was a good shot," Wilson said. "They're a small target."

"Is it a worth-while head?" Macomber asked.

"It's excellent," Wilson told him. "You shoot like that and you'll have no trouble."

"Do you think we'll find buffalo tomorrow?"

"There's a good chance of it. They feed out early in the morning and with luck we may catch them in the open."

"I'd like to clear away that lion business," Macomber said. "It's not very pleasant to have your wife see you do something like that."

I should think it would be even more unpleasant to do it, Wilson thought, wife or no wife, or to talk about it having done it. But he said, "I wouldn't think about that any more. Any one could be upset by his first lion. That's all over."

But that night after dinner and a whisky and soda by the fire before going to bed, as Francis Macomber lay on his cot with the mosquito bar over him and listened to the night noises it was not all over. It was neither all over nor was it beginning. It was there exactly as it happened with some parts of it indelibly emphasized and he was miserably ashamed at it. But more than shame he felt cold, hollow fear in him. The fear was still there like a cold slimy hollow in all the emptiness where once his confidence had been and it made him feel sick. It was still there with him now.

It had started the night before when he had wakened and heard the lion roaring somewhere up along the river. It was a deep sound and at the end there were sort of coughing grunts that made him seem just outside the tent, and when Francis Macomber woke in the night to hear it he was afraid. He could hear his wife breathing quietly, asleep. There was no one to tell he was afraid, nor to be afraid with him, and, lying alone, he did not know the Somali proverb that says a brave man is always frightened three times by a lion; when he first sees his track, when he first hears

him roar and when he first confronts him. Then while they were
eating breakfast by lantern light out in the dining tent, before the
sun was up, the lion roared again and Francis thought he was just
at the edge of camp.

"Sounds like an old-timer," Robert Wilson said, looking up
from his kippers and coffee. "Listen to him cough."

"Is he very close?"

"A mile or so up the stream."

"Will we see him?"

"We'll have a look."

"Does his roaring carry that far? It sounds as though he were
right in camp."

"Carries a hell of a long way," said Robert Wilson. "It's
strange the way it carries. Hope he's a shootable cat. The boys
said there was a very big one about here."

"If I get a shot, where should I hit him," Macomber asked, "to
stop him?"

"In the shoulders," Wilson said. "In the neck if you can make
it. Shoot for bone. Break him down."

"I hope I can place it properly," Macomber said.

"You shoot very well," Wilson told him. "Take your time.
Make sure of him. The first one in is the one that counts."

"What range will it be?"

"Can't tell. Lion has something to say about that. Won't shoot
unless it's close enough so you can make sure."

"At under a hundred yards?" Macomber asked.

Wilson looked at him quickly.

"Hundred's about right. Might have to take him a bit under.
Shouldn't chance a shot at much over that. A hundred's a decent
range. You can hit him wherever you want at that. Here comes
the Memsahib."

"Good morning," she said. "Are we going after that lion?"

"As soon as you deal with your breakfast," Wilson said. "How
are you feeling?"

"Marvellous," she said. "I'm very excited."

"I'll just go and see that everything is ready," Wilson went off. As he left the lion roared again.

"Noisy beggar," Wilson said. "We'll put a stop to that."

"What's the matter, Francis?" his wife asked him.

"Nothing," Macomber said.

"Yes, there is," she said. "What are you upset about?"

"Nothing," he said.

"Tell me," she looked at him. "Don't you feel well?"

"It's that damned roaring," he said. "It's been going on all night, you know."

"Why didn't you wake me," she said. "I'd love to have heard it."

"I've got to kill the damned thing," Macomber said, miserably.

"Well, that's what you're out here for, isn't it?"

"Yes. But I'm nervous. Hearing the thing roar gets on my nerves."

"Well then, as Wilson said, kill him and stop his roaring."

"Yes, darling," said Francis Macomber. "It sounds easy, doesn't it?"

"You're not afraid, are you?"

"Of course not. But I'm nervous from hearing him roar all night."

"You'll kill him marvellously," she said. "I know you will. I'm awfully anxious to see it."

"Finish your breakfast and we'll be starting."

"It's not light yet," she said. "This is a ridiculous hour."

Just then the lion roared in a deep-chested moaning, suddenly guttural, ascending vibration that seemed to shake the air and ended in a sigh and a heavy, deep-chested grunt.

"He sounds almost here," Macomber's wife said.

"My God," said Macomber. "I hate that damned noise."

"It's very impressive."

"Impressive. It's frightful."

Robert Wilson came up then carrying his short, ugly, shockingly big-bored .505 Gibbs and grinning.

"Come on," he said. "Your gun-bearer has your Springfield and the big gun. Everything's in the car. Have you solids?"

"Yes."

"I'm ready," Mrs. Macomber said.

"Must make him stop that racket," Wilson said. "You get in front. The Memsahib can sit back here with me."

They climbed into the motor car and, in the gray first daylight, moved off up the river through the trees. Macomber opened the breech of his rifle and saw he had metal-cased bullets, shut the bolt and put the rifle on safety. He saw his hand was trembling. He felt in his pocket for more cartridges and moved his fingers over the cartridges in the loops of his tunic front. He turned back to where Wilson sat in the rear seat of the doorless, box-bodied motor car beside his wife, them both grinning with excitement, and Wilson leaned forward and whispered,

"See the birds dropping. Means the old boy has left his kill."

On the far bank of the stream Macomber could see, above the trees, vultures circling and plummeting down.

"Chances are he'll come to drink along here," Wilson whispered. "Before he goes to lay up. Keep an eye out."

They were driving slowly along the high bank of the stream which here cut deeply to its boulder-filled bed, and they wound in and out through big trees as they drove. Macomber was watching the opposite bank when he felt Wilson take hold of his arm. The car stopped.

"There he is," he heard the whisper. "Ahead and to the right. Get out and take him. He's a marvellous lion."

Macomber saw the lion now. He was standing almost broadside, his great head up and turned toward them. The early morning breeze that blew toward them was just stirring his dark mane, and the lion looked huge, silhouetted on the rise of bank in the gray morning light, his shoulders heavy, his barrel of a body bulking smoothly.

"How far is he?" asked Macomber, raising his rifle.

"About seventy-five. Get out and take him."

"Why not shoot from where I am?"

"You don't shoot them from cars," he heard Wilson saying in his ear. "Get out. He's not going to stay there all day."

Macomber stepped out of the curved opening at the side of the front seat, onto the step and down onto the ground. The lion still stood looking majestically and coolly toward this object that his eyes only showed in silhouette, bulking like some super-rhino. There was no man smell carried toward him and he watched the object, moving his great head a little from side to side. Then watching the object, not afraid, but hesitating before going down the bank to drink with such a thing opposite him, he saw a man figure detach itself from it and he turned his heavy head and swung away toward the cover of the trees as he heard a cracking crash and felt the slam of a .30–06 220-grain solid bullet that bit his flank and ripped in sudden hot scalding nausea through his stomach. He trotted, heavy, big-footed, swinging wounded full-bellied, through the trees toward the tall grass and cover, and the crash came again to go past him ripping the air apart. Then it crashed again and he felt the blow as it hit his lower ribs and ripped on through, blood sudden hot and frothy in his mouth, and he galloped toward the high grass where he could crouch and not be seen and make them bring the crashing thing close enough so he could make a rush and get the man that held it.

Macomber had not thought how the lion felt as he got out of the car. He only knew his hands were shaking and as he walked away from the car it was almost impossible for him to make his legs move. They were stiff in the thighs, but he could feel the muscles fluttering. He raised the rifle, sighted on the junction of the lion's head and shoulders and pulled the trigger. Nothing happened though he pulled until he thought his finger would break. Then he knew he had the safety on and as he lowered the rifle to move the safety over he moved another frozen pace forward, and the lion seeing his silhouette now clear of the silhouette of the car, turned and started off at a trot, and, as Macomber fired, he heard a whunk that meant that the bullet was home; but the lion kept on going. Macomber shot again and every one saw the bullet throw a spout of dirt beyond the trotting lion. He shot again, remembering to lower his aim, and they all heard the bullet hit, and the lion went into a gallop and was in the tall grass before he had the bolt pushed forward.

Macomber stood there feeling sick at his stomach, his hands that held the Springfield still cocked, shaking, and his wife and Robert Wilson were standing by him. Beside him too were the two gun-bearers chattering in Wakamba.

"I hit him," Macomber said. "I hit him twice."

"You gut-shot him and you hit him somewhere forward," Wilson said without enthusiasm. The gun-bearers looked very grave. They were silent now.

"You may have killed him," Wilson went on. "We'll have to wait a while before we go in to find out."

"What do you mean?"

"Let him get sick before we follow him up."

"Oh," said Macomber.

"He's a hell of a fine lion," Wilson said cheerfully. "He's gotten into a bad place though."

"Why is it bad?"

"Can't see him until you're on him."

"Oh," said Macomber.

"Come on," said Wilson. "The Memsahib can stay here in the car. We'll go to have a look at the blood spoor."

"Stay here, Margot," Macomber said to his wife. His mouth was very dry and it was hard for him to talk.

"Why?" she asked.

"Wilson says to."

"We're going to have a look," Wilson said. "You stay here. You can see even better from here."

"All right."

Wilson spoke in Swahili to the driver. He nodded and said, "Yes, Bwana."

Then they went down the steep bank and across the stream,

climbing over and around the boulders and up the other bank, pulling up by some projecting roots, and along it until they found where the lion had been trotting when Macomber first shot. There was dark blood on the short grass that the gun-bearers pointed out with grass stems, and that ran away behind the river bank trees.

"What do we do?" asked Macomber.

"Not much choice," said Wilson. "We can't bring the car over. Bank's too steep. We'll let him stiffen up a bit and then you and I'll go in and have a look for him."

"Can't we set the grass on fire?" Macomber asked.

"Too green."

"Can't we send beaters?"

Wilson looked at him appraisingly. "Of course we can," he said. "But it's just a touch murderous. You see we know the lion's wounded. You can drive an unwounded lion—he'll move on ahead of a noise—but a wounded lion's going to charge. You can't see him until you're right on him. He'll make himself perfectly flat in cover you wouldn't think would hide a hare. You can't very well send boys in there to that sort of a show. Somebody bound to get mauled."

"What about the gun-bearers?"

"Oh, they'll go with us. It's their *shauri*. You see, they signed on for it. They don't look too happy though, do they?"

"I don't want to go in there," said Macomber. It was out before he knew he'd said it.

"Neither do I," said Wilson very cheerily. "Really no choice though." Then, as an afterthought, he glanced at Macomber and saw suddenly how he was trembling and the pitiful look on his face.

"You don't have to go in, of course," he said. "That's what I'm hired for, you know. That's why I'm so expensive."

"You mean you'd go in by yourself? Why not leave him there?"

Robert Wilson, whose entire occupation had been with the lion and the problem he presented, and who had not been thinking about Macomber except to note that he was rather windy, suddenly felt as though he had opened the wrong door in a hotel and seen something shameful.

"What do you mean?"

"Why not just leave him?"

"You mean pretend to ourselves he hasn't been hit?"

"No. Just drop it."

"It isn't done."

"Why not?"

"For one thing, he's certain to be suffering. For another, some one else might run onto him."

"I see."

"But you don't have to have anything to do with it."

"I'd like to," Macomber said. "I'm just scared, you know."

"I'll go ahead when we go in," Wilson said, "with Kongoni tracking. You keep behind me and a little to one side. Chances are we'll hear him growl. If we see him we'll both shoot. Don't worry about anything. I'll keep you backed up. As a matter of fact, you know, perhaps you'd better not go. It might be much better. Why don't you go over and join the Memsahib while I just get it over with?"

"No, I want to go."

"All right," said Wilson. "But don't go in if you don't want to. This is my *shauri* now, you know."

"I want to go," said Macomber.

They sat under a tree and smoked.

"Want to go back and speak to the Memsahib while we're waiting?" Wilson asked.

"No."

"I'll just step back and tell her to be patient."

"Good," said Macomber. He sat there, sweating under his arms, his mouth dry, his stomach hollow feeling, wanting to find courage to tell Wilson to go on and finish off the lion without him. He could not know that Wilson was furious because he had not noticed the state he was in earlier and sent him back to his wife.

While he sat there Wilson came up. "I have your big gun," he said. "Take it. We've given him time, I think. Come on."

Macomber took the big gun and Wilson said:

"Keep behind me and about five yards to the right and do exactly as I tell you." Then he spoke in Swahili to the two gun-bearers who looked the picture of gloom.

"Let's go," he said.

"Could I have a drink of water?" Macomber asked. Wilson spoke to the older gun-bearer, who wore a canteen on his belt, and the man unbuckled, unscrewed the top and handed it to Macomber, who took it noticing how heavy it seemed and how hairy and shoddy the felt covering was in his hand. He raised it to drink and looked ahead at the high grass with the flat-topped trees behind it. A breeze was blowing toward them and the grass rippled gently in the wind. He looked at the gun-bearer and he could see the gun-bearer was suffering too with fear.

Thirty-five yards into the grass the big lion lay flattened out along the ground. His ears were back and his only movement was a slight twitching up and down of his long, black-tufted tail. He had turned at bay as soon as he had reached this cover and he was sick with the wound through his full belly, and weakening with the wound through his lungs that brought a thin foamy red to his mouth each time he breathed. His flanks were wet and hot and flies were on the little openings the solid bullets had made in his tawny hide, and his big yellow eyes, narrowed with hate, looked straight ahead, only blinking when the pain came as he breathed, and his claws dug in the soft baked earth. All of him, pain, sickness, hatred and all of his remaining strength, was tightening into an absolute concentration for a rush. He could hear the men talking and he waited, gathering all of himself into this preparation for a charge as soon as the men would come into the grass. As he heard their voices his tail stiffened to twitch up and down, and, as they came into the edge of the grass, he made a coughing grunt and charged.

Kongoni, the old gun-bearer, in the lead watching the blood

spoor, Wilson watching the grass for any movement, his big gun ready, the second gun-bearer looking ahead and listening, Macomber close to Wilson, his rifle cocked, they had just moved into the grass when Macomber heard the blood-choked coughing grunt, and saw the swishing rush in the grass. The next thing he knew he was running; running wildly, in panic in the open, running toward the stream.

He heard the *ca-ra-wong!* of Wilson's big rifle, and again in a second a crashing *carawong!* and turning saw the lion, horrible-looking now, with half his head seeming to be gone, crawling toward Wilson in the edge of the tall grass while the red-faced man worked the bolt on the short ugly rifle and aimed carefully as another blasting *carawong!* came from the muzzle, and the crawling, heavy, yellow bulk of the lion stiffened and the huge, mutilated head slid forward and Macomber, standing by himself in the clearing where he had run, holding a loaded rifle, while two black men and a white man looked back at him in contempt, knew the lion was dead. He came toward Wilson, his tallness all seeming a naked reproach, and Wilson looked at him and said:

"Want to take pictures?"

"No," he said.

That was all any one had said until they reached the motor car. Then Wilson had said:

"Hell of a fine lion. Boys will skin him out. We might as well stay here in the shade."

Macomber's wife had not looked at him nor he at her and he had sat by her in the back seat with Wilson sitting in the front seat. Once he had reached over and taken his wife's hand without looking at her and she had removed her hand from his. Looking across the stream to where the gun-bearers were skinning out the lion he could see that she had been able to see the whole thing. While they sat there his wife had reached forward and put her hand on Wilson's shoulder. He turned and she had leaned forward over the low seat and kissed him on the mouth.

"Oh, I say," said Wilson, going redder than his natural baked color.

"Mr. Robert Wilson," she said. "The beautiful red-faced Mr. Robert Wilson."

Then she sat down beside Macomber again and looked away across the stream to where the lion lay, with uplifted, white-muscled, tendon-marked naked forearms, and white bloating belly, as the black men fleshed away the skin. Finally the gun-bearers brought the skin over, wet and heavy, and climbed in behind with it, rolling it up before they got in, and the motor car started. No one had said anything more until they were back in camp.

That was the story of the lion. Macomber did not know how the lion had felt before he started his rush, nor during it when the unbelievable smash of the .505 with a muzzle velocity of two tons had hit him in the mouth, nor what kept him coming after that, when the second ripping crash had smashed his hind quarters and he had come crawling on toward the crashing, blasting thing that had destroyed him. Wilson knew something about it and only expressed it by saying, "Damned fine lion," but Macomber did not know how Wilson felt about things either. He did not know how his wife felt except that she was through with him.

His wife had been through with him before but it never lasted. He was very wealthy, and would be much wealthier, and he knew she would not leave him ever now. That was one of the few things that he really knew. He knew about that, about motor cycles—that was earliest—about motor cars, about duck-shooting, about fishing, trout, salmon and big-sea, about sex in books, many books, too many books, about all court games, about dogs, not much about horses, about hanging on to his money, about most of the other things his world dealt in, and about his wife not leaving him. His wife had been a great beauty and she was still a great beauty in Africa, but she was not a great enough beauty any more at home to be able to leave him and better herself and she knew it and he knew it. She had missed the chance to leave him and he knew it. If he had been better with women she would probably have started to worry about him getting another new, beautiful wife; but she knew too much about him to worry about him either. Also, he had always had a great tolerance which seemed the nicest thing about him if it were not the most sinister.

All in all they were known as a comparatively happily married couple, one of those whose disruption is often rumored but never occurs, and as the society columnist put it, they were adding more than a spice of *adventure* to their much envied and ever-enduring *Romance* by a *Safari* in what was known as *Darkest Africa* until the Martin Johnsons lighted it on so many silver screens where they were pursuing *Old Simba* the lion, the buffalo, *Tembo* and the elephant and as well collecting specimens for the Museum of Natural History. This same columnist had reported them *on the verge* at least three times in the past and they had been. But they always made it up. They had a sound basis of union. Margot was too beautiful for Macomber to divorce her and Macomber had too much money for Margot ever to leave him.

It was now about three o'clock in the morning and Francis Macomber, who had been asleep a little while after he had stopped thinking about the lion, wakened and then slept again, woke suddenly, frightened in a dream of the bloody-headed lion standing over him, and listening while his heart pounded, he realized that his wife was not in the other cot in the tent. He lay awake with that knowledge for two hours.

At the end of that time his wife came into the tent, lifted her mosquito bar and crawled cozily into bed.

"Where have you been?" Macomber asked in the darkness.

"Hello," she said. "Are you awake?"

"Where have you been?"

"I just went out to get a breath of air."

"You did, like hell."

"What do you want me to say, darling?"

"Where have you been?"

"Out to get a breath of air."

"That's a new name for it. You *are* a bitch."

"Well, you're a coward."

"All right," he said. "What of it?"

"Nothing as far as I'm concerned. But please let's not talk, darling, because I'm very sleepy."

"You think that I'll take anything."

"I know you will, sweet."

"Well, I won't."

"Please, darling, let's not talk. I'm so very sleepy."

"There wasn't going to be any of that. You promised there wouldn't be."

"Well, there is now," she said sweetly.

"You said if we made this trip that there would be none of that. You promised."

"Yes, darling. That's the way I meant it to be. But the trip was spoiled yesterday. We don't have to talk about it, do we?"

"You don't wait long when you have an advantage, do you?"

"Please let's not talk. I'm so sleepy, darling."

"I'm going to talk."

"Don't mind me then, because I'm going to sleep." And she did.

At breakfast they were all three at the table before daylight and Francis Macomber found that, of all the many men that he had hated, he hated Robert Wilson the most.

"Sleep well?" Wilson asked in his throaty voice, filling a pipe.

"Did you?"

"Topping," the white hunter told him.

You bastard, thought Macomber, you insolent bastard.

So she woke him when she came in, Wilson thought, looking at them both with his flat, cold eyes. Well, why doesn't he keep his wife where she belongs? What does he think I am, a bloody plaster saint? Let him keep her where she belongs. It's his own fault.

"Do you think we'll find buffalo?" Margot asked, pushing away a dish of apricots.

"Chance of it," Wilson said and smiled at her. "Why don't you stay in camp?"

"Not for anything," she told him.

"Why not order her to stay in camp?" Wilson said to Macomber.

"You order her," said Macomber coldly.

"Let's not have any ordering, nor," turning to Macomber, "any silliness, Francis," Margot said quite pleasantly.

"Are you ready to start?" Macomber asked.

"Any time," Wilson told him. "Do you want the Memsahib to go?"

"Does it make any difference whether I do or not?"

The hell with it, thought Robert Wilson. The utter complete hell with it. So this is what it's going to be like. Well, this is what it's going to be like, then.

"Makes no difference," he said.

"You're sure you wouldn't like to stay in camp with her yourself and let me go out and hunt the buffalo?" Macomber asked.

"Can't do that," said Wilson. "Wouldn't talk rot if I were you."

"I'm not talking rot. I'm disgusted."

"Bad word, disgusted."

"Francis, will you please try to speak sensibly?" his wife said.

"I speak too damned sensibly," Macomber said. "Did you ever eat such filthy food?"

"Something wrong with the food?" asked Wilson quietly.

"No more than with everything else."

"I'd pull yourself together, laddybuck," Wilson said very quietly. "There's a boy waits at table that understands a little English."

"The hell with him."

Wilson stood up and puffing on his pipe strolled away, speaking a few words in Swahili to one of the gun-bearers who was standing waiting for him. Macomber and his wife sat on at the table. He was staring at his coffee cup.

"If you make a scene I'll leave you, darling," Margot said quietly.

"No, you won't."

"You can try it and see."

"You won't leave me."

"No," she said. "I won't leave you and you'll behave yourself."

"Behave myself? That's a way to talk. Behave myself."

"Yes. Behave yourself."

"Why don't *you* try behaving?"

"I've tried it so long. So very long."

"I hate that red-faced swine," Macomber said. "I loathe the sight of him."

"He's really *very* nice."

"Oh, *shut up*," Macomber almost shouted. Just then the car came up and stopped in front of the dining tent and the driver and the two gun-bearers got out. Wilson walked over and looked at the husband and wife sitting there at the table.

"Going shooting?" he asked.

"Yes," said Macomber, standing up. "Yes."

"Better bring a woolly. It will be cool in the car," Wilson said.

"I'll get my leather jacket," Margot said.

"The boy has it," Wilson told her. He climbed into the front with the driver and Francis Macomber and his wife sat, not speaking, in the back seat.

Hope the silly beggar doesn't take a notion to blow the back of my head off, Wilson thought to himself. Women *are* a nuisance on safari.

The car was grinding down to cross the river at a pebbly ford in the gray daylight and then climbed, angling up the steep bank, where Wilson had ordered a way shovelled out the day before so they could reach the parklike wooded rolling country on the far side.

It was a good morning, Wilson thought. There was a heavy dew and as the wheels went through the grass and low bushes he could smell the odor of the crushed fronds. It was an odor like

verbena and he liked this early morning smell of the dew, the
crushed bracken and the look of the tree trunks showing black
through the early morning mist, as the car made its way through
the untracked, parklike country. He had put the two in the back
seat out of his mind now and was thinking about buffalo. The
buffalo that he was after stayed in the daytime in a thick swamp
where it was impossible to get a shot, but in the night they fed
out into an open stretch of country and if he could come between
them and their swamp with the car, Macomber would have a
good chance at them in the open. He did not want to hunt buff
with Macomber in thick cover. He did not want to hunt buff or
anything else with Macomber at all, but he was a professional
hunter and he had hunted with some rare ones in his time. If they
got buff today there would only be rhino to come and the poor
man would have gone through his dangerous game and things
might pick up. He'd have nothing more to do with the woman
and Macomber would get over that too. He must have gone
through plenty of that before by the look of things. Poor beggar.
He must have a way of getting over it. Well, it was the poor sod's
own bloody fault.

He, Robert Wilson, carried a double size cot on safari to ac-
commodate any windfalls he might receive. He had hunted for a
certain clientele, the international, fast, sporting set, where the
women did not feel they were getting their money's worth unless
they had shared that cot with the white hunter. He despised
them when he was away from them although he liked some of
them well enough at the time, but he made his living by them;
and their standards were his standards as long as they were hiring
him.

They were his standards in all except the shooting. He had his
own standards about the killing and they could live up to them
or get some one else to hunt them. He knew, too, that they all
respected him for this. This Macomber was an odd one though.
Damned if he wasn't. Now the wife. Well, the wife. Yes, the
wife. Hm, the wife. Well he'd dropped all that. He looked around

at them. Macomber sat grim and furious. Margot smiled at him. She looked younger today, more innocent and fresher and not so professionally beautiful. What's in her heart God knows, Wilson thought. She hadn't talked much last night. At that it was a pleasure to see her.

The motor car climbed up a slight rise and went on through the trees and then out into a grassy prairie-like opening and kept in the shelter of the trees along the edge, the driver going slowly and Wilson looking carefully out across the prairie and all along its far side. He stopped the car and studied the opening with his field glasses. Then he motioned to the driver to go on and the car moved slowly along, the driver avoiding wart-hog holes and driving around the mud castles ants had built. Then, looking across the opening, Wilson suddenly turned and said,

"By God, there they are!"

And looking where he pointed, while the car jumped forward and Wilson spoke in rapid Swahili to the driver, Macomber saw three huge, black animals looking almost cylindrical in their long heaviness, like big black tank cars, moving at a gallop across the far edge of the open prairie. They moved at a stiff-necked, stiff-bodied gallop and he could see the upswept wide black horns on their heads as they galloped heads out; the heads not moving.

"They're three old bulls," Wilson said. "We'll cut them off before they get to the swamp."

The car was going a wild forty-five miles an hour across the open and as Macomber watched, the buffalo got bigger and bigger until he could see the gray, hairless, scabby look of one huge bull and how his neck was a part of his shoulders and the shiny black of his horns as he galloped a little behind the others that were strung out in that steady plunging gait; and then, the car swaying as though it had just jumped a road, they drew up close and he could see the plunging hugeness of the bull, and the dust in his sparsely haired hide, the wide boss of horn and his outstretched, wide-nostrilled muzzle, and he was raising his rifle when Wilson shouted, "Not from the car, you fool!" and he had no fear, only hatred of Wilson, while the brakes clamped on and the car skidded, plowing sideways to an almost stop and Wilson was out on one side and he on the other, stumbling as his feet hit the still speeding-by of the earth, and then he was shooting at the bull as he moved away, hearing the bullets whunk into him, emptying his rifle at him as he moved steadily away, finally remembering to get his shots forward into the shoulder, and as he fumbled to re-load, he saw the bull was down. Down on his knees, his big head tossing, and seeing the other two still galloping he shot at the leader and hit him. He shot again and missed and he heard the *carawonging* roar as Wilson shot and saw the leading bull slide forward onto his nose.

"Get that other," Wilson said. "Now you're shooting!"

But the other bull was moving steadily at the same gallop and he missed, throwing a spout of dirt, and Wilson missed and the dust rose in a cloud and Wilson shouted, "Come on. He's too far!" and grabbed his arm and they were in the car again, Macomber and Wilson hanging on the sides and rocketing swayingly over the uneven ground, drawing up on the steady, plunging, heavy-necked, straight-moving gallop of the bull.

They were behind him and Macomber was filling his rifle, dropping shells onto the ground, jamming it, clearing the jam, then they were almost up with the bull when Wilson yelled "Stop," and the car skidded so that it almost swung over and Macomber fell forward onto his feet, slammed his bolt forward and fired as far forward as he could aim into the galloping, rounded black back, aimed and shot again, then again, then again, and the bullets, all of them hitting, had no effect on the buffalo that he could see. Then Wilson shot, the roar deafening him, and he could see the bull stagger. Macomber shot again, aiming carefully, and down he came, onto his knees.

"All right," Wilson said. "Nice work. That's three."

Macomber felt a drunken elation.

"How many times did you shoot?" he asked.

"Just three," Wilson said. "You killed the first bull. The big-

gest one. I helped you finish the other two. Afraid they might
have got into cover. You had them killed. I was just mopping up
a little. You shot damn well."

"Let's go to the car," said Macomber. "I want a drink."

"Got to finish off that buff first," Wilson told him. The buffalo
was on his knees and he jerked his head furiously and bellowed
in pig-eyed, roaring rage as they came toward him.

"Watch he doesn't get up," Wilson said. Then, "Get a little
broadside and take him in the neck just behind the ear."

Macomber aimed carefully at the center of the huge, jerking,
rage-driven neck and shot. At the shot the head dropped forward.

"That does it," said Wilson. "Got the spine. They're a hell of
a looking thing, aren't they?"

"Let's get the drink," said Macomber. In his life he had never
felt so good.

In the car Macomber's wife sat very white faced. "You were
marvellous, darling," she said to Macomber. "What a ride."

"Was it rough?" Wilson asked.

"It was frightful. I've never been more frightened in my life."

"Let's all have a drink," Macomber said.

"By all means," said Wilson. "Give it to the Memsahib." She
drank the neat whisky from the flask and shuddered a little when
she swallowed. She handed the flask to Macomber who handed
it to Wilson.

"It was frightfully exciting," she said. "It's given me a dreadful
headache. I didn't know you were allowed to shoot them from
cars though."

"No one shot from cars," said Wilson coldly.

"I mean chase them from cars."

"Wouldn't ordinarily," Wilson said. "Seemed sporting enough
to me though while we were doing it. Taking more chance driving that way across the plain full of holes and one thing and
another than hunting on foot. Buffalo could have charged us
each time we shot if he liked. Gave him every chance. Wouldn't
mention it to any one though. It's illegal if that's what you mean."

"It seemed very unfair to me," Margot said, "chasing those big helpless things in a motor car."

"Did it?" said Wilson.

"What would happen if they heard about it in Nairobi?"

"I'd lose my licence for one thing. Other unpleasantnesses," Wilson said, taking a drink from the flask. "I'd be out of business."

"Really?"

"Yes, really."

"Well," said Macomber, and he smiled for the first time all day. "Now she has something on you."

"You have such a pretty way of putting things, Francis," Margot Macomber said. Wilson looked at them both. If a four-letter man marries a five-letter woman, he was thinking, what number of letters would their children be? What he said was, "We lost a gun-bearer. Did you notice it?"

"My God, no," Macomber said.

"Here he comes," Wilson said. "He's all right. He must have fallen off when we left the first bull."

Approaching them was the middle-aged gun-bearer, limping along in his knitted cap, khaki tunic, shorts and rubber sandals, gloomy-faced and disgusted looking. As he came up he called out to Wilson in Swahili and they all saw the change in the white hunter's face.

"What does he say?" asked Margot.

"He says the first bull got up and went into the bush," Wilson said with no expression in his voice.

"Oh," said Macomber blankly.

"Then it's going to be just like the lion," said Margot, full of anticipation.

"It's not going to be a damned bit like the lion," Wilson told her. "Did you want another drink, Macomber?"

"Thanks, yes," Macomber said. He expected the feeling he had had about the lion to come back but it did not. For the first time in his life he really felt wholly without fear. Instead of fear he had a feeling of definite elation.

"We'll go and have a look at the second bull," Wilson said. "I'll tell the driver to put the car in the shade."

"What are you going to do?" asked Margaret Macomber.

"Take a look at the buff," Wilson said.

"I'll come."

"Come along."

The three of them walked over to where the second buffalo bulked blackly in the open, head forward on the grass, the massive horns swung wide.

"He's a very good head," Wilson said. "That's close to a fifty-inch spread."

Macomber was looking at him with delight.

"He's hateful looking," said Margot. "Can't we go into the shade?"

"Of course," Wilson said. "Look," he said to Macomber, and pointed. "See that patch of bush?"

"Yes."

"That's where the first bull went in. The gun-bearer said when he fell off the bull was down. He was watching us helling along and the other two buff galloping. When he looked up there was the bull up and looking at him. Gun-bearer ran like hell and the bull went off slowly into that bush."

"Can we go in after him now?" asked Macomber eagerly.

Wilson looked at him appraisingly. Damned if this isn't a strange one, he thought. Yesterday he's scared sick and today he's a ruddy fire eater.

"No, we'll give him a while."

"Let's please go into the shade," Margot said. Her face was white and she looked ill.

They made their way to the car where it stood under a single, wide-spreading tree and all climbed in.

"Chances are he's dead in there," Wilson remarked. "After a little we'll have a look."

Macomber felt a wild unreasonable happiness that he had never known before.

"By God, that was a chase," he said. "I've never felt any such feeling. Wasn't it marvellous, Margot?"

"I hated it."

"Why?"

"I hated it," she said bitterly. "I loathed it."

"You know I don't think I'd ever be afraid of anything again," Macomber said to Wilson. "Something happened in me after we first saw the buff and started after him. Like a dam bursting. It was pure excitement."

"Cleans out your liver," said Wilson. "Damn funny things happen to people."

Macomber's face was shining. "You know something did happen to me," he said. "I feel absolutely different."

His wife said nothing and eyed him strangely. She was sitting far back in the seat and Macomber was sitting forward talking to Wilson who turned sideways talking over the back of the front seat.

"You know, I'd like to try another lion," Macomber said. "I'm really not afraid of them now. After all, what can they do to you?"

"That's it," said Wilson. "Worst one can do is kill you. How does it go? Shakespeare. Damned good. See if I can remember. Oh, damned good. Used to quote it to myself at one time. Let's see. 'By my troth, I care not; a man can die but once; we owe God a death and let it go which way it will, he that dies this year is quit for the next.' Damned fine, eh?"

He was very embarrassed, having brought out this thing he had lived by, but he had seen men come of age before and it always moved him. It was not a matter of their twenty-first birthday.

It had taken a strange chance of hunting, a sudden precipitation into action without opportunity for worrying beforehand, to bring this about with Macomber, but regardless of how it had happened it had most certainly happened. Look at the beggar now, Wilson thought. It's that some of them stay little boys so long, Wilson thought. Sometimes all their lives. Their figures stay boyish when they're fifty. The great American boy-men.

Damned strange people. But he liked this Macomber now. Damned strange fellow. Probably meant the end of cuckoldry too. Well, that would be a damned good thing. Damned good thing. Beggar had probably been afraid all his life. Don't know what started it. But over now. Hadn't had time to be afraid with the buff. That and being angry too. Motor car too. Motor cars made it familiar. Be a damn fire eater now. He'd seen it in the war work the same way. More of a change than any loss of virginity. Fear gone like an operation. Something else grew in its place. Main thing a man had. Made him into a man. Women knew it too. No bloody fear.

From the far corner of the seat Margaret Macomber looked at the two of them. There was no change in Wilson. She saw Wilson as she had seen him the day before when she had first realized what his great talent was. But she saw the change in Francis Macomber now.

"Do you have that feeling of happiness about what's going to happen?" Macomber asked, still exploring his new wealth.

"You're not supposed to mention it," Wilson said, looking in the other's face. "Much more fashionable to say you're scared. Mind you, you'll be scared too, plenty of times."

"But you *have* a feeling of happiness about action to come?"

"Yes," said Wilson. "There's that. Doesn't do to talk too much about all this. Talk the whole thing away. No pleasure in anything if you mouth it up too much."

"You're both talking rot," said Margot. "Just because you've chased some helpless animals in a motor car you talk like heroes."

"Sorry," said Wilson. "I have been gassing too much." She's worried about it already, he thought.

"If you don't know what we're talking about why not keep out of it?" Macomber asked his wife.

"You've gotten awfully brave, awfully suddenly," his wife said contemptuously, but her contempt was not secure. She was very afraid of something.

Macomber laughed, a very natural hearty laugh. "You know I *have*," he said. "I really have."

"Isn't it sort of late?" Margot said bitterly. Because she had done the best she could for many years back and the way they were together now was no one person's fault.

"Not for me," said Macomber.

Margot said nothing but sat back in the corner of the seat.

"Do you think we've given him time enough?" Macomber asked Wilson cheerfully.

"We might have a look," Wilson said. "Have you any solids left?"

"The gun-bearer has some."

Wilson called in Swahili and the older gun-bearer, who was skinning out one of the heads, straightened up, pulled a box of solids out of his pocket and brought them over to Macomber, who filled his magazine and put the remaining shells in his pocket.

"You might as well shoot the Springfield," Wilson said. "You're used to it. We'll leave the Mannlicher in the car with the Memsahib. Your gun-bearer can carry your heavy gun. I've this damned cannon. Now let me tell you about them." He had saved this until the last because he did not want to worry Macomber. "When a buff comes he comes with his head high and thrust straight out. The boss of the horns covers any sort of a brain shot. The only shot is straight into the nose. The only other shot is into his chest or, if you're to one side, into the neck or the shoulders. After they've been hit once they take a hell of a lot of killing. Don't try anything fancy. Take the easiest shot there is. They've finished skinning out that head now. Should we get started?"

He called to the gun-bearers, who came up wiping their hands, and the older one got into the back.

"I'll only take Kongoni," Wilson said. "The other can watch to keep the birds away."

As the car moved slowly across the open space toward the island of brushy trees that ran in a tongue of foliage along a dry water course that cut the open swale, Macomber felt his heart pounding and his mouth was dry again, but it was excitement, not fear.

"Here's where he went in," Wilson said. Then to the gun-bearer in Swahili, "Take the blood spoor."

The car was parallel to the patch of bush. Macomber, Wilson and the gun-bearer got down. Macomber, looking back, saw his wife, with the rifle by her side, looking at him. He waved to her and she did not wave back.

The brush was very thick ahead and the ground was dry. The middle-aged gun-bearer was sweating heavily and Wilson had his hat down over his eyes and his red neck showed just ahead of Macomber. Suddenly the gun-bearer said something in Swahili to Wilson and ran forward.

"He's dead in there," Wilson said. "Good work," and he turned to grip Macomber's hand and as they shook hands, grinning at each other, the gun-bearer shouted wildly and they saw him coming out of the bush sideways, fast as a crab, and the bull coming, nose out, mouth tight closed, blood dripping, massive head straight out, coming in a charge, his little pig eyes bloodshot as he looked at them. Wilson, who was ahead, was kneeling shooting, and Macomber, as he fired, unhearing his shot in the roaring of Wilson's gun, saw fragments like slate burst from the huge boss of the horns, and the head jerked, he shot again at the wide nostrils and saw the horns jolt again and fragments fly, and he did not see Wilson now and, aiming carefully, shot again with the buffalo's huge bulk almost on him and his rifle almost level with the on-coming head, nose out, and he could see the little wicked eyes and the head started to lower and he felt a sudden white-hot, blinding flash explode inside his head and that was all he ever felt.

Wilson had ducked to one side to get in a shoulder shot. Macomber had stood solid and shot for the nose, shooting a touch high each time and hitting the heavy horns, splintering and chipping them like hitting a slate roof, and Mrs. Macomber, in the car, had shot at the buffalo with the 6.5 Mannlicher as it seemed about to gore Macomber and had hit her husband about two inches up and a little to one side of the base of his skull.

Francis Macomber lay now, face down, not two yards from where the buffalo lay on his side and his wife knelt over him with Wilson beside her.

"I wouldn't turn him over," Wilson said.

The woman was crying hysterically.

"I'd get back in the car," Wilson said. "Where's the rifle?"

She shook her head, her face contorted. The gun-bearer picked up the rifle.

"Leave it as it is," said Wilson. Then, "Go get Abdulla so that he may witness the manner of the accident."

He knelt down, took a handkerchief from his pocket, and spread it over Francis Macomber's crew-cropped head where it lay. The blood sank into the dry, loose earth.

Wilson stood up and saw the buffalo on his side, his legs out, his thinly-haired belly crawling with ticks. "Hell of a good bull," his brain registered automatically. "A good fifty inches, or better. Better." He called to the driver and told him to spread a blanket over the body and stay by it. Then he walked over to the motor car where the woman sat crying in the corner.

"That was a pretty thing to do," he said in a toneless voice. "He *would* have left you too."

"Stop it," she said.

"Of course it's an accident," he said. "I know that."

"Stop it," she said.

"Don't worry," he said. "There will be a certain amount of unpleasantness but I will have some photographs taken that will be very useful at the inquest. There's the testimony of the gun-bearers and the driver too. You're perfectly all right."

"Stop it," she said.

"There's a hell of a lot to be done," he said. "And I'll have to send a truck off to the lake to wireless for a plane to take the three of us into Nairobi. Why didn't you poison him? That's what they do in England."

"Stop it. Stop it. Stop it," the woman cried.

Wilson looked at her with his flat blue eyes.

"I'm through now," he said. "I was a little angry. I'd begun to like your husband."

"Oh, please stop it," she said. "Please, please stop it."

"That's better," Wilson said. "Please is much better. Now I'll stop."

Dry September

WILLIAM FAULKNER (1897–   )

THROUGH the bloody September twilight, aftermath of sixty-two rainless days, it had gone like a fire in dry grass—the rumor, the story, whatever it was. Something about Miss Minnie Cooper and a negro. Attacked, insulted, frightened: none of them, gathered in the barbershop on that Saturday evening where the ceiling fan stirred, without freshening it, the vitiated air, sending back upon them, in recurrent surges of stale pomade and lotion, their own stale breath and odors, knew exactly what had happened.

"Except it wasn't Will Mayes," a barber said. He was a man of middle age; a thin, sand-colored man with a mild face, who was shaving a client. "I know Will Mayes. He's a good nigger. And I know Miss Minnie Cooper, too."

"What do you know about her?" a second barber said.

"Who is she?" the client said. "A girl?"

"No," the barber said. "She's about forty, I reckon. She ain't married. That's why I don't believe—"

"Believe hell!" a hulking youth in a sweat-stained silk shirt said. "Won't you take a white woman's word before a nigger's?"

"I don't believe Will Mayes did it," the barber said. "I know Will Mayes."

"Maybe you know who did it, then. Maybe you already got him out of town, you damn nigger-lover."

"I don't believe anybody did anything. I don't believe anything happened. I leave it to you fellows if them ladies that gets old without getting married don't have notions that a man can't—"

"Then you're a hell of a white man," the client said. He moved under the cloth. The youth had sprung to his feet.

"You don't?" he said. "Do you accuse a white woman of telling a lie?"

The barber held the razor poised above the half-risen client. He did not look around.

"It's this durn weather," another said. "It's enough to make any man do anything. Even to her."

Nobody laughed. The barber said in his mild, stubborn tone: "I ain't accusing nobody of nothing. I just know and you fellows know how a woman that never—"

"You damn nigger-lover!" the youth said.

"Shut up, Butch," another said. "We'll get the facts in plenty of time to act."

"Who is? Who's getting them?" the youth said. "Facts, hell! I—"

"You're a fine white man," the client said. "Ain't you?" In his frothy beard he looked like a desert-rat in the moving pictures. "You tell them, Jack," he said to the youth. "If they ain't any white men in this town, you can count on me, even if I ain't only a drummer and a stranger."

"That's right, boys," the barber said. "Find out the truth first. I know Will Mayes."

"Well, by God!" the youth shouted. "To think that a white man in this town—"

"Shut up, Butch," the second speaker said. "We got plenty of time."

The client sat up. He looked at the speaker. "Do you claim that anything excuses a nigger attacking a white woman? Do you mean to tell me that you're a white man and you'll stand for it? You better go back North where you come from. The South don't want your kind here."

"North what?" the second said. "I was born and raised in this town."

"Well, by God!" the youth said. He looked about with a strained, baffled gaze, as if he was trying to remember what it was he wanted to say or do. He drew his sleeve across his sweating face. "Damn if I'm going to let a white woman—"

"You tell them, Jack," the drummer said. "By God, if they—"

The screen-door crashed open. A man stood in the floor, his feet apart and his heavy-set body poised easily. His white shirt was open at the throat; he wore a felt hat. His hot, bold glance swept the group. His name was Plunkett. He had commanded troops at the front in France and had been decorated for valor.

"Well," he said, "are you going to sit there and let a black son rape a white woman on the streets of Jefferson?"

Butch sprang up again. The silk of his shirt clung flat to his heavy shoulders. At each armpit was a dark half-moon. "That's what I been telling them! That's what I—"

"Did it really happen?" a third said. "This ain't the first man-scare she ever had, like Hawkshaw says. Wasn't there something about a man on the kitchen roof, watching her undress, about a year ago?"

"What?" the client said. "What's that?" The barber had been slowly forcing him back into the chair; he arrested himself reclining, his head lifted, the barber still pressing him down.

Plunkett whirled on the third speaker. "Happen? What the hell difference does it make? Are you going to let the black sons get away with it until one really does it?"

"That's what I'm telling them!" Butch shouted. He cursed, long and steady, pointless.

"Here, here," a fourth said. "Not so loud. Don't talk so loud."

"Sure," Plunkett said; "no talking necessary at all. I've done my talking. Who's with me?" He poised on the balls of his feet, roving his gaze.

The barber held the client's face down, the razor poised. "Find out the facts first, boys. I know Willy Mayes. It wasn't him. Let's get the sheriff and do this thing right."

Plunkett whirled upon him his furious, rigid face. The barber did not look away. They looked like men of different races. The other barbers had ceased also above their prone clients. "You mean to tell me," Plunkett said, "that you'd take a nigger's word before a white woman's? Why, you damn nigger-loving—"

The third rose and grasped Plunkett's arm; he too had been a soldier. "Now, now! Let's figure this thing out. Who knows anything about what really happened?"

"Figure out hell!" Plunkett jerked his arm free. "All that're with me get up from there. The ones that ain't—" He roved his gaze, dragging his sleeve across his face.

Three men rose. The client in the chair sat up. "Here," he said, jerking at the cloth around his neck; "get this rag off me. I'm with him. I don't live here, but, by God, if our mothers and wives and sisters—" He smeared the cloth over his face and flung it to the floor. Plunkett stood in the floor and cursed the others. Another rose and moved toward him. The remainder sat uncomfortably, not looking at one another, then one by one they rose and joined him.

The barber picked the cloth from the floor. He began to fold it neatly. "Boys, don't do that. Will Mayes never done it. I know."

"Come on," Plunkett said. He whirled. From his hip pocket protruded the butt of a heavy automatic pistol. They went out. The screen-door crashed behind them reverberant in the dead air.

The barber wiped the razor carefully and swiftly, and put it away, and ran to the rear, and took his hat from the wall. "I'll be back soon as I can," he said to the other barbers. "I can't let—" He went out, running. The two other barbers followed him to the door and caught it on the rebound, leaning out and looking up the street after him. The air was flat and dead. It had a metallic taste at the base of the tongue.

"What can he do?" the first said. The second one was saying "Jees Christ, Jees Christ" under his breath. "I'd just as lief be Will Mayes as Hawk, if he gets Plunkett riled."

"Jees Christ, Jees Christ," the second whispered.

"You reckon he really done it to her?" the first said.

II

She was thirty-eight or thirty-nine. She lived in a small frame house with her invalid mother and a thin, sallow, unflagging aunt, where each morning, between ten and eleven, she would appear on the porch in a lace-trimmed boudoir cap, to sit swinging in the porch swing until noon. After dinner she lay down for a while, until the afternoon began to cool. Then, in one of the three or four new voile dresses which she had each summer, she would go down-town to spend the afternoon in the stores with the other ladies, where they would handle the goods and haggle over prices in cold, immediate voices, without any intention of buying.

She was of comfortable people—not the best in Jefferson, but good people enough—and she was still on the slender side of ordinary-looking, with a bright, faintly haggard manner and dress. When she was young she had had a slender, nervous body and a sort of hard vivacity which had enabled her to ride for the time upon the crest of the town's social life as exemplified by the high-school party and church-social period of her contemporaries while still children enough to be un-classconscious.

She was the last to realize that she was losing ground; that those among whom she had been a little brighter and louder flame than any other were beginning to learn the pleasure of snobbery—male —and retaliation—female. That was when her face began to wear that bright, haggard look. She still carried it to parties on shadowy porticos and summer lawns, like a mask or a flag, with that bafflement and furious repudiation of truth in her eyes. One evening at a party she heard a boy and two girls, all schoolmates, talking. She never accepted another invitation.

She watched the girls with whom she had grown up as they married and got houses and children, but no man ever called on her steadily until the children of the other girls had been calling her "aunty" for several years, the while their mothers told them in bright voices about how popular Minnie had been as a girl. Then the town began to see her driving on Sunday afternoons with the cashier in the bank. He was a widower of about forty— a high-colored man, smelling always faintly of the barbershop or of whiskey. He owned the first automobile in town, a red run-about; Minnie had the first motoring bonnet and veil the town ever saw. Then the town began to say: "Poor Minnie!" "But she is old enough to take care of herself," others said. That was when she first asked her schoolmates that the children call her "cousin" instead of "aunty."

It was twelve years now since she had been relegated into adultery by public opinion, and eight years since the cashier had gone to a Memphis bank, returning for one day each Christmas, which he spent at an annual bachelors' party in a hunting-club on the river. From behind their curtains the neighbors would see him pass, and during the across-the-street Christmas-day visiting they would tell her about him, about how well he looked, and how they heard that he was prospering in the city, watching with bright, secret eyes her haggard, bright face. Usually by that hour there would be the scent of whiskey on her breath. It was supplied her by a youth, a clerk at the soda-fountain: "Sure; I buy it for the old gal. I reckon she's entitled to a little fun."

Her mother kept to her room altogether now; the gaunt aunt ran the house. Against that background Minnie's bright dresses, her idle and empty days, had a quality of furious unreality. She went out in the evenings only with women now, neighbors, to the moving pictures. Each afternoon she dressed in one of the new dresses and went down-town alone, where her young cousins were already strolling in the late afternoons with their delicate, silken heads and thin, awkward arms and conscious hips, clinging to one another or shrieking and giggling with paired boys in the soda-fountain when she passed and went on along the serried stores, in the doors of which sitting and lounging men did not even follow her with their eyes any more.

III

The barber went swiftly up the street where the sparse lights, insect-swirled, glared in rigid and violent suspension in the lifeless air. The day had died in a pall of dust; above the darkened square, shrouded by the spent dust, the sky was clear as the inside of a brass bell. Below the east was a rumor of the twice-waxed moon.

When he overtook them Plunkett and three others were getting into a car parked in an alley. Plunkett stooped his thick head, peering out beneath the top. "Changed your mind, did you?" he said. "Damn good thing; by God, to-morrow when this town hears about how you talked to-night—"

"Now, now," the other ex-soldier said. "Hawkshaw's all right. Come on, Hawk; jump in!"

"Will Mayes never done it, boys," the barber said. "If anybody done it. Why, you all know well as I do there ain't any town where they got better niggers than us. And you know how a lady will kind of think things about men when there ain't any reason to, and Miss Minnie anyway—"

"Sure, sure," the soldier said. "We're just going to talk to him a little; that's all."

"Talk hell!" Butch said. "When we're done with the—"

"Shut up, for God's sake!" the soldier said. "Do you want everybody in town—"

"Tell them, by God!" Plunkett said. "Tell every one of the sons that'll let a white woman—"

"Let's go; let's go: here's the other car." The second car slid squealing out of a cloud of dust at the alley-mouth. Plunkett started his car and backed out and took the lead. Dust lay like fog in the street. The street lights hung nimbused as in water. They drove on out of town.

A rutted lane turned at right angles. Dust hung above it too, and above all the land. The dark bulk of the ice-plant, where the negro Mayes was night-watchman, rose against the sky. "Better stop here, hadn't we?" the soldier said. Plunkett did not reply. He hurled the car up and slammed to a stop, the headlights glaring on the blank wall.

"Listen here, boys," the barber said; "if he's here, don't that prove he never done it? Don't it? If it was him, he would run. Don't you see he would?" The second car came up and stopped. Plunkett got down; Butch sprang down beside him. "Listen, boys," the barber said.

"Cut the lights off!" Plunkett said. The breathless darkness rushed down. There was no sound in it save their lungs as they sought air in the parched dust in which for two months they had lived; then the diminishing crunch of Plunkett's and Butch's feet, and a moment later Plunkett's voice:

"Will! . . . Will!"

Below the east the wan hemorrhage of the moon increased. It heaved above the ridge, silvering the air, the dust, so that they seemed to breathe, live, in a bowl of molten lead. There was no sound of night-bird nor insect, no sound save their breathing and a faint ticking of contracting metal about the cars. Where their bodies touched one another they seemed to sweat dryly, for no more moisture came. "Christ!" a voice said; "let's get out of here."

But they didn't move until vague noises began to grow out of the darkness ahead; then they got out and waited tensely in the breathless dark. There was another sound: a blow, a hissing expulsion of breath and Plunkett cursing in undertone. They stood a moment longer, then they ran forward. They ran in a stumbling clump, as though they were fleeing something. "Kill him, kill the son!" a voice whispered. Plunkett flung them back.

"Not here," he said. "Get him into the car." They hauled the negro up. "Kill him, kill the black son!" the voice murmured.

They dragged the negro to the car. The barber had waited beside the car. He could feel himself sweating and he knew he was going to be sick at the stomach.

"What is it, captains?" the negro said. "I ain't done nothing. 'Fore God, Mr. John." Some one produced handcuffs. They worked busily about him as though he were a post, quiet, intent, getting in one another's way. He submitted to the handcuffs, looking swiftly and constantly from dim face to face. "Who's here, captains?" he said, leaning to peer into the faces until they could feel his breath and smell his sweaty reek. He spoke a name or two. "What you-all say I done, Mr. John?"

Plunkett jerked the car-door open. "Get in!" he said.

The negro did not move. "What you-all going to do with me, Mr. John? I ain't done nothing. White folks, captains, I ain't done nothing: I swear 'fore God." He called another name.

"Get in!" Plunkett said. He struck the negro. The others expelled their breath in a dry hissing and struck him with random blows, and he whirled and cursed them, and swept his manacled hands across their faces and slashed the barber upon the mouth, and the barber struck him also. "Get him in there," Plunkett said. They pushed at him. He ceased struggling and got in, and sat quietly as the others took their places. He sat between the barber and the soldier, drawing his limbs in so as not to touch them, his eyes going swiftly and constantly from face to face. Butch clung to the running-board. The car moved on. The barber nursed his mouth in his handkerchief.

"What's the matter, Hawk?" the soldier said.

"Nothing," the barber said. They regained the high road and turned away from town. The second car dropped back out of the dust. They went on, gaining speed; the final fringe of houses dropped behind.

"Goddam, he stinks!" the soldier said.

"We'll fix that," the man in front beside Plunkett said. On the running-board Butch cursed into the hot rush of air. The barber leaned suddenly forward and touched Plunkett's shoulder.

"Let me out, John."

"Jump out, nigger-lover," Plunkett said without turning his head. He drove swiftly. Behind them the sourceless lights of the second car glared in the dust. Presently Plunkett turned into a narrow road. It too was rutted in disuse. It led back to an old brick-kiln—a series of reddish mounds and weed-and-vine-choked vats without bottom. It had been used for pasture once, until one day the owner missed one of his mules. Although he prodded carefully in the vats with a long pole, he could not even find the bottom of them.

"John," the barber said.

"Jump out, then," Plunkett said, hurling the car along the ruts. Beside the barber the negro spoke:

"Mr. Henry."

The barber sat forward. The narrow tunnel of the road rushed up and past. Their motion was like an extinct furnace blast: cooler, but utterly dead. The car bounded from rut to rut.

"Mr. Henry," the negro said.

The barber began to tug furiously at the door. "Look out, there!" the soldier said, but he had already kicked the door open and swung onto the running-board. The soldier leaned across the negro and grasped at him, but he had already jumped. The car went on without checking speed.

The impetus hurled him crashing, through dust-sheathed weeds, into the ditch. Dust puffed about him, and in a thin, vicious crackling of sapless stems he lay choking and retching until the second car passed and died away. Then he rose and limped on until he reached the high road and turned toward town, brushing at his clothes with his hands. The moon was higher, riding high and clear of the dust at last, and after a while the town began to glare beneath the dust. He went on, limping. Presently he heard the cars and the glow of them grew in the dust behind him and he left the road and crouched again in the weeds until they passed. Plunkett's car came last now. There were four people in it and Butch was not on the running-board.

They went on; the dust swallowed them; the glare and the sound died away. The dust of them hung for a while, but soon the eternal dust absorbed it again. The barber climbed back onto the road and limped on toward town.

IV

As she dressed after supper, on that Saturday evening, her own flesh felt like fever. Her hands trembled among the hooks and eyes, and her eyes had a feverish look, and her hair swirled crisp and crackling under the comb. While she was still dressing, the friends called for her and sat while she donned her sheerest under-things and stockings and a new voile dress. "Do you feel strong enough to go out?" they said, their eyes bright too, with a dark glitter. "When you have had time to get over the shock, you must tell us what happened. What he said and did; everything."

In the leafed darkness, as they walked toward the square, she began to breathe deeply, something like a swimmer preparing to dive, until she ceased trembling, the four of them walking slowly because of the terrible heat and out of solicitude for her. But as they neared the square she began to tremble again, walking with her head up, her hands clinched at her sides, their voices about her murmurous, also with that feverish, glittering quality of their eyes.

They entered the square, she in the centre of the group, fragile in her fresh dress. She was trembling worse. She walked slower and slower, as children eat ice-cream, her head up and her eyes bright in the haggard banner of her face, passing the hotel and the coatless drummers in chairs along the curb looking around at her: "That's the one: see? The one in pink in the middle." "Is that her? What did they do with the nigger? Did they—?" "Sure. He's all right." "All right, is he?" "Sure. He went on a little trip." Then the drug-store, where even the young men lounging in the door-way tipped their hats and followed with their eyes the motion of her hips and legs when she passed.

They went on, passing the lifted hats of the gentlemen, the

suddenly ceased voices, protective, deferent. "Do you see?" the friends said. Their voices sounded like long hovering sighs of hissing exultation. "There's not a negro on the square. Not one."

They reached the picture-show. It was like a miniature fairy-land with its lighted lobby and colored lithographs of life caught in its terrible and beautiful mutations. Her lips began to tingle. In the dark, when the picture began, it would be all right; she could hold back the laughing so it would not waste away so fast and so soon. So she hurried on before the turning faces, the under-tones of low astonishment, and they took their accustomed places where she could see the aisle against the silver glare and the young men and girls coming in two and two against it.

The lights flicked away; the screen glowed silver, and soon life began to unfold, beautiful and passionate and sad, while still the young men and girls entered, scented and sibilant in the half-dark, their paired backs in silhouette delicate and sleek, their slim, quick bodies awkward, divinely young, while beyond them the silver dream accumulated, inevitably on and on. She began to laugh. In trying to suppress it, it made more noise than ever; heads began to turn. Still laughing, her friends raised her and led her out, and she stood at the curb, laughing on a high, sustained note, until the taxi came up and they helped her in.

They removed the pink voile and the sheer underthings, and the stockings, and put her to bed, and cracked ice for her temples, and sent for the doctor. He was hard to locate, so they ministered to her with hushed ejaculations, renewing the ice and fanning her. While the ice was fresh and cold she stopped laughing and lay still for a time, moaning only a little. But soon the laughing welled again and her voice rose screaming.

"Shhhhhhhhhhh! Shhhhhhhhhhh!" they said, freshening the ice-pack, smoothing her hair, examining it for gray; "poor girl!" Then to one another: "Do you suppose anything really happened?" their eyes darkly aglitter, secret and passionate. "Shhhhhhhhhhh! Poor girl! Poor Minnie!"

V

It was midnight when Plunkett drove up to his neat new house. It was trim and fresh as a bird-cage and almost as small, with its clean green-and-white paint. He locked the car and mounted the porch and entered. His wife rose from a chair beside the reading-lamp. Plunkett stopped in the floor and stared at her until she looked down.

"Look at that clock!" he said, lifting his arm, pointing. She stood before him, her face lowered, a magazine in her hands. Her face was pale, strained, and weary-looking. "Haven't I told you about sitting up like this, waiting to see when I come in?"

"John!" she said. She laid the magazine down. Poised on the balls of his feet, he glared at her with his hot eyes, his sweating face.

"Didn't I tell you?" He went toward her. She looked up then. He caught her shoulder. She stood passive, looking at him.

"Don't, John. I couldn't sleep. . . . The heat; something. Please, John. You're hurting me."

"Didn't I tell you?" He released her and half struck, half flung her across the chair, and she lay there and watched him quietly as he left the room.

He went on through the house, ripping off his shirt, and on the dark, screened porch at the rear he stood and mopped his head and shoulders with the shirt and flung it away. He took the pistol from his hip and laid it on the table beside the bed, and sat on the bed and removed his shoes, and rose and slipped his trousers off. He was sweating again already, and he stooped and hunted furiously for the shirt. At last he found it and wiped his body again, and, with his body pressed against the dusty screen, he stood panting. There was no movement, no sound, not even an insect. The dark world seemed to lie stricken beneath the cold moon and the lidless stars.

Noon Wine

KATHERINE ANNE PORTER (1894–   )

Time: 1896–1905
Place: Small South Texas Farm

THE TWO grubby small boys with tow-colored hair who were digging among the ragweed in the front yard sat back on their heels and said, "Hello," when the tall bony man with straw-colored hair turned in at their gate. He did not pause at the gate; it had swung back, conveniently half open, long ago, and was now sunk so firmly on its broken hinges no one thought of trying to close it. He did not even glance at the small boys, much less give them good-day. He just clumped down his big square dusty shoes one after the other steadily, like a man following a plow, as if he knew the place well and knew where he was going and what he would find there. Rounding the right-hand corner of the house under the row of chinaberry trees, he walked up to the side porch where Mr. Thompson was pushing a big swing churn back and forth.

Mr. Thompson was a tough weather-beaten man with stiff black hair and a week's growth of black whiskers. He was a noisy proud man who held his neck so straight his whole face stood

NOON WINE is reprinted from *Pale Horse, Pale Rider* by Katherine Anne Porter. Copyright 1939 by Katherine Anne Porter. Reprinted by permission of Harcourt, Brace and Company, Inc.

level with his Adam's apple, and the whiskers continued down his neck and disappeared into a black thatch under his open collar. The churn rumbled and swished like the belly of a trotting horse, and Mr. Thompson seemed somehow to be driving a horse with one hand, reining it in and urging it forward; and every now and then he turned halfway around and squirted a tremendous spit of tobacco juice out over the steps. The door stones were brown and gleaming with fresh tobacco juice. Mr. Thompson had been churning quite a while and he was tired of it. He was just fetching a mouthful of juice to squirt again when the stranger came around the corner and stopped. Mr. Thompson saw a narrow-chested man with blue eyes so pale they were almost white, looking and not looking at him from a long gaunt face, under white eyebrows. Mr. Thompson judged him to be another of these Irishmen, by his long upper lip.

"Howdy do, sir," said Mr. Thompson politely, swinging his churn.

"I need work," said the man, clearly enough but with some kind of foreign accent Mr. Thompson couldn't place. It wasn't Cajun and it wasn't Nigger and it wasn't Dutch, so it had him stumped. "You need a man here?"

Mr. Thompson gave the churn a great shove and it swung back and forth several times on its own momentum. He sat on the steps, shot his quid into the grass, and said, "Set down. Maybe we can make a deal. I been kinda lookin' round for somebody. I had two niggers but they got into a cutting scrape up the creek last week, one of 'em dead now and the other in the hoosegow at Cold Springs. Neither one of 'em worth killing, come right down to it. So it looks like I'd better get somebody. Where'd you work last?"

"North Dakota," said the man, folding himself down on the other end of the steps, but not as if he were tired. He folded up and settled down as if it would be a long time before he got up again. He never had looked at Mr. Thompson, but there wasn't anything sneaking in his eye, either. He didn't seem to be looking anywhere else. His eyes sat in his head and let things pass by them. They didn't seem to be expecting to see anything worth looking at. Mr. Thompson waited a long time for the man to say something more, but he had gone into a brown study.

"North Dakota," said Mr. Thompson, trying to remember where that was. "That's a right smart distance off, seems to me."

"I can do everything on farm," said the man; "cheap. I need work."

Mr. Thompson settled himself to get down to business. "My name's Thompson, Mr. Royal Earle Thompson," he said.

"I'm Mr. Helton," said the man, "Mr. Olaf Helton." He did not move.

"Well, now," said Mr. Thompson in his most carrying voice, "I guess we'd better talk turkey."

When Mr. Thompson expected to drive a bargain he always grew very hearty and jovial. There was nothing wrong with him except that he hated like the devil to pay wages. He said so himself. "You furnish grub and a shack," he said, "and then you got to pay 'em besides. It ain't right. Besides the wear and tear on your implements," he said, "they just let everything go to rack and ruin." So he began to laugh and shout his way through the deal.

"Now, what I want to know is, how much you fixing to gouge outa me?" he brayed, slapping his knee. After he had kept it up as long as he could, he quieted down, feeling a little sheepish, and cut himself a chew. Mr. Helton was staring out somewhere between the barn and the orchard, and seemed to be sleeping with his eyes open.

"I'm good worker," said Mr. Helton as from the tomb. "I get dollar a day."

Mr. Thompson was so shocked he forgot to start laughing again at the top of his voice until it was nearly too late to do any good. "Haw, haw," he bawled. "Why, for a dollar a day I'd hire out myself. What kinda work is it where they pay you a dollar a day?"

"Wheatfields, North Dakota," said Mr. Helton, not even smiling.

Mr. Thompson stopped laughing. "Well, this ain't any wheat-field by a long shot. This is more of a dairy farm," he said, feeling apologetic. "My wife, she was set on a dairy, she seemed to like working around with cows and calves, so I humored her. But it was a mistake," he said. "I got nearly everything to do, anyhow. My wife ain't very strong. She's sick today, that's a fact. She's been porely for the last few days. We plant a little feed, and a corn patch, and there's the orchard, and a few pigs and chickens, but our main hold is the cows. Now just speakin' as one man to another, there ain't any money in it. Now I can't give you no dollar a day because ackshally I don't make that much out of it. No, sir, we get along on a lot less than a dollar a day, I'd say, if we figger up everything in the long run. Now, I paid seven dollars a month to the two niggers, three-fifty each, and grub, but what I say is, one middlin'-good white man ekals a whole passel of niggers any day in the week, so I'll give you seven dollars and you eat at the table with us, and you'll be treated like a white man, as the feller says—"

"That's all right," said Mr. Helton. "I take it."

"Well, now I guess we'll call it a deal, hey?" Mr. Thompson jumped up as if he had remembered important business. "Now, you just take hold of that churn and give it a few swings, will you, while I ride to town on a coupla little errands. I ain't been able to leave the place all week. I guess you know what to do with butter after you get it, don't you?"

"I know," said Mr. Helton without turning his head. "I know butter business." He had a strange drawling voice, and even when he spoke only two words his voice waved slowly up and down and the emphasis was in the wrong place. Mr. Thompson wondered what kind of foreigner Mr. Helton could be.

"Now just where did you say you worked last?" he asked, as if he expected Mr. Helton to contradict himself.

"North Dakota," said Mr. Helton.

"Well, one place is good as another once you get used to it," said Mr. Thompson, amply. "You're a forriner, ain't you?"

"I'm a Swede," said Mr. Helton, beginning to swing the churn.

Mr. Thompson let forth a booming laugh, as if this was the best joke on somebody he'd ever heard. "Well, I'll be damned," he said at the top of his voice. "A Swede: well, now, I'm afraid you'll get pretty lonesome around here. I never seen any Swedes in this neck of the woods."

"That's all right," said Mr. Helton. He went on swinging the churn as if he had been working on the place for years.

"In fact, I might as well tell you, you're practically the first Swede I ever laid eyes on."

"That's all right," said Mr. Helton.

Mr. Thompson went into the front room where Mrs. Thompson was lying down, with the green shades drawn. She had a bowl of water by her on the table and a wet cloth over her eyes. She took the cloth off at the sound of Mr. Thompson's boots and said, "What's all the noise out there? Who is it?"

"Got a feller out there says he's a Swede, Ellie," said Mr. Thompson; "says he knows how to make butter."

"I hope it turns out to be the truth," said Mrs. Thompson. "Looks like my head never will get any better."

"Don't you worry," said Mr. Thompson. "You fret too much. Now I'm gointa ride into town and get a little order of groceries."

"Don't you linger, now, Mr. Thompson," said Mrs. Thompson. "Don't go to the hotel." She meant the saloon; the proprietor also had rooms for rent upstairs.

"Just a coupla little toddies," said Mr. Thompson, laughing loudly, "never hurt anybody."

"I never took a dram in my life," said Mrs. Thompson, "and what's more I never will."

"I wasn't talking about the womenfolks," said Mr. Thompson.

The sound of the swinging churn rocked Mrs. Thompson first into a gentle doze, then a deep drowse from which she waked suddenly knowing that the swinging had stopped a good while ago. She sat up shading her weak eyes from the flat strips of late summer sunlight between the sill and the lowered shades. There she was, thank God, still alive, with supper to cook but no churning on hand, and her head still bewildered, but easy. Slowly she realized she had been hearing a new sound even in her sleep. Somebody was playing a tune on the harmonica, not merely shrilling up and down making a sickening noise, but really playing a pretty tune, merry and sad.

She went out through the kitchen, stepped off the porch, and stood facing the east, shading her eyes. When her vision cleared and settled, she saw a long, pale-haired man in blue jeans sitting in the doorway of the hired man's shack, tilted back in a kitchen chair, blowing away at the harmonica with his eyes shut. Mrs. Thompson's heart fluttered and sank. Heavens, he looked lazy and worthless, he did, now. First a lot of no-count fiddling darkies and then a no-count white man. It was just like Mr. Thompson to take on that kind. She did wish he would be more considerate, and take a little trouble with his business. She wanted to believe in her husband, and there were too many times when she couldn't. She wanted to believe that tomorrow, or at least the day after, life, such a battle at best, was going to be better.

She walked past the shack without glancing aside, stepping carefully, bent at the waist because of the nagging pain in her side, and went to the springhouse, trying to harden her mind to speak very plainly to that new hired man if he had not done his work.

The milk house was only another shack of weather-beaten boards nailed together hastily years before because they needed a milk house; it was meant to be temporary, and it was; already shapeless, leaning this way and that over a perpetual cool trickle of water that fell from a little grot, almost choked with pallid ferns. No one else in the whole countryside had such a spring on his land. Mr. and Mrs. Thompson felt they had a fortune in that spring, if ever they got around to doing anything with it.

Rickety wooden shelves clung at hazard in the square around the small pool where the larger pails of milk and butter stood, fresh and sweet in the cold water. One hand supporting her flat, pained side, the other shading her eyes, Mrs. Thompson leaned over and peered into the pails. The cream had been skimmed and set aside, there was a rich roll of butter, the wooden molds and shallow pans had been scrubbed and scalded for the first time in who knows when, the barrel was full of buttermilk ready for the pigs and the weanling calves, the hard packed-dirt floor had been swept smooth. Mrs. Thompson straightened up again, smiling tenderly. She had been ready to scold him, a poor man who needed a job, who had just come there and who might not have been expected to do things properly at first. There was nothing she could do to make up for the injustice she had done him in her thoughts but to tell him how she appreciated his good clean work, finished already, in no time at all. She ventured near the door of the shack with her careful steps; Mr. Helton opened his eyes, stopped playing, and brought his chair down straight, but did not look at her, or get up. She was a little frail woman with long thick brown hair in a braid, a suffering patient mouth and diseased eyes which cried easily. She wove her fingers into an eyeshade, thumbs on temples, and winking her tearful lids, said with a polite little manner, "Howdy do, sir. I'm Miz Thompson, and I wanted to tell you I think you did real well in the milk house. It's always been a hard place to keep."

He said, "That's all right," in a slow voice, without moving.

Mrs. Thompson waited a moment. "That's a pretty tune you're playing. Most folks don't seem to get much music out of a harmonica."

Mr. Helton sat humped over, long legs sprawling, his spine in a bow, running his thumb over the square mouth-stops; except for his moving hand he might have been asleep. The harmonica was a big shiny new one, and Mrs. Thompson, her gaze wandering about, counted five others, all good and expensive, standing in a row on the shelf beside his cot. "He must carry them around in his jumper pocket," she thought, and noted there was not a sign of any other possession lying about. "I see you're mighty fond of music," she said. "We used to have an old accordion, and Mr. Thompson could play it right smart, but the little boys broke it up."

Mr. Helton stood up rather suddenly, the chair clattered under him, his knees straightened though his shoulders did not, and he looked at the floor as if he were listening carefully. "You know how little boys are," said Mrs. Thompson. "You'd better set them harmonicas on a high shelf or they'll be after them. They're great hands for getting into things. I try to learn 'em, but it don't do much good."

Mr. Helton, in one wide gesture of his long arms, swept his harmonicas up against his chest, and from there transferred them in a row to the ledge where the roof joined to the wall. He pushed them back almost out of sight.

"That'll do, maybe," said Mrs. Thompson. "Now I wonder," she said, turning and closing her eyes helplessly against the stronger western light, "I wonder what became of them little tads. I can't keep up with them." She had a way of speaking about her children as if they were rather troublesome nephews on a prolonged visit.

"Down by the creek," said Mr. Helton, in his hollow voice. Mrs. Thompson, pausing confusedly, decided he had answered her question. He stood in silent patience, not exactly waiting for her to go, perhaps, but pretty plainly not waiting for anything else. Mrs. Thompson was perfectly accustomed to all kinds of men full of all kinds of cranky ways. The point was, to find out just how Mr. Helton's crankiness was different from any other man's, and then get used to it, and let him feel at home. Her father had been cranky, her brothers and uncles had all been set in their ways and none of them alike; and every hired man she'd ever seen had quirks and crotchets of his own. Now here was Mr. Helton, who was a Swede, who wouldn't talk, and who played the harmonica besides.

"They'll be needing something to eat," said Mrs. Thompson in a vague friendly way, "pretty soon. Now I wonder what I ought to be thinking about for supper? Now what do you like to eat, Mr. Helton? We always have plenty of good butter and milk and cream, that's a blessing. Mr. Thompson says we ought to sell all of it, but I say my family comes first." Her little face went all out of shape in a pained blind smile.

"I eat anything," said Mr. Helton, his words wandering up and down.

He *can't* talk, for one thing, thought Mrs. Thompson; it's a shame to keep at him when he don't know the language good. She took a slow step away from the shack, looking back over her shoulder. "We usually have cornbread except on Sundays," she told him. "I suppose in your part of the country you don't get much good cornbread."

Not a word from Mr. Helton. She saw from her eye-corner that he had sat down again, looking at his harmonica, chair tilted. She hoped he would remember it was getting near milking time. As she moved away, he started playing again, the same tune.

Milking time came and went. Mrs. Thompson saw Mr. Helton going back and forth between the cow barn and the milk house. He swung along in an easy lope, shoulders bent, head hanging, the big buckets balancing like a pair of scales at the ends of his bony arms. Mr. Thompson rode in from town sitting straighter than usual, chin in, a towsack full of supplies swung behind the saddle. After a trip to the barn, he came into the kitchen full of good will, and gave Mrs. Thompson a hearty smack on the cheek after dusting her face off with his tough whiskers. He had been to the hotel, that was plain. "Took a look around the premises, Ellie," he shouted. "That Swede sure is grinding out the labor. But he is the closest mouthed feller I ever met up with in all my days. Looks like he's scared he'll crack his jaw if he opens his front teeth."

Mrs. Thompson was stirring up a big bowl of buttermilk cornbread. "You smell like a toper, Mr. Thompson," she said with perfect dignity. "I wish you'd get one of the little boys to bring me in an extra load of firewood. I'm thinking about baking a batch of cookies tomorrow."

Mr. Thompson, all at once smelling the liquor on his own breath, sneaked out, justly rebuked, and brought in the firewood himself. Arthur and Herbert, grubby from thatched head to toes, from skin to shirt, came stamping in yelling for supper. "Go wash your faces and comb your hair," said Mrs. Thompson, automatically. They retired to the porch. Each one put his hand under the pump and wet his forelock, combed it down with his fingers, and returned at once to the kitchen, where all the fair prospects of life were centered. Mrs. Thompson set an extra plate and commanded Arthur, the eldest, eight years old, to call Mr. Helton for supper.

Arthur, without moving from the spot, bawled like a bull calf, "Saaaaaay, Hellllllton, suuuuuupper's ready!" and added in a lower voice, "You big Swede!"

"Listen to me," said Mrs. Thompson, "that's no way to act. Now you go out there and ask him decent, or I'll get your daddy to give you a good licking."

Mr. Helton loomed, long and gloomy, in the doorway. "Sit right there," boomed Mr. Thompson, waving his arm. Mr. Helton swung his square shoes across the kitchen in two steps, slumped onto the bench and sat. Mr. Thompson occupied his chair at the head of the table, the two boys scrambled into place opposite Mr. Helton, and Mrs. Thompson sat at the end nearest the stove. Mrs. Thompson clasped her hands, bowed her head and said aloud hastily, "Lord, for all these and Thy other blessings we thank Thee in Jesus' name, amen," trying to finish before Herbert's rusty little paw reached the nearest dish. Otherwise she would be duty-bound to send him away from the table, and growing children need their meals. Mr. Thompson and Arthur always waited, but Herbert, aged six, was too young to take training yet.

Mr. and Mrs. Thompson tried to engage Mr. Helton in conversation, but it was a failure. They tried first the weather, and then the crops, and then the cows, but Mr. Helton simply did not reply.

Mr. Thompson then told something funny he had seen in town. It was about some of the other old grangers at the hotel, friends of his, giving beer to a goat, and the goat's subsequent behavior. Mr. Helton did not seem to hear. Mrs. Thompson laughed dutifully, but she didn't think it was very funny. She had heard it often before, though Mr. Thompson, each time he told it, pretended it had happened that self-same day. It must have happened years ago if it ever happened at all, and it had never been a story that Mrs. Thompson thought suitable for mixed company. The whole thing came of Mr. Thompson's weakness for a dram too much now and then, though he voted for local option at every election. She passed the food to Mr. Helton, who took a helping of everything, but not much, not enough to keep him up to his full powers if he expected to go on working the way he had started.

At last, he took a fair-sized piece of cornbread, wiped his plate up as clean as if it had been licked by a hound dog, stuffed his mouth full, and, still chewing, slid off the bench and started for the door.

"Good night, Mr. Helton," said Mrs. Thompson, and the other Thompsons took it up in a scattered chorus. "Good night, Mr. Helton!"

"Good night," said Mr. Helton's wavering voice grudgingly from the darkness.

"Gude not," said Arthur, imitating Mr. Helton.

"Gude not," said Herbert, the copy-cat.

"You don't do it right," said Arthur. "Now listen to me. Guuuuuude naht," and he ran a hollow scale in a luxury of successful impersonation. Herbert almost went into a fit with joy.

"Now you *stop* that," said Mrs. Thompson. "He can't help the way he talks. You ought to be ashamed of yourselves, both of you, making fun of a poor stranger like that. How'd you like to be a stranger in a strange land?"

"I'd like it," said Arthur. "I think it would be fun."

"They're both regular heathens, Ellie," said Mr. Thompson. "Just plain ignoramuses." He turned the face of awful fatherhood upon his young. "You're both going to get sent to school next year, and that'll knock some sense into you."

"I'm going to git sent to the 'formatory when I'm old enough," piped up Herbert. "That's where I'm goin'."

"Oh, you are, are you?" asked Mr. Thompson. "Who says so?"

"The Sunday School Supintendant," said Herbert, a bright boy showing off.

"You see?" said Mr. Thompson, staring at his wife. "What did I tell you?" He became a hurricane of wrath. "Get to bed, you two," he roared until his Adam's apple shuddered. "Get now before I take the hide off you!" They got, and shortly from their attic bedroom the sounds of scuffling and snorting and giggling and growling filled the house and shook the kitchen ceiling.

Mrs. Thompson held her head and said in a small uncertain voice, "It's no use picking on them when they're so young and tender. I can't stand it."

"My goodness, Ellie," said Mr. Thompson, "we've got to raise 'em. We can't just let 'em grow up hog wild."

She went on in another tone. "That Mr. Helton seems all right, even if he can't be made to talk. Wonder how he comes to be so far from home."

"Like I said, he isn't no whamper-jaw," said Mr. Thompson, "but he sure knows how to lay out the work. I guess that's the main thing around here. Country's full of fellers trampin' round looking for work."

Mrs. Thompson was gathering up the dishes. She now gathered up Mr. Thompson's plate from under his chin. "To tell you the honest truth," she remarked, "I think it's a mighty good change to have a man round the place who knows how to work and keep his mouth shut. Means he'll keep out of our business. Not that we've got anything to hide, but it's convenient."

"That's a fact," said Mr. Thompson. "Haw, haw," he shouted suddenly. "Means you can do all the talking, huh?"

"The only thing," went on Mrs. Thompson, "is this: he don't eat hearty enough to suit me. I like to see a man set down and relish a good meal. My granma used to say it was no use putting dependence on a man who won't set down and make out his dinner. I hope it won't be that way this time."

"Tell *you* the truth, Ellie," said Mr. Thompson, picking his teeth with a fork and leaning back in the best of good humors, "I always thought your granma was a ter'ble ole fool. She'd just say the first thing that popped into her head and call it God's wisdom."

"My granma wasn't anybody's fool. Nine times out of ten she knew what she was talking about. I always say, the first thing you think is the best thing you can say."

"Well," said Mr. Thompson, going into another shout, "you're so reefined about that goat story, you just try speaking out in mixed comp'ny sometime! You just try it. S'pose you happened to be thinking about a hen and a rooster, hey? I reckon you'd shock the Babtist preacher!" He gave her a good pinch on her thin little rump. "No more meat on you than a rabbit," he said, fondly. "Now I like 'em cornfed."

Mrs. Thompson looked at him open-eyed and blushed. She could see better by lamplight. "Why, Mr. Thompson, sometimes I think you're the evilest-minded man that ever lived." She took a handful of hair on the crown of his head and gave it a good, slow pull. "That's to show you how it feels, pinching so hard when you're supposed to be playing," she said, gently.

In spite of his situation in life, Mr. Thompson had never been able to outgrow his deep conviction that running a dairy and chasing after chickens was woman's work. He was fond of saying that he could plow a furrow, cut sorghum, shuck corn, handle a team, build a corn crib, as well as any man. Buying and selling, too, were man's work. Twice a week he drove the spring wagon to market with the fresh butter, a few eggs, fruits in their proper season, sold them, pocketed the change, and spent it as seemed best, being careful not to dig into Mrs. Thompson's pin money.

But from the first the cows worried him, coming up regularly twice a day to be milked, standing there reproaching him with their smug female faces. Calves worried him, fighting the rope and strangling themselves until their eyes bulged, trying to get at the teat. Wrestling with a calf unmanned him, like having to change a baby's diaper. Milk worried him, coming bitter sometimes, drying up, turning sour. Hens worried him, cackling, clucking, hatching out when you least expected it and leading their broods into the barnyard where the horses could step on them; dying of roup and wryneck and getting plagues of chicken lice; laying eggs all over God's creation so that half of them were spoiled before a man could find them, in spite of a rack of nests Mrs. Thompson had set out for them in the feed room. Hens were a blasted nuisance.

Slopping hogs was hired man's work, in Mr. Thompson's opinion. Killing hogs was a job for the boss, but scraping them and cutting them up was for the hired man again; and again woman's proper work was dressing meat, smoking, pickling, and making lard and sausage. All his carefully limited fields of activity were related somehow to Mr. Thompson's feeling for the appearance of things, his own appearance in the sight of God and man. "It don't *look* right," was his final reason for not doing anything he did not wish to do.

It was his dignity and his reputation that he cared about, and there were only a few kinds of work manly enough for Mr. Thompson to undertake with his own hands. Mrs. Thompson, to whom so many forms of work would have been becoming, had simply gone down on him early. He saw, after a while, how short-sighted it had been of him to expect much from Mrs. Thompson; he had fallen in love with her delicate waist and lace-trimmed petticoats and big blue eyes, and, though all those charms had disappeared, she had in the meantime become Ellie to him, not at all the same person as Miss Ellen Bridges, popular Sunday School teacher in the Mountain City First Baptist Church, but his dear wife, Ellie, who was not strong. Deprived as he was, however, of the main support in life which a man might expect in marriage, he had almost without knowing it resigned himself to failure. Head erect, a prompt payer of taxes, yearly subscriber to the preacher's salary, land owner and father of a family, employer, a hearty good fellow among men, Mr. Thompson knew, without putting it into words, that he had been going steadily down hill. God amighty, it did look like somebody around the place might take a rake in hand now and then and clear up the clutter around the barn and the kitchen steps. The wagon shed was so full of broken-down machinery and ragged harness and old wagon wheels and battered milk pails and rotting lumber you could hardly drive in there any more. Not a soul on the place would raise a hand to it, and as for him, he had all he could do with his regular work. He would sometimes in the slack season sit for hours worrying about it, squirting tobacco on the ragweeds growing in a thicket against the wood pile, wondering what a fellow could do, handicapped as he was. He looked forward to the boys growing up soon; he was going to put them through the mill just as his own father had done with him when he was a boy; they were going to learn how to take hold and run the place right. He wasn't going to overdo it, but those two boys were going to earn their salt, or he'd know why. Great big lubbers sitting around whittling! Mr. Thompson sometimes grew quite enraged with them, when imagining their possible future, big lubbers sitting around whittling or thinking about fishing trips. Well, he'd put a stop to that, mighty damn quick.

As the seasons passed, and Mr. Helton took hold more and more, Mr. Thompson began to relax in his mind a little. There seemed to be nothing the fellow couldn't do, all in the day's work and as a matter of course. He got up at five o'clock in the morning, boiled his own coffee and fried his own bacon and was out in the cow lot before Mr. Thompson had even begun to yawn, stretch, groan, roar and thump around looking for his jeans. He milked the cows, kept the milk house, and churned the butter; rounded the hens up and somehow persuaded them to lay in the nests, not under the house and behind the haystacks; he fed them regularly and they hatched out until you couldn't set a foot down for them. Little by little the piles of trash around the barns and house disappeared. He carried buttermilk and corn to the hogs, and curried cockleburs out of the horses' manes. He was gentle with the calves, if a little grim with the cows and hens; judging by his conduct, Mr. Helton had never heard of the difference between man's and woman's work on a farm.

In the second year, he showed Mr. Thompson the picture of a cheese press in a mail order catalogue, and said, "This is a good thing. You buy this, I make cheese." The press was bought and Mr. Helton did make cheese, and it was sold, along with the increased butter and the crates of eggs. Sometimes Mr. Thompson felt a little contemptuous of Mr. Helton's ways. It did seem kind of picayune for a man to go around picking up half a dozen ears of corn that had fallen off the wagon on the way from the field, gathering up fallen fruit to feed to the pigs, storing up old nails and stray parts of machinery, spending good time stamping a fancy pattern on the butter before it went to market. Mr. Thompson, sitting up high on the spring-wagon seat, with the decorated butter in a five-gallon lard can wrapped in wet towsack, driving to town, chirruping to the horses and snapping the reins over their backs, sometimes thought that Mr. Helton was a pretty meeching sort of fellow; but he never gave way to these feelings, he knew a good thing when he had it. It was a fact the hogs were in better shape and sold for more money. It was a fact that Mr. Thompson stopped buying feed, Mr. Helton managed the crops so well. When beef- and hog-slaughtering time came, Mr. Helton knew how to save the scraps that Mr. Thompson had thrown away, and wasn't above scraping guts and filling them with sausages that he made by his own methods. In all, Mr. Thompson had no grounds for complaint. In the third year, he raised Mr. Helton's wages, though Mr. Helton had not asked for a raise. The fourth year, when Mr. Thompson was not only out of debt but had a little cash in the bank, he raised Mr. Helton's wages again, two dollars and a half a month each time.

"The man's worth it, Ellie," said Mr. Thompson, in a glow

of self-justification for his extravagance. "He's made this place pay, and I want him to know I appreciate it."

Mr. Helton's silence, the pallor of his eyebrows and hair, his long, glum jaw and eyes that refused to see anything, even the work under his hands, had grown perfectly familiar to the Thompsons. At first, Mrs. Thompson complained a little. "It's like sitting down at the table with a disembodied spirit," she said. "You'd think he'd find something to say, sooner or later."

"Let him alone," said Mr. Thompson. "When he gets ready to talk, he'll talk."

The years passed, and Mr. Helton never got ready to talk. After his work was finished for the day, he would come up from the barn or the milk house or the chicken house, swinging his lantern, his big shoes clumping like pony hoofs on the hard path. They, sitting in the kitchen in the winter, or on the back porch in summer, would hear him drag out his wooden chair, hear the creak of it tilted back, and then for a little while he would play his single tune on one or another of his harmonicas. The harmonicas were in different keys, some lower and sweeter than the others, but the same changeless tune went on, a strange tune, with sudden turns in it, night after night, and sometimes even in the afternoons when Mr. Helton sat down to catch his breath. At first the Thompsons liked it very much, and always stopped to listen. Later there came a time when they were fairly sick of it, and began to wish to each other that he would learn a new one. At last they did not hear it any more, it was as natural as the sound of the wind rising in the evenings, or the cows lowing, or their own voices.

Mrs. Thompson pondered now and then over Mr. Helton's soul. He didn't seem to be a church-goer, and worked straight through Sunday as if it were any common day of the week. "I think we ought to invite him to go to hear Dr. Martin," she told Mr. Thompson. "It isn't very Christian of us not to ask him. He's not a forward kind of man. He'd wait to be asked."

"Let him alone," said Mr. Thompson. "The way I look at

it, his religion is every man's own business. Besides, he ain't got any Sunday clothes. He wouldn't want to go to church in them jeans and jumpers of his. I don't know what he does with his money. He certainly don't spend it foolishly."

Still, once the notion got into her head, Mrs. Thompson could not rest until she invited Mr. Helton to go to church with the family next Sunday. He was pitching hay into neat little piles in the field back of the orchard. Mrs. Thompson put on smoked glasses and a sunbonnet and walked all the way down there to speak to him. He stopped and leaned on his pitchfork, listening, and for a moment Mrs. Thompson was almost frightened at his face. The pale eyes seemed to glare past her, the eyebrows frowned, the long jaw hardened. "I got work," he said bluntly, and lifting his pitchfork he turned from her and began to toss the hay. Mrs. Thompson, her feelings hurt, walked back thinking that by now she should be used to Mr. Helton's ways, but it did seem like a man, even a foreigner, could be just a little polite when you gave him a Christian invitation. "He's not polite, that's the only thing I've got against him," she said to Mr. Thompson. "He just can't seem to behave like other people. You'd think he had a grudge against the world," she said. "I sometimes don't know what to make of it."

In the second year something had happened that made Mrs. Thompson uneasy, the kind of thing she could not put into words, hardly into thoughts, and if she had tried to explain to Mr. Thompson it would have sounded worse than it was, or not bad enough. It was that kind of queer thing that seems to be giving a warning, and yet, nearly always nothing comes of it. It was on a hot, still spring day, and Mrs. Thompson had been down to the garden patch to pull some new carrots and green onions and string beans for dinner. As she worked, sunbonnet low over her eyes, putting each kind of vegetable in a pile by itself in her basket, she noticed how neatly Mr. Helton weeded, and how rich the soil was. He had spread it all over with manure from the barns, and worked it in, in the fall, and the vegetables were

coming up fine and full. She walked back under the nubbly little
fig trees where the unpruned branches leaned almost to the
ground, and the thick leaves made a cool screen. Mrs. Thompson
was always looking for shade to save her eyes. So she, looking
idly about, saw through the screen a sight that struck her as very
strange. If it had been a noisy spectacle, it would have been quite
natural. It was the silence that struck her. Mr. Helton was shaking Arthur by the shoulders, ferociously, his face most terribly
fixed and pale. Arthur's head snapped back and forth and he had
not stiffened in resistance, as he did when Mrs. Thompson tried
to shake him. His eyes were rather frightened, but surprised, too,
probably more surprised than anything else. Herbert stood by
meekly, watching. Mr. Helton dropped Arthur, and seized Herbert, and shook him with the same methodical ferocity, the same
face of hatred. Herbert's mouth crumpled as if he would cry,
but he made no sound. Mr. Helton let him go, turned and strode
into the shack, and the little boys ran, as if for their lives, without
a word. They disappeared around the corner to the front of
the house.

Mrs. Thompson took time to set her basket on the kitchen
table, to push her sunbonnet back on her head and draw it forward again, to look in the stove and make certain the fire was
going, before she followed the boys. They were sitting huddled
together under a clump of chinaberry trees in plain sight of her
bedroom window, as if it were a safe place they had discovered.

"What are you doing?" asked Mrs. Thompson.

They looked hang-dog from under their foreheads and Arthur
mumbled, "Nothin'."

"Nothing *now*, you mean," said Mrs. Thompson, severely.
"Well, I have plenty for you to do. Come right in here this minute and help me fix vegetables. This minute."

They scrambled up very eagerly and followed her close. Mrs.
Thompson tried to imagine what they had been up to; she did
not like the notion of Mr. Helton taking it on himself to correct
her little boys, but she was afraid to ask them for reasons. They

might tell her a lie, and she would have to overtake them in it, and whip them. Or she would have to pretend to believe them, and they would get in the habit of lying. Or they might tell her the truth, and it would be something she would have to whip them for. The very thought of it gave her a headache. She supposed she might ask Mr. Helton, but it was not her place to ask. She would wait and tell Mr. Thompson, and let him get at the bottom of it. While her mind ran on, she kept the little boys hopping. "Cut those carrot tops closer, Herbert, you're just being careless. Arthur, stop breaking up the beans so little. They're little enough already. Herbert, you go get an armload of wood. Arthur, you take these onions and wash them under the pump. Herbert, as soon as you're done here, you get a broom and sweep out this kitchen. Arthur, you get a shovel and take up the ashes. Stop picking your nose, Herbert. How often must I tell you? Arthur, you go look in the top drawer of my bureau, left-hand side, and bring me the vaseline for Herbert's nose. Herbert, come here to me. . . ."

They galloped through their chores, their animal spirits rose with activity, and shortly they were out in the front yard again, engaged in a wrestling match. They sprawled and fought, scrambled, clutched, rose and fell shouting, as aimlessly, noisily, monotonously as two puppies. They imitated various animals, not a human sound from them, and their dirty faces were streaked with sweat. Mrs. Thompson, sitting at her window, watched them with baffled pride and tenderness, they were so sturdy and healthy and growing so fast; but uneasily, too, with her pained little smile and the tears rolling from her eyelids that clinched themselves against the sunlight. They were so idle and careless, as if they had no future in this world, and no immortal souls to save, and oh, what had they been up to that Mr. Helton had shaken them, with his face positively dangerous?

In the evening before supper, without a word to Mr. Thompson of the curious fear the sight had caused her, she told him that Mr. Helton had shaken the little boys for some reason. He stepped out to the shack and spoke to Mr. Helton. In five minutes he was back, glaring at his young. "He says them brats been fooling with his harmonicas, Ellie, blowing in them and getting them all dirty and full of spit and they don't play good."

"Did he say all that?" asked Mrs. Thompson. "It doesn't seem possible."

"Well, that's what he meant, anyhow," said Mr. Thompson. "He didn't say it just that way. But he acted pretty worked up about it."

"That's a shame," said Mrs. Thompson, "a perfect shame. Now we've got to do something so they'll remember they mustn't go into Mr. Helton's things."

"I'll tan their hides for them," said Mr. Thompson. "I'll take a calf rope to them if they don't look out."

"Maybe you'd better leave the whipping to me," said Mrs. Thompson. "You haven't got a light enough hand for children."

"That's just what's the matter with them now," shouted Mr. Thompson, "rotten spoiled and they'll wind up in the penitentiary. You don't half whip 'em. Just little love taps. My pa used to knock me down with a stick of stove wood or anything else that came handy."

"Well, that's not saying it's right," said Mrs. Thompson. "I don't hold with that way of raising children. It makes them run away from home. I've seen too much of it."

"I'll break every bone in 'em," said Mr. Thompson, simmering down, "if they don't mind you better and stop being so bull-headed."

"Leave the table and wash your face and hands," Mrs. Thompson commanded the boys, suddenly. They slunk out and dabbled at the pump and slunk in again, trying to make themselves small. They had learned long ago that their mother always made them wash when there was trouble ahead. They looked at their plates. Mr. Thompson opened up on them.

"Well, now, what you got to say for yourselves about going into Mr. Helton's shack and ruining his harmonicas?"

The two little boys wilted, their faces drooped into the grieved hopeless lines of children's faces when they are brought to the terrible bar of blind adult justice; their eyes telegraphed each other in panic, "Now we're really going to catch a licking"; in despair, they dropped their buttered cornbread on their plates, their hands lagged on the edge of the table.

"I ought to break your ribs," said Mr. Thompson, "and I'm a good mind to do it."

"Yes, sir," whispered Arthur, faintly.

"Yes, sir," said Herbert, his lip trembling.

"Now, papa," said Mrs. Thompson in a warning tone. The children did not glance at her. They had no faith in her good will. She had betrayed them in the first place. There was no trusting her. Now she might save them and she might not. No use depending on her.

"Well, you ought to get a good thrashing. You deserve it, don't you, Arthur?"

Arthur hung his head. "Yes, sir."

"And the next time I catch either of you hanging around Mr. Helton's shack, I'm going to take the hide off *both* of you, you hear me, Herbert?"

Herbert mumbled and choked, scattering his cornbread. "Yes, sir."

"Well, now sit up and eat your supper and not another word out of you," said Mr. Thompson, beginning on his own food. The little boys perked up somewhat and started chewing, but every time they looked around they met their parents' eyes, regarding them steadily. There was no telling when they would think of something new. The boys ate warily, trying not to be seen or heard, the cornbread sticking, the buttermilk gurgling, as it went down their gullets.

"And something else, Mr. Thompson," said Mrs. Thompson after a pause. "Tell Mr. Helton he's to come straight to us when they bother him, and not to trouble shaking them himself. Tell him we'll look after that."

"They're so mean," answered Mr. Thompson, staring at them. "It's a wonder he don't just kill 'em off and be done with it." But there was something in the tone that told Arthur and Herbert that nothing more worth worrying about was going to happen this time. Heaving deep sighs, they sat up, reaching for the food nearest them.

"Listen," said Mrs. Thompson, suddenly. The little boys stopped eating. "Mr. Helton hasn't come for his supper. Arthur, go and tell Mr. Helton he's late for supper. Tell him nice, now."

Arthur, miserably depressed, slid out of his place and made for the door, without a word.

There were no miracles of fortune to be brought to pass on a small dairy farm. The Thompsons did not grow rich, but they kept out of the poor house, as Mr. Thompson was fond of saying, meaning he had got a little foothold in spite of Ellie's poor health, and unexpected weather, and strange declines in market prices, and his own mysterious handicaps which weighed him down. Mr. Helton was the hope and the prop of the family, and all the Thompsons became fond of him, or at any rate they ceased to regard him as in any way peculiar, and looked upon him, from a distance they did not know how to bridge, as a good man and a good friend. Mr. Helton went his way, worked, played his tune. Nine years passed. The boys grew up and learned to work. They could not remember the time when Ole Helton hadn't been there: a grouchy cuss, Brother Bones; Mr. Helton, the dairymaid; that Big Swede. If he had heard them, he might have been annoyed at some of the names they called him. But he did not hear them, and besides they meant no harm—or at least such harm as existed was all there, in the names; the boys referred to their father as the Old Man, or the Old Geezer, but not to his face. They lived through by main strength all the grimy, secret, oblique phases of growing up and got past the crisis safely if anyone does. Their parents could see they were good solid boys with hearts of gold in spite of their rough ways. Mr. Thompson was relieved to find that, without knowing how he had done it, he had succeeded in raising a set of boys who were not trifling whittlers. They were such good boys Mr. Thompson began to believe they were born that way, and that he had never spoken a harsh word to them in their lives, much less thrashed them. Herbert and Arthur never disputed his word.

Mr. Helton, his hair wet with sweat, plastered to his dripping forehead, his jumper streaked dark and light blue and clinging to his ribs, was chopping a little firewood. He chopped slowly, struck the ax into the end of the chopping log, and piled the wood up neatly. He then disappeared round the house into his shack, which shared with the wood pile a good shade from a row of mulberry trees. Mr. Thompson was lolling in a swing chair on the front porch, a place he had never liked. The chair was new, and Mrs. Thompson had wanted it on the front porch, though the side porch was the place for it, being cooler; and Mr. Thompson wanted to sit in the chair, so there he was. As soon as the new wore off of it, and Ellie's pride in it was exhausted, he would move it round to the side porch. Meantime the August heat was almost unbearable, the air so thick you could poke a hole in it. The dust was inches thick on everything, though Mr. Helton sprinkled the whole yard regularly every night. He even shot the hose upward and washed the tree tops and the roof of the house. They had laid waterpipes to the kitchen and an outside faucet. Mr. Thompson must have dozed, for he opened his eyes and shut his mouth just in time to save his face before a stranger who had driven up to the front gate. Mr. Thompson stood up, put on his hat, pulled up his jeans, and watched while the stranger tied his team, attached to a light spring wagon, to the hitching post. Mr. Thompson recognized the team and wagon. They were from a livery stable in Buda. While the stranger was opening the gate, a strong gate that Mr. Helton had built and set firmly on its hinges several years back, Mr. Thompson strolled down the path to greet him and find out what in God's world a man's business might be that would bring him out at this time of day, in all this dust and welter.

He wasn't exactly a fat man. He was more like a man who had been fat recently. His skin was baggy and his clothes were too big for him, and he somehow looked like a man who should be fat, ordinarily, but who might have just got over a spell of sickness. Mr. Thompson didn't take to his looks at all, he couldn't say why.

The stranger took off his hat. He said in a loud hearty voice, "Is this Mr. Thompson, Mr. Royal Earle Thompson?"

"That's my name," said Mr. Thompson, almost quietly, he was so taken aback by the free manner of the stranger.

"My name is Hatch," said the stranger, "Mr. Homer T. Hatch, and I've come to see you about buying a horse."

"I reckon you've been misdirected," said Mr. Thompson. "I haven't got a horse for sale. Usually if I've got anything like that to sell," he said, "I tell the neighbors and tack up a little sign on the gate."

The fat man opened his mouth and roared with joy, showing rabbit teeth brown as shoeleather. Mr. Thompson saw nothing to laugh at, for once. The stranger shouted, "That's just an old joke of mine." He caught one of his hands in the other and shook hands with himself heartily. "I always say something like that when I'm calling on a stranger, because I've noticed that when a feller says he's come to buy something nobody takes him for a suspicious character. You see? Haw, haw, haw."

His joviality made Mr. Thompson nervous, because the expression in the man's eyes didn't match the sounds he was making. "Haw, haw," laughed Mr. Thompson obligingly, still not seeing the joke. "Well, that's all wasted on me because I never take any man for a suspicious character 'til he shows hisself to be one. Says or does something," he explained. "Until that happens, one man's as good as another, so far's *I'm* concerned."

"Well," said the stranger, suddenly very sober and sensible, "I ain't come neither to buy nor sell. Fact is, I want to see you about something that's of interest to us both. Yes, sir, I'd like to have a little talk with you, and it won't cost you a cent."

"I guess that's fair enough," said Mr. Thompson, reluctantly. "Come on around the house where there's a little shade."

They went round and seated themselves on two stumps under a chinaberry tree.

"Yes, sir, Homer T. Hatch is my name and America is my nation," said the stranger. "I reckon you must know the name? I used to have a cousin named Jameson Hatch lived up the country a ways."

"Don't think I know the name," said Mr. Thompson. "There's some Hatchers settled somewhere around Mountain City."

"Don't know the old Hatch family," cried the man in deep concern. He seemed to be pitying Mr. Thompson's ignorance. "Why, we came over from Georgia fifty years ago. Been here long yourself?"

"Just all my whole life," said Mr. Thompson, beginning to feel peevish. "And my pa and my grampap before me. Yes, sir, we've been right here all along. Anybody wants to find a Thompson knows where to look for him. My grampap immigrated in 1836."

"From Ireland, I reckon?" said the stranger.

"From Pennsylvania," said Mr. Thompson. "Now what makes you think we came from Ireland?"

The stranger opened his mouth and began to shout with merriment, and he shook hands with himself as if he hadn't met himself for a long time. "Well, what I always says is, a feller's got to come from *somewhere*, ain't he?"

While they were talking, Mr. Thompson kept glancing at the face near him. He certainly did remind Mr. Thompson of somebody, or maybe he really had seen the man himself somewhere. He couldn't just place the features. Mr. Thompson finally decided it was just that all rabbit-teethed men looked alike.

"That's right," acknowledged Mr. Thompson, rather sourly, "but what I always say is, Thompsons have been settled here for so long it don't make much difference any more *where* they come from. Now a course, this is the slack season, and we're all just laying round a little, but nevertheless we've all got our chores to do, and I don't want to hurry you, and so if you've come to see me on business maybe we'd better get down to it."

"As I said, it's not in a way, and again in a way it is," said the fat man. "Now I'm looking for a man named Helton, Mr. Olaf Eric Helton, from North Dakota, and I was told up around the country a ways that I might find him here, and I wouldn't mind having a little talk with him. No, siree, I sure wouldn't mind, if it's all the same to you."

"I never knew his middle name," said Mr. Thompson, "but Mr. Helton is right here, and been here now for going on nine years. He's a mighty steady man, and you can tell anybody I said so."

"I'm glad to hear that," said Mr. Homer T. Hatch. "I like to hear of a feller mending his ways and settling down. Now when I knew Mr. Helton he was pretty wild, yes, sir, wild is what he was, he didn't know his own mind atall. Well, now, it's going to be a great pleasure to me to meet up with an old friend and find him all settled down and doing well by hisself."

"We've all got to be young once," said Mr. Thompson. "It's like the measles, it breaks out all over you, and you're a nuisance to yourself and everybody else, but it don't last, and it usually don't leave no ill effects." He was so pleased with this notion he forgot and broke into a guffaw. The stranger folded his arms over his stomach and went into a kind of fit, roaring until he had tears in his eyes. Mr. Thompson stopped shouting and eyed the stranger uneasily. Now he liked a good laugh as well as any man, but there ought to be a little moderation. Now this feller laughed like a perfect lunatic, that was a fact. And he wasn't laughing because he really thought things were funny, either. He was laughing for reasons of his own. Mr. Thompson fell into a moody silence, and waited until Mr. Hatch settled down a little.

Mr. Hatch got out a very dirty blue cotton bandanna and wiped his eyes. "That joke just about caught me where I live," he said, almost apologetically. "Now I wish I could think up things as funny as that to say. It's a gift. It's . . ."

"If you want to speak to Mr. Helton, I'll go and round him up," said Mr. Thompson, making motions as if he might get up. "He may be in the milk house and he may be setting in his shack this time of day." It was drawing towards five o'clock. "It's right around the corner," he said.

"Oh, well, there ain't no special hurry," said Mr. Hatch. "I've been wanting to speak to him for a good long spell now and I guess a few minutes more won't make no difference. I just more wanted to locate him, like. That's all."

Mr. Thompson stopped beginning to stand up, and unbuttoned one more button of his shirt, and said, "Well, he's here, and he's this kind of man, that if he had any business with you he'd like to get it over. He don't dawdle, that's one thing you can say for him."

Mr. Hatch appeared to sulk a little at these words. He wiped his face with the bandanna and opened his mouth to speak, when round the house there came the music of Mr. Helton's harmonica. Mr. Thompson raised a finger. "There he is," said Mr. Thompson. "Now's your time."

Mr. Hatch cocked an ear towards the east side of the house and listened for a few seconds, a very strange expression on his face.

"I know that tune like I know the palm of my own hand," said Mr. Thompson, "but I never heard Mr. Helton say what it was."

"That's a kind of Scandahoovian song," said Mr. Hatch. "Where I come from they sing it a lot. In North Dakota, they sing it. It says something about starting out in the morning feeling so good you can't hardly stand it, so you drink up all your likker before noon. All the likker, y' understand, that you was saving for the noon lay-off. The words ain't much, but it's a pretty tune. It's a kind of drinking song." He sat there drooping a little, and Mr. Thompson didn't like his expression. It was a satisfied expression, but it was more like the cat that et the canary.

"So far as I know," said Mr. Thompson, "he ain't touched a

drop since he's been on the place, and that's nine years this coming September. Yes, sir, nine years, so far as I know, he ain't wetted his whistle once. And that's more than I can say for myself," he said, meekly proud.

"Yes, that's a drinking song," said Mr. Hatch. "I used to play 'Little Brown Jug' on the fiddle when I was younger than I am now," he went on, "but this Helton, he just keeps it up. He just sits and plays it by himself."

"He's been playing it off and on for nine years right here on the place," said Mr. Thompson, feeling a little proprietary.

"And he was certainly singing it as well, fifteen years before that, in North Dakota," said Mr. Hatch. "He used to sit up in a straitjacket, practically, when he was in the asylum—"

"What's that you say?" said Mr. Thompson. "What's that?"

"Shucks, I didn't mean to tell you," said Mr. Hatch, a faint leer of regret in his drooping eyelids. "Shucks, that just slipped out. Funny, now I'd made up my mind I wouldn' say a word, because it would just make a lot of excitement, and what I say is, if a man has lived harmless and quiet for nine years it don't matter if he *is* loony, does it? So long's he keeps quiet and don't do nobody harm."

"You mean they had him in a straitjacket?" asked Mr. Thompson, uneasily. "In a lunatic asylum?"

"They sure did," said Mr. Hatch. "That's right where they had him, from time to time."

"They put my Aunt Ida in one of them things in the State asylum," said Mr. Thompson. "She got vi'lent, and they put her in one of these jackets with long sleeves and tied her to an iron ring in the wall, and Aunt Ida got so wild she broke a blood vessel and when they went to look after her she was dead. I'd think one of them things was dangerous."

"Mr. Helton used to sing his drinking song when he was in a straitjacket," said Mr. Hatch. "Nothing ever bothered him, except if you tried to make him talk. That bothered him, and he'd get vi'lent, like your Aunt Ida. He'd get vi'lent and then they'd put him in the jacket and go off and leave him, and he'd lay there perfickly contented, so far's you could see, singing his song. Then one night he just disappeared. Left, you might say, just went, and nobody ever saw hide or hair of him again. And then I come along and find him here," said Mr. Hatch, "all settled down and playing the same song."

"He never acted crazy to me," said Mr. Thompson. "He always acted like a sensible man, to me. He never got married, for one thing, and he works like a horse, and I bet he's got the first cent I paid him when he landed here, and he don't drink, and he never says a word, much less swear, and he don't waste time runnin' around Saturday nights, and if he's crazy," said Mr. Thompson, "why, I think I'll go crazy myself for a change."

"Haw, ha," said Mr. Hatch, "heh, he, that's good! Ha, ha, ha, I hadn't thought of it jes like that. Yeah, that's right. Let's all go crazy and get rid of our wives and save our money, hey?" He smiled unpleasantly, showing his little rabbit teeth.

Mr. Thompson felt he was being misunderstood. He turned around and motioned toward the open window back of the honeysuckle trellis. "Let's move off down here a little," he said. "I oughta thought of that before." His visitor bothered Mr. Thompson. He had a way of taking the words out of Mr. Thompson's mouth, turning them around and mixing them up until Mr. Thompson didn't know himself what he had said. "My wife's not very strong," said Mr. Thompson. "She's been kind of invalid now goin' on fourteen years. It's mighty tough on a poor man, havin' sickness in the family. She had four operations," he said proudly, "one right after the other, but they didn't do any good. For five years handrunnin', I just turned every nickel I made over to the doctors. Upshot is, she's a mighty delicate woman."

"My old woman," said Mr. Homer T. Hatch, "had a back like a mule, yes, sir. That woman could have moved the barn with her bare hands if she'd ever took the notion. I used to say, it was a good thing she didn't know her own stren'th. She's dead now, though. That kind wear out quicker than the puny ones. I never had much use for a woman always complainin'. I'd get rid of her mighty quick, yes, sir, mighty quick. It's just as you say: a dead loss, keepin' one of 'em up."

This was not at all what Mr. Thompson had heard himself say; he had been trying to explain that a wife as expensive as his was a credit to a man. "She's a mighty reasonable woman," said Mr. Thompson, feeling baffled, "but I wouldn't answer for what she'd say or do if she found out we'd had a lunatic on the place all this time." They had moved away from the window; Mr. Thompson took Mr. Hatch the front way, because if he went the back way they would have to pass Mr. Helton's shack. For some reason he didn't want the stranger to see or talk to Mr. Helton. It was strange, but that was the way Mr. Thompson felt.

Mr. Thompson sat down again, on the chopping log, offering his guest another tree stump. "Now, I mighta got upset myself at such a thing, once," said Mr. Thompson, "but now I *deefy* anything to get me lathered up." He cut himself an enormous plug of tobacco with his horn-handled pocketknife, and offered it to Mr. Hatch, who then produced his own plug and, opening a huge bowie knife with a long blade sharply whetted, cut off a large wad and put it in his mouth. They then compared plugs and both of them were astonished to see how different men's ideas of good chewing tobacco were.

"Now, for instance," said Mr. Hatch, "mine is lighter colored. That's because, for one thing, there ain't any sweetenin' in this plug. I like it dry, natural leaf, medium strong."

"A little sweetenin' don't do no harm so far as I'm concerned," said Mr. Thompson, "but it's got to be mighty little. But with me, now, I want a strong leaf, I want it heavy-cured, as the feller says. There's a man near here, named Williams, Mr. John Morgan Williams, who chews a plug—well, sir, it's black as your hat and soft as melted tar. It fairly drips with molasses, jus' plain molasses, and it chews like licorice. Now, I don't call that a good chew."

"One man's meat," said Mr. Hatch, "is another man's poison.

Now, such a chew would simply gag me. I couldn't begin to put it in my mouth."

"Well," said Mr. Thompson, a tinge of apology in his voice, "I jus' barely tasted it myself, you might say. Just took a little piece in my mouth and spit it out again."

"I'm dead sure I couldn't even get that far," said Mr. Hatch. "I like a dry natural chew without any artificial flavorin' of any kind."

Mr. Thompson began to feel that Mr. Hatch was trying to make out he had the best judgment in tobacco, and was going to keep up the argument until he proved it. He began to feel seriously annoyed with the fat man. After all, who was he and where did he come from? Who was he to go around telling other people what kind of tobacco to chew?

"Artificial flavorin'," Mr. Hatch went on, doggedly, "is jes put in to cover up a cheap leaf and make a man think he's gettin' somethin' more than he *is* gettin'. Even a little sweetenin' is a sign of a cheap leaf, you can mark my words."

"I've always paid a fair price for my plug," said Mr. Thompson, stiffly. "I'm not a rich man and I don't go round settin' myself up for one, but I'll say this, when it comes to such things as tobacco, I buy the best on the market."

"Sweetenin', even a little," began Mr. Hatch, shifting his plug and squirting tobacco juice at a dry-looking little rose bush that was having a hard enough time as it was, standing all day in the blazing sun, its roots clenched in the baked earth, "is the sign of—"

"About this Mr. Helton, now," said Mr. Thompson, determinedly, "I don't see no reason to hold it against a man because he went loony once or twice in his lifetime and so I don't expect to take no steps about it. Not a step. I've got nothin' against the man, he's always treated me fair. They's things and people," he went on, " 'nough to drive any man loony. The wonder to me is, more men don't wind up in straitjackets, the way things are going these days and times."

"That's right," said Mr. Hatch, promptly, entirely too promptly, as if he were turning Mr. Thompson's meaning back on him. "You took the words right out of my mouth. There ain't every man in a straitjacket that ought to be there. Ha, ha, you're right all right. You got the idea."

Mr. Thompson sat silent and chewed steadily and stared at a spot on the ground about six feet away and felt a slow muffled resentment climbing from somewhere deep down in him, climbing and spreading all through him. What was this fellow driving at? What was he trying to say? It wasn't so much his words, but his looks and his way of talking: that droopy look in the eye, that tone of voice, as if he was trying to mortify Mr. Thompson about something. Mr. Thompson didn't like it, but he couldn't get hold of it either. He wanted to turn around and shove the fellow off the stump, but it wouldn't look reasonable. Suppose something happened to the fellow when he fell off the stump, just for instance, if he fell on the ax and cut himself, and then someone should ask Mr. Thompson why he shoved him, and what could a man say? It would look mighty funny, it would sound mighty strange to say, Well, him and me fell out over a plug of tobacco. He might just shove him anyhow and then tell people he was a fat man not used to the heat and while he was talking he got dizzy and fell off by himself, or something like that, and it wouldn't be the truth either, because it wasn't the heat and it wasn't the tobacco. Mr. Thompson made up his mind to get the fellow off the place pretty quick, without seeming to be anxious, and watch him sharp till he was out of sight. It doesn't pay to be friendly with strangers from another part of the country. They're always up to something, or they'd stay at home where they belong.

"And they's some people," said Mr. Hatch, "would jus' as soon have a loonatic around their house as not, they can't see no difference between them and anybody else. I always say, if that's the way a man feels, don't care who he associates with, why, why, that's his business, not mine. I don't wanta have a thing to do with it. Now back home in North Dakota, we don't feel that way. I'd like to a seen anybody hiring a loonatic there, aspecially after what he done."

"I didn't understand your home was North Dakota," said Mr. Thompson. "I thought you said Georgia."

"I've got a married sister in North Dakota," said Mr. Hatch, "married a Swede, but a white man if ever I saw one. So I say *we* because we got into a little business together out that way. And it seems like home, kind of."

"What did he do?" asked Mr. Thompson, feeling very uneasy again.

"Oh, nothin' to speak of," said Mr. Hatch, jovially, "jus' went loony one day in the hayfield and shoved a pitchfork right square through his brother, when they was makin' hay. They was goin' to execute him, but they found out he had went crazy with the heat, as the feller says, and so they put him in the asylum. That's all he done. Nothin' to get lathered up about, ha, ha, ha!" he said, and taking out his sharp knife he began to slice off a chew as carefully as if he were cutting cake.

"Well," said Mr. Thompson, "I don't deny that's news. Yes, sir, news. But I still say somethin' must have drove him to it. Some men make you feel like giving 'em a good killing just by lookin' at you. His brother may a been a mean ornery cuss."

"Brother was going to get married," said Mr. Hatch; "used to go courtin' his girl nights. Borrowed Mr. Helton's harmonica to give her a serenade one evenin', and lost it. Brand new harmonica."

"He thinks a heap of his harmonicas," said Mr. Thompson. "Only money he ever spends, now and then he buys hisself a new one. Must have a dozen in that shack, all kinds and sizes."

"Brother wouldn't buy him a new one," said Mr. Hatch, "so Mr. Helton just ups, as I says, and runs his pitchfork through his brother. Now you know he musta been crazy to get all worked up over a little thing like that."

"Sounds like it," said Mr. Thompson, reluctant to agree in anything with this intrusive and disagreeable fellow. He kept thinking he couldn't remember when he had taken such a dislike to a man on first sight.

"Seems to me you'd get pretty sick of hearin' the same tune year in, year out," said Mr. Hatch.

"Well, sometimes I think it wouldn't do no harm if he learned a new one," said Mr. Thompson, "but he don't, so there's nothin' to be done about it. It's a pretty good tune, though."

"One of the Scandahoovians told me what it meant, that's how I come to know," said Mr. Hatch. "Especially that part about getting so gay you jus' go ahead and drink up all the likker you got on hand before noon. It seems like up in them Swede countries a man carries a bottle of wine around with him as a matter of course, at least that's the way I understood it. Those fellers will tell you anything, though—" He broke off and spat.

The idea of drinking any kind of liquor in this heat made Mr. Thompson dizzy. The idea of anybody feeling good on a day like this, for instance, made him tired. He felt he was really suffering from the heat. The fat man looked as if he had grown to the stump; he slumped there in his damp, dark clothes too big for him, his belly slack in his pants, his wide black felt hat pushed off his narrow forehead red with prickly heat. A bottle of good cold beer, now, would be a help, thought Mr. Thompson, remembering the four bottles sitting deep in the pool at the spring-house, and his dry tongue squirmed in his mouth. He wasn't going to offer this man anything, though, not even a drop of water. He wasn't even going to chew any more tobacco with him. He shot out his quid suddenly, and wiped his mouth on the back of his hand, and studied the head near him attentively. The man was no good, and he was there for no good, but what was he up to? Mr. Thompson made up his mind he'd give him a little more time to get his business, whatever it was, with Mr. Helton over, and then if he didn't get off the place he'd kick him off.

Mr. Hatch, as if he suspected Mr. Thompson's thoughts, turned his eyes, wicked and pig-like, on Mr. Thompson. "Fact is," he said, as if he had made up his mind about something, "I might need your help in the little matter I've got on hand, but it won't cost you any trouble. Now, this Mr. Helton here, like I tell you, he's a dangerous escaped loonatic, you might say. Now fact is, in the last twelve years or so I musta rounded up twenty-odd escaped loonatics, besides a couple of escaped convicts that I just run into by accident, like. I don't make a business of it, but if there's a re-ward, and there usually is a reward, of course, I get it. It amounts to a tidy little sum in the long run, but that ain't the main ques-tion. Fact is, I'm for law and order, I don't like to see lawbreakers and loonatics at large. It ain't the place for them. Now I reckon you're bound to agree with me on that, aren't you?"

Mr. Thompson said, "Well, circumstances alters cases, as the feller says. Now, what I know of Mr. Helton, he ain't dangerous, as I told you." Something serious was going to happen, Mr. Thompson could see that. He stopped thinking about it. He'd just let this fellow shoot off his head and then see what could be done about it. Without thinking he got out his knife and plug and started to cut a chew, then remembered himself and put them back in his pocket.

"The law," said Mr. Hatch, "is solidly behind me. Now this Mr. Helton, he's been one of my toughest cases. He's kept my record from being practically one hundred per cent. I knew him before he went loony, and I know the fam'ly, so I undertook to help out rounding him up. Well, sir, he was gone slick as a whistle, for all we knew the man was as good as dead long while ago. Now we never might have caught up with him, but do you know what he did? Well, sir, about two weeks ago his old mother gets a letter from him, and in that letter, what do you reckon she found? Well, it was a check on that little bank in town for eight hundred and fifty dollars, just like that; the letter wasn't nothing much, just said he was sending her a few little savings, she might need something, but there it was, name, postmark, date, everything. The old woman practically lost her mind with joy. She's gettin' childish, and it looked like she kinda forgot that her only living son killed his brother and went loony. Mr.

Helton said he was getting along all right, and for her not to tell nobody. Well, natchally, she couldn't keep it to herself, with that check to cash and everything. So that's how I come to know." His feelings got the better of him. "You coulda knocked me down with a feather." He shook hands with himself and rocked, wagging his head, going "Heh, heh," in his throat. Mr. Thompson felt the corners of his mouth turning down. Why, the dirty low-down hound, sneaking around spying into other people's business like that. Collecting blood money, that's what it was! Let him talk!

"Yea, well, that musta been a surprise all right," he said, trying to hold his voice even. "I'd say a surprise."

"Well, siree," said Mr. Hatch, "the more I got to thinking about it, the more I just come to the conclusion that I'd better look into the matter a little, and so I talked to the old woman. She's pretty decrepit, now, half blind and all, but she was all for taking the first train out and going to see her son. I put it up to her square—how she was too feeble for the trip, and all. So, just as a favor to her, I told her for my expenses I'd come down and see Mr. Helton and bring her back all the news about him. She gave me a new shirt she made herself by hand, and a big Swedish kind of cake to bring to him, but I musta mislaid them along the road somewhere. It don't reely matter, though, he prob'ly ain't in any state of mind to appreciate 'em."

Mr. Thompson sat up and turning round on the log looked at Mr. Hatch and asked as quietly as he could, "And now what are you aiming to do? That's the question."

Mr. Hatch slouched up to his feet and shook himself. "Well, I come all prepared for a little scuffle," he said. "I got the hand-cuffs," he said, "but I don't want no violence if I can help it. I didn't want to say nothing around the countryside, making an uproar. I figured the two of us could overpower him." He reached into his big inside pocket and pulled them out. Handcuffs, for God's sake, thought Mr. Thompson. Coming round on a peace-able afternoon worrying a man, and making trouble, and fishing handcuffs out of his pocket on a decent family homestead, as if it was all in the day's work.

Mr. Thompson, his head buzzing, got up too. "Well," he said, roundly, "I want to tell you I think you've got a mighty sorry job on hand, you sure must be hard up for something to do, and now I want to give you a good piece of advice. You just drop the idea that you're going to come here and make trouble for Mr. Helton, and the quicker you drive that hired rig away from my front gate the better I'll be satisfied."

Mr. Hatch put one handcuff in his outside pocket, the other dangling down. He pulled his hat down over his eyes, and reminded Mr. Thompson of a sheriff, somehow. He didn't seem in the least nervous, and didn't take up Mr. Thompson's words. He said, "Now listen just a minute, it ain't reasonable to suppose that a man like yourself is going to stand in the way of getting an escaped loonatic back to the asylum where he belongs. Now I know it's enough to throw you off, coming sudden like this, but fact is I counted on your being a respectable man and helping me out to see that justice is done. Now a course, if you won't help, I'll have to look around for help somewheres else. It won't look very good to your neighbors that you was harbring an escaped loonatic who killed his own brother, and then you refused to give him up. It will look mighty funny."

Mr. Thompson knew almost before he heard the words that it would look funny. It would put him in a mighty awkward position. He said, "But I've been trying to tell you all along that the man ain't loony now. He's been perfectly harmless for nine years. He's—he's—"

Mr. Thompson couldn't think how to describe how it was with Mr. Helton. "Why, he's been like one of the family," he said, "the best standby a man ever had." Mr. Thompson tried to see his way out. It was a fact Mr. Helton might go loony again any minute, and now this fellow talking around the country would put Mr. Thompson in a fix. It was a terrible position. He couldn't think of any way out. "You're crazy," Mr. Thompson roared suddenly, "you're the crazy one around here, you're crazier than he ever was! You get off this place or I'll handcuff you and turn you over to the law. You're trespassing," shouted Mr. Thompson. "Get out of here before I knock you down!"

He took a step towards the fat man, who backed off, shrinking, "Try it, try it, go ahead!" and then something happened that Mr. Thompson tried hard afterwards to piece together in his mind, and in fact it never did come straight. He saw the fat man with his long bowie knife in his hand, he saw Mr. Helton come round the corner on the run, his long jaw dropped, his arms swinging, his eyes wild. Mr. Helton came in between them, fists doubled up, then stopped short, glaring at the fat man, his big frame seemed to collapse, he trembled like a shied horse; and then the fat man drove at him, knife in one hand, handcuffs in the other. Mr. Thompson saw it coming, he saw the blade going into Mr. Helton's stomach, he knew he had the ax out of the log in his own hands, felt his arms go up over his head and bring the ax down on Mr. Hatch's head as if he were stunning a beef.

Mrs. Thompson had been listening uneasily for some time to the voices going on, one of them strange to her, but she was too tired at first to get up and come out to see what was going on. The confused shouting that rose so suddenly brought her up to her feet and out across the front porch without her slippers, hair half-braided. Shading her eyes, she saw first Mr. Helton, running all stooped over through the orchard, running like a man with dogs after him; and Mr. Thompson supporting himself on the ax handle was leaning over shaking by the shoulder a man Mrs. Thompson had never seen, who lay doubled up with the top of his head smashed and the blood running away in a greasy-looking puddle. Mr. Thompson without taking his hand from the man's shoulder, said in a thick voice, "He killed Mr. Helton, he killed him, I saw him do it. I had to knock him out," he called loudly, "but he won't come to."

Mrs. Thompson said in a faint scream, "Why, yonder goes Mr. Helton," and she pointed. Mr. Thompson pulled himself up and looked where she pointed. Mrs. Thompson sat down slowly against the side of the house and began to slide forward on her face; she felt as if she were drowning, she couldn't rise to the top somehow, and her only thought was she was glad the boys were not there, they were out, fishing at Halifax, oh, God, she was glad the boys were not there.

Mr. and Mrs. Thompson drove up to their barn about sunset. Mr. Thompson handed the reins to his wife, got out to open the big door, and Mrs. Thompson guided old Jim in under the roof. The buggy was gray with dust and age, Mrs. Thompson's face was gray with dust and weariness, and Mr. Thompson's face, as he stood at the horse's head and began unhitching, was gray except for the dark blue of his freshly shaven jaws and chin, gray and blue and caved in, but patient, like a dead man's face.

Mrs. Thompson stepped down to the hard packed manure of the barn floor, and shook out her light flower-sprigged dress. She wore her smoked glasses, and her wide shady leghorn hat with the wreath of exhausted pink and blue forget-me-nots hid her forehead, fixed in a knot of distress.

The horse hung his head, raised a huge sigh and flexed his stiffened legs. Mr. Thompson's words came up muffled and hollow. "Poor ole Jim," he said, clearing his throat, "he looks pretty sunk in the ribs. I guess he's had a hard week." He lifted the harness up in one piece, slid it off and Jim walked out of the shafts halting a little. "Well, this is the last time," Mr. Thompson said, still talking to Jim. "Now you can get a good rest."

Mrs. Thompson closed her eyes behind her smoked glasses. The last time, and high time, and they should never have gone at all. She did not need her glasses any more, now the good darkness was coming down again, but her eyes ran full of tears steadily, though she was not crying, and she felt better with the glasses, safer, hidden away behind them. She took out her handkerchief with her hands shaking as they had been shaking ever since *that day*, and blew her nose. She said, "I see the boys have lighted the lamps. I hope they've started the stove going."

She stepped along the rough path holding her thin dress and starched petticoats around her, feeling her way between the sharp small stones, leaving the barn because she could hardly bear to be near Mr. Thompson, advancing slowly towards the house because she dreaded going there. Life was all one dread, the faces of her neighbors, of her boys, of her husband, the face of the whole world, the shape of her own house in the darkness, the very smell of the grass and the trees were horrible to her. There was no place to go, only one thing to do, bear it somehow—but how? She asked herself that question often. How was she going to keep on living now? Why had she lived at all? She wished now she had died one of those times when she had been so sick, instead of living on for this.

The boys were in the kitchen; Herbert was looking at the funny pictures from last Sunday's newspapers, the Katzenjammer Kids and Happy Hooligan. His chin was in his hands and his elbows on the table, and he was really reading and looking at the pictures, but his face was unhappy. Arthur was building the fire, adding kindling a stick at a time, watching it catch and blaze. His face was heavier and darker than Herbert's, but he was a little sullen by nature; Mrs. Thompson thought, he takes things harder, too. Arthur said, "Hello, Momma," and went on with his work. Herbert swept the papers together and moved over on the bench. They were big boys—fifteen and seventeen, and Arthur as tall as his father. Mrs. Thompson sat down beside Herbert, taking off her hat. She said, "I guess you're hungry. We were late today. We went the Log Hollow road, it's rougher than ever." Her pale mouth drooped with a sad fold on either side.

"I guess you saw the Mannings, then," said Herbert.

"Yes, and the Fergusons, and the Allbrights, and that new family McClellan."

"Anybody say anything?" asked Herbert.

"Nothing much, you know how it's been all along, some of them keeps saying, yes, they know it was a clear case and a fair trial and they say how glad they are your papa came out so well, and all that, some of 'em do, anyhow, but it looks like they don't really take sides with him. I'm about wore out," she said, the tears rolling again from under her dark glasses. "I don't know what good it does, but your papa can't seem to rest unless he's telling how it happened. I don't know."

"I don't think it does any good, not a speck," said Arthur, moving away from the stove. "It just keeps the whole question stirred up in people's minds. Everybody will go round telling what he heard, and the whole thing is going to get worse mixed up than ever. It just makes matters worse. I wish you could get Papa to stop driving round the country talking like that."

"Your papa knows best," said Mrs. Thompson. "You oughtn't to criticize him. He's got enough to put up with without that."

Arthur said nothing, his jaw stubborn. Mr. Thompson came in, his eyes hollowed out and dead-looking, his thick hands gray white and seamed from washing them clean every day before he started out to see the neighbors to tell them his side of the story. He was wearing his Sunday clothes, a thick pepper-and-salt-colored suit with a black string tie.

Mrs. Thompson stood up, her head swimming. "Now you-all get out of the kitchen, it's too hot in here and I need room. I'll get us a little bite of supper, if you'll just get out and give me some room."

They went as if they were glad to go, the boys outside, Mr. Thompson into his bedroom. She heard him groaning to himself as he took off his shoes, and heard the bed creak as he lay down. Mrs. Thompson opened the icebox and felt the sweet coldness flow out of it; she had never expected to have an icebox, much less did she hope to afford to keep it filled with ice. It still seemed like a miracle, after two or three years. There was the food, cold and clean, all ready to be warmed over. She would never have had that icebox if Mr. Helton hadn't happened along one day, just by the strangest luck; so saving, and so managing, so good, thought Mrs. Thompson, her heart swelling until she feared she would faint again, standing there with the door open and leaning her head upon it. She simply could not bear to remember Mr. Helton, with his long sad face and silent ways, who had always been so quiet and harmless, who had worked so hard and helped Mr. Thompson so much, running through the hot fields and woods, being hunted like a mad dog, everybody turning out with ropes and guns and sticks to catch and tie him. Oh, God, said Mrs. Thompson in a long dry moan, kneeling before the icebox and fumbling inside for the dishes, even if they did pile mattresses all over the jail floor and against the walls, and five men there to hold him to keep him from hurting himself any more, he was already hurt too badly, he couldn't have lived anyway. Mr. Barbee, the sheriff, told her about it. He said, well, they didn't aim to harm him but they had to catch him, he was crazy as a loon; he picked up rocks and tried to brain every man that got near him. He had two harmonicas in his jumper pocket, said the sheriff, but they fell out in the scuffle, and Mr. Helton tried to pick 'em up again, and that's when they finally got him. "They *had* to be rough, Miz Thompson, he fought like a wildcat." Yes, thought Mrs. Thompson again with the same bitterness, of course, they had to be rough. They always have to be rough. Mr. Thompson can't argue with a man and get him off the place peaceably; no, she thought, standing up and shutting the icebox, he has to kill somebody, he has to be a murderer and ruin his boys' lives and cause Mr. Helton to be killed like a mad dog.

Her thoughts stopped with a little soundless explosion, cleared and began again. The rest of Mr. Helton's harmonicas were still in the shack, his tune ran in Mrs. Thompson's head at certain times of the day. She missed it in the evenings. It seemed so strange she had never known the name of that song, nor what it meant, until after Mr. Helton was gone. Mrs. Thompson, trembling in the knees, took a drink of water at the sink and poured the red beans into the baking dish, and began to roll the pieces of chicken in flour to fry them. There was a time, she said to herself, when I thought I had neighbors and friends, there was a time when we could hold up our heads, there was a time when my husband hadn't killed a man and I could tell the truth to anybody about anything.

Mr. Thompson, turning on his bed, figured that he had done all he could, he'd just try to let the matter rest from now on. His lawyer, Mr. Burleigh, had told him right at the beginning, "Now you keep calm and collected. You've got a fine case, even if you haven't got witnesses. Your wife must sit in court, she'll be a powerful argument with the jury. You just plead not guilty and I'll do the rest. The trial is going to be a mere formality, you haven't got a thing to worry about. You'll be clean out of this before you know it." And to make talk Mr. Burleigh had got to telling about all the men he knew around the country who for one reason or another had been forced to kill somebody, always in self-defense, and there just wasn't anything to it at all. He even told about how his own father in the old days had shot and killed a man just for setting foot inside his gate when he told him not to. "Sure, I shot the scoundrel," said Mr. Burleigh's father, "in self-defense; I *told* him I'd shoot him if he set his foot in my yard, and he did, and I did." There had been bad blood between them for years, Mr. Burleigh said, and his father had waited a long time to catch the other fellow in the wrong, and when he did he certainly made the most of his opportunity.

"But Mr. Hatch, as I told you," Mr. Thompson had said, "made a pass at Mr. Helton with his bowie knife. That's why I took a hand."

"All the better," said Mr. Burleigh. "That stranger hadn't any right coming to your house on such an errand. Why, hell," said Mr. Burleigh, "that wasn't even manslaughter you committed. So now you just hold your horses and keep your shirt on. And don't say one word without I tell you."

Wasn't even manslaughter. Mr. Thompson had to cover Mr.

Hatch with a piece of wagon canvas and ride to town to tell the
sheriff. It had been hard on Ellie. When they got back, the
sheriff and the coroner and two deputies, they found her sitting
beside the road, on a low bridge over a gulley, about half a mile
from the place. He had taken her up behind his saddle and got her
back to the house. He had already told the sheriff that his wife
had witnessed the whole business, and now he had time, getting
her to her room and in bed, to tell her what to say if they asked
anything. He had left out the part about Mr. Helton being crazy
all along, but it came out at the trial. By Mr. Burleigh's advice
Mr. Thompson had pretended to be perfectly ignorant; Mr. Hatch
hadn't said a word about that. Mr. Thompson pretended to believe that Mr. Hatch had just come looking for Mr. Helton to
settle old scores, and the two members of Mr. Hatch's family who
had come down to try to get Mr. Thompson convicted didn't
get anywhere at all. It hadn't been much of a trial, Mr. Burleigh
saw to that. He had charged a reasonable fee, and Mr. Thompson had paid him and felt grateful, but after it was over Mr.
Burleigh didn't seem pleased to see him when he got to dropping
into the office to talk it over, telling him things that had slipped
his mind at first: trying to explain what an ornery low hound
Mr. Hatch had been, anyhow. Mr. Burleigh seemed to have lost
his interest; he looked sour and upset when he saw Mr. Thompson at the door. Mr. Thompson kept saying to himself that he'd
got off, all right, just as Mr. Burleigh had predicted, but, but
—and it was right there that Mr. Thompson's mind stuck, squirm-
ing like an angleworm on a fishhook: he had killed Mr. Hatch,
and he was a murderer. That was the truth about himself that
Mr. Thompson couldn't grasp, even when he said the word to
himself. Why, he had not even once *thought* of killing anybody,
much less Mr. Hatch, and if Mr. Helton hadn't come out so unexpectedly, hearing the row, why, then—but then, Mr. Helton
had come on the run that way to help him. What he couldn't
understand was what happened next. He had seen Mr. Hatch go
after Mr. Helton with the knife, he had seen the point, blade

up, go into Mr. Helton's stomach and slice up like you slice a hog, but when they finally caught Mr. Helton there wasn't a knife scratch on him. Mr. Thompson knew he had the ax in his own hands and felt himself lifting it, but he couldn't remember hitting Mr. Hatch. He couldn't remember it. He couldn't. He remembered only that he had been determined to stop Mr. Hatch from cutting Mr. Helton. If he was given a chance he could explain the whole matter. At the trial they hadn't let him talk. They just asked questions and he answered yes or no, and they never did get to the core of the matter. Since the trial, now, every day for a week he had washed and shaved and put on his best clothes and had taken Ellie with him to tell every neighbor he had that he never killed Mr. Hatch on purpose, and what good did it do? Nobody believed him. Even when he turned to Ellie and said, "You was there, you saw it, didn't you?" and Ellie spoke up, saying, "Yes, that's the truth. Mr. Thompson was trying to save Mr. Helton's life," and he added, "If you don't believe me, you can believe my wife. She won't lie," Mr. Thompson saw something in all their faces that disheartened him, made him feel empty and tired out. They didn't believe he was not a murderer.

Even Ellie never said anything to comfort him. He hoped she would say finally, "I remember now, Mr. Thompson, I really did come round the corner in time to see everything. It's not a lie, Mr. Thompson. Don't you worry." But as they drove together in silence, with the days still hot and dry, shortening for fall, day after day, the buggy jolting in the ruts, she said nothing; they grew to dread the sight of another house, and the people in it: all houses looked alike now, and the people—old neighbors or new—had the same expression when Mr. Thompson told them why he had come and began his story. Their eyes looked as if someone had pinched the eyeball at the back; they shriveled and the light went out of them. Some of them sat with fixed tight smiles trying to be friendly. "Yes, Mr. Thompson, we know how you must feel. It must be terrible for you, Mrs. Thompson. Yes, you know, I've about come to the point where I believe in such a thing as killing in self-defense. Why, certainly, we believe you, Mr. Thompson, why shouldn't we believe you? Didn't you have a perfectly fair and above-board trial? Well, now, natchally, Mr. Thompson, we think you done right."

Mr. Thompson was satisfied they didn't think so. Sometimes the air around him was so thick with their blame he fought and pushed with his fists, and the sweat broke out all over him, he shouted his story in a dust-choked voice, he would fairly bellow at last: "My wife, here, you know her, she was there, she saw and heard it all, if you don't believe me, ask her, she won't lie!" and Mrs. Thompson, with her hands knotted together, aching, her chin trembling, would never fail to say: "Yes, that's right, that's the truth—"

The last straw had been laid on today, Mr. Thompson decided. Tom Allbright, an old beau of Ellie's, why, he had squired Ellie around a whole summer, had come out to meet them when they drove up, and standing there bareheaded had stopped them from getting out. He had looked past them with an embarrassed frown on his face, telling them his wife's sister was there with a raft of young ones, and the house was pretty full and everything upset, or he'd ask them to come in. "We've been thinking of trying to get up to your place one of these days," said Mr. Allbright, moving away trying to look busy, "we've been mighty occupied up here of late." So they had to say, "Well, we just happened to be driving this way," and go on. "The Allbrights," said Mrs. Thompson, "always was fair-weather friends." "They look out for number one, that's a fact," said Mr. Thompson. But it was cold comfort to them both.

Finally Mrs. Thompson had given up. "Let's go home," she said. "Old Jim's tired and thirsty, and we've gone far enough."

Mr. Thompson said, "Well, while we're out this way, we might as well stop at the McClellans'." They drove in, and asked a little cotton-haired boy if his mamma and papa were at home. Mr. Thompson wanted to see them. The little boy stood gazing with his mouth open, then galloped into the house shouting, "Mommer, Popper, come out hyah. That man that kilt Mr. Hatch has come ter see yer!"

The man came out in his sock feet, with one gallus up, the other broken and dangling, and said, "Light down, Mr. Thompson, and come in. The ole woman's washing, but she'll git here." Mrs. Thompson, feeling her way, stepped down and sat in a broken rocking-chair on the porch that sagged under her feet. The woman of the house, barefooted, in a calico wrapper, sat on the edge of the porch, her fat sallow face full of curiosity. Mr. Thompson began, "Well, as I reckon you happen to know, I've had some strange troubles lately, and, as the feller says, it's not the kind of trouble that happens to a man every day in the year, and there's some things I don't want no misunderstanding about in the neighbors' minds, so—" He halted and stumbled forward, and the two listening faces took on a mean look, a greedy, despising look, a look that said plain as day, "My, you must be a purty sorry feller to come round worrying about what *we* think, *we* know you wouldn't be here if you had anybody else to turn to—my, I wouldn't lower myself that much, myself." Mr. Thompson was ashamed of himself, he was suddenly in a rage, he'd like to knock their dirty skunk heads together, the low-down white trash—but he held himself down and went on to the end. "My wife will tell you," he said, and this was the hardest place, because Ellie always without moving a muscle seemed to stiffen as if somebody had threatened to hit her; "ask my wife, she won't lie."

"It's true, I saw it—"

"Well, now," said the man, drily, scratching his ribs inside his shirt, "that sholy is too bad. Well, now, I kaint see what we've got to do with all this here, however. I kaint see no good reason for us to git mixed up in these murder matters, I shore kaint. Whichever way you look at it, it ain't none of my business. However, it's mighty nice of you-all to come around and give us the straight of it, fur we've heerd some mighty queer yarns about it, mighty queer, I golly you couldn't hardly make head ner tail of it."

"Evvybody goin' round shootin' they heads off," said the woman. "Now we don't hold with killin'; the Bible says—"

"Shet yer trap," said the man, "and keep it shet 'r I'll shet it fer yer. Now it shore looks like to me—"

"We mustn't linger," said Mrs. Thompson, unclasping her hands. "We've lingered too long now. It's getting late, and we've far to go." Mr. Thompson took the hint and followed her. The man and the woman lolled against their rickety porch poles and watched them go.

Now lying on his bed, Mr. Thompson knew the end had come. Now, this minute, lying in the bed where he had slept with Ellie for eighteen years; under this roof where he had laid the shingles when he was waiting to get married; there as he was with his whiskers already sprouting since his shave that morning; with his fingers feeling his bony chin, Mr. Thompson felt he was a dead man. He was dead to his other life, he had got to the end of something without knowing why, and he had to make a fresh start, he did not know how. Something different was going to begin, he didn't know what. It was in some way not his business. He didn't feel he was going to have much to do with it. He got up, aching, hollow, and went out to the kitchen where Mrs. Thompson was just taking up the supper.

"Call the boys," said Mrs. Thompson. They had been down to the barn, and Arthur put out the lantern before hanging it on a nail near the door. Mr. Thompson didn't like their silence. They had hardly said a word about anything to him since that day. They seemed to avoid him, they ran the place together as if he wasn't there, and attended to everything without asking him for any advice. "What you boys been up to?" he asked, trying to be hearty. "Finishing your chores?"

"No, sir," said Arthur, "there ain't much to do. Just greasing some axles." Herbert said nothing. Mrs. Thompson bowed her head: "For these and all Thy blessings. . . . Amen," she whis-

pered weakly, and the Thompsons sat there with their eyes down
and their faces sorrowful, as if they were at a funeral.

Every time he shut his eyes, trying to sleep, Mr. Thompson's
mind started up and began to run like a rabbit. It jumped from
one thing to another, trying to pick up a trail here or there that
would straighten out what had happened that day he killed Mr.
Hatch. Try as he might, Mr. Thompson's mind would not go
anywhere that it had not already been, he could not see anything
but what he had seen once, and he knew that was not right.
If he had not seen straight that first time, then everything about
his killing Mr. Hatch was wrong from start to finish, and there
was nothing more to be done about it, he might just as well give
up. It still seemed to him that he had done, maybe not the right
thing, but the only thing he could do, that day, but had he? *Did
he have to kill Mr. Hatch?* He had never seen a man he hated more,
the minute he laid eyes on him. He knew in his bones the fellow
was there for trouble. What seemed so funny now was this: Why
hadn't he just told Mr. Hatch to get out before he ever even got in?
  Mrs. Thompson, her arms crossed on her breast, was lying beside him, perfectly still, but she seemed awake, somehow. "Asleep,
Ellie?"
  After all, he might have got rid of him peaceably, or maybe he
might have had to overpower him and put those handcuffs on him
and turn him over to the sheriff for disturbing the peace. The
most they could have done was to lock Mr. Hatch up while he
cooled off for a few days, or fine him a little something. He would
try to think of things he might have said to Mr. Hatch. Why,
let's see, I could just have said, Now look here, Mr. Hatch, I want
to talk to you as man to man. But his brain would go empty. What
could he have said or done? But if he *could* have done anything
else almost except kill Mr. Hatch, then nothing would have happened to Mr. Helton. Mr. Thompson hardly ever thought of Mr.
Helton. His mind just skipped over him and went on. If he stopped
to think about Mr. Helton he'd never in God's world get any-

where. He tried to imagine how it might all have been, this very night even, if Mr. Helton were still safe and sound out in his shack playing his tune about feeling so good in the morning, drinking up all the wine so you'd feel even better; and Mr. Hatch safe in jail somewhere, mad as hops, maybe, but out of harm's way and ready to listen to reason and to repent of his meanness, the dirty, yellow-livered hound coming around persecuting an innocent man and ruining a whole family that never harmed him! Mr. Thompson felt the veins of his forehead start up, his fists clutched as if they seized an ax handle, the sweat broke out on him, he bounded up from the bed with a yell smothered in his throat, and Ellie started up after him, crying out, "Oh, oh, don't! Don't! Don't!" as if she were having a nightmare. He stood shaking until his bones rattled in him, crying hoarsely, "Light the lamp, light the lamp, Ellie."

Instead, Mrs. Thompson gave a shrill weak scream, almost the same scream he had heard on that day she came around the house when he was standing there with the ax in his hand. He could not see her in the dark, but she was on the bed, rolling violently. He felt for her in horror, and his groping hands found her arms, up, and her own hands pulling her hair straight out from her head, her neck strained back, and the tight screams strangling her. He shouted out for Arthur, for Herbert. "Your mother!" he bawled, his voice cracking. As he held Mrs. Thompson's arms, the boys came tumbling in, Arthur with the lamp above his head. By this light Mr. Thompson saw Mrs. Thompson's eyes, wide open, staring dreadfully at him, the tears pouring. She sat up at sight of the boys, and held out one arm towards them, the hand wagging in a crazy circle, then dropped on her back again, and suddenly went limp. Arthur set the lamp on the table and turned on Mr. Thompson. "She's scared," he said, "she's scared to death." His face was in a knot of rage, his fists were doubled up, he faced his father as if he meant to strike him. Mr. Thompson's jaw fell, he was so surprised he stepped back from the bed. Herbert went to the other side. They stood on each side of Mrs. Thompson and watched Mr. Thompson as if he were a dangerous wild beast. "What did you do to her?" shouted Arthur, in a grown man's voice. "You touch her again and I'll blow your heart out!" Herbert was pale and his cheek twitched, but he was on Arthur's side; he would do what he could to help Arthur.

Mr. Thompson had no fight left in him. His knees bent as he stood, his chest collapsed. "Why, Arthur," he said, his words crumbling and his breath coming short. "She's fainted again. Get the ammonia." Arthur did not move. Herbert brought the bottle, and handed it, shrinking, to his father.

Mr. Thompson held it under Mrs. Thompson's nose. He poured a little in the palm of his hand and rubbed it on her forehead. She gasped and opened her eyes and turned her head away from him. Herbert began a doleful hopeless sniffling. "Mamma," he kept saying, "Mamma, don't die."

"I'm all right," Mrs. Thompson said. "Now don't you worry around. Now Herbert, you mustn't do that. I'm all right." She closed her eyes. Mr. Thompson began pulling on his best pants; he put on his socks and shoes. The boys sat on each side of the bed, watching Mrs. Thompson's face. Mr. Thompson put on his shirt and coat. He said, "I reckon I'll ride over and get the doctor. Don't look like all this fainting is a good sign. Now you just keep watch until I get back." They listened, but said nothing. He said, "Don't you get any notions in your head. I never did your mother any harm in my life, on purpose." He went out, and, looking back, saw Herbert staring at him from under his brows, like a stranger. "You'll know how to look after her," said Mr. Thompson.

Mr. Thompson went through the kitchen. There he lighted the lantern, took a thin pad of scratch paper and a stub pencil from the shelf where the boys kept their schoolbooks. He swung the lantern on his arm and reached into the cupboard where he kept the guns. The shotgun was there to his hand, primed and ready, a man never knows when he may need a shotgun. He went out of the house without looking around, or looking back when he had left it, passed his barn without seeing it, and struck out to the farthest end of his fields, which ran for half a mile to the east. So many blows had been struck at Mr. Thompson and from so many directions he couldn't stop any more to find out where he was hit. He walked on, over plowed ground and over meadow, going through barbed wire fences cautiously, putting his gun through first; he could almost see in the dark, now his eyes were used to it. Finally he came to the last fence; here he sat down, back against a post, lantern at his side, and, with the pad on his knee, moistened the stub pencil and began to write:

"Before Almighty God, the great judge of all before who I am about to appear, I do hereby solemnly swear that I did not take the life of Mr. Homer T. Hatch on purpose. It was done in defense of Mr. Helton. I did not aim to hit him with the ax but only to keep him off Mr. Helton. He aimed a blow at Mr. Helton who was not looking for it. It was my belief at the time that Mr. Hatch would of taken the life of Mr. Helton if I did not interfere. I have told all this to the judge and the jury and they let me off but nobody believes it. This is the only way I can prove I am not a cold blooded murderer like everybody seems to think. If I had been in Mr. Helton's place he would of done the same for me. I still think I done the only thing there was to do. My wife—"

Mr. Thompson stopped here to think a while. He wet the pencil point with the tip of his tongue and marked out the last two words. He sat a while blacking out the words until he had made a neat oblong patch where they had been, and started again:

"It was Mr. Homer T. Hatch who came to do wrong to a harmless man. He caused all this trouble and he deserved to die but I am sorry it was me who had to kill him."

He licked the point of his pencil again, and signed his full name carefully, folded the paper and put it in his outside pocket. Taking off his right shoe and sock, he set the butt of the shotgun along the ground with the twin barrels pointed towards his head. It was very awkward. He thought about this a little, leaning his head against the gun mouth. He was trembling and his head was drumming until he was deaf and blind, but he lay down flat on the earth on his side, drew the barrel under his chin and fumbled for the trigger with his great toe. That way he could work it.

In the Zoo

JEAN STAFFORD (1915–   )

KEENING HARSHLY in his senility, the blind polar bear slowly and ceaselessly shakes his head in the stark heat of the July and mountain noon. His open eyes are blue. No one stops to look at him; an old farmer, in passing, sums up the old bear's situation by observing, with a ruthless chuckle, that he is a "back number." Patient and despairing, he sits on his yellowed haunches on the central rock of his pool, his huge toy paws wearing short boots of mud.

The grizzlies to the right of him, a conventional family of father and mother and two spring cubs, alternately play the clown and sleep. There is a blustery, scoundrelly, half-likable bravado in the manner of the black bear on the polar's left; his name, according to the legend on his cage, is Clancy, and he is a rough-and-tumble, brawling blowhard, thundering continually as he paces back and forth, or pauses to face his audience of children and mothers and release from his great, gray-tongued mouth a perfectly Vesuvian roar. If he were to be reincarnated in human form, he would be a man of action, possibly a football coach, probably a politician. One expects to see his black hat hanging from a branch of one of his trees; at any moment he will light a cigar.

Reprinted from *Stories* by Jean Stafford, by permission of Farrar, Straus & Cudahy, Inc. Copyright © 1956 by Farrar, Straus & Cudahy, Inc.

The polar bear's next-door neighbors are not the only ones who offer so sharp and sad a contrast to him. Across a reach of scrappy grass and litter is the convocation of conceited monkeys, burrowing into each other's necks and chests for fleas, picking their noses with their long, black, finicky fingers, swinging by their gifted tails on the flying trapeze, screaming bloody murder. Even when they mourn—one would think the male orangutan was on the very brink of suicide—they are comedians; they only fake depression, for they are firmly secure in their rambunctious tribalism and in their appalling insight and contempt. Their flibbertigibbet gambolling is a sham, and, stealthily and shiftily, they are really watching the pitiful polar bear ("Back number," they quote the farmer. "That's *his* number all right," they snigger), and the windy black bear ("Life of the party. Gasbag. Low I.Q.," they note scornfully on his dossier), and the stupid, bourgeois grizzlies ("It's feed the face and hit the sack for them," the monkeys say). And they are watching my sister and me, two middle-aged women, as we sit on a bench between the exhibits, eating popcorn, growing thirsty. We are thoughtful.

A chance remark of Daisy's a few minutes before has turned us to memory and meditation. "I don't know why," she said, "but that poor blind bear reminds me of Mr. Murphy." The name "Mr. Murphy" at once returned us both to childhood, and we were floated far and fast, our later lives diminished. So now we eat our popcorn in silence with the ritualistic appetite of childhood, which has little to do with hunger; it is not so much food as a sacrament, and in tribute to our sisterliness and our friendliness I break the silence to say that this is the best popcorn I have ever eaten in my life. The extravagance of my statement instantly makes me feel self-indulgent, and for some time I uneasily avoid looking at the blind bear. My sister does not agree or disagree; she simply says that popcorn is the only food she has ever really liked. For a long time, then, we eat without a word, but I know, because I know her well and know her similarity to me, that Daisy is thinking what I am thinking; both of us are mournfully remembering Mr. Murphy, who, at one time in our lives, was our only friend.

This zoo is in Denver, a city that means nothing to my sister and me except as a place to take or meet trains. Daisy lives two hundred miles farther west, and it is her custom, when my every-other-year visit with her is over, to come across the mountains to see me off on my eastbound train. We know almost no one here, and because our stays are short, we have never bothered to learn the town in more than the most desultory way. We know the Burlington uptown office and the respectable hotels, a restaurant or two, the Union Station, and, beginning today, the zoo in the city park.

But since the moment that Daisy named Mr. Murphy by name our situation in Denver has been only corporeal; our minds and our hearts are in Adams, fifty miles north, and we are seeing, under the white sun at its pitiless meridian, the streets of that ugly town, its parks and trees and bridges, the bandstand in its dreary park, the roads that lead away from it, west to the mountains and east to the plains, its mongrel and multitudinous churches, its high school shaped like a loaf of bread, the campus of its college, an oasis of which we had no experience except to walk through it now and then, eying the woodbine on the impressive buildings. These things are engraved forever on our minds with a legibility so insistent that you have only to say the name of the town aloud to us to rip the rinds from our nerves and leave us exposed in terror and humiliation.

We have supposed in later years that Adams was not so bad as all that, and we know that we magnified its ugliness because we looked upon it as the extension of the possessive, unloving, scornful, complacent foster mother, Mrs. Placer, to whom, at the death of our parents within a month of each other, we were sent like Dickensian grotesqueries—cowardly, weak-stomached, given to tears, backward in school. Daisy was ten and I was eight when, unaccompanied, we made the long trip from Marblehead to our benefactress, whom we had never seen and, indeed, never heard of until the pastor of our church came to tell us of the arrangement our father had made on his deathbed, seconded by our mother on hers. This man, whose name and face I have forgotten and whose parting speeches to us I have not forgiven, tried to dry our tears with talk of Indians and of buffaloes; he spoke, however, at much greater length, and in preaching cadences, of the Christian goodness of Mrs. Placer. She was, he said, childless and fond of children, and for many years she had been a widow, after the lingering demise of her tubercular husband, for whose sake she had moved to the Rocky Mountains. For his support and costly medical care, she had run a boarding house, and after his death, since he had left her nothing, she was obliged to continue running it. She had been a girlhood friend of our paternal grandmother, and our father, in the absence of responsible relatives, had made her the beneficiary of his life insurance on the condition that she lodge and rear us. The pastor, with a frankness remarkable considering that he was talking to children, explained to us that our father had left little more than a drop in the bucket for our care, and he enjoined us to give Mrs. Placer, in return for her hospitality and sacrifice, courteous help and eternal thanks. "Sacrifice" was a word we were never allowed to forget.

And thus it was, in grief for our parents, that we came cringing to the dry Western town and to the house where Mrs. Placer lived, a house in which the square, uncushioned furniture was cruel and the pictures on the walls were either dour or dire and the lodgers, who lived in the upper floors among shadowy wardrobes and chiffoniers, had come through the years to resemble their landlady in appearance as well as in deportment.

After their ugly-colored evening meal, Gran—as she bade us call her—and her paying guests would sit, rangy and aquiline, rocking on the front porch on spring and summer and autumn nights, tasting their delicious grievances: those slights delivered by ungrateful sons and daughters, those impudences committed by trolley-car conductors and uppity salegirls in the ready-to-wear, all those slurs and calculated elbow-jostlings that were their daily crucifixion and their staff of life. We little girls, washing the dishes in the cavernous kitchen, listened to their even, martyred voices, fixed like leeches to their solitary subject and their solitary creed—that life was essentially a matter of being done in, let down, and swindled.

At regular intervals, Mrs. Placer, chairwoman of the victims, would say, "Of course, I don't care; I just have to laugh," and then would tell a shocking tale of an intricate piece of skulduggery perpetrated against her by someone she did not even know. Sometimes, with her avid, partial jury sitting there on the porch behind the bitter hopvines in the heady mountain air, the cases she tried involved Daisy and me, and, listening, we travailed, hugging each other, whispering, "I wish she wouldn't! Oh, how did she find out?" How *did* she? Certainly we never told her when we were snubbed or chosen last on teams, never admitted to a teacher's scolding or to the hoots of laughter that greeted us when we bit on silly, unfair jokes. But she knew. She knew about the slumber parties we were not invited to, the beefsteak fries at which we were pointedly left out; she knew that the singing teacher had said in so many words that I could not carry a tune in a basket and that the sewing superintendent had said that Daisy's fingers were all thumbs. With our teeth chattering in the cold of our isolation, we would hear her protestant, litigious voice defending our right to be orphans, paupers, wholly dependent on her—except for the really ridiculous pittance from our father's life insurance—when it was all she could do to make ends meet. She did not care, but she had to laugh that people in general were so small-minded that they looked down on fatherless, motherless waifs like us and, by association, looked down on her. It seemed funny to her that people gave her no credit for taking on these sickly youngsters who were not even kin but only the grandchildren of a friend.

If a child with braces on her teeth came to play with us, she was, according to Gran, slyly lording it over us because our teeth were crooked, but there was no money to have them straightened. And what could be the meaning of our being asked to come for supper at the doctor's house? Were the doctor and his la-di-da New York wife and those pert girls with their solid-gold barrettes and their Shetland pony going to shame her poor darlings? Or shame their poor Gran by making them sorry to come home to the plain but honest life that was all she could provide for them?

There was no stratum of society not reeking with the effluvium of fraud and pettifoggery. And the school system was almost the worst of all: if we could not understand fractions, was that not our teacher's fault? And therefore what right had she to give us F? It was as plain as a pikestaff to Gran that the teacher was only covering up her own inability to teach. It was unlikely, too—highly unlikely—that it was by accident that time and time again the free medical clinic was closed for the day just as our names were about to be called out, so that nothing was done about our bad tonsils, which meant that we were repeatedly sick in the winter, with Gran fetching and carrying for us, climbing those stairs a jillion times a day with her game leg and her heart that was none too strong.

Steeped in these mists of accusation and hidden plots and double meanings, Daisy and I grew up like worms. I think no one could have withstood the atmosphere in that house where everyone trod on eggs that a little bird had told them were bad. They spied on one another, whispered behind doors, conjectured, drew parallels beginning "With all due respect . . ." or "It is a matter of indifference to *me* but . . ." The vigilantes patrolled our town by day, and by night returned to lay their goodies at their priestess's feet and wait for her oracular interpretation of the innards of the butcher, the baker, the candlestick maker, the soda jerk's girl, and the barber's unnatural deaf white cat.

Consequently, Daisy and I also became suspicious. But it was suspicion of ourselves that made us mope and weep and grimace with self-judgment. Why were we not happy when Gran had sacrificed herself to the bone for us? Why did we not cut dead the paper boy who had called her a filthy name? Why did we persist in our willful friendliness with the grocer who had tried, unsuccessfully, to overcharge her on a case of pork and beans?

Our friendships were nervous and surreptitious; we sneaked and lied, and as our hungers sharpened, our debasement deepened; we were pitied; we were shifty-eyed, always on the lookout for Mrs. Placer or one of her tattletale lodgers; we were hypocrites.

Nevertheless, one thin filament of instinct survived, and Daisy and I in time found asylum in a small menagerie down by the railroad tracks. It belonged to a gentle alcoholic ne'er-do-well, who did nothing all day long but drink bathtub gin in rickeys and play solitaire and smile to himself and talk to his animals. He had a little, stunted red vixen and a deodorized skunk, a parrot from Tahiti that spoke Parisian French, a woebegone coyote, and two capuchin monkeys, so serious and humanized, so small and sad and sweet, and so religious-looking with their tonsured heads that it was impossible not to think their gibberish was really an ordered language with a grammar that someday some philologist would understand.

Gran knew about our visits to Mr. Murphy and she did not object, for it gave her keen pleasure to excoriate him when we came home. His vice was not a matter of guesswork; it was an established fact that he was half-seas over from dawn till midnight. "With the black Irish," said Gran, "the taste for drink is taken in with the mother's milk and is never mastered. Oh, I know all about those promises to join the temperance movement and not to touch another drop. The way to Hell is paved with good intentions."

We were still little girls when we discovered Mr. Murphy,

before the shattering disease of adolescence was to make our
bones and brains ache even more painfully than before, and we
loved him and we hoped to marry him when we grew up. We
loved him, and we loved his monkeys to exactly the same degree
and in exactly the same way; they were husbands and fathers
and brothers, these three little, ugly, dark, secret men who
minded their own business and let us mind ours. If we stuck
our fingers through the bars of the cage, the monkeys would
sometimes take them in their tight, tiny hands and look into our
faces with a tentative, somehow absent-minded sorrow, as if
they terribly regretted that they could not place us but were
glad to see us all the same. Mr. Murphy, playing a solitaire game
of cards called "once in a blue moon" on a kitchen table in his
back yard beside the pens, would occasionally look up and blink
his beautiful blue eyes and say, "You're peaches to make over
my wee friends. I love you for it." There was nothing demand-
ing in his voice, and nothing sticky; on his lips the word "love"
was jocose and forthright, it had no strings attached. We would
sit on either side of him and watch him regiment his ranks of
cards and stop to drink as deeply as if he were dying of thirst
and wave to his animals and say to them, "Yes, lads, you're
dandies."

Because Mr. Murphy was as reserved with us as the capuchins
were, as courteously noncommittal, we were surprised one spring
day when he told us that he had a present for us, which he hoped
Mrs. Placer would let us keep; it was a puppy, for whom the
owner had asked him to find a home—half collie and half
Labrador retriever, blue-blooded on both sides.

"You might tell Mrs. Placer—" he said, smiling at the name,
for Gran was famous in the town. "You might tell Mrs. Placer,"
said Mr. Murphy, "that this lad will make a fine watchdog.
She'll never have to fear for her spoons again. Or her honor."
The last he said to himself, not laughing but tucking his chin
into his collar; lines sprang to the corners of his eyes. He would
not let us see the dog, whom we could hear yipping and squealing

inside his shanty, for he said that our disappointment would weigh on his conscience if we lost our hearts to the fellow and then could not have him for our own.

That evening at supper, we told Gran about Mr. Murphy's present. A dog? In the first place, why a dog? Was it possible that the news had reached Mr. Murphy's ears that Gran had just this very day finished planting her spring garden, the very thing that a rampageous dog would have in his mind to destroy? What sex was it? A male! Females, she had heard, were more trustworthy; males roved and came home smelling of skunk; such a consideration as this, of course, would not have crossed Mr. Murphy's fuddled mind. Was this young male dog house-broken? We had not asked? That was the limit!

Gran appealed to her followers, too raptly fascinated by Mr. Murphy's machinations to eat their Harvard beets. "Am I being farfetched or does it strike you as decidedly queer that Mr. Murphy is trying to fob off on my little girls a young cur that has not been trained?" she asked them. "If it were housebroken, he would have said so, so I feel it is safe to assume that it is not. Perhaps cannot *be* housebroken. I've heard of such cases."

The fantasy spun on, richly and rapidly, with all the skilled helping hands at work at once. The dog was tangibly in the room with us, shedding his hair, biting his fleas, shaking rain off himself to splatter the walls, dragging some dreadful carcass across the floor, chewing up slippers, knocking over chairs with his tail, gobbling the chops from the platter, barking, biting, fathering, fighting, smelling to high heaven of carrion, staining the rug with his muddy feet, scratching the floor with his claws. He developed rabies; he bit a child, two children! Three! Every-one in town! And Gran and her poor darlings went to jail for harboring this murderous, odoriferous, drunk, Roman Catholic dog.

And yet, astoundingly enough, she came around to agreeing to let us have the dog. It was, as Mr. Murphy had predicted, the word "watchdog" that deflected the course of the trial. The

moment Daisy uttered it, Gran halted, marshalling her reverse
march; while she rallied and tacked and reconnoitred, she sent
us to the kitchen for the dessert. And by the time this course
was under way, the uses of a dog, the enormous potentialities
for investigation and law enforcement in a dog trained by Mrs.
Placer, were being minutely and passionately scrutinized by
the eight upright bloodhounds sitting at the table wolfing their
brown Betty as if it were fresh-killed rabbit. The dog now sat
at attention beside his mistress, fiercely alert, ears cocked, nose
aquiver, the protector of widows, of orphans, of lonely people
who had no homes. He made short shrift of burglars, homicidal
maniacs, Peeping Toms, gypsies, bogus missionaries, Fuller
Brush men with a risqué spiel. He went to the store and brought
back groceries, retrieved the evening paper from the awkward
place the boy had meanly thrown it, rescued cripples from burning houses, saved children from drowning, heeled at command,
begged, lay down, stood up, sat, jumped through a hoop, ratted.

Both times—when he was a ruffian of the blackest delinquency
and then a pillar of society—he was full-grown in his prefigura-
tion, and when Laddy appeared on the following day, small,
unsteady, and whimpering lonesomely, Gran and her lodgers
were taken aback; his infant, clumsy paws embarrassed them,
his melting eyes were unapropos. But it could never be said of
Mrs. Placer, as Mrs. Placer her own self said, that she was a
woman who went back on her word, and her darlings were
going to have their dog, softheaded and feckless as he might
be. All the first night, in his carton in the kitchen, he wailed
for his mother, and in the morning, it was true, he had made a
shambles of the room—fouled the floor, and pulled off the tablecloth together with a ketchup bottle, so that thick gore lay
everywhere. At breakfast, the lodgers confessed they had had a
most amusing night, for it had actually been funny the way the
dog had been determined not to let anyone get a wink of sleep.
After that first night, Laddy slept in our room, receiving from
us, all through our delighted, sleepless nights, pats and embraces

and kisses and whispers. He was our baby, our best friend, the smartest, prettiest, nicest dog in the entire wide world. Our soft and rapid blandishments excited him to yelp at us in pleased bewilderment, and then we would playfully grasp his muzzle, so that he would snarl, deep in his throat like an adult dog, and shake his head violently, and, when we freed him, nip us smartly with great good will.

He was an intelligent and genial dog and we trained him quickly. He steered clear of Gran's radishes and lettuce after she had several times given him a brisk comeuppance with a strap across the rump, and he soon left off chewing shoes and the laundry on the line, and he outgrew his babyish whining. He grew like a weed; he lost his spherical softness, and his coat, which had been sooty fluff, came in stiff and rusty black; his nose grew aristocratically long, and his clever, pointed ears stood at attention. He was all bronzy, lustrous black except for an Elizabethan ruff of white and a tip of white at the end of his perky tail. No one could deny that he was exceptionally handsome and that he had as well, great personal charm and style. He escorted Daisy and me to school in the morning, laughing interiorly out of the enormous pleasure of his life as he gracefully cantered ahead of us, distracted occasionally by his private interest in smells or unfamiliar beings in the grass but, on the whole, engrossed in his role of chaperon. He made friends easily with other dogs, and sometimes he went for a long hunting weekend into the mountains with a huge and bossy old red hound named Mess, who had been on the country most of his life and had made a good thing of it, particularly at the fire station.

It was after one of these three-day excursions into the high country that Gran took Laddy in hand. He had come back spent and filthy, his coat a mass of cockleburs and ticks, his eyes bloodshot, loud *râles* in his chest; for half a day he lay motionless before the front door like someone in a hangover, his groaning eyes explicitly saying "Oh, for God's sake, leave

me be" when we offered him food or bowls of water. Gran
was disapproving, then affronted, and finally furious. Not, of
course, with Laddy, since all inmates of her house enjoyed im-
munity, but with Mess, whose caddish character, together with
that of his nominal masters, the firemen, she examined closely
under a strong light, with an air of detachment, with her not
caring but her having, all the same, to laugh. A lodger who
occupied the back west room had something to say about the
fire chief and his nocturnal visits to a certain house occupied
by a certain group of young women, too near the same age to
be sisters and too old to be the daughters of the woman who
claimed to be their mother. What a story! The exophthalmic
librarian—she lived in one of the front rooms—had some interesting insinuations to make about the deputy marshal, who
had borrowed, significantly, she thought, a book on hypnotism.
She also knew—she was, of course, in a most useful position in
the town, and from her authoritative pen in the middle of the
library her mammiform and azure eyes and her eager ears missed
nothing—that the fire chief's wife was not as scrupulous as she
might be when she was keeping score on bridge night at the
Sorosis.

There was little at the moment that Mrs. Placer and her
disciples could do to save the souls of the Fire Department and
their families, and therefore save the town from holocaust (a
very timid boarder—a Mr. Beaver, a newcomer who was not
to linger long—had sniffed throughout this recitative as if he
were smelling burning flesh), but at least the unwholesome bond
between Mess and Laddy could and would be severed once
and for all. Gran looked across the porch at Laddy, who lay
stretched at full length in the darkest corner, shuddering and
baying abortively in his throat as he chased jack rabbits in his
dreams, and she said, "A dog can have morals like a human."
With this declaration Laddy's randy, manly holidays were
finished. It may have been telepathy that woke him; he lifted
his heavy head from his paws, laboriously got up, hesitated for

a moment, and then padded languidly across the porch to Gran. He stood docilely beside her chair, head down, tail drooping as if to say, "O.K., Mrs. Placer, show me how and I'll walk the straight and narrow."

The very next day, Gran changed Laddy's name to Caesar, as being more dignified, and a joke was made at the supper table that he had come, seen, and conquered Mrs. Placer's heart —for within her circle, where the magnanimity she lavished upon her orphans was daily demonstrated, Mrs. Placer's heart was highly thought of. On that day also, although we did not know it yet, Laddy ceased to be our dog. Before many weeks passed, indeed, he ceased to be anyone we had ever known. A week or so after he became Caesar, he took up residence in her room, sleeping alongside her bed. She broke him of the habit of taking us to school (temptation to low living was rife along those streets; there was a chow—well, never mind) by the simple expedient of chaining him to a tree as soon as she got up in the morning. This discipline, together with the stamina-building cuffs she gave his sensitive ears from time to time, gradually but certainly remade his character. From a sanguine, affectionate, easygoing Gael (with the fits of melancholy that alternated with the larkiness), he turned into an overbearing, military, efficient, loud-voiced Teuton. His bark, once wide of range, narrowed to one dark, glottal tone.

Soon the paper boy flatly refused to serve our house after Caesar efficiently removed the bicycle clip from his pants leg; the skin was not broken, or even bruised, but it was a matter of principle with the boy. The milkman approached the back door in a seizure of shakes like St. Vitus's dance. The meter-men, the coal men, and the garbage collector crossed themselves if they were Catholics and, if they were not, tried whistling in the dark. "Good boy, good Caesar," they carolled, and, unctuously lying, they said they knew his bark was worse than his bite, knowing full well that it was not, considering the very nasty nip, requiring stitches, he had given a representative of

the Olson Rug Company, who had had the folly to pat him on
the head. Caesar did not molest the lodgers, but he disdained
them and he did not brook being personally addressed by anyone except Gran. One night, he wandered into the dining room,
appearing to be in search of something he had mislaid, and, for
some reason that no one was ever able to divine, suddenly stood
stock-still and gave the easily upset Mr. Beaver a long and
penetrating look. Mr. Beaver, trembling from head to toe,
stammered, "Why—er, hello there, Caesar, old boy, old boy,"
and Caesar charged. For a moment, it was touch and go, but
Gran saved Mr. Beaver, only to lose him an hour later when he
departed, bag and baggage, for the Y.M.C.A. This rout and the
consequent loss of revenue would more than likely have meant
Caesar's downfall and his deportation to the pound if it had not
been that a newly widowed druggist, very irascible and very
much Gran's style, had applied for a room in her house a week
or so before, and now he moved in delightedly, as if he were
coming home.

Finally, the police demanded that Caesar be muzzled and
they warned that if he committed any major crime again—
they cited the case of the Olson man—he would be shot on
sight. Mrs. Placer, although she had no respect for the law,
knowing as much as she did about its agents, obeyed. She obeyed,
that is, in part; she put the muzzle on Caesar for a few hours a
day, usually early in the morning when the traffic was light and
before the deliveries had started, but the rest of the time his
powerful jaws and dazzling white sabre teeth were free and
snapping. There was between these two such preternatural rapport, such an impressive conjugation of suspicion, that he, sens-
ing the approach of a policeman, could convey instantly to her
the immediate necessity of clapping his nose cage on. And the
policeman, sent out on the complaint of a terrorized neighbor,
would be greeted by this law-abiding pair at the door.

Daisy and I wished we were dead. We were divided between
hating Caesar and loving Laddy, and we could not give up the

hope that something, someday, would change him back into the loving animal he had been before he was appointed vice-president of the Placerites. Now at the meetings after supper on the porch he took an active part, standing rigidly at Gran's side except when she sent him on an errand. He carried out these assignments not with the air of a servant but with that of an accomplice. "Get me the paper, Caesar," she would say to him, and he, dismayingly intelligent and a shade smart-alecky, would open the screen door by himself and in a minute come back with the *Bulletin*, from which Mrs. Placer would then read an item, like the Gospel of the day, and then read between the lines of it, scandalized.

In the deepening of our woe and our bereavement and humiliation, we mutely appealed to Mr. Murphy. We did not speak outright to him, for Mr. Murphy lived in a state of indirection, and often when he used the pronoun "I," he seemed to be speaking of someone standing a little to the left of him, but we went to see him and his animals each day during the sad summer, taking what comfort we could from the cozy, quiet indolence of his back yard, where small black eyes encountered ours politely and everyone was half asleep. When Mr. Murphy inquired about Laddy in his bland, inattentive way, looking for a stratagem whereby to shift the queen of hearts into position by the king, we would say, "Oh, he's fine," or "Laddy is a nifty dog." And Mr. Murphy, reverently slaking the thirst that was his talent and his concubine, would murmur, "I'm glad."

We wanted to tell him, we wanted his help, or at least his sympathy, but how could we cloud his sunny world? It was awful to see Mr. Murphy ruffled. Up in the calm clouds as he generally was, he could occasionally be brought to earth with a thud, as we had seen and heard one day. Not far from his house, there lived a bad troublemaking boy of twelve, who was forever hanging over the fence trying to teach the parrot obscene words. He got nowhere, for she spoke no English and she would flabber-

gast him with her cold eye and sneer, "*Tant pis.*" One day, this
boorish fellow went too far; he suddenly shot his head over the
fence like a jack-in-the-box and aimed a water pistol at the
skunk's face. Mr. Murphy leaped to his feet in a scarlet rage;
he picked up a stone and threw it accurately, hitting the boy
square in the back, so hard that he fell right down in a mud
puddle and lay there kicking and squalling and, as it turned out,
quite badly hurt. "If you ever come back here again, I'll kill
you!" roared Mr. Murphy. I think he meant it, for I have seldom
seen an anger so resolute, so brilliant, and so voluble. "How
dared he!" he cried, scrambling into Mallow's cage to hug and
pet and soothe her. "He must be absolutely mad! He must be the
Devil!" He did not go back to his game after that but paced the
yard, swearing a blue streak and only pausing to croon to his
animals, now as frightened by him as they had been by the in-
truder, and to drink straight from the bottle, not bothering with
fixings. We were fascinated by this unfamiliar side of Mr. Murphy, but we did not want to see it ever again, for his face had
grown so dangerously purple and the veins of his forehead
seemed ready to burst and his eyes looked scorched. He was the
closest thing to a maniac we had ever seen. So we did not tell
him about Laddy; what he did not know would not hurt him,
although it was hurting us, throbbing in us like a great, bleating
wound.

But eventually Mr. Murphy heard about our dog's conversion,
one night at the pool hall, which he visited from time to time
when he was seized with a rare but compelling garrulity, and
the next afternoon when he asked us how Laddy was and we
replied that he was fine, he tranquilly told us, as he deliberated
whether to move the jack of clubs now or to bide his time, that
we were sweet girls but we were lying in our teeth. He did not
seem at all angry but only interested, and all the while he questioned us, he went on about his business with the gin and the
hearts and spades and diamonds and clubs. It rarely happened
that he won the particular game he was playing, but that day he

did, and when he saw all the cards laid out in their ideal pattern, he leaned back, looking disappointed, and he said, "I'm damned." He then scooped up the cards, in a gesture unusually quick and tidy for him, stacked them together, and bound them with a rubber band. Then he began to tell us what he thought of Gran. He grew as loud and apoplectic as he had been that other time, and though he kept repeating that he knew *we* were innocent and he put not a shred of the blame on us, we were afraid he might suddenly change his mind, and, speechless, we cowered against the monkeys' cage. In dread, the monkeys clutched the fingers we offered to them and made soft, protesting noises, as if to say, "Oh, stop it, Murphy! Our nerves!"

As quickly as it had started, the tantrum ended. Mr. Murphy paled to his normal complexion and said calmly that the only practical thing was to go and have it out with Mrs. Placer. "At once," he added, although he said he bitterly feared that it was too late and there would be no exorcising the fiend from Laddy's misused spirit. And because he had given the dog to us and not to her, he required that we go along with him, stick up for our rights, stand on our mettle, get up our Irish, and give the old bitch something to put in her pipe and smoke.

Oh, it was hot that day! We walked in a kind of delirium through the simmer, where only the grasshoppers had the energy to move, and I remember wondering if ether smelled like the gin on Mr. Murphy's breath. Daisy and I, in one way or another, were going to have our gizzards cut out along with our hearts and our souls and our pride, and I wished I were as drunk as Mr. Murphy, who swam effortlessly through the heat, his lips parted comfortably, his eyes half closed. When we turned in to the path at Gran's house, my blood began to scald my veins. It was so futile and so dangerous and so absurd. Here we were on a high moral mission, two draggletailed, gumptionless little girls and a toper whom no one could take seriously, partly because he was little more than a gurgling bottle of booze and partly because of the clothes he wore. He was a sight, as he always was when he was out of his own yard. There, somehow, in the care-free disorder, his clothes did not look especially strange, but on the streets of the town, in the barbershop or the post office or on Gran's path, they were fantastic. He wore a pair of hound's tooth pants, old but maintaining a vehement pattern, and with them he wore a collarless blue flannelette shirt. His hat was the silliest of all, because it was a derby three sizes too big. And as if Shannon, too, was a part of his funny-paper costume, the elder capuchin rode on his shoulder, tightly embracing his thin red neck.

Gran and Caesar were standing side by side behind the screen door, looking as if they had been expecting us all along. For a moment, Gran and Mr. Murphy faced each other across the length of weedy brick between the gate and the front porch, and no one spoke. Gran took no notice at all of Daisy and me. She adjusted her eyeglasses, using both hands, and then looked down at Caesar and matter-of-factly asked, "Do you want out?"

Caesar flung himself full-length upon the screen and it sprang open like a jaw. I ran to meet and head him off, and Daisy threw a library book at his head, but he was on Mr. Murphy in one split second and had his monkey off his shoulder and had broken Shannon's neck in two shakes. He would have gone on nuzzling and mauling and growling over the corpse for hours if Gran had not marched out of the house and down the path and slapped him lightly on the flank and said, in a voice that could not have deceived an idiot, "Why, Caesar, you scamp! You've hurt Mr. Murphy's monkey! Aren't you ashamed!"

Hurt the monkey! In one final, apologetic shudder, the life was extinguished from the little fellow. Bloody and covered with slather, Shannon lay with his arms suppliantly stretched over his head, his leather fingers curled into loose, helpless fists. His hind legs and his tail lay limp and helter-skelter on the path. And Mr. Murphy, all of a sudden reeling drunk, burst into the kind of tears that Daisy and I knew well—the kind that time alone could stop. We stood aghast in the dark-red sunset, killed by our horror and our grief for Shannon and our unforgivable disgrace. We stood upright in a dead faint, and an eon passed before Mr. Murphy picked up Shannon's body and wove away, sobbing, "I don't believe it! I don't *believe it!*"

The very next day, again at morbid, heavy sunset, Caesar died in violent convulsions, knocking down two tall hollyhocks in his throes. Long after his heart had stopped, his right hind leg continued to jerk in aimless reflex. Madly methodical, Mr. Murphy had poisoned some meat for him, had thoroughly envenomed a whole pound of hamburger, and early in the morning, before sunup, when he must have been near collapse with his hangover, he had stolen up to Mrs. Placer's house and put it by the kitchen door. He was so stealthy that Caesar never stirred in his fool's paradise there on the floor by Gran. We knew these to be the facts, for Mr. Murphy made no bones about them. Afterward, he had gone home and said a solemn Requiem for Shannon in so loud a voice that someone sent for the police, and they took him away in the Black Maria to sober him up on strong green tea. By the time he was in the lockup and had confessed what he had done, it was far too late, for Caesar had already gulped down the meat. He suffered an undreamed-of agony in Gran's flower garden, and Daisy and I, unable to bear the sight of it, hiked up to the red rocks and shook there, wretchedly ripping to shreds the sand lilies that grew in the cracks. Flight was the only thing we could think of, but where could we go? We stared west at the mountains and quailed at the look of the stern white glacier; we wildly scanned the prairies for escape. "If only we were something besides kids! Besides girls!" mourned Daisy. I could not speak at all; I huddled in a niche of the rocks and cried.

No one in town, except, of course, her lodgers, had the slightest sympathy for Gran. The townsfolk allowed that Mr. Murphy was a drunk and was fighting Irish, but he had a heart and this was something that could never be said of Mrs. Placer. The neighbor who had called the police when he was chanting the

Dies Irae before breakfast in that deafening monotone had said, "The poor guy is having some kind of a spell, so don't be rough on him, hear?" Mr. Murphy became, in fact, a kind of hero; some people, stretching a point, said he was a saint for the way that every day and twice on Sunday he sang a memorial Mass over Shannon's grave, now marked with a chipped, cheap plaster figure of Saint Francis. He withdrew from the world more and more, seldom venturing into the streets at all, except when he went to the bootlegger to get a new bottle to snuggle into. All summer, all fall, we saw him as we passed by his yard, sitting at his dilapidated table, enfeebled with gin, graying, withering, turning his head ever and ever more slowly as he maneuvered the protocol of the kings and the queens and the knaves. Daisy and I could never stop to visit him again.

It went on like this, year after year. Daisy and I lived in a mesh of lies and evasions, baffled and mean, like rats in a maze. When we were old enough for beaux, we connived like sluts to see them, but we would never admit to their existence until Gran caught us out by some trick. Like this one, for example: Once, at the end of a long interrogation, she said to me, "I'm more relieved than I can tell you that you *don't* have anything to do with Jimmy Gilmore, because I happen to know that he is after only one thing in a girl," and then, off guard in the loving memory of sitting in the movies the night before with Jimmy, not even holding hands, I defended him and defeated myself, and Gran, smiling with success, said, "I *thought* you knew him. It's a pretty safe rule of thumb that where there's smoke there's fire." That finished Jimmy and me, for afterward I was nervous with him and I confounded and alarmed and finally bored him by trying to convince him, although the subject had not come up, that I did not doubt his good intentions.

Daisy and I would come home from school, or, later, from our jobs, with a small triumph or an interesting piece of news, and if we forgot ourselves and, in our exuberance, told Gran, we were hustled into court at once for cross-examination. Once, I remember, while I was still in high school, I told her about getting a part in a play. How very nice for me, she said, if that kind of make-believe seemed to me worth while. But what was my role? An old woman! A widow woman believed to be a witch? She did not care a red cent, but she did have to laugh in view of the fact that Miss Eccles, in charge of dramatics, had almost run her down in her car. And I would forgive her, would I not, if she did not come to see the play, and would not think her eccentric for not wanting to see herself ridiculed in public?

My pleasure strangled, I crawled, joy-killed, to our third-floor room. The room was small and its monstrous furniture was too big and the rag rugs were repulsive, but it was bright. We would not hang a blind at the window, and on this day I stood there staring into the mountains that burned with the sun. I feared the mountains, but at times like this their massiveness consoled me; they, at least, could not be gossiped about.

Why did we stay until we were grown? Daisy and I ask ourselves this question as we sit here on the bench in the municipal zoo, reminded of Mr. Murphy by the polar bear, reminded by the monkeys not of Shannon but of Mrs. Placer's insatiable gossips at their postprandial feast.

"But how could we have left?" says Daisy, wringing her buttery hands. "It was the depression. We had no money. We had nowhere to go."

"All the same, we could have gone," I say, resentful still of the waste of all those years. "We could have come here and got jobs as waitresses. Or prostitutes, for that matter."

"I wouldn't have wanted to be a prostitute," says Daisy.

We agreed that under the circumstances it would have been impossible for us to run away. The physical act would have been simple, for the city was not far and we could have stolen the bus fare or hitched a ride. Later, when we began to work as salesgirls in Kress's, it would have been no trick at all to vanish one Saturday afternoon with our week's pay, without so much as going home to say goodbye. But it had been infinitely harder than that, for Gran, as we now see, held us trapped by our sense of guilt. We were vitiated, and we had no choice but to wait, flaccidly, for her to die.

You may be sure we did not unlearn those years as soon as we put her out of sight in the cemetery and sold her house for a song to the first boob who would buy it. Nor did we forget when we left the town for another one, where we had jobs at a dude camp—the town where Daisy now lives with a happy husband and two happy sons. The succubus did not relent for years, and I can still remember, in the beginning of our days at the Lazy S 3, overhearing an edgy millionaire say to his wife, naming my name, "That girl gives me the cold shivers. One would think she had just seen a murder." Well, I had. For years, whenever I woke in the night in fear or pain or loneliness, I would increase my suffering by the memory of Shannon, and my tears were as bitter as poor Mr. Murphy's.

We have never been back to Adams. But we see that house plainly, with the hopvines straggling over the porch. The windows are hung with the cheapest grade of marquisette, dipped into coffee to impart to it an unwilling color, neither white nor tan but individual and spitefully unattractive. We see the wicker rockers and the swing, and through the screen door we dimly make out the slightly veering corridor, along one wall of which stands a glass-doored bookcase; when we were children, it had contained not books but stale old cardboard boxes filled with such things as W.C.T.U. tracts and anti-cigarette literature and newspaper clippings related to sexual sin in the Christianized islands of the Pacific.

Even if we were able to close our minds' eyes to the past, Mr. Murphy would still be before us in the apotheosis of the polar bear. My pain becomes intolerable, and I am relieved when Daisy rescues us. "We've got to go," she says in a sudden panic. "I've got asthma coming on." We rush to the nearest exit of the city park and hail a cab, and, once inside it, Daisy gives herself an injection of adrenalin and then leans back. We are heartbroken and infuriated, and we cannot speak.

Two hours later, beside my train, we clutch each other as if we were drowning. We ought to go out to the nearest policeman and say, "We are not responsible women. You will have to take care of us because we cannot take care of ourselves." But gradually the storm begins to lull.

"You're sure you've got your ticket?" says Daisy. "You'll surely be able to get a roomette once you're on."

"I don't know about that," I say. "If there are any V.I.P.s on board, I won't have a chance. 'Spinisters and Orphans Last' is the motto of this line."

Daisy smiles. "I didn't care," she says, "but I had to laugh when I saw that woman nab the redcap you had signalled to. I had a good notion to give her a piece of my mind."

"It will be a miracle if I ever see my bags again," I say, mounting the steps of the train. "Do you suppose that blackguardly porter knows about the twenty-dollar gold piece in my little suitcase?"

"Anything's possible!" cries Daisy, and begins to laugh. She is so pretty, standing there in her bright-red linen suit and her black velvet hat. A solitary ray of sunshine comes through a broken pane in the domed vault of the train shed and lies on her shoulder like a silver arrow.

"So long, Daisy!" I call as the train begins to move.

She walks quickly along beside the train. "Watch out for pickpockets!" she calls.

"You, too!" My voice is thin and lost in the increasing noise of the speeding train wheels. "Goodbye, old dear!"

I go at once to the club car and I appropriate the writing

table, to the vexation of a harried priest, who snatches up the telegraph pad and gives me a sharp look. I write Daisy approximately the same letter I always write her under this particular set of circumstances, the burden of which is that nothing for either of us can ever be as bad as the past before Gran mercifully died. In a postscript I add: "There is a Roman Catholic priest (that is to say, he is *dressed* like one) sitting behind me although all the chairs on the opposite side of the car are empty. I can only conclude that he is looking over my shoulder, and while I do not want to cause you any alarm, I think you would be advised to be on the lookout for any appearance of miraculous medals, scapulars, papist booklets, etc., in the shops of your town. It really makes me laugh to see the way he is pretending that all he wants is for me to finish this letter so that he can have the table."

I sign my name and address the envelope, and I give up my place to the priest, who smiles nicely at me, and then I move across the car to watch the fields as they slip by. They are alfalfa fields, but you can bet your bottom dollar that they are chockablock with marijuana.

I begin to laugh. The fit is silent but it is devastating; it surges and rattles in my rib cage, and I turn my face to the window to avoid the narrow gaze of the Filipino bar boy. I must think of something sad to stop this unholy giggle, and I think of the polar bear. But even his bleak tragedy does not sober me. Wildly I fling open the newspaper I have brought and I pretend to be reading something screamingly funny. The words I see are in a Hollywood gossip column: "How a well-known starlet can get a divorce in Nevada without her crooner husband's consent, nobody knows. It won't be worth a plugged nickel here."

Keela, the Outcast Indian Maiden

EUDORA WELTY (1909–   )

ONE MORNING in summertime, when all his sons and daughters were off picking plums and Little Lee Roy was all alone, sitting on the porch and only listening to the screech owls away down in the woods, he had a surprise.

First he heard white men talking. He heard two white men coming up the path from the highway. Little Lee Roy ducked his head and held his breath; then he patted all around back of him for his crutches. The chickens all came out from under the house and waited attentively on the steps.

The men came closer. It was the young man who was doing all of the talking. But when they got through the fence, Max, the older man, interrupted him. He tapped him on the arm and pointed his thumb toward Little Lee Roy.

He said, "Bud? Yonder he is."

But the younger man kept straight on talking, in an explanatory voice.

"Bud?" said Max again. "Look, Bud, yonder's the only little clubfooted nigger man was ever around Cane Springs. Is he the party?"

They came nearer and nearer to Little Lee Roy and then stopped and stood there in the middle of the yard. But the young man was so excited he did not seem to realize that they had arrived anywhere. He was only about twenty years old, very sunburned. He talked constantly, making only one gesture—raising his hand stiffly and then moving it a little to one side.

"They dressed it in a red dress, and it ate chickens alive," he said. "I sold tickets and I thought it was worth a dime, honest. They gimme a piece of paper with the thing wrote off I had to say. That was easy. 'Keela, the Outcast Indian Maiden!' I call it out through a pasteboard megaphone. Then ever' time it was fixin' to eat a live chicken, I blowed the sireen out front."

"Just tell me, Bud," said Max, resting back on the heels of his perforated tan-and-white sport shoes. "Is this nigger the one? Is that him sittin' there?"

Little Lee Roy sat huddled and blinking, a smile on his face. . . . But the young man did not look his way.

"Just took the job that time. I didn't mean to—I mean, I meant to go to Port Arthur because my brother was on a boat," he said. "My name is Steve, mister. But I worked with this show selling tickets for three months, and I never would of knowed it was like that if it hadn't been for that man." He arrested his gesture.

"Yeah, what man?" said Max in a hopeless voice.

Little Lee Roy was looking from one white man to the other, excited almost beyond respectful silence. He trembled all over, and a look of amazement and sudden life came into his eyes.

"Two years ago," Steve was saying impatiently. "And we was travelin' through Texas in those ole trucks.—See, the reason nobody ever come clost to it before was they give it a iron bar this long. And tole it if anybody come near, to shake the bar good at 'em, like this. But it couldn't say nothin'. Turned out they'd tole it it couldn't say nothin' to anybody ever, so it just kind of mumbled and growled, like a animal."

"Hee! hee!" This from Little Lee Roy, softly.

"Tell me again," said Max, and just from his look you could tell that everybody knew old Max. "Somehow I can't get it straight in my mind. Is this the boy? Is this little nigger boy the same as this Keela, the Outcast Indian Maiden?"

Up on the porch, above them, Little Lee Roy gave Max a glance full of hilarity, and then bent the other way to catch Steve's next words.

"Why, if anybody was to even come near it or even bresh their shoulder against the rope it'd growl and take on and shake its iron rod. When it would eat the live chickens it'd growl somethin' awful—you ought to heard it."

"Hee! hee!" It was a soft, almost incredulous laugh that began to escape from Little Lee Roy's tight lips, a little mew of delight.

"They'd throw it this chicken, and it would reach out an' grab it. Would sort of rub over the chicken's neck with its thumb an' press on it good, an' then it would bite its head off."

"O.K.," said Max.

"It skint back the feathers and stuff from the neck and sucked the blood. But ever'body said it was still alive." Steve drew closer to Max and fastened his light-colored, troubled eyes on his face.

"O.K."

"Then it would pull the feathers out easy and neat-like, awful fast, an' growl the whole time, kind of moan, an' then it would commence to eat all the white meat. I'd go in an' look at it. I reckon I seen it a thousand times."

"That was you, boy?" Max demanded of Little Lee Roy unexpectedly.

But Little Lee Roy could only say, "Hee! hee!" The little man at the head of the steps where the chickens sat, one on each step, and the two men facing each other below made a pyramid.

Steve stuck his hand out for silence. "They said—I mean, I said it, out front through the megaphone, I said it myself, that it wouldn't eat nothin' but only live meat. It was supposed to be a Indian woman, see, in this red dress an' stockin's. It didn't have on no shoes, so when it drug its foot ever'body could see. . . . When it come to the chicken's heart, it would eat that too, real fast, and the heart would still be jumpin'."

"Wait a second, Bud," said Max briefly. "Say, boy, is this white man here crazy?"

Little Lee Roy burst into hysterical, deprecatory giggles. He said, "Naw suh, don't think so." He tried to catch Steve's eye, seeking appreciation, crying, "Naw suh, don't think he crazy, mista."

Steve gripped Max's arm. "Wait! Wait!" he cried anxiously. "You ain't listenin'. I want to tell you about it. You didn't catch my name—Steve. You never did hear about that little nigger—all that happened to him? Lived in Cane Springs, Miss'ippi?"

"But," said Max, disengaging himself, "I don't hear anything. I got a juke box, see, so I don't have to listen."

"Look—I was really the one," said Steve more patiently, but nervously, as if he had been slowly breaking bad news. He walked up and down the bare-swept ground in front of Little Lee Roy's porch, along the row of princess feathers and snow-on-the-mountain. Little Lee Roy's turning head followed him. "I was the one—that's what I'm tellin' you."

"Suppose I was to listen to what every dope comes in Max's Place got to say, *I'd* be nuts," said Max.

"It's all me, see," said Steve. "I know that. I was the one was the cause for it goin' on an' on an' not bein' found out—such an awful thing. It was me, what I said out front through the mega-phone."

He stopped still and stared at Max in despair.

"Look," said Max. He sat on the steps, and the chickens hopped off. "I know I ain't nobody but Max. I got Max's Place. I only run a place, understand, fifty yards down the highway. Liquor buried twenty feet from the premises, and no trouble yet. I ain't ever been up here before. I don't claim to been anywhere. People come to my place. Now. You're the hitchhiker. You're tellin' me, see. You claim a lot of information. If I don't get it I don't get it and I ain't complainin' about it, see. But I think you're nuts, and did from the first. I only come up here with you because I figured you's crazy."

"Maybe you don't believe I remember every word of it even now," Steve was saying gently. "I think about it at night—that an' drums on the midway. You ever hear drums on the midway?" He paused and stared politely at Max and Little Lee Roy.

"Yeh," said Max.

"Don't it make you feel sad? I remember how the drums was goin' and I was yellin', 'Ladies and gents! Do not try to touch Keela, the Outcast Indian Maiden—she will only beat your brains out with her iron rod, and eat them alive!' " Steve waved his arm gently in the air, and Little Lee Roy drew back and squealed. " 'Do not go near her, ladies and gents! I'm warnin' you!' So nobody ever did. Nobody ever come near her. Until that man."

"Sure," said Max. "That fella." He shut his eyes.

"Afterwards when he come up so bold, I remembered seein' him walk up an' buy the ticket an' go in the tent. I'll never forget that man as long as I live. To me he's a sort of—well—"

"Hero," said Max.

"I wish I could remember what he looked like. Seem like he was a tallish man with a sort of white face. Seem like he had bad teeth, but I may be wrong. I remember he frowned a lot. Kept frownin'. Whenever he'd buy a ticket, why, he'd frown."

"Ever seen him since?" asked Max cautiously, still with his eyes closed. "Ever hunt him up?"

"No, never did," said Steve. Then he went on. "He'd frown an' buy a ticket ever' day we was in these two little smelly towns in Texas, sometimes three-four times a day, whether it was fixin' to eat a chicken or not."

"O.K., so he gets in the tent," said Max.

"Well, what the man finally done was, he walked right up to the little stand where it was tied up and laid his hand out open on the planks in the platform. He just laid his hand out open there and said, 'Come here,' real low and quick, that-a-way."

Steve laid his open hand on Little Lee Roy's porch and held it there, frowning in concentration.

"I get it," said Max. "He'd caught on it was a fake."

Steve straightened up. "So ever'body yelled to git away, git away," he continued, his voice rising, "because it was growlin' an' carryin' on an' shakin' its iron bar like they tole it. When I heard all that commotion—boy! I was scared."

"You didn't know it was a fake."

Steve was silent for a moment, and Little Lee Roy held his breath, for fear everything was all over.

"Look," said Steve finally, his voice trembling. "I guess I was supposed to feel bad like this, and you wasn't. I wasn't supposed to ship out on that boat from Port Arthur and all like that. This other had to happen to me—not you all. Feelin' responsible. You'll be O.K., mister, but I won't. I feel awful about it. That poor little old thing."

"Look, you got him right here," said Max quickly. "See him? Use your eyes. He's O.K., ain't he? Looks O.K. to me. It's just you. You're nuts, is all."

"You know—when that man laid out his open hand on the boards, why, it just let go the iron bar," continued Steve, "let it fall down like that—bang—and act like it didn't know what to do. Then it drug itself over to where the fella was standin' an' leaned down an' grabbed holt onto that white man's hand as tight as it could an' cried like a baby. It didn't want to hit him!"

"Hee! hee! hee!"

"No sir, it didn't want to hit him. You know what it wanted?" Max shook his head.

"It wanted him to help it. So the man said, 'Do you wanta get out of this place, whoever you are?' An' it never answered—none of us knowed it could talk—but it just wouldn't let that man's hand a-loose. It hung on, cryin' like a baby. So the man says, 'Well, wait here till I come back.'"

"Uh-huh?" said Max.

"Went off an' come back with the sheriff. Took us all to jail. But just the man owned the show and his son got took to the pen. They said I could go free. I kep' tellin' 'em I didn't know it wouldn't hit me with the iron bar an' kep' tellin' 'em I didn't know it could tell what you was sayin' to it."

"Yeh, guess you told 'em," said Max.

"By that time I felt bad. Been feelin' bad ever since. Can't hold onto a job or stay in one place for nothin' in the world. They

made it stay in jail to see if it could talk or not, and the first night
it wouldn't say nothin'. Some time it cried. And they undressed
it an' found out it wasn't no outcast Indian woman a-tall. It
was a little clubfooted nigger man."

"Hee! hee!"

"You mean it was this boy here—yeh. It was him."

"Washed its face, and it was paint all over it made it look red.
It all come off. And it could talk—as good as me or you. But
they'd tole it not to, so it never did. They'd tole it if anybody
was to come near it they was comin' to git it—and for it to hit
'em quick with that iron bar an' growl. So nobody ever come
near it—until that man. I was yellin' outside, tellin' 'em to keep
away, keep away. You could see where they'd whup it. They
had to whup it some to make it eat all the chickens. It was awful
dirty. They let it go back home free, to where they got it in the
first place. They made them pay its ticket from Little Oil, Texas,
to Cane Springs, Miss'ippi."

"You got a good memory," said Max.

"The way it *started* was," said Steve, in a wondering voice,
"the show was just travelin' along in ole trucks through the
country, and just seen this little deformed nigger man, sittin' on
a fence, and just took it. It couldn't help it."

Little Lee Roy tossed his head back in a frenzy of amusement.

"I found it all out later. I was up on the Ferris wheel with one
of the boys—got to talkin' up yonder in the peace an' quiet—an'
said they just kind of happened up on it. Like a cyclone happens:
it wasn't nothin' it could do. It was just took up." Steve suddenly paled through his sunburn. "An' they found out that back
in Miss'ippi it had it a little bitty pair of crutches an' could just
go runnin' on 'em!"

"And there they are," said Max.

Little Lee Roy held up a crutch and turned it about, and then
snatched it back like a monkey.

"But if it hadn't been for that man, I wouldn't of knowed it till yet. If it wasn't for him bein' so bold. If he hadn't knowed what he was doin'."

"You remember that man this fella's talkin' about, boy?" asked Max, eying Little Lee Roy.

Little Lee Roy, in reluctance and shyness, shook his head gently.

"Naw suh, I can't say as I remembas that ve'y man, suh," he said softly, looking down where just then a sparrow alighted on his child's shoe. He added happily, as if on inspiration, "Now I remembas *this* man."

Steve did not look up, but when Max shook with silent laughter, alarm seemed to seize him like a spasm in his side. He walked painfully over and stood in the shade for a few minutes, leaning his head on a sycamore tree.

"Seemed like that man just studied it out an' knowed it was somethin' wrong," he said presently, his voice coming more remotely than ever. "But I didn't know. I can't look at nothin' an' be sure what it is. Then afterwards I know. Then I see how it was."

"Yeh, but you're nuts," said Max affably.

"You wouldn't of knowed it either!" cried Steve in sudden boyish, defensive anger. Then he came out from under the tree and stood again almost pleadingly in the sun, facing Max where he was sitting below Little Lee Roy on the steps. "You'd of let it go on an' on when they made it do those things—just like I did."

"Bet I could tell a man from a woman and an Indian from a nigger though," said Max.

Steve scuffed the dust into little puffs with his worn shoe. The chickens scattered, alarmed at last.

Little Lee Roy looked from one man to the other radiantly, his hands pressed over his grinning gums.

Then Steve sighed, and as if he did not know what else he

could do, he reached out and without any warning hit Max in the jaw with his fist. Max fell off the steps.

Little Lee Roy suddenly sat as still and dark as a statue, looking on.

"Say! Say!" cried Steve. He pulled shyly at Max where he lay on the ground, with his lips pursed up like a whistler, and then stepped back. He looked horrified. "How you feel?"

"Lousy," said Max thoughtfully. "Let me alone." He raised up on one elbow and lay there looking all around, at the cabin, at Little Lee Roy sitting cross-legged on the porch, and at Steve with his hand out. Finally he got up.

"I can't figure out how I could of ever knocked down an athaletic guy like you. I had to do it," said Steve. "But I guess you don't understand. I had to hit you. First you didn't believe me, and then it didn't bother you."

"That's all O.K., only hush," said Max, and added, "Some dope is always giving me the lowdown on something, but this is the first time one of 'em ever got away with a thing like this. I got to watch out."

"I hope it don't stay black long," said Steve.

"I got to be going," said Max. But he waited. "What you want to transact with Keela? You come a long way to see him." He stared at Steve with his eyes wide open now, and interested.

"Well, I was goin' to give him some money or somethin', I guess, if I ever found him, only now I ain't got any," said Steve defiantly.

"O.K.," said Max. "Here's some change for you, boy. Just take it. Go on back in the house. Go on."

Little Lee Roy took the money speechlessly, and then fell upon his yellow crutches and hopped with miraculous rapidity away through the door. Max stared after him for a moment.

"As for you"—he brushed himself off, turned to Steve and then said, "When did you eat last?"

"Well, I'll tell you," said Steve.

"Not here," said Max. "I didn't go to ask you a question. Just

follow me. We serve eats at Max's Place, and I want to play the
juke box. You eat, and I'll listen to the juke box."

"Well . . ." said Steve. "But when it cools off I got to catch
a ride some place."

"Today while all you all was gone, and not a soul in de house,"
said Little Lee Roy at the supper table that night, "two white
mens come heah to de house. Wouldn't come in. But talks to me
about de ole times when I use to be wid de circus—"

"Hush up, Pappy," said the children.

Critical Questions

NOTE THAT in "The Gioconda Smile" Huxley uses an omniscient
point of view; that is, he does not limit himself to what it would
be possible for a spectator to observe. He gets at the thoughts
of his characters, especially the thoughts of the chief character,
Mr. Hutton; and he is aware of and comments on the meaning
of actions and emotions. Generally speaking the comments seem
to be Mr. Hutton's; but some are obviously Huxley's, in his own
person. What does Huxley gain by this shifting point of view?
Is the device justified by the gain?

In "Keela, the Outcast Indian Maiden," on the other hand,
Eudora Welty limits herself to recording what an observer might
see. In the stage directions accompanying the dialogue, she seldom
gives more than a gesture or a description of a voice tone. The
reader has to reconstruct the emotions and motivations of the
characters. How does this opacity affect the tone of the story?
Note that Eudora Welty sets the characters of Max and Steve
quite explicitly in the passage beginning, " 'Look,' said Steve
finally, his voice trembling. 'I guess I was supposed to feel bad like
this, and you wasn't' " (page 520).

Note the first two speeches of Max. Explain the repeated
" 'Bud?' " That is, what emotion is implied by the question?

Note Max's speech (page 516): " 'Yeah, what man?' said Max in a hopeless voice." Why is he hopeless?

What is the effect of the final conversation between Little Lee Roy and his children?

The Rocking-Horse Winner

D. H. LAWRENCE (1885–1930)

THERE WAS a woman who was beautiful, who started with all the advantages, yet she had no luck. She married for love, and the love turned to dust. She had bonny children, yet she felt they had been thrust upon her, and she could not love them. They looked at her coldly, as if they were finding fault with her. And hurriedly she felt she must cover up some fault in herself. Yet what it was that she must cover up she never knew. Nevertheless, when her children were present, she always felt the centre of her heart go hard. This troubled her, and in her manner she was all the more gentle and anxious for her children, as if she loved them very much. Only she herself knew that at the centre of her heart was a hard little place that could not feel love, no, not for anybody. Everybody else said of her: "She is such a good mother. She adores her children." Only she herself, and her children themselves, knew it was not so. They read it in each other's eyes.

There were a boy and two little girls. They lived in a pleasant house, with a garden, and they had discreet servants, and felt themselves superior to anyone in the neighbourhood.

Although they lived in style, they felt always an anxiety in the house. There was never enough money. The mother had a small income, and the father had a small income, but not nearly enough for the social position which they had to keep up. The father went into town to some office. But though he had good prospects, these prospects never materialized. There was always the grinding sense of the shortage of money, though the style was always kept up.

At last the mother said: "I will see if I can't make something." But she did not know where to begin. She racked her brains, and tried this thing and the other, but could not find anything successful. The failure made deep lines come into her face. Her children were growing up, they would have to go to school. There must be more money, there must be more money. The father, who was always very handsome and expensive in his tastes, seemed as if he never would be able to do anything worth doing. And the mother, who had a great belief in herself, did not succeed any better, and her tastes were just as expensive.

And so the house came to be haunted by the unspoken phrase: There must be more money! There must be more money! The children could hear it all the time, though nobody said it aloud. They heard it at Christmas, when the expensive and splendid toys filled the nursery. Behind the shining modern rocking-horse, behind the smart doll's-house, a voice would start whispering: "There must be more money! There must be more money!" And the children would stop playing, to listen for a moment. They would look into each other's eyes, to see if they had all heard. And each one saw in the eyes of the other two that they too had heard. "There must be more money! There must be more money!"

It came whispering from the springs of the still-swaying rocking-horse, and even the horse, bending his wooden, champing head, heard it. The big doll, sitting so pink and smirking in her new pram, could hear it quite plainly, and seemed to be smirking all the more self-consciously because of it. The foolish puppy, too, that took the place of the teddy-bear, he was looking so extraordinarily foolish for no other reason but that he heard the secret whisper all over the house: "There must be more money!"

Yet nobody ever said it aloud. The whisper was everywhere, and therefore no one spoke it. Just as no one ever says: "We are breathing!" in spite of the fact that breath is coming and going all the time.

"Mother," said the boy Paul one day, "why don't we keep a car of our own? Why do we always use uncle's, or else a taxi?"

"Because we're the poor members of the family," said the mother.

"But why are we, mother?"

"Well—I suppose," she said slowly and bitterly, "it's because your father has no luck."

The boy was silent for some time.

"Is luck money, mother?" he asked, rather timidly.

"No, Paul. Not quite. It's what causes you to have money."

"Oh!" said Paul vaguely. "I thought when Uncle Oscar said filthy lucker, it meant money."

"Filthy lucre does mean money," said the mother. "But it's lucre, not luck."

"Oh!" said the boy. "Then what is luck, mother?"

"It's what causes you to have money. If you're lucky you have money. That's why it's better to be born lucky than rich. If you're rich, you may lose your money. But if you're lucky, you will always get more money."

"Oh! Will you? And is father not lucky?"

"Very unlucky, I should say," she said bitterly.

The boy watched her with unsure eyes.

"Why?" he asked.

"I don't know. Nobody ever knows why one person is lucky and another unlucky."

"Don't they? Nobody at all? Does nobody know?"

"Perhaps God. But He never tells."

"He ought to, then. And aren't you lucky either, mother?"

"I can't be, if I married an unlucky husband."

"But by yourself, aren't you?"

"I used to think I was, before I married. Now I think I am very unlucky indeed."

"Why?"

"Well—never mind! Perhaps I'm not really," she said.

The child looked at her, to see if she meant it. But he saw, by the lines of her mouth, that she was only trying to hide something from him.

"Well, anyhow," he said stoutly, "I'm a lucky person."

"Why?" said his mother, with a sudden laugh.

He stared at her. He didn't even know why he had said it.

"God told me," he asserted, brazening it out.

"I hope He did, dear!" she said, again with a laugh, but rather bitter.

"He did, mother!"

"Excellent!" said the mother, using one of her husband's exclamations.

The boy saw she did not believe him; or, rather, that she paid no attention to his assertion. This angered him somewhat, and made him want to compel her attention.

He went off by himself, vaguely, in a childish way, seeking for the clue to "luck." Absorbed, taking no heed of other people, he went about with a sort of stealth, seeking inwardly for luck. He wanted luck, he wanted it, he wanted it. When the two girls were playing dolls in the nursery, he would sit on his big rocking-horse, charging madly into space, with a frenzy that made the little girls peer at him uneasily. Wildly the horse careered, the waving dark hair of the boy tossed, his eyes had a strange glare in them. The little girls dared not speak to him.

When he had ridden to the end of his mad little journey, he climbed down and stood in front of his rocking-horse, staring fixedly into its lowered face. Its red mouth was slightly open, its big eye was wide and glassy-bright.

"Now!" he would silently command the snorting steed. "Now, take me to where there is luck! Now take me!"

And he would slash the horse on the neck with the little whip
he had asked Uncle Oscar for. He knew the horse could take
him to where there was luck, if only he forced it. So he would
mount again, and start on his furious ride, hoping at last to get
there. He knew he could get there.

"You'll break your horse, Paul!" said the nurse.

"He's always riding like that! I wish he'd leave off!" said his
elder sister Joan.

But he only glared down on them in silence. Nurse gave him
up. She could make nothing of him. Anyhow he was growing
beyond her.

One day his mother and his Uncle Oscar came in when he
was on one of his furious rides. He did not speak to them.

"Hallo, you young jockey! Riding a winner?" said his uncle.

"Aren't you growing too big for a rocking-horse? You're not
a very little boy any longer, you know," said his mother.

But Paul only gave a blue glare from his big, rather close-set
eyes. He would speak to nobody when he was in full tilt. His
mother watched him with an anxious expression on her face.

At last he suddenly stopped forcing his horse into the mechanical gallop, and slid down.

"Well, I got there!" he announced fiercely, his blue eyes still
flaring, and his sturdy long legs straddling apart.

"Where did you get to?" asked his mother.

"Where I wanted to go," he flared back at her.

"That's right, son!" said Uncle Oscar. "Don't you stop till you
get there. What's the horse's name?"

"He doesn't have a name," said the boy.

"Gets on without all right?" asked the uncle.

"Well, he has different names. He was called Sansovino last
week."

"Sansovino, eh? Won the Ascot. How did you know his
name?"

"He always talks about horse-races with Bassett," said Joan.

The uncle was delighted to find that his small nephew was

posted with all the racing news. Bassett, the young gardener, who had been wounded in the left foot in the war and had got his present job through Oscar Cresswell, whose batman he had been, was a perfect blade of the "turf." He lived in the racing events, and the small boy lived with him.

Oscar Cresswell got it all from Bassett.

"Master Paul comes and asks me, so I can't do more than tell him, sir," said Bassett, his face terribly serious, as if he were speaking of religious matters.

"And does he ever put anything on a horse he fancies?"

"Well—I don't want to give him away—he's a young sport, a fine sport, sir. Would you mind asking him yourself? He sort of takes a pleasure in it, and perhaps he'd feel I was giving him away, sir, if you don't mind."

Bassett was serious as a church.

The uncle went back to his nephew, and took him off for a ride in the car.

"Say, Paul, old man, do you ever put anything on a horse?" the uncle asked.

The boy watched the handsome man closely.

"Why, do you think I oughtn't to?" he parried.

"Not a bit of it! I thought perhaps you might give me a tip for the Lincoln."

The car sped on into the country, going down to Uncle Oscar's place in Hampshire.

"Honour bright?" said the nephew.

"Honour bright, son!" said the uncle.

"Well, then, Daffodil."

"Daffodil! I doubt it, sonny. What about Mirza?"

"I only know the winner," said the boy. "That's Daffodil."

"Daffodil, eh?"

There was a pause. Daffodil was an obscure horse comparatively.

"Uncle!"

"Yes, son?"

"You won't let it go any further, will you? I promised Bassett."

"Bassett be damned, old man! What's he got to do with it?"

"We're partners. We've been partners from the first. Uncle, he lent me my first five shillings, which I lost. I promised him, honour bright, it was only between me and him; only you gave me that ten-shilling note I started winning with, so I thought you were lucky. You won't let it go any further, will you?"

The boy gazed at his uncle from those big, hot, blue eyes, set rather close together. The uncle stirred and laughed uneasily.

"Right you are, son! I'll keep your tip private. Daffodil, eh? How much are you putting on him?"

"All except twenty pounds," said the boy. "I keep that in reserve."

The uncle thought it a good joke.

"You keep twenty pounds in reserve, do you, you young romancer? What are you betting, then?"

"I'm betting three hundred," said the boy gravely. "But it's between you and me, Uncle Oscar! Honour bright?"

The uncle burst into a roar of laughter.

"It's between you and me all right, you young Nat Gould," he said, laughing. "But where's your three hundred?"

"Bassett keeps it for me. We're partners."

"You are, are you! And what is Bassett putting on Daffodil?"

"He won't go quite as high as I do, I expect. Perhaps he'll go a hundred and fifty."

"What, pennies?" laughed the uncle.

"Pounds," said the child, with a surprised look at his uncle. "Bassett keeps a bigger reserve than I do."

Between wonder and amusement Uncle Oscar was silent. He pursued the matter no further, but he determined to take his nephew with him to the Lincoln races.

"Now, son," he said, "I'm putting twenty on Mirza, and I'll put five for you on any horse you fancy. What's your pick?"

"Daffodil, uncle."

"No, not the fiver on Daffodil!"

"I should if it was my own fiver," said the child.

"Good! Good! Right you are! A fiver for me and a fiver for you on Daffodil."

The child had never been to a race-meeting before, and his eyes were blue fire. He pursed his mouth tight, and watched. A Frenchman just in front had put his money on Lancelot. Wild with excitement, he flayed his arms up and down, yelling "Lancelot! Lancelot!" in his French accent.

Daffodil came in first, Lancelot second, Mirza third. The child, flushed and with eyes blazing, was curiously serene. His uncle brought him four five-pound notes, four to one.

"What am I to do with these?" he cried, waving them before the boy's eyes.

"I suppose we'll talk to Bassett," said the boy. "I expect I have fifteen hundred now; and twenty in reserve; and this twenty."

His uncle studied him for some moments.

"Look here, son!" he said. "You're not serious about Bassett and that fifteen hundred, are you?"

"Yes, I am. But it's between you and me, uncle. Honour bright!"

"Honour bright all right, son! But I must talk to Bassett."

"If you'd like to be a partner, uncle, with Bassett and me, we could all be partners. Only, you'd have to promise, honour bright, uncle, not to let it go beyond us three. Bassett and I are lucky, and you must be lucky, because it was your ten shillings I started winning with. . . ."

Uncle Oscar took both Bassett and Paul into Richmond Park for an afternoon, and there they talked.

"It's like this, you see, sir," Bassett said. "Master Paul would get me talking about racing events, spinning yarns, you know, sir. And he was always keen on knowing if I'd made or if I'd lost. It's about a year since, now, that I put five shillings on Blush of Dawn for him—and we lost. Then the luck turned, with that ten shillings he had from you, that we put on Singhalese. And since that time, it's been pretty steady, all things considering. What do you say, Master Paul?"

"We're all right when we're sure," said Paul. "It's when we're not quite sure that we go down."

"Oh, but we're careful then," said Bassett.

"But when are you sure?" smiled Uncle Oscar.

"It's Master Paul, sir," said Bassett, in a secret, religious voice. "It's as if he had it from heaven. Like Daffodil, now, for the Lincoln. That was as sure as eggs."

"Did you put anything on Daffodil?" asked Oscar Cresswell.

"Yes, sir. I made my bit."

"And my nephew?"

Bassett was obstinately silent, looking at Paul.

"I made twelve hundred, didn't I, Bassett? I told uncle I was putting three hundred on Daffodil."

"That's right," said Bassett, nodding.

"But where's the money?" asked the uncle.

"I keep it safe locked up, sir. Master Paul he can have it any minute he likes to ask for it."

"What, fifteen hundred pounds?"

"And twenty! And forty, that is, with the twenty he made on the course."

"It's amazing!" said the uncle.

"If Master Paul offers you to be partners, sir, I would, if I were you; if you'll excuse me," said Bassett.

Oscar Cresswell thought about it.

"I'll see the money," he said.

They drove home again, and sure enough, Bassett came round to the garden-house with fifteen hundred pounds in notes. The twenty pounds reserve was left with Joe Glee, in the Turf Commission deposit.

"You see, it's all right, uncle, when I'm sure! Then we go strong, for all we're worth. Don't we, Bassett?"

"We do that, Master Paul."

"And when are you sure?" said the uncle, laughing.

"Oh, well, sometimes I'm absolutely sure, like about Daffodil," said the boy; "and sometimes I have an idea; and sometimes I

haven't even an idea, have I, Bassett? Then we're careful, because we mostly go down."

"You do, do you! And when you're sure, like about Daffodil,
what makes you sure, sonny?"

"Oh, well, I don't know," said the boy uneasily. "I'm sure, you
know, uncle; that's all."

"It's as if he had it from heaven, sir," Bassett reiterated.

"I should say so!" said the uncle.

But he became a partner. And when the Leger was coming
on, Paul was "sure" about Lively Spark, which was a quite in-
considerable horse. The boy insisted on putting a thousand on
the horse, Bassett went for five hundred, and Oscar Cresswell
two hundred. Lively Spark came in first, and the betting had
been ten to one against him. Paul had made ten thousand.

"You see," he said, "I was absolutely sure of him."

Even Oscar Cresswell had cleared two thousand.

"Look here, son," he said, "this sort of thing makes me nervous."

"It needn't, uncle! Perhaps I shan't be sure again for a long
time."

"But what are you going to do with your money?" asked the
uncle.

"Of course," said the boy, "I started it for mother. She said
she had no luck, because father is unlucky, so I thought if I was
lucky, it might stop whispering."

"What might stop whispering?"

"Our house. I hate our house for whispering."

"What does it whisper?"

"Why—why"—the boy fidgeted—"why, I don't know. But
it's always short of money, you know, uncle."

"I know it, son, I know it."

"You know people send mother writs, don't you, uncle?"

"I'm afraid I do," said the uncle.

"And then the house whispers, like people laughing at you
behind your back. It's awful, that is! I thought if I was lucky . . ."

"You might stop it," added the uncle.

The boy watched him with big blue eyes that had an uncanny cold fire in them, and he said never a word.

"Well, then!" said the uncle. "What are we doing?"

"I shouldn't like mother to know I was lucky," said the boy.

"Why not, son?"

"She'd stop me."

"I don't think she would."

"Oh!"—and the boy writhed in an odd way—"I don't want her to know, uncle."

"All right, son! We'll manage it without her knowing."

They managed it very easily. Paul, at the other's suggestion, handed over five thousand pounds to his uncle, who deposited it with the family lawyer, who was then to inform Paul's mother that a relative had put five thousand pounds into his hands, which sum was to be paid out a thousand pounds at a time, on the mother's birthday, for the next five years.

"So she'll have a birthday present of a thousand pounds for five successive years," said Uncle Oscar. "I hope it won't make it all the harder for her later."

Paul's mother had her birthday in November. The house had been "whispering" worse than ever lately, and, even in spite of his luck, Paul could not bear up against it. He was very anxious to see the effect of the birthday letter, telling his mother about the thousand pounds.

When there were no visitors, Paul now took his meals with his parents, as he was beyond the nursery control. His mother went into town nearly every day. She had discovered that she had an odd knack of sketching furs and dress materials, so she worked secretly in the studio of a friend who was the chief "artist" for the leading drapers. She drew the figures of ladies in furs and ladies in silk and sequins for the newspaper advertisements. This young woman artist earned several thousand pounds a year, but Paul's mother only made several hundreds, and she was again dissatisfied. She so wanted to be first in something, and she did not succeed, even in making sketches for drapery advertisements.

She was down to breakfast on the morning of her birthday. Paul watched her face as she read her letters. He knew the lawyer's letter. As his mother read it, her face hardened and became more expressionless. Then a cold, determined look came on her mouth. She hid the letter under the pile of others, and said not a word about it.

"Didn't you have anything nice in the post for your birthday, mother?" said Paul.

"Quite moderately nice," she said, her voice cold and absent.

She went away to town without saying more.

But in the afternoon Uncle Oscar appeared. He said Paul's mother had had a long interview with the lawyer, asking if the whole five thousand could be advanced at once, as she was in debt.

"What do you think, uncle?" said the boy.

"I leave it to you, son."

"Oh, let her have it, then! We can get some more with the other," said the boy.

"A bird in the hand is worth two in the bush, laddie!" said Uncle Oscar.

"But I'm sure to know for the Grand National; or the Lincolnshire; or else the Derby. I'm sure to know for one of them," said Paul.

So Uncle Oscar signed the agreement, and Paul's mother touched the whole five thousand. Then something very curious happened. The voices in the house suddenly went mad, like a chorus of frogs on a spring evening. There were certain new furnishings, and Paul had a tutor. He was really going to Eton, his father's school, in the following autumn. There were flowers in the winter, and a blossoming of the luxury Paul's mother had been used to. And yet the voices in the house, behind the sprays of mimosa and almond blossom, and from under the piles of iridescent cushions, simply trilled and screamed in a sort of ecstasy: "There must be more money! Oh-h-h, there must be more money. Oh, now, now-w! Now-w-w—there must be more money!—more than ever! More than ever!"

It frightened Paul terribly. He studied away at his Latin and Greek with his tutors. But his intense hours were spent with Bassett. The Grand National had gone by: he had not "known," and had lost a hundred pounds. Summer was at hand. He was in agony for the Lincoln. But even for the Lincoln he didn't "know" and he lost fifty pounds. He became wild-eyed and strange, as if something were going to explode in him.

"Let it alone, son! Don't you bother about it!" urged Uncle Oscar. But it was as if the boy couldn't really hear what his uncle was saying.

"I've got to know for the Derby! I've got to know for the Derby!" the child reiterated, his big blue eyes blazing with a sort of madness.

His mother noticed how overwrought he was.

"You'd better go to the seaside. Wouldn't you like to go now to the seaside, instead of waiting? I think you'd better," she said, looking down at him anxiously, her heart curiously heavy because of him.

But the child lifted his uncanny blue eyes.

"I couldn't possibly go before the Derby, mother!" he said. "I couldn't possibly!"

"Why not?" she said, her voice becoming heavy when she was opposed. "Why not? You can still go from the seaside to see the Derby with your Uncle Oscar, if that's what you wish. No need for you to wait here. Besides, I think you care too much about these races. It's a bad sign. My family has been a gambling family, and you won't know till you grow up how much damage it has done. But it has done damage. I shall have to send Bassett away, and ask Uncle Oscar not to talk racing to you, unless you promise to be reasonable about it; go away to the seaside and forget it. You're all nerves!"

"I'll do what you like, mother, so long as you don't send me away till after the Derby," the boy said.

"Send you away from where? Just from this house?"

"Yes," he said, gazing at her.

"Why, you curious child, what makes you care about this house so much, suddenly? I never knew you loved it."

He gazed at her without speaking. He had a secret within a secret, something he had not divulged, even to Bassett or to his Uncle Oscar.

But his mother, after standing undecided and a little bit sullen for some moments, said:

"Very well, then! Don't go to the seaside till after the Derby, if you don't wish it. But promise me you won't let your nerves go to pieces. Promise you won't think so much about horse-racing and events, as you call them!"

"Oh, no," said the boy casually. "I won't think much about them, mother. You needn't worry. I wouldn't worry, mother, if I were you."

"If you were me and I were you," said his mother, "I wonder what we should do!"

"But you know you needn't worry, mother, don't you?" the boy repeated.

"I should be awfully glad to know it," she said wearily.

"Oh, well, you can, you know. I mean, you ought to know you needn't worry," he insisted.

"Ought I? Then I'll see about it," she said.

Paul's secret of secrets was his wooden horse, that which had no name. Since he was emancipated from a nurse and a nursery-governess, he had had his rocking-horse removed to his own bedroom at the top of the house.

"Surely, you're too big for a rocking-horse!" his mother had remonstrated.

"Well, you see, mother, till I can have a real horse, I like to have some sort of animal about," had been his quaint answer.

"Do you feel he keeps you company?" she laughed.

"Oh, yes! He's very good, he always keeps me company, when I'm there," said Paul.

So the horse, rather shabby, stood in an arrested prance in the boy's bedroom.

The Derby was drawing near, and the boy grew more and more tense. He hardly heard what was spoken to him, he was very frail, and his eyes were really uncanny. His mother had sudden seizures of uneasiness about him. Sometimes, for half-an-hour, she would feel a sudden anxiety about him that was almost anguish. She wanted to rush to him at once, and know he was safe.

Two nights before the Derby, she was at a big party in town, when one of her rushes of anxiety about her boy, her first-born, gripped her heart till she could hardly speak. She fought with the feeling, might and main, for she believed in common sense. But it was too strong. She had to leave the dance and go downstairs to telephone to the country. The children's nursery-governess was terribly surprised and startled at being rung up in the night.

"Are the children all right, Miss Wilmot?"

"Oh, yes, they are quite all right."

"Master Paul? Is he all right?"

"He went to bed as right as a trivet. Shall I run up and look at him?"

"No," said Paul's mother reluctantly. "No! Don't trouble. It's all right. Don't sit up. We shall be home fairly soon." She did not want her son's privacy intruded upon.

"Very good," said the governess.

It was about one o'clock when Paul's mother and father drove up to their house. All was still. Paul's mother went to her room and slipped off her white fur coat. She had told her maid not to wait up for her. She heard her husband downstairs, mixing a whisky-and-soda.

And then, because of the strange anxiety at her heart, she stole upstairs to her son's room. Noiselessly she went along the upper corridor. Was there a faint noise? What was it?

She stood, with arrested muscles, outside his door, listening. There was a strange, heavy, and yet not loud noise. Her heart stood still. It was a soundless noise, yet rushing and powerful.

Something huge, in violent, hushed motion. What was it? What in God's name was it? She ought to know. She felt that she knew the noise. She knew what it was.

Yet she could not place it. She couldn't say what it was. And on and on it went, like a madness.

Softly, frozen with anxiety and fear, she turned the door-handle.

The room was dark. Yet in the space near the window, she heard and saw something plunging to and fro. She gazed in fear and amazement.

Then suddenly she switched on the light, and saw her son, in his green pyjamas, madly surging on the rocking-horse. The blaze of light suddenly lit him up, as he urged the wooden horse, and lit her up, as she stood, blonde, in her dress of pale green and crystal, in the doorway.

"Paul!" she cried. "Whatever are you doing?"

"It's Malabar!" he screamed, in a powerful, strange voice. "It's Malabar."

His eyes blazed at her for one strange and senseless second, as he ceased urging his wooden horse. Then he fell with a crash to the ground, and she, all her tormented motherhood flooding upon her, rushed to gather him up.

But he was unconscious, and unconscious he remained, with some brain-fever. He talked and tossed, and his mother sat stonily by his side.

"Malabar! It's Malabar! Bassett, Bassett, I know! It's Malabar!"

So the child cried, trying to get up and urge the rocking-horse that gave him his inspiration.

"What does he mean by Malabar?" asked the heart-frozen mother.

"I don't know," said the father stonily.

"What does he mean by Malabar?" she asked her brother Oscar.

"It's one of the horses running for the Derby," was the answer.

And, in spite of himself, Oscar Cresswell spoke to Bassett, and himself put a thousand on Malabar: at fourteen to one.

The third day of the illness was critical: they were waiting for a change. The boy, with his rather long, curly hair, was tossing ceaselessly on the pillow. He neither slept nor regained consciousness, and his eyes were like blue stones. His mother sat, feeling her heart had gone, turned actually into a stone.

In the evening, Oscar Cresswell did not come, but Bassett sent a message, saying could he come up for one moment, just one moment? Paul's mother was very angry at the intrusion, but on second thought she agreed. The boy was the same. Perhaps Bassett might bring him to consciousness.

The gardener, a shortish fellow with a little brown moustache, and sharp little brown eyes, tiptoed into the room, touched his imaginary cap to Paul's mother, and stole to the bedside, staring with glittering, smallish eyes, at the tossing, dying child.

"Master Paul!" he whispered. "Master Paul! Malabar come in first all right, a clean win. I did as you told me. You've made over seventy thousand pounds, you have; you've got over eighty thousand. Malabar came in all right, Master Paul."

"Malabar! Malabar! Did I say Malabar, mother? Did I say Malabar? Do you think I'm lucky, mother? I knew Malabar, didn't I? Over eighty thousand pounds! I call that lucky, don't you, mother? Over eighty thousand pounds! I knew, didn't I know I knew? Malabar came in all right. If I ride my horse till I'm sure, then I tell you, Bassett, you can go as high as you like. Did you go for all you were worth, Bassett?"

"I went a thousand on it, Master Paul."

"I never told you, mother, that if I can ride my horse, and get there, then I'm absolutely sure—oh, absolutely! Mother, did I ever tell you? I am lucky."

"No, you never did," said the mother.

But the boy died in the night.

And even as he lay dead, his mother heard her brother's voice saying to her: "My God, Hester, you're eighty-odd thousand to the good and a poor devil of a son to the bad. But, poor devil, poor devil, he's best gone out of a life where he rides his rocking-horse to find a winner."

Critical Analysis

THIS STORY could be described, on one level, as a tale of a boy who gave his life in a futile attempt to provide his insatiable mother with enough money. Approached differently, it might be seen as a kind of ghost story in which the main interest lies in the mystery of the unexplained power which enabled the boy to pick the winner in a horse race. Incomplete or distorted analyses of the story might pursue either of these directions and neglect the other. A close examination of Lawrence's methods, however, will show how the two elements fit together and how the story at once arouses and satisfies the reader's interest in a melodramatic suspense, in "psychology," and in a theme.

The story begins very simply: "There was a woman who was beautiful, who started with all the advantages, yet she had no luck." It is almost the style of a fairy tale, and the fresh, naive style is important in putting the reader in the frame of mind necessary for the story which is to follow. We must, in fact, believe something which has no obvious natural explanation, so we are urged subtly to adopt for a moment that kind of wonder and suspension of disbelief which we used to feel when we read Grimm or Hans Christian Andersen. As the story progresses, however, this style changes and becomes more intense. It is directly related to the mounting excitement of the story, with the psychological element in it.

How much is psychological and how much is moral? In the first place, the reader must recognize that the attitude toward horse racing and betting on the horses is thoroughly British; there is no hint in the story of disapproval of betting *as such*. The moral concern is rather over the quality in some people which always makes them want more money. This moral concern is developed psychologically: the need for more money in the family is presented, not as something that anybody says, not as an external fact established in the story by a glance at the family bank book or the mention of a pile of bills on the first of the month, but as something *felt*.

And so the house came to be haunted by the unspoken phrase: There must be more money! There must be more money!

This is the kind of haunted house which even the most skeptical reader will be prepared to accept, and Lawrence reinforces the effect by relating the whisper to the children's expensive toys:

The children could hear it all the time, though nobody said it aloud. They heard it at Christmas, when the expensive and splendid toys filled the nursery. Behind the shining modern rocking-horse, behind the smart doll's house, a voice would start whispering. . . .

It is a short step from this point to attributing the feeling to the toys themselves: ". . . even the horse, bending his wooden, champing head, heard it." By this innocent and subtle method the reader is prepared for the tremendous role of the rocking horse in the climax of the story. But even more important, the *antagonist* in the story has been created. Here is the force against which the hero is to throw himself and perish.

If such a disembodied force is to be a character in the story, there must be careful handling of the characters who are people, so that the composition does not become confused. Notice how vague are the outlines of Paul's mother and father. The father is described as going into town to "some office," and when the mother tries to earn money, she is said to try "this thing and the other." The mother is not even named—she is always Paul's mother—until the very end of the story, when she is no longer Paul's mother and the author allows Oscar to call her by her name, Hester.

The central role of Paul in the story demands careful atten-

tion. Frequently Lawrence takes us close to the point of view of
Paul, and some readers might say that the vagueness about his
father's business or his mother's attempts to make money merely
indicates the normal child's vagueness about such matters. But the
story cannot really be told from Paul's point of view, for several
reasons. The suspense of the story would be ruined if the reader
knew immediately all that went on in Paul's mind. The "secret
within a secret" could not be held back from the reader. Moreover, the emotional quality of the ending would be changed; if
we had followed the story exclusively through Paul's eyes and
feelings, the ending would be pathetic and maudlin. As it is, there
is enough distance so that a tragic feeling is possible.

As mediators between the reader's natural skepticism and the
fantasy element in the plot stand Uncle Oscar and Bassett. They
are both men of practical common sense, Bassett with his repeated
"It's as if he had it from heaven" and his respectful suggestion to
his social superior that when you have a good thing you shouldn't
refuse it just because you don't understand it—"If Master Paul
offers you to be partners, sir, I would, if I were you; if you'll excuse me"—and Uncle Oscar with his sense of humor and his cautious indulgence of his nephew. Oscar is developed very fully.
He is introduced first unobtrusively, as the owner of the car
which Paul's family borrows, as the source of the phrase "filthy
lucre" which confused Paul, as the donor of the whip, the unconscious planter of the idea of "riding a winner" and the donor of
the ten shillings which started Paul on his winning streak. When
Oscar emerges into the foreground as an important character,
he serves the purpose of expressing the reader's doubts. "Oscar
Cresswell thought about it. 'I'll see the money,' he said." But the
joke is on Uncle Oscar, as it will be on the reader if he is too
skeptical. When the Leger is run, Oscar bets only two hundred
pounds, while the humble and conservative Bassett bets five hundred and the boy a thousand. When their horse wins at the odds
of ten to one, Paul is not a bit surprised: " 'You see,' he said, 'I was

absolutely sure of him.' Even Oscar Cresswell had cleared two thousand. 'Look here, son,' he said, 'this sort of thing makes me nervous.'" Lawrence exploits the comic irony of Cresswell's situation, but not to the extent of forfeiting our sympathy with him. So his final bet, on Malabar in the Derby, is made "in spite of himself." And Uncle Oscar is saved to be the speaker of the epitaph for Paul.

Despite the skill and subtlety with which the characters are presented, this is not primarily a story of character. Certain symbols in the story have much more vitality than any of the people in it, and as we have already pointed out, one of the chief characters is not a person but a feeling, a fear, expressed in the unspoken whispers which are as real as breathing. From the very first sentence of the story, "luck" is used as a symbol. In the story as a whole, it seems to be the opposite of, or a substitute for, love. Paul's pursuit of "luck" might be translated as a pursuit of love, if he had been able to understand rightly what he wanted. Then why, if this is what Lawrence means, does he not say so? The answer must be that love is not a concept, to be understood rationally, any more than "luck" is. It must be felt. And he very carefully shows that the absence of love on the part of Paul's mother is not mere failure in kindness, gentleness, or consideration: she is a good mother in these respects, and everybody says so. It is "a hard little place" at the center of her heart; she knows it is there and her children know it is there. "They read it in each other's eyes."

The dialogue between Paul and his mother on the subject of luck is very interesting. Superficially, it is merely a step in the education of the boy; he is learning about an adult idea. But notice how much more Lawrence conveys in this dialogue than is actually expressed in the speeches of the characters; the mother's answers are given "slowly and bitterly," "bitterly," "again with a laugh, but rather bitter." Paul, on the other hand, shows more from his silences than he does from his words. "The boy was

546

silent for some time." "The boy watched her with unsure eyes."
"The child looked at her, to see if she meant it." It is in this
dialogue that the boy's hunger for love is betrayed, distorted into
the pursuit of luck. But Lawrence is writing a story in which
suspense is important, and the revelations here are carefully controlled. Very unobtrusively he prepares for the bitter irony of
the end:

> "Well, anyhow," he said stoutly, "I'm a lucky person."
> "Why?" said his mother, with a sudden laugh.

Paul's last words, as he lies dying, return to this:

> "Mother, did I ever tell you? I am lucky."
> "No, you never did," said the mother.
> But the boy died in the night.

The condemnation of the mother could hardly be more violent,
but the irony does not stop here. It continues, to underline Oscar's
last words and to force upon us the feeling that Paul was luckier
than he knew.

The last three-fourths of the story is devoted to the discovery
of Paul's secret; this is done gradually, with some humor, as the
character of Uncle Oscar emerges. But at the same time the des-
peration of the mother increases, the whispering increases so
that after the birthday and the mother's receipt of five thousand
pounds the voices are screaming. What we have is a building up
of Paul's confidence and strength as Uncle Oscar and Bassett
seem mere attendants on him, but at the same time the antagonist
is growing in strength too, and the way is prepared for the great
tragic climax. Lawrence does full justice to the theatrical quality
of the scene; the mother's uneasiness at the party, the vague, mysterious noise, the dark bedroom and the sudden blaze of light
bringing out the two figures, the boy in his green pyjamas "madly
surging" and the mother "as she stood, blonde, in her dress of
pale green and crystal, in the doorway." The difference between
them is immediately shown in their lines,

"Paul!" she cried. "Whatever are you doing?"
"It's Malabar!" he screamed, in a powerful, strange voice.

Even in all this theatricality the values of the symbols are not lost. Paul's fever and the mother's coldness (now become a coldness of the heart somewhat different from her first state) show us the equivalents in feeling of love and luck.

The Rocking-Horse Winner is not a cheap story with the obvious sentimental moral that life without love is worse than death; it is not a psychological thriller about a boy with extrasensory perception who dies in the act of trying to predict the outcome of the Derby; it is not merely a satire on people who never have enough money, no matter how much they have. Each of these descriptions is wrong because it is incomplete, because it does violence to the particular and individual character of the story. A satisfactory analysis must be one which responds to the way in which Lawrence has woven together character and symbol, theme and plot tension. These elements do not exist separately, they must be seen in relationship to each other. The only reason for taking them apart is to put them back together again and appreciate them more fully.

The Celestial Omnibus

E. M. FORSTER (1879–   )

THE BOY who resided at Agathox Lodge, 28, Buckingham Park Road, Surbiton, had often been puzzled by the old sign-post that stood almost opposite. He asked his mother about it, and she replied that it was a joke, and not a very nice one, which had been

THE CELESTIAL OMNIBUS is reprinted from *The Celestial Omnibus* by E. M. Forster, by permission of Alfred A. Knopf, Inc.

made many years back by some naughty young men, and that the police ought to remove it. For there were two strange things about this sign-post: firstly, it pointed up a blank alley, and, secondly, it had painted on it, in faded characters, the words, "To Heaven."

"What kind of young men were they?" he asked.

"I think your father told me that one of them wrote verses, and was expelled from the University and came to grief in other ways. Still, it was a long time ago. You must ask your father about it. He will say the same as I do, that it was put up as a joke."

"So it doesn't mean anything at all?"

She sent him upstairs to put on his best things, for the Bonses were coming to tea, and he was to hand the cakestand.

It struck him, as he wrenched on his tightening trousers, that he might do worse than ask Mr. Bons about the sign-post. His father, though very kind, always laughed at him—shrieked with laughter whenever he or any other child asked a question or spoke. But Mr. Bons was serious as well as kind. He had a beautiful house and lent one books, he was a churchwarden, and a candidate for the County Council; he had donated to the Free Library enormously, he presided over the Literary Society, and had Members of Parliament to stop with him—in short, he was probably the wisest person alive.

Yet even Mr. Bons could only say that the sign-post was a joke —the joke of a person named Shelley.

"Of course!" cried the mother; "I told you so, dear. That was the name."

"Had you ever heard of Shelley?" asked Mr. Bons.

"No," said the boy, and hung his head.

"But is there no Shelley in the house?"

"Why, yes!" exclaimed the lady, in much agitation. "Dear Mr. Bons, we aren't such Philistines as that. Two at the least. One a wedding present, and the other, smaller print, in one of the spare rooms."

"I believe we have seven Shelleys," said Mr. Bons, with a slow smile. Then he brushed the cake crumbs off his stomach, and, together with his daughter, rose to go.

The boy, obeying a wink from his mother, saw them all the way to the garden gate, and when they had gone he did not at once return to the house, but gazed for a little up and down Buckingham Park Road.

His parents lived at the right end of it. After No. 39 the quality of the houses dropped very suddenly, and 64 had not even a separate servants' entrance. But at the present moment the whole road looked rather pretty, for the sun had just set in splendour, and the inequalities of rent were drowned in a saffron afterglow. Small birds twittered, and the breadwinners' train shrieked musically down through the cutting—that wonderful cutting which has drawn to itself the whole beauty out of Surbiton, and clad itself, like any Alpine valley, with the glory of the fir and the silver birch and the primrose. It was this cutting that had first stirred desires within the boy—desires for something just a little different, he knew not what, desires that would return whenever things were sunlit, as they were this evening, running up and down inside him, up and down, up and down, till he would feel quite unusual all over, and as likely as not would want to cry. This evening he was even sillier, for he slipped across the road towards the sign-post and began to run up the blank alley.

The alley runs between high walls—the walls of the gardens of "Ivanhoe" and "Bella Vista," respectively. It smells a little all the way, and is scarcely twenty yards long, including the turn at the end. So not unnaturally the boy soon came to a standstill. "I'd like to kick that Shelley," he exclaimed, and glanced idly at a piece of paper which was pasted on the wall. Rather an odd piece of paper, and he read it carefully before he turned back. This is what he read:

S. AND C.R.C.C.

ALTERATION IN SERVICE

Owing to lack of patronage the Company are regretfully compelled to suspend the hourly service, and to retain only the

Sunrise and Sunset Omnibuses,

which will run as usual. It is to be hoped that the public will patronize an arrangement which is intended for their convenience. As an extra inducement, the Company will, for the first time, now issue

Return Tickets!

(available one day only), which may be obtained of the driver. Passengers are again reminded that *no tickets are issued at the other end,* and that no complaints in this connection will receive consideration from the Company. Nor will the Company be responsible for any negligence or stupidity on the part of Passengers, nor for Hailstorms, Lightning, Loss of Tickets, nor for any Act of God.

For the Direction.

Now he had never seen this notice before, nor could he imagine where the omnibus went to. S. of course was for Surbiton, and R.C.C. meant Road Car Company. But what was the meaning of the other C.? Coombe and Malden, perhaps, or possibly "City." Yet it could not hope to compete with the South-Western. The whole thing, the boy reflected, was run on hopelessly unbusinesslike lines. Why no tickets from the other end? And what an hour to start! Then he realized that unless the notice was a hoax, an omnibus must have been starting just as he was wishing the Bonses good-bye. He peered at the ground through the gathering dusk, and there he saw what might or might not be the marks of wheels. Yet nothing had come out of the alley. And he had never seen an omnibus at any time in the Buckingham Park Road. No:

it must be a hoax, like the sign-post, like the fairy tales, like the dreams upon which he would wake suddenly in the night. And with a sigh he stepped from the alley—right into the arms of his father.

Oh, how his father laughed! "Poor, poor Popsey!" he cried. "Diddums! Diddums! Diddums think he'd walky-palky up to Evink!" And his mother, also convulsed with laughter, appeared on the steps of Agathox Lodge.

"Don't, Bob!" she gasped. "Don't be so naughty! Oh, you'll kill me! Oh, leave the boy alone!"

But all that evening the joke was kept up. The father implored to be taken too. Was it a very tiring walk? Need one wipe one's shoes on the door-mat? And the boy went to bed feeling faint and sore, and thankful for only one thing—that he had not said a word about the omnibus. It was a hoax, yet through his dreams it grew more and more real, and the streets of Surbiton, through which he saw it driving, seemed instead to become hoaxes and shadows. And very early in the morning he woke with a cry, for he had had a glimpse of its destination.

He struck a match, and its light fell not only on his watch but also on his calendar, so that he knew it to be half-an-hour to sunrise. It was pitch dark, for the fog had come down from London in the night, and all Surbiton was wrapped in its embraces. Yet he sprang out and dressed himself, for he was determined to settle once for all which was real: the omnibus or the streets. "I shall be a fool one way or the other," he thought, "until I know." Soon he was shivering in the road under the gas lamp that guarded the entrance to the alley.

To enter the alley itself required some courage. Not only was it horribly dark, but he now realized that it was an impossible terminus for an omnibus. If it had not been for a policeman, whom he heard approaching through the fog, he would never have made the attempt. The next moment he had made the attempt and failed. Nothing. Nothing but a blank alley and a very silly boy gaping at its dirty floor. It *was* a hoax. "I'll tell papa and mamma," he decided. "I deserve it. I deserve that they should know. I am too silly to be alive." And he went back to the gate of Agathox Lodge.

There he remembered that his watch was fast. The sun was not risen; it would not rise for two minutes. "Give the bus every chance," he thought cynically, and returned into the alley.

But the omnibus was there.

II

It had two horses, whose sides were still smoking from their journey, and its two great lamps shone through the fog against the alley's walls, changing their cobwebs and moss into tissues of fairyland. The driver was huddled up in a cape. He faced the blank wall, and how he had managed to drive in so neatly and so silently was one of the many things that the boy never discovered. Nor could he imagine how ever he would drive out.

"Please," his voice quavered through the foul brown air, "please, is that an omnibus?"

"Omnibus est," said the driver, without turning round. There was a moment's silence. The policeman passed, coughing, by the entrance of the alley. The boy crouched in the shadow, for he did not want to be found out. He was pretty sure, too, that it was a Pirate; nothing else, he reasoned, would go from such odd places and at such odd hours.

"About when do you start?" He tried to sound nonchalant.

"At sunrise."

"How far do you go?"

"The whole way."

"And can I have a return ticket which will bring me all the way back?"

"You can."

"Do you know, I half think I'll come." The driver made no answer. The sun must have risen, for he unhitched the brake. And scarcely had the boy jumped in before the omnibus was off.

How? Did it turn? There was no room. Did it go forward?

There was a blank wall. Yet it was moving—moving at a stately pace through the fog, which had turned from brown to yellow. The thought of warm bed and warmer breakfast made the boy feel faint. He wished he had not come. His parents would not have approved. He would have gone back to them if the weather had not made it impossible. The solitude was terrible; he was the only passenger. And the omnibus, though well-built, was cold and somewhat musty. He drew his coat round him, and in so doing chanced to feel his pocket. It was empty. He had forgotten his purse.

"Stop!" he shouted. "Stop!" And then, being of a polite disposition, he glanced up at the painted notice-board so that he might call the driver by name. "Mr. Browne! stop; oh, do please stop!"

Mr. Browne did not stop, but he opened a little window and looked in at the boy. His face was a surprise, so kind it was and modest.

"Mr. Browne, I've left my purse behind. I've not got a penny. I can't pay for the ticket. Will you take my watch, please? I am in the most awful hole."

"Tickets on this line," said the driver, "whether single or return, can be purchased by coinage from no terrene mint. And a chronometer, though it had solaced the vigils of Charlemagne, or measured the slumbers of Laura, can acquire by no mutation the double-cake that charms the fangless Cerberus of Heaven!" So saying, he handed in the necessary ticket, and, while the boy said "Thank you," continued, "Titular pretensions, I know it well, are vanity. Yet they merit no censure when uttered on a laughing lip, and in an homonymous world are in some sort useful, since they do serve to distinguish one Jack from his fellow. Remember me, therefore, as Sir Thomas Browne."

"Are you a Sir? Oh, sorry!" He had heard of these gentlemen drivers. "It *is* good of you about the ticket. But if you go on at this rate, however does your bus pay?"

"It does not pay. It was not intended to pay. Many are the

faults of my equipage; it is compounded too curiously of foreign woods; its cushions tickle erudition rather than promote repose; and my horses are nourished not on the evergreen pastures of the moment, but on the dried bents and clovers of Latinity. But that it pays!—that error at all events was never intended and never attained."

"Sorry again," said the boy rather hopelessly. Sir Thomas looked sad, fearing that, even for a moment, he had been the cause of sadness. He invited the boy to come up and sit beside him on the box, and together they journeyed on through the fog, which was now changing from yellow to white. There were no houses by the road; so it must be either Putney Heath or Wimbledon Common.

"Have you been a driver always?"

"I was a physician once."

"But why did you stop? Weren't you good?"

"As a healer of bodies I had scant success, and several score of my patients preceded me. But as a healer of the spirit I have succeeded beyond my hopes and my deserts. For though my draughts were not better nor subtler than those of other men, yet, by reason of the cunning goblets wherein I offered them, the queasy soul was ofttimes tempted to sip and be refreshed."

"The queasy soul," the boy murmured; "if the sun sets with trees in front of it, and you suddenly come strange all over, is that a queasy soul?"

"Have you felt that?"

"Why, yes."

After a pause he told the boy a little, a very little, about the journey's end. But they did not chatter much, for the boy, when he liked a person, would as soon sit silent in his company as speak, and this, he discovered, was also the mind of Sir Thomas Browne and of many others with whom he was to be acquainted. He heard, however, about the young man Shelley, who was now quite a famous person, with a carriage of his own, and about some of the other drivers who are in the service of the Company.

Meanwhile the light grew stronger, though the fog did not disperse. It was now more like mist than fog, and at times would travel quickly across them, as if it was part of a cloud. They had been ascending, too, in a most puzzling way; for over two hours the horses had been pulling against the collar, and even if it were Richmond Hill they ought to have been at the top long ago. Perhaps it was Epsom, or even the North Downs; yet the air seemed keener than that which blows on either. And as to the name of their destination, Sir Thomas Browne was silent.

Crash!

"Thunder, by Jove!" said the boy, "and not so far off either. Listen to the echoes! It's more like mountains."

He thought, not very vividly, of his father and mother. He saw them sitting down to sausages and listening to the storm. He saw his own empty place. Then there would be questions, alarms, theories, jokes, consolations. They would expect him back at lunch. To lunch he would not come, nor to tea, but he would be in for dinner, and so his day's truancy would be over. If he had had his purse he would have bought them presents— not that he should have known what to get them.

Crash!

The peal and the lightning came together. The cloud quivered as if it were alive, and torn streamers of mist rushed past. "Are you afraid?" asked Sir Thomas Browne.

"What is there to be afraid of? Is it much farther?"

The horses of the omnibus stopped just as a ball of fire burst up and exploded with a ringing noise that was deafening but clear, like the noise of a blacksmith's forge. All the cloud was shattered.

"Oh, listen, Sir Thomas Browne! No, I mean look; we shall get a view at last. No, I mean listen; that sounds like a rainbow!"

The noise had died into the faintest murmur, beneath which another murmur grew, spreading stealthily, steadily, in a curve that widened but did not vary. And in widening curves a rainbow was spreading from the horses' feet into the dissolving mists.

"But how beautiful! What colours! Where will it stop? It is more like the rainbows you can tread on. More like dreams."

The colour and the sound grew together. The rainbow spanned an enormous gulf. Clouds rushed under it and were pierced by it, and still it grew, reaching forward, conquering the darkness, until it touched something that seemed more solid than a cloud.

The boy stood up. "What is that out there?" he called. "What does it rest on, out at that other end?"

In the morning sunshine a precipice shone forth beyond the gulf. A precipice—or was it a castle? The horses moved. They set their feet upon the rainbow.

"Oh, look!" the boy shouted. "Oh, listen! Those caves—or are they gateways? Oh, look between those cliffs at those ledges. I see people! I see trees!"

"Look also below," whispered Sir Thomas. "Neglect not the diviner Acheron."

The boy looked below, past the flames of the rainbow that licked against their wheels. The gulf also had cleared, and in its depths there flowed an everlasting river. One sunbeam entered and struck a green pool, and as they passed over he saw three maidens rise to the surface of the pool, singing, and playing with something that glistened like a ring.

"You down in the water—" he called.

They answered, "You up on the bridge—" There was a burst of music. "You up on the bridge, good luck to you. Truth in the depth, truth on the height."

"You down in the water, what are you doing?"

Sir Thomas Browne replied: "They sport in the mancipiary possession of their gold"; and the omnibus arrived.

III

The boy was in disgrace. He sat locked up in the nursery of Agathox Lodge, learning poetry for a punishment. His father had said, "My boy! I can pardon anything but untruthfulness," and had caned him, saying at each stroke, "There is *no* omnibus, *no* driver, *no* bridge, *no* mountain; you are a *truant*, a *gutter snipe*, a *liar*." His father could be very stern at times. His mother had begged him to say he was sorry. But he could not say that. It was the greatest day of his life, in spite of the caning and the poetry at the end of it.

He had returned punctually at sunset—driven not by Sir Thomas Browne, but by a maiden lady who was full of quiet fun. They had talked of omnibuses and also of barouche landaus. How far away her gentle voice seemed now! Yet it was scarcely three hours since he had left her up the alley.

His mother called through the door. "Dear, you are to come down and to bring your poetry with you."

He came down, and found that Mr. Bons was in the smoking-room with his father. It had been a dinner party.

"Here is the great traveller!" said his father grimly. "Here is the young gentleman who drives in an omnibus over rain-bows, while young ladies sing to him." Pleased with his wit, he laughed.

"After all," said Mr. Bons, smiling, "there is something a little like it in Wagner. It is odd how, in quite illiterate minds, you will find glimmers of Artistic Truth. The case interests me. Let me plead for the culprit. We have all romanced in our time, haven't we?"

"Hear how kind Mr. Bons is," said his mother, while his father said, "Very well. Let him say his Poem, and that will do. He is going away to my sister on Tuesday, and *she* will cure him of this alley-slopering." (Laughter.) "Say your Poem."

The boy began. " 'Standing aloof in giant ignorance.' "

His father laughed again—roared. "One for you, my son! 'Standing aloof in giant ignorance!' I never knew these poets talked sense. Just describes you. Here, Bons, you go in for poetry. Put him through it, will you, while I fetch up the whisky?"

"Yes, give me the Keats," said Mr. Bons. "Let him say his Keats to me."

So for a few moments the wise man and the ignorant boy were left alone in the smoking-room.

" 'Standing aloof in giant ignorance, of thee I dream and of the Cyclades, as one who sits ashore and longs perchance to visit—' " [1]

"Quite right. To visit what?"

" 'To visit dolphin coral in deep seas,' " said the boy, and burst into tears.

"Come, come! why do you cry?"

"Because—because all these words that only rhymed before, now that I've come back they're me."

Mr. Bons laid the Keats down. The case was more interesting than he had expected. "*You?*" he exclaimed. "This sonnet, *you?*"

"Yes—and look further on: 'Aye, on the shores of darkness there is light, and precipices show untrodden green.' It *is* so, sir. All these things are true."

"I never doubted it," said Mr. Bons, with closed eyes.

"You—then you believe me? You believe in the omnibus and the driver and the storm and that return ticket I got for nothing and—"

"Tut, tut! No more of your yarns, my boy. I meant that I never doubted the essential truth of Poetry. Some day, when you have read more, you will understand what I mean."

"But, Mr. Bons, it *is* so. There *is* light upon the shores of darkness. I have seen it coming. Light and a wind."

"Nonsense," said Mr. Bons.

"If I had stopped! They tempted me. They told me to give up my ticket—for you cannot come back if you lose your ticket. They called from the river for it, and indeed I was tempted, for I have never been so happy as among those precipices. But I thought of my mother and father, and that I must fetch them. Yet they will not come, though the road starts opposite our house. It has all happened as the people up there warned me, and Mr.

[1] *Editors' note:* The boy is reciting Keats's sonnet *To Homer*, given in full in the last part of this book.

Bons has disbelieved me like everyone else. I have been caned. I shall never see that mountain again."

"What's that about me?" said Mr. Bons, sitting up in his chair very suddenly.

"I told them about you, and how clever you were, and how many books you had, and they said, 'Mr. Bons will certainly disbelieve you.'"

"Stuff and nonsense, my young friend. You grow impertinent. I—well—I will settle the matter. Not a word to your father. I will cure you. Tomorrow evening I will myself call here to take you for a walk, and at sunset we will go up this alley opposite and hunt for your omnibus, you silly little boy."

His face grew serious, for the boy was not disconcerted, but leapt about the room singing, "Joy! joy! I told them you would believe me. We will drive together over the rainbow. I told them that you would come." After all, could there be anything in the story? Wagner? Keats? Shelley? Sir Thomas Browne? Certainly the case was interesting.

And on the morrow evening, though it was pouring with rain, Mr. Bons did not omit to call at Agathox Lodge.

The boy was ready, bubbling with excitement, and skipping about in a way that rather vexed the President of the Literary Society. They took a turn down Buckingham Park Road, and then—having seen that no one was watching them—slipped up the alley. Naturally enough (for the sun was setting) they ran straight against the omnibus.

"Good heavens!" exclaimed Mr. Bons. "Good gracious heavens!"

It was not the omnibus in which the boy had driven first, nor yet that in which he had returned. There were three horses—black, gray, and white, the gray being the finest. The driver, who turned round at the mention of goodness and of heaven, was a sallow man with terrifying jaws and sunken eyes. Mr. Bons, on seeing him, gave a cry as if of recognition, and began to tremble violently.

The boy jumped in.

"Is it possible?" cried Mr. Bons. "Is the impossible possible?"

"Sir; come in, sir. It is such a fine omnibus. Oh, here is his name —Dan someone."

Mr. Bons sprang in too. A blast of wind immediately slammed the omnibus door, and the shock jerked down all the omnibus blinds, which were very weak on their springs.

"Dan . . . Show me. Good gracious heavens! We're moving."

"Hooray!" said the boy.

Mr. Bons became flustered. He had not intended to be kidnapped. He could not find the door-handle nor push up the blinds. The omnibus was quite dark, and by the time he had struck a match, night had come on outside also. They were moving rapidly.

"A strange, a memorable adventure," he said, surveying the interior of the omnibus, which was large, roomy, and constructed with extreme regularity, every part exactly answering to every other part. Over the door (the handle of which was outside) was written, "Lasciate ogni baldanza voi che entrate"—at least, that was what was written, but Mr. Bons said that it was Lashy arty something, and that baldanza was a mistake for speranza. His voice sounded as if he was in church. Meanwhile, the boy called to the cadaverous driver for two return tickets. They were handed in without a word. Mr. Bons covered his face with his hand and again trembled. "Do you know who that is!" he whispered, when the little window had shut upon them. "It is the impossible."

"Well, I don't like him as much as Sir Thomas Browne, though I shouldn't be surprised if he had even more in him."

"More in him?" He stamped irritably. "By accident you have made the greatest discovery of the century, and all you can say is that there is more in this man. Do you remember those vellum books in my library, stamped with red lilies? This—sit still, I bring you stupendous news!—*this is the man who wrote them*."

The boy sat quite still. "I wonder if we shall see Mrs. Gamp?" he asked, after a civil pause.

"Mrs.—?"

"Mrs. Gamp and Mrs. Harris. I like Mrs. Harris. I came upon them quite suddenly. Mrs. Gamp's bandboxes have moved over the rainbow so badly. All the bottoms have fallen out, and two of the pippins off her bedstead tumbled into the stream."

"Out there sits the man who wrote my vellum books!" thundered Mr. Bons, "and you talk to me of Dickens and of Mrs. Gamp?"

"I know Mrs. Gamp so well," he apologized. "I could not help being glad to see her. I recognized her voice. She was telling Mrs. Harris about Mrs. Prig."

"Did you spend the whole day in her elevating company?"

"Oh, no. I raced. I met a man who took me out beyond to a race-course. You run, and there are dolphins out at sea."

"Indeed. Do you remember the man's name?"

"Achilles. No; he was later. Tom Jones."

Mr. Bons sighed heavily. "Well, my lad, you have made a miserable mess of it. Think of a cultured person with your opportunities! A cultured person would have known all these characters and known what to have said to each. He would not have wasted his time with a Mrs. Gamp or a Tom Jones. The creations of Homer, of Shakespeare, and of Him who drives us now, would alone have contented him. He would not have raced. He would have asked intelligent questions."

"But, Mr. Bons," said the boy humbly, "you will be a cultured person. I told them so."

"True, true, and I beg you not to disgrace me when we arrive. No gossiping. No running. Keep close to my side, and never speak to these Immortals unless they speak to you. Yes, and give me the return tickets. You will be losing them."

The boy surrendered the tickets, but felt a little sore. After all, he had found the way to this place. It was hard first to be disbelieved and then to be lectured. Meanwhile, the rain had stopped, and moonlight crept into the omnibus through the cracks in the blinds.

"But how is there to be a rainbow?" cried the boy.

"You distract me," snapped Mr. Bons. "I wish to meditate on beauty. I wish to goodness I was with a reverent and sympathetic person."

The lad bit his lip. He made good resolutions. He would imitate Mr. Bons all the visit. He would not laugh, or run, or sing, or do any of the vulgar things that must have disgusted his new friends last time. He would be very careful to pronounce their names properly, and to remember who knew whom. Achilles did not know Tom Jones—at least, so Mr. Bons said. The Duchess of Malfi was older than Mrs. Gamp—at least, so Mr. Bons said. He would be self-conscious, reticent, and prim. He would never say he liked anyone. Yet, when the blind flew up at a chance touch of his head, all these good resolutions went to the winds, for the omnibus had reached the summit of a moonlit hill, and there was the chasm, and there, across it, stood the old precipices, dreaming, with their feet in the everlasting river. He exclaimed, "The mountain! Listen to the new tune in the water! Look at the camp fires in the ravines," and Mr. Bons, after a hasty glance, retorted, "Water? Camp fires? Ridiculous rubbish. Hold your tongue. There is nothing at all."

Yet, under his eyes, a rainbow formed, compounded not of sunlight and storm, but of moonlight and the spray of the river. The three horses put their feet upon it. He thought it the finest rainbow he had seen, but did not dare to say so, since Mr. Bons said that nothing was there. He leant out—the window had opened—and sang the tune that rose from the sleeping waters.

"The prelude of Rhinegold?" said Mr. Bons suddenly. "Who taught you these *leit motifs*?" He, too, looked out of the window. Then he behaved very oddly. He gave a choking cry and fell back onto the omnibus floor. He writhed and kicked. His face was green.

"Does the bridge make you dizzy?" the boy asked.

"Dizzy!" gasped Mr. Bons. "I want to go back. Tell the driver."

But the driver shook his head.

"We are nearly there," said the boy. "They are asleep. Shall I call? They will be so pleased to see you, for I have prepared them."

Mr. Bons moaned. They moved over the lunar rainbow, which ever and ever broke away behind their wheels. How still the night was! Who would be sentry at the Gate?

"I am coming," he shouted, again forgetting the hundred resolutions. "I am returning—I, the boy."

"The boy is returning," cried a voice to other voices, who repeated, "The boy is returning."

"I am bringing Mr. Bons with me."

Silence.

"I should have said Mr. Bons is bringing me with him."

Profound silence.

"Who stands sentry?"

"Achilles."

And on the rocky causeway, close to the springing of the rainbow bridge, he saw a young man who carried a wonderful shield.

"Mr. Bons, it is Achilles, armed."

"I want to go back," said Mr. Bons.

The last fragment of the rainbow melted, the wheels sang upon the living rock, the door of the omnibus burst open. Out leapt the boy—he could not resist—and sprang to meet the warrior, who, stooping suddenly, caught him on his shield.

"Achilles!" he cried, "let me get down, for I am ignorant and vulgar, and I must wait for that Mr. Bons of whom I told you yesterday."

But Achilles raised him aloft. He crouched on the wonderful shield, on heroes and burning cities, on vineyards graven in gold, on every dear passion, every joy, on the entire image of the Mountain that he had discovered, encircled, like it, with an everlasting stream. "No, no," he protested, "I am not worthy. It is Mr. Bons who must be up here."

But Mr. Bons was whimpering, and Achilles trumpeted and cried, "Stand upright upon my shield!"

"Sir, I did not mean to stand! something made me stand. Sir, why do you delay? Here is only the great Achilles, whom you knew."

Mr. Bons screamed, "I see no one. I see nothing. I want to go back." Then he cried to the driver, "Save me! Let me stop in your chariot. I have honoured you. I have quoted you. I have bound you in vellum. Take me back to my world."

The driver replied, "I am the means and not the end. I am the food and not the life. Stand by yourself, as that boy has stood. I cannot save you. For poetry is a spirit; and they that would worship it must worship in spirit and in truth."

Mr. Bons—he could not resist—crawled out of the beautiful omnibus. His face appeared, gaping horribly. His hands followed, one gripping the step, the other beating the air. Now his shoulders emerged, his chest, his stomach. With a shriek of "I see London," he fell—fell against the hard, moonlit rock, fell into it as if it were water, fell through it, vanished, and was seen by the boy no more.

"Where have you fallen to, Mr. Bons? Here is a procession arriving to honour you with music and torches. Here come the men and women whose names you know. The mountain is awake, the river is awake, over the race-course the sea is awaking those dolphins, and it is all for you. They want you—"

There was the touch of fresh leaves on his forehead. Someone had crowned him.

ΤΕΛΟΣ

✦

From the *Kingston Gazette, Surbiton Times*, and *Raynes Park Observer*.

The body of Mr. Septimus Bons has been found in a shockingly mutilated condition in the vicinity of the Bermondsey gasworks. The deceased's pockets contained a sovereign-purse, a silver cigar-case, a bijou pronouncing dictionary, and a couple of omnibus tickets. The unfortunate gentleman had apparently been hurled from a considerable height. Foul play is suspected, and a thorough investigation is pending by the authorities.

The Dead

JAMES JOYCE (1882–1941)

LILY, the caretaker's daughter, was literally run off her feet. Hardly had she brought one gentleman into the little pantry behind the office on the ground floor and helped him off with his overcoat than the wheezy hall-door bell clanged again and she had to scamper along the bare hallway to let in another guest. It was well for her she had not to attend to the ladies also. But Miss Kate and Miss Julia had thought of that and had converted the bathroom upstairs into a ladies' dressing-room. Miss Kate and Miss Julia were there, gossiping and laughing and fussing, walking after each other to the head of the stairs, peering down over the banisters and calling down to Lily to ask her who had come.

It was always a great affair, the Misses Morkan's annual dance. Everybody who knew them came to it, members of the family, old friends of the family, the members of Julia's choir, any of Kate's pupils that were grown up enough, and even some of Mary Jane's pupils too. Never once had it fallen flat. For years and years it had gone off in splendid style, as long as anyone could remember; ever since Kate and Julia, after the death of their brother

Pat, had left the house in Stoney Batter and taken Mary Jane, their only niece, to live with them in the dark, gaunt house on Usher's Island, the upper part of which they had rented from Mr. Fulham, the corn-factor on the ground floor. That was a good thirty years ago if it was a day. Mary Jane, who was then a little girl in short clothes, was now the main prop of the household, for she had the organ in Haddington Road. She had been through the Academy and gave a pupils' concert every year in the upper room of the Antient Concert Rooms. Many of her pupils belonged to the better-class families on the Kingstown and Dalkey line. Old as they were, her aunts also did their share. Julia, though she was quite grey, was still the leading soprano in Adam and Eve's, and Kate, being too feeble to go about much, gave music lessons to beginners on the old square piano in the back room. Lily, the caretaker's daughter, did housemaid's work for them. Though their life was modest, they believed in eating well; the best of everything: diamond-bone sirloins, three-shilling tea and the best bottled stout. But Lily seldom made a mistake in the orders, so that she got on well with her three mistresses. They were fussy, that was all. But the only thing they would not stand was back answers.

Of course, they had good reason to be fussy on such a night. And then it was long after ten o'clock and yet there was no sign of Gabriel and his wife. Besides they were dreadfully afraid that Freddy Malins might turn up screwed. They would not wish for worlds that any of Mary Jane's pupils should see him under the influence; and when he was like that it was sometimes very hard to manage him. Freddy Malins always came late, but they wondered what could be keeping Gabriel: and that was what brought them every two minutes to the banisters to ask Lily had Gabriel or Freddy come.

"O, Mr. Conroy," said Lily to Gabriel when she opened the door for him, "Miss Kate and Miss Julia thought you were never coming. Good-night, Mrs. Conroy."

"I'll engage they did," said Gabriel, "but they forget that my wife here takes three mortal hours to dress herself."

He stood on the mat, scraping the snow from his goloshes, while Lily led his wife to the foot of the stairs and called out:

"Miss Kate, here's Mrs. Conroy."

Kate and Julia came toddling down the dark stairs at once. Both of them kissed Gabriel's wife, said she must be perished alive, and asked was Gabriel with her.

"Here I am as right as the mail, Aunt Kate! Go on up. I'll follow," called out Gabriel from the dark.

He continued scraping his feet vigorously while the three women went upstairs, laughing, to the ladies' dressing-room. A light fringe of snow lay like a cape on the shoulders of his overcoat and like toecaps on the toes of his goloshes; and, as the buttons of his overcoat slipped with a squeaking noise through the snow-stiffened frieze, a cold, fragrant air from out-of-doors escaped from crevices and folds.

"Is it snowing again, Mr. Conroy?" asked Lily.

She had preceded him into the pantry to help him off with his overcoat. Gabriel smiled at the three syllables she had given his surname and glanced at her. She was a slim, growing girl, pale in complexion and with hay-coloured hair. The gas in the pantry made her look still paler. Gabriel had known her when she was a child and used to sit on the lowest step nursing a rag doll.

"Yes, Lily," he answered, "and I think we're in for a night of it."

He looked up at the pantry ceiling, which was shaking with the stamping and shuffling of feet on the floor above, listened for a moment to the piano and then glanced at the girl, who was folding his overcoat carefully at the end of a shelf.

"Tell me, Lily," he said in a friendly tone, "do you still go to school?"

"O no, sir," she answered. "I'm done schooling this year and more."

"O, then," said Gabriel gaily, "I suppose we'll be going to your wedding one of these fine days with your young man, eh?"

The girl glanced back at him over her shoulder and said with great bitterness:

"The men that is now is only all palaver and what they can get out of you."

Gabriel coloured, as if he felt he had made a mistake and, without looking at her, kicked off his goloshes and flicked actively with his muffler at his patent-leather shoes.

He was a stout, tallish young man. The high colour of his cheeks pushed upwards even to his forehead, where it scattered itself in a few formless patches of pale red; and on his hairless face there scintillated restlessly the polished lenses and the bright gilt rims of the glasses which screened his delicate and restless eyes. His glossy black hair was parted in the middle and brushed in a long curve behind his ears where it curled slightly beneath the groove left by his hat.

When he had flicked lustre into his shoes he stood up and pulled his waistcoat down more tightly on his plump body. Then he took a coin rapidly from his pocket.

"O Lily," he said, thrusting it into her hands, "it's Christmas-time, isn't it? Just . . . here's a little . . ."

He walked rapidly towards the door.

"O no, sir!" cried the girl, following him. "Really, sir, I wouldn't take it."

"Christmas-time! Christmas-time!" said Gabriel, almost trotting to the stairs and waving his hand to her in deprecation.

The girl, seeing that he had gained the stairs, called out after him:

"Well, thank you, sir."

He waited outside the drawing-room door until the waltz should finish, listening to the skirts that swept against it and to the shuffling of feet. He was still discomposed by the girl's bitter and sudden retort. It had cast a gloom over him which he tried to dispel by arranging his cuffs and the bows of his tie. He then took from his waistcoat pocket a little paper and glanced at the headings he had made for his speech. He was undecided about the lines from Robert Browning, for he feared they would be above the heads of his hearers. Some quotation that they would recognise from Shakespeare or from the Melodies would be better. The indelicate clacking of the men's heels and the shuffling of their soles reminded him that their grade of culture differed from his. He would only make himself ridiculous by quoting poetry to them which they could not understand. They would think that he was airing his superior education. He would fail with them just as he had failed with the girl in the pantry. He had taken up a wrong tone. His whole speech was a mistake from first to last, an utter failure.

Just then his aunts and his wife came out of the ladies' dressing-room. His aunts were two small, plainly dressed old women. Aunt Julia was an inch or so the taller. Her hair, drawn low over the tops of her ears, was grey; and grey also, with darker shadows, was her large flaccid face. Though she was stout in build and stood erect, her slow eyes and parted lips gave her the appearance of a woman who did not know where she was or where she was going. Aunt Kate was more vivacious. Her face, healthier than her sister's, was all puckers and creases, like a shrivelled red apple, and her hair, braided in the same old-fashioned way, had not lost its ripe nut colour.

They both kissed Gabriel frankly. He was their favourite nephew, the son of their dead elder sister, Ellen, who had married T. J. Conroy of the Port and Docks.

"Gretta tells me you're not going to take a cab back to Monks-town tonight, Gabriel," said Aunt Kate.

"No," said Gabriel, turning to his wife, "we had quite enough of that last year, hadn't we? Don't you remember, Aunt Kate, what a cold Gretta got out of it? Cab windows rattling all the way, and the east wind blowing in after we passed Merrion. Very jolly it was. Gretta caught a dreadful cold."

Aunt Kate frowned severely and nodded her head at every word.

"Quite right, Gabriel, quite right," she said. "You can't be too careful."

"But as for Gretta there," said Gabriel, "she'd walk home in the snow if she were let."

Mrs. Conroy laughed.

"Don't mind him, Aunt Kate," she said. "He's really an awful bother, what with green shades for Tom's eyes at night and making him do the dumb-bells, and forcing Eva to eat the stirabout. The poor child! And she simply hates the sight of it! . . . O, but you'll never guess what he makes me wear now!"

She broke out into a peal of laughter and glanced at her husband, whose admiring and happy eyes had been wandering from her dress to her face and hair. The two aunts laughed heartily, too, for Gabriel's solicitude was a standing joke with them.

"Goloshes!" said Mrs. Conroy. "That's the latest. Whenever it's wet underfoot I must put on my goloshes. Tonight even, he wanted me to put them on, but I wouldn't. The next thing he'll buy me will be a diving suit."

Gabriel laughed nervously and patted his tie reassuringly, while Aunt Kate nearly doubled herself, so heartily did she enjoy the joke. The smile soon faded from Aunt Julia's face and her mirthless eyes were directed towards her nephew's face. After a pause she asked:

"And what are goloshes, Gabriel?"

"Goloshes, Julia!" exclaimed her sister. "Goodness me, don't you know what goloshes are? You wear them over your . . . over your boots, Gretta, isn't it?"

"Yes," said Mrs. Conroy. "Guttapercha things. We both have a pair now. Gabriel says everyone wears them on the Continent."

"O, on the Continent," murmured Aunt Julia, nodding her head slowly.

Gabriel knitted his brows and said, as if he were slightly angered:

"It's nothing very wonderful, but Gretta thinks it very funny because she says the word reminds her of Christy Minstrels."

"But tell me, Gabriel," said Aunt Kate, with brisk tact. "Of course, you've seen about the room. Gretta was saying . . ."

"O, the room is all right," replied Gabriel. "I've taken one in the Gresham."

"To be sure," said Aunt Kate, "by far the best thing to do. And the children, Gretta, you're not anxious about them?"

"O, for one night," said Mrs. Conroy. "Besides, Bessie will look after them."

"To be sure," said Aunt Kate again. "What a comfort it is to have a girl like that, one you can depend on! There's that Lily, I'm sure I don't know what has come over her lately. She's not the girl she was at all."

Gabriel was about to ask his aunt some questions on this point, but she broke off suddenly to gaze after her sister, who had wandered down the stairs and was craning her neck over the banisters.

"Now, I ask you," she said almost testily, "where is Julia going? Julia! Julia! Where are you going?"

Julia, who had gone half way down one flight, came back and announced blandly: "Here's Freddy."

At the same moment a clapping of hands and a final flourish of the pianist told that the waltz had ended. The drawing-room door was opened from within and some couples came out. Aunt Kate drew Gabriel aside hurriedly and whispered into his ear:

"Slip down, Gabriel, like a good fellow and see if he's all right, and don't let him up if he's screwed. I'm sure he's screwed. I'm sure he is."

Gabriel went to the stairs and listened over the banisters. He could hear two persons talking in the pantry. Then he recognised Freddy Malins' laugh. He went down the stairs noisily.

"It's such a relief," said Aunt Kate to Mrs. Conroy, "that Gabriel is here. I always feel easier in my mind when he's here. . . . Julia, there's Miss Daly and Miss Power will take some refreshment. Thanks for your beautiful waltz, Miss Daly. It made lovely time."

A tall wizen-faced man, with a stiff grizzled moustache and swarthy skin, who was passing out with his partner, said:

"And may we have some refreshment, too, Miss Morkan?"

"Julia," said Aunt Kate summarily, "and here's Mr. Browne and Miss Furlong. Take them in, Julia, with Miss Daly and Miss Power."

"I'm the man for the ladies," said Mr. Browne, pursing his lips until his moustache bristled and smiling in all his wrinkles. "You know, Miss Morkan, the reason they are so fond of me is—"

He did not finish his sentence, but, seeing that Aunt Kate was out of earshot, at once led the three young ladies into the back room. The middle of the room was occupied by two square tables placed end to end, and on these Aunt Julia and the caretaker were straightening and smoothing a large cloth. On the sideboard were arrayed dishes and plates, and glasses and bundles of knives and forks and spoons. The top of the closed square piano served also as a sideboard for viands and sweets. At a smaller sideboard in one corner two young men were standing, drinking hop-bitters.

Mr. Browne led his charges thither and invited them all, in jest, to some ladies' punch, hot, strong and sweet. As they said they never took anything strong, he opened three bottles of lemonade for them. Then he asked one of the young men to move aside, and, taking hold of the decanter, filled out for himself a goodly measure of whisky. The young men eyed him respectfully while he took a trial sip.

"God help me," he said, smiling, "it's the doctor's orders."

His wizened face broke into a broader smile, and the three young ladies laughed in musical echo to his pleasantry, swaying their bodies to and fro, with nervous jerks of their shoulders. The boldest said:

"O, now, Mr. Browne, I'm sure the doctor never ordered anything of the kind."

Mr. Browne took another sip of his whisky and said, with sidling mimicry:

"Well, you see, I'm like the famous Mrs. Cassidy, who is reported to have said: 'Now, Mary Grimes, if I don't take it, make me take it, for I feel I want it.' "

His hot face had leaned forward a little too confidentially and he had assumed a very low Dublin accent so that the young ladies, with one instinct, received his speech in silence. Miss Furlong, who was one of Mary Jane's pupils, asked Miss Daly what was the name of the pretty waltz she had played; and Mr. Browne, seeing that he was ignored, turned promptly to the two young men who were more appreciative.

A red-faced young woman, dressed in pansy, came into the room, excitedly clapping her hands and crying:

"Quadrilles! Quadrilles!"

Close on her heels came Aunt Kate, crying:

"Two gentlemen and three ladies, Mary Jane!"

"O, here's Mr. Bergin and Mr. Kerrigan," said Mary Jane. "Mr. Kerrigan, will you take Miss Power? Miss Furlong, may I get you a partner, Mr. Bergin. O, that'll just do now."

"Three ladies, Mary Jane," said Aunt Kate.

The two young gentlemen asked the ladies if they might have the pleasure, and Mary Jane turned to Miss Daly.

"O, Miss Daly, you're really awfully good, after playing for the last two dances, but really we're so short of ladies tonight."

"I don't mind in the least, Miss Morkan."

"But I've a nice partner for you, Mr. Bartell D'Arcy, the tenor. I'll get him to sing later on. All Dublin is raving about him."

"Lovely voice, lovely voice!" said Aunt Kate.

As the piano had twice begun the prelude to the first figure Mary Jane led her recruits quickly from the room. They had hardly gone when Aunt Julia wandered slowly into the room, looking behind her at something.

"What is the matter, Julia?" asked Aunt Kate anxiously. "Who is it?"

Julia, who was carrying in a column of table-napkins, turned to her sister and said, simply, as if the question had surprised her:

"It's only Freddy, Kate, and Gabriel with him."

In fact right behind her Gabriel could be seen piloting Freddy Malins across the landing. The latter, a young man of about forty, was of Gabriel's size and build, with very round shoulders. His face was fleshy and pallid, touched with colour only at the thick hanging lobes of his ears and at the wide wings of his nose. He had coarse features, a blunt nose, a convex and receding brow, tumid and protruded lips. His heavy-lidded eyes and the disorder of his scanty hair made him look sleepy. He was laughing heartily in a high key at a story which he had been telling Gabriel on the stairs and at the same time rubbing the knuckles of his left fist backwards and forwards into his left eye.

"Good evening, Freddy," said Aunt Julia.

Freddy Malins bade the Misses Morkan good-evening in what seemed an offhand fashion by reason of the habitual catch in his voice and then, seeing that Mr. Browne was grinning at him from the sideboard, crossed the room on rather shaky legs and began to repeat in an undertone the story he had just told to Gabriel.

"He's not so bad, is he?" said Aunt Kate to Gabriel.

Gabriel's brows were dark but he raised them quickly and answered:

"O, no, hardly noticeable."

"Now, isn't he a terrible fellow!" she said. "And his poor mother made him take the pledge on New Year's Eve. But come on, Gabriel, into the drawing-room."

Before leaving the room with Gabriel she signalled to Mr. Browne by frowning and shaking her forefinger in warning to and fro. Mr. Browne nodded in answer and, when she had gone, said to Freddy Malins:

"Now, then, Teddy, I'm going to fill you out a good glass of lemonade just to buck you up."

Freddy Malins, who was nearing the climax of his story, waved the offer aside impatiently but Mr. Browne, having first called Freddy Malins' attention to a disarray in his dress, filled out and handed him a full glass of lemonade. Freddy Malins' left hand accepted the glass mechanically, his right hand being engaged in the mechanical readjustment of his dress. Mr. Browne, whose face was once more wrinkling with mirth, poured out for himself a glass of whisky while Freddy Malins exploded, before he had well reached the climax of his story, in a kink of high-pitched bronchitic laughter and, setting down his untasted and overflowing glass, began to rub the knuckles of his left fist backwards and forwards into his left eye, repeating words of his last phrase as well as his fit of laughter would allow him.

. . . .

Gabriel could not listen while Mary Jane was playing her Academy piece, full of runs and difficult passages, to the hushed drawing-room. He liked music but the piece she was playing had no melody for him and he doubted whether it had any melody for the other listeners, though they had begged Mary Jane to play something. Four young men, who had come from the refreshment-room to stand in the doorway at the sound of the piano, had gone away quietly in couples after a few minutes. The only persons who seemed to follow the music were Mary Jane herself, her hands racing along the key-board or lifted from it at the pauses like those of a priestess in momentary imprecation, and Aunt Kate standing at her elbow to turn the page.

Gabriel's eyes, irritated by the floor, which glittered with bees-wax under the heavy chandelier, wandered to the wall above the piano. A picture of the balcony scene in *Romeo and Juliet* hung there and beside it was a picture of the two murdered princes in the Tower which Aunt Julia had worked in red, blue and brown wools when she was a girl. Probably in the school they had gone to as girls that kind of work had been taught for one year. His mother had worked for him as a birthday present a waistcoat of purple tabinet, with little foxes' heads upon it, lined with brown satin and having round mulberry buttons. It was strange that his mother had had no musical talent though Aunt Kate used to call her the brains carrier of the Morkan family. Both she and Julia had always seemed a little proud of their serious and matronly sister. Her photograph stood before the pierglass. She held an open book on her knees and was pointing out something in it to Constantine who, dressed in a man-o'-war suit, lay at her feet. It was she who had chosen the names of her sons for she was very sensible of the dignity of family life. Thanks to her, Constantine was now senior curate in Balbriggan and, thanks to her, Gabriel himself had taken his degree in the Royal University. A shadow passed over his face as he remembered her sullen opposition to his marriage. Some slighting phrases she had used still rankled in his memory; she had once spoken of Gretta as being country cute and that was not true of Gretta at all. It was Gretta who had nursed her during all her last long illness in their house at Monkstown.

He knew that Mary Jane must be near the end of her piece for she was playing again the opening melody with runs of scales after every bar and while he waited for the end the resentment died down in his heart. The piece ended with a trill of octaves in the treble and a final deep octave in the bass. Great applause greeted Mary Jane as, blushing and rolling up her music nervously, she escaped from the room. The most vigorous clapping came from the four young men in the doorway who had gone away to the refreshment-room at the beginning of the piece but had come back when the piano had stopped.

Lancers were arranged. Gabriel found himself partnered with Miss Ivors. She was a frank-mannered talkative young lady, with a freckled face and prominent brown eyes. She did not wear a low-cut bodice and the large brooch which was fixed in the front of her collar bore on it an Irish device and motto.

When they had taken their places she said abruptly:

"I have a crow to pluck with you."

"With me?" said Gabriel.

She nodded her head gravely.

"What is it?" asked Gabriel, smiling at her solemn manner.

"Who is G. C.?" answered Miss Ivors, turning her eyes upon him.

Gabriel coloured and was about to knit his brows, as if he did not understand, when she said bluntly:

"O, innocent Amy! I have found out that you write for *The Daily Express*. Now, aren't you ashamed of yourself?"

"Why should I be ashamed of myself?" asked Gabriel, blinking his eyes and trying to smile.

"Well, I'm ashamed of you," said Miss Ivors frankly. "To say you'd write for a paper like that. I didn't think you were a West Briton."

A look of perplexity appeared on Gabriel's face. It was true that he wrote a literary column every Wednesday in *The Daily Express*, for which he was paid fifteen shillings. But that did not make him a West Briton surely. The books he received for review were almost more welcome than the paltry cheque. He loved to feel the covers and turn over the pages of newly printed books. Nearly every day when his teaching in the college was ended he used to wander down the quays to the second-hand booksellers, to Hickey's on Bachelor's Walk, to Webb's or Massey's on Aston's Quay, or to O'Clohissey's in the by-street. He did not know how to meet her charge. He wanted to say that literature was above politics. But they were friends of many years' standing and their careers had been parallel, first at the University and then as teachers: he could not risk a grandiose phrase with her. He continued blinking his eyes and trying to smile and murmured lamely that he saw nothing political in writing reviews of books.

When their turn to cross had come he was still perplexed and inattentive. Miss Ivors promptly took his hand in a warm grasp and said in a soft friendly tone:

"Of course, I was only joking. Come, we cross now."

When they were together again she spoke of the University question and Gabriel felt more at ease. A friend of hers had shown her his review of Browning's poems. That was how she had found out the secret: but she liked the review immensely. Then she said suddenly:

"O, Mr. Conroy, will you come for an excursion to the Aran

Isles this summer? We're going to stay there a whole month. It will be splendid out in the Atlantic. You ought to come. Mr. Clancy is coming, and Mr. Kilkelly and Kathleen Kearney. It would be splendid for Gretta too if she'd come. She's from Connacht, isn't she?"

"Her people are," said Gabriel shortly.

"But you will come, won't you?" said Miss Ivors, laying her warm hand eagerly on his arm.

"The fact is," said Gabriel, "I have just arranged to go—"

"Go where?" asked Miss Ivors.

"Well, you know, every year I go for a cycling tour with some fellows and so—"

"But where?" asked Miss Ivors.

"Well, we usually go to France or Belgium or perhaps Germany," said Gabriel awkwardly.

"And why do you go to France and Belgium," said Miss Ivors, "instead of visiting your own land?"

"Well," said Gabriel, "it's partly to keep in touch with the languages and partly for a change."

"And haven't you your own language to keep in touch with—Irish?" asked Miss Ivors.

"Well," said Gabriel, "if it comes to that, you know, Irish is not my language."

Their neighbours had turned to listen to the cross-examination. Gabriel glanced right and left nervously and tried to keep his good humour under the ordeal which was making a blush invade his forehead.

"And haven't you your own land to visit," continued Miss Ivors, "that you know nothing of, your own people, and your own country?"

"O, to tell you the truth," retorted Gabriel suddenly, "I'm sick of my own country, sick of it!"

"Why?" asked Miss Ivors.

Gabriel did not answer for his retort had heated him.

"Why?" repeated Miss Ivors.

They had to go visiting together and, as he had not answered her, Miss Ivors said warmly:

"Of course, you've no answer."

Gabriel tried to cover his agitation by taking part in the dance with great energy. He avoided her eyes for he had seen a sour expression on her face. But when they met in the long chain he was surprised to feel his hand firmly pressed. She looked at him from under her brows for a moment quizzically until he smiled. Then, just as the chain was about to start again, she stood on tiptoe and whispered into his ear:

"West Briton!"

When the lancers were over Gabriel went away to a remote corner of the room where Freddy Malins' mother was sitting. She was a stout feeble old woman with white hair. Her voice had a catch in it like her son's and she stuttered slightly. She had been told that Freddy had come and that he was nearly all right. Gabriel asked her whether she had had a good crossing. She lived with her married daughter in Glasgow and came to Dublin on a visit once a year. She answered placidly that she had had a beautiful crossing and that the captain had been most attentive to her. She spoke also of the beautiful house her daughter kept in Glasgow, and of all the friends they had there. While her tongue rambled on Gabriel tried to banish from his mind all memory of the unpleasant incident with Miss Ivors. Of course the girl or woman, or whatever she was, was an enthusiast but there was a time for all things. Perhaps he ought not to have answered her like that. But she had no right to call him a West Briton before people, even in joke. She had tried to make him ridiculous before people, heckling him and staring at him with her rabbit's eyes.

He saw his wife making her way towards him through the waltzing couples. When she reached him she said into his ear:

"Gabriel, Aunt Kate wants to know won't you carve the goose as usual. Miss Daly will carve the ham and I'll do the pudding."

"All right," said Gabriel.

"She's sending in the younger ones first as soon as this waltz is over so that we'll have the table to ourselves."

"Were you dancing?" asked Gabriel.

"Of course I was. Didn't you see me? What row had you with Molly Ivors?"

"No row. Why? Did she say so?"

"Something like that. I'm trying to get that Mr. D'Arcy to sing. He's full of conceit, I think."

"There was no row," said Gabriel moodily, "only she wanted me to go for a trip to the west of Ireland and I said I wouldn't."

His wife clasped her hands excitedly and gave a little jump.

"O, do go, Gabriel," she cried. "I'd love to see Galway again."

"You can go if you like," said Gabriel coldly.

She looked at him for a moment, then turned to Mrs. Malins and said:

"There's a nice husband for you, Mrs. Malins."

While she was threading her way back across the room Mrs. Malins, without adverting to the interruption, went on to tell Gabriel what beautiful places there were in Scotland and beautiful scenery. Her son-in-law brought them every year to the lakes and they used to go fishing. Her son-in-law was a splendid fisher. One day he caught a beautiful big fish and the man in the hotel cooked it for their dinner.

Gabriel hardly heard what she said. Now that supper was coming near he began to think again about his speech and about the quotation. When he saw Freddy Malins coming across the room to visit his mother Gabriel left the chair free for him and retired into the embrasure of the window. The room had already cleared and from the back room came the clatter of plates and knives. Those who still remained in the drawing-room seemed tired of dancing and were conversing quietly in little groups. Gabriel's warm trembling fingers tapped the cold pane of the window. How cool it must be outside! How pleasant it would be to walk out alone, first along by the river and then through the park! The snow would be lying on the branches of the trees and forming a bright cap on the top of the Wellington Monument. How much more pleasant it would be there than at the supper-table!

He ran over the headings of his speech: Irish hospitality, sad memories, the Three Graces, Paris, the quotation from Browning. He repeated to himself a phrase he had written in his review: "One feels that one is listening to a thought-tormented music." Miss Ivors had praised the review. Was she sincere? Had she really any life of her own behind all her propagandism? There had never been any ill-feeling between them until that night. It unnerved him to think that she would be at the supper-table, looking up at him while he spoke with her critical quizzing eyes. Perhaps she would not be sorry to see him fail in his speech. An idea came into his mind and gave him courage. He would say, alluding to Aunt Kate and Aunt Julia: "Ladies and Gentlemen, the generation which is now on the wane among us may have had its faults but for my part I think it had certain qualities of hospitality, of humour, of humanity, which the new and very serious and hyper-educated generation that is growing up around us seems to me to lack." Very good: that was one for Miss Ivors. What did he care that his aunts were only two ignorant old women?

A murmur in the room attracted his attention. Mr. Browne was advancing from the door, gallantly escorting Aunt Julia, who leaned upon his arm, smiling and hanging her head. An irregular musketry of applause escorted her also as far as the piano and then, as Mary Jane seated herself on the stool, and Aunt Julia, no longer smiling, half turned so as to pitch her voice fairly into the room, gradually ceased. Gabriel recognised the prelude. It was that of an old song of Aunt Julia's—*Arrayed for the Bridal*. Her voice, strong and clear in tone, attacked with great spirit the runs which embellish the air and though she sang very rapidly she did not miss even the smallest of the grace notes. To follow the voice, without looking at the singer's face, was to feel and share the excitement of swift and secure flight. Gabriel applauded loudly with all the others at the close of the song and loud ap-

plause was borne in from the invisible supper-table. It sounded
so genuine that a little colour struggled into Aunt Julia's face as
she bent to replace in the music-stand the old leather-bound song-
book that had her initials on the cover. Freddy Malins, who had
listened with his head perched sideways to hear her better, was
still applauding when everyone else had ceased and talking ani-
matedly to his mother who nodded her head gravely and slowly
in acquiescence. At last, when he could clap no more, he stood up
suddenly and hurried across the room to Aunt Julia whose hand
he seized and held in both his hands, shaking it when words failed
him or the catch in his voice proved too much for him.

"I was just telling my mother," he said, "I never heard you
sing so well, never. No, I never heard your voice so good as it
is tonight. Now! Would you believe that now? That's the truth.
Upon my word and honour that's the truth. I never heard your
voice sound so fresh and so . . . so clear and fresh, never."

Aunt Julia smiled broadly and murmured something about
compliments as she released her hand from his grasp. Mr. Browne
extended his open hand towards her and said to those who were
near him in the manner of a showman introducing a prodigy
to an audience:

"Miss Julia Morkan, my latest discovery!"

He was laughing very heartily at this himself when Freddy
Malins turned to him and said:

"Well, Browne, if you're serious you might make a worse
discovery. All I can say is I never heard her sing half so well
as long as I am coming here. And that's the honest truth."

"Neither did I," said Mr. Browne. "I think her voice has
greatly improved."

Aunt Julia shrugged her shoulders and said with meek pride:

"Thirty years ago I hadn't a bad voice as voices go."

"I often told Julia," said Aunt Kate emphatically, "that she
was simply thrown away in that choir. But she never would be
said by me."

She turned as if to appeal to the good sense of the others

against a refractory child while Aunt Julia gazed in front of her, a vague smile of reminiscence playing on her face.

"No," continued Aunt Kate, "she wouldn't be said or led by anyone, slaving there in that choir night and day, night and day. Six o'clock on Christmas morning! And all for what?"

"Well, isn't it for the honour of God, Aunt Kate?" asked Mary Jane, twisting round on the piano-stool and smiling.

Aunt Kate turned fiercely on her niece and said:

"I know all about the honour of God, Mary Jane, but I think it's not at all honourable for the pope to turn out the women out of the choirs that have slaved there all their lives and put little whipper-snappers of boys over their heads. I suppose it is for the good of the Church if the pope does it. But it's not just, Mary Jane, and it's not right."

She had worked herself into a passion and would have continued in defence of her sister for it was a sore subject with her but Mary Jane, seeing that all the dancers had come back, intervened pacifically:

"Now, Aunt Kate, you're giving scandal to Mr. Browne who is of the other persuasion."

Aunt Kate turned to Mr. Browne, who was grinning at this allusion to his religion, and said hastily:

"O, I don't question the pope's being right. I'm only a stupid old woman and I wouldn't presume to do such a thing. But there's such a thing as common everyday politeness and gratitude. And if I were in Julia's place I'd tell that Father Healey straight up to his face . . ."

"And besides, Aunt Kate," said Mary Jane, "we really are all hungry and when we are hungry we are all very quarrelsome."

"And when we are thirsty we are also quarrelsome," added Mr. Browne.

"So that we had better go to supper," said Mary Jane, "and finish the discussion afterwards."

On the landing outside the drawing-room Gabriel found his wife and Mary Jane trying to persuade Miss Ivors to stay for supper. But Miss Ivors, who had put on her hat and was buttoning her cloak, would not stay. She did not feel in the least hungry and she had already overstayed her time.

"But only for ten minutes, Molly," said Mrs. Conroy. "That won't delay you."

"To take a pick itself," said Mary Jane, "after all your dancing."

"I really couldn't," said Miss Ivors.

"I am afraid you didn't enjoy yourself at all," said Mary Jane hopelessly.

"Ever so much, I assure you," said Miss Ivors, "but you really must let me run off now."

"But how can you get home?" asked Mrs. Conroy.

"O, it's only two steps up the quay."

Gabriel hesitated a moment and said:

"If you will allow me, Miss Ivors, I'll see you home if you are really obliged to go."

But Miss Ivors broke away from them.

"I won't hear of it," she cried. "For goodness' sake go in to your suppers and don't mind me. I'm quite well able to take care of myself."

"Well, you're the comical girl, Molly," said Mrs. Conroy frankly.

"*Beannacht libh,*" cried Miss Ivors, with a laugh, as she ran down the staircase.

Mary Jane gazed after her, a moody puzzled expression on her face, while Mrs. Conroy leaned over the banisters to listen for the hall-door. Gabriel asked himself was he the cause of her abrupt departure. But she did not seem to be in ill humour: she had gone away laughing. He stared blankly down the staircase.

At the moment Aunt Kate came toddling out of the supper-room, almost wringing her hands in despair.

"Where is Gabriel?" she cried. "Where on earth is Gabriel? There's everyone waiting in there, stage to let, and nobody to carve the goose!"

"Here I am, Aunt Kate!" cried Gabriel, with sudden animation, "ready to carve a flock of geese, if necessary."

A fat brown goose lay at one end of the table and at the other end, on a bed of creased paper strewn with sprigs of parsley, lay a great ham, stripped of its outer skin and peppered over with crust crumbs, a neat paper frill round its shin and beside this was a round of spiced beef. Between these rival ends ran parallel lines of side-dishes: two little minsters of jelly, red and yellow; a shallow dish full of blocks of blancmange and red jam, a large green leaf-shaped dish with a stalk-shaped handle, on which lay bunches of purple raisins and peeled almonds, a companion dish on which lay a solid rectangle of Smyrna figs, a dish of custard topped with grated nutmeg, a small bowl full of chocolates and sweets wrapped in gold and silver papers and a glass vase in which stood some tall celery stalks. In the centre of the table there stood, as sentries to a fruit-stand which upheld a pyramid of oranges and American apples, two squat old-fashioned de-canters of cut glass, one containing port and the other dark sherry. On the closed square piano a pudding in a huge yellow dish lay in waiting and behind it were three squads of bottles of stout and ale and minerals, drawn up according to the colours of their uniforms, the first two black, with brown and red labels, the third and smallest squad white, with transverse green sashes.

Gabriel took his seat boldly at the head of the table and, having looked to the edge of the carver, plunged his fork firmly into the goose. He felt quite at ease now for he was an expert carver and liked nothing better than to find himself at the head of a well-laden table.

"Miss Furlong, what shall I send you?" he asked. "A wing or a slice of the breast?"

"Just a small slice of the breast."

"Miss Higgins, what for you?"

"O, anything at all, Mr. Conroy."

While Gabriel and Miss Daly exchanged plates of goose and plates of ham and spiced beef Lily went from guest to guest with a dish of hot floury potatoes wrapped in a white napkin. This was Mary Jane's idea and she had also suggested apple sauce for the goose but Aunt Kate had said that plain roast goose without any apple sauce had always been good enough for her and she hoped she might never eat worse. Mary Jane waited on her pupils and saw that they got the best slices and Aunt Kate and Aunt Julia opened and carried across from the piano bottles of stout and ale for the gentlemen and bottles of minerals for the ladies. There was a great deal of confusion and laughter and noise, the noise of orders and counter-orders, of knives and forks, of corks and glass-stoppers. Gabriel began to carve second helpings as soon as he had finished the first round without serving himself. Everyone protested loudly so that he compromised by taking a long draught of stout for he had found the carving hot work. Mary Jane settled down quietly to her supper but Aunt Kate and Aunt Julia were still toddling round the table, walking on each other's heels, getting in each other's way and giving each other unheeded orders. Mr. Browne begged of them to sit down and eat their suppers and so did Gabriel but they said there was time enough, so that, at last, Freddy Malins stood up and, capturing Aunt Kate, plumped her down on her chair amid general laughter.

When everyone had been well served Gabriel said, smiling:

"Now, if anyone wants a little more of what vulgar people call stuffing let him or her speak."

A chorus of voices invited him to begin his own supper and Lily came forward with three potatoes which she had reserved for him.

"Very well," said Gabriel amiably, as he took another preparatory draught, "kindly forget my existence, ladies and gentlemen, for a few minutes."

He set to his supper and took no part in the conversation with which the table covered Lily's removal of the plates. The subject of talk was the opera company which was then at the Theatre Royal. Mr. Bartell D'Arcy, the tenor, a dark-complexioned young man with a smart moustache, praised very highly the leading contralto of the company but Miss Furlong thought she had a rather vulgar style of production. Freddy Malins said there was a Negro chieftain singing in the second part of the Gaiety pantomime who had one of the finest tenor voices he had ever heard.

"Have you heard him?" he asked Mr. Bartell D'Arcy across the table.

"No," answered Mr. Bartell D'Arcy carelessly.

"Because," Freddy Malins explained, "now I'd be curious to hear your opinion of him. I think he has a grand voice."

"It takes Teddy to find out the really good things," said Mr. Browne familiarly to the table.

"And why couldn't he have a voice too?" asked Freddy Malins sharply. "Is it because he's only a black?"

Nobody answered this question and Mary Jane led the table back to the legitimate opera. One of her pupils had given her a pass for *Mignon*. Of course it was very fine, she said, but it made her think of poor Georgina Burns. Mr. Browne could go back farther still, to the old Italian companies that used to come to Dublin—Tietjens, Ilma de Murzka, Campanini, the great Trebelli, Giuglini, Ravelli, Aramburo. Those were the days, he said, when there was something like singing to be heard in Dublin. He told too of how the top gallery of the old Royal used to be packed night after night, of how one night an Italian tenor had sung five encores to *Let me like a Soldier fall*, introducing a high C every time, and of how the gallery boys would sometimes in their enthusiasm unyoke the horses from the carriage of some great *prima donna* and pull her themselves through the streets to her hotel. Why did they never play the grand old operas now, he asked, *Dinorah, Lucrezia Borgia?* Because they could not get the voices to sing them: that was why.

"O, well," said Mr. Bartell D'Arcy, "I presume there are as good singers today as there were then."

"Where are they?" asked Mr. Browne defiantly.

"In London, Paris, Milan," said Mr. Bartell D'Arcy warmly. "I suppose Caruso, for example, is quite as good, if not better than any of the men you have mentioned."

"Maybe so," said Mr. Browne. "But I may tell you I doubt it strongly."

"O, I'd give anything to hear Caruso sing," said Mary Jane.

"For me," said Aunt Kate, who had been picking a bone, "there was only one tenor. To please me, I mean. But I suppose none of you ever heard of him."

"Who was he, Miss Morkan?" asked Mr. Bartell D'Arcy politely.

"His name," said Aunt Kate, "was Parkinson. I heard him when he was in his prime and I think he had then the purest tenor voice that was ever put into a man's throat."

"Strange," said Mr. Bartell D'Arcy. "I never even heard of him."

"Yes, yes, Miss Morkan is right," said Mr. Browne. "I remember hearing of old Parkinson but he's too far back for me."

"A beautiful, pure, sweet, mellow English tenor," said Aunt Kate with enthusiasm.

Gabriel having finished, the huge pudding was transferred to the table. The clatter of forks and spoons began again. Gabriel's wife served out spoonfuls of the pudding and passed the plates down the table. Midway down they were held up by Mary Jane, who replenished them with raspberry or orange jelly or with blancmange and jam. The pudding was of Aunt Julia's making and she received praises for it from all quarters. She herself said that it was not quite brown enough.

"Well, I hope, Miss Morkan," said Mr. Browne, "that I'm brown enough for you because, you know, I'm all brown."

All the gentlemen, except Gabriel, ate some of the pudding out of compliment to Aunt Julia. As Gabriel never ate sweets the celery had been left for him. Freddy Malins also took a stalk of celery and ate it with his pudding. He had been told that celery was a capital thing for the blood and he was just then under doctor's care. Mrs. Malins, who had been silent all through the supper, said that her son was going down to Mount Melleray in a week or so. The table then spoke of Mount Melleray, how bracing the air was down there, how hospitable the monks were and how they never asked for a penny-piece from their guests.

"And do you mean to say," asked Mr. Browne incredulously, "that a chap can go down there and put up there as if it were a hotel and live on the fat of the land and then come away without paying anything?"

"O, most people give some donation to the monastery when they leave," said Mary Jane.

"I wish we had an institution like that in our Church," said Mr. Browne candidly.

He was astonished to hear that the monks never spoke, got up at two in the morning and slept in their coffins. He asked what they did it for.

"That's the rule of the order," said Aunt Kate firmly.

"Yes, but why?" asked Mr. Browne.

Aunt Kate repeated that it was the rule, that was all. Mr. Browne still seemed not to understand. Freddy Malins explained to him, as best he could, that the monks were trying to make up for the sins committed by all the sinners in the outside world. The explanation was not very clear for Mr. Browne grinned and said:

"I like that idea very much but wouldn't a comfortable spring bed do them as well as a coffin?"

"The coffin," said Mary Jane, "is to remind them of their last end."

As the subject had grown lugubrious it was buried in a silence of the table during which Mrs. Malins could be heard saying to her neighbour in an indistinct undertone:

"They are very good men, the monks, very pious men."

The raisins and almonds and figs and apples and oranges and chocolates and sweets were now passed about the table and Aunt Julia invited all the guests to have either port or sherry. At first Mr. Bartell D'Arcy refused to take either but one of his neighbours nudged him and whispered something to him upon which he allowed his glass to be filled. Gradually as the last glasses were being filled the conversation ceased. A pause followed, broken only by the noise of the wine and by unsettlings of chairs. The Misses Morkan, all three, looked down at the tablecloth. Someone coughed once or twice and then a few gentlemen patted the table gently as a signal for silence. The silence came and Gabriel pushed back his chair and stood up.

The patting at once grew louder in encouragement and then ceased altogether. Gabriel leaned his ten trembling fingers on the tablecloth and smiled nervously at the company. Meeting a row of upturned faces he raised his eyes to the chandelier. The piano was playing a waltz tune and he could hear the skirts sweeping against the drawing-room door. People, perhaps, were standing in the snow on the quay outside, gazing up at the lighted windows and listening to the waltz music. The air was pure there. In the distance lay the park where the trees were weighted with snow. The Wellington Monument wore a gleaming cap of snow that flashed westward over the white field of Fifteen Acres.

He began:

"Ladies and Gentlemen,

"It has fallen to my lot this evening, as in years past, to perform a very pleasing task but a task for which I am afraid my poor powers as a speaker are all too inadequate."

"No, no!" said Mr. Browne.

"But, however that may be, I can only ask you tonight to take the will for the deed and to lend me your attention for a few moments while I endeavour to express to you in words what my feelings are on this occasion.

"Ladies and Gentlemen, it is not the first time that we have gathered together under this hospitable roof, around this hospitable board. It is not the first time that we have been the recipients—or perhaps, I had better say, the victims—of the hospitality of certain good ladies."

He made a circle in the air with his arm and paused. Everyone laughed or smiled at Aunt Kate and Aunt Julia and Mary Jane who all turned crimson with pleasure. Gabriel went on more boldly:

"I feel more strongly with every recurring year that our country has no tradition which does it so much honour and which it should guard so jealously as that of its hospitality. It is a tradition that is unique as far as my experience goes (and I have visited not a few places abroad) among the modern nations. Some would say, perhaps, that with us it is rather a failing than anything to be boasted of. But granted even that, it is, to my mind, a princely failing, and one that I trust will long be cultivated among us. Of one thing, at least, I am sure. As long as this one roof shelters the good ladies aforesaid—and I wish from my heart it may do so for many and many a long year to come—the tradition of genuine warm-hearted courteous Irish hospitality, which our forefathers have handed down to us and which we in turn must hand down to our descendants, is still alive among us."

A hearty murmur of assent ran round the table. It shot through Gabriel's mind that Miss Ivors was not there and that she had gone away discourteously: and he said with confidence in himself:

"Ladies and Gentlemen,

"A new generation is growing up in our midst, a generation actuated by new ideas and new principles. It is serious and enthusiastic for these new ideas and its enthusiasm, even when it is misdirected, is, I believe, in the main sincere. But we are living in a sceptical and, if I may use the phrase, a thought-tormented age: and sometimes I fear that this new generation, educated or hypereducated as it is, will lack those qualities of humanity, of hospitality, of kindly humour which belonged to an older day. Listening tonight to the names of all those great singers of the past it seemed to me, I must confess, that we were living in a less spacious age. Those days might, without exaggeration, be called spacious days: and if they are gone beyond recall let us hope, at least, that in gatherings such as this we shall still speak of them with pride and affection, still cherish in our hearts the memory of those dead and gone great ones whose fame the world will not willingly let die."

"Hear, hear!" said Mr. Browne loudly.

"But yet," continued Gabriel, his voice falling into a softer inflection, "there are always in gatherings such as this sadder thoughts that will recur to our minds: thoughts of the past, of youth, of changes, of absent faces that we miss here tonight. Our path through life is strewn with many such sad memories: and were we to brood upon them always we could not find the heart to go on bravely with our work among the living. We have all of us living duties and living affections which claim, and rightly claim, our strenuous endeavours.

"Therefore, I will not linger on the past. I will not let any gloomy moralising intrude upon us here tonight. Here we are gathered together for a brief moment from the bustle and rush of our everyday routine. We are met here as a friends, in the spirit of good-fellowship, as colleagues, also to a certain extent, in the true spirit of *camaraderie*, and as the guests of—what shall I call them?—the Three Graces of the Dublin musical world."

The table burst into applause and laughter at this allusion. Aunt Julia vainly asked each of her neighbours in turn to tell her what Gabriel had said.

"He says we are the Three Graces, Aunt Julia," said Mary Jane.

Aunt Julia did not understand but she looked up, smiling, at Gabriel, who continued in the same vein:

"Ladies and Gentlemen,

"I will not attempt to play tonight the part that Paris played on another occasion. I will not attempt to choose between them. The task would be an invidious one and one beyond my poor powers. For when I view them in turn, whether it be our chief hostess herself, whose good heart, whose too good heart, has become a byword with all who know her, or her sister, who seems to be gifted with perennial youth and whose singing must have been a surprise and a revelation to us all tonight, or, last but

not least, when I consider our youngest hostess, talented, cheerful, hard-working and the best of nieces, I confess, Ladies and
Gentlemen, that I do not know to which of them I should award
the prize."

Gabriel glanced down at his aunts and, seeing the large smile
on Aunt Julia's face and the tears which had risen to Aunt Kate's
eyes, hastened to his close. He raised his glass of port gallantly,
while every member of the company fingered a glass expectantly,
and said loudly:

"Let us toast them all three together. Let us drink to their
health, wealth, long life, happiness and prosperity and may they
long continue to hold the proud and self-won position which
they hold in their profession and the position of honour and
affection which they hold in our hearts."

All the guests stood up, glass in hand, and turning towards the
three seated ladies, sang in unison, with Mr. Browne as leader:

> *For they are jolly gay fellows,*
> *For they are jolly gay fellows,*
> *For they are jolly gay fellows,*
> *Which nobody can deny.*

Aunt Kate was making frank use of her handkerchief and even
Aunt Julia seemed moved. Freddy Malins beat time with his
pudding-fork and the singers turned towards one another, as if in
melodious conference, while they sang with emphasis:

> *Unless he tells a lie,*
> *Unless he tells a lie,*

Then, turning once more towards their hostesses, they sang:

> *For they are jolly gay fellows,*
> *For they are jolly gay fellows,*
> *For they are jolly gay fellows,*
> *Which nobody can deny.*

The acclamation which followed was taken up beyond the
door of the supper-room by many of the other guests and renewed

time after time, Freddy Malins acting as officer with his fork on
high.

.   .   .   .

The piercing morning air came into the hall where they were
standing so that Aunt Kate said:

"Close the door, somebody. Mrs. Malins will get her death of
cold."

"Browne is out there, Aunt Kate," said Mary Jane.

"Browne is everywhere," said Aunt Kate, lowering her voice.

Mary Jane laughed at her tone.

"Really," she said archly, "he is very attentive."

"He has been laid on here like the gas," said Aunt Kate in the
same tone, "all during the Christmas."

She laughed herself this time good-humouredly and then added
quickly:

"But tell him to come in, Mary Jane, and close the door. I hope
to goodness he didn't hear me."

At that moment the hall-door was opened and Mr. Browne
came in from the doorstep, laughing as if his heart would break.
He was dressed in a long green overcoat with mock astrakhan
cuffs and collar and wore on his head an oval fur cap. He pointed
down the snow-covered quay from where the sound of shrill prolonged whistling was borne in.

"Teddy will have all the cabs in Dublin out," he said.

Gabriel advanced from the little pantry behind the office, struggling into his overcoat and, looking round the hall,
said:

"Gretta not down yet?"

"She's getting on her things, Gabriel," said Aunt Kate.

"Who's playing up there?" asked Gabriel.

"Nobody. They're all gone."

"O no, Aunt Kate," said Mary Jane. "Bartell D'Arcy and Miss
O'Callaghan aren't gone yet."

"Someone is fooling at the piano anyhow," said Gabriel.

Mary Jane glanced at Gabriel and Mr. Browne and said with a shiver:

"It makes me feel cold to look at you two gentlemen muffled up like that. I wouldn't like to face your journey home at this hour."

"I'd like nothing better this minute," said Mr. Browne stoutly, "than a rattling fine walk in the country or a fast drive with a good spanking goer between the shafts."

"We used to have a very good horse and trap at home," said Aunt Julia sadly.

"The never-to-be-forgotten Johnny," said Mary Jane, laughing.

Aunt Kate and Gabriel laughed too.

"Why, what was wonderful about Johnny?" asked Mr. Browne.

"The late lamented Patrick Morkan, our grandfather, that is," explained Gabriel, "commonly known in his later years as the old gentleman, was a glue-boiler."

"O, now, Gabriel," said Aunt Kate, laughing, "he had a starch mill."

"Well, glue or starch," said Gabriel, "the old gentleman had a horse by the name of Johnny. And Johnny used to work in the old gentleman's mill, walking round and round in order to drive the mill. That was all very well; but now comes the tragic part about Johnny. One fine day the old gentleman thought he'd like to drive out with the quality to a military review in the park."

"The Lord have mercy on his soul," said Aunt Kate compassionately.

"Amen," said Gabriel. "So the old gentleman, as I said, harnessed Johnny and put on his very best tall hat and his very best stock collar and drove out in grand style from his ancestral mansion somewhere near Back Lane, I think."

Everyone laughed, even Mrs. Malins, at Gabriel's manner and Aunt Kate said:

"O, now, Gabriel, he didn't live in Back Lane, really. Only the mill was there."

"Out from the mansion of his forefathers," continued Gabriel, "he drove with Johnny. And everything went on beautifully until Johnny came in sight of King Billy's statue: and whether he fell in love with the horse King Billy sits on or whether he thought he was back again in the mill, anyhow he began to walk round the statue."

Gabriel paced in a circle round the hall in his goloshes amid the laughter of the others.

"Round and round he went," said Gabriel, "and the old gentleman, who was a very pompous old gentleman, was highly indignant. 'Go on, sir! What do you mean, sir? Johnny! Johnny! Most extraordinary conduct! Can't understand the horse!' "

The peal of laughter which followed Gabriel's imitation of the incident was interrupted by a resounding knock at the hall door. Mary Jane ran to open it and let in Freddy Malins. Freddy Malins, with his hat well back on his head and his shoulders humped with cold, was puffing and steaming after his exertions.

"I could only get one cab," he said.

"O, we'll find another along the quay," said Gabriel.

"Yes," said Aunt Kate. "Better not keep Mrs. Malins standing in the draught."

Mrs. Malins was helped down the front steps by her son and Mr. Browne and, after many manœuvres, hoisted into the cab. Freddy Malins clambered in after her and spent a long time settling her on the seat, Mr. Browne helping him with advice. At last she was settled comfortably and Freddy Malins invited Mr. Browne into the cab. There was a good deal of confused talk, and then Mr. Browne got into the cab. The cabman settled his rug over his knees, and bent down for the address. The confusion grew greater and the cabman was directed differently by Freddy Malins and Mr. Browne, each of whom had his head out through a window of the cab. The difficulty was to know where to drop Mr. Browne along the route, and Aunt Kate, Aunt Julia and Mary Jane helped the discussion from the doorstep with cross-

directions and contradictions and abundance of laughter. As for
Freddy Malins he was speechless with laughter. He popped his
head in and out of the window every moment to the great danger
of his hat, and told his mother how the discussion was progressing,
till at last Mr. Browne shouted to the bewildered cabman above
the din of everybody's laughter:

"Do you know Trinity College?"

"Yes, sir," said the cabman.

"Well, drive bang up against Trinity College gates," said Mr.
Browne, "and then we'll tell you where to go. You understand
now?"

"Yes, sir," said the cabman.

"Make like a bird for Trinity College."

"Right, sir," said the cabman.

The horse was whipped up and the cab rattled off along the
quay amid a chorus of laughter and adieus.

Gabriel had not gone to the door with the others. He was in
a dark part of the hall gazing up the staircase. A woman was
standing near the top of the first flight, in the shadow also. He
could not see her face but he could see the terra-cotta and salmon-
pink panels of her skirt which the shadow made appear black
and white. It was his wife. She was leaning on the banisters, listening to something. Gabriel was surprised at her stillness and strained
his ear to listen also. But he could hear little save the noise of
laughter and dispute on the front steps, a few chords struck on
the piano and a few notes of a man's voice singing.

He stood still in the gloom of the hall, trying to catch the air
that the voice was singing and gazing up at his wife. There was
grace and mystery in her attitude as if she were a symbol of
something. He asked himself what is a woman standing on the
stairs in the shadow, listening to distant music, a symbol of.
If he were a painter he would paint her in that attitude. Her
blue felt hat would show off the bronze of her hair against the
darkness and the dark panels of her skirt would show off the

light ones. *Distant Music* he would call the picture if he were a painter.

The hall-door was closed; and Aunt Kate, Aunt Julia and Mary Jane came down the hall, still laughing.

"Well, isn't Freddy terrible?" said Mary Jane. "He's really terrible."

Gabriel said nothing but pointed up the stairs towards where his wife was standing. Now that the hall-door was closed the voice and the piano could be heard more clearly. Gabriel held up his hand for them to be silent. The song seemed to be in the old Irish tonality and the singer seemed uncertain both of his words and of his voice. The voice, made plaintive by distance and by the singer's hoarseness, faintly illuminated the cadence of the air with words expressing grief:

> *O, the rain falls on my heavy locks*
> *And the dew wets my skin,*
> *My babe lies cold . . .*

"O," exclaimed Mary Jane. "It's Bartell D'Arcy singing and he wouldn't sing all the night. O, I'll get him to sing a song before he goes."

"O, do, Mary Jane," said Aunt Kate.

Mary Jane brushed past the others and ran to the staircase, but before she reached it the singing stopped and the piano was closed abruptly.

"O, what a pity!" she cried. "Is he coming down, Gretta?"

Gabriel heard his wife answer yes and saw her come down towards them. A few steps behind her were Mr. Bartell D'Arcy and Miss O'Callaghan.

"O, Mr. D'Arcy," cried Mary Jane, "it's downright mean of you to break off like that when we were all in raptures listening to you."

"I have been at him all the evening," said Miss O'Callaghan, "and Mrs. Conroy, too, and he told us he had a dreadful cold and couldn't sing."

"O, Mr. D'Arcy," said Aunt Kate, "now that was a great fib to tell."

"Can't you see that I'm as hoarse as a crow?" said Mr. D'Arcy roughly.

He went into the pantry hastily and put on his overcoat. The others, taken aback by his rude speech, could find nothing to say. Aunt Kate wrinkled her brows and made signs to the others to drop the subject. Mr. D'Arcy stood swathing his neck carefully and frowning.

"It's the weather," said Aunt Julia, after a pause.

"Yes, everybody has colds," said Aunt Kate readily, "everybody."

"They say," said Mary Jane, "we haven't had snow like it for thirty years; and I read this morning in the newspapers that the snow is general all over Ireland."

"I love the look of snow," said Aunt Julia sadly.

"So do I," said Miss O'Callaghan. "I think Christmas is never really Christmas unless we have the snow on the ground."

"But poor Mr. D'Arcy doesn't like the snow," said Aunt Kate, smiling.

Mr. D'Arcy came from the pantry, fully swathed and buttoned, and in a repentant tone told them the history of his cold. Everyone gave him advice and said it was a great pity and urged him to be very careful of his throat in the night air. Gabriel watched his wife, who did not join in the conversation. She was standing right under the dusty fanlight and the flame of the gas lit up the rich bronze of her hair, which he had seen her drying at the fire a few days before. She was in the same attitude and seemed unaware of the talk about her. At last she turned towards them and Gabriel saw that there was colour on her cheeks and that her eyes were shining. A sudden tide of joy went leaping out of his heart.

"Mr. D'Arcy," she said, "what is the name of that song you were singing?"

"It's called *The Lass of Aughrim*," said Mr. D'Arcy, "but

I couldn't remember it properly. Why? Do you know it?"

"*The Lass of Aughrim*," she repeated. "I couldn't think of the name."

"It's a very nice air," said Mary Jane. "I'm sorry you were not in voice tonight."

"Now, Mary Jane," said Aunt Kate, "don't annoy Mr. D'Arcy. I won't have him annoyed."

Seeing that all were ready to start she shepherded them to the door, where good-night was said:

"Well, good-night, Aunt Kate, and thanks for the pleasant evening."

"Good-night, Gabriel. Good-night, Gretta!"

"Good-night, Aunt Kate, and thanks ever so much. Good-night, Aunt Julia."

"O, good-night, Gretta, I didn't see you."

"Good-night, Mr. D'Arcy. Good-night, Miss O'Callaghan."

"Good-night, Miss Morkan."

"Good-night, again."

"Good-night, all. Safe home."

"Good-night. Good night."

The morning was still dark. A dull, yellow light brooded over the houses and the river; and the sky seemed to be descending. It was slushy underfoot; and only streaks and patches of snow lay on the roofs, on the parapets of the quay and on the area railings. The lamps were still burning redly in the murky air and, across the river, the palace of the Four Courts stood out menacingly against the heavy sky.

She was walking on before him with Mr. Bartell D'Arcy, her shoes in a brown parcel tucked under one arm and her hands holding her skirt up from the slush. She had no longer any grace of attitude, but Gabriel's eyes were still bright with happiness. The blood went bounding along his veins; and the thoughts went rioting through his brain, proud, joyful, tender, valorous.

She was walking on before him so lightly and so erect that he longed to run after her noiselessly, catch her by the shoulders and say something foolish and affectionate into her ear. She seemed to him so frail that he longed to defend her against something and then to be alone with her. Moments of their secret life together burst like stars upon his memory. A heliotrope envelope was lying beside his breakfast-cup and he was caressing it with his hand. Birds were twittering in the ivy and the sunny web of the curtain was shimmering along the floor: he could not eat for happiness. They were standing on the crowded platform and he was placing a ticket inside the warm palm of her glove. He was standing with her in the cold, looking in through a grated window at a man making bottles in a roaring furnace. It was very cold. Her face, fragrant in the cold air, was quite close to his; and suddenly he called out to the man at the furnace:

"Is the fire hot, sir?"

But the man could not hear with the noise of the furnace. It was just as well. He might have answered rudely.

A wave of yet more tender joy escaped from his heart and went coursing in warm flood along his arteries. Like the tender fire of stars moments of their life together, that no one knew of or would ever know of, broke upon and illumined his memory. He longed to recall to her those moments, to make her forget the years of their dull existence together and remember only their moments of ecstasy. For the years, he felt, had not quenched his soul or hers. Their children, his writing, her household cares had not quenched all their souls' tender fire. In one letter that he had written to her then he had said: "Why is it that words like these seem to me so dull and cold? Is it because there is no word tender enough to be your name?"

Like distant music these words that he had written years before were borne towards him from the past. He longed to be alone with her. When the others had gone away, when he and she were in the room in the hotel, then they would be alone together. He would call her softly:

"Gretta!"

Perhaps she would not hear at once: she would be undressing.

Then something in his voice would strike her. She would turn and look at him. . . .

At the corner of Winetavern Street they met a cab. He was glad of its rattling noise as it saved him from conversation. She was looking out of the window and seemed tired. The others spoke only a few words, pointing out some building or street. The horse galloped along wearily under the murky morning sky, dragging his old rattling box after his heels, and Gabriel was again in a cab with her, galloping to catch the boat, galloping to their honeymoon.

As the cab drove across O'Connell Bridge Miss O'Callaghan said:

"They say you never cross O'Connell Bridge without seeing a white horse."

"I see a white man this time," said Gabriel.

"Where?" asked Mr. Bartell D'Arcy.

Gabriel pointed to the statue, on which lay patches of snow. Then he nodded familiarly to it and waved his hand.

"Good-night, Dan," he said gaily.

When the cab drew up before the hotel, Gabriel jumped out and, in spite of Mr. Bartell D'Arcy's protest, paid the driver. He gave the man a shilling over his fare. The man saluted and said:

"A prosperous New Year to you, sir."

"The same to you," said Gabriel cordially.

She leaned for a moment on his arm in getting out of the cab and while standing at the curbstone, bidding the others good-night. She leaned lightly on his arm, as lightly as when she had danced with him a few hours before. He had felt proud and happy then, happy that she was his, proud of her grace and wifely carriage. But now, after the kindling again of so many memories, the first touch of her body, musical and strange and perfumed, sent through him a keen pang of lust. Under cover of her silence he pressed her arm closely to his side; and, as they stood at the hotel door, he felt that they had escaped from their lives and duties, escaped from home and friends and run away together with wild and radiant hearts to a new adventure.

An old man was dozing in a great hooded chair in the hall. He lit a candle in the office and went before them to the stairs. They followed him in silence, their feet falling in soft thuds on the thickly carpeted stairs. She mounted the stairs behind the porter, her head bowed in the ascent, her frail shoulders curved as with a burden, her skirt girt tightly about her. He could have flung his arms about her hips and held her still, for his arms were trembling with desire to seize her and only the stress of his nails against the palms of his hands held the wild impulse of his body in check. The porter halted on the stairs to settle his guttering candle. They halted, too, on the steps below him. In the silence Gabriel could hear the falling of the molten wax into the tray and the thumping of his own heart against his ribs.

The porter led them along a corridor and opened a door. Then he set his unstable candle down on a toilet-table and asked at what hour they were to be called in the morning.

"Eight," said Gabriel.

The porter pointed to the tap of the electric-light and began a muttered apology, but Gabriel cut him short.

"We don't want any light. We have light enough from the street. And I say," he added, pointing to the candle, "you might remove that handsome article, like a good man."

The porter took up his candle again, but slowly, for he was surprised by such a novel idea. Then he mumbled good-night and went out. Gabriel shot the lock to.

A ghastly light from the street lamp lay in a long shaft from one window to the door. Gabriel threw his overcoat and hat on a couch and crossed the room towards the window. He looked down into the street in order that his emotion might calm a little. Then he turned and leaned against a chest of drawers with his back to the light. She had taken off her hat and cloak and was standing before a large swinging mirror, unhooking her waist. Gabriel paused for a few moments, watching her, and then said:

"Gretta!"

She turned away from the mirror slowly and walked along the shaft of light towards him. Her face looked so serious and weary that the words would not pass Gabriel's lips. No, it was not the moment yet.

"You looked tired," he said.

"I am a little," she answered.

"You don't feel ill or weak?"

"No, tired: that's all."

She went on to the window and stood there, looking out. Gabriel waited again and then, fearing that diffidence was about to conquer him, he said abruptly:

"By the way, Gretta!"

"What is it?"

"You know that poor fellow Malins?" he said quickly.

"Yes. What about him?"

"Well, poor fellow, he's a decent sort of chap, after all," continued Gabriel in a false voice. "He gave me back that sovereign I lent him, and I didn't expect it, really. It's a pity he wouldn't keep away from that Browne, because he's not a bad fellow, really."

He was trembling now with annoyance. Why did she seem so abstracted? He did not know how he could begin. Was she annoyed, too, about something? If she would only turn to him or come to him of her own accord! To take her as she was would be brutal. No, he must see some ardour in her eyes first. He longed to be master of her strange mood.

"When did you lend him the pound?" she asked, after a pause.

Gabriel strove to restrain himself from breaking out into brutal language about the sottish Malins and his pound. He longed to cry to her from his soul, to crush her body against his, to overmaster her. But he said:

"O, at Christmas, when he opened that little Christmas-card shop in Henry Street."

He was in such a fever of rage and desire that he did not

hear her come from the window. She stood before him for an instant, looking at him strangely. Then, suddenly raising herself on tiptoe and resting her hands lightly on his shoulders, she kissed him.

"You are a very generous person, Gabriel," she said.

Gabriel, trembling with delight at her sudden kiss and at the quaintness of her phrase, put his hands on her hair and began smoothing it back, scarcely touching it with his fingers. The washing had made it fine and brilliant. His heart was brimming over with happiness. Just when he was wishing for it she had come to him of her own accord. Perhaps her thoughts had been running with his. Perhaps she had felt the impetuous desire that was in him, and then the yielding mood had come upon her. Now that she had fallen to him so easily, he wondered why he had been so diffident.

He stood, holding her head between his hands. Then, slipping one arm swiftly about her body and drawing her towards him, he said softly:

"Gretta, dear, what are you thinking about?"

She did not answer nor yield wholly to his arm. He said again, softly:

"Tell me what it is, Gretta. I think I know what is the matter. Do I know?"

She did not answer at once. Then she said in an outburst of tears:

"O, I am thinking about that song, *The Lass of Aughrim*."

She broke loose from him and ran to the bed and, throwing her arms across the bed-rail, hid her face. Gabriel stood stock-still for a moment in astonishment and then followed her. As he passed in the way of the cheval-glass he caught sight of himself in full length, his broad, well-filled shirt-front, the face whose expression always puzzled him when he saw it in a mirror, and his glimmering gilt-rimmed eyeglasses. He halted a few paces from her and said:

"What about the song? Why does that make you cry?"

She raised her head from her arms and dried her eyes with the back of her hand like a child. A kinder note than he had intended went into his voice.

"Why, Gretta?" he asked.

"I am thinking about a person long ago who used to sing that song."

"And who was the person long ago?" asked Gabriel, smiling.

"It was a person I used to know in Galway when I was living with my grandmother," she said.

The smile passed away from Gabriel's face. A dull anger began to gather again at the back of his mind and the dull fires of his lust began to glow angrily in his veins.

"Someone you were in love with?" he asked ironically.

"It was a young boy I used to know," she answered, "named Michael Furey. He used to sing that song, *The Lass of Aughrim*. He was very delicate."

Gabriel was silent. He did not wish her to think that he was interested in this delicate boy.

"I can see him so plainly," she said, after a moment. "Such eyes as he had: big, dark eyes! And such an expression in them—an expression!"

"O, then, you are in love with him?" said Gabriel.

"I used to go out walking with him," she said, "when I was in Galway."

A thought flew across Gabriel's mind.

"Perhaps that was why you wanted to go to Galway with that Ivors girl?" he said coldly.

She looked at him and asked in surprise:

"What for?"

Her eyes made Gabriel feel awkward. He shrugged his shoulders and said:

"How do I know? To see him, perhaps."

She looked away from him along the shaft of light towards the window in silence.

"He is dead," she said at length. "He died when he was only seventeen. Isn't it a terrible thing to die so young as that?"

"What was he?" asked Gabriel, still ironically.

"He was in the gasworks," she said.

Gabriel felt humiliated by the failure of his irony and by the evocation of this figure from the dead, a boy in the gasworks. While he had been full of memories of their secret life together, full of tenderness and joy and desire, she had been comparing him in her mind with another. A shameful consciousness of his own person assailed him. He saw himself as a ludicrous figure, acting as a pennyboy for his aunts, a nervous, well-meaning sentimentalist, orating to vulgarians and idealising his own clownish lusts, the pitiable fatuous fellow he had caught a glimpse of in the mirror. Instinctively he turned his back more to the light lest she might see the shame that burned upon his forehead.

He tried to keep up his tone of cold interrogation, but his voice when he spoke was humble and indifferent.

"I suppose you were in love with this Michael Furey, Gretta," he said.

"I was great with him at that time," she said.

Her voice was veiled and sad. Gabriel, feeling now how vain it would be to try to lead her whither he had purposed, caressed one of her hands and said, also sadly:

"And what did he die of so young, Gretta? Consumption, was it?"

"I think he died for me," she answered.

A vague terror seized Gabriel at this answer, as if, at that hour when he had hoped to triumph, some impalpable and vindictive being was coming against him, gathering forces against him in its vague world. But he shook himself free of it with an effort of reason and continued to caress her hand. He did not question her again, for he felt that she would tell him of herself. Her hand was warm and moist: it did not respond to his touch, but he continued to caress it just as he had caressed her first letter to him that spring morning.

"It was in the winter," she said, "about the beginning of the winter when I was going to leave my grandmother's and come up here to the convent. And he was ill at the time in his lodgings in Galway and wouldn't be let out, and his people in Oughterard were written to. He was in decline, they said, or something like that. I never knew rightly."

She paused for a moment and sighed.

"Poor fellow," she said. "He was very fond of me and he was such a gentle boy. We used to go out together, walking, you know, Gabriel, like the way they do in the country. He was going to study singing only for his health. He had a very good voice, poor Michael Furey."

"Well; and then?" asked Gabriel.

"And then when it came to the time for me to leave Galway and come up to the convent he was much worse and I wouldn't be let see him so I wrote him a letter saying I was going up to Dublin and would be back in the summer, and hoping he would be better then."

She paused for a moment to get her voice under control, and then went on:

"Then the night before I left, I was in my grandmother's house in Nuns' Island, packing up, and I heard gravel thrown up against the window. The window was so wet I couldn't see, so I ran downstairs as I was and slipped out the back into the garden and there was the poor fellow at the end of the garden, shivering."

"And did you not tell him to go back?" asked Gabriel.

"I implored of him to go home at once and told him he would get his death in the rain. But he said he did not want to live. I can see his eyes as well as well! He was standing at the end of the wall where there was a tree."

"And did he go home?" asked Gabriel.

"Yes, he went home. And when I was only a week in the convent he died and he was buried in Oughterard, where his people came from. O, the day I heard that, that he was dead!"

She stopped, choking with sobs, and, overcome by emotion, flung herself face downward on the bed, sobbing in the quilt. Gabriel held her hand for a moment longer, irresolutely, and then, shy of intruding on her grief, let it fall gently and walked quietly to the window.

She was fast asleep.

Gabriel, leaning on his elbow, looked for a few moments unresentfully on her tangled hair and half-open mouth, listening to her deep-drawn breath. So she had had that romance in her life: a man had died for her sake. It hardly pained him now to think how poor a part he, her husband, had played in her life. He watched her while she slept, as though he and she had never lived together as man and wife. His curious eyes rested long upon her face and on her hair: and, as he thought of what she must have been then, in that time of her first girlish beauty, a strange, friendly pity for her entered his soul. He did not like to say even to himself that her face was no longer beautiful, but he knew that it was no longer the face for which Michael Furey had braved death.

Perhaps she had not told him all the story. His eyes moved to the chair over which she had thrown some of her clothes. A petticoat string dangled to the floor. One boot stood upright, its limp upper fallen down: the fellow of it lay upon its side. He wondered at his riot of emotions of an hour before. From what had it proceeded? From his aunt's supper, from his own foolish speech, from the wine and dancing, the merry-making when saying good-night in the hall, the pleasure of the walk along the river in the snow. Poor Aunt Julia! She, too, would soon be a shade with the shade of Patrick Morkan and his horse. He had caught that haggard look upon her face for a moment when she was singing *Arrayed for the Bridal*. Soon, perhaps, he would be sitting in that same drawing-room, dressed in black, his silk hat on his knees. The blinds would be drawn down and Aunt Kate would be sitting beside him, crying and blowing her nose and telling him how Julia had died. He would cast about in his mind for some words that might console her, and would find only lame and useless ones. Yes, yes: that would happen very soon.

The air of the room chilled his shoulders. He stretched himself cautiously along under the sheets and lay down beside his wife. One by one, they were all becoming shades. Better pass boldly into that other world, in the full glory of some passion, than fade and wither dismally with age. He thought of how she who lay beside him had locked in her heart for so many years that image of her lover's eyes when he had told her that he did not wish to live.

Generous tears filled Gabriel's eyes. He had never felt like that himself towards any woman, but he knew that such a feeling must be love. The tears gathered more thickly in his eyes and in the partial darkness he imagined he saw the form of a young man standing under a dripping tree. Other forms were near. His soul had approached that region where dwell the vast hosts of the dead. He was conscious of, but could not apprehend, their wayward and flickering existence. His own identity was fading out into a grey impalpable world: the solid world itself, which these dead had one time reared and lived in, was dissolving and dwindling.

A few light taps upon the pane made him turn to the window. It had begun to snow again. He watched sleepily the flakes, silver and dark, falling obliquely against the lamplight. The time had come for him to set out on his journey westward. Yes, the newspapers were right: snow was general all over Ireland. It was falling on every part of the dark central plain, on the treeless hills, falling softly upon the Bog of Allen and, farther westward, softly falling into the dark mutinous Shannon waves. It was falling, too, upon every part of the lonely churchyard on the hill where Michael Furey lay buried. It lay thickly drifted on the crooked crosses and headstones, on the spears of the little gate, on the barren thorns. His soul swooned slowly as he heard the snow falling faintly through the universe and faintly falling, like the descent of their last end, upon all the living and the dead.

Critical Questions

WHAT ARE the moments when emotion is most poignantly felt in the story? What is the stimulus for the emotion in each instance? Could the expression be called sentimental? (Distinguish between sentimental treatment and sentimental subject.)

At what points in the story does Gabriel Conroy reveal himself most clearly? Is Joyce's treatment of Gabriel sympathetic, neutral or satirical?

Do the characters strike you as free or frustrated? Consider Lily, Aunt Kate and Aunt Julia, Miss Ivors, Bartell D'Arcy, Gretta, Gabriel. What do Freddy Malins and Mr. Browne contribute to the story?

Discuss the possible symbolic value in the story of Johnny (Grandfather's horse), the snow, Michael Furey.

How do you account for the length and the proportions of the story, its narrative method, and the considerable attention to apparently insignificant details?

What effect is created by the last three paragraphs? Consider in some detail the style of the last paragraph.

Joyce said that in *The Dubliners,* of which "The Dead" (1907) is the last story, his intention was to write "a chapter of the moral history of my country and I chose Dublin for the scene because that city seemed to me to be the centre of paralysis." What are the most important surface features of the life of the city seen in "The Dead"? The most important profound traits?

Although "The Dead" can be read with enjoyment without reference to its autobiographical elements or its relation to all the stories in *The Dubliners,* a student of the story should know that *The Dubliners,* like Joyce's *Ulysses,* has analogues in Homer's *Odyssey.* The understanding of Joyce's creative method in the story will be increased by a knowledge of the parts of the original tale that Joyce retells. (For an interesting article on the analogues see Richard Levin and Charles Shattuck's "A New Reading of Joyce's *Dubliners*," reprinted from *Accent*, Winter, 1944, in Seon Givens, ed.; *James Joyce: Two Decades of Criticism* [1948], pp. 87–92.)

The Poems

~~~~~~

POETRY MAKES the greatest demands on the critical reader and it offers him the greatest rewards. To read poetry sensitively, skillfully and relevantly requires practice and it requires some understanding of the ways in which poetry differs from other forms of discourse. In poetry language is used for all of its functions: for its sound, its rhythmic arrangement, its plain prose meaning or denotation, and its suggestiveness or connotation. It is impossible to know beforehand which of these functions the language of a poem will be fulfilling at any given time, and very often it will be found that the language is operating in several ways simultaneously. Accordingly, the good reader must be alert with his ears, with his understanding and with his imagination. For him the printed poem is something like a musical score and he must know how to play it if it is to yield his meaning to him.

We need not worry too much about the nature of poetry. Two poets, writing in the essay section of this volume, give apparently contradictory views. E. E. Cummings declares in his "Nonlecture" that "poetry is being, not doing"; Archibald MacLeish, lecturing on "The Poet and the Press," maintains that "Poetry, despite the almost magical powers of the greatest poets, is a human labor." In a sense they are both right. Poetry essentially produces states of mind, not actions; yet a poem is a constructed thing, an art work, a piece of craftsmanship, or it is nothing. If we ask the question, "To what class of things do successful poems belong?" the answer might be given, "To the class of moments of most highly significant consciousness."

What kind of thought or statement do we find in poetry?

Most commonly, not the ordinary logical statement of prose. Poetry deals largely in figurative language; its most common vehicle is metaphor. We hear a typical poet talking when Dylan Thomas says

> I would be tickled by the rub that is:
> Man be my metaphor.

It is sometimes said that poetry is the art of calling names, which does not suggest that it is very important. But when Shakespeare says

> That time of year thou mayst in me behold
> When yellow leaves, or none, or few, do hang
> Upon those boughs which shake against the cold,
> Bare ruin'd choirs, where late the sweet birds sang

he is doing some elaborate name-calling. The aging man is like the autumn of the year, more specifically like the tree which has lost most of its leaves; the tree in turn is like a ruined chapel formerly occupied by sweet singers. This metaphorical thinking evokes qualities and attributes for the speaker's age and also expresses in a subtle way his attitude toward it.

The critical reader of poetry must be aware of tone. It is easy enough to respond to exclamation, as when the poet Hopkins exults in the beauty of a bird in flight,

> And the fire that breaks from thee then, a billion
> Times told lovelier, more dangerous, O my chevalier!

Just so when Keats exclaims in awe at the permanent beauty of the carved figures in the marble of the Grecian urn:

> Ah, happy, happy boughs! that cannot shed
> Your leaves, nor ever bid the spring adieu;
> And, happy melodist, unweariëd,
> Forever piping songs forever new;

Or the tone may result from solemn pronouncement, as when Milton says of God

> His state
> Is kingly: thousands at his bidding speed
> And post o'er land and ocean without rest.

Such tone of certainty and finality does not have to be associated with a divine subject; it may even occur in the humble context of pastoral:

> Time drives the flocks from field to fold
> When rivers rage and rocks grow cold

says Raleigh's nymph in her reply to the carefree invitations of a passionate shepherd.

Poetry most often involves emotion, but it may also present the more rational activities of the mind, such as reflection and the kind of logical thought that produces paradox. Pope is a good example:

> Wise wretch! with pleasures too refin'd to please;
> With too much spirit to be e'er at ease;
> With too much quickness ever to be taught;
> With too much thinking to have common thought:
> You purchase pain with all that joy can give,
> And die of nothing but a rage to live.

This kind of reflective, epigrammatic, witty discourse does not require always the highly polished, sophisticated urbanity of Pope; it can be present in the homely, colloquial diction of Robert Frost:

> Men of the woods and lumberjacks,
> They judged me by their appropriate tool.
> Except as a fellow handled an ax,
> They had no way of knowing a fool.

And finally, of course, poetry may sing or dance. The contagious lilt of a chorus in Dryden's "Secular Masque" may serve to illustrate:

> Then our age was in its prime,
> Free from rage, and free from crime,

A very merry, dancing, drinking,
Laughing, quaffing, and unthinking time.

What a poem says, what it means, what final effect it produces—these are by no means easy questions. Language is both
direct and oblique. Coleridge described this quality of poetry in
the twenty-second chapter of *Biographia Literaria:*

> In poetry, in which every line, every phrase, may pass the ordeal
> of deliberation and deliberate choice, it is possible, and barely pos-
> sible, to attain that ultimatum which I have ventured to propose as
> the infallible test of a blameless style; its *untranslatableness* in words
> of the same language without injury to the meaning. Be it observed,
> however, that I include in the *meaning* of a word not only its cor-
> respondent object, but likewise all the associations which it recalls.
> For language is framed to convey not the object alone, but likewise
> the character, mood and intentions of the person who is representing
> it.

Any sensitive reader who takes to heart Coleridge's wisdom
on the subject of meaning and words will soon find that as he
reads poems, he is uncertain where to draw the line at the in-
clusion of associations. "All the associations which it recalls,"
says Coleridge. But surely some associations in the mind of
everyone are accidental and irrelevant, not really a part of the
language of the poem at all. "How can I be sure I'm not reading
into the poem something that isn't there—or that *you're* not
reading into it?" It is a valid question. And the answer is complex.
We can only say that to test his own reading, his own series of
suggestions and associations called up by the poem, the reader
must study what is sometimes called the poem's "strategy"—
its form, organization, style and scope; its approach to the reader
through its diction and verse form; its symmetry and proportion. These elements of the poem, properly studied, supply
a control over the associations admitted and a criterion of their
relevance. Finally, the critical reader needs a native tact in these
matters; critical reading is after all an art.

Terence, This Is Stupid Stuff

A. E. HOUSMAN (1859–1936)

"Terence, this is stupid stuff:
You eat your victuals fast enough;
There can't be much amiss, 'tis clear,
To see the rate you drink your beer.
But oh, good Lord, the verse you make,　　　　5
It gives a chap the belly-ache.
The cow, the old cow, she is dead;
It sleeps well, the hornèd head:
We poor lads, 'tis our turn now
To hear such tunes as killed the cow.　　　　10
Pretty friendship 'tis to rhyme
Your friends to death before their time
Moping melancholy mad:
Come, pipe a tune to dance to, lad."

Why, if 'tis dancing you would be,　　　　15
There's brisker pipes than poetry.
Say, for what were hop-yards meant,
Or why was Burton built on Trent?
Oh, many a peer of England brews
Livelier liquor than the Muse,　　　　20
And malt does more than Milton can
To justify God's ways to man.
Ale, man, ale's the stuff to drink
For fellows whom it hurts to think:
Look into the pewter pot　　　　25
To see the world as the world's not.

TERENCE, THIS IS STUPID STUFF is reprinted from *A Shropshire Lad* by A. E. Housman. Used by permission of Henry Holt and Company, Inc.

And faith, 'tis pleasant till 'tis past:
The mischief is that 'twill not last.
Oh, I have been to Ludlow fair
And left my necktie God knows where,   30
And carried half-way home, or near,
Pints and quarts of Ludlow beer:
Then the world seemed none so bad,
And I myself a sterling lad;
And down in lovely muck I've lain,   35
Happy till I woke again.
Then I saw the morning sky:
Heigho, the tale was all a lie;
The world, it was the old world yet,
I was I, my things were wet,   40
And nothing now remained to do
But begin the game anew.

Therefore, since the world has still
Much good, but much less good than ill,
And while the sun and moon endure
Luck's a chance, but trouble's sure,   45
I'd face it as a wise man would,
And train for ill and not for good.
'Tis true, the stuff I bring for sale
Is not so brisk a brew as ale: 50
Out of a stem that scored the hand
I wrung it in a weary land.
But take it: if the smack is sour,
The better for the embittered hour;
It should do good to heart and head   55
When your soul is in my soul's stead;
And I will friend you, if I may,
In the dark and cloudy day.

There was a king reigned in the East:
There, when kings will sit to feast,   60

They get their fill before they think
With poisoned meat and poisoned drink.
He gathered all that springs to birth
From the many-venomed earth;
First a little, thence to more,   65
He sampled all her killing store;
And easy, smiling, seasoned sound,
Sate the king when healths went round,
They put arsenic in his meat
And stared aghast to watch him eat;   70
They poured strychnine in his cup
And shook to see him drink it up:
They shook, they stared as white's their shirt:
Them it was their poison hurt.
—I tell the tale that I heard told.   75
Mithridates, he died old.

In My Craft or Sullen Art

DYLAN THOMAS (1914-1953)

In my craft or sullen art
Exercised in the still night
When only the moon rages
And the lovers lie abed
With all their griefs in their arms.   5
I labour by singing light
Not for ambition or bread
Or the strut and trade of charms
On the ivory stages

But for the common wages   10
Of their most secret heart.

Not for the proud man apart
From the raging moon I write
On these spindrift pages
Nor for the towering dead   15
With their nightingales and psalms
But for the lovers, their arms
Round the griefs of the ages,
Who pay no praise or wages
Nor heed my craft or art.   20

Poetry

MARIANNE MOORE (1887–   )

~~~~~~

I too, dislike it: there are things that are important
    beyond all this fiddle.
Reading it, however, with a perfect contempt for it,
    one discovers in
it after all, a place for the genuine.   5
    Hands that can grasp, eyes
    that can dilate, hair that can rise
        if it must, these things are important not because a

high sounding interpretation can be put upon them
    but because they are   10
useful. When they become so derivative
    as to become unintelligible,
the same thing may be said for all of us, that we

do not admire what
we cannot understand: the bat,   15
   holding on upside down or in quest of something to

eat, elephants pushing, a wild horse taking a roll,
  a tireless wolf under
a tree, the immovable critic twitching his skin
  like a horse that feels a flea, the base-   20
ball fan, the statistician—
  nor is it valid
   to discriminate against "business documents and

school-books"; all these phenomena are important.
  One must make a distinction   25
however: when dragged into prominence by half poets,
  the result is not poetry,
nor till the poets among us can be
  "literalists of
  the imagination"—above   30
   insolence and triviality and can present

for inspection, imaginary gardens with real toads in them,
  shall we have
it. In the meantime, if you demand on the one hand,
  the raw material of poetry in   35
   all its rawness and
   that which is on the other hand
    genuine, then you are interested in poetry.

On First Looking into Chapman's Homer

JOHN KEATS (1795–1821)

Much have I travelled in the realms of gold,
  And many goodly states and kingdoms seen;
  Round many western islands have I been
Which bards in fealty to Apollo hold.
Oft of one wide expanse had I been told   5
  That deep-browed Homer ruled as his demesne;
  Yet did I never breathe its pure serene
Till I heard Chapman speak out loud and bold:
Then felt I like some watcher of the skies
  When a new planet swims into his ken;   10
Or like stout Cortez when with eagle eyes
  He stared at the Pacific—and all his men
Looked at each other with a wild surmise—
  Silent, upon a peak in Darien.

Two Tramps in Mud Time

ROBERT FROST (1875–   )

Out of the mud two strangers came
And caught me splitting wood in the yard.

And one of them put me off my aim
By hailing cheerily "Hit them hard!"
I knew pretty well why he dropped behind 5
And let the other go on a way.
I knew pretty well what he had in mind:
He wanted to take my job for pay.

Good blocks of beech it was I split,
As large around as the chopping block; 10
And every piece I squarely hit
Fell splinterless as a cloven rock.
The blows that a life of self-control
Spares to strike for the common good
That day, giving a loose to my soul, 15
I spent on the unimportant wood.

The sun was warm but the wind was chill.
You know how it is with an April day
When the sun is out and the wind is still,
You're one month on in the middle of May. 20
But if you so much as dare to speak,
A cloud comes over the sunlit arch,
A wind comes off a frozen peak,
And you're two months back in the middle of March.

A bluebird comes tenderly up to alight 25
And fronts the wind to unruffle a plume,
His song so pitched as not to excite
A single flower as yet to bloom.
It is snowing a flake: and he half knew
Winter was only playing possum. 30
Except in color he isn't blue,
But he wouldn't advise a thing to blossom.

The water for which we may have to look
In summertime with a witching-wand,
In every wheelrut's now a brook, 35
In every print of a hoof a pond.
Be glad of water, but don't forget
The lurking frost in the earth beneath
That will steal forth after the sun is set
And show on the water its crystal teeth. 40

The time when most I loved my task
These two must make me love it more
By coming with what they came to ask.
You'd think I never had felt before
The weight of an ax-head poised aloft, 45
The grip on earth of outspread feet,
The life of muscles rocking soft
And smooth and moist in vernal heat.

Out of the woods two hulking tramps
(From sleeping God knows where last night, 50
But not long since in the lumber camps).
They thought all chopping was theirs of right.
Men of the woods and lumberjacks,
They judged me by their appropriate tool.
Except as a fellow handled an ax, 55
They had no way of knowing a fool.

Nothing on either side was said.
They knew they had but to stay their stay
And all their logic would fill my head:
As that I had no right to play 60
With what was another man's work for gain.
My right might be love but theirs was need.
And where the two exist in twain
Theirs was the better right—agreed.

But yield who will to their separation, 65
My object in living is to unite
My avocation and my vocation
As my two eyes make one in sight.
Only where love and need are one,
And the work is play for mortal stakes, 70
Is the deed ever really done
For Heaven and the future's sakes.

Miniver Cheevy

EDWIN ARLINGTON ROBINSON (1869–1935)

Miniver Cheevy, child of scorn,
    Grew lean while he assailed the seasons;
He wept that he was ever born,
    And he had reasons.

Miniver loved the days of old 5
    When swords were bright and steeds were prancing;
The vision of a warrior bold
    Would set him dancing.

Miniver sighed for what was not,
    And dreamed, and rested from his labors; 10
He dreamed of Thebes and Camelot,
    And Priam's neighbors.

Miniver mourned the ripe renown
    That made so many a name so fragrant;

He mourned Romance, now on the town,   15
    And Art, a vagrant.

Miniver loved the Medici,
    Albeit he had never seen one;
He would have sinned incessantly
    Could he have been one.   20

Miniver cursed the commonplace
    And eyed a khaki suit with loathing;
He missed the mediæval grace
    Of iron clothing.

Miniver scorned the gold he sought,   25
    But sore annoyed was he without it;
Miniver thought, and thought, and thought,
    And thought about it.

Miniver Cheevy, born too late,
    Scratched his head and kept on thinking;   30
Miniver coughed, and called it fate,
    And kept on drinking.

Moral Essays: Epistle II, To a Lady
Of the Characters of Women

ALEXANDER POPE (1688–1744)

Nothing so true as what you once let fall,
"Most women have no characters at all."
Matter too soft a lasting mark to bear,
And best distinguish'd by black, brown, or fair.
How many pictures of one nymph we view,   5
All how unlike each other, all how true!
Arcadia's countess here, in ermin'd pride,
Is there Pastora by a fountain side;
Here Fannia, leering on her own good man,
And there a naked Leda with a swan.   10
Let then the fair one beautifully cry,
In Magdalen's loose hair and lifted eye,
Or, dress'd in smiles of sweet Cecilia shine,
With simp'ring angels, palms, and harps divine;
Whether the charmer sinner it, or saint it,   15
If folly grow romantic I must paint it.
    Come then, the colours and the ground prepare!
Dip in the rainbow, trick her off in air;
Choose a firm cloud, before it fall, and in it
Catch, ere she change, the Cynthia of this minute.   20
    Rufa, whose eye quick-glancing o'er the park,
Attracts each light gay meteor of a spark,
Agrees as ill with Rufa studying Locke
As Sappho's di'monds with her dirty smock;
Or Sappho at her toilet's greasy task,   25
With Sappho fragrant at an ev'ning mask:
So morning insects that in muck begun
Shine, buzz, and fly-blow in the setting sun.

How soft is Silia! fearful to offend,
The frail one's advocate, the weak one's friend: 30
To her Calista prov'd her conduct nice,
And good Simplicius asks of her advice.
Sudden, she storms! she raves! You tip the wink,
But spare your censure; Silia does not drink:
All eyes may see from what the change arose,   35
All eyes may see—a pimple on her nose.

    Papillia, wedded to her am'rous spark,
Sighs for the shades—"How charming is a park!"
A park is purchas'd, but the fair he sees
All bath'd in tears—"Oh, odious, odious trees!"   40

    Ladies, like variegated tulips, show;
'Tis to their changes half their charms we owe;
Fine by defect, and delicately weak,
Their happy spots the nice admirer take;
'Twas thus Calypso once each heart alarm'd,   45
Aw'd without virtue, without beauty charm'd;
Her tongue bewitch'd as oddly as her eyes,
Less wit than mimic, more a wit than wise;
Strange graces still, and stranger flights she had,
Was just not ugly, and was just not mad;   50
Yet ne'er so sure our passion to create,
As when she touch'd the brink of all we hate.

    Narcissa's nature, tolerably mild,
To make a wash, would hardly stew a child;
Has ev'n been prov'd to grant a lover's pray'r,   55
And paid a tradesman once to make him stare;
Gave alms at Easter, in a Christian trim,
And made a widow happy, for a whim.
Why then declare good-nature is her scorn,
When 'tis by that alone she can be borne?   60
Why pique all mortals, yet affect a name?
A fool to pleasure, yet a slave to fame:
Now deep in Taylor and the Book of Martyrs,

Now drinking citron with his Grace and Chartres:
Now conscience chills her, and now passion burns;   65
And atheism and religion take their turns;
A very heathen in the carnal part,
Yet still a sad, good Christian at her heart.
　　See Sin in state, majestically drunk;
Proud as a peeress, prouder as a punk;   70
Chaste to her husband, frank to all beside,
A teeming mistress, but a barren bride.
What then? let blood and body bear the fault,
Her head's untouch'd, that noble seat of thought:
Such this day's doctrine—in another fit   75
She sins with poets through pure love of wit.
What has not fir'd her bosom or her brain?
Cæsar and Tall-boy, Charles and Charlemagne.
As Helluo, late dictator of the feast,
The nose of *haut-gout*, and the tip of taste,   80
Critiqu'd your wine, and analyz'd your meat,
Yet on plain pudding deign'd at home to eat;
So Philomedé, lect'ring all mankind
On the soft passion, and the taste refin'd,
Th' address, the delicacy—stoops at once,   85
And makes her hearty meal upon a dunce.
　　Flavia's a wit, has too much sense to pray;
To toast our wants and wishes, is her way;
Nor asks of God, but of her stars, to give
The mighty blessing, "while we live, to live."   90
Then all for death, that opiate of the soul!
Lucretia's dagger, Rosamonda's bowl.
Say, what can cause such impotence of mind?
A spark too fickle, or a spouse too kind.
Wise wretch! with pleasures too refin'd to please;   95
With too much spirit to be e'er at ease;
With too much quickness ever to be taught;
With too much thinking to have common thought:

You purchase pain with all that joy can give,
And die of nothing but a rage to live.   100
    Turn then from wits; and look on Simo's mate,
No ass so meek, no ass so obstinate.
Or her, that owns her faults, but never mends,
Because she's honest, and the best of friends.
Or her, whose life the church and scandal share,   105
Forever in a passion, or a pray'r.
Or her, who laughs at hell, but (like her Grace)
Cries, "Ah! how charming, if there's no such place!"
Or who in sweet vicissitude appears
Of mirth and opium, ratafia and tears,   110
The daily anodyne, and nightly draught,
To kill those foes to fair ones, time and thought.
Woman and fool are two hard things to hit;
For true no-meaning puzzles more than wit.
    But what are these to great Atossa's mind?   115
Scarce once herself, by turns all womankind!
Who, with herself, or others, from her birth
Finds all her life one warfare upon earth:
Shines in exposing knaves, and painting fools,
Yet is whate'er she hates and ridicules.   120
No thought advances, but her eddy brain
Whisks it about, and down it goes again.
Full sixty years the world has been her trade,
The wisest fool much time has ever made.
From loveless youth to unrespected age,   125
No passion gratified except her rage.
So much the fury still outran the wit,
The pleasure miss'd her, and the scandal hit.
Who breaks with her, provokes revenge from hell,
But he's a bolder man who dares be well.   130
Her ev'ry turn with violence pursu'd,
No more a storm her hate than gratitude:
To that each passion turns, or soon or late;

Love, if it makes her yield, must make her hate:
Superiors? death! and equals? what a curse! 135
But an inferior not dependent? worse.
Offend her, and she knows not to forgive;
Oblige her, and she'll hate you while you live:
But die, and she'll adore you—Then the bust
And temple rise—then fall again to dust. 140
Last night, her lord was all that's good and great;
A knave this morning, and his will a cheat.
Strange! by the means defeated of the ends,
By spirit robb'd of pow'r, by warmth of friends,
By wealth of follow'rs! without one distress, 145
Sick of herself through very selfishness!
Atossa, curs'd with ev'ry granted pray'r,
Childless with all her children, wants an heir.
To heirs unknown descends th' unguarded store,
Or wanders, Heav'n-directed, to the poor. 150
    Pictures like these, dear Madam, to design,
Asks no firm hand, and no unerring line;
Some wand'ring touches, some reflected light,
Some flying stroke alone can hit 'em right:
For how should equal colours do the knack? 155
Chameleons who can paint in white and black?
    "Yet Chloe sure was form'd without a spot"—
Nature in her then err'd not, but forgot.
"With ev'ry pleasing, ev'ry prudent part,
Say, what can Chloe want?"—She wants a heart. 160
She speaks, behaves, and acts just as she ought;
But never, never, reach'd one gen'rous thought.
Virtue she finds too painful an endeavour,
Content to dwell in decencies forever.
So very reasonable, so unmov'd, 165
As never yet to love, or to be lov'd.
She, while her lover pants upon her breast,
Can mark the figures on an Indian chest;

And when she sees her friend in deep despair,
Observes how much a chintz exceeds mohair.   170
Forbid it Heav'n, a favour or a debt
She e'er should cancel—but she may forget.
Safe is your secret still in Chloe's ear;
But none of Chloe's shall you ever hear.
Of all her dears she never slander'd one,   175
But cares not if a thousand are undone.
Would Chloe know if you're alive or dead?
She bids her footman put it in her head.
Chloe is prudent—Would you too be wise?
Then never break your heart when Chloe dies.   180
    One certain portrait may (I grant) be seen,
Which Heav'n has varnish'd out, and made a queen;
The same forever! and describ'd by all
With truth and goodness, as with crown and ball.
Poets heap virtues, painters gems at will,   185
And show their zeal, and hide their want of skill.
'Tis well—but, artists! who can paint or write,
To draw the naked is your true delight.
That robe of quality so struts and swells,
None see what parts of nature it conceals: 190
Th' exactest traits of body or of mind,
We owe to models of an humble kind.
If Queensberry to strip there's no compelling,
'Tis from a handmaid we must take a Helen.
From peer or bishop 'tis no easy thing   195
To draw the man who loves his God, or king:
Alas! I copy (or my draught would fail)
From honest Mah'met, or plain Parson Hale.
    But grant, in public men sometimes are shown,
A woman's seen in private life alone: 200
Our bolder talents in full light display'd;
Your virtues open fairest in the shade.
Bred to disguise, in public 'tis you hide;

There, none distinguish 'twixt your shame or pride,
Weakness or delicacy; all so nice,   205
That each may seem a virtue, or a vice.
    In men, we various ruling passions find;
In women, two almost divide the kind;
Those, only fix'd, they first or last obey,
The love of pleasure, and the love of sway.   210
    That, Nature gives; and where the lesson taught
Is but to please, can pleasure seem a fault?
Experience, this; by man's oppression curst,
They seek the second not to lose the first.
    Men, some to bus'ness, some to pleasure take;   215
But ev'ry woman is at heart a rake:
Men, some to quiet, some to public strife;
But ev'ry lady would be queen for life.
    Yet mark the fate of a whole sex of queens!
Pow'r all their end, but beauty all the means: 220
In youth they conquer, with so wild a rage,
As leaves them scarce a subject in their age:
For foreign glory, foreign joy, they roam:
No thought of peace or happiness at home.
But wisdom's triumph is well-tim'd retreat,   225
As hard a science to the fair as great!
Beauties, like tyrants, old and friendless grown,
Yet hate repose, and dread to be alone,
Worn out in public, weary ev'ry eye,
Nor leave one sigh behind them when they die.   230
    Pleasures the sex, as children birds, pursue,
Still out of reach, yet never out of view;
Sure, if they catch, to spoil the toy at most,
To covet flying, and regret when lost:
At last, to follies youth could scarce defend,   235
It grows their age's prudence to pretend;
Asham'd to own they gave delight before,
Reduc'd to feign it, when they give no more:

As hags hold sabbaths, less for joy than spite,
So these their merry, miserable night;   240
Still round and round the ghosts of beauty glide,
And haunt the places where their honour died.
　See how the world its veterans rewards!
A youth of frolics, an old age of cards;
Fair to no purpose, artful to no end,   245
Young without lovers, old without a friend;
A fop their passion, but their prize a sot;
Alive, ridiculous, and dead, forgot!
　Ah! Friend! to dazzle let the vain design;
To raise the thought and touch the heart, be thine!   250
That charm shall grow, while what fatigues the Ring,
Flaunts and goes down, an unregarded thing:
So when the sun's broad beam has tir'd the sight,
All mild ascends the moon's more sober light,
Serene in virgin modesty she shines,   255
And unobserv'd the glaring orb declines.
　Oh! blest with temper, whose unclouded ray
Can make to-morrow cheerful as to-day;
She, who can love a sister's charms, or hear
Sighs for a daughter with unwounded ear;   260
She, who ne'er answers till a husband cools,
Or, if she rules him, never shows she rules;
Charms by accepting, by submitting sways,
Yet has her humour most, when she obeys;
Let fops or fortune fly which way they will;   265
Disdains all loss of tickets, or codille;
Spleen, vapours, or smallpox, above them all,
And mistress of herself, though china fall.
　And yet, believe me, good as well as ill,
Woman's at best a contradiction still.   270
Heav'n, when it strives to polish all it can
Its last best work, but forms a softer man;
Picks from each sex, to make the fav'rite blest,

Your love of pleasure, our desire of rest:
Blends, in exception to all gen'ral rules,   275
Your taste of follies, with our scorn of fools:
Reserve with frankness, art with truth allied,
Courage with softness, modesty with pride;
Fix'd principles, with fancy ever new;
Shakes all together, and produces—You.   280
    Be this a woman's fame: with this unblest,
Toasts live a scorn, and queens may die a jest.
This Phœbus promis'd (I forget the year)
When those blue eyes first open'd on the sphere;
Ascendant Phœbus watch'd that hour with care,   285
Averted half your parents' simple pray'r;
And gave you beauty, but denied the pelf
That buys your sex a tyrant o'er itself.
The gen'rous god, who wit and gold refines,
And ripens spirits as he ripens mines,   290
Kept dross for duchesses, the world shall know it,
To you gave sense, good-humour, and a poet.

Critical Analysis

THE SUBTITLE "Of the Characters of Women" describes generally
Pope's poem, but the first five-sixths of the epistle is a satirical
portrait gallery in verse, and the last part is an enthusiastic favorable portrait—a compliment to the Lady of the title, Martha
Blount. Pope contrasts her character, manner, and disposition to
an array of eighteenth-century court women. No one in the group
is named except the Duchess of Queensberry (line 193), but they
are given distinguishing classical names, some of which suggest
particular features or qualities.

    The poem develops as a series of illustrations of the truth of
Martha Blount's remark, "Most women have no characters at all."
What this means is that women, unlike men, are not controlled

by a ruling passion or principle; they are changeable, self-
contradictory, inconsistent. Any definite description you apply
to a woman is immediately contradicted by something else in her
behavior or temperament. This complaint, by no means original
with Pope or Martha Blount, of course, is made fresh and vivid
by the metaphor of painting portraits. Most society ladies, says
Pope, have to be portrayed in a series of roles—as a countess in
court costume and as a shepherdess; as a good and loving wife
and as the naked pagan Leda with her swan-lover; as the immoral
Magdalen and the pure St. Cecilia. How then is the poet to cap-
ture them in a single verse portrait apiece? This is the all but impossible task Pope sets himself, and the answer he gives to the
question of how to do it develops the painting metaphor and
incidentally characterizes his own style and manner:

> Come then, the colours and the ground prepare!
> Dip in the rainbow, trick her off in air;
> Choose a firm cloud, before it fall, and in it
> Catch, ere she change, the Cynthia of this minute. (17–20)

The idea that the material itself is evanescent is of course a phras-
ing of the main theme, but the suggestion that the treatment is to
be all delicate and airy is in part a deliberate deception of the
reader: he is all the more shocked when he finds that very frequently the ladies are sketched not with cloud-stuff and rainbow
tints, but with acid, sharply and firmly etched. But Pope's model
in this poem and others like it is Horace, and the epistles of Horace
are satires which are never heavy-footed and violent, but witty,
urbane, and smooth. The conventional "epistle" or letter gives an
air of informality, and the poet is not setting himself up as the
formal indignant castigator of the vices and follies of mankind.
The instrument of this kind of satirist is the rapier and not the
whip.

But neither "rapier" nor "paintbrush" adequately conveys an
idea of Pope's technique. It is first of all a kind of thinking, and

the intellectual power of the poem should not be underestimated. Take Calypso, for example, she who

> once each heart alarm'd,
> Awed without virtue, without beauty charm'd; (45–46)

what is the mysterious source of her attractiveness? If she is neither good nor beautiful, what is it that she has? Pope pretends that it is a mystery, but he shows by his manner of describing it that he knows that we are sometimes drawn or attracted by those things that are just this side of the repulsive:

> Strange graces still, and stranger flights she had,
> Was just not ugly, and was just not mad;
> Yet ne'er so sure our passion to create,
> As when she touch'd the brink of all we hate. (49–52)

For all the emphasis on female vanity, on social foibles, on fashionable affectations, this epistle is fundamentally a Moral Essay; it probes deeply into the relationship between motives and deeds. Narcissa is not a "bad" woman; she wouldn't stew a child, in the fashion of witches making their broth, just to prepare a cosmetic "wash" for her face; she is even generous, if you recite some of her deeds—but what about the motives? She

> Has ev'n been prov'd to grant a lover's pray'r,
> And paid a tradesman once to make him stare;
> Gave alms at Easter, in a Christian trim,
> And made a widow happy, for a whim. (55–58)

As a matter of fact, she is another example of that combination of irreconcilable opposites which constitutes the female character:

> Now conscience chills her, and now passion burns;
> And atheism and religion take their turns;
> A very heathen in the carnal part,
> Yet still a sad, good Christian at her heart. (65–67)

Pope's moral insight is exhibited even more impressively in the rhetoric and logical syntax of passages which appear on the surface to be mere wit:

> See Sin in state, majestically drunk;
> Proud as a peeress, prouder as a punk; (69–70)

Here the paradox in the phrase "majestically drunk" not only expresses contempt for the degradation of majestic qualities in drunkenness; it also prepares the reader's mind for some such phrase as "drunk as a lord." And the phrase follows, satisfyingly: "Proud as a peeress," but by a verbal trick Pope converts what seems like a superlative into a mere positive, and the comparative "prouder as a punk" explodes in a marvelous anticlimax. The rhetorical progression in the description of Flavia, the epicurean, reveals the same degree of profundity:

> Wise wretch! with pleasures too refin'd to please;
> With too much spirit to be e'er at ease;
> With too much quickness ever to be taught;
> With too much thinking to have common thought:
> You purchase pain with all that joy can give,
> And die of nothing but a rage to live. (95–100)

The thrice-repeated "with too much . . ." and the metaphor of purchasing develop a sense of opulence and wealth to give a terrible significance to the word "nothing" in the last line.

To temper this moral seriousness and to keep the poem on the level of the well-bred, cultivated letter from one friend to another, to suggest a tone of gallant frankness rather than zealous misogyny, Pope returns, after one hundred and fifty lines, to a comment on his technique:

> Pictures like these, dear Madam, to design,
> Asks no firm hand, and no unerring line;
> Some wand'ring touches, some reflected light,
> Some flying stroke alone can hit 'em right: (151–154)

Any analysis of Pope's style might take this passage as its point of departure. Is there really no firm hand or unerring line in these portraits? Are they really just flying strokes?

The versification of this poem is of course connected with its wit. But the iambic pentameter couplet which Pope so polished and developed, which he made so capable of variety and so fluent in a poem of almost three hundred lines, is not to be considered the source of the wit. It is the sharpening of something which already cuts. So many illustrations offer themselves to show Pope's skill in the technique of versification that it is hard to make a choice. Is he most remarkable for his variation of the normal iambic movement to make a sudden special effect, as in the second line of

> A very heathen in the carnal part,
> Yet still a sad, good Christian at her heart. (67–68)

or is he to be praised for the compactness of his summarizing couplets, when he conveys the matter of an epic in an epigram?

> From loveless youth to unrespected age,
> No passion gratified except her rage. (125–126)

One might point out the extraordinary precision in the choice of the specific detail to contrast with a general emotion:

> She, while her lover pants upon her breast,
> Can mark the figures on an Indian chest;
> And when she sees her friend in deep despair,
> Observes how much a chintz exceeds mohair. (167–170)

This is in reality a perfect realization of balance, intellectually and imaginatively, and the same poise is evident in Pope's prosody. The quotability of his general statements is often due to this balance:

> In men, we various ruling passions find;
> In women, two almost divide the kind;

> Those, only fix'd, they first or last obey,
> The love of pleasure, and the love of sway. (207–210)

Here the unbalance of the third line, in the placing of caesuras, prepares the ear for the satisfaction of the perfect balance of the fourth, and even the parallel structure of the first and second lines, with the early caesura, has its effect on the last line.

The end of the poem, progressing from the character of "Queensberry" through some general reflections on the female sex, leads up to the good advice and gallant compliment paid to Martha Blount. Yet in paying this compliment Pope does not retract his general contention about the contradictions in feminine character; he only makes it clear that one combination of disparate traits, the best from each sex, has resulted in the creation of an ideal woman and friend. As the poet makes his exit, he separates Martha Blount from the women of the world he has been describing. She has beauty but not wealth; hence she is unspoiled. And in the final lines, as he shows the compensations for lack of wealth, he produces the same retarding effect in the last line that we are accustomed to at the end of a piece of music:

> The gen'rous god, who wit and gold refines,
> And ripens spirits as he ripens mines,
> Kept dross for duchesses, the world shall know it,
> To you gave sense, good-humour, and a poet. (289–292)

Anyone who walks through an art gallery and looks at the portraits of eighteenth-century ladies by Lely, Kneller and Reynolds is not quite satisfied until he goes up to the pictures of the ladies, in their roles as the goddess Diana, the Tragic Muse, or St. Cecilia, to read on the little brass plates the names of the actual subjects of the pictures. So, in Pope's poem, it may be of some interest to know that Philomede is supposed to represent Henrietta, Duchess of Marlborough, in succession to her father, the first Duke; Atossa is traditionally supposed to be Sarah, Duchess of Marlborough, widow of the first Duke; Chloe is thought to be the Countess of Suffolk (Mrs. Howard), a neighbor of

Pope's at Twickenham and formerly mistress to King George II.
There is some point to "dross for *duchesses*" in the next-to-last
line.

Sir Patrick Spence

ANONYMOUS

    The king sits in Dumferling toune,
        Drinking the blude-reid wine:
    "O whar will I get guid sailor,
        To sail this schip of mine?"

    Up and spak an eldern knicht,   5
        Sat at the kings richt kne:
    "Sir Patrick Spence is the best sailor
        That sails upon the se."

    The king has written a braid letter,
        And signd it wi his hand,   10
    And sent it to Sir Patrick Spence,
        Was walking on the sand.

    The first line that Sir Patrick red,
        A loud lauch lauchèd he;
    The next line that Sir Patrick red,   15
        The teir blinded his ee.

    "O wha is this has don this deid,
        This ill deid don to me,
    To send me out this time o' the yeir,
        To sail upon the se!   20

"Mak hast, mak haste, my mirry men all,
　　Our guid schip sails the morne":
"O say na sae, my master deir,
　　For I feir a deadlie storme.

"Late late yestreen I saw the new moone,　　25
　　Wi the auld moone in hir arme,
And I feir, I feir, my deir master,
　　That we will cum to harme."

O our Scots nobles wer richt laith
　　To weet their cork-heild schoone;　　30
Bot lang owre a' the play wer playd,
　　Thair hats they swam aboone.

O lang, lang may their ladies sit,
　　Wi thair fans into their hand,
Or eir they se Sir Patrick Spence　　35
　　Cum sailing to the land.

O lang, lang may the ladies stand,
　　Wi thair gold kems in their hair,
Waiting for thair ain deir lords,
　　For they'll se thame na mair.　　40

Haf owre, haf owre to Aberdour,
　　It's fiftie fadom deip,
And thair lies guid Sir Patrick Spence,
　　Wi the Scots lords at his feit.

Edward

ANONYMOUS

"Why dois your brand sae drap wi bluid,
   Edward, Edward,
Why dois your brand sae drap wi bluid,
 And why sae sad gang yee O?"
"O I hae killed my hauke sae guid,   5
   Mither, mither,
O I hae killed my hauke sae guid,
 And I had nae mair bot hee O."

"Your haukis bluid was nevir sae reid,
   Edward, Edward,   10
Your haukis bluid was nevir sae reid,
 My deir son I tell thee O."
"O I hae killed my reid-roan steid,
   Mither, mither,
O I hae killed my reid-roan steid,   15
 That erst was sae fair and frie O."

"Your steid was auld, and ye hae got mair,
   Edward, Edward,
Your steid was auld, and ye hae got mair,
 Sum other dule ye drie O."   20
"O I hae killed my fadir deir,
   Mither, mither,
O I hae killed my fadir deir,
 Alas, and wae is mee O!"

"And whatten penance wul ye drie for that,   25
   Edward, Edward,

643

And whatten penance will ye drie for that?
　　　My deir son, now tell me O."
"Ile set my feit in yonder boat,
　　　　　Mither, mither,   30
Ile set my feit in yonder boat,
　　　And Ile fare ovir the sea O."

"And what wul ye doe wi your towirs and your ha,
　　　　　Edward, Edward?
And what wul ye doe wi your towirs and your ha,   35
　　　That were sae fair to see O?"
"Ile let thame stand tul they doun fa,
　　　　　Mither, mither,
Ile let thame stand tul they doun fa,
　　　For here nevir mair maun I bee O."   40

"And what wul ye leive to your bairns and your wife,
　　　　　Edward, Edward?
And what wul ye leive to your bairns and your wife,
　　　Whan ye gang ovir the sea O?"
"The warldis room, late them beg thrae life,   45
　　　　　Mither, mither,
The warldis room, late them beg thrae life,
　　　For thame nevir mair wul I see O."

"And what wul ye leive to your ain mither deir,
　　　　　Edward, Edward?   50
And what wul ye leive to your ain mither deir?
　　　My deir son, now tell me O."
"The curse of hell frae me sall ye beir,
　　　　　Mither, mither,
The curse of hell frae me sall ye beir,   55
　　　Sic counseils ye gave to me O."

Lord Randal

ANONYMOUS

"O where hae ye been, Lord Randal, my son?
O where hae ye been, my handsome young man?"
"I hae been to the wild wood; mother, make my bed soon,
For I'm weary wi hunting, and fain wald lie down."

"Where gat ye your dinner, Lord Randal, my son?   5
Where gat ye your dinner, my handsome young man?"
"I din'd wi my true-love; mother, make my bed soon,
For I'm weary wi hunting, and fain wald lie down."

"What gat ye to your dinner, Lord Randal, my son?
What gat ye to your dinner, my handsome young man?"   10
"I gat eels boiled in broo; mother, make my bed soon,
For I'm weary wi hunting, and fain wald lie down."

"What became of your bloodhounds, Lord Randal, my son?
What became of your bloodhounds, my handsome young man?"
"O they swelld and they died; mother, make my bed soon,   15
For I'm weary wi hunting, and fain wald lie down."

"O I fear ye are poisond, Lord Randal, my son!
O I fear ye are poisond, my handsome young man!"
"O yes! I am poisond; mother, make my bed soon,
For I'm sick at the heart and I fain wald lie down."   20

645

Ballad of the Goodly Fere

(Simon Zelotes speaketh it somewhile after the Crucifixion)

EZRA POUND (1885–   )

Ha' we lost the goodliest fere o' all
For the priests and the gallows tree?
Aye, lover he was of brawny men,
O' ships and the open sea.

When they came wi' a host to take Our Man   5
His smile was good to see,
"First let these go!" quo' our Goodly Fere,
"Or I'll see ye damned," says he.

Aye, he sent us out through the crossed high spears,
And the scorn of his laugh rang free,   10
"Why took ye not me when I walked about
Alone in the town?" says he.

Oh we drank his "Hale" in the good red wine
When we last made company,
No capon priest was the Goodly Fere   15
But a man o' men was he.

I ha' seen him drive a hundred men
Wi' a bundle o' cords swung free,
When they took the high and holy house
For their pawn and treasury.   20

They'll no get him a' in a book I think
Though they write it cunningly;
No mouse of the scrolls was the Goodly Fere
But aye loved the open sea.

If they think they ha' snared our Goodly Fere   25
They are fools to the last degree.
"I'll go to the feast," quo' our Goodly Fere,
"Though I go to the gallows tree."

"Ye ha' seen me heal the lame and the blind,
And wake the dead," says he,   30
"Ye shall see one thing to master all:
'Tis how a brave man dies on the tree."

A son of God was the Goodly Fere
That bade us his brothers be.
I ha' seen him cow a thousand men.   35
I ha' seen him upon the tree.

He cried no cry when they drave the nails
And the blood gushed hot and free,
The hounds of the crimson sky gave tongue
But never a cry cried he.   40

I ha' seen him cow a thousand men
On the hills o' Galilee,
They whined as he walked out calm between,
Wi' his eyes like the gray o' the sea.

Like the sea that brooks no voyaging   45
With the winds unleashed and free,
Like the sea that he cowed at Gennesaret
Wi' twey words spoke' suddenly.

A master of men was the Goodly Fere,
A mate of the wind and sea,   50
If they think they ha' slain our Goodly Fere
They are fools eternally.

I ha' seen him eat o' the honey-comb
Sin' they nailed him to the tree.

Journey of the Magi

T. S. ELIOT (1888–   )

'A cold coming we had of it,
Just the worst time of the year
For a journey, and such a long journey:
The ways deep and the weather sharp,
The very dead of winter.'   5
And the camels galled, sore-footed, refractory,
Lying down in the melting snow.
There were times we regretted
The summer palaces on slopes, the terraces,
And the silken girls bringing sherbet.   10
Then the camel men cursing and grumbling
And running away, and wanting their liquor and women,
And the night-fires going out, and the lack of shelters,
And the cities hostile and the towns unfriendly
And the villages dirty and charging high prices: 15
A hard time we had of it.
At the end we preferred to travel all night,
Sleeping in snatches,

With the voices singing in our ears, saying
That this was all folly.   20

Then at dawn we came down to a temperate valley,
Wet, below the snow line, smelling of vegetation;
With a running stream and a water-mill beating the darkness,
And three trees on the low sky,
And an old white horse galloped away in the meadow.   25
Then we came to a tavern with vine-leaves over the lintel,
Six hands at an open door dicing for pieces of silver,
And feet kicking the empty wine-skins.
But there was no information, and so we continued
And arrived at evening, not a moment too soon   30
Finding the place; it was (you may say) satisfactory.

All this was a long time ago, I remember,
And I would do it again, but set down
This set down
This: were we led all that way for   35
Birth or Death? There was a Birth, certainly,
We had evidence and no doubt. I had seen birth and death,
But had thought they were different; this Birth was
Hard and bitter agony for us, like Death, our death.
We returned to our places, these Kingdoms,   40
But no longer at ease here, in the old dispensation,
With an alien people clutching their gods.
I should be glad of another death.

The Chariot

EMILY DICKINSON (1830–1886)

Because I could not stop for Death,
He kindly stopped for me;
The carriage held but just ourselves
And Immortality.

We slowly drove, he knew no haste,   5
And I had put away
My labour, and my leisure too,
For his civility.

We passed the school where children played,
Their lessons scarcely done;   10
We passed the fields of gazing grain,
We passed the setting sun.

We paused before a house that seemed
A swelling on the ground;
The roof was scarcely visible,   15
The cornice but a mound.

Since then 'tis centuries; but each
Feels shorter than the day
I first surmised the horses' heads
Were toward eternity.   20

THE CHARIOT by Emily Dickinson is reprinted from *The Poems of Emily Dickinson*, edited by Martha Dickinson Bianchi and Alfred Leete Hampson, by permission of Little Brown & Company.

The Scholar-Gypsy

MATTHEW ARNOLD (1822–1888)

Go, for they call you, shepherd, from the hill;
   Go, shepherd, and untie the wattled cotes!
      No longer leave thy wistful flock unfed,
   Nor let thy bawling fellows rack their throats,
      Nor the cropped herbage shoot another head.   5
        But when the fields are still,
   And the tired men and dogs all gone to rest,
      And only the white sheep are sometimes seen
      Cross and recross the strips of moon-blanched green,
   Come, shepherd, and again begin the quest!   10

Here, where the reaper was at work of late—
   In this high field's dark corner, where he leaves
      His coat, his basket, and his earthen cruse,
   And in the sun all morning binds the sheaves,
      Then here, at noon, comes back his stores to use—   15
        Here will I sit and wait,
   While to my ear from uplands far away
      The bleating of the folded flocks is borne,
      With distant cries of reapers in the corn—
   All the live murmur of a summer's day.   20

Screened is this nook o'er the high, half-reaped field,
   And here till sun-down, shepherd! will I be.
      Through the thick corn the scarlet poppies peep,
   And round green roots and yellowing stalks I see
      Pale pink convolvulus in tendrils creep;   25
        And air-swept lindens yield
   Their scent, and rustle down their perfumed showers

Of bloom on the bent grass where I am laid,
And bower me from the August sun with shade;
And the eye travels down to Oxford's towers.   30

And near me on the grass lies Glanvil's book—
Come, let me read the oft-read tale again!
The story of the Oxford scholar poor,
Of pregnant parts and quick inventive brain,
Who, tired of knocking at preferment's door,   35
One summer-morn forsook
His friends, and went to learn the gypsy-lore,
And roamed the world with that wild brotherhood,
And came, as most men deemed, to little good,
But came to Oxford and his friends no more.   40

But once, years after, in the country-lanes,
Two scholars, whom at college erst he knew,
Met him, and of his way of life inquired;
Whereat he answered that the gypsy-crew,
His mates, had arts to rule as they desired   45
The workings of men's brains,
And they can bind them to what thoughts they will.
"And I," he said, "the secret of their art,
When fully learned, will to the world impart;
But it needs heaven-sent moments for this skill."   50

This said, he left them, and returned no more.—
But rumors hung about the country-side,
That the lost Scholar long was seen to stray,
Seen by rare glimpses, pensive and tongue-tied,
In hat of antique shape, and cloak of gray,   55
The same the gypsies wore.
Shepherds had met him on the Hurst in spring;
At some lone alehouse in the Berkshire moors,
On the warm ingle-bench, the smock-frocked boors
Had found him seated at their entering.   60

But, 'mid their drink and clatter, he would fly.
   And I myself seem half to know thy looks,
     And put the shepherds, wanderer! on thy trace;
   And boys who in lone wheatfields scare the rooks
     I ask if thou hast passed their quiet place; 65
       Or in my boat I lie
Moored to the cool bank in the summer-heats,
   'Mid wide grass meadows which the sunshine fills,
   And watch the warm, green-muffled Cumner hills,
   And wonder if thou haunt'st their shy retreats. 70

For most, I know, thou lov'st retired ground!
   Thee at the ferry Oxford riders blithe,
     Returning home on summer-nights, have met
   Crossing the stripling Thames at Bab-lock-hithe,
     Trailing in the cool stream thy fingers wet, 75
       As the punt's rope chops round;
And leaning backward in a pensive dream,
   And fostering in thy lap a heap of flowers
   Plucked in shy fields and distant Wychwood bowers,
   And thine eyes resting on the moonlit stream. 80

And then they land, and thou art seen no more!—
   Maidens, who from the distant hamlets come
     To dance around the Fyfield elm in May,
   Oft through the darkening fields have seen thee roam,
     Or cross a stile into the public way. 85
       Oft thou hast given them store
Of flowers—the frail-leafed, white anemone,
   Dark bluebells drenched with dews of summer eves,
   And purple orchises with spotted leaves—
   But none hath words she can report of thee. 90

And, above Godstow Bridge, when hay-time's here
   In June, and many a scythe in sunshine flames,
     Men who through those wide fields of breezy grass

Where black-winged swallows haunt the glittering Thames,
   To bathe in the abandoned lasher pass,   95
      Have often passed thee near
Sitting upon the river bank o'ergrown;
   Marked thine outlandish garb, thy figure spare,
   Thy dark vague eyes, and soft abstracted air—
But, when they came from bathing, thou wast gone!   100

At some lone homestead in the Cumner hills,
   Where at her open door the housewife darns,
      Thou hast been seen, or hanging on a gate
To watch the threshers in the mossy barns.
      Children, who early range these slopes and late   105
         For cresses from the rills,
Have known thee eying, all an April-day,
   The springing pastures and the feeding kine;
   And marked thee, when the stars come out and shine,
Through the long dewy grass move slow away.   110

In autumn, on the skirts of Bagley Wood—
   Where most the gypsies by the turf-edged way
      Pitch their smoked tents, and every bush you see
With scarlet patches tagged and shreds of gray,
      Above the forest-ground called Thessaly—   115
         The blackbird, picking food,
Sees thee, nor stops his meal, nor fears at all;
   So often has he known thee past him stray,
   Rapt, twirling in thy hand a withered spray,
And waiting for the spark from heaven to fall.   120

And once, in winter, on the causeway chill
   Where home through flooded fields foot-travelers go,
      Have I not passed thee on the wooden bridge,
Wrapped in thy cloak and battling with the snow,
      Thy face tow'rd Hinksey and its wintry ridge?   125

And thou hast climbed the hill,
And gained the white brow of the Cumner range;
   Turned once to watch, while thick the snowflakes fall,
   The line of festal light in Christ-Church hall—
Then sought thy straw in some sequestered grange.				130

But what—I dream! Two hundred years are flown
   Since first thy story ran through Oxford halls,
      And the grave Glanvil did the tale inscribe
   That thou wert wandered from the studious walls
      To learn strange arts, and join a gypsy tribe;			135
         And thou from earth art gone
   Long since, and in some quiet churchyard laid—
      Some country-nook, where o'er thy unknown grave
      Tall grasses and white flowering nettles wave,
Under a dark, red-fruited yew-tree's shade.				140

—No, no, thou hast not felt the lapse of hours!
   For what wears out the life of mortal men?
      'Tis that from change to change their being rolls;
   'Tis that repeated shocks, again, again,
      Exhaust the energy of strongest souls				145
         And numb the elastic powers,
   Till having used our nerves with bliss and teen,
      And tired upon a thousand schemes our wit,
      To the just-pausing Genius we remit
Our worn-out life, and are—what we have been.				150

Thou hast not lived, why should'st thou perish, so?
   Thou hadst *one* aim, *one* business, *one* desire;
      Else wert thou long since numbered with the dead!
   Else hadst thou spent, like other men, thy fire!
      The generations of thy peers are fled,				155
         And we ourselves shall go;
But thou possessest an immortal lot,

And we imagine thee exempt from age
And living as thou liv'st on Glanvil's page,
Because thou hadst—what we, alas! have not.   160

For early didst thou leave the world, with powers
    Fresh, undiverted to the world without,
        Firm to their mark, not spent on other things;
    Free from the sick fatigue, the languid doubt,
        Which much to have tried, in much been baffled, brings.   165
            O life unlike to ours!
    Who fluctuate idly without term or scope,
        Of whom each strives, nor knows for what he strives,
        And each half lives a hundred different lives;
    Who wait like thee, but not, like thee, in hope.   170

Thou waitest for the spark from heaven! and we,
    Light half-believers of our casual creeds,
        Who never deeply felt, nor clearly willed,
    Whose insight never has borne fruit in deeds,
        Whose vague resolves never have been fulfilled;   175
            For whom each year we see
    Breeds new beginnings, disappointments new;
        Who hesitate and falter life away,
        And lose tomorrow the ground won today—
    Ah! do not we, wanderer! await it too?   180

Yes, we await it!—but it still delays,
    And then we suffer! and amongst us one,
        Who most hast suffered, takes dejectedly
    His seat upon the intellectual throne;
        And all his store of sad experience he   185
            Lays bare of wretched days;
    Tells us his misery's birth and growth and signs,
        And how the dying spark of hope was fed,
        And how the breast was soothed, and how the head,
    And all his hourly varied anodynes.   190

This for our wisest! and we others pine,
    And wish the long unhappy dream would end,
      And waive all claim to bliss, and try to bear;
    With close-lipped patience for our only friend,
        Sad patience, too near neighbor to despair—   195
          But none has hope like thine!
Thou through the fields and through the woods dost stray,
    Roaming the country-side, a truant boy,
    Nursing thy project in unclouded joy,
    And every doubt long blown by time away.   200

O born in days when wits were fresh and clear,
    And life ran gayly as the sparkling Thames;
      Before this strange disease of modern life,
    With its sick hurry, its divided aims,
        Its head o'ertaxed, its palsied hearts, was rife—   205
          Fly hence, our contact fear!
Still fly, plunge deeper in the bowering wood!
    Averse, as Dido did with gesture stern
    From her false friend's approach in Hades turn,
    Wave us away, and keep thy solitude!   210

Still nursing the unconquerable hope,
    Still clutching the inviolable shade,
      With a free, onward impulse brushing through,
    By night, the silvered branches of the glade—
        Far on the forest-skirts, where none pursue,   215
          On some mild pastoral slope
    Emerge, and resting on the moonlit pales
      Freshen thy flowers as in former years
      With dew, or listen with enchanted ears,
    From the dark dingles, to the nightingales!   220

But fly our paths, our feverish contact fly!
    For strong the infection of our mental strife,

Which, though it gives no bliss, yet spoils for rest;
And we should win thee from thy own fair life,
   Like us distracted, and like us unblest.   225
      Soon, soon thy cheer would die,
Thy hopes grow timorous, and unfixed thy powers,
   And thy clear aims be cross and shifting made;
   And then thy glad perennial youth would fade,
Fade, and grow old at last, and die like ours.   230

Then fly our greetings, fly our speech and smiles!
   —As some grave Tyrian trader, from the sea,
   Descried at sunrise an emerging prow
Lifting the cool-haired creepers stealthily,
   The fringes of a southward-facing brow   235
      Among the Ægæan isles;
And saw the merry Grecian coaster come,
   Freighted with amber grapes, and Chian wine,
   Green, bursting figs, and tunnies steeped in brine—
And knew the intruders on his ancient home,   240

The young light-hearted masters of the waves—
   And snatched his rudder, and shook out more sail;
   And day and night held on indignantly
O'er the blue Midland waters with the gale,
   Betwixt the Syrtes and soft Sicily,   245
      To where the Atlantic raves
Outside the western straits; and unbent sails
   There, where down cloudy cliffs, through sheets of foam,
   Shy traffickers, the dark Iberians come;
And on the beach undid his corded bales.   250

Critical Analysis

ARNOLD'S POEM is famous for various virtues, and it may impress
different readers in different ways, but a good critical analysis

will see to it that all the major elements in the poem are considered and that the relationship between Arnold's method and the total effect of the poem is adequately accounted for.

It is perhaps most obviously a pastoral poem celebrating the quiet beauties of the countryside around Oxford, and it is so faithful to the locality that it can be used as a kind of guidebook for walks among the Cumner Hills and Berkshire moors. Arnold's scenes which convey the feeling of the countryside are precise and specific: the shaded top of the half-reaped field (stanzas 2–3), the punt which serves as a ferry over the "stripling Thames" at Bablockhithe, the housewife darning at the open door of some homestead, the gypsies camped on the edge of Bagley Wood, the blackbird undisturbed by the familiar figure going by. They are rich in suggestion, they are chosen in a very satisfying way from that area halfway between the ideal and the actual, and they exhibit wide variety and compass, consciously reflecting different seasons of the year—May, harvest-time, autumn, winter.

To give this descriptive poetry life we have a figure moving through it—the scholar gypsy whose story is told in a seventeenth-century book, Joseph Glanvill's *The Vanity of Dogmatizing*. Arnold introduces the source directly into the poem. Stanza 4 summarizes it, and stanza 5 describes the lesson the scholar was trying to learn from the gypsies. For the most part, the scholar's relationship to the countryside is emphasized as one of shy familiarity, and it is only toward the end of the first thirteen stanzas, which fill out the description, that the more general and significant meaning of the scholar's search is mentioned:

And waiting for the spark from heaven to fall. (line 120)

The transition to the next section is strongly marked by rhetorical devices: "But what—I dream!" and the exclamation and question of the first lines of the succeeding stanzas.

Arnold now begins the development of his theme, for this is not a mere celebration of the Oxford countryside or a narrative from Oxford folklore, but a serious criticism of contemporary life. The essence of the scholar gypsy was unity of purpose, the poet says, and because of this unity of purpose he has gained immortality and youth, though perhaps he never succeeded in his search. A strong and explicit contrast is drawn between the scholar and us moderns, including the poet, who also wait for the spark from heaven, but "hesitate and falter life away." In fact, modern life is called a disease, "with its sick hurry, its divided aims," and the shy retiring avoidance of the world practiced by the scholar is now commended, for the quarrels ("mental strife"), indecision, and pessimism of the modern world are like an infection which it is only prudent to avoid. If he did not escape from life, in its modern form at any rate, the scholar would become "like us distracted, and like us unblest."

Here is a structural link between the first, descriptive section of the poem and the didactic second part. The justification for rejecting and escaping from modern life, or Arnold's interpretation of the nineteenth century, rests now upon the beauty of the pastoral Oxford countryside as given in the first section and the arguments of the second section. They reinforce each other.

Finally, since the scholar gypsy is something of a legend anyhow, now dead two hundred years and probably buried in some quiet country churchyard but still alive and youthful in the pages of Glanvill's book (and indeed much more so in Arnold's poem), he is associated with, or transformed into, a figure even farther back and more remote, an anonymous figure of the classical world. The "grave Tyrian trader" simile at the end of the poem is extended, in the epic manner; but its artistic significance is not that it shows Arnold's mastery of Greek material and his ability to handle it romantically without distortion; it is rather that the Tyrian, with his bold independence and his avoidance of the competition with Greek intruders, sails to the west across the Mediterranean. He is a symbol of the youth, optimism, independence which Arnold admired in the scholar gypsy. When we recover from the captivating intensity of the little narrative we see that it is a satisfying and consistent conclusion to the poem.

It returns our response to the level of beauty, where it started; it subsumes the critical didacticism of the second section, and it provides us with a remarkable example of the great range of Arnold's style—from the exotic richness of Keats to the simple, stark effectiveness of Wordsworth:

> There, where down cloudy cliffs, through sheets of foam,
>   Shy traffickers, the dark Iberians come;
> And on the beach undid his corded bales.

Hymn to Earth

ELINOR WYLIE (1886–1929)

> Farewell, incomparable element,
> Whence man arose, where he shall not return;
> And hail, imperfect urn
> Of his last ashes, and his firstborn fruit;
> Farewell, the long pursuit,   5
> And all the adventures of his discontent;
> The voyages which sent
> His heart averse from home:
> Metal of clay, permit him that he come
> To thy slow-burning fire as to a hearth;   10
> Accept him as a particle of earth.
>
> Fire, being divided from the other three,
> It lives removed, or secret at the core;
> Most subtle of the four,
> When air flies not, nor water flows,   15

It disembodied goes,
Being light, elixir of the first decree,
More volatile than he;
With strength and power to pass
Through space, where never his least atom was: 20
He has no part in it, save as his eyes
Have drawn its emanation from the skies.

A wingless creature heavier than air,
He is rejected of its quintessence;
Coming and going hence,   25
In the twin minutes of his birth and death,
He may inhale as breath,
As breath relinquish heaven's atmosphere,
Yet in it have no share,
Nor can survive therein   30
Where its outer edge is filtered pure and thin:
It doth but lend its crystal to his lungs
For his early crying, and his final songs.

The element of water has denied
Its child; it is no more his element;   35
It never will relent;
Its silver harvests are more sparsely given
Than the rewards of heaven,
And he shall drink cold comfort at its side:
The water is too wide: 40
The seamew and the gull
Feather a nest made soft and pitiful
Upon its foam; he has not any part
In the long swell of sorrow at its heart.

Hail and farewell, beloved element,   45
Whence he departed, and his parent once;
See where thy spirit runs

Which for so long hath had the moon to wife;
Shall this support his life
Until the arches of the waves be bent 50
And grow shallow and spent?
Wisely it cast him forth
With his dead weight of burdens nothing worth,
Leaving him, for the universal years,
A little seawater to make his tears. 55

Hail, element of earth, receive thy own,
And cherish, at thy charitable breast,
This man, this mongrel beast:
He plows the sand, and, at his hardest need,
He sows himself for seed; 60
He plows the furrow, and in this lies down
Before the corn is grown;
Between the apple bloom
And the ripe apple is sufficient room
In time, and matter, to consume his love 65
And make him parcel of a cypress grove.

Receive him as thy lover for an hour
Who will not weary, by a longer stay,
The kind embrace of clay;
Even within thine arms he is dispersed 70
To nothing, as at first;
The air flings downward from its four-quartered tower
Him whom the flames devour;
At the full tide, at the flood,
The sea is mingled with his salty blood: 75
The traveller dust, although the dust be vile,
Sleeps as thy lover for a little while.

Spring and Winter

WILLIAM SHAKESPEARE (1564–1616)

Spring

When daisies pied and violets blue
  And lady-smocks all silver-white
And cuckoo-buds of yellow hue
  Do paint the meadows with delight,
The cuckoo then, on every tree,   5
Mocks married men; for thus sings he,
           Cuckoo;
Cuckoo, cuckoo: O, word of fear,
Unpleasing to a married ear!

When shepherds pipe on oaten straws,   10
  And merry larks are ploughmen's clocks,
When turtles tread, and rooks, and daws,
  And maidens bleach their summer smocks,
The cuckoo then, on every tree,
Mocks married men; for thus sings he,   15
           Cuckoo;
Cuckoo, cuckoo: O, word of fear,
Unpleasing to a married ear!

Winter

When icicles hang by the wall,
  And Dick the shepherd blows his nail,
And Tom bears logs into the hall,
  And milk comes frozen home in pail,
When blood is nipp'd, and ways be foul,   5
Then nightly sings the staring owl,

Tu-who;

Tu-whit, tu-who—a merry note,
While greasy Joan doth keel the pot.

When all aloud the wind doth blow,   10
   And coughing drowns the parson's saw,
And birds sit brooding in the snow,
   And Marian's nose looks red and raw,
When roasted crabs hiss in the bowl,
Then nightly sings the staring owl,   15
Tu-who;

Tu-whit, tu-who—a merry note,
While greasy Joan doth keel the pot.

(Love's Labour's Lost, V, iii)

Full Fathom Five

WILLIAM SHAKESPEARE (1564–1616)

Full fathom five thy father lies;
   Of his bones are coral made;
Those are pearls that were his eyes:
   Nothing of him that doth fade,
But doth suffer a sea change   5
Into something rich and strange.
Sea nymphs hourly ring his knell:
Burthen. Ding-dong.

Hark! now I hear them,—Ding-dong, bell.

(The Tempest, I, ii)

Call for the Robin Redbreast and the Wren

JOHN WEBSTER (circa 1580–1634)

Call for the robin redbreast and the wren,
Since o'er shady groves they hover,
And with leaves and flowers do cover
The friendless bodies of unburied men.
Call unto his funeral dole   5
The ant, the field mouse, and the mole,
To rear him hillocks that shall keep him warm,
And, when gay tombs are robbed, sustain no harm;
But keep the wolf far thence, that's foe to men,
For with his nails he'll dig them up again.   10

(*The White Devil*, V, iv)

To Althea, from Prison

RICHARD LOVELACE (1618–1658)

When Love with unconfined wings
    Hovers within my gates,
And my divine Althea brings
    To whisper at the grates;
When I lie tangled in her hair   5
    And fettered to her eye,
The birds that wanton in the air
    Know no such liberty.

When flowing cups run swiftly round,
   With no allaying Thames,   10
Our careless heads with roses bound,
   Our hearts with loyal flames;
When thirsty grief in wine we steep,
   When healths and draughts go free,
Fishes that tipple in the deep   15
   Know no such liberty.

When, like committed linnets, I
   With shriller throat shall sing
The sweetness, mercy, majesty,
   And glories of my king;   20
When I shall voice aloud how good
   He is, how great should be,
Enlarged winds that curl the flood
   Know no such liberty.

Stone walls do not a prison make,   25
   Nor iron bars a cage:
Minds innocent and quiet take
   That for an hermitage.
If I have freedom in my love,
   And in my soul am free,   30
Angels alone, that soar above,
   Enjoy such liberty.

Like as the Waves Make towards the Pebbled Shore

WILLIAM SHAKESPEARE (1564–1616)

Like as the waves make towards the pebbled shore,
So do our minutes hasten to their end;
Each changing place with that which goes before,
In sequent toil all forwards do contend.
Nativity, once in the main of light,   5
Crawls to maturity, wherewith being crown'd,
Crooked eclipses 'gainst his glory fight,
And Time that gave doth now his gift confound.
Time doth transfix the flourish set on youth
And delves the parallels in beauty's brow,   10
Feeds on the rarities of nature's truth,
And nothing stands but for his scythe to mow:
    And yet to times in hope my verse shall stand,
    Praising thy worth, despite his cruel hand.

Critical Analysis

THIS SONNET seems to be a conventional poem on the well-worn
theme of the passage of time and the ability of poetry to survive
when other things are destroyed. Its subject matter offers nothing novel or unexpected; it is one of the most commonplace of
themes. Yet the sonnet is one of the greatest, even among Shakespeare's. Why?

To answer this question we must respond first of all to the
metaphorical language in the poem and take it seriously, for the
essence of the poem lies in its metaphorical thinking. Because a

Shakespearean sonnet is composed of three quatrains and a couplet, it is natural to look first to see if the metaphors are adapted to this structure.

The first quatrain presents a clear image of "our minutes" (that is, time allotted to us, considered in particles) represented as waves of the sea, each succeeding another in steady, rapid, incessant progression. The movement is rapid ("hasten") but labored ("toil" and "contend"). "Make towards" is a nautical expression, used of a ship. (See Shakespeare's *Comedy of Errors* I, i, 93 for another example.) The fourth line, a summary of time considered as the sea, is full of abstract words ("sequent toil," "forwards," which Shakespeare here uses as a noun, etc.), and it stresses the verbal ideas heavily, as indeed the whole quatrain does. See how many of the words are verbs or near-verbs: "make towards," "do," "hasten," "end" (near-verb), "changing place," "goes," "sequent" (near-verb, especially if the Latin *sequor* is recalled), "toil" (near-verb), "forwards" (near-verb), "contend." All this motion and action in the space of four lines! The first quatrain, then, adopts the basic image of minutes as waves and then reinforces it by conveying to the reader a powerful sense of surging and continuing motion.

The metaphor of the second quatrain is not so clear, because the thing acting is an abstract, "nativity." To the modern reader this word has associations from religion, or from religious painting, but in the time of Shakespeare it had a much more common reference —that of any person's birth, a time at which it was usual to cast a horoscope and tell the infant's fortune from the situation of the stars at the moment of "nativity." In the fifth line nativity is said to have been once in the "main" or sea of light (the word is used as in the expression "the Spanish Main"), and then in the sixth line, he "crawls" to maturity. The image here is a curious but not illogical one, of a baby. But as the quatrain develops, we see more clearly that it is also the sun. Expanding the quatrain very crudely, we might say something like this: "Our time passes by as a baby grows to be a man, or as the sun climbs up the sky, *or as both,* because the birth, growth, and decline of the sun every day is merely a model of what happens to all of us." "Crooked eclipses," which blot out part of the sun's perfect circle and are therefore crooked, are said to come after noon, or maturity. (We will not bother with the astronomical accuracy of this, because what is important is the metaphor, the image.) The eighth line, the last of this quatrain, is again more general and summary in nature: Time, that gave (the gift was "glory" and "maturity") now confounds his own gift, that is, mars or destroys it.

The third quatrain is tied closely to the second by a repetition of the statement about time, and the first three lines of this quatrain are all declarations of time's actions. He transfixes the flourish set on youth, a general statement equivalent to line 8 but more positive and direct. Then he "delves the parallels" or digs the furrows in beauty's brow, feeds on the rarities, mows with his scythe. The metaphor is agricultural, and time has become not only the grim reaper with his scythe, but the plowman and the consumer of the rarities of the garden as well. (Some readers may be too squeamish to accept Shakespeare's image of the wrinkles in the brow of a beautiful person as the furrows dug by time's plow; the poet does not force the image very hard, but because of the next two lines he clearly intends it.) In abstract terms, Youth, Beauty and Nature all perish in time.

The progression of the general images in the three quatrains is full of interest: first the sea, then the sky, and finally the earth; this gives a sense of the whole world's being involved and serves as a background to the final statement. Moreover, there is *dramatic* progression: in the first quatrain time exerts no action on us; they are "our" minutes, to be sure, but the struggle seems one merely of movement, not of opposition. In the second quatrain the struggle is more active, but directed against nativity, or the sun, and does not directly implicate the reader. But cruelty is already apparent as a characteristic of time, in fighting against glory and in confounding the gift given. In the third quatrain the victims are, respectively, youth, beauty, and nature's truth, so the conclusion that nothing escapes the scythe is justified, and it includes us.

This feeling is so marked that the turn in the couplet must be very strong: *And yet!* Granting everything the three quatrains have established, still poetry will survive. "Shall" is strongly emphasized by the *s* sounds surrounding it, and the word order is carefully arranged to give the "despite" statement after the declaration, not before it. The couplet is tied to the last quatrain by the repetition of "stands—stand."

If we glance back through the quatrains we may also notice a fleeting suggestion here and there of riches, jewelry, magnificence —a suggestion coming from relationships between "crowned," "glory," "flourish," "rarities." The full purpose of these words cannot be seen until the couplet is reached. Then we become conscious of how fully prepared for is the word "worth" in the last line.

The metaphors in this poem fit the structure beautifully, they build up the strength of feeling which the sonnet reaches at its conclusion, and they illuminate the subject of time and change by converting them from abstract conceptions into realized imaginative experience. On these grounds one may assert that Shakespeare's sonnet is a great poem.

That Time of Year Thou Mayst in Me Behold

WILLIAM SHAKESPEARE (1564–1616)

That time of year thou mayst in me behold
When yellow leaves, or none, or few, do hang
Upon those boughs which shake against the cold,
Bare ruin'd choirs, where late the sweet birds sang.

In me thou see'st the twilight of such day, 5
As after sunset fadeth in the west,
Which by and by black night doth take away,
Death's second self, that seals up all in rest.
In me thou see'st the glowing of such fire,
That on the ashes of his youth doth lie, 10
As the death-bed whereon it must expire,
Consum'd with that which it was nourish'd by.
    This thou perceiv'st, which makes thy love more strong,
    To love that well which thou must leave ere long.

Let Me Not to the Marriage of True Minds

WILLIAM SHAKESPEARE (1564–1616)

Let me not to the marriage of true minds
Admit impediments. Love is not love
Which alters when it alteration finds,
Or bends with the remover to remove:
O, no! it is an ever-fixed mark, 5
That looks on tempests and is never shaken;
It is the star to every wandering bark,
Whose worth's unknown, although his height be taken.
Love's not Time's fool, though rosy lips and cheeks
Within his bending sickle's compass come; 10
Love alters not with his brief hours and weeks,
But bears it out even to the edge of doom.
    If this be error, and upon me prov'd,
    I never writ, nor no man ever lov'd.

When in the Chronicle of Wasted Time

WILLIAM SHAKESPEARE (1564–1616)

When in the chronicle of wasted time
I see descriptions of the fairest wights,
And beauty making beautiful old rime,
In praise of ladies dead and lovely knights;
Then, in the blazon of sweet beauty's best,   5
Of hand, of foot, of lip, of eye, of brow,
I see their antique pen would have express'd
Even such a beauty as you master now.
So all their praises are but prophecies
Of this our time, all you prefiguring;   10
And, for they look'd but with divining eyes,
They had not skill enough your worth to sing:
    For we, which now behold these present days,
    Have eyes to wonder, but lack tongues to praise.

Tired with All These

WILLIAM SHAKESPEARE (1564–1616)

Tired with all these, for restful death I cry,
As, to behold desert a beggar born,
And needy nothing trimmed in jollity,
And purest faith unhappily forsworn,
And gilded honor shamefully misplaced,   5
And maiden virtue rudely strumpeted,

And right perfection wrongfully disgraced,
And strength by limping sway disabled,
And art made tongue-tied by authority,
And folly, doctorlike, controlling skill,   10
And simple truth miscalled simplicity,
And captive good attending captain ill.
    Tired with all these, from these would I be gone,
    Save that, to die I leave my love alone.

A Valediction Forbidding Mourning

JOHN DONNE (1572–1631)

As virtuous men pass mildly away,
   And whisper to their souls to go,
Whilst some of their sad friends do say,
   "The breath goes now," and some say, "No";

So let us melt, and make no noise,   5
   No tear-floods nor sigh-tempests move;
'Twere profanation of our joys
   To tell the laity our love.

Moving of the earth brings harms and fears;
   Men reckon what it did and meant;   10
But trepidation of the spheres,
   Though greater far, is innocent.

Dull sublunary lovers' love,
   Whose soul is sense, cannot admit
Absence, because it doth remove   15
   Those things which elemented it.

But we, by a love so much refined
    That ourselves know not what it is,
Inter-assured of the mind,
    Care less eyes, lips, and hands to miss.   20

Our two souls, therefore, which are one,
    Though I must go, endure not yet
A breach, but an expansion,
    Like gold to airy thinness beat.

If they be two, they are two so   25
    As stiff twin compasses are two;
Thy soul, the fixed foot, makes no show
    To move, but doth if the other do.

And though it in the center sit,
    Yet when the other far doth roam,   30
It leans, and hearkens after it,
    And grows erect as that comes home.

Such wilt thou be to me, who must,
    Like the other foot, obliquely run;
Thy firmness makes my circle just,   35
    And makes me end where I begun.

When Our Two Souls Stand Up Erect and Strong

ELIZABETH BARRETT BROWNING (1806–1861)

When our two souls stand up erect and strong,
Face to face, silent, drawing nigh and nigher,
Until the lengthening wings break into fire
At either curved point,—what bitter wrong

Can the earth do to us, that we should not long   5
Be here contented? Think! In mounting higher,
The angels would press on us and aspire
To drop some golden orb of perfect song
Into our deep, dear silence. Let us stay
Rather on earth, Beloved,—where the unfit,   10
Contrarious moods of men recoil away
And isolate pure spirits, and permit
A place to stand and love in for a day,
With darkness and the death-hour rounding it.

Song

WILLIAM BLAKE (1757–1827)

My silks and fine array,
My smiles and languished air,
By love are driven away;
And mournful lean Despair
Brings me yew to deck my grave: 5
Such end true lovers have.

His face is fair as heaven,
When springing buds unfold;
O why to him was't given
Whose heart is wintry cold?   10
His breast is love's all-worshiped tomb,
Where all love's pilgrims come.

Bring me an axe and spade,
Bring me a winding-sheet;

When I my grave have made   15
Let winds and tempests beat:
Then down I'll lie as cold as clay.
True love doth pass away!

To Autumn

JOHN KEATS (1795–1821)

Season of mists and mellow fruitfulness,
    Close bosom-friend of the maturing sun;
Conspiring with him how to load and bless
    With fruit the vines that round the thatch-eaves run;
To bend with apples the mossed cottage-trees,   5
    And fill all fruit with ripeness to the core;
    To swell the gourd, and plump the hazel shells
With a sweet kernel; to set budding more,
    And still more, later flowers for the bees,
    Until they think warm days will never cease,   10
        For Summer has o'er-brimmed their clammy cells.

Who hath not seen thee oft amid thy store?
    Sometimes whoever seeks abroad may find
Thee sitting careless on a granary floor,
    Thy hair soft-lifted by the winnowing wind;   15
Or on a half-reaped furrow sound asleep,
    Drowsed with the fume of poppies, while thy hook
        Spares the next swath and all its twinèd flowers:
And sometimes like a gleaner thou dost keep
    Steady thy laden head across a brook;   20
    Or by a cider-press, with patient look,
        Thou watchest the last oozings hours by hours.

Where are the songs of Spring? Ay, where are they?
    Think not of them, thou hast thy music too,—
While barrèd clouds bloom the soft-dying day,   25
    And touch the stubble-plains with rosy hue;
Then in a wailful choir the small gnats mourn
    Among the river shallows, borne aloft
        Or sinking as the light wind lives or dies;
And full-grown lambs loud bleat from hilly bourn;   30
    Hedge-crickets sing; and now with treble soft
    The red-breast whistles from a garden-croft;
        And gathering swallows twitter in the skies.

The Garden

ANDREW MARVELL (1621–1678)

        How vainly men themselves amaze
    To win the palm, the oak, or bays,
    And their incessant labors see
    Crowned from some single herb, or tree,
    Whose short and narrow-verged shade   5
    Does prudently their toils upbraid;
    While all flowers and all trees do close
    To weave the garlands of repose!

        Fair Quiet, have I found thee here,
    And Innocence, thy sister dear?   10
    Mistaken long, I sought you then
    In busy companies of men.
    Your sacred plants, if here below,
    Only among the plants will grow;
    Society is all but rude   15
    To this delicious solitude.

No white nor red was ever seen
So amorous as this lovely green.
Fond lovers, cruel as their flame,
Cut in these trees their mistress' name: 20
Little, alas, they know or heed
How far these beauties hers exceed!
Fair trees, wheresoe'er your barks I wound,
No name shall but your own be found.

When we have run our passion's heat,   25
Love hither makes his best retreat.
The gods, that mortal beauty chase,
Still in a tree did end their race:
Apollo hunted Daphne so,
Only that she might laurel grow;   30
And Pan did after Syrinx speed,
Not as a nymph, but for a reed.

What wondrous life is this I lead!
Ripe apples drop about my head;
The luscious clusters of the vine   35
Upon my mouth do crush their wine;
The nectarine and curious peach
Into my hands themselves do reach;
Stumbling on melons, as I pass,
Insnared with flowers, I fall on grass.   40

Meanwhile the mind, from pleasure less
Withdraws into its happiness;
The mind, that ocean where each kind
Does straight its own resemblance find;
Yet it creates, transcending these,   45
Far other worlds and other seas,
Annihilating all that's made
To a green thought in a green shade.

Here at the fountain's sliding foot,
Or at some fruit-tree's mossy root,   50
Casting the body's vest aside,
My soul into the boughs does glide:
There, like a bird, it sits and sings,
Then whets and combs its silver wings,
And, till prepared for longer flight,   55
Waves in its plumes the various light.

Such was that happy garden-state,
While man there walked without a mate:
After a place so pure and sweet,
What other help could yet be meet!   60
But 'twas beyond a mortal's share
To wander solitary there:
Two paradises 'twere in one
To live in paradise alone.

How well the skilful gardener drew   65
Of flowers and herbs this dial new,
Where, from above, the milder sun
Does through a fragrant zodiac run;
And as it works, the industrious bee
Computes its time as well as we!   70
How could such sweet and wholesome hours
Be reckoned but with herbs and flowers?

Critical Analysis

THE TITLE of Marvell's poem might lead a reader to expect a description of flowers, fruits, and the contents of a garden. But the
opening lines come as a shock to any such expectation. Neverthe-

less, the most cursory reading will reveal the central conceit: the garden is all experience; it is time. The experience of the speaker is the experience of the world (stanzas 1 and 2), and of love and passion (stanzas 3 and 4). Stanza 5, which is pivotal in the poem, continues with the experience of the physical sensation of the garden; stanzas 6 and 7 with the experience of intellectual and spiritual contemplation. The last stanza abstracts all experience in terms of time and the garden. Yet the poem is actually well named; for throughout, the scene is either before the speaker's eye or in his mind, and the imagery is centered on the selected aspects of this garden.

The first four stanzas develop skillfully and are almost a tour de force of wit. Actually, Marvell keeps presenting us with a series of apparent reversals of our common ideas and justifies each one by the logic of the poem. The paradoxes make our process of readjusting to Marvell's harmony a continual one, not a thing done once and for all, as in Keats' ode, "To Autumn," where the readers' presuppositions are attacked only once. (We expect spring to be glorified, and Keats glorifies autumn, but once we make that shift, everything is in harmony.) Marvell asks us to accept such apparently outrageous propositions as:

Stanza 1. Ambition is less well rewarded than laziness.

Stanza 2. Society, usually thought of as refined and polished, is really *ruder* (rougher, more uncouth) than solitude.

Stanza 3. Red and white, the colors of female beauty, are less *amorous* than green, and a tree is a more suitable object of a lover's ecstasies than a lady.

Stanza 4. The myths of Apollo and Pan mean the opposite of what they seem to. Apollo and Pan were not disappointed when their nymphs turned into plants. They were delighted; that is why they chased them.

Once he has made the reader swallow these reversals, he shifts his strategy. In stanzas 5–7, Marvell sweeps the reader into the ecstasy of the garden, first physical, then mental, then spiritual. Yet even these mental and spiritual ecstasies are conveyed by

garden-images—by "green thought," and by the image of the
soul as a bird. The shift to mental and spiritual ecstasy contains
the only complicated imagery of the poem, but the shift is not
abrupt. It has been prepared for in the imaginative treatment
of the garden in previous stanzas, especially 2 and 3. The garden,
even where it appears to be most physical (stanza 5), is a world
of imagination.

The mind (stanza 6) moving from the lesser pleasures (line 41)
withdraws into its own happiness, since (as we learn from the
succeeding image) it is the essence or idea of happiness. The
speaker then introduces a vast metaphor (lines 43–48). The mind
is an ocean. The mind is to the body as the ocean is to the land,
an idea based on the notion that for every kind or genus on land
there is a parallel in marine life. The mind has all the counter-
parts of the body, but extending from these ("transcending" not
in the sense of "separation" but of "extension") creates new es-
sences ("Far other worlds and other seas") and reduces all ordinary creation in a material world to pure thought in solitude ("To
a *green* thought in a *green* shade") which has all the basic color
symbolism of the garden as well as the color of the transforming
sea. In perfect solitude, the mind can transcend even vast reality.
To a believer in only what he sees before him, this proposition
is a difficult one; it is an abstraction of reality.

The seventh stanza considers the projection—almost the trans-
figuration—of the speaker from the body to the state of the soul
in the form of a bird. The scene of the mind's or soul's power to
do this is the fountain, the source of growth in the garden, or the
foot of the fruit tree. The soul leaves the body, glides like a bird
into the tree. The bird is not delineated beyond its silver wings,
although its action is described ("sits and sings," "whets [preens]
and combs its silver wings," "Waves in its plumes the various
light"). There is no need to give the bird individual quality. It
is simply a new form of the soul, liberated from the body under
the influence of the garden—the state of solitude.

The two final paradoxes could not be sustained without the

erion

preparatory rhapsody. They are the great ones—that solitude in a garden out-paradises paradise (for perfect paradise, which is *solitude* in the Garden of Eden, existed only when Adam was alone and was lost with the advent of Eve) and that time, usually thought of as the great destroyer of pastoral, idyllic life (cf. Ralegh's "The Nymph's Reply to the Shepherd," page 686) is really not inimical to it at all, but is suitably measured and ordered *only* by herbs, flowers, and insects.

The last stanza, which draws attention to one part of the garden in the form of a sundial, gives Marvell opportunity to display the benevolence of the largest aspect of nature, the sun. The conclusive effect of the stanza is seen in the speaker's return to the world. He has had an imaginative, almost mystical vision of escape, but his place in the world remains, and he understands through the garden his own position in time.

The whole treatment of the garden is contemplative and imaginative and, in several cases, intellectual. Although the tone is complex, the imagery and form are not complicated. In a poem of this sort one might have expected to find the verses more loaded with imagery. In fact, the images, although occasionally extended (as in stanzas 6–7), are few. The floral rewards for civic achievement (palm), military achievement (oak), and literary prowess (bays) are striking symbols in contrast to men's deeds (stanza 1). Quiet and Innocence are personified in stanza 2 and Love in stanza 4. The mind as an ocean and the soul like a bird constitute the imagery of stanzas 6–7, already discussed, but it should be noted that the most fanciful stanzas of the poem contain the most concrete imagery.

Effects akin to those of imagery are obtained by literary allusion—to the Apollo-Daphne and Pan-Syrinx legends (stanza 4). The allusions are in keeping with a classical quality which the poem has and give it a sense of timelessness. The eighth stanza, which culminates what might be called the Christian or philosophical imagery begun in stanzas 6 and 7, is a witty treatment of the Garden of Eden legend in a way well suited to the movement and tone of the poem already established.

As the reader looks back over the poem, he can see that its structure is governed by the experience of the speaker. The speaker ends where he begins, in the garden, but he has sounded joys, real and imaginative, in his contact with the garden and with his view of his own soul, temporarily freed by the situation of the garden.

The stanzas (eight-line tetrameter couplets) form individual paragraphs, but their relation to each other and the idea of the world is clear. Stanzas 1 and 2 deal with the themes of ambition and solitude and are verbally connected by lines 8 and 9. The last lines of both stanzas have similar pictorial quality: "garlands of repose" and "delicious solitude." Stanzas 3 and 4 are closely related and deal with love and physical beauty. Stanza 5 concentrates on the physical effects of the garden on the speaker. The next two stanzas form a unit in content; the eighth, powerful in its paradox, is allusive and transitional. The last stanza returns to the garden itself, which becomes a symbol for the final contraction of all experience. In addition to the clarity provided by the paragraphing of the poem, the versification itself gives the effect of simplicity and directness which encourages the reader to move through the complications of the thought and the imagery.

Further analysis of the poem, in the light of seventeenth-century thought and of stanzas 6 and 7, particularly, in their relation to Neo-Platonic ideas, would be valuable and interesting. But even without such study the poem is rich in meaning. Skillful and controlled, it presents through a series of paradoxes, through imagination and symbolic action, a view of all experience, of time itself, from the vantage point of solitude—the garden. This analysis, though extensive, is obviously an incomplete record of the total effect of "The Garden."

The Passionate Shepherd to His Love

CHRISTOPHER MARLOWE (1564–1593)

Come live with me and be my love,
And we will all the pleasures prove
That valleys, groves, hills, and fields,
Woods, or steepy mountain yields.

And we will sit upon the rocks, 5
Seeing the shepherds feed their flocks,
By shallow rivers to whose falls
Melodious birds sing madrigals.

And I will make thee beds of roses
And a thousand fragrant posies, 10
A cap of flowers, and a kirtle
Embroidered all with leaves of myrtle;

A gown made of the finest wool
Which from our pretty lambs we pull;
Fair linèd slippers for the cold, 15
With buckles of the purest gold;

A belt of straw and ivy buds,
With coral clasps and amber studs:
And if these pleasures may thee move,
Come live with me and be my love. 20

The shepherds' swains shall dance and sing
For thy delight each May morning:
If these delights thy mind may move,
Then live with me and be my love.

The Nymph's Reply to the Shepherd

SIR WALTER RALEGH (1552–1618)

If all the world and love were young,
And truth in every shepherd's tongue,
These pretty pleasures might me move
To live with thee and be thy love.

Time drives the flocks from field to fold   5
When rivers rage and rocks grow cold,
And Philomel becometh dumb;
The rest complains of cares to come.

The flowers do fade, and wanton fields
To wayward winter reckoning yields;   10
A honey tongue, a heart of gall,
Is fancy's spring, but sorrow's fall.

Thy gowns, thy shoes, thy beds of roses,
Thy cap, thy kirtle, and thy posies
Soon break, soon wither, soon forgotten,—   15
In folly ripe, in reason rotten.

Thy belt of straw and ivy buds,
Thy coral clasps and amber studs,
All these in me no means can move
To come to thee and be thy love.   20

But could youth last and love still breed,
Had joys no date nor age no need,
Then these delights my mind might move
To live with thee and be thy love.

Rose Aylmer

WALTER SAVAGE LANDOR (1775–1864)

Ah, what avails the sceptred race,
Ah, what the form divine!
What every virtue, every grace!
Rose Aylmer, all were thine.

Rose Aylmer, whom these wakeful eyes   5
May weep, but never see,
A night of memories and sighs
I consecrate to thee.

Here Lies a Lady

JOHN CROWE RANSOM (1888–   )

Here lies a lady of beauty and high degree.
Of chills and fever she died, of fever and chills,
The delight of her husband, her aunts, an infant of three,
And of medicos marvelling sweetly on her ills.

For either she burned, and her confident eyes would blaze,   5
And her fingers fly in a manner to puzzle their heads—

HERE LIES A LADY is reprinted from *Selected Poems of John Crowe Ransom* by permission of Alfred A. Knopf, Inc. Copyright 1924, 1945 by Alfred A. Knopf, Inc.

What was she making? Why, nothing; she sat in a maze
Of old scraps of laces, snipped into curious shreds—

Or this would pass, and the light of her fire decline
Till she lay discouraged and cold as a thin stalk white and blown,
And would not open her eyes, to kisses, to wine;   11
The sixth of these states was her last; the cold settled down.

Sweet ladies, long may ye bloom, and toughly I hope ye may thole,
But was she not lucky? In flowers and lace and mourning,
In love and great honour we bade God rest her soul   15
After six little spaces of chill, and six of burning.

The Exequy

HENRY KING (1592–1669)

~~~~~~

Accept, thou shrine of my dead saint,
Instead of dirges, this complaint;
And for sweet flowers to crown thy hearse,
Receive a strew of weeping verse
From thy grieved friend, whom thou might'st see   5
Quite melted into tears for thee.

Dear loss! since thy untimely fate
My task hath been to meditate
On thee, on thee; thou art the book,
The library whereon I look,   10
Though almost blind. For thee, loved clay,
I languish out, not live, the day,
Using no other exercise

But what I practise with mine eyes;
By which wet glasses I find out   15
How lazily time creeps about
To one that mourns; this, only this,
My exercise and business is.
So I compute the weary hours
With sighs dissolved into showers.   20

Nor wonder if my time go thus
Backward and most preposterous;
Thou hast benighted me; thy set
This eve of blackness did beget,
Who wast my day, though overcast   25
Before thou hadst thy noon-tide passed;
And I remember must in tears,
Thou scarce hadst seen so many years
As day tells hours. By thy clear sun
My love and fortune first did run;   30
But thou wilt never more appear
Folded within my hemisphere,
Since both thy light and motion
Like a fled star is fallen and gone;
And 'twixt me ànd my soul's dear wish   35
An earth now interposed is,
Which such a strange eclipse doth make
As ne'er was read in almanac.

I could allow thee for a time
To darken me and my sad clime;   40
Were it a month, a year, or ten,
I would thy exile live till then,
And all that space my mirth adjourn,
So thou wouldst promise to return,
And putting off thy ashy shroud,   45
At length disperse this sorrow's cloud.

But woe is me! the longest date
Too narrow is to calculate
These empty hopes; never shall I
Be so much blest as to descry   50
A glimpse of thee, till that day come
Which shall the earth to cinders doom,
And a fierce fever must calcine
The body of this world—like thine,
My little world. That fit of fire   55
Once off, our bodies shall aspire
To our souls' bliss; then we shall rise
And view ourselves with clearer eyes
In that calm region where no night
Can hide us from each other's sight.   60

Meantime, thou hast her, earth; much good
May my harm do thee. Since it stood
With heaven's will I might not call
Her longer mine, I give thee all
My short-lived right and interest   65
In her whom living I loved best;
With a most free and bounteous grief
I give thee what I could not keep.
Be kind to her, and prithee look
Thou write into thy doomsday book   70
Each parcel of this rarity
Which in thy casket shrined doth lie.
See that thou make thy reckoning straight,
And yield her back again by weight;
For thou must audit on thy trust   75
Each grain and atom of this dust,
As thou wilt answer Him that lent,
Not gave thee, my dear monument.
So close the ground, and 'bout her shade
Black curtains draw; my bride is laid.   80

Sleep on, my love, in thy cold bed,
Never to be disquieted!
My last good-night! Thou wilt not wake
Till I thy fate shall overtake;
Till age, or grief, or sickness must   85
Marry my body to that dust
It so much loves, and fill the room
My heart keeps empty in thy tomb.
Stay for me there; I will not fail
To meet thee in that hollow vale.   90
And think not much of my delay;
I am already on the way,
And follow thee with all the speed
Desire can make, or sorrows breed.
Each minute is a short degree,   95
And every hour a step towards thee.
At night when I betake to rest,
Next morn I rise nearer my west
Of life, almost by eight hours' sail,
Than when sleep breathed his drowsy gale.   100

Thus from the sun my bottom steers,
And my day's compass downward bears;
Nor labor I to stem the tide
Through which to thee I swiftly glide.

'Tis true, with shame and grief I yield,   105
Thou like the van first took'st the field,
And gotten hath the victory
In thus adventuring to die
Before me, whose more years might crave
A just precedence in the grave.   110
But hark! my pulse like a soft drum
Beats my approach, tells thee I come;
And slow howe'er my marches be,
I shall at last sit down by thee.

And slow howe'er my marches be,
I shall at last sit down by thee.

The thought of this bids me go on,   115
And wait my dissolution
With hope and comfort. Dear (forgive
The crime) I am content to live
Divided, with but half a heart,
Till we shall meet and never part.   120

On His Blindness

JOHN MILTON (1608–1674)

When I consider how my light is spent
Ere half my days in this dark world and wide,
And that one talent which is death to hide
Lodged with me useless, though my soul more bent
To serve therewith my Maker, and present   5
My true account, lest He returning chide,
"Doth God exact day-labor, light denied?"
I fondly ask. But Patience, to prevent
That murmur, soon replies, "God doth not need
Either man's work or his own gifts. Who best   10
Bear his mild yoke, they serve him best. His state
Is kingly: thousands at his bidding speed,
And post o'er land and ocean without rest;
They also serve who only stand and wait."

To Homer

JOHN KEATS (1795–1821)

Standing aloof in giant ignorance,
　　Of thee I hear and of the Cyclades,
As one who sits ashore and longs perchance
　　To visit dolphin-coral in deep seas.
So thou wast blind!—but then the veil was rent,　　　5
　　For Jove uncurtain'd Heaven to let thee live,
And Neptune made for thee a spumy tent,
　　And Pan made sing for thee his forest-hive;
Aye, on the shores of darkness there is light,
　　And precipices show untrodden green;　　　10
There is a budding morrow in midnight;
　　There is a triple sight in blindness keen;
Such seeing hadst thou, as it once befel
To Dian, Queen of Earth, and Heaven, and Hell.

An Irish Airman Foresees His Death

WILLIAM BUTLER YEATS (1865–1939)

I know that I shall meet my fate
Somewhere among the clouds above;
Those that I fight I do not hate,
Those that I guard I do not love;

My country is Kiltartan Cross,   5
My countrymen Kiltartan's poor,
No likely end could bring them loss
Or leave them happier than before.
Nor law, nor duty bade me fight,
Nor public men, nor cheering crowds,   10
A lonely impulse of delight
Drove to this tumult in the clouds;
I balanced all, brought all to mind,
The years to come seemed waste of breath,
A waste of breath the years behind   15
In balance with this life, this death.

Ode
Written in the Beginning of the Year 1746

WILLIAM COLLINS (1721–1759)

I

How sleep the brave, who sink to rest,
By all their country's wishes blest!
When Spring, with dewy fingers cold,
Returns to deck their hallow'd mold,
She there shall dress a sweeter sod,   5
Than Fancy's feet have ever trod.

II

By fairy hands their knell is rung,
By forms unseen their dirge is sung;
There Honour comes, a pilgrim grey,
To bless the turf that wraps their clay,   10
And Freedom shall a while repair,
To dwell a weeping hermit there!

Still to Be Neat

BEN JONSON (1572–1637)

Still to be neat, still to be dressed,
As you were going to a feast;
Still to be powdered, still perfumed:
Lady, it is to be presumed,
Though art's hid causes are not found,   5
All is not sweet, all is not sound.

Give me a look, give me a face,
That makes simplicity a grace;
Robes loosely flowing, hair as free:
Such sweet neglect more taketh me   10
Than all the adulteries of art;
They strike mine eyes, but not my heart.

Delight in Disorder

ROBERT HERRICK (1591–1674)

A sweet disorder in the dress
Kindles in clothes a wantonness;
A lawn about the shoulders thrown
Into a fine distractiòn;
An erring lace, which here and there   5
Enthralls the crimson stomacher;
A cuff neglectful, and thereby

Ribands to flow confusèdly;
A winning wave (deserving note)
In the tempestuous petticoat;   10
A careless shoe-string, in whose tie
I see a wild civility:
Do more bewitch me, than when art
Is too precise in every part.

Never Love unless You Can

THOMAS CAMPION (1567–1620)

Never love unless you can
Bear with all the faults of man;
Men sometimes will jealous be,
Though but little cause they see,
And hang the head, as discontent,   5
And speak what straight they will repent.

Men that but one saint adore
Make a show of love to more;
Beauty must be scorned in none,
Though but truly served in one;   10
For what is courtship but disguise?
True hearts may have dissembling eyes.

Men when their affairs require
Must a while themselves retire,
Sometimes hunt, and sometimes hawk,   15
And not ever sit and talk.
If these and such like you can bear,
Then like, and love, and never fear.

A Pretty a Day

E. E. CUMMINGS (1894–   )

a pretty a day
(and every fades)
is here and away
(but born are maids
to flower an hour   5
in all,all)

o yes to flower
until so blithe
a doer a wooer
some limber and lithe   10
some very fine mower
a tall;tall

some jerry so very
(and nellie and fan)
some handsomest harry   15
(and sally and nan
they tremble and cower
so pale:pale)

for betty was born
to never say nay   20
but lucy could learn
and lily could pray
and fewer were shyer
than doll.   doll

A PRETTY A DAY is reprinted from *50 Poems* by E. E. Cummings. Copyright 1939, 1940 by E. E. Cummings. Used by permission of Duell, Sloan and Pearce, Inc.

The Night Piece, to Julia

ROBERT HERRICK (1591–1674)

Her eyes the glowworm lend thee;
The shooting stars attend thee;
 And the elves also,
 Whose little eyes glow
Like the sparks of fire, befriend thee.   5

No will-o'-the-wisp mislight thee;
Nor snake or slowworm bite thee;
 But on, on thy way,
 Not making a stay,
Since ghost there's none to affright thee.   10

Let not the dark thee cumber;
What though the moon does slumber?
 The stars of the night
 Will lend thee their light,
Like tapers clear without number.   15

Then, Julia, let me woo thee,
Thus, thus to come unto me;
 And when I shall meet
 Thy silvery feet,
My soul I'll pour into thee.   20

Critical Analysis

HERRICK's "Night Piece, to Julia" is a poem of invitation, addressed to a lady. It asks her, in the fourth stanza, to come to the poet, who will, he says, pour his soul into her. Nothing is said directly about the poet's feeling for Julia, and no arguments are given to overcome her possible reluctance to meet him. Instead, the first three stanzas develop a description of the night. The poem is a "Night Piece."

But the reader soon perceives that not much is told specifically about the night except that it is dark, with no moon shining, and only glowworms and stars for light. The first two stanzas, and perhaps also the third, take the form of a charm—something spoken to ward off danger, as one knocks on wood to avert bad luck. In the first stanza, the poet invokes guardians and friends for the lady—the glowworm, the shooting stars, and the elves. Both natural and supernatural things are thus in the picture, but the identity of the guardians suggests that the superstitious fears are not to be taken too seriously. But it *is* dark, and there are elves, so possibly there may be other inhabitants of the night who are rather to be feared than trusted. The second stanza is a conjuring of these dangers not to harm the lady—either will-o'-the-wisp, snake, or slowworm. And ghosts, perhaps the greatest terror of the night, are declared not to exist—at least not here.

By this time the poem has turned from a charm into a more direct appeal to the lady. The effect of the first two stanzas has been to give a curious mixed feeling, of awareness of the soft and tender beauties of the night with a slight nervousness and fear, somewhat feminine in quality. We seem to share the lady's apprehensions even as we hear the charm, for after all, will-o'-the-wisps, snakes, and ghosts are brought into the picture, even if only to be exorcised. In the middle of stanza 2 we even feel the hesitation of her step in the repetition of "But on, on thy way."

Therefore the third stanza is more urgent, more confident. We are led out of the atmosphere of elves and will-o'-the-wisps to starlight that is just as secure as indoors—"like tapers clear without number." The final stanza is most direct, with the urging repetition "thus, thus" and the promise of the last line.

If all this is so, there remains a question about the nature of the lady's timidity. Is it really simple fear of the dark? The delicacy and intimacy of the first two stanzas suggest something else. (Notice the feminine rhymes of lines 1, 2 and 5. How does this feature of versification affect the tone?) Finally, the wooing and the promise of the last line suggest that the feeling even in the first part of the poem is more personal, and has perhaps more to do with her waiting lover than with the night.

The tenderness and delicacy of the poem suggest that what appears to be said about the night is really said about the lady. This is then an oblique poem, meaning a good deal more than it says and concentrating that meaning in a specific direction—that of Julia's coyness. Julia is surrounded by intimate, tender feelings, yet in the midst of them there is still a sense of mild alarm and excitement. The poem woos her.

If the poem is primarily a wooing poem, why talk about the night? The qualities of the night have somehow become identified with those of Julia herself. So it is no shock, for example, to encounter her *silvery* feet in the next to the last line. In the context of the night the word is perfect, but one can think of other contexts in which the effect of this word's connotations would be unpleasant.

The last line of the poem is prepared for metrically. In the corresponding line of each of the previous stanzas, an anapestic foot is substituted for one of the normal iambs, giving a tripping effect. But the final line is simple, strong iambic throughout: "My soul I'll pour into thee." This might be interpreted as suggesting the stability of her arrival as contrasted with the light-footed skipping of her journey to her lover. But it has also another effect. The reader wonders about an innuendo in the last line, and begins to translate it into something else, but its straightforward simplicity (aided perhaps by the assonance of *soul* and *pour*) pulls him back into the statement of the line itself. The movement here might be said to give an air of sincerity.

The physical and sensual impressions in the poem are carefully controlled. The poet is not saying one thing and leering at the reader to show he means something else; this is no vulgar exercise in *double entendre*. The quality of "The Night Piece, to Julia" depends upon the fine balance between statement and suggestion, the complete integration of feelings about the girl and the night, and the firm control the poet maintains over sensations and suggestions vividly called up in the reader's mind.

Much of value could be learned from an analysis of the metrical elements of the poem—scansion, line length, and sound effects. This poem is especially interesting to study because Herrick took the verse form, the rhetorical device of the charm, and even an image or two from one of Ben Jonson's gypsy songs in *The Gipsies Metamorphosed;* it is sung just before the fortune-telling begins:

> The faery beam upon you,
> The stars to-glister on you,
> A moon of light
> In the noon of night
> Till the fire-drake hath o'ergone you!
>
> The wheel of fortune guide you,
> The boy with the bow beside you
> Run aye in the way,
> Till the bird of day
> And the luckier lot betide you!

("To-glister" in line 2 means "glitter brightly." The "fire-drake" in line 5 is a meteor—presumably the original of Herrick's shooting stars.)

In what ways has Herrick changed the poem? What are the

purposes and effect of these changes? What did he see in Jonson's poem that prompted him to use it as a model? What should be our final verdict about Herrick's originality?

To His Coy Mistress

ANDREW MARVELL (1621–1678)

Had we but world enough, and time,
This coyness, Lady, were no crime.
We would sit down, and think which way
To walk, and pass our long love's day.
Thou by the Indian Ganges' side   5
Shouldst rubies find; I by the tide
Of Humber would complain. I would
Love you ten years before the Flood,
And you should, if you please, refuse
Till the conversion of the Jews.   10
My vegetable love should grow
Vaster than empires and more slow;
An hundred years should go to praise
Thine eyes, and on thy forehead gaze;
Two hundred to adore each breast,   15
But thirty thousand to the rest;
An age at least to every part,
And the last age should show your heart.
For, Lady, you deserve this state,
Nor would I love at lower rate.   20
   But at my back I always hear
Time's wingèd chariot hurrying near;
And yonder all before us lie
Deserts of vast eternity.

Thy beauty shall no more be found, 25
Nor, in thy marble vault, shall sound
My echoing song; then worms shall try
That long-preserved virginity,
And your quaint honor turn to dust,
And into ashes all my lust: 30
The grave's a fine and private place,
But none, I think, do there embrace.
   Now therefore, while the youthful hue
Sits on thy skin like morning dew,
And while thy willing soul transpires 35
At every pore with instant fires,
Now let us sport us while we may.
And now, like amorous birds of prey,
Rather at once our time devour
Than languish in his slow-chapped power. 40
Let us roll all our strength and all
Our sweetness up into one ball,
And tear our pleasures with rough strife
Thorough the iron gates of life;
Thus, though we cannot make our sun 45
Stand still, yet we will make him run.

If I Were Tickled by the Rub of Love

DYLAN THOMAS (1914–1953)

If I were tickled by the rub of love,
A rooking girl who stole me for her side,
Broke through her straws, breaking my bandaged string,

IF I WERE TICKLED BY THE RUB OF LOVE (from *18 Poems*, 1934) by Dylan Thomas is reprinted from *The World I Breathe*. Copyright 1939, New Directions. Used by permission of the publisher.

If the red tickle as the cattle calve
Still set to scratch a laughter from my lung,   5
I would not fear the apple nor the flood
Nor the bad blood of spring.

Shall it be male or female? say the cells,
And drop the plum like fire from the flesh.
If I were tickled by the hatching hair,   10
The winging bone that sprouted in the heels,
The itch of man upon the baby's thigh,
I would not fear the gallows nor the axe
Nor the crossed sticks of war.

Shall it be male or female? say the fingers   15
That chalk the walls with green girls and their men.
I would not fear the muscling-in of love
If I were tickled by the urchin hungers
Rehearsing heat upon a raw-edged nerve.
I would not fear the devil in the loin   20
Nor the outspoken grave.

If I were tickled by the lovers' rub
That wipes away not crow's-foot nor the lock
Of sick old manhood on the fallen jaws,
Time and the crabs and the sweethearting crib   25
Would leave me cold as butter for the flies,
The sea of scums could drown me as it broke
Dead on the sweethearts' toes.

This world is half the devil's and my own,
Daft with the drug that's smoking in a girl   30
And curling round the bud that forks her eye.
An old man's shank one-marrowed with my bone,
And all the herrings smelling in the sea,
I sit and watch the worm beneath my nail
Wearing the quick away.   35

And that's the rub, the only rub that tickles.
The knobbly ape that swings along his sex
From damp love-darkness and the nurse's twist
Can never raise the midnight of a chuckle,
Nor when he finds a beauty in the breast   40
Of lover, mother, lovers, or his six
Feet in the rubbing dust.

And what's the rub? Death's feather on the nerve?
Your mouth, my love, the thistle in the kiss?
My Jack of Christ born thorny on the tree?   45
The words of death are dryer than his stiff,
My wordy wounds are printed with your hair.
I would be tickled by the rub that is:
Man be my metaphor.

Pied Beauty

GERARD MANLEY HOPKINS (1844–1889)

Glory be to God for dappled things—
    For skies of couple-color as a brinded cow;
        For rose-moles all in stipple upon trout that swim;
Fresh-firecoal chestnut-falls; finches' wings;
    Landscape plotted and pieced—fold, fallow, and plough;   5
        And all trades, their gear and tackle and trim.
All things counter, original, spare, strange;
    Whatever is fickle, freckled (who knows how?)
        With swift, slow; sweet, sour; adazzle, dim;
He fathers-forth whose beauty is past change: 10
                    Praise him.

The Windhover—To Christ Our Lord

GERARD MANLEY HOPKINS (1844–1889)

I caught this morning morning's minion, king-
    dom of daylight's dauphin, dapple-dawn-drawn Falcon, in his
        riding
    Of the rolling level underneath him steady air, and striding
High there, how he rung upon the rein of a wimpling wing

In his ecstasy! then off, off forth on swing,   5
    As a skate's heel sweeps smooth on a bow-bend: the hurl and
        gliding
    Rebuffed the big wind. My heart in hiding
Stirred for a bird,—the achieve of, the mastery of the thing!

Brute beauty and valor and act, oh, air, pride, plume, here
    Buckle! And the fire that breaks from thee then, a billion   10
Times told lovelier, more dangerous, O my chevalier!

No wonder of it: sheer plod makes plough down sillion
Shine, and blue-bleak embers, ah my dear,
    Fall, gall themselves, and gash gold-vermilion.

The Great Lover

RUPERT BROOKE (1887–1915)

I have been so great a lover: filled my days
So proudly with the splendor of Love's praise,
The pain, the calm, and the astonishment,
Desire illimitable, and still content,
And all dear names men use, to cheat despair,   5
For the perplexed and viewless streams that bear
Our hearts at random down the dark of life.
Now, ere the unthinking silence on that strife
Steals down, I would cheat drowsy Death so far,
My night shall be remembered for a star   10
That outshone all the suns of all men's days.
Shall I not crown them with immortal praise
Whom I have loved, who have given me, dared with me
High secrets, and in darkness knelt to see
The inenarrable godhead of delight?   15
Love is a flame;—we have beaconed the world's night.
A city:—and we have built it, these and I.
An emperor:—we have taught the world to die.
So, for their sakes I loved, ere I go hence,
And the high cause of Love's magnificence,   20
And to keep loyalties young, I'll write those names
Golden for ever, eagles, crying flames,
And set them as a banner, that men may know,
To dare the generations, burn, and blow
Out on the wind of Time, shining and streaming . . .   25

THE GREAT LOVER is reprinted by permission of Dodd, Mead & Company from
The Collected Poems of Rupert Brooke. Copyright 1915 by Dodd, Mead &
Company, Inc.

These I have loved:
    White plates and cups, clean-gleaming,
Ringed with blue lines; and feathery, faery dust;
Wet roofs, beneath the lamp-light; the strong crust
Of friendly bread; and many-tasting food;
Rainbows; and the blue bitter smoke of wood;   30
And radiant raindrops couching in cool flowers;
And flowers themselves, that sway through sunny hours,
Dreaming of moths that drink them under the moon;
Then, the cool kindliness of sheets, that soon
Smooth away trouble; and the rough male kiss   35
Of blankets; grainy wood; live hair that is
Shining and free; blue-massing clouds; the keen
Unpassioned beauty of a great machine;
The benison of hot water; furs to touch;
The good smell of old clothes; and other such—   40
The comfortable smell of friendly fingers,
Hair's fragrance, and the musty reek that lingers
About dead leaves and last year's ferns . . .
                        Dear names,
And thousand others throng to me! Royal flames;
Sweet water's dimpling laugh from tap or spring;   45
Holes in the ground; and voices that do sing;
Voices in laughter, too; and body's pain,
Soon turned to peace; and the deep-panting train;
Firm sands; the little dulling edge of foam
That browns and dwindles as the wave goes home;   50
And washen stones, gay for an hour; the cold
Graveness of iron; moist black earthen mould;
Sleep; and high places; footprints in the dew;
And oaks; and brown horse-chestnuts, glossy-new;
And new-peeled sticks; and shining pools on grass;—   55
All these have been my loves. And these shall pass,
Whatever passes not, in the great hour,
Nor all my passion, all my prayers, have power

To hold them with me through the gate of Death.
They'll play deserter, turn with the traitor breath,   60
Break the high bond we made, and sell Love's trust
And sacramented covenant to the dust.
—Oh, never a doubt but, somewhere, I shall wake,
And give what's left of love again, and make
New friends, now strangers. . . .
                But the best I've known,   65
Stays here, and changes, breaks, grows old, is blown
About the winds of the world, and fades from brains
Of living men and dies.
                    Nothing remains.
O dear my loves, O faithless, once again
This one last gift I give: that after men   70
Shall know, and later lovers, far-removed,
Praise you, "All these were lovely"; say, "He loved."

The Secular Masque

JOHN DRYDEN (1631–1700)

Enter JANUS.

JANUS.

Chronos, Chronos, mend thy pace,
A hundred times the rolling sun
Around the radiant belt has run
In his revolving race.
Behold, behold, the goal in sight,   5
Spread thy fans, and wing thy flight.

Enter CHRONOS, *with a scythe in his hand, and a globe on his
back, which he sets down at his entrance.*

CHRONOS.

Weary, weary of my weight,
Let me, let me drop my freight,
  And leave the world behind.
I could not bear,   10
Another year,
The load of humankind.

Enter MOMUS *laughing.*

MOMUS.

Ha! ha! ha! ha! ha! ha! well hast thou done
  To lay down thy pack,
  And lighten thy back,   15
The world was a fool, e'er since it begun,
And since neither Janus, nor Chronos, nor I
  Can hinder the crimes,
  Or mend the bad times,
'Tis better to laugh than to cry.   20
     CHORUS OF ALL THREE.
'Tis better to laugh than to cry.
        JANUS.
Since Momus comes to laugh below,
  Old Time begin the show,
That he may see, in every scene,
What changes in this age have been.   25
      CHRONOS.
Then goddess of the silver bow begin.
      [*Horns, or hunting music within.*

Enter DIANA.

DIANA.

With horns and with hounds I waken the day;
  And hie to the woodland-walks away:

I tuck up my robe, and am buskin'd soon,
And tie to my forehead a wexing moon. 30
I course the fleet stag, unkennel the fox,
And chase the wild goats o'er summits of rocks,
With shouting and hooting we pierce through the sky,
And Echo turns hunter, and doubles the cry.

CHORUS OF ALL.

With shouting and hooting we pierce thro' the sky, 35
And Echo turns hunter, and doubles the cry.

JANUS.

Then our age was in its prime:

CHRONOS.

Free from rage:

DIANA.

And free from crime:

MOMUS.

A very merry, dancing, drinking, 40
Laughing, quaffing, and unthinking time.

CHORUS OF ALL.

Then our age was in its prime,
Free from rage, and free from crime,
A very merry, dancing, drinking,
Laughing, quaffing, and unthinking time. 45

[*Dance of Diana's attendants.*

Enter MARS.

MARS.

Inspire the vocal brass, inspire;
The world is past its infant age:
    Arms and honour,
    Arms and honour,
Set the martial mind on fire, 50
And kindle manly rage.
Mars has look'd the sky to red;

And Peace, the lazy god, is fled.
Plenty, peace, and pleasure fly;
 The sprightly green,   55
In woodland-walks, no more is seen;
The sprightly green has drunk the Tyrian dye.

CHORUS OF ALL.

Plenty, peace, &c.

MARS.

Sound the trumpet, beat the drum;
Through all the world around,   60
Sound a reveillé, sound, sound,
The warrior god is come.

CHORUS OF ALL.

Sound the trumpet, &c.

MOMUS.

Thy sword within the scabbard keep,
 And let mankind agree;   65
Better the world were fast asleep,
Than kept awake by thee.
The fools are only thinner,
 With all our cost and care;
But neither side a winner,   70
 For things are as they were.

CHORUS OF ALL.

The fools are only, &c.

Enter VENUS.

VENUS.

Calms appear when storms are past;
Love will have his hour at last:
Nature is my kindly care;   75
Mars destroys, and I repair;
Take me, take me, while you may,
Venus comes not every day.

CHORUS OF ALL.

Take her, take her, &c.

CHRONOS.

The world was then so light, 80
I scarcely felt the weight;
Joy rul'd the day, and Love the night.
But, since the queen of pleasure left the ground,
I faint, I lag,
And feebly drag 85
The ponderous orb around.

MOMUS.

All, all of a piece throughout:
Thy chase had a beast in view;
[Pointing to Diana.
Thy wars brought nothing about; [To Mars.
Thy lovers were all untrue. [To Venus.

JANUS.

'Tis well an old age is out. 91

CHRONOS.

And time to begin a new.

CHORUS OF ALL.

All, all of a piece throughout;
Thy chase had a beast in view:
Thy wars brought nothing about; 95
Thy lovers were all untrue.
'Tis well an old age is out,
And time to begin a new.
[Dance of huntsmen, nymphs, warriors,
and lovers.

Ozymandias

PERCY BYSSHE SHELLEY (1792-1822)

I met a traveller from an antique land
Who said: Two vast and trunkless legs of stone
Stand in the desert. Near them, on the sand,
Half sunk, a shattered visage lies, whose frown,
And wrinkled lip, and sneer of cold command,   5
Tell that its sculptor well those passions read
Which yet survive, (stamped on these lifeless things,)
The hand that mocked them and the heart that fed:
And on the pedestal these words appear:
"My name is Ozymandias, king of kings: 10
Look on my works, ye Mighty, and despair!"
Nothing beside remains. Round the decay
Of that colossal wreck, boundless and bare
The lone and level sands stretch far away.

Kubla Khan

SAMUEL TAYLOR COLERIDGE (1772-1834)

In Xanadu did Kubla Khan
A stately pleasure-dome decree:
Where Alph, the sacred river, ran
Through caverns measureless to man
   Down to a sunless sea.   5

So twice five miles of fertile ground
With walls and towers were girdled round:
And there were gardens bright with sinuous rills,
Where blossomed many an incense-bearing tree;
And here were forests ancient as the hills,   10
Enfolding sunny spots of greenery.

But oh! that deep romantic chasm which slanted
Down the green hill athwart a cedarn cover!
A savage place! as holy and enchanted
As e'er beneath a waning moon was haunted   15
By woman wailing for her demon-lover!
And from this chasm, with ceaseless turmoil seething,
As if this earth in fast thick pants were breathing,
A mighty fountain momently was forced:
Amid whose swift half-intermitted burst   20
Huge fragments vaulted like rebounding hail,
Or chaffy grain beneath the thresher's flail:
And 'mid these dancing rocks at once and ever
It flung up momently the sacred river.
Five miles meandering with a mazy motion   25
Through wood and dale the sacred river ran,
Then reached the caverns measureless to man,
And sank in tumult to a lifeless ocean:
  And 'mid this tumult Kubla heard from far
  Ancestral voices prophesying war!   30
  The shadow of the dome of pleasure
  Floated midway on the waves;
  Where was heard the mingled measure
  From the fountain and the caves.
It was a miracle of rare device,   35
A sunny pleasure-dome with caves of ice!

  A damsel with a dulcimer
  In a vision once I saw:

It was an Abyssinian maid,
And on her dulcimer she played, 40
Singing of Mount Abora.
Could I revive within me
Her symphony and song,
   To such a deep delight 'twould win me,
That with music loud and long, 45
I would build that dome in air,
That sunny dome! those caves of ice!
And all who heard should see them there,
And all should cry, Beware! Beware!
His flashing eyes, his floating hair! 50
Weave a circle round him thrice,
And close your eyes with holy dread,
For he on honey-dew hath fed,
And drunk the milk of Paradise.

Ode on a Grecian Urn

JOHN KEATS (1795–1821)

Thou still unravish'd bride of quietness,
   Thou foster-child of silence and slow time,
Sylvan historian, who canst thus express
   A flowery tale more sweetly than our rhyme:
What leaf-fring'd legend haunts about thy shape 5
   Of deities or mortals, or of both,
      In Tempe or the dales of Arcady?
   What men or gods are these? What maidens loth?
What mad pursuit? What struggle to escape?
      What pipes and timbrels? What wild ecstasy? 10

Heard melodies are sweet, but those unheard
  Are sweeter; therefore, ye soft pipes, play on;
Not to the sensual ear, but, more endear'd,
  Pipe to the spirit ditties of no tone:
Fair youth, beneath the trees, thou canst not leave   15
  Thy song, nor ever can those trees be bare;
    Bold lover, never, never canst thou kiss,
Though winning near the goal—yet, do not grieve;
    She cannot fade, though thou hast not thy bliss,
  Forever wilt thou love, and she be fair!   20

Ah, happy, happy boughs! that cannot shed
  Your leaves, nor ever bid the spring adieu;
And, happy melodist, unwearied,
  Forever piping songs forever new;
More happy love! more happy, happy love!   25
  Forever warm and still to be enjoy'd,
    Forever panting, and forever young;
All breathing human passion far above,
    That leaves a heart high-sorrowful and cloy'd,
    A burning forehead, and a parching tongue.   30

Who are these coming to the sacrifice?
  To what green altar, O mysterious priest,
Lead'st thou that heifer lowing at the skies,
  And all her silken flanks with garlands drest?
What little town by river or sea-shore,   35
  Or mountain-built with peaceful citadel,
    Is emptied of this folk, this pious morn?
And, little town, thy streets forevermore
    Will silent be; and not a soul to tell
    Why thou art desolate, can e'er return.   40

O Attic shape! fair attitude! with brede
  Of marble men and maidens overwrought,

With forest branches and the trodden weed;
   Thou, silent form! dost tease us out of thought
As doth eternity. Cold Pastoral!   45
   When old age shall this generation waste,
      Thou shalt remain, in midst of other woe
   Than ours, a friend to man, to whom thou say'st,
'Beauty is truth, truth beauty,' that is all
      Ye know on earth, and all ye need to know.   50

Tithonus

ALFRED, LORD TENNYSON (1809–1892)

The woods decay, the woods decay and fall,
The vapors weep their burthen to the ground;
Man comes and tills the field and lies beneath,
And after many a summer dies the swan.
Me only cruel immortality   5
Consumes; I wither slowly in thine arms,
Here at the quiet limit of the world,
A white-haired shadow roaming like a dream
The ever-silent spaces of the East,
Far-folded mists, and gleaming halls of morn.   10
   Alas! for this gray shadow, once a man—
So glorious in his beauty and thy choice,
Who madest him thy chosen, that he seemed
To his great heart none other than a god!
I asked thee, "Give me immortality."   15
Then didst thou grant mine asking with a smile,
Like wealthy men who care not how they give.
But thy strong Hours indignant worked their wills,
And beat me down and marred and wasted me,
And though they could not end me, left me maimed   20
To dwell in presence of immortal youth,

Immortal age beside immortal youth,
And all I was in ashes. Can thy love,
Thy beauty, make amends, though even now,
Close over us, the silver star, thy guide,   25
Shines in those tremulous eyes that fill with tears
To hear me? Let me go; take back thy gift.
Why should a man desire in any way
To vary from the kindly race of men,
Or pass beyond the goal of ordinance   30
Where all should pause, as is most meet for all?
   A soft air fans the cloud apart; there comes
A glimpse of that dark world where I was born.
Once more the old mysterious glimmer steals
From thy pure brows, and from thy shoulders pure,   35
And bosom beating with a heart renewed.
Thy cheek begins to redden through the gloom,
Thy sweet eyes brighten slowly close to mine,
Ere yet they blind the stars, and the wild team
Which love thee, yearning for thy yoke, arise,   40
And shake the darkness from their loosened manes,
And beat the twilight into flakes of fire.
   Lo! ever thus thou growest beautiful
In silence; then, before thine answer given,
Departest, and thy tears are on my cheek.   45
   Why wilt thou ever scare me with thy tears,
And make me tremble lest a saying learnt,
In days far-off, on that dark earth, be true?
"The gods themselves cannot recall their gifts."
   Ay me! ay me! with what another heart   50
In days far-off, and with what other eyes
I used to watch—if I be he that watched—
The lucid outline forming round thee; saw
The dim curls kindle into sunny rings;
Changed with thy mystic change, and felt my blood   55
Glow with the glow that slowly crimsoned all

Thy presence and thy portals, while I lay,
Mouth, forehead, eyelids, growing dewy-warm
With kisses balmier than half-opening buds
Of April, and could hear the lips that kissed   60
Whispering I knew not what of wild and sweet,
Like that strange song I heard Apollo sing,
While Ilion like a mist rose into towers.
    Yet hold me not forever in thine East;
How can my nature longer mix with thine?   65
Coldly thy rosy shadows bathe me, cold
Are all thy lights, and cold my wrinkled feet
Upon thy glimmering thresholds, when the steam
Floats up from those dim fields about the homes
Of happy men that have the power to die,   70
And grassy barrows of the happier dead.
Release me, and restore me to the ground.
Thou seest all things, thou wilt see my grave;
Thou wilt renew thy beauty morn by morn,
I earth in earth forget these empty courts,   75
And thee returning on thy silver wheels.

Critical Analysis

"TITHONUS" presents a simple theme: the apparent glory of being apart from men and the ordinary course of human life, even in a state of immortality, does not yield happiness. The theme is dramatized in a monologue by Tithonus, a figure in Greek legend, on whom the goddess of dawn has bestowed immortal life. From the barest incidents of the legend Tennyson has developed a moving lament. The lament is not just a gasp and a sigh; the interjections (Alas! Ay me! Ay me!) are few. Tithonus pictures himself in a cycle of decay through age, recalls his bright days of youth and love, and makes a plea for release from the burdens of living forever. In one place only does the theme stand out from the texture and movement of the poem, and even here the lines are dramatically consistent with the character of Tithonus.

> Why should a man desire in any way
> To vary from the kindly race of men,
> Or pass beyond the goal of ordinance
> Where all should pause, as is most meet for all?

Through these direct and simple lines Tennyson voices in general terms a late Victorian sentiment: the worship of conformity. Immortal life, such as Tithonus has been granted, is simply an aberration from normal human existence: it is outside the ordered grooves of society. The theme offers nothing searching or new, but through the sheer magical effect of most of the verse the poem is a satisfying artistic experience.

Although the legend itself, when known to the reader, helps to establish the background of the poem, it contributes only a small part to the total effect of the poem. "Tithonus," though using figures in the legend, is purely a work of dramatic imagination. The legend concerns Tithonus, the son of Laodemon, King of Troy, who was beloved for his beauty by Aurora, the goddess of dawn. Aurora prevailed on Jupiter to grant Tithonus immortality but forgot to ask for perpetual youth. Tithonus grew old and feeble and finally asked to be allowed to die. Unable to retract the gift, Aurora changed Tithonus into a grasshopper.

The poem is not a reworking of the legend, but is a selected dramatic plea in the life of Tithonus. What distinguishes "Tithonus" is that in movement, diction, and the controlled richness of its imagery the verse is in almost perfect accord with the dramatic situation and the theme. The result is a tone poem, at once rich and hymn-like in quality.

The emotional effect of the contrasts of color (gray and silver) and contrasts of time and action (youth and age; love and death) is produced mainly through the imagery. The poem opens with the imagery of death: the decaying woods, weeping vapors, dying swan. The contrast to the cycle of death is in Tithonus' paradoxical statement: "Me only cruel immortality consumes." Immortality, not death, is personified as a devouring creature. Tithonus characterizes himself through images: "white-hair'd shadow roaming like a dream," and sets himself against the brilliant background of dawn with its "ever-silent spaces of the East," "far-folded mists," "gleaming halls of morn." The poem continues the contrasting images of brightness of dawn and youth and the gray of wornout life. Tithonus is "a white-hair'd shadow," a "gray shadow," "in ashes." Dawn is "gleaming," shining, soft, pure, of sweet eyes, glowing. The event of dawn as seen in sections III, V, and VII is packed with imagery which gives a strong impressionistic effect: "old mysterious glimmer," "dim curls kindle into sunny rings."

All the imagery is bound into the dramatic situation of "Tithonus." In not a single section is the "I" or "me" lost. Furthermore, there is little abstract conception of age and youth in the poem. Consequently the texture of the poem, though opulent, is not a profusion of extraneous imagery to dazzle the reader but a conscious, controlled development of the theme and situation through all the poetic devices and rich materials used. The poem follows a pattern which alternates reflection or contemplation and expression of immediate feeling. The irony of the dramatic situation is emphasized by the fact that the poem is addressed to Aurora, goddess of dawn, and hence of rebirth. Tithonus' strong final plea is a startling example of this irony:

> Release me, and restore me to the ground.
> Thou seest all things, thou wilt see my grave;
> Thou wilt renew thy beauty morn by morn,
> I earth in earth forget these empty courts,
> And thee returning on thy silver wheels.

It is interesting also to see how Tennyson can enhance what otherwise might be a rather pedestrian line by putting it into juxtaposition with a striking line. Read outside the poem, the line, "Man comes and tills the field and lies beneath," for all its effective conciseness, could have been written by the imitators of Thomas Gray, but the next line gives brilliance to the idea:

> And after many a summer dies the swan.

The importance of imagery in the impression the poem creates is great, but it has a splendid concomitant in the use of rhythm and sound. The movement of the blank verse is slow and regular, but not monotonous. The impression of reflection is created by the regular iambic movement of the first four lines:

> The woods | decay, || | the woods | decay | and fall, || |
>
> The va|pors weep | their bur|then to | the ground; || |
>
> Man comes | and tills | the field | and lies | beneath, || |
>
> And af|ter ma|ny a sum|mer dies | the swan. || |

The fifth line comes with a shock because of the inversion:

> Me on|ly cru|el im|mortal|ity |
>
> Consumes; || |

and the spondaic opening of the line; and Tithonus' feeling as he sees the glow of dawn is intensified in the verse by devices of sound: by alliteration, assonance and onomatopoetic effects in the last two lines of the first section:

> The ever-silent spaces of the East,
> Far-folded mists, and gleaming halls of morn.

The stately tone of the second section is created by diction which has strong reminiscences of Virgil and the English Bible:

> Who madest him thy chosen, that he seemed
> To his great heart none other than a god!

and by the prominence of spondees in the rhythm. Rhythm, sound, diction, and imagery, working in perfect harmony, produce section VI, which, although it comes close to over-sweetness and lushness in tone and pictorial quality, is highly effective. The pace of the section is characterized by a continuously forward drive because of run-on lines. In lines 55–58 intensity is achieved through repetition of open *o* sounds and by the skillful piling up of caesuras.

> Changed with thy mystic change, and felt my blood
> Glow with the glow that slowly crimsoned all
> Thy presence and thy portals, while I lay,
> Mouth,||forehead,||eyelids,||growing dewy-warm

The preceding remarks—by no means a complete analysis of the poem—merely indicate how an awareness of the values of rhythm, sound, and imagery can increase the critical reader's appreciation of the poem, provided, of course, that the analysis of any of the elements is made with regard to the total emotional effect.

The reader who dwells on the theme might well ask, "Why all this elaboration? Why use a legend and all this consciously artistic imagery and decoration to say such a simple thing?" The answer is that the poem is not simply a communication of the theme we have stated at the beginning of this analysis. It is, like a symphony, a dramatic expression of theme, and the theme *and* the whole poem, not the theme alone, are the artistic experience of value.

Though "Tithonus" survives as a masterpiece of verbal music, poetic texture and sensitive control of mood and atmosphere, it is also interesting as an example of the way a poet can convert personal emotions into art. It was written in the fall of 1833, when Tennyson was plunged into almost suicidal grief over the death of his friend Arthur Henry Hallam. Tennyson's sister Emily, who was engaged to Hallam, exclaimed bitterly, "None of the Tennyson's ever die!" On this hint Tennyson took the classical legend of Tithonus, who could not die, and fashioned his poem. He published it more than a quarter of a century later (1860) when asked for a poem by his friend Thackeray, the editor of the *Cornhill Magazine*.

Sailing to Byzantium

WILLIAM BUTLER YEATS (1865–1939)

That is no country for old men. The young
In one another's arms, birds in the trees
(Those dying generations) at their song,
The salmon-falls, the mackerel-crowded seas,
Fish, flesh, or fowl, commend all summer long   5
Whatever is begotten, born, and dies.
Caught in that sensual music, all neglect
Monuments of unaging intellect.

An aged man is but a paltry thing,
A tattered coat upon a stick, unless   10
Soul clap its hands and sing, and louder sing
For every tatter in its mortal dress;
Nor is there singing school but studying
Monuments of its own magnificence;
And therefore I have sailed the seas and come   15
To the holy city of Byzantium.

O sages, standing in God's holy fire
As in the gold mosaic of a wall,
Come from the holy fire, perne in a gyre,
And be the singing-masters of my soul.   20
Consume my heart away—sick with desire
And fastened to a dying animal
It knows not what it is—and gather me
Into the artifice of eternity.

SAILING TO BYZANTIUM is reprinted from *Collected Poems* by William Butler Yeats. Copyright 1919, 1928 by The Macmillan Company. Used by permission of The Macmillan Company.

The quotations from the early drafts of "Sailing to Byzantium" by William Butler Yeats are used by permission of Mrs. W. B. Yeats.

Once out of nature I shall never take   25
My bodily form from any natural thing,
But such a form as Grecian goldsmiths make
Of hammered gold and gold enamelling
To keep a drowsy emperor awake;
Or set upon a golden bough to sing   30
To lords and ladies of Byzantium
Of what is past, or passing, or to come.

Critical Analysis

THIS POEM presents striking contrasts between two themes: the
curse of old age and the "artifice of eternity" or an ageless existence of beauty and art, as opposed to nature. Its method is that of
symbols, a method more easily illustrated than defined.

In the first stanza, for example, old men are said to be out of
place in a country which is represented by the flesh—young
lovers, birds singing in the trees, fish in the seas and rivers. These
three kinds, fish, flesh, and fowl, represent all nature, and they are
so intent upon life (celebrating "whatever is begotten, born, and
dies") that they neglect monuments of unaging intellect. Their
concern is with "that sensual music." So, starting with the abstraction of "youth," we have progressed to concrete examples, people,
birds and fish, and they in turn have somehow come to be represented by what they are interested in—"that sensual music." This
last phrase is then a symbol, standing not only for a meaning or
denotation, but also for an attitude which is large enough to be a
view of life.

Stanza 2 picks up the symbol and applies it to the old man. He
can sing, but not with the body, only with the soul; there is no way
to learn this singing except by studying "monuments of its own
magnificence," the same monuments referred to in the last line
of stanza 1. Therefore, the speaker says, he has come to Byzantium,
the holy city of the Eastern empire in the early Middle Ages. By-

zantium represents a degree of balance, of achievement and perfection in art. Byzantine art is conventionalized, not "natural" or representational, and it seems free from the more modern obsession with time and its passage, wholly devoted to the permanent and immortal. Byzantium is also a symbol, of course. It does not mean merely "Constantinople in earlier times."

The third stanza is a prayer, addressed to the saints in a Byzantine mosaic, to come from the wall and "perne in a gyre" (move upward in a spiral) and teach the speaker this singing, or in other words to gather him into the artifice of eternity.

Finally, in the last stanza, the speaker finds a form for himself when he is "once out of nature," beyond this dying animal life; it will be an artificial form, that of a golden bird, skillfully made so that it can sing. The music, which was introduced in the first stanza, has now gone through three phases—the flesh, the old man, and the golden bird. There are contrasts between the golden bird and those natural birds of the first stanza, and with the scarecrow in the second stanza. The gold of the mosaic wall ("God's holy fire") is also associated with the gold of the artificial bird at the end. The "monuments" of the first two stanzas are also related by contrast to the scarecrow and by similarity to the golden bird.

Many other relationships in the poem can be discovered by the attentive and sensitive reader. After he has explored the poem further, he should turn to the early drafts of the first two stanzas, to see how this magnificent imagery developed in Yeats' mind. The first draft of the first stanza is as follows:

> All in this land—my Maker that is play
> Or else asleep upon His Mother's knees,
> Others that as the mountain people say
> Are at their hunting and their gallantries
> Under the hills, as in our fathers' day
> The changing colours of the hills and seas
> All that men know or think they know, being young,
> Cry that my tale is told, my story sung.

This is a much more plaintive and personal wail of an old man. Even religion portrays Christ as a child, and all the popular folk tales and nature itself suggest that the old man is through. The tone of the stanza might almost be called that of a whimper. Yeats revised the stanza in a second draft:

> Here all is young; the chapel walls display
> An infant sleeping on his Mother's knees,
> Weary with toil Teig sleeps till break of day
> This other wearied with night's gallantries
> Sleeps the morning and the noon away
> And I have toiled and loved until I slept
> A slumbering labyrinth and leaves a snail
> Scrawl upon the mirror of the soul.

Here the speaker is less sentimental; he has objectified himself by making use of two invented characters, Teig the worker and "this other," the lover. He combines in himself the activities of the two, but his resulting sleep, however "poetically" it is described, is somewhat obscure and he has got off the track of the youth-age contrast. So in the third and published version, Yeats returns to the picture of youth and the sensual music. By now he has succeeded in avoiding the whining tone of the first draft and the irrelevances of the second. Notice what he has been willing to sacrifice of his original idea.

The second stanza has a similar history. At first it was direct, and again personal:

> I therefore travel towards Byzantium
> Among these sun-brown pleasant mariners
> Another dozen days and we shall come
> Under the jetty and the marble stair

But he revised it to give a more complete picture of Byzantium:

> But now these pleasant dark-skinned mariners
> Carry me towards that great Byzantium
> Where all is ancient, singing at the oars
> That I may look in the great church's dome
> On gold-embedded saints and emperors

> After the mirroring waters and the foam
> Where the dark drowsy fins a moment rise
> Of fish that carry souls to paradise.

Finally, however (perhaps after the creation of the "sensual music" in the first stanza), the poet saw that what was needed was a principle of contrast and, rhetorically, another declarative statement like that with which the first stanza begins. The lovely description of Byzantium could be postponed. So the published draft of the second stanza begins

> An aged man is but a paltry thing,
> A tattered coat upon a stick, unless
> Soul clap its hands and sing . . .

Again the reader is astonished at what Yeats has been willing to cut out. The rejected lines of these early drafts would be enough to make the reputation of a lesser poet.

A study of the successive stages of the poem (from which much more could be learned than is indicated here) makes clear that Yeats did not start with the symbols—he arrived at them. What constitutes the poem, then, changes in the process of writing it. Some of the details of the poem may be regarded as the happy results of direct inspiration: the surprising parenthesis of "those dying generations" in the first stanza, for example, or the continuance of the scarecrow image into the passage "and louder sing / For every tatter in its mortal dress" in the third. But the essential quality of the poem, its marvelous richness and compression, its rhetorical variety and its great compass in diction, from the plainest prose of "a tattered coat upon a stick" to the serene music of "And therefore I have sailed the seas and come / To the holy city of Byzantium" all derive from architecture and craftsmanship, like the "hammered gold and gold enamelling" of the Grecian goldsmiths. In fact the poem, surely one of the greatest of modern works of the imagination, continues to satisfy the reader because of its perfect fusion of subject and form; "Sailing to Byzantium" is itself an "artifice of eternity."

A Prayer for My Daughter

WILLIAM BUTLER YEATS (1865–1939)

Once more the storm is howling, and half hid
Under this cradle-hood and coverlid
My child sleeps on. There is no obstacle
But Gregory's wood and one bare hill
Whereby the haystack- and roof-levelling wind,   5
Bred on the Atlantic, can be stayed;
And for an hour I have walked and prayed
Because of the great gloom that is in my mind.

I have walked and prayed for this young child an hour
And heard the sea-wind scream upon the tower,   10
And under the arches of the bridge, and scream
In the elms above the flooded stream;
Imagining in excited reverie
That the future years had come,
Dancing to a frenzied drum,   15
Out of the murderous innocence of the sea.

May she be granted beauty and yet not
Beauty to make a stranger's eye distraught,
Or hers before a looking-glass, for such,
Being made beautiful overmuch,   20
Consider beauty a sufficient end,
Lose natural kindness and maybe
The heart-revealing intimacy
That chooses right, and never find a friend.

Helen being chosen found life flat and dull 25
And later had much trouble from a fool,
While that great Queen, that rose out of the spray,
Being fatherless could have her way
Yet chose a bandy-leggèd smith for man.
It's certain that fine women eat 30
A crazy salad with their meat
Whereby the Horn of Plenty is undone.

In courtesy I'd have her chiefly learned;
Hearts are not had as a gift but hearts are earned
By those that are not entirely beautiful; 35
Yet many, that have played the fool
For beauty's very self, has charm made wise,
And many a poor man that has roved,
Loved and thought himself beloved,
From a glad kindness cannot take his eyes. 40

May she become a flourishing hidden tree
That all her thoughts may like the linnet be,
And have no business but dispensing round
Their magnanimities of sound,
Nor but in merriment begin a chase, 45
Nor but in merriment a quarrel.
O may she live like some green laurel
Rooted in one dear perpetual place.

My mind, because the minds that I have loved,
The sort of beauty that I have approved, 50
Prosper but little, has dried up of late,
Yet knows that to be choked with hate
May well be of all evil chances chief.
If there's no hatred in a mind
Assault and battery of the wind 55
Can never tear the linnet from the leaf.

An intellectual hatred is the worst,
So let her think opinions are accursed.

Have I not seen the loveliest woman born
Out of the mouth of Plenty's horn,   60
Because of her opinionated mind
Barter that horn and every good
By quiet natures understood
For an old bellows full of angry wind?

Considering that, all hatred driven hence,   65
The soul recovers radical innocence
And learns at last that it is self-delighting,
Self-appeasing, self-affrighting,
And that its own sweet will is Heaven's will;
She can, though every face should scowl   70
And every windy quarter howl
Or every bellows burst, be happy still.

And may her bridegroom bring her to a house
Where all's accustomed, ceremonious;
For arrogance and hatred are the wares   75
Peddled in the thoroughfares.
How but in custom and in ceremony
Are innocence and beauty born?
Ceremony's a name for the rich horn,
And custom for the spreading laurel tree.   80

Whence Had They Come?

WILLIAM BUTLER YEATS (1865–1939)

Eternity is passion, girl or boy
Cry at the onset of their sexual joy
'For ever and for ever'; then awake
Ignorant what Dramatis Personae spake;

A passion-driven exultant man sings out 5
Sentences that he has never thought;
The Flagellant lashes those submissive loins
Ignorant what that dramatist enjoins,
What master made the lash. Whence had they come,
The hand and lash that beat down frigid Rome? 10
What sacred drama through her body heaved
When world-transforming Charlemagne was conceived?

The Eye

ROBINSON JEFFERS (1887–   )

The Atlantic is a stormy moat, and the Mediterranean,
The blue pool in the old garden,
More than five thousand years has drunk sacrifice
Of ships and blood and shines in the sun; but here the Pacific:
The ships, planes, wars are perfectly irrelevant. 5
Neither our present blood-feud with the brave dwarfs
Nor any future world-quarrel of westering
And eastering man, the bloody migrations, greed of power, battle-
    falcons,
Are a mote of dust in the great scale-pan.
Here from this mountain shore, headland beyond stormy headland
    plunging like dolphins through the gray sea-smoke 10
Into pale sea, look west at the hill of water: it is half the planet:
    this dome, this half-globe, this bulging
Eyeball of water, arched over to Asia,
Australia and white Antarctica: those are the eyelids that never
    close; this is the staring unsleeping
Eye of the earth, and what it watches is not our wars.

THE EYE is reprinted from *The Double Axe* by Robinson Jeffers. Copyright 1948 by Robinson Jeffers. Reprinted by permission of Random House, Inc.

The Love Song of J. Alfred Prufrock

T. S. ELIOT (1888–   )

Let us go then, you and I,
When the evening is spread out against the sky
Like a patient etherised upon a table;
Let us go, through certain half-deserted streets,
The muttering retreats   5
Of restless nights in one-night cheap hotels
And sawdust restaurants with oyster-shells:
Streets that follow like a tedious argument
Of insidious intent
To lead you to an overwhelming question . . .   10
Oh, do not ask, "What is it?"
Let us go and make our visit.

In the room the women come and go
Talking of Michelangelo.

The yellow fog that rubs its back upon the window-panes,   15
The yellow smoke that rubs its muzzle on the window-panes
Licked its tongue into the corners of the evening,
Lingered upon the pools that stand in drains,
Let fall upon its back the soot that falls from chimneys,
Slipped by the terrace, made a sudden leap,   20
And seeing that it was a soft October night,
Curled once about the house, and fell asleep.

And indeed there will be time
For the yellow smoke that slides along the street,
Rubbing its back upon the window-panes;   25
There will be time, there will be time

To prepare a face to meet the faces that you meet;
There will be time to murder and create,
And time for all the works and days of hands
That lift and drop a question on your plate;   30
Time for you and time for me,
And time yet for a hundred indecisions,
And for a hundred visions and revisions,
Before the taking of a toast and tea.

In the room the women come and go   35
Talking of Michelangelo.

And indeed there will be time
To wonder, "Do I dare?" and, "Do I dare?"
Time to turn back and descend the stair,
With a bald spot in the middle of my hair—   40
(They will say: "How his hair is growing thin!")
My morning coat, my collar mounting firmly to the chin,
My necktie rich and modest, but asserted by a simple pin—
(They will say: "But how his arms and legs are thin!")
Do I dare   45
Disturb the universe?
In a minute there is time
For decisions and revisions which a minute will reverse.

For I have known them all already, known them all:
Have known the evenings, mornings, afternoons,   50
I have measured out my life with coffee spoons;
I know the voices dying with a dying fall
Beneath the music from a farther room.
    So how should I presume?

And I have known the eyes already, known them all—   55
The eyes that fix you in a formulated phrase,
And when I am formulated, sprawling on a pin,

When I am pinned and wriggling on the wall,
Then how should I begin
To spit out all the butt-ends of my days and ways?   60
   And how should I presume?

And I have known the arms already, known them all—
Arms that are braceleted and white and bare
(But in the lamplight, downed with light brown hair!)
Is it perfume from a dress   65
That makes me so digress?
Arms that lie along a table, or wrap about a shawl.
   And should I then presume?
   And how should I begin?

           *   *   *   *   *

Shall I say, I have gone at dusk through narrow streets   70
And watched the smoke that rises from the pipes
Of lonely men in shirt-sleeves, leaning out of windows? . . .

I should have been a pair of ragged claws
Scuttling across the floors of silent seas.

           *   *   *   *   *

And the afternoon, the evening, sleeps so peacefully!   75
Smoothed by long fingers,
Asleep . . . tired . . . or it malingers,
Stretched on the floor, here beside you and me.
Should I, after tea and cakes and ices,
Have the strength to force the moment to its crisis?   80
But though I have wept and fasted, wept and prayed,
Though I have seen my head (grown slightly bald) brought in
      upon a platter,
I am no prophet—and here's no great matter;
I have seen the moment of my greatness flicker,

And I have seen the eternal Footman hold my coat, and snicker,   85
And in short, I was afraid.

And would it have been worth it, after all,
After the cups, the marmalade, the tea,
Among the porcelain, among some talk of you and me,
Would it have been worth while,   90
To have bitten off the matter with a smile,
To have squeezed the universe into a ball
To roll it toward some overwhelming question,
To say: "I am Lazarus, come from the dead,
Come back to tell you all, I shall tell you all"—   95
If one, settling a pillow by her head,
   Should say: "That is not what I meant at all;
   That is not it, at all."

And would it have been worth it, after all,
Would it have been worth while,   100
After the sunsets and the dooryards and the sprinkled streets,
After the novels, after the teacups, after the skirts that trail along
   the floor—
And this, and so much more?—
It is impossible to say just what I mean!
But as if a magic lantern threw the nerves in patterns on a screen:
Would it have been worth while   106
If one, settling a pillow or throwing off a shawl,
And turning toward the window, should say:
   "That is not it at all,
   That is not what I meant, at all."   110

*   *   *   *   *

No! I am not Prince Hamlet, nor was meant to be;
Am an attendant lord, one that will do
To swell a progress, start a scene or two,

Advise the prince; no doubt, an easy tool,
Deferential, glad to be of use,   115
Politic, cautious, and meticulous;
Full of high sentence, but a bit obtuse;
At times, indeed, almost ridiculous—
Almost, at times, the Fool.

I grow old . . . I grow old . . .   120
I shall wear the bottoms of my trousers rolled.

Shall I part my hair behind? Do I dare to eat a peach?
I shall wear white flannel trousers, and walk upon the beach.
I have heard the mermaids singing, each to each.

I do not think that they will sing to me.   125

I have seen them riding seaward on the waves
Combing the white hair of the waves blown back
When the wind blows the water white and black.

We have lingered in the chambers of the sea
By sea-girls wreathed with seaweed red and brown   130
Till human voices wake us, and we drown.

Street Song

EDITH SITWELL (1887–   )

"Love my heart for an hour, but my bone for a day—
At least the skeleton smiles, for it has a morrow:
But the hearts of the young are now the dark treasure of Death,
And summer is lonely.

Comfort the lonely light and the sun in its sorrow,   5
Come like the night, for terrible is the sun
As truth, and the dying light shows only the skeleton's hunger
For peace, under the flesh like the summer rose.

Come through the darkness of death, as once through the branches
Of youth you came, through the shade like the flowering door   10
That leads into Paradise, far from the street,—you, the unborn
City seen by the homeless, the night of the poor.

You walk in the city ways, where Man's threatening shadow
Red-edged by the sun like Cain, has a changing shape—
Elegant like the Skeleton, crouched like the Tiger,   15
With the age-old wisdom and aptness of the Ape.

The pulse that beats in the heart is changed to the hammer
That sounds in the Potter's Field where they build a new world
From our Bone, and the carrion-bird days' foul droppings and
          clamour—
But you are my night, and my peace,—   20

The holy night of conception, of rest, the consoling
Darkness when all men are equal,—the wrong and the right,
And the rich and the poor are no longer separate nations,—
They are brothers in night."

This was the song I heard; but the Bone is silent!   25
Who knows if the sound was that of the dead light calling,—
Of Caesar rolling onward his heart, that stone,
Or the burden of Atlas falling.

Tract

WILLIAM CARLOS WILLIAMS (1883–   )

~~~~~~

I will teach you my townspeople
how to perform a funeral—
for you have it over a troop
of artists—
unless one should scour the world—   5
you have the ground sense necessary.

See! the hearse leads.
I begin with a design for a hearse.
For Christ's sake not black—
nor white either—and not polished!   10
Let it be weathered—like a farm wagon—
with gilt wheels (this could be
applied fresh at small expense)
or no wheels at all:
a rough dray to drag over the ground.   15

Knock the glass out!
My God—glass, my townspeople!
For what purpose? Is it for the dead
to look out or for us to see
how well he is housed or to see   20
the flowers or the lack of them—
or what?
To keep the rain and snow from him?
He will have a heavier rain soon:
pebbles and dirt and what not.   25

Let there be no glass—
and no upholstery! phew!
and no little brass rollers
and small easy wheels on the bottom—
my townspeople what are you thinking of!   30

A rough plain hearse then
with gilt wheels and no top at all.
On this the coffin lies
by its own weight.   35

                    No wreaths please—
especially no hot-house flowers.
Some common memento is better,
something he prized and is known by:
his old clothes—a few books perhaps—
God knows what! You realize   40
how we are about these things,
my townspeople—
something will be found—anything—
even flowers if he had come to that.
So much for the hearse.   45

For heaven's sake though see to the driver!
Take off the silk hat! In fact
that's no place at all for him
up there unceremoniously
dragging our friend out to his own dignity!   50
Bring him down—bring him down!
Low and inconspicuous! I'd not have him ride
on the wagon at all—damn him—
the undertaker's understrapper!
Let him hold the reins   55
and walk at the side
and inconspicuously too!

Then briefly as to yourselves:
Walk behind—as they do in France,
seventh class, or if you ride   60
Hell take curtains! Go with some show
of inconvenience; sit openly—
to the weather as to grief.
Or do you think you can shut grief in?
What—from us? We who have perhaps   65
nothing to lose? Share with us
share with us—it will be money
in your pockets.
                              Go now
I think you are ready.   70

Petition

                                              W. H. AUDEN (1907-   )

Sir, no man's enemy, forgiving all
But will his negative inversion, be prodigal:
Send to us power and light, a sovereign touch
Curing the intolerable neural itch,
The exhaustion of weaning, the liar's quinsy,   5
And the distortions of ingrown virginity.
Prohibit sharply the rehearsed response
And gradually correct the coward's stance;
Cover in time with beams those in retreat
That, spotted, they turn though the reverse were great;   10
Publish each healer that in city lives
Or country houses at the end of drives;
Harrow the house of the dead; look shining at
New styles of architecture, a change of heart.

Boy-Man

KARL SHAPIRO (1913–   )

England's lads are miniature men
To start with, grammar in their shiny hats,
And serious: in America who knows when
Manhood begins? Presidents dance and hug
And while the kind King waves and gravely chats   5
America wets on England's old green rug.

The boy-man roars. Worry alone will give
This one the verisimilitude of age.
Those white teeth are his own, for he must live
Longer, grow taller than the Texas race.   10
Fresh are his eyes, his darkening skin the gauge
Of bloods that freely mix beneath his face.

He knows the application of the book
But not who wrote it; shuts it like a shot.
Rather than read he thinks that he will look,   15
Rather than look he thinks that he will talk,
Rather than talk he thinks that he will not
Bother at all; would rather ride than walk.

His means of conversation is the joke,
Humor his language underneath which lies   20
The undecoded dialect of the folk.
Abroad he scorns the foreigner: what's old
Is worn, what's different bad, what's odd unwise.

Is worn, what's different bad, what's odd unwise.
He gives off heat and is enraged by cold.

Charming, becoming to the suits he wears,   25
The boy-man, younger than his eldest son,
Inherits the state; upon his silver hairs
Time like a panama hat sits at a tilt
And smiles. To him the world has just begun
And every city waiting to be built.   30

Mister, remove your shoulder from the wheel
And say this prayer, "Increase my vitamins,
Make my decisions of the finest steel,
Pour motor oil upon my troubled spawn,
Forgive the Europeans for their sins,   35
Establish them, that values may go on."

I Think Continually of Those

STEPHEN SPENDER (1909–   )

I think continually of those who were truly great.
Who, from the womb, remembered the soul's history
Through corridors of light where the hours are suns
Endless and singing. Whose lovely ambition

Was that their lips, still touched with fire,   5
Should tell of the Spirit clothed from head to foot in song.
And who hoarded from the Spring branches
The desires falling across their bodies like blossoms.

What is precious is never to forget
The essential delight of the blood drawn from ageless springs   10
Breaking through rocks in worlds before our earth.
Never to deny its pleasure in the morning simple light
Nor its grave evening demand for love.
Never to allow gradually the traffic to smother
With noise and fog the flowering of the spirit.   15

Near the snow, near the sun, in the highest fields
See how these names are feted by the waving grass
And by the streamers of white cloud
And whispers of wind in the listening sky.
The names of those who in their lives fought for life   20
Who wore at their hearts the fire's center.
Born of the sun they travelled a short while towards the sun,
And left the vivid air signed with their honor.

The Express

STEPHEN SPENDER (1909–   )

After the first powerful plain manifesto
The black statement of pistons, without more fuss
But gliding like a queen, she leaves the station.
Without bowing and with restrained unconcern
She passes the houses which humbly crowd outside,   5
The gasworks and at last the heavy page
Of death, printed by gravestones in the cemetery.
Beyond the town there lies the open country
Where, gathering speed, she acquires mystery,

THE EXPRESS is reprinted from *Poems* by Stephen Spender. Copyright 1934
by Modern Library. Used by permission of Random House, Inc.

The luminous self-possession of ships on ocean.   10
It is now she begins to sing—at first quite low
Then loud, and at last with a jazzy madness—
The song of her whistle screaming at curves,
Of deafening tunnels, brakes, innumerable bolts.
And always light, aerial, underneath   15
Goes the elate meter of her wheels.
Steaming through metal landscape on her lines
She plunges new eras of wild happiness
Where speed throws up strange shapes, broad curves
And parallels clean like the steel of guns.   20
At last, further than Edinburgh or Rome,
Beyond the crest of the world, she reaches night
Where only a low streamline brightness
Of phosphorus on the tossing hills is white.
Ah, like a comet through flames she moves entranced   25
Wrapt in her music no bird song, no, nor bough
Breaking with honey buds, shall ever equal.

Critical Analysis

SPENDER'S poem presents few difficulties, and the reader may
miss something by thinking he has absorbed all of it at a first
reading. The main effect of *The Express* is descriptive, with vivid
evocation of the motion and sound of a train. The poem is an
example of the celebration of an object of the machine age in
terms as enthusiastic as any of those used by poets of the Romantic
Movement for objects of nature. The real question for the critical
reader of the poem is whether the heightened feeling at the end
is really justified:

> Ah, like a comet through flame she moves entranced
> Wrapt in her music no bird song, no, nor bough
> Breaking with honey buds, shall ever equal.

The exclamation, "Ah," the repetition of "no," and the extremely romantic atmosphere of the comparison between the train and the "bough breaking with honey buds," the positive form of the future tense, "*shall* ever equal," all mark a high and unusual state of excitement about the train. And it is of course no justification to say, "Well, that is the way the poet felt. He likes trains more than most people do." For the poem to succeed, it is necessary to have this excitement prepared for and justified within the poem itself.

What are the attributes of the express train in which the poet shows us meaning and significance? There is first the authority of the engine: it issues a "manifesto"; the action of its pistons is a "black statement." Then the train, in motion, becomes a queen, gliding gracefully, without bowing, receiving with regal dignity the homage of the humbler houses which crowd outside. After ten lines the elements of dignity and majesty are dropped and the train in its speed becomes a thing of mystery. The poet plays with the contrast between the train's lightness and speed and its fierceness, its noise. It is, after all, an iron monster, but it has the cleanness and value of speed. The gradually amplifying song of the train, interpreted as it is, makes the mood heighten also, and the "jazzy madness" is perhaps an attribute of the style of the poem as well as of the express. Finally, since the train in her song has been made a thing of mystery, that mystery can best be apprehended by the concept of distance, of the leaving of lesser things behind. Therefore the poet moves from literal landscape, which he had only allegorized slightly and in details such as the "heavy page of death printed by gravestones in the cemetery" to a landscape which is "new eras of wild happiness," and the train moves "beyond the crest of the world" where the unseen and imagined country, dark except for a white line on the hills, is far enough away to be romantic. This is further than Edinburgh and Rome in the sense that now the train has moved out of our world of common recognition into a world of the imagination. Then, finally, the poet passes judgment on her, and we are prepared to share with him in the extravagance of the feeling at the end, without being aware that it is extravagant.

For all of his romantic treatment, Spender uses a diction which is disarming because of its easy colloquial quality. "Without more fuss," for example, or the frank description of "a jazzy madness," holds us back from a too serious or "poetic" attitude toward the subject until we are ready for it.

The poem is not a very ambitious one; the experience contained in it is not complex, and the subject and its attributes are easy to apprehend. But failure in such a limited effort is very easy, and a less sure sense of pace or control of the reader's response would have made it a bad minor poem instead of a good one. The importance of the right epithet, the exact adjective, can often better be illustrated in a poem of this sort than in a more complicated one. Consider, for example, the word "elate" to describe the "meter of her wheels." It is of some interest that Spender did not arrive at this word until the fourth draft of his poem. He at first wrote "tapping meter," changed it to "raving" when he wanted the word "tapping" for another line, which he later canceled, and then finally arrived at "elate" for the right description of the meter of the wheels. Consider the adjectives in the line preceding this, and comment on the poet's changes. (The various drafts of this poem, in a workbook of the poet's in the Lockwood Library at the University of Buffalo, are printed in Thomas and Brown, *Reading Poems*, pp. 624–629.)

The Emperor of Ice-Cream

WALLACE STEVENS (1879–   )

~~~~~~

Call the roller of big cigars,
The muscular one, and bid him whip
In kitchen cups concupiscent curds.
Let the wenches dawdle in such dress

As they are used to wear, and let the boys   5
Bring flowers in last month's newspapers.
Let be be finale of seem.
The only emperor is the emperor of ice-cream.

Take from the dresser of deal,
Lacking the three glass knobs, that sheet   10
On which she embroidered fantails once
And spread it so as to cover her face.
If her horny feet protrude, they come
To show how cold she is, and dumb.
Let the lamp affix its beam.   15
The only emperor is the emperor of ice-cream.

Anecdote of the Jar

WALLACE STEVENS (1879–1955)

I placed a jar in Tennessee,
And round it was, upon a hill.
It made the slovenly wilderness
Surround that hill.

The wilderness rose up to it,   5
And sprawled around, no longer wild.
The jar was round upon the ground
And tall and of a port in air.

It took dominion everywhere.
The jar was gray and bare.   10
It did not give of bird or bush,
Like nothing else in Tennessee.

Appendix: Metrics

ANALYSIS of the technical aspects of a poem will illuminate its craftsmanship, but it is simply one step, not an end, in critical reading. A reader may be able to scan a poem without gaining a glint of its meaning or without feeling its power as a work of art. Yet if the craft (the verse technique) is considered as organic in the total effect of the poem, that is, one of the elements which make the poem an artistic experience and not just an ordinary, though perhaps useful, communication of fact or idea, then the analysis of sound and meter becomes a vital part of the understanding of poetry.

Basic in the study of the craft of poetry is an awareness of the rhythms, for verse has, in contrast to prose, more highly organized or more systematic arrangement of rhythm. Some prose has its own recognizable rhythm, as anyone will see who reads aloud such sentences as this one in James Agee's essay "At the Gudgers'" (p. 83), in which he is describing the taste of field peas: "Their taste is a cross between lentils and boiled beans; their broth is bright with seasoning of pork, and of this also they taste." The importance of rhythm in every aspect of the universe from the motion of the planets to the buzzing of an insect is clear to anyone who has looked at the world about him. Both the accentual quality and the very sound of English poetry derive from rhythm.

It is of basic importance to remember that in English verse, with certain exceptions, words take their normal speech accents. Thus in scanning English verse, the first step would be to mark the accents which the words would usually receive when pronounced with their full values; that is, as separate words, not as words in a context: the múl-tĭ-tú-dĭ-noŭs seas ĭn-cár-nă-dĭne. (Note that the passage does not "scan" when so marked. But it can be scanned as soon as one notices that in actual speech, the *i*

750

of the penult does not receive its full value, so that we say *túd-nous.*) These normal speech accents will by no means give the actual rhythm of the passage, but they do provide the structure on which the rhythm is built. After this step, the words should be reread as part of the context, in order to determine to what extent the sense (rhetorical emphasis) of the passage modifies the usual speech accents. Here, of course, individual differences in interpretation will have their effect on the scansion.

Since verse is rhythmically arranged sound, rhythm establishes through stress the arrangement or pattern which the reader will expect and recognize as it recurs. In the following stanza,

> Queen and huntress, chaste and fair,
> Now the sun is laid to sleep,
> Seated in thy silver chair,
> State in wonted manner keep:
>   Hesperus entreats thy light,
>   Goddess excellently bright.

the first line begins with a vocative, an address to the goddess Diana. The opening word "Queen" is stressed and is followed by "and," which receives far less stress. The rhythmical pattern is simple and clearly heard. The same pattern follows for the rest of the lines.

> stress stress stress stress
> Queen and huntress, chaste and fair,

The pattern thus set up (trochaic: ´ ˘) may continue in the reader's mind beyond the reading of the line to the point where it becomes a desired pattern for another experience like the first line. The poem does not disappoint this wish, for the rest of the lines follow the pattern. There are other elements, such as rhyme, which develop expected patterns, but these are not under discussion here.

But all verse is not just the fulfillment of established or expected rhythmic patterns. Within a poem the rhythmic movement may vary or "counterpoint" the expected pattern. Some of the most interesting rhythmical effects are produced by this "counterpointing," or apparent violation of the expected pattern. In such cases the poet may play against the rhythm which is being heard in the reader's mind. A simple parallel in music is syncopation; many of the interesting characteristics of modern dance music—swing and bebop—are built on variation of the basic rhythmic patterns set up in the listener's consciousness.

In the following stanza from Part IV of *The Ancient Mariner*, describing the water snakes, the first two lines set up a simple rhythmic pattern (iambic: ˘ ´) in which a stressed syllable regularly follows an unstressed syllable. (The stressed syllables are marked with an accent: ´.)

> Withín the shádow óf the shíp
> I wátch'd their rích attíre:
> Blúe, glóssy gréen, and vélvet bláck,
> They cóil'd and swám; and évery tráck
> Was a flásh of gólden fíre.

The third line comes as a kind of shock. It begins with stress on "Blue" and follows with another stressed syllable, "glóssy." The expected pattern is violated, but the effect created is dramatic; it draws attention to striking color. The fourth line returns to the iambic pattern, but the fifth line provides another variant of interest in opening with two unstressed syllables, "Was a," followed by a strong stress on "flash." The effect of this variation is to give a sense of speed to the line, in perfect accord with the picture Coleridge is creating.

For purposes of study some general features of rhythm in English verse, seen in broadest terms as alternation of stress and less stress or lack of stress in syllables, can be marked by accepted graphic symbols: ˘ for an unaccented syllable; ´ for an accented syllable. But the application of these signs to verse, a practice called scansion, only generally and loosely indicates the real quality and effects; and most of the descriptive terms, derived from classical Greek and Latin principles of versification, are, in fact, misnomers. Too often readers are content to think they have understood the craftsmanship of a line of verse if they have scanned it or can say glibly, "iambic pentameter."

Although no two people read a line of a poem the same way, intelligent reading aloud is an essential step toward understanding the craft of poetry. The ear must be used as the responsive, critical, and appreciative instrument it really is. Intelligent reading will reveal the main stresses or accents in the lines as no optical analysis will. Only after careful reading should a student begin a graphic though approximate record of the rhythm of the poem. No attempt should be made to fit iambic or trochaic or other measures and accents until the main accents are indicated. The opening stanza of Gray's "Elegy Written in a Country Churchyard" will serve as an example.

> The curfew tolls the knell of parting day,
> The lowing herd wind slowly o'er the lea,
> The plowman homeward plods his weary way,
> And leaves the world to darkness and to me.

The regularity of the movement should be immediately apparent when the unstressed syllables are also marked:

> The curfew tolls the knell of parting day.

Lines 3 and 4 show the same regularity. In line 2, properly read, the word "wind" seems to require greater stress than the unaccented words like "the," perhaps almost the same stress as "slowly." Here the slight variation from the plain iambic (˘ ′) pattern is also a matter of time as well as accent. The graphic symbol to mark the value of "wind" exactly does not exist. The necessary approach to it might be a secondary accent (`) or a full accent. The effect of slowness is strongly established and then reinforced by the rhythmical quality and the placing of the central words in the line. The line could thus be scanned: "The lowing herd wind slowly o'er the lea." Time values expressed by musical notes might give a more graphic idea of the line.

The lowing herd wind slowly o'er the lea.

♪ ♩. ♪ ♩ ♩ ♩ ♩ ♩. ♪ ♩.

The whole stanza has a feeling of calmness and quiet, not only because of the details of atmosphere ("curfew tolls") or the pictorial details ("lowing herd," "plowman") but because of the regularity in iambic pentameter of the rhythm and because of various devices of sound (rhyme, *abab*; alliteration in "*pl*owman . . . *pl*ods"; "*w*eary *w*ay"; assonance in "l*ow*ing" and "sl*ow*ly," "slow*ly*" and "*lea*"; consonance in "*l*owing," "s*l*owly," "*l*ea").

The stanza contains almost no pauses within the line, the main caesuras (or pauses) coming regularly at the end of each line. In line 4, a light caesura after "darkness" gives a dramatic effect to the final verse. The suitability of the rhythm to the tone of the stanza is apparent. The rhythm in all its aspects is not *imposed* on the stanza. It is an integral part of the stanza.

Gray's stanza offers almost no metrical complexities; its atmosphere has been derived in part from the simplicity of its meter. The following song of Ben Jonson's from a masque called *Cynthia's Revels* (1601) is a good example of the use of a more complicated metrical and sound pattern to produce the dramatic effect of grief. The verses are Echo's song over the death of her love, Narcissus, who melted away into a spring and eventually, in Jonson's use of the legend, became a daffodil.

> Slow, slow, fresh fount, keep time with my salt tears;
> > Yet slower yet, oh, faintly, gentle springs;
> List to the heavy part the music bears,
> > Woe weeps out her division when she sings.
> > > Droop herbs and flowers,
> > > Fall grief in showers;
> > > Our beauties are not ours.
> > > > Oh, I could still,
> Like melting snow upon some craggy hill,
> > Drop, drop, drop, drop,
> Since nature's pride is now a withered daffodil.

A reading of the poem will reveal how completely the poet has control over the mood and the movement of the poem. Even the least experienced reader cannot destroy the essentially deliberate slow tempo of the lines. The reason is that Jonson has made full use of devices of rhythm and sound.

In the first place Jonson has combined spondaic movement (´´) with a frequent use of strategically placed pauses or caesuras. The first six syllables of the ten in the opening line are almost equally stressed; three pauses occur: the first after the first syllable, the second after the second syllable and the third after the fourth syllable.

Slow, || slow, || | fresh fount, || | keep time | with my | salt tears; || |

The effect of the line is one of gravity and grief.

The second line intensifies the dramatic situation with a feeling of anxiety and pleading. The rhythm of the line differs from the first line, but the tempo is just as thoroughly controlled by the caesuras after "yet" and "faintly." Although the basic meter of the line is iambic, the secondary accent on "oh" and the ceasuras break up any completely iambic movement.

Yet slow|er yet, || oh, faint|ly, || gen|tle springs; || |

The third line, essentially trochaic in movement, is a mild command to attention to the mournful quality of the fountain; and the fourth line by a combination of alliteration and consecutively stressed syllables produces an effect which exactly illustrates what is called for in line 3 and corresponds generally with the rhythmical characteristics of line 1.

List to the | heavy | part the | music | bears, || |
Woe weeps | out her | divi|sion when | she sings. || |

Repetition and assonance (Sl*ow*, sl*ow*, line 1; sl*ow*er, line 2; *Woe* in line 4;), and alliteration (*W*oe *w*eeps . . . *w*hen in line 4) are a few of the devices of sound which help to create here the emotional effect of grief.

The next three lines form a triplet in which the feminine rhymes (flówers, shówers, oúrs; "ours" in line 7 is read as two syllables), the short lines, and the consequent quick return of the rhymes maintain the tone of the poem, but also seem to provide a contemplative quality by the formal tripartite division.

The last four lines contain a personal wish. Their outstanding sound device is, of course, the onomatopoetic words "Drop, drop, drop, drop" (line 10) with their even stresses and regular pauses. The last line, which gives the reason for the situation of grief, is the longest line of the poem, containing six feet, and has a conclusive effect because of its length and its iambic regularity.

Since náture's príde ĭs nŏw ă wíthĕrĕd dáffŏdíl.

Although this brief survey of the meter and sound of Jonson's poem may seem detailed to a critical reader at first, it does not attempt to cover all the technical aspects of the poem. Enough has been noticed, however, to show how carefully the small song is made and how effectively its technical qualities suit its delicacy, mood, and emotional effect.

The variety of effects which a line of verse or a stanza or a whole poem may have are in part attributable to the basic rhythmical and vocal qualities of the poem itself. These elements can be temporarily isolated for study but can be finally appreciated only in terms of the whole work; in a good poem, style, which involves craftmanship in meter and sound, cannot be separated from substance. Remember that the terms and symbols used to describe and scan verse are only approximate. A scientific record of anyone's reading of a line of verse could of course be made, but an oscillograph is not a necessary piece of equipment for the average reader.

For the sake of convenience the following list of terms and definitions is supplied. The arrangement is according to rhythm and meter and devices of sound.

RHYTHM AND METER

FOOT: The metrical unit of a poem; consists of one accented and one or more unaccented syllables. Common types of feet in English verse are:

IAMB (˘ ´ *compel*): An unaccented syllable followed by an accented syllable; the most common meter in English.

TROCHEE (´ ˘ *neatly*): One accented followed by one unaccented syllable.

ANAPEST (˘ ˘ ´ *interfere*): Two unaccented syllables followed by an accented syllable.

DACTYL (´ ˘ ˘ *happiness*): One accented syllable followed by two unaccented syllables.

SPONDEE (´ ´ *sunset*): The term really describes a foot in classical meter composed of two long syllables, but it is often used in English verse to describe a situation in which two accents or a secondary and a full accent are in succession.

And one | clear call | for me! |

VERSE: A line of poetry. A line of verse is composed of one or more feet.

> One foot: monometer
> Two feet: dimeter
> Three feet: trimeter
> Four feet: tetrameter
> Five feet: pentameter
> Six feet: hexameter or alexandrine
> Seven feet: heptameter

CAESURA: The main pause in a line of verse, which is sometimes marked ‖ to distinguish it from the mark used to designate a foot |. Other pauses are sometimes called secondary pauses.

> Tears, idle tears, || I know not what they mean,||
> Tears from the depth of some divine despair
> Rise in the heart, || and gather to the eyes, . . .

RUN-ON LINES: The carrying over of sense and grammatical structure from one verse to a succeeding one for completion; the process is often called enjambement. The opening lines of Shakespeare's 116th sonnet will illustrate:

> Let me not to the marriage of true minds
> Admit impediments. Love is not love
> Which alters when it alteration finds, . . .

END-STOPPED LINES: Lines of verse in which both the grammatical structure and the sense are complete at the end of the line. A couplet from Pope's *An Essay on Criticism* may serve:

> True ease in writing comes from art, not chance,
> As those move easiest who have learned to dance.

SOUND

The quality and relationships of sounds in poetry are often called *verse texture*. Among these relationships are alliteration, assonance, consonance, and rhyme.

ALLITERATION: Repetition of consonants, especially initial consonants, in a line. A stanza from Coleridge's *The Rime of the Ancient Mariner* gives examples:

> The fair breeze blew, the white foam flew,
> The furrow followed free;
> We were the first that ever burst
> Into that silent sea.

ASSONANCE: The identity of vowel sounds in a line or stanza.

> To dying ears, when unto dying eyes, . . .

CONSONANCE: The identity of consonant patterns in a line or stanza. Consonance is found more rarely than assonance in English verse. A line from Shelley's "To Night" illustrates consonance within a line:

Where *all* the *long* and *lon*e daylight

ONOMATOPOEIA: The use of words which suggest their meaning through their pronunciation: *buzz, whirr, sizzle.*

> And more to lull him in his slumber soft,
> A *trickling* stream from high rock tumbling down
> And *ever-drizzling* rain upon the loft,
> Mixed with a *murmuring* wind, much like the sound
> Of swarming bees, did cast him in a swoon:
> No other noise, nor people's troublous cries,
> As still are wont t'annoy the walled town,
> Might there be heard: but careless Quiet lies,
> Wrapped in eternal silence far from enemies.
> (Spenser's *Faerie Queene*, Bk. I)

RHYME: Actually the similarity or identity of sounds based on the vowels of accented syllables and the consonants and vowels following within a line or lines of verse. (Assonance, consonance, and alliteration may all be considered forms of rhyme.) The term *rhyme* is most often used to designate *end rhyme*, which occurs at the ends of the verses. *End rhyme* is often classified as *masculine rhyme*, in which the final syllable of the line is the rhymed syllable:

obey, decay

and *feminine*, in which the rhymed syllables are followed by identical unaccented syllables:

fighting, writing

This is sometimes called *double rhyme*. When the correspondence of sound occurs in three syllables it is called *triple rhyme:*

malicious, nutritious

RHYME SCHEME: The patterns of end rhymes in a stanza, usually designated by indicating each similar sound by the same letter of the alphabet. The pattern of the Spenserian stanza quoted under ONOMATOPOEIA is *ababbcbcc*.

STANZA FORMS

The most commonly used forms are defined briefly below:

COUPLET: A stanza of two lines. *Tetrameter couplet:* also called octosyllabic couplet; usually iambic tetrameter, *aa*. *Heroic couplet:* Usually iambic pentameter, *aa*.

TERCET: A stanza of three lines, a triplet, *aaa*.

TERZA RIMA: Iambic pentameter tercets in linked rhyme, *ababcb-cdc*, etc.

QUATRAIN: A stanza of four lines. Ballad measure; lines 1 and 3 have eight syllables each and lines 2 and 4 six syllables. Usually iambic; rhyme is *abcb*. The ordinary quatrain is iambic pentameter, *abab*, as in Gray's *Elegy*, but there are variants of the rhyme scheme, such as *abba, aaba*.

RHYME ROYAL: A stanza of seven lines, pentameter, *ababbcc*.

OTTAVA RIMA: A stanza of eight lines, pentameter, *abababcc*.

SPENSERIAN STANZA: A stanza of nine lines, pentameter, except for last line, which is an alexandrine, *ababbcbcc*.

SONNET: A stanza of fourteen lines, pentameter.
  1. Italian sonnet, pentameter, *abbaabba cdecde*. The first eight lines, which usually present the theme of the sonnet, are called an *octave*. The last six lines, in which the conclusion of the theme is given, are called a *sestet*. The sestet often varies in rhyme scheme.
  2. The Shakespearean (or English) sonnet, pentameter, *ababcdcdefefgg*. The division is by three quatrains and a concluding couplet. Often the proposition of

the poem is presented in the first three quatrains and concluded or commented on in the couplet, but the first two quatrains are sometimes used as the octave in the Italian sonnet.

BLANK VERSE: Not a stanza form. It is a line of unrhymed pentameter verse, usually iambic. It can of course form lines which may constitute a stanza pattern.

FREE VERSE: Verse which does not conform to any conventional or regular pattern.